SHELLY CASHMAN SERIES®

COMPREHENSIVE

Microsoft® Office 365® & ACCESS® 2019

SANDRA E. CABLE | ELLEN F. MONK

 CENGAGE

SHELLY CASHMAN SERIES®

Australia • Brazil • Canada • Mexico • Singapore • United Kingdom • United States

Shelly Cashman Series® Microsoft® Office 365® & Access® 2019 Comprehensive
Sandra E. Cable and Ellen F. Monk

SVP, GM Skills & Global Product Management: Jonathan Lau

Product Director: Lauren Murphy

Product Assistant: Veronica Moreno-Nestojko

Executive Director, Content Design: Marah Bellegarde

Director, Learning Design: Leigh Hefferon

Learning Designer: Courtney Cozzy

Vice President, Marketing - Science, Technology, and Math: Jason R. Sakos

Senior Marketing Director: Michele McTighe

Marketing Manager: Timothy J. Cali

Director, Content Delivery: Patty Stephan

Senior Content Manager: Anne Orgren

Digital Delivery Lead: Laura Ruschman

Designer: Lizz Anderson

Cover image(s): Sergey Kelin/ShutterStock.com (Ocean), nikkytok/ShutterStock.com (Crystal), PARINKI/ShutterStock.com (Marble), Erika Kirkpatrick/ShutterStock.com (Driftwood), Vladitto/ShutterStock.com (Skyscraper), Roman Sigaev/ShutterStock.com (Clouds)

Mac Users: If you're working through this product using a Mac, some of the steps may vary. Additional information for Mac users is included with the Data files for this product.

Disclaimer: This text is intended for instructional purposes only; data is fictional and does not belong to any real persons or companies.

Disclaimer: The material in this text was written using Microsoft Windows 10 and Office 365 Professional Plus and was Quality Assurance tested before the publication date. As Microsoft continually updates the Windows 10 operating system and Office 365, your software experience may vary slightly from what is presented in the printed text.

Windows, Access, Excel, and PowerPoint are registered trademarks of Microsoft Corporation. Microsoft and the Office logo are either registered trademarks or trademarks of Microsoft Corporation in the United States and/or other countries. This product is an independent publication and is neither affiliated with, nor authorized, sponsored, or approved by, Microsoft Corporation.

Some of the product names and company names used in this book have been used for identification purposes only and may be trademarks or registered trademarks of Microsoft Corporation in the United States and/or other countries.

Unless otherwise noted, all non-Microsoft clip art is courtesy of openclipart.org.

For product information and technology assistance, contact us at **Cengage Customer & Sales Support, 1-800-354-9706** or **support.cengage.com.**

For permission to use material from this text or product, submit all requests online at **www.cengage.com/permissions**

Library of Congress Control Number: 2019939820

Student Edition ISBN: 978-0-357-02639-7
Looseleaf available as part of a digital bundle

Cengage
200 Pier 4 Boulevard
Boston, MA 02210
USA

Cengage is a leading provider of customized learning solutions with employees residing in nearly 40 different countries and sales in more than 125 countries around the world. Find your local representative at **www.cengage.com.**

To learn more about Cengage platforms and services, visit **www.cengage.com.**

Notice to the Reader

Publisher does not warrant or guarantee any of the products described herein or perform any independent analysis in connection with any of the product information contained herein. Publisher does not assume, and expressly disclaims, any obligation to obtain and include information other than that provided to it by the manufacturer. The reader is expressly warned to consider and adopt all safety precautions that might be indicated by the activities described herein and to avoid all potential hazards. By following the instructions contained herein, the reader willingly assumes all risks in connection with such instructions. The publisher makes no representations or warranties of any kind, including but not limited to, the warranties of fitness for particular purpose or merchantability, nor are any such representations implied with respect to the material set forth herein, and the publisher takes no responsibility with respect to such material. The publisher shall not be liable for any special, consequential, or exemplary damages resulting, in whole or part, from the readers' use of, or reliance upon, this material.

Printed at CLDPC, USA, 10-23

Microsoft® Office 365® & ACCESS® 2019

COMPREHENSIVE

Brief Contents

Access 2019

Microsoft® Office 365® & ACCESS® 2019

COMPREHENSIVE

Contents

Microsoft® Office 365®
ACCESS® 2019

COMPREHENSIVE

Getting to Know Microsoft Office Versions

Cengage is proud to bring you the next edition of Microsoft Office. This edition was designed to provide a robust learning experience that is not dependent upon a specific version of Office.

Microsoft supports several versions of Office:

- **Office 365:** A cloud-based subscription service that delivers Microsoft's most up-to-date, feature-rich, modern productivity tools direct to your device. There are variations of Office 365 for business, educational, and personal use. Office 365 offers extra online storage and cloud-connected features, as well as updates with the latest features, fixes, and security updates.

- **Office 2019:** Microsoft's "on-premises" version of the Office apps, available for both PCs and Macs, offered as a static, one-time purchase and outside of the subscription model.

- **Office Online:** A free, simplified version of Office web applications (Word, Excel, PowerPoint, and OneNote) that facilitates creating and editing files collaboratively.

Office 365 (the subscription model) and Office 2019 (the one-time purchase model) had only slight differences between them at the time this content was developed. Over time, Office 365's cloud interface will continuously update, offering new application features and functions, while Office 2019 will remain static. Therefore, your onscreen experience may differ from what you see in this product. For example, the more advanced features and functionalities covered in this product may not be available in Office Online or may have updated from what you see in Office 2019.

For more information on the differences between Office 365, Office 2019, and Office Online, please visit the Microsoft Support site.

Cengage is committed to providing high-quality learning solutions for you to gain the knowledge and skills that will empower you throughout your educational and professional careers.

Thank you for using our product, and we look forward to exploring the future of Microsoft Office with you!

Using SAM Projects and Textbook Projects

SAM and *MindTap* are interactive online platforms designed to transform students into Microsoft Office and Computer Concepts masters. Practice with simulated SAM Trainings and MindTap activities and actively apply the skills you learned live in Microsoft Word, Excel, PowerPoint, or Access. Become a more productive student and use these skills throughout your career.

If your instructor assigns SAM Projects:

1. Launch your SAM Project assignment from SAM or MindTap.
2. Click the links to download your **Instructions file**, **Start file**, and **Support files** (when available).
3. Open the Instructions file and follow the step-by-step instructions.
4. When you complete the project, upload your file to SAM or MindTap for immediate feedback.

To use SAM Textbook Projects:

1. Launch your SAM Project assignment from SAM or MindTap.
2. Click the links to download your **Start file** and **Support files** (when available).
3. Locate the module indicated in your book or eBook.
4. Read the module and complete the project.

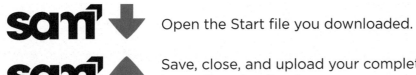

Open the Start file you downloaded.

Save, close, and upload your completed project to receive immediate feedback.

IMPORTANT: To receive full credit for your Textbook Project, you must complete the activity using the Start file you downloaded from SAM or MindTap.

1 Databases and Database Objects: An Introduction

Objectives

You will have mastered the material in this module when you can:

- Describe the features of the Access window
- Create a database
- Create tables in Datasheet and Design views
- Add records to a table
- Close a database

- Open a database
- Create and use a query
- Create and use a form
- Create a report
- Perform special database operations

Introduction

The term **database** describes a collection of data organized in a manner that allows access, retrieval, and use of that data. Microsoft Access 2019, usually referred to as simply Access, is a database management system. A **database management system** is software that allows you to use a computer to create a database; add, change, and delete data in the database; ask and answer questions concerning the data; and create forms and reports using the data.

Project—Database Creation

CanisMajorFelis Veterinary, or CMF Vets as its commonly known, is a veterinary practice that takes care of all cat and dog pet needs. Up until now, the appointment system has been paper-based. The staff records appointments in a large book with each page containing a specific date and time. Each page has slots for appointments, which are made in pencil to allow for changes. CMF Vets wants to computerize the appointment system with an Access database. The practice owns multiple veterinary clinics in the southwest. The practice wants to make the appointment system easier to use and more efficient. To accomplish that goal, the practice needs better record keeping.

CMF Vets needs to record all information about the pet owners. Name and full mailing address are essential pieces of information. In addition, the practice must be able to contact pet owners quickly. The staff needs to record home phone numbers, mobile phone numbers, and email addresses for appointment reminders, test results, and emergency calls.

Patient information is paramount. The patient's breed, animal type, name, and owner should be always recorded so that information can be easily retrieved. The database should also contain each patient's appointments with specific date, time, and procedure. For example, the staffing requirements of a surgical procedure will differ from those of a check-up.

Each treatment has a specific cost, which needs to be recorded and applied as patients undergo these treatments. The database system must also track the veterinarians who perform these treatments.

By recording all of its practice information, CMF Vets keeps its data current and accurate and can analyze it for trends. Using a database also allows CMF Vets to create a variety of useful reports; for example, tracking the frequency of certain procedures. These reports are vital for planning purposes.

In a **relational database,** such as those maintained by Access, a database consists of a collection of tables, each of which contains information on a specific subject. Figure 1–1 shows the database for CMF Vets. It consists of five tables: the Owners table (Figure 1–1a) contains information about the pet owners, the Patients table (Figure 1–1b) contains contact information for each pet's owner, the Appointments table (Figure 1–1c) contains information about the scheduling of appointments, the Treatment Cost table (Figure 1–1d) contains information about the cost of each treatment, and the Veterinarians table (Figure 1–1e) contains a listing of the veterinarians in the practice.

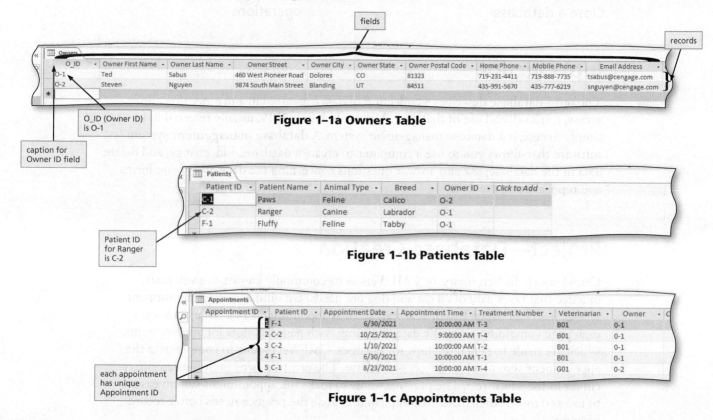

fields

records

Owners

O_ID	Owner First Name	Owner Last Name	Owner Street	Owner City	Owner State	Owner Postal Code	Home Phone	Mobile Phone	Email Address
O-1	Ted	Sabus	460 West Pioneer Road	Dolores	CO	81323	719-231-4411	719-888-7735	tsabus@cengage.com
O-2	Steven	Nguyen	9874 South Main Street	Blanding	UT	84511	435-991-5670	435-777-6219	snguyen@cengage.com

Figure 1–1a Owners Table

O_ID (Owner ID) is O-1

caption for Owner ID field

Patients

Patient ID	Patient Name	Animal Type	Breed	Owner ID	Click to Add
C-1	Paws	Feline	Calico	O-2	
C-2	Ranger	Canine	Labrador	O-1	
F-1	Fluffy	Feline	Tabby	O-1	

Patient ID for Ranger is C-2

Figure 1–1b Patients Table

Appointments

Appointment ID	Patient ID	Appointment Date	Appointment Time	Treatment Number	Veterinarian	Owner	
1	F-1	6/30/2021	10:00:00 AM	T-3	B01	O-1	
2	C-2	10/25/2021	9:00:00 AM	T-4	B01	O-1	
3	C-2	1/10/2021	10:00:00 AM	T-2	B01	O-1	
4	F-1	6/30/2021	10:00:00 AM	T-1	B01	O-1	
5	C-1	8/23/2021	10:00:00 AM	T-4	G01	O-2	

each appointment has unique Appointment ID

Figure 1–1c Appointments Table

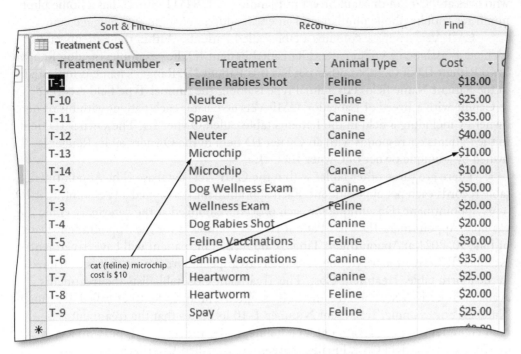

Figure 1–1d Treatment Cost Table

Figure 1–1e Veterinarians Table

The rows in the tables are called **records**. A record contains information about a given person (or in this case, pet), product, or event. A row in the Owners table, for example, contains information about a specific owner, such as the owner's name, address, and other data.

The columns in the tables are called fields. A **field** contains a specific piece of information within a record. In the Owners table, for example, the fifth field, Owner City, contains the name of the city where the owner is located.

The first field in the Owners table is Owner ID, which is an abbreviation for Owner Identification Number. CMF Vets assigns each owner an identifying number; the Owner ID consists of one uppercase letter followed by a number.

The Owner IDs are unique; that is, no two owners have the same number. Such a field is a **unique identifier**. A unique identifier, as its name suggests, is a way of uniquely identifying each record in the database. A given owner number will appear only in a single record in the table. Only one record exists, for example, in which the Owner ID is O-2. A unique identifier is also called a **primary key**. Thus, the Owner ID field is the primary key for the Owners table. This means the Owner ID field can be used to uniquely identify a record in the table. No two records can have the same value in the Owner ID field.

The next nine fields in the Owners table are Owner First Name, Owner Last Name, Owner Street, Owner City, Owner State, Owner Postal Code, Home Phone, Mobile Phone, and Email Address. For example, Owner ID O-2 is Steven Nguyen,

BTW
Captions
You can change a field's caption, or the wording that appears as the field's name, to language that is more descriptive, shorter, or meets some other requirement.

BTW
Naming Fields
Access 2019 has a number of reserved words, words that have a special meaning to Access. You cannot use these reserved words as field names. For example, Name is a reserved word and could not be used in the Owners table to describe a pet owner's name. For a complete list of reserved words in Access 2019, consult Access Help.

who lives at 9874 South Main Street in Blanding UT, 84511. Steven has a home phone number, a mobile phone number, and an email address of snguyen@cengage.com.

CMF Vets database contains a table called Patients. Within the Patients table, each pet is assigned a unique identifier called Patient ID. For example, the dog Ranger has a Patient ID of C-2. No other pet has this Patient ID. Ranger's name is indicated in the Patient Name field. His animal type is under the Animal Type field recorded as Canine with a Breed of Labrador. CMF Vets associates each patient with his or her owner by including a field in the Patients table called Owner ID. The Owner ID field in the Patients corresponds with an Owner ID field in the Owners table. Ranger is owned by a unique owner of Owner ID O-1.

There are three other tables within the CMF Vets database. The Appointments table records each pet appointment. Each appointment is assigned an Appointment ID. This Appointment ID is unique for each procedure booked at the veterinary clinic. For example, Appointment ID 1 has Patient ID F-1 coming in for the Appointment Date of June 30, 2021 at Appointment Time 10:00 A.M. This patient will have Treatment Number T-3. Treatment Number T-3 refers to a specific treatment that is explained in the fourth table, Treatment Cost. The Treatment Cost table lists the treatments available at CMF Vets. Each treatment is assigned a unique identifier called Treatment Number. For example, Treatment Number T-10 indicates that the treatment is a Neuter, under the field Treatment, of a Feline, under the Animal Type, with a cost of $25, under the field Cost. Finally, there is a table called Veterinarians that lists the veterinarians in the practice. Each doctor has a unique Veterinarian ID that is associated with the veterinarian's contact details. For example, Veterinarian ID G01 is Teresa Gomez, in Blanding, Utah, with a cell phone number of 435-229-5612.

CONSIDER THIS

How would you find the owner of a specific patient?
If CMF Vets had a test result of a specific patient, Ranger, Patient ID C-2, and the veterinarian wanted to telephone the owner with the test results, the vet could easily find that telephone number by looking in the Patients table and then in Owners table. In the Patients table, locate the Patient C-2 and read across until you come to the Owner ID field, which is O-1. Then, in the Owner table, locate the record which has the Owner ID O-1, and read across to find the owners name, Ted Sabus, and his phone numbers, home and mobile.

CONSIDER THIS

How would you find appointment information for a specific patient?
First, look in the Patients table to identify the specific pet and its Patient ID. Assume that the Patient's Owner is O-1 and the Patient's name is Fluffy. Fluffy's Patient ID is F-1. Next, look in the appointments table for Patient F-1 and find that Fluffy is scheduled to come into the clinic on June 30, 2021 at 10:00 A.M.

Creating a Database

In Access, all the tables, reports, forms, and queries that you create are stored in a single file called a database. A database is a structure that can store information about multiple types of objects, the properties of those objects, and the relationships among the objects. The first step is to create the database that will hold your tables, reports, forms, and queries. You can use either the Blank desktop database option or a template to create a new database. If you already know the tables and fields you want in your database, you would use the Blank desktop database option. If not, you can use a template. Templates can guide you by suggesting some commonly used databases.

To Create a Database

Because you already know the tables and fields you want in the CMF Vets database, you will use the Blank desktop database option rather than a template to create the database. *Why? The Blank desktop database is the most efficient way to create a database for which you already know the intended data needs.* The following steps create the database.

- Click the Windows Start button to display the Windows menu.
- Click the Access button to start Access (Figure 1–2a).

Figure 1–2a

2

- Click the Blank database button to specify the type of database to create.
- **sam** ⬇ Type `CMF Vets` in the File Name text box, and then click the Create button to create the database (Figure 1–2).

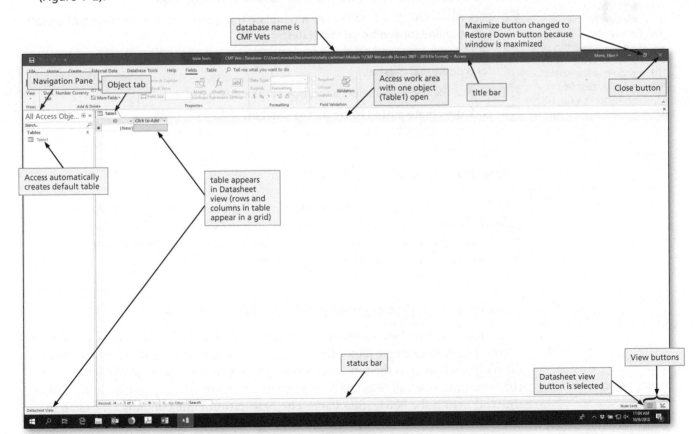

Figure 1–2

CONSIDER THIS

Saving a Microsoft Access Database File
Unlike other Microsoft Office applications, the Access app allocates storage space when the database is created, even before any tables have been designed and data has been entered. In other Microsoft Office applications, you can enter data before saving. In Access, as you are working and saving each object, such as a table, the entire database is being saved in the app's designated storage space.

Q&A

The title bar for my Navigation Pane contains All Tables rather than All Access Objects, as in the figure. Is that a problem?
It is not a problem. The title bar indicates how the Navigation Pane is organized. You can carry out the steps in the text with either organization. To make your screens match the ones in the text, click the Navigation Pane arrow and then click Object Type.

I do not have the Search bar that appears in the figure. Is that a problem?
It is not a problem. If your Navigation Pane does not display a Search bar and you want your screens to match the ones in the text, right-click the Navigation Pane title bar arrow to display a shortcut menu, and then click Search Bar.

BTW
Available Templates
The templates gallery includes both desktop and web-based templates. If you are creating an Access database for your own use, select a desktop template. Web-based templates allow you to create databases that you can publish to a SharePoint server.

To Create a Database Using a Template

Ideally, you will design your own database, create a blank database, and then create the tables you have determined that your database should contain. If you are not sure what database design you will need, you can use a template. Templates can guide you by suggesting some commonly used databases. To create a database using a template, you would use the following steps.

BTW
Organizing Files and Folders
You should organize and store files in folders so that you easily can find the files later. For example, if you are taking an introductory computer class called CIS 101, a good practice would be to save all Access files in an Access folder in a CIS 101 folder.

1 If you have another database open, close it without exiting Access by clicking File on the ribbon to open the Backstage view and then clicking Close.

2 Click File – New. If you do not see a template that you want, you can search Microsoft Office online for additional templates.

3 Click the template you want to use. Be sure you have selected one that indicates it is for a desktop database.

4 Enter a file name and select a location for the database.

5 Click the Create button to create the database.

The Access Window

The Access window consists of a variety of components to make your work more efficient. These include the Navigation Pane, Access work area, ribbon, shortcut menus, and Quick Access Toolbar. Some of these components are common to other Microsoft Office apps; others are unique to Access.

BTW
Access Screen Resolution
If you are using a computer or mobile device to step through the project in this module and you want your screens to match the figures in this book, you should change your screen's resolution to 1366 x 768.

Navigation Pane and Access Work Area

You work on objects such as tables, forms, and reports in the **Access work area**. Figure 1–2 shows a single table, Table1, open in the work area. **Object tabs** for the open objects appear at the top of the work area. If you have multiple objects open at the same time, you can select one of the open objects by clicking its tab. To the left of the work area is the Navigation Pane. The **Navigation Pane** contains a list of all the objects in the database. You use this pane to open an object. You can also customize the way objects are displayed in the Navigation Pane.

The **status bar**, located at the bottom of the Access window, presents information about the database object, the progress of current tasks, and the status of certain commands and keys; it also provides controls for viewing the object. As you type text or perform certain commands, various indicators might appear on the status bar. The left edge of the status bar in Figure 1–2 shows that the table object is open in **Datasheet view**. In Datasheet view, the table is represented as a collection of rows and columns called a **datasheet**. Toward the right edge are View buttons, which you can use to change the view that currently appears.

Determining Tables and Fields

Once you have created the database, you need to create the tables and fields that your database will contain. Before doing so, however, you need to make some decisions regarding the tables and fields.

Naming Tables and Fields

In creating your database, you must name tables, fields, and other objects. Before beginning the design process, you must understand the rules Access applies to table and field names. These rules are:

1. Names can be up to 64 characters in length.
2. Names can contain letters, digits, and spaces, as well as most of the punctuation symbols.
3. Names cannot contain periods (.), exclamation points (!), accent graves (`), or square brackets ([ ]).
4. Each field in a table must have a unique name.

The approach to naming tables and fields used in this text is to begin all names with an uppercase letter. In multiple-word names, each word begins with an uppercase letter, and there is a space between words (for example, Owner Street).

Determining the Primary Key

For each table, you need to determine the primary key, the unique identifier. In many cases, you will have obvious choices, such as Patient ID or Owner ID. If you do not have an obvious choice, you can use the primary key that Access creates automatically. It is a field called ID. It is an **autonumber field**, which means that Access will assign the value 1 to the first record, 2 to the second record, and so on.

Determining Data Types for the Fields

For each field in your database, you must determine the field's **data type**, that is, the type of data that can be stored in the field. Four of the most commonly used data types in Access are:

1. **Short Text** — The field can contain any characters. A maximum number of 255 characters is allowed in a field whose data type is Short Text.
2. **Number** — The field can contain only numbers. The numbers can be either positive or negative. Fields assigned this type can be used in arithmetic

BTW
AutoNumber Fields
AutoNumber fields also are
called AutoIncrement fields.
In Design view, the New
Values field property allows
you to increment the field
sequentially (Increment) or
randomly (Random). The
default is sequential.

operations. You usually assign fields that contain numbers but will not
be used for arithmetic operations (such as postal codes) a data type of
Short Text.

3. **Currency** — The field can contain only monetary data. The values will appear
   with currency symbols, such as dollar signs, commas, and decimal points, and
   with two digits following the decimal point. Like numeric fields, you can use
   currency fields in arithmetic operations. Access assigns a size to currency fields
   automatically.

4. **Date & Time** — The field can contain dates and/or times.

Table 1–1 shows the other data types that are available in Access.

Table 1–1 Additional Data Types	
Data Type	**Description**
Long Text	Field can store up to a gigabyte of text.
AutoNumber	Field can store a unique sequential number that Access assigns to a record. Access will increment the number by 1 as each new record is added.
Yes/No	Field can store only one of two values. The choices are Yes/No, True/False, or On/Off.
OLE Object	Field can store an OLE object, which is an object linked to or embedded in the table.
Hyperlink	Field can store text that can be used as a hyperlink address.
Attachment	Field can contain an attached file. Images, spreadsheets, documents, charts, and other elements can be attached to this field in a record in the database. You can view and edit the attached file.
Calculated	Field specified as a calculation based on other fields. The value is not actually stored.

BTW
Currency Symbols
To show the symbol for the
Euro (€) instead of the dollar
sign, change the Format
property for the field whose
data type is currency. To
change the default symbols
for currency, change the
settings in Windows.

In the Owners table, because the Owner ID, Owner First Name, Owner Last
Name, Owner Street, Owner City, Owner State, Owner Postal Code, Home Phone,
Mobile Phone, and Email Address can all contain letters or symbols, their data types
should be Short Text. The data type for Owner Postal Code is Short Text instead of
Number because you typically do not use postal codes in arithmetic operations; you do
not add postal codes or find an average postal code, for example. The Owner ID field
contains numbers, but you will not use these numbers in arithmetic operations, so its
data type should be Short Text.

Similarly, in the Appointments table, the data type for the Account Manager
Appointment ID, Patient ID and Treatment Number fields should all be Short Text.
The Appointment Date and Appointment Time fields should have a data type of Date
& Time. In the Treatment Cost table, the Cost contains monetary amounts, so its data
type should be Currency.

For fields whose data type is Short Text, you can change the field size, that is, the
maximum number of characters that can be entered in the field. If you set the field size
for the State field to 2, for example, Access will not allow the user to enter more than
two characters in the field. On the other hand, fields whose data type is Number often
require you to change the field size, which is the storage space assigned to the field by
Access. Table 1–2 shows the possible field sizes for Number fields.

Table 1–2 Field Sizes for Number Fields	
Field Size	**Description**
Byte	Integer value in the range of 0 to 255
Integer	Integer value in the range of -32,768 to 32,767
Long Integer	Integer value in the range of -2,147,483,648 to 2,147,483,647
Single	Numeric values with decimal places to seven significant digits—requires 4 bytes of storage
Double	Numeric values with decimal places to more accuracy than Single—requires 8 bytes of storage
Replication ID	Special identifier required for replication
Decimal	Numeric values with decimal places to more accuracy than Single or Double—requires 12 bytes of storage

What is the appropriate size for the Owner Postal Code field?
A Short Text field created will allocate 255 spaces for data. However, a postal code normally would only take up 9 spaces. It is more accurate to change the Short Text field size to limit to 9 spaces to account for the postal code plus 4 (5 numbers, a dash, followed by 4 numbers).

Creating a Table in Datasheet View

To create a table in Access, you must define its structure. That is, you must define all the fields that make up the table and their characteristics. You must also indicate the primary key.

In Access, you can use two different views to create a table: Datasheet view and Design view. Although the main reason to use Datasheet view is to add or update records in a table, you can also use it to create a table or to later modify its structure. The other view, **Design view**, is only used to create a table or to modify the structure of a table.

As you might expect, Design view has more functionality for creating a table than Datasheet view. That is, there are certain actions that can only be performed in Design view. One such action is assigning Short Text as the field size for the Owner ID. In this module, you will create the first table, the Owners table, in Datasheet view. Once you have created the table in Datasheet view, you will use Design view to change the field size.

Whichever view you choose to use, before creating the table, you need to know the names and data types of the fields that will make up the table. You can also decide to enter a description for a particular field to explain important details about the field. When you select this field, this description will appear on the status bar. You might also choose to assign a **caption** to a particular field. If you assign a caption, Access will display the value you assign, rather than the field name, in datasheets and in forms. If you do not assign a caption, Access will display the field name.

BTW
Naming Files
The following characters cannot be used in a file name: question mark (?), quotation mark ("), slash (/), backslash (\ ), colon (:), asterisk (*), vertical bar (|), greater than symbol (>), and less than symbol (<).

When would you want to use a caption?
You would use a caption whenever you wanted something other than the field name displayed. One common example is when the field name is relatively long and the data in the field is relatively short. In the Owners table, the name of the first field is Owner ID, but the field contains data that is only at most five characters long. You will change the caption for this field to O_ID, which is much shorter than Owner ID, yet still describes the field. Doing so will enable you to greatly reduce the width of the column.

The results of these decisions for the fields in the Owners table are shown in Table 1–3. The table also shows the data types and field sizes of the fields as well as any special properties that need to be changed. The Owner ID short text field has a caption of O_ID, enabling the width of the Owner ID column to be reduced in the datasheet.

Table 1–3 Structure of Owners Table			
Field Name	**Data Type**	**Field Size**	**Description**
Owner ID	Short Text	5	Primary Key **Description:** Unique identifier of pet owner **Caption:** O_ID
Owner First Name	Short Text	50	
Owner Last Name	Short Text	50	
Owner Street	Short Text	255	
Owner City	Short Text	50	
Owner State	Short Text	2	
Owner Postal Code	Short Text	9	
Home Phone	Short Text	25	
Mobile Phone	Short Text	25	
Email Address	Short Text	50	

CONSIDER THIS

How do you determine the field size?
You need to determine the maximum number of characters that can be entered in the field. In some cases, it is obvious. Field sizes of 2 for the State field and 9 for the Postal Code field are certainly the appropriate choices. In other cases, you need to determine how many characters you want to allow. In the list shown in Table 1–3, CMF Vets decided allowing 50 characters was sufficient for last names. You can change this field size later if it proves to be insufficient.

To Modify the Primary Key

When you first create a database, Access automatically creates a table for you. You can immediately begin defining the fields. If, for any reason, you do not have this table or inadvertently delete it, you can create the table by clicking Create on the ribbon and then clicking the Table button (Create tab | Tables group). In either case, you are ready to define the fields.

The following steps change the name, data type, and other properties of the first field to match the Owner ID field in Table 1–3, which is the primary key. *Why? Access has already created the first field as the primary key field, which it has named ID. Owner ID is a more appropriate name.*

1

• Right-click the column heading for the ID field to display a shortcut menu (Figure 1–3).

Q&A Why does my shortcut menu look different?
You displayed a shortcut menu for the column instead of the column heading. Be sure you right-click the column heading.

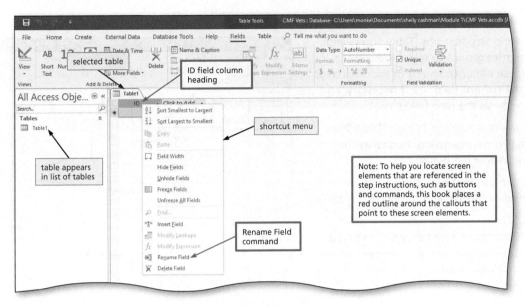

Figure 1–3

❷
- Click Rename Field on the shortcut menu to highlight the current name.

- Type **Owner ID** to assign a name to the new field.

- Click the white space immediately below the field name to complete the addition of the field (Figure 1–4).

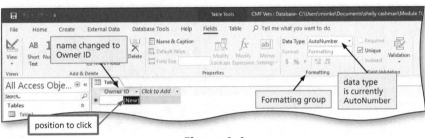

Figure 1–4

Q&A | Why does the full name of the field not appear?

The default column size might not be large enough for Owner ID, or a later field such as Owner Last Name, to be displayed in its entirety. If necessary, you will address this issue in later steps.

❸
- Because the data type needs to be changed from AutoNumber to Short Text, click the Data Type arrow (Table Tools Fields tab | Formatting group) to display a menu of available data types (Figure 1–5).

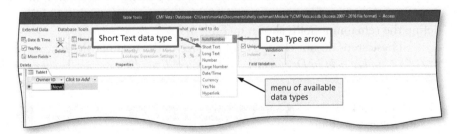

Figure 1–5

 Click Short Text to select the data type for the field (Figure 1–6).

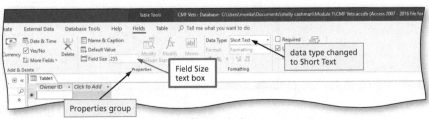

Figure 1–6

5

- Click the Field Size text box (Table Tools Fields tab | Properties group) to select the current field size, use either the DELETE or BACKSPACE key to erase the current field size if necessary, and then type 5 as the new field size.

- Click the Name & Caption button (Table Tools Fields tab | Properties group) to display the Enter Field Properties dialog box.

- Click the Caption text box (Enter Field Properties dialog box), and then type O_ID as the caption.

- Click the Description text box, and then type **Unique identifier of pet owner** as the description (Figure 1–7).

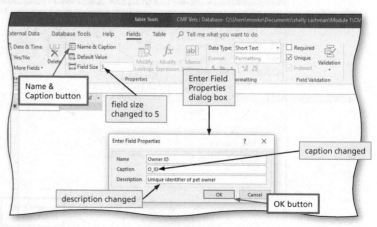

Figure 1–7

 6

- Click OK (Enter Field Properties dialog box) to change the caption and description (Figure 1–8).

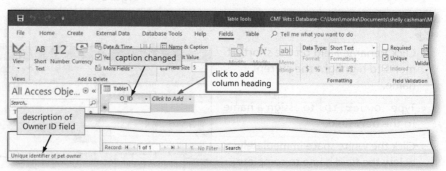

Figure 1–8

To Define the Remaining Fields in a Table

   To define an additional field, you click the Click to Add column heading, select the data type, and then type the field name. This is different from the process you used to modify the ID field. The following steps define the remaining fields shown in Table 1–3.

   These steps do not change the field size of the number field, however. *Why? You can only change the field size of a Number field in Design view. Later, you will use Design view to change field size and change the format.*

 1

- Click the Click to Add column heading to display a menu of available data types (Figure 1–9).

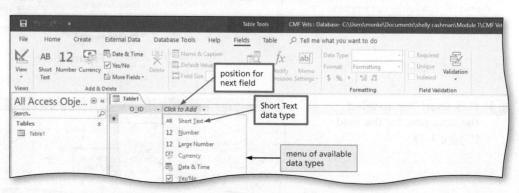

Figure 1–9

- Click Short Text in the menu of available data types to select the Short Text data type.

- Type `Owner First Name` to enter a field name.

- Click the blank space below the field name to complete the change of the name. Click the blank space a second time to select the field (Figure 1–10).

- If necessary, enlarge the field name box to display the entire

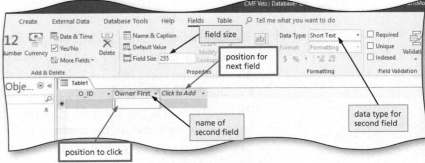

Figure 1–10

name by clicking between Owner First Name and the Click to Add box. Drag the pointer, which is now a double-tipped arrow, to the right so that the entire field name of Owner First Name is visible.

Q&A

After entering the field name, I realized that I selected the wrong data type. How can I correct it?
Click the Data Type arrow, and then select the correct type.

I inadvertently clicked the blank space before entering the field name. How can I correct the name?
Right-click the field name, click Rename Field on the shortcut menu, and then type the new name.

- Change the field size to 50 just as you changed the field size of the Owner ID field.

- Using the same technique, add the remaining fields in the Owners table. For the Owner

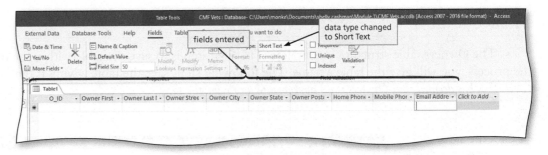

Figure 1–11

Last Name, Owner Street, Owner City, Owner State, Owner Postal Code, Home Phone, Mobile Phone, and Email Address fields, use the Short Text data type, but change the field sizes to match Table 1–3. Your Owners table should look like Figure 1–11.

Q&A

I have an extra row between the row containing the field names and the row that begins with the asterisk. What happened? Is this a problem? If so, how do I fix it?
You inadvertently added a record to the table by pressing a key. Even pressing the SPACEBAR adds a record. You now have an unwanted record. To fix it, press the ESC key or click the Undo button to undo the action. You may need to do this more than once.

When I try to move on to specify another field, I get an error message indicating that the primary key cannot contain a null value. How do I correct this?
First, click the OK button to remove the error message. Next, press the ESC key or click the Undo button to undo the action. You may need to do this more than once.

Making Changes to the Structure

When creating a table, check the entries carefully to ensure they are correct. If you discover a mistake while still typing the entry, you can correct the error by repeatedly pressing the BACKSPACE key until the incorrect characters are removed. Then, type the correct characters. If you do not discover a mistake until later, you can use the following techniques to make the necessary changes to the structure:

BTW
Touch Screen Differences
The Office and Windows interfaces may vary if you are using a touch screen. For this reason, you might notice that the function or appearance of your touch screen differs slightly from this module's presentation.

- To undo your most recent change, click the Undo button on the Quick Access Toolbar. If there is nothing that Access can undo, this button will be dim, and clicking it will have no effect.
- To delete a field, right-click the column heading for the field (the position containing the field name), and then click Delete Field on the shortcut menu.
- To change the name of a field, right-click the column heading for the field, click Rename Field on the shortcut menu, and then type the desired field name.
- To insert a field as the last field, click the Click to Add column heading, click the appropriate data type on the menu of available data types, type the desired field name, and, if necessary, change the field size.
- To insert a field between existing fields, right-click the column heading for the field that will follow the new field, and click Insert Field on the shortcut menu. Right-click the column heading for the field, click Rename Field on the shortcut menu, and then type the desired field name.
- To move a field, click the column heading for the field to be moved to select the field, and then drag the field to the desired position.

As an alternative to these steps, you might want to start over. To do so, click the Close button for the table, and then click the No button in the Microsoft Access dialog box. Click Create on the ribbon, and then click the Table button to create a table. You then can repeat the process you used earlier to define the fields in the table.

To Save a Table

The Owners table structure is complete. The final step is to save the table within the database. As part of the process, you will give the table a name. The following steps save the table, giving it the name Owners. *Why? CMF Vets has decided that Owners is an appropriate name for the table.*

- Click the Save button on the Quick Access Toolbar to display the Save As dialog box (Figure 1–12).

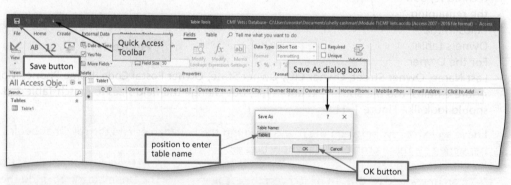

Figure 1–12

- Type `Owners` to change the name assigned to the table.
- Click OK (Save As dialog box) to save the table (Figure 1–13).

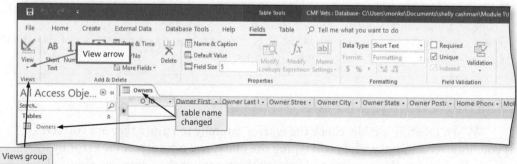

Figure 1–13

Other Ways

1. Click File on the ribbon, click Save in the Backstage view
2. Right-click tab for table, click Save on shortcut menu
3. Press CTRL+S

To View the Table in Design View

Even when creating a table in Datasheet view, Design view can be helpful. *Why? You easily can view the fields, data types, and properties to ensure you have entered them correctly. It is also easier to determine the primary key in Design view.* The following steps display the structure of the Owner table in Design view so that you can verify the design is correct.

1

• Click the View arrow (Table Tools Fields tab | Views group) to display the View menu (Figure 1–14).

Q&A Could I just click the View button rather than the arrow?
Yes. Clicking the button is equivalent to clicking the command represented by the icon that currently appears on the button. Because the icon on the button in Figure 1–14 is for Design view, clicking the button would display the table in Design view. If you are uncertain, you can always click the arrow and select Design View from the menu.

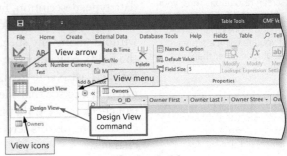

Figure 1–14

2

• Click Design View on the View menu to view the table in Design view (Figure 1–15).

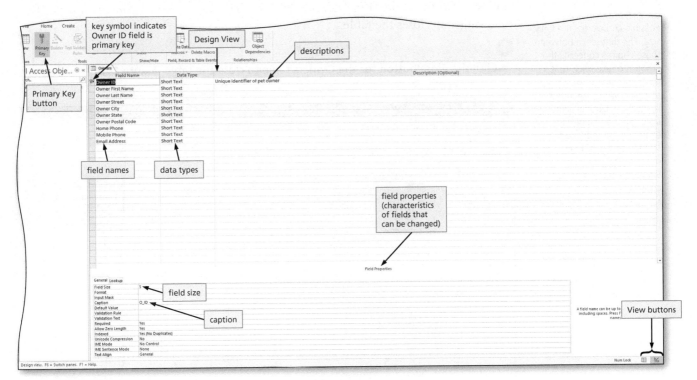

Figure 1–15

Other Ways

1. Click Design View button on status bar

BTW
The Ribbon and Screen Resolution
Access may change how the groups and buttons within the groups appear on the ribbon, depending on the computer or mobile device's screen resolution. Thus, your ribbon may look different from the ones in this book if you are using a screen resolution other than 1366 × 768.

BTW
Changing a Field Size in Design View
Most field size changes can be made in either Datasheet view or Design view. However, changing the field size for Number fields can only be done in Design view. If field values have decimal places, only Single, Double, or Decimal are possible choices for the field size. The difference between these choices concerns the amount of accuracy, that is, the number of decimal places to which the number is accurate. Double is more accurate than Single, for example, but requires more storage space. If a field has only two decimal places, Single is an acceptable choice.

Checking the Structure in Design View

You should use Design view to carefully check the entries you have made. In Figure 1–15, for example, the key symbol in front of the Owner ID field name indicates that the Owner ID field is the primary key of the Owners table. If your table does not have a key symbol, you can click the Primary Key button (Table Tools Design tab | Tools group) to designate a field as the primary key. You can also check that the data type, description, field size, and caption are all correct.

For the other fields, you can see the field name, data type, and description without taking any special action. To see the field size and/or caption for a field, click the field's **row selector**, the small box to the left of the field. Clicking the row selector for the Last Name field, for example, displays the properties for that field. You then can check to see that the field size is correct. In addition, if the field has a caption, you can check to see if that is correct. If you find any mistakes, you can make the necessary corrections on this screen. When you have finished, click the Save button to save your changes.

To Close the Table

Once you are sure that your entries are correct and you have saved your changes, you can close the table. *Why? Closing database objects keeps the workspace uncluttered.* The following step closes the table.

1
- Click the Close button for the Owners table to close the table (Figure 1–16).

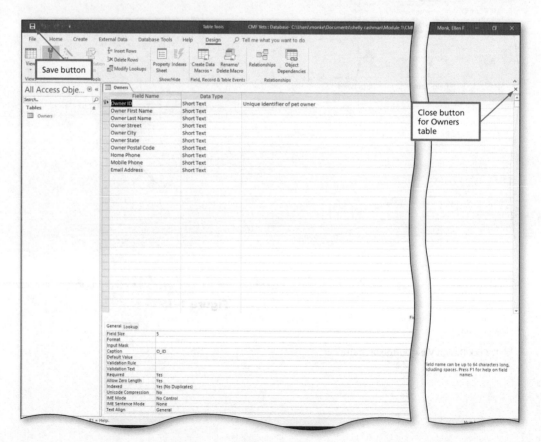

Figure 1–16

- If necessary, click Yes to save changes to the design of the table and then close the table. The dialog box will not appear if you did not make any changes.

Other Ways

1. Right-click tab for table, click Close on shortcut menu

To Add Records to a Table

Creating a table by building the structure and saving the table is the first step in the two-step process of using a table in a database. The second step is to add records to the table. To add records to a table, the table must be open. When making changes to records, you work in Datasheet view.

You often add records in phases. *Why? You might not have enough time to add all the records in one session, or you might not have all the records currently available.* The following steps open the Owners table in Datasheet view and then add the two records in the Owners table (Figure 1–17).

O_ID	Owner First Name	Owner Last Name	Owner Street	Owner City	Owner State	Owner Postal Code	Home Phone	Mobile Phone	Email Address
O-1	Ted	Sabus	460 West Pioneer Road	Dolores	CO	81323	719-231-4411	719-888-7735	tsabus@cengage.com
O-2	Steven	Nguyen	9874 South Main Street	Blanding	UT	84511	435-991-5670	435-777-6219	snguyen@cengage.com

Figure 1–17

1

- Right-click the Owners table in the Navigation Pane to display the shortcut menu (Figure 1–18).

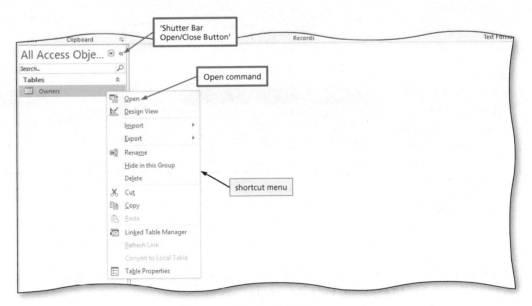

Figure 1–18

2

- Click Open on the shortcut menu to open the table in Datasheet view.

- Click the 'Shutter Bar Open/Close Button' to close the Navigation Pane (Figure 1–19).

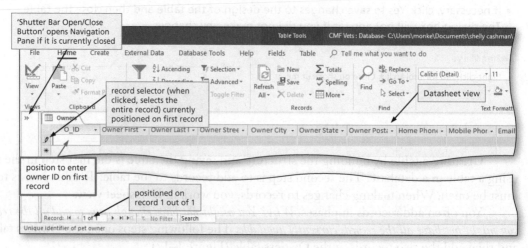

Figure 1–19

3

- Click the first row in the O_ID field if necessary to display an insertion point, and type O-1 (the letter "O" followed by a hyphen and the number 1) to enter the first owner ID (Figure 1–20).

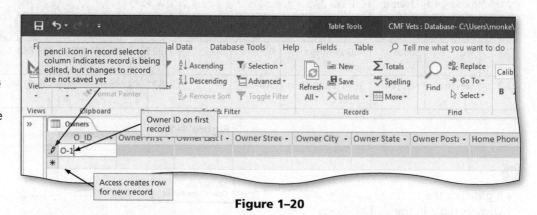

Figure 1–20

4

- Press TAB to move to the next field.

- Enter the first name, last name, street, city, state, postal code, home phone, mobile phone, and email address by typing the following entries, as shown in Figure 1–21, pressing TAB after each entry: Ted as the first name, Sabus as the last name, 460 West Pioneer Road as the street, Dolores as the city, CO as the state, 81323 as the postal code, 719-231-4411 as the home phone, and 719-888-7735 as the mobile phone.

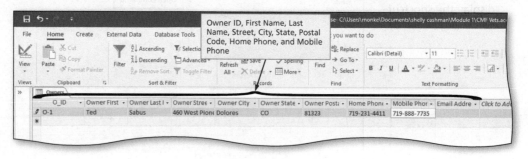

Figure 1–21

- If requested by your instructor, enter your address instead of 460 West Pioneer Road as the street. If your address is longer than 50 characters, enter the first 50 characters.

5

- Press TAB to complete the entry for the Email Address field.

- If requested by your instructor, enter your email address instead of tsabus@cengage.com in the Email Address field. If your email address is longer than 50 characters, shorten the part of the Email Address field so that it ends before the @ symbol.

- Press the TAB key to complete the entry of the first record (Figure 1–22).

Q&A How and when do I save the record?

As soon as you have entered or modified a record and moved to another record, Access saves the original record. This is different from other applications. The rows entered in an Excel worksheet, for example, are not saved until the entire worksheet is saved.

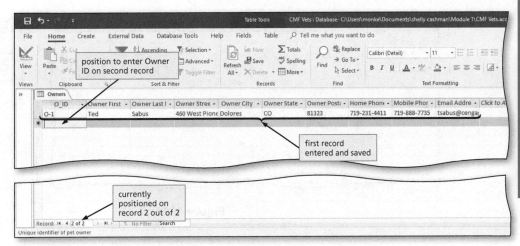

Figure 1–22

6

- Use the techniques in Steps 3 through 5 to enter the owner data (found in Figure 1–17) to complete the second record (Figure 1–23).

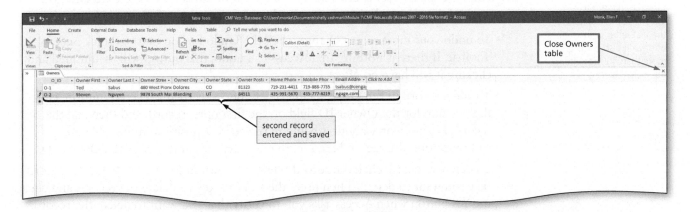

Figure 1–23

Q&A Does it matter that I entered Owner ID O-1 after I entered Owner ID O-2? Should the Owner IDs be in order?

The order in which you enter the records is not important. When you close and later reopen the table, the records will be in Owner ID order, because the Owner ID field is the primary key.

I made a mistake in entering the data. When should I fix it?

It is a good idea to fix it now, although you can fix it later as well. In any case, the following section gives you the techniques you can use to make any necessary corrections. If you want to fix it now, read that section and make your corrections before proceeding to the next step.

7

- Click the Close button for the Owners table, shown in Figure 1–23, to close the table (Figure 1–24).
- Exit Access.

Q&A Is it necessary for me to exit Access at this point?

No. The step is here for two reasons. First, you will often not be able to add all the records you need to add in one sitting. In such a case, you will add some records, and then exit Access. When you are ready to resume adding the records, you will run Access, open the table, and then continue the addition process. Second, there is a break point coming up in the module. If you want to take advantage of that break, you need to first exit Access.

clicking 'Shutter Bar Open/Close Button' opens the Navigation Pane

Owners table no longer appears

Close button for Access

Figure 1–24

Making Changes to the Data

As you enter data in the datasheet view, check your entries carefully to ensure they are correct. If you make a mistake and discover it before you press the TAB key, correct it by pressing the BACKSPACE key until the incorrect characters are removed, and then type the correct characters. If you do not discover a mistake until later, you can use the following techniques to make the necessary corrections to the data:

- To undo your most recent change, click the Undo button on the Quick Access Toolbar. If there is nothing that Access can undo, this button will be dimmed and clicking it will have no effect.

- To add a record in the Owners table, click the 'New (blank) record' button, click the position for the Owner ID field on the first open record, and then add the record. Do not worry about it being in the correct position in the table. Access will reposition the record based on the primary key, in this case, the Owner ID.

- To delete a record, click the record selector, shown in Figure 1–19, for the record that you want to delete. Then press the DELETE key to delete the record, and click the Yes button when Access asks you to verify that you want to delete the record.

- To change the contents of one or more fields in a record, the record must be on the screen. If it is not, use any appropriate technique, such as the UP ARROW and DOWN ARROW keys or the vertical scroll bar, to move to the record. If the field you want to correct is not visible on the screen, use the horizontal scroll bar along the bottom of the screen to shift all the fields until the one you want appears. If the value in the field is currently highlighted, you can simply type the new value. If you would rather edit the existing value, you must have an insertion point in the field. You can place the insertion point by clicking in the field or by pressing the F2 key. You then can use the arrow keys, the DELETE key, and the BACKSPACE key for making the correction. You can also use the INSERT key to switch between Insert and Overtype mode. When you have made the change, press the TAB key to move to the next field.

CONSIDER THIS

Duplicate Key Fields
When typing in new records, if you inadvertently type in the same key field as another record, Access will display a dialog box saying that the changes were not successful because they would create duplicate values in the index, primary key, or relationship. To correct this problem, change the primary key to a different field that has already been entered. You can then delete the record if you no longer need this.

If you cannot determine how to correct the data, you may find that you are "stuck" on the record, in which case Access neither allows you to move to another record nor allows you to close the table until you have made the correction. If you encounter this situation, simply press the ESC key. Pressing the ESC key will remove from the screen the record you are trying to add. You then can move to any other record, close the table, or take any other action you desire.

Break Point: If you wish to take a break, this is a good place to do so. You can exit Access now. To resume at a later time, run Access, open the database called CMF Vets, and continue following the steps from this location forward.

Navigation Buttons

You will often need to update tables with new records. You can open a table that already contains data and add records using a process similar to that used to add records to an empty table. The only difference is that you place the insertion point after the last record before you enter the additional data. To position the insertion point after the last record, you can use the **Navigation buttons**, which are buttons used to move within a table, found near the lower-left corner of the screen when a table is open. It is a good habit to use the 'New (blank) record' button. Once a table contains more records than will fit on the screen, it is easier to click the 'New (blank) record' button. The purpose of each Navigation button is described in Table 1–4.

Table 1–4 Navigation Buttons in Datasheet View	
Button	**Purpose**
First record	Moves to the first record in the table
Previous record	Moves to the previous record
Next record	Moves to the next record
Last record	Moves to the last record in the table
New (blank) record	Moves to the end of the table to a position for entering a new record

To Resize Columns in a Datasheet

Access assigns default column sizes, which do not always provide space to display all the data in the field. In some cases, the data might appear but the entire field name is not visible. You can correct this problem by resizing the column (changing its size) in the datasheet. In some instances, you might want to reduce the size of a column. *Why? Some fields, such as the Owner State field, are short enough that they do not require all the space on the screen that is allotted to them.* Changing a column width changes the layout, or design, of a table. The following steps resize the columns in the Owners table and save the changes to the layout.

BTW
Other AutoCorrect Options
Using the Office AutoCorrect feature, you can create entries that will replace abbreviations with spelled-out names and phrases automatically. To specify AutoCorrect rules, click File on the ribbon to open the Backstage view, click Options, and then click Proofing in the Access Options dialog box.

BTW
Enabling Content
If the database is one that you created, or if it comes from a trusted source, you can enable the content. You should disable the content of a database if you suspect that your database might contain harmful content or damaging macros.

- Run Access, unless it is already running.
- Open the CMF Vets database from your hard drive, OneDrive, or other storage location (Figure 1–25).
- If a Security Warning appears, click the Enable Content button.

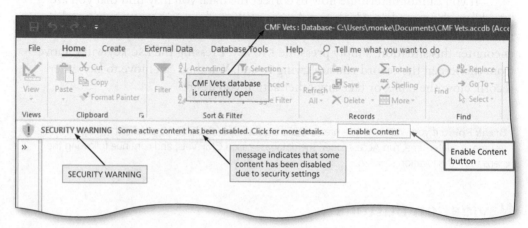

Figure 1–25

- If the Navigation Pane is closed, click the 'Shutter Bar Open/Close Button,' shown in Figure 1–24, to open the Navigation Pane (Figure 1–26).

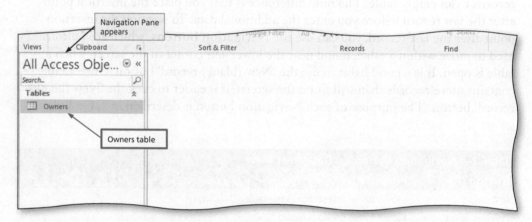

Figure 1–26

- Right-click the Owners table in the Navigation Pane to display a shortcut menu.
- Click Open on the shortcut menu to open the table in Datasheet view.

Q&A | Why do the records appear in a different order from how I entered them?
When you open the table, they are sorted in the order of the primary key. In this case, that means they will appear in Owner ID order.

- Point to the right boundary of the field selector for the Owner First Name field (Figure 1–27) so that the pointer becomes a two-headed arrow.

Q&A | I am using touch and I cannot see the pointer. Is this a problem?
It is not a problem. Remember that if you are using your finger on a touch screen, you will not see the pointer.

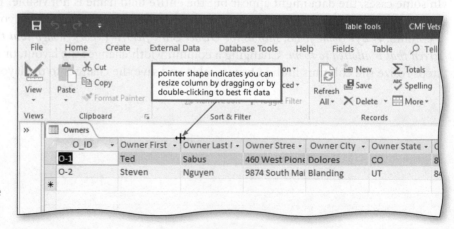

Figure 1–27

5

- Double-click the right boundary of the field selector to resize the field so that it best fits the data.

- Use the same technique to resize all the other fields to best fit the data.

- Save the changes to the layout by clicking the Save button on the Quick Access Toolbar (Figure 1–28).

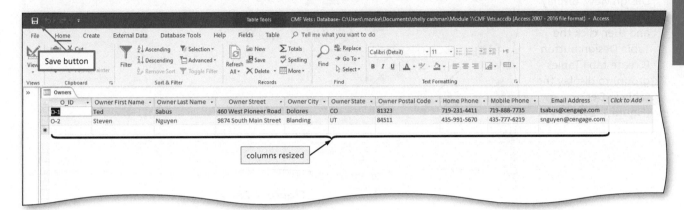

Figure 1–28

6

- Click the table's Close button (shown in Figure 1–23) to close the table.

Q&A What if I closed the table without saving the layout changes?
You would be asked if you want to save the changes.

Other Ways

1. Right-click field name, click Field Width

What is the best method for distributing database objects?

The traditional method of distributing database objects such as tables, reports, and forms uses a printer to produce a hard copy. A hard copy or printout is information that exists on a physical medium such as paper. Hard copies can be useful for the following reasons:

- Some people prefer proofreading a hard copy of a document rather than viewing it on the screen to check for errors and readability.

- Hard copies can serve as a backup reference if your storage medium is lost or becomes corrupted and you need to recreate the document. Instead of distributing a hard copy, users can distribute the document as an electronic image that mirrors the original document's appearance. The electronic image of the document can be emailed, posted on a website, or copied to a portable storage medium such as a USB flash drive. Two popular electronic image formats, sometimes called fixed formats, are PDF by Adobe Systems and XPS by Microsoft.

In Access, you can create electronic image files through the External Data tab on the ribbon. Electronic images of documents, such as PDF and XPS, can be useful for the following reasons:

- Users can view electronic images of documents without the software that created the original document (e.g., Access). Specifically, to view a PDF file, you use a program called Adobe Reader, which can be downloaded free from Adobe's website. Similarly, to view an XPS file, you use a program called XPS Viewer, which is included in the latest versions of Windows and Edge.

- Sending electronic documents saves paper and printer supplies. Society encourages users to contribute to **green computing**, which involves reducing the electricity consumed and environmental waste generated when using computers, mobile devices, and related technologies.

CONSIDER THIS

To Create a Table in Design View

The following steps use Design view to create a table. *Why? Instead of using Datasheet view, Design view is the most efficient way to create a table because you specify field name, data type, and size all in one view.*

1
- To create a table in Design view, display the Create tab, and then click the Table Design button (Create tab | Tables group) to display the table in Design view (Figure 1–29).

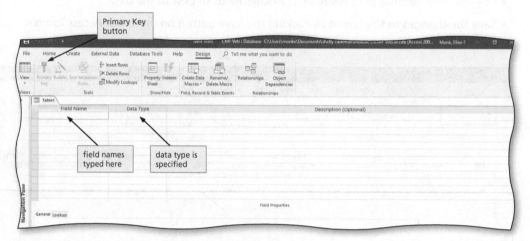

Figure 1–29

2
- Click in the empty field below Field Name, and then type **Patient ID** to enter the data for the first field. Continue entering the data for the Patients table, as shown in Figure 1–30.

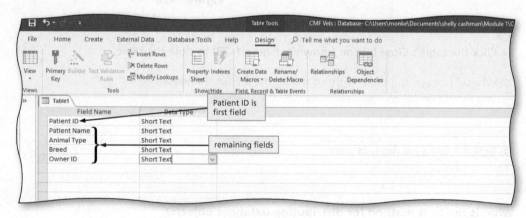

Figure 1–30

3
- Click the Patient ID row selector, if necessary, and then click the Primary Key button to assign Patient ID as the primary key field (Figure 1–31).

- Click the Save button on the Quick Access toolbar and enter **Patients** in the text box to save the table with the name, Patients.

Q&A
How do I rename a field in Design view?
In Design view, place your pointer on the end of the field you want to rename and press the BACKSPACE key until the name is removed. Enter the correct name.

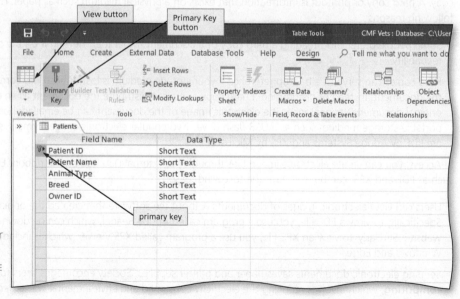

Figure 1–31

Correcting Errors in the Structure

Whenever you create or modify a table in Design view, you should check the entries carefully to ensure they are correct. If you make a mistake and discover it before you press the TAB key, you can correct the error by repeatedly pressing the BACKSPACE key until the incorrect characters are removed. Then, type the correct characters. If you do not discover a mistake until later, you can click the entry, type the correct value, and then press the ENTER key. You can use the following techniques to make changes to the structure:

- If you accidentally add an extra field to the structure, select the field by clicking the row selector (the leftmost column on the row that contains the field to be deleted). Once you have selected the field, press the DELETE key. This will remove the field from the structure.
- If you forget to include a field, select the field that will follow the one you want to add by clicking the row selector, and then press the INSERT key. The remaining fields move down one row, making room for the missing field. Make the entries for the new field in the usual manner.
- If you made the wrong field a primary key field, click the correct primary key entry for the field and then click the Primary Key button (Table Tools Design tab | Tools group).
- To move a field, click the row selector for the field to be moved to select the field, and then drag the field to the desired position.

As an alternative to these steps, you might want to start over. To do so, click the Close button for the window containing the table, and then click the No button in the Microsoft Access dialog box. You then can repeat the process you used earlier to define the fields in the table.

Populating the Patients Table

Now that you have created the Patients table, you can populate the table by entering the data in Datasheet view. Populating the table means entering data into the tables.

1 Click the View button (Table Tools Design tab | Views group) to change to Datasheet view.

2 If necessary, click the View button (Table Tools Fields tab | Views group) to confirm that you are in Datasheet view (see Figure 1–31).

3 Enter the patient data, as shown in Figure 1–32.

Patients				
Patient ID	Patient Name	Animal Type	Breed	Owner ID
C-1	Paws	Feline	Calico	O-2
C-2	Ranger	Canine	Labrador	O-1
F-1	Fluffy	Feline	Tabby	O-1

Figure 1–32

To Close the Table

Now that you have completed and saved the Patients table, you can close it. The following step closes the table.

1 Click the Close button for the Patients table (Figure 1–33) to close the table.

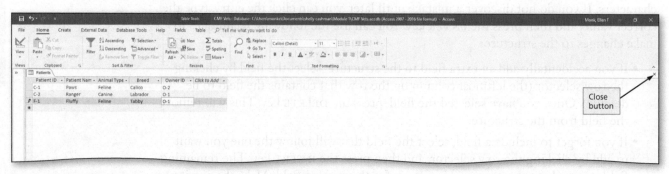

Figure 1–33

To Resize Columns in a Datasheet

BTW
Resizing Columns
To resize all columns in a datasheet to best fit simultaneously, select the column heading for the first column, hold down SHIFT and select the last column in the datasheet. Then, double-click the right boundary of any field selector.

You can resize the columns in the datasheet for the Patients table just as you resized the columns in the datasheet for the Owners table. The following steps resize the columns in the Patients table to best fit the data.

1 Open the Patients table in Datasheet view.

2 Double-click the right boundary of the field selectors of each of the fields to resize the columns so that they best fit the data.

3 Save the changes to the layout by clicking the Save button on the Quick Access Toolbar.

4 Close the table.

Importing Additional Access Database Tables into an Existing Database

Access users frequently need to import tables that contain data into an existing database. *Why? Organizations have data in tables that needs to be used in other databases. Importing tables ensures efficiency and accuracy.* In addition to owners and patients, CMF Vets must also keep track of its procedures and appointments, and the veterinarians assigned to those appointments. This information exists in another database. The following steps import three tables into the CMF Vets database.

- Open the database file Support_AC_CMF Vets Extra Tables from the Data Files and save it to the storage location specified by your instructor.
- Open the CMF Vets database.
- Click External Data on the ribbon to display the External Data tab (Figure 1–34).

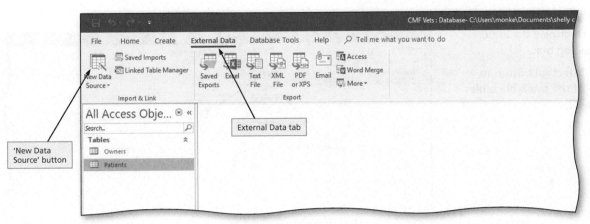

Figure 1–34

2

- Click the 'New Data Source' button (External Data tab | Import & Link group) to open a menu.

- Point to From Database to display a menu (Figure 1–35) and then click Access to display the Get External Data, Access Database dialog box.

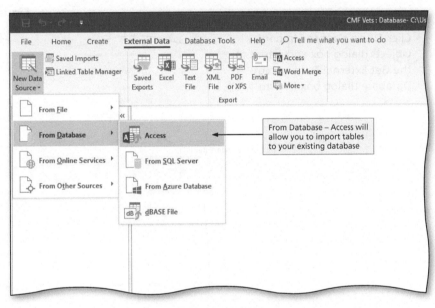

Figure 1–35

3

- Click the Browse button, and then navigate to the storage location for the CMF Vets Extra Tables file to specify the source of the data you are importing.

- Click the 'Import tables, queries, forms, reports, macros, and modules into the current database' option box to specify how and where you want to store the data. (Figure 1–36).

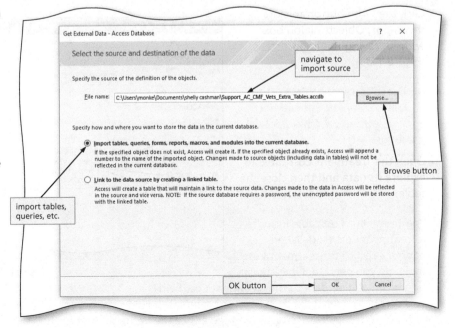

Figure 1–36

- Click OK to display the Import Objects dialog box.
- Click the Select All button to select all of the available tables (Figure 1–37).

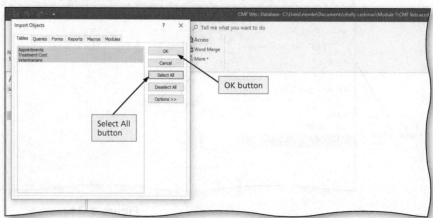
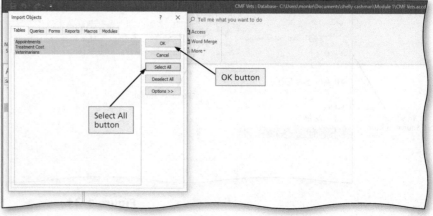

Figure 1–37

⑤
- Click OK to close the Import Objects dialog box and return to the Get External Data - Access Database dialog box (Figure 1–38)

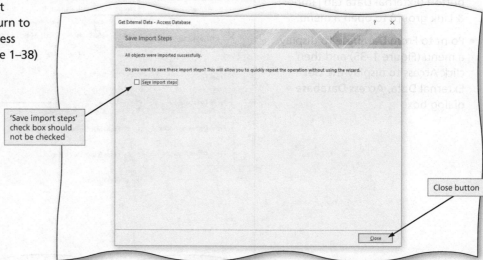

Figure 1–38

⑥
- Click the Close button to close the Import Objects dialog box without saving the Import steps (Figure 1–39).

Q&A Do I need to repeat this process?
You have completed the import and will not repeat this import procedure.

- Open the Treatment Cost table to explore its data and then close the table.

Q&A The Treatment Cost table includes a Treatment Cost field. When adding a record to Treatment Cost table, do you need to type a dollar sign when adding data to the Treatment Cost field?
You do not need to type dollar signs or commas. In addition, because the digits to the right of the decimal point are both zeros, you do not need to type either the decimal point or the zeros.

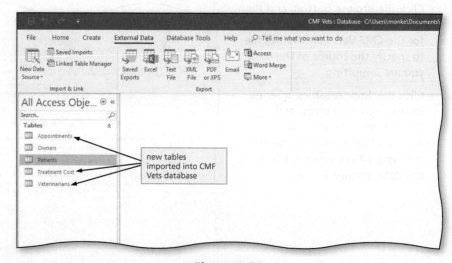

Figure 1–39

Break Point: If you wish to take a break, this is a good place to do so. You can exit Access now. To resume at a later time, start Access, open the database called CMF Vets, and continue following the steps from this location forward.

Additional Database Objects

A database contains many types of objects. Tables are the objects you use to store and manipulate data. Access supports other important types of objects as well; each object has a specific purpose that helps maximize the benefits of a database. Through queries (questions), Access makes it possible to ask complex questions concerning the data in the database and then receive instant answers. Access also allows the user to produce attractive and useful forms for viewing and updating data. Additionally, Access includes report creation tools that make it easy to produce sophisticated reports for presenting data.

BTW

Creating Queries
The Simple Query Wizard is a convenient way to create straightforward queries. It is a good method to learn about queries, although you will find that many of the queries you create require more control than the wizard provides.

Creating Queries

Queries are simply questions, the answers to which are in the database. Access contains a powerful query feature that helps you find the answers to a wide variety of questions. Once you have examined the question you want to ask to determine the fields involved in the question, you can begin creating the query. If the query involves no special sort order, restrictions, or calculations, you can use the Simple Query Wizard.

To Use the Simple Query Wizard to Create a Query

The following steps use the Simple Query Wizard to create a query that CMF Vets can use to obtain a list of their owners to send out a mailing. *Why? The Simple Query Wizard is the quickest and easiest way to create a query.* This query displays the Owner's first and last name, the street address, city, state, and postal code.

- If the Navigation Pane is closed, click the 'Shutter Bar Open/Close Button' to open the Navigation Pane.

- If necessary, click the Owners table to select it.

- Click Create on the ribbon to display the Create tab.

- Click the Query Wizard button (Create tab | Queries group) to display the New Query dialog box (Figure 1–40).

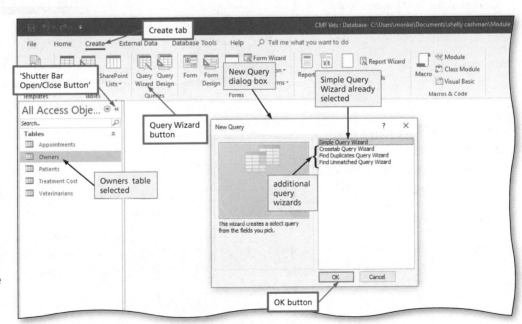

Figure 1–40

2

- Be sure Simple Query Wizard is selected, and then click OK (New Query dialog box) to display the Simple Query Wizard dialog box (Figure 1–41).

What would happen if the Patients table were selected instead of the Owners table?
The list of available fields would contain fields from the Patients table rather than the Owners table.

If the list contained Patients table fields, how could I make it contain Owners table fields?
Click the arrow in the Tables/Queries box, and then click the Owners table in the list that appears.

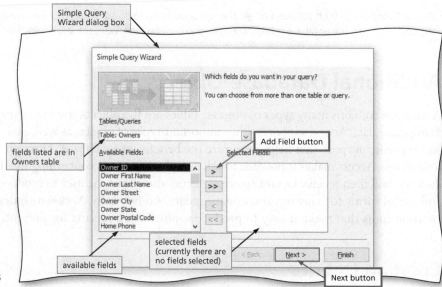

Figure 1–41

3

- If necessary, select the Owner First Name field, and then click the Add Field button to add the field to the query.

- With the Owner Last Name field selected, click the Add Field button a second time to add the field.

- Using the same technique, add the Owner Street, Owner City, Owner State, and Owner Postal Code fields (Figure 1–42).

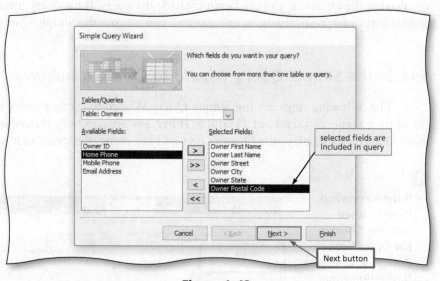

Figure 1–42

4

- Click Next to move to the next screen.

- Confirm that the title of the query is Owners Query (Figure 1–43).

What should I do if the title is incorrect?
Click the box containing the title to produce an insertion point. Erase the current title and then type Owners Query.

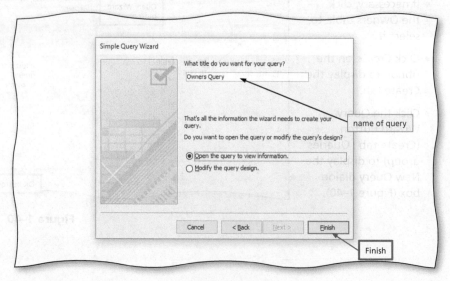

Figure 1–43

5

- Click the Finish button to create the query (Figure 1–44).

- Click the Close button for the Owners Query to remove the query results from the screen.

If I want to use this query in the future, do I need to save the query?
Normally you would. The one exception is a query created by the wizard. The wizard automatically saves the query it creates.

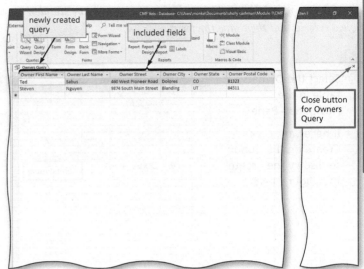

Figure 1–44

Using Queries

After you have created and saved a query, Access stores it as a database object and makes it available for use in a variety of ways:

- If you want to change the design of the query, right-click the query in the Navigation Pane and then click Design View on the shortcut menu to open the query in Design view.

- To view the results of the query from Design view, click the Run button to instruct Access to **run** the query, that is, to perform the necessary actions to produce and display the results in Datasheet view.

- To view the results of the query from the Navigation Pane, open it by right-clicking the query and clicking Open on the shortcut menu. Access automatically runs the query and displays the results in Datasheet view.

You can switch between views of a query using the View button (Home tab | Views group). Clicking the arrow in the bottom of the button produces the View button menu. You then click the desired view in the menu. The two query views you will use in this module are Datasheet view (which displays the query results) and Design view (for changing the query design). You can also click the top part of the View button, in which case you will switch to the view identified by the icon on the button. For the most part, the icon on the button represents the view you want, so you can usually simply click the button.

Creating Forms

In Datasheet view, you can view many records at once. If there are many fields, however, only some of the fields in each record might be visible at a time. In **Form view**, where data is displayed in a form on the screen, you can usually see all the fields, but only for one record.

To Create a Form

Like a paper form, a **form** in a database is a formatted document with fields that contain data. Forms allow you to view and maintain data. Forms can also be used to print data, but reports are more commonly used for that purpose. The simplest type of form in Access is one that includes all the fields in a table stacked one above the other, which can be achieved by simply clicking the Form button. The following steps use the Form button to create a form. *Why? Using the Form button is the simplest way to create this type of form. The steps use the form to view records and then save the form.*

- Select the Owners table in the Navigation Pane.

- If necessary, click Create on the ribbon to display the Create tab (Figure 1–45).

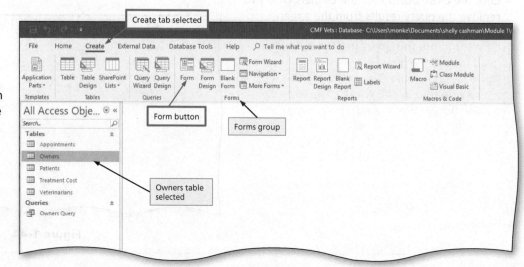

Figure 1–45

- Click the Form button (Create tab | Forms group) to create a simple form (Figure 1–46).

Q&A
A Field list appeared on my screen. What should I do?

Click the 'Add Existing Fields' button (Form Layout Tools Design tab | Tools group) to remove the Field list from the screen.

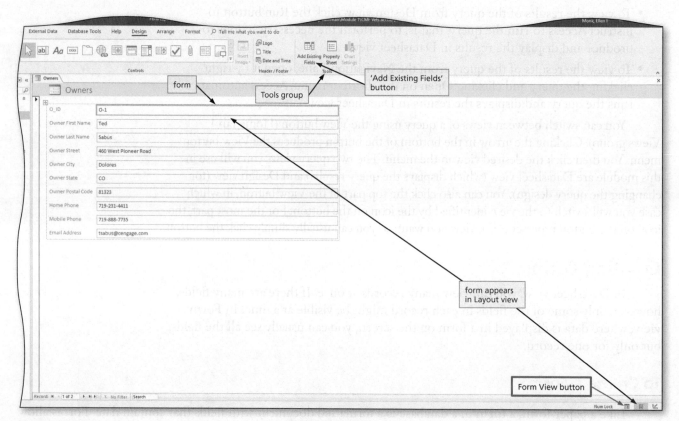

Figure 1–46

3

- Click the Form View button on the Access status bar to display the form in Form view rather than Layout view.

What is the difference between Layout view and Form view?
Layout view allows you to make changes to the look of the form. Form view is the view you use to examine or make changes to the data.

How can I tell when I am in Layout view?
Access identifies

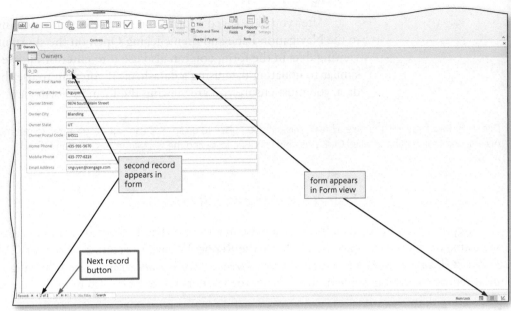

Figure 1–47

Layout view in three ways. The left side of the status bar will contain the words Layout View, shading will appear around the outside of the selected field in the form, and the Layout View button will be selected on the right side of the status bar.

- Click the Next record button once to advance through the records (Figure 1–47).

4

- Click the Save button on the Quick Access Toolbar to display the Save As dialog box (Figure 1–48).

Do I have to click the Next record button before saving?
No. The only reason you were asked to click the button was so that you could experience navigation within the form.

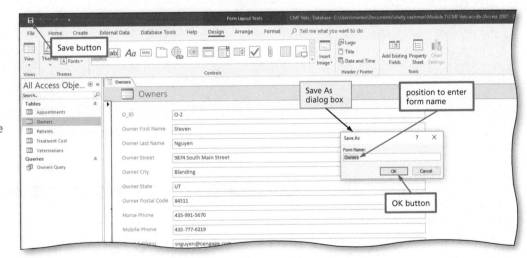

Figure 1–48

5

- Type **Owners Form** as the form name, and then click OK to save the form.

- Click Close for the form to close the form.

Other Ways

1. Click View button (Form Layout Tools Design tab | Views group)

Using a Form

After you have saved a form, you can use it at any time by right-clicking the form in the Navigation Pane and then clicking Open on the shortcut menu. In addition to viewing data in the form, you can also use it to enter or update data, a process that is similar to updating data using a datasheet. If you plan to use the form to enter or revise data, you must ensure you are viewing the form in Form view.

Break Point: If you wish to take a break, this is a good place to do so. You can exit Access now. To resume at a later time, start Access, open the database called CMF Vets, and continue following the steps from this location forward.

To Create a Report Using the Report Wizard

Reports present the data from a database in a format that is easily distributed, either as hard copy (printouts) or in other formats. You will use the Report Wizard to create a report for CMF Vets. *Why? Using the Report Wizard is an easy way to get started in creating professional reports.* The following steps create and save an initial report containing some of the fields in the Owners table. They also modify the report title.

- Be sure the Owners table is selected in the Navigation Pane.
- Click Create on the ribbon to display the Create tab (Figure 1–49).

Q&A
Do I need to select the Owners table prior to clicking Create on the ribbon?
You do not need to select the table at that point. You do need to select a table prior to clicking the Report Wizard button, because Access will include all the fields in whichever table or query is currently selected.

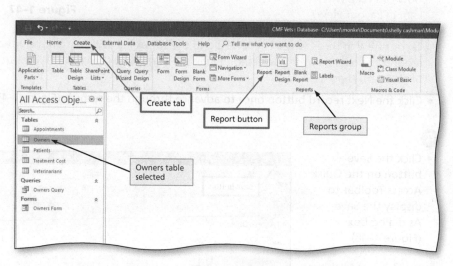

Figure 1–49

- Click the Report Wizard button (Create tab | Reports group) to display the Report Wizard dialog box (Figure 1–50).

Q&A
Why is the report title Owners?
Access automatically assigns the name of the table or query as the title of the report. It also automatically includes the date and time. You can change either of these later.

Figure 1–50

- In Available Fields area, select Owner First Name and then click the Add Field button to add the field to the Selected Fields area.

- Click the arrow button a second time to move the Owner Last Name field to the Selected Fields area.

- Move the Owner Street, Owner City, and Owner State to the Selected Fields box. (Figure 1–51)

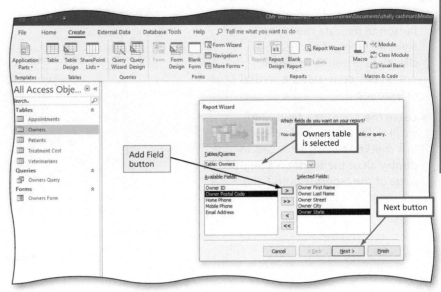

Figure 1–51

- Click Next, and select Owner State, and then click the Add Field button In the Do you want to add any grouping levels area to indicate that the report will be grouped by Owner State. (Figure 1–52).

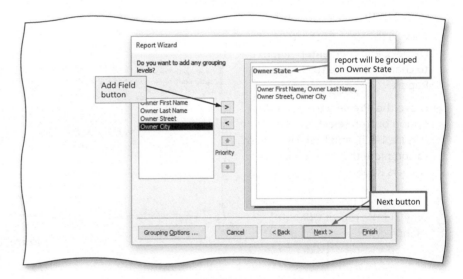

Figure 1–52

- Click Next to move to the next screen in the Report Wizard.

Q&A How do I correct a mistake I made in the Report Wizard?
The Report Wizard lets you click the Back button at any time to undo an action.

- Click Next again to move to the next screen without indicating a sort order for detail records. (Figure 1–53).

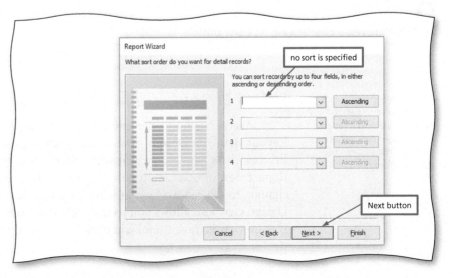

Figure 1–53

- Click the Stepped layout option button to indicate the layout style, and then, if necessary, click the Portrait Orientation option button to select a vertical orientation.

- Leave the Adjust the field width so all fields fit on a page check box checked to instruct Access to display all of the fields on a single page of the report (Figure 1–54).

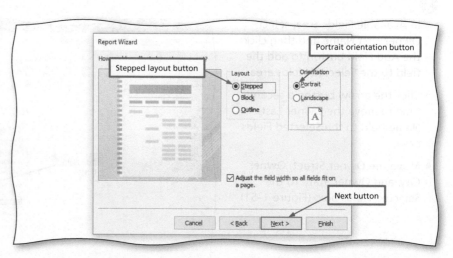

Figure 1–54

- Click Next to move to the next screen of the Report Wizard.

- Click to the right of the word, Owners, and then enter **Report** to change the title to Owners Report.

- Leave the 'Preview the report' option button selected (Figure 1–55), and then click Finish to complete the creation of the Owners Report.

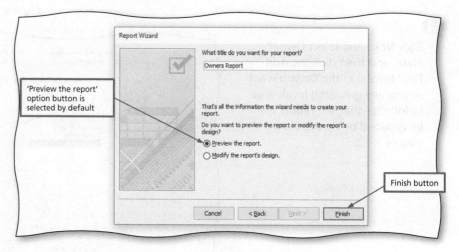

Figure 1–55

Q&A

The name of the report changed. Why did the report title not change?
The report title is assigned the same name as the report by default. Changing the name of the report does not change the report title. You can change the title at any time to anything you like.

- Close the report by clicking its Close button.

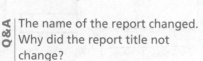

BTW
Report Navigation
When previewing a report, you can use the Navigation buttons on the status bar to move from one page to another.

Using Layout View in a Report

Access has four different ways to view reports: Report view, Print Preview, Layout view, and Design view. Report view shows the report on the screen. Print Preview shows the report as it will appear when printed. Layout view is similar to Report view in that it shows the report on the screen, but it also allows you to make changes to the report. Layout view is usually the easiest way to make such changes. Design view also allows you to make changes, but does not show you the actual report. Design view is most useful when the changes you need to make are especially complex.

Database Properties

Access helps you organize and identify your databases by using **database properties**, which are the details about a file. Database properties, also known as **metadata**, can include such information as the project author, title, or subject. **Keywords** are words or phrases that further describe the database. For example, a class name or database topic can describe the file's purpose or content.

Five different types of database properties exist, but the more common ones used in this book are standard and automatically updated properties. **Standard properties** are associated with all Microsoft Office documents and include author, title, and subject. **Automatically updated properties** include file system properties, such as the date you create or change a file, and statistics, such as the file size.

Why would you want to assign database properties to a database?
Database properties are valuable for a variety of reasons:

- Users can save time locating a particular file because they can view a file's database properties without opening the database.

- By creating consistent properties for files having similar content, users can better organize their databases.

- Some organizations require Access users to add database properties so that other employees can view details about these files.

To Change Database Properties

To change database properties, you would follow these steps.

1. Click File on the ribbon to open the Backstage view and then, if necessary, click the Info tab in the Backstage view to display the Info gallery.

2. Click the 'View and edit database properties' link in the right pane of the Info gallery to display the CMF Vets Properties dialog box.

Q&A | Why are some of the database properties already filled in?
The person who installed Office 2019 on your computer or network might have set or customized the properties.

3. If the property you want to change is displayed in the Properties dialog box, click the text box for the property and make the desired change. Skip the remaining steps.

4. If the property you want to change is not displayed in the Properties dialog box, click the appropriate tab so the property is displayed and then make the desired change.

5. Click the OK button in the Properties dialog box to save your changes and remove the dialog box from the screen.

Special Database Operations

Additional operations involved in maintaining a database are backup, recovery, compacting, and repairing.

Backup and Recovery

It is possible to damage or destroy a database. Users can enter data that is incorrect, programs that are updating the database can end abnormally during an update, a hardware problem can occur, and so on. After any such event has occurred, the database might contain invalid data or it might be totally destroyed.

BTW
Tabbed Documents Versus Overlapping Windows
By default, Access 2019 displays database objects in tabbed documents instead of in overlapping windows. If your database is in overlapping windows mode, click File on the ribbon, click Options in the Backstage view, click Current Database in the Access Options dialog box, and select the 'Display Document Tabs' check box and the Tabbed Documents option button.

Obviously, you cannot allow a situation in which data has been damaged or destroyed to go uncorrected. You must somehow return the database to a correct state. This process is called recovery; that is, you **recover** the database.

The simplest approach to recovery involves periodically making a copy of the database (called a **backup copy** or a **save copy**). This is referred to as **backing up** the database. If a problem occurs, you correct the problem by overwriting the actual database—often referred to as the **live database**—with the backup copy.

To back up the database that is currently open, you use the Back Up Database command on the Save As tab in the Backstage view. In the process, Access suggests a name that is a combination of the database name and the current date. For example, if you back up the CMF Vets database on October 20, 2021, Access will suggest the name, CMF Vets_2021-10-20. You can change this name if you desire, although it is a good idea to use this name. By doing so, it will be easy to distinguish between all the backup copies you have made to determine which is the most recent. In addition, if you discover that a critical problem occurred on October 18, 2021, you might want to go back to the most recent backup before October 18. If, for example, the database was not backed up on October 17 but was backed up on October 16, you would use CMF Vets_2021-10-16.

TO BACK UP A DATABASE

You would use the following steps to back up a database to a file on a hard drive, high-capacity removable disk, or other storage location.

1. Open the database to be backed up.
2. Click File on the ribbon to open the Backstage view, and then click the Save As tab.
3. With Save Database As selected in the File Types area, click 'Back Up Database' in the Save Database As area, and then click the Save As button.
4. Navigate to the desired location in the Save As box. If you do not want the name Access has suggested, enter the desired name in the File name text box.
5. Click the Save button to back up the database.

Access creates a backup copy with the desired name in the desired location. Should you ever need to recover the database using this backup copy, you can simply copy it over the live version.

Compacting and Repairing a Database

As you add more data to a database, it naturally grows larger. When you delete an object (records, tables, forms, or queries), the space previously occupied by the object does not become available for additional objects. Instead, the additional objects are given new space; that is, space that was not already allocated. To remove this empty space from the database, you must **compact** the database. The same option that compacts the database also repairs problems that might have occurred in the database.

TO COMPACT AND REPAIR A DATABASE

You would use the following steps to compact and repair a database.

1. Open the database to be compacted.
2. Click File on the ribbon to open the Backstage view, and then, if necessary, select the Info tab.
3. Click the 'Compact & Repair Database' button in the Info gallery to compact and repair the database.

The database now is the compacted form of the original.

Additional Operations

Additional special operations include opening another database, closing a database without exiting Access, and saving a database with another name. They also include deleting a table (or another object) as well as renaming an object.

When you are working in a database and you open another database, Access will automatically close the database that was previously open. Before deleting or renaming an object, you should ensure that the object has no dependent objects; that is, other objects that depend on the object you want to delete.

To Close a Database without Exiting Access

You would use the following steps to close a database without exiting Access.

1. Click File on the ribbon to open the Backstage view.
2. Click Close.

To Save a Database with Another Name

To save a database with another name, you would use the following steps.

1. Click File on the ribbon to open the Backstage view, and then select the Save As tab.
2. With Save Database As selected in the File Types area and Access Database selected in the Save Database As area, click the Save As button.
3. Enter a name and select a location for the new version.
4. Click the Save button.

If you want to make a backup, could you just save the database with another name?
You could certainly do that. Using the backup procedure discussed earlier is useful because doing so automatically includes the current database name and the date in the name of the file it creates.

CONSIDER THIS

To Delete a Table or Other Object in the Database

You would use the following steps to delete a database object.

1. Right-click the object in the Navigation Pane.
2. Click Delete on the shortcut menu.
3. Click the Yes button in the Microsoft Access dialog box.

To Rename an Object in the Database

You would use the following steps to rename a database object.

1. Right-click the object in the Navigation Pane.
2. Click Rename on the shortcut menu.
3. Type the new name and press the ENTER key.

To Exit Access

All the steps in this module are now complete.

1 If desired, sign out of your Microsoft account.

2 sam↑ Exit Access.

BTW
Access Help
At any time while using Access, you can find answers to questions and display information about various topics through Access Help. Used properly, this form of assistance can increase your productivity and reduce your frustration by minimizing the time you spend learning how to use Access. For instructions about Access Help and exercises that will help you gain confidence in using it, read the Office and Windows module at the beginning of this book.

Summary

In this module you have learned to create an Access database, create tables and add records to a database, import tables, create queries, create forms, create reports, and change database properties.

CONSIDER THIS

What decisions will you need to make when creating your next database?

Use these guidelines as you complete the assignments in this module and create your own databases outside of this class.

1. Identify the information you want to record in the tables.
2. Determine the fields within those tables.
3. Determine the primary key for each table.
4. Determine the data types for the fields in the table.
5. Determine additional properties for fields.
   a. Determine if a caption if warranted.
   b. Determine if a description of the field is warranted.
   c. Determine field sizes.
   d. Determine formats.
6. Determine a storage location for the database.
7. Determine any simple queries, forms, or reports needed.

Apply Your Knowledge

Reinforce the skills and apply the concepts you learned in this module.

Adding a Caption, Changing a Data Type, and Creating a Query, Form, and Report

Note: To complete this assignment, you will be required to use the Data Files. Please contact your instructor for information about accessing the Data Files.

Instructions: Financial Services provides financial planning advice to the community. The company employs a number of trained and certified financial advisors to help their clients navigate the complex world of financial investing. Financial Services has a database that keeps track of its advisors and its clients. Each client is assigned to a single advisor; each advisor may be assigned many clients. The database has two tables. The Client table contains data on the clients who use Financial Services. The Advisor table contains data on the advisors. You will add a caption, change a data type, and create a query, a form, and a report, as shown in Figure 1–56.

Perform the following tasks:

1. Start Access, open the Support_AC_Financial Services database from the Data Files, and enable the content.

2. Open the Advisor table in Datasheet view, add AU # as the caption for the Advisor Number field, and resize all columns to best fit the data. Save the changes to the layout of the table and close the table.

3. Open the Client table in Design view and change the data type for the Advisor Number field to Short Text. Change the field size for the field to 4 and add AU # as the caption for the Advisor Number field. Save the changes to the table and close the table.

4. Use the Simple Query Wizard to create a query for the Client table that contains the Client Number, Client Name, and Advisor Number. Use the name Client Query for the query and close the query.

5. Create a simple form for the Advisor table. Save the form and use the name Advisor for the form. Close the form.

6. Create the report shown in Figure 1–56 for the Client table. Move the page number so that it is within the margins. Save the report as Client Advisor Report.

7. If requested by your instructor, add your last name to the title of the report, that is, change the title to Client Advisor Report LastName where LastName is your actual last name.

8. Compact and repair the database.

9. Submit the revised database in the format specified by your instructor.

10. ✳ How would you change the field name of the Street field in the Client table to Address?

Continued >

Apply Your Knowledge *continued*

Client Advisor Report

Advisor Number	Client Name	Street	City
103			
	Kirk D'Elia	378 Stout Ave.	Carlton
	Heidi Croft	245 Beard St.	Kady
	Cindy Platt	178 Fletcher Rd.	Conradt
	Alton Repart	220 Beard St.	Kady
	Patricia Singer	254 Hartwell Dr.	Carlton
	Moss Manni	109 Fletcher Dr.	Carlton
	Carly Cohen	87 Fletcher Rd.	Conradt
120			
	Timothy Edwards	876 Redfern Rd.	Kady
	Katy Cline	255 Main St.	Kady
	Bob Schwartz	443 Cheddar St.	Kady

Figure 1–56

Extend Your Knowledge

Extend the skills you learned in this module and experiment with new skills. You may need to use Help to complete the assignment.

Using a Database Template to Create a Student Database

Instructions: Access includes both desktop database templates and web-based templates. You can use a template to create a beginning database that can be modified to meet your specific needs. You will use a template to create a Students database. The database template includes sample tables, queries, forms, and reports. You will modify the database and create the Guardians Relationship Query shown in Figure 1–57.

Perform the following tasks:

1. Run Access.
2. Select the Students template in the template gallery and create a new database with the file name Students.
3. Close the welcome dialog box, and then close the Student List form.
4. Open the Navigation Pane and change the organization to Object Type.
5. Open the Guardians table in Datasheet view and delete the Attachments field in the table. The Attachments field has a paperclip as the column heading.
6. Add the Guardian Relationship field to the end of the table. Assign the Short Text data type with a field size of 15.
7. Save the changes to the Guardians table and close the table.
8. Use the Simple Query Wizard to create the Guardian Relationship Query shown in Figure 1–57. Close the query.

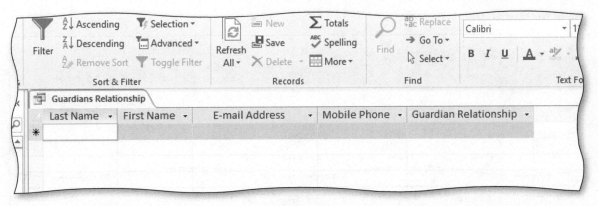

Figure 1–57

9. Open the Emergency Contact Information report in Layout view. Delete the controls containing the current date and current time in the upper-left corner of the report. Change the title of the report to Student Emergency Contact List.

10. Save the changes to the report.

11. If requested to do so by your instructor, add your first and last names to the end of the title and save the changes to the report.

12. Submit the revised database in the format specified by your instructor.

13. ✳ a. Why would you use a template instead of creating a database from scratch with just the fields you need?

   b. The Attachment data type allows you to attach files to a database record. If you were using this database to keep track of students, what specific documents might you attach to a Guardian record?

Expand Your World

Create a solution, which uses cloud and web technologies, by learning and investigating on your own from general guidance.

Problem: As a volunteer project, you and a few friends are creating a database for a local physical therapy clinic that provides therapy to the elderly in their homes. You want to be able to share query results and reports, so you have decided to store the items in the cloud. You are still learning Access, so you are going to create a sample query and the report shown in Figure 1–58, export the results, and save them to a cloud storage location, such as Microsoft OneDrive, Dropbox, or Google Drive.

Note: To complete this assignment, you will be required to use the Data Files. Please contact your instructor for information about accessing the Data Files.

Instructions:

1. Open the Support_AC_Physical Therapy database from the Data Files and enable the content.

   If your instructor wants you to submit your work as a SAM Project for automatic grading, you must download the Data Files from the assignment launch page.

2. Use the Simple Query Wizard to create a query that includes the Client Number, First Name, Last Name, and Therapist Number. Save the query as Client Query.

3. Export the Client Query as an XPS document to a cloud-based storage location of your choice.

4. Create the report shown in Figure 1–58. Save the report as Client Therapist Report.

Continued >

Expand Your World *continued*

Client Therapist Report				
Client Number	Last Name	First Name	Phone	Therapist Number
AB10	Autley	Francis	555-4321	203
BR16	Behrens	Alexa	555-6987	205
FE45	Ferdon	Jean	555-3412	207
KL12	Klingman	Cynthia	555-4576	203
MA34	Marston	Libby	555-8787	207
PR80	Priestly	Martin	555-4454	205
SA23	Sanders	Marya	555-9780	207
TR35	Teeter	Rich	555-2222	205

Figure 1–58

5. Export the Client Status Report as a PDF document to a cloud-based storage location of your choice. You do not need to change any optimization or export settings. Do not save the export steps.

6. If requested to do so by your instructor, open the Therapist table and change the last name and first name for Therapist 203 to your last name and your first name.

7. Submit the assignment in the format specified by your instructor.

8. ✳ Which cloud-based storage location did you use for this assignment? Why?

In the Lab

Design, create, modify, and/or use a database following the guidelines, concepts, and skills presented in this module. This Lab requires you to create solutions based on what you learned in the module.

Lab: Creating Objects for the Lancaster College Intramural Sports Database

Problem: Lancaster College runs an intramural sports program. One of the students attending Lancaster College is familiar with Microsoft Access and created a database to use to keep track of the program. This database keeps track of all aspects of the intramural program such as the equipment, the fields, the maintenance personnel, the coaches, the teams, the students and their participation. The database and the Coach table have been created, but the Sport field needs to be added to the table. The records shown in Figure 1–59 must be added to the Coach table. The Lancaster College Intramural Sports department would like to finish storing this data in a database and has asked you to help.

Note: To complete this assignment, you will be required to use the Data Files. Please contact your instructor for information about accessing the Data Files.

Part 1:   Open the Support_AC_1_Lab Lancaster College database from the Data Files, and enable the content. If your instructor wants you to submit your work as a SAM Project for automatic grading, you must download the Data Files from the assignment launch page. Add a field SportName to the Coach table. Assign the correct data type and a caption to the field.

Add the records shown in Figure 1–59.

Coach ID	FirstName	LastName	Office	Phone	Cell	SportName
17893	Lakisha	Black	WM-18	7178798787	7172451245	Track
18797	Bill	Brinkly	SM-1	7178798797	7175643751	Tennis
18798	Tom	Smith	SM-0	7178795467	7175432495	Wrestling
18990	William	Gutierez	WM-10	7178798789	7174597655	Football
18999	Sharon	Stone	WM-10	7178794681	7174231021	Softball
78978	Frank	Terranova	SM-10	7178798798	7172031543	Pool
78979	Gail	French	SM-12	7178792543	7172468713	Ping Pong
79798	Daniel	Costner	SM-15	7178798793	7172403120	Swimming
79879	Gary	Faulkner	SM-18	7178795432	7178965532	Soccer
82374	Jean	Epperson	JK-18	7178795402	7179845411	Basketball

Figure 1–59

Change the Student table's fields to be the correct data type and length. Add an appropriate caption to the Student ID field. Save your changes. Create a query that displays the StudentID, FirstName, LastName and Waiver, and save the query. Create the report shown in Figure 1–60 for the Coach table. Save the report.

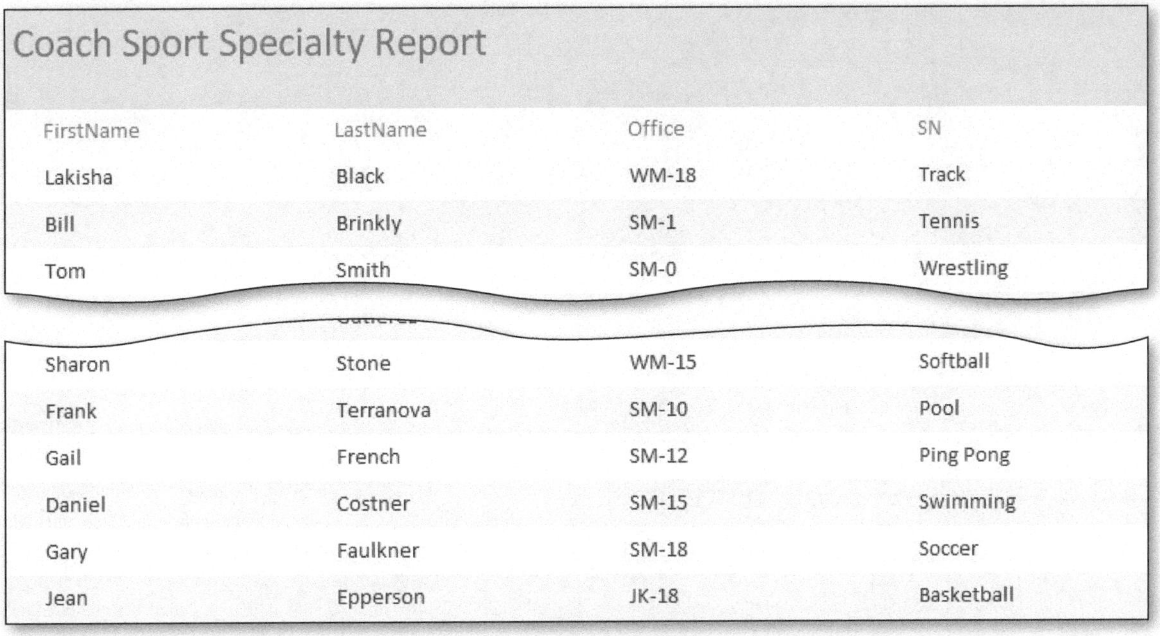

Coach Sport Specialty Report

FirstName	LastName	Office	SN
Lakisha	Black	WM-18	Track
Bill	Brinkly	SM-1	Tennis
Tom	Smith	SM-0	Wrestling
	Gutierez		
Sharon	Stone	WM-15	Softball
Frank	Terranova	SM-10	Pool
Gail	French	SM-12	Ping Pong
Daniel	Costner	SM-15	Swimming
Gary	Faulkner	SM-18	Soccer
Jean	Epperson	JK-18	Basketball

Figure 1–60

Continued >

If requested to do so by your instructor, change any data in the database to reflect your own personal information. Submit the revised database in the format specified by your instructor.

Part 2:   The Waiver and the Academic fields in the Student table are Yes/No Data Types. Why is this appropriate?

2 | Querying a Database

Objectives

You will have mastered the material in this module when you can:

- Create queries using Design view
- Include fields in the design grid
- Use text and numeric data in criteria
- Save a query and use the saved query
- Create and use parameter queries
- Use compound criteria in queries
- Sort data in queries

- Join tables in queries
- Create a report and a form from a query
- Export data from a query to another application
- Perform calculations and calculate statistics in queries
- Create crosstab queries
- Customize the Navigation Pane

Introduction

One of the primary benefits of using a database management system such as Access is having the ability to find answers to questions related to data stored in the database. When you pose a question to Access, or any other database management system, the question is called a query. A query is simply a question presented in a way that Access can process.

To find the answer to a question, you first create a corresponding query using the techniques illustrated in this module. After you have created the query, you instruct Access to run the query, that is, to perform the steps necessary to obtain the answer. Access then displays the answer in Datasheet view.

Project — Querying a Database

Examples of questions related to the data in the CMF Vets database are shown in Figure 2–1. In addition to these questions, CMF Vets managers need to find information about a patient like the animal type, such as canine or feline. The managers can use a parameter query to accomplish this task. A **parameter query** prompts you to enter a search term and then displays the results based on the search term you entered. CMF Vets managers also want to summarize data in a specific way, such as by animal type or treatment cost, which might involve performing calculations, and they can use a crosstab query to present the data in the desired form.

In this module, you will learn how to create and use the queries shown in Figure 2–1.

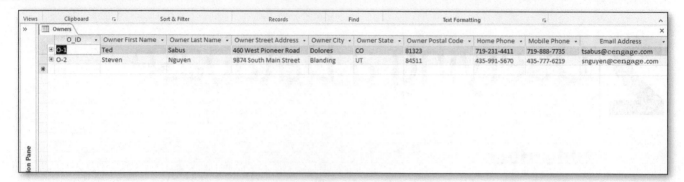

Figure 2–1a Pet Owner Addresses

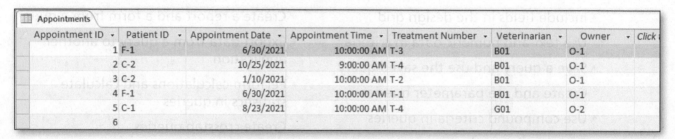

Figure 2–1b Appointment Dates and Times

Figure 2–1c Treatments and their Costs

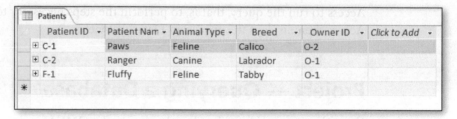

Figure 2–1d Patient Names, Types, and Breeds

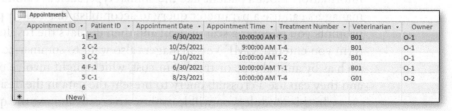

Figure 2–1e Owners and Pet Treatments

Figure 2–1f Pet Owners and Their Contact Information

Figure 2–1g Veterinarians

Figure 2–1h Treatments for Pets

Creating Queries

As you learned previously, you can use queries in Access to find answers to questions about the data contained in the database. *Note:* In this module, you will save each query example. When you use a query for another task, such as to create a form or report, you will assign a specific name to a query, for example, Manager-Appointments Query. In situations in which you will not use the query again, you will assign a name using a convention that includes the module number and a query number, for example, m02q01. Queries are numbered consecutively.

To Add Records to the Database

Because the practice continues to grow, with new patients and their owners coming to CMF Vets for care, the managers need to add records to reflect the growth of the business. The following steps open the Owners, Patients, and Veterinarians tables and add data.

1 Open the Owners table in Datasheet view, and then close the Navigation Pane.

2 Click the open cell below O-2 to enter a new owner ID. Enter the data for owner O-3, Liz O'Brien, as shown in Figure 2–2a.

new owners to be added to Owners table

Figure 2–2a

3 Enter the data for the additional owners shown in Figure 2-2a.

4 Close the Owners table.

5 Open the Patients table in Datasheet view, and then close the Navigation Pane.

6 Click the open cell below Patient ID to enter an ID for Patient P-1, Pepper. Enter Pepper's information as shown in Figure 2–2b.

7 Change the Patient ID numbers for the existing patients so that they are consistent with Figure 2–2b.

8 Enter the data for the remaining patients as shown in the figure.

9 Close the Patients table.

patients in Patients table

Figure 2–2b

10 Open the Veterinarians table in Datasheet view, and then close the Navigation Pane.

11 Click the open cell below Gomez to enter a new veterinarian last name. Enter the data for Calvin Bennett as shown in Figure 2–2c, and then enter the data for Mia Rahn-Lee.

12 Close the Veterinarians table.

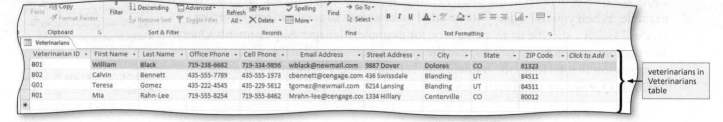

veterinarians in Veterinarians table

Figure 2–2c

To Create a Query in Design View

You have already used the Simple Query Wizard to create a query. Most of the time, however, you will use Design view, which is the primary option for creating queries. *Why? Once you have created a new query in Design view, you have more options than with the wizard and can specify fields, criteria, sorting, calculations, and so on.* The following steps create a new query in Design view.

1

- **sam'** ✦ Start Access and open the database named CMF Vets from your hard drive, OneDrive, or other storage location.

- Click the 'Shutter Bar Open/Close Button' to close the Navigation Pane.

- Click Create on the ribbon to display the Create tab (Figure 2–3).

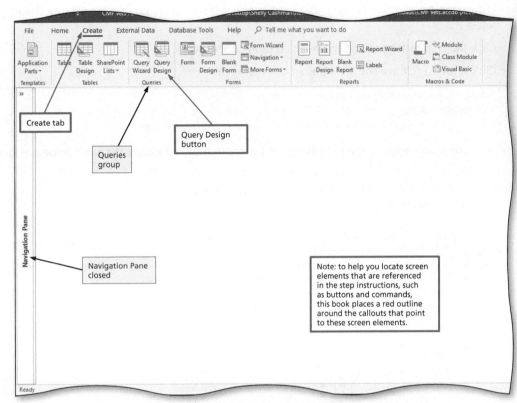

Figure 2–3

2

- Click the Query Design button (Create tab | Queries group) to create a new query (Figure 2–4).

Q&A Is it necessary to close the Navigation Pane?
No. Closing the pane gives you more room for the query, however, so it is usually a good practice.

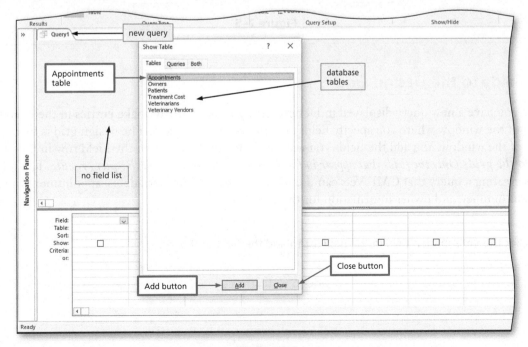

Figure 2–4

3
- Ensure the Appointments table (Show Table dialog box) is selected. If it is not, click the Appointments table to select it.
- Click the Add button to add the selected table to the query.
- Click Close to remove the dialog box from the screen.

Q&A What if I inadvertently add the wrong table?

Right-click the table that you added in error and click Remove Table on the shortcut menu. You also can just close the query, indicate that you do not want to save it, and then start over.

- Drag the lower edge of the field list down far enough so all fields in the table appear (Figure 2–5).

Q&A Is it essential that I resize the field list?

No. You can always scroll through the list of fields using the scroll bar. Resizing the field list so that all fields appear is usually more convenient.

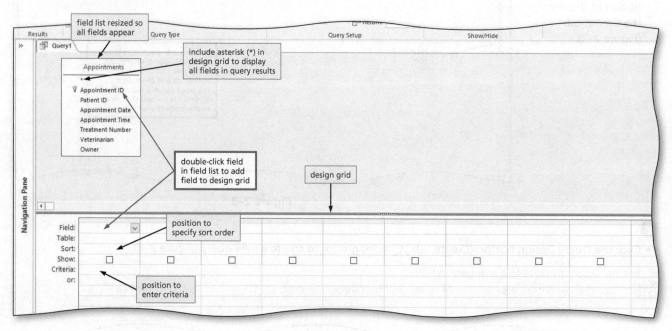

Figure 2–5

To Add Fields to the Design Grid

Once you have a new query displayed in Design view, you are ready to make entries in the **design grid**, the portion of the window where you specify fields and criteria for the query. The design grid is located in the lower pane of the window. You add the fields you want included in the query to the Field row in the grid. **Why add fields to the grid?** *Only the fields that appear in the design grid are included in the query results.* The following step begins creating a query that CMF Vets can use to obtain the appointment dates, appointment times, patient ID, treatment number, and owner information for the veterinarians.

1
- Double-click the Veterinarian field in the field list to add the field to the query.

Q&A What if I add the wrong field?

Click just above the field name in the design grid to select the column, and then press DELETE to remove the field.

- Double-click the Appointment Date field in the field list to add the field to the query.

- Add the Appointment Time, Patient ID, Treatment Number, and Owner fields to the query (Figure 2–6).

Q&A

What if I want to include all fields? Do I have to add each field individually?
No. Instead of adding individual fields, you can double-click the asterisk (*) to add the asterisk to the design grid. The asterisk is a shortcut indicating all fields are to be included.

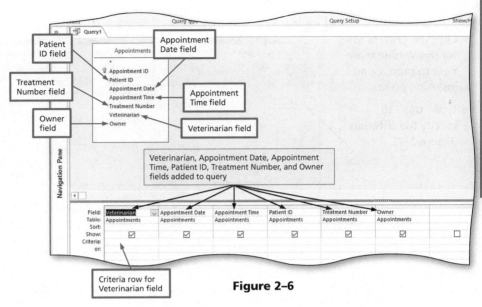

Figure 2–6

Determining Criteria

When you use queries, usually you are looking for those records that satisfy some criterion. For example, you might want to see appointment dates, appointment times, patient ID, types of treatments, and owner information for one of the veterinarians. You enter criteria in the Criteria row in the design grid below the field name to which the criterion applies. For example, to find appointments for Dr. Gomez, you first must add the Veterinarian field to the design grid. For ease of typing, the veterinarians were given ID numbers, for example, Dr. Teresa Gomez's ID is G01, and Dr. William Black's ID is B01. Therefore, when you enter the Veterinarian ID, you will only need to type G01 or B01 in the Criteria row. For example, you only need to type G01 for Gomez in the Criteria row below the Veterinarian field.

Running the Query

After adding the appropriate fields and defining the query's criteria, you must run the query to get the results. To view the results of the query from Design view, click the Run button to instruct Access to run the query, that is, to perform the necessary actions to produce and display the results in Datasheet view.

To Use Text Data in a Criterion

To use **text data** (data in a field whose data type is Short Text) in criteria, simply type the text in the Criteria row below the corresponding field name, just as you did previously. In Access, you typically do not need to enclose text data in quotation marks as you do in many other database management systems. *Why? Access will enter the quotation marks automatically, so you can simply type the desired text.* The following steps finish creating a query that CMF Vets managers might use to obtain Dr. Gomez's appointment dates, appointment times, patient IDs, types of treatments, and pet owner information. These steps also save the query.

BTW
Touch Screen Differences
The Office and Windows interfaces may vary if you are using a touch screen. For this reason, you might notice that the function or appearance of your touch screen differs slightly from this module's presentation.

BTW
Access Screen Resolution
If you are using a computer or mobile device to step through the project in this module and you want your screens to match the figures in this book, you should change your screen's resolution to 1366 × 768.

1

- Click the Criteria row for the Veterinarian field to produce an insertion point.

- Type `G01` to specify the criterion (Figure 2–7).

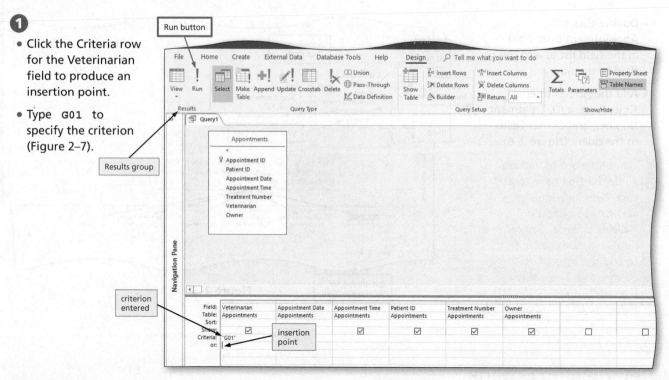

Figure 2–7

2

- Click the Run button (Query Tools Design tab | Results group) to run the query (Figure 2–8) and display Dr. Gomez's appointments.

Q&A Can I also use the View button in the Results group to run the query?

Yes. You can click the View button to view the query results in Datasheet view.

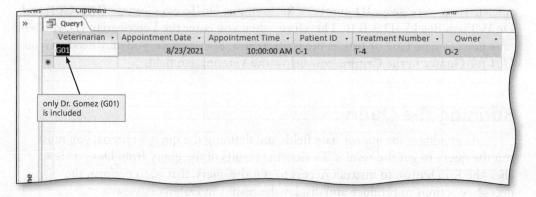

Figure 2–8

3

- Click the Save button on the Quick Access Toolbar to display the Save As dialog box.

- Type `m02q01` as the name of the query (Figure 2–9).

Q&A Can I also save from Design view?

Yes. You can save the query when you view it in Design view just as you can save it when you view query results in Datasheet view.

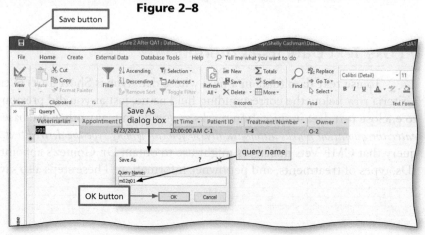

Figure 2–9

4
- Click OK (Save As dialog box) to save the query (Figure 2–10), and then click Close for the m02q01 query to close the query.

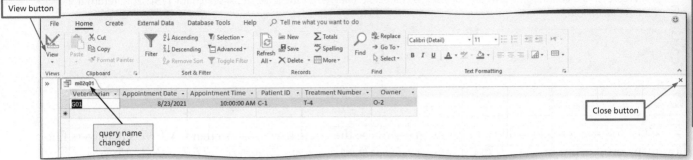

Figure 2–10

Other Ways

1. Right-click query tab, click Save on shortcut menu or Press CTRL+S.

Using Saved Queries

After you have created and saved a query, you can use it in a variety of ways:

- To view the results of a query that is not currently open, open it by right-clicking the query in the Navigation Pane and clicking Open on the shortcut menu.
- If you want to change the design of a query that is already open, return to Design view and make the changes.
- If you want to change the design of a query that is not currently open, right-click the query in the Navigation Pane and then click Design View on the shortcut menu to open the query in Design view.
- To print the results with a query open, click File on the ribbon, click the Print tab in the Backstage view, and then click Quick Print.
- To print a query without first opening it, be sure the query is selected in the Navigation Pane and click File on the ribbon, click the Print tab in the Backstage view, and then click Quick Print.
- You can switch between views of a query using the View button (Home tab | Views group). Clicking the arrow at the bottom of the button produces the View button menu. You then click the desired view in the menu. The two query views you use in this module are Datasheet view (to see the results) and Design view (to change the design). You can also click the top part of the View button, in which case you will switch to the view identified by the icon on the button. In Figure 2–10, the View button displays the icon for Design view, so clicking the button would change to Design view. For the most part, the icon on the button represents the view you want, so you can usually simply click the button.

Wildcards

Microsoft Access supports wildcards. **Wildcards** are symbols that represent any character or combination of characters. One common wildcard, the **asterisk (*)**, represents any collection of characters. Another wildcard symbol is the **question mark (?)**, which represents any individual character.

BTW

The Ribbon and Screen Resolution
Access may change how the groups and buttons within the groups appear on the ribbon, depending on the computer or mobile device's screen resolution. Thus, your ribbon may look different from the ones in this book if you are using a screen resolution other than 1366 × 768.

BTW

Organizing Files and Folders
You should organize and store files in folders so that you easily can find the files later. For example, if you are taking an introductory computer class called CIS 101, a good practice would be to save all Access files in an Access folder in a CIS 101 folder.

What does S* represent? What does T?m represent?

S* represents the letter, S, followed by any collection of characters. A search for S* might return System, So, or Superlative. T?m represents the letter, T, followed by any single character, followed by the letter, m. A search for T?m might return the names Tim or Tom.

To Use a Wildcard

The following steps modify an existing query to use the asterisk wildcard so that CMF Vets managers find how many owners live in Utah. *Why? Because you do not know how many characters will follow the U, the asterisk wildcard symbol is appropriate.* The steps also save the query with a new name using Save As.

1

- Open the Owners Query in Design View.

- Click the Criteria row below the Owner State field to produce an insertion point.

- If there were any existing data in the Criteria row, you would use the DELETE or BACKSPACE key. But, since there is no existing criteria, you can simply type the criteria.

- Type U* as the criterion (Figure 2–11).

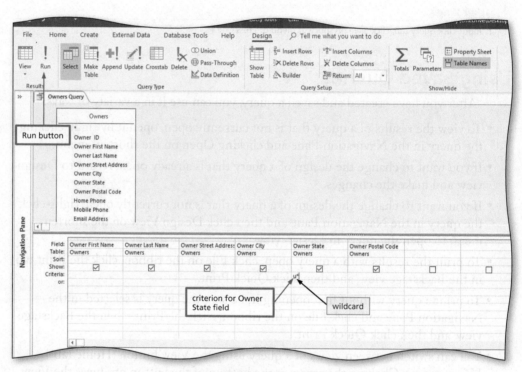

Figure 2–11

2

- Run the query by clicking the Run button (Query Tools Design tab | Results group) (Figure 2–12).

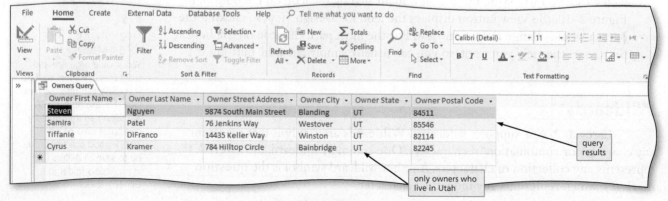

Figure 2–12

⌕ Experiment

- Change the letter U to lowercase in the criterion and run the query to determine whether case makes a difference when entering a wildcard.

❸

- Click File on the ribbon to open the Backstage view.
- Click the Save As tab in the Backstage view to display the Save As gallery.
- Click 'Save Object As' in the File Types area (Figure 2–13).

Q&A The text I entered is now preceded by the word, Like. What happened?

Criteria that include wildcards need to be preceded by the word, Like. However, you do not have to type it; Access adds the word automatically to any criterion involving a wildcard.

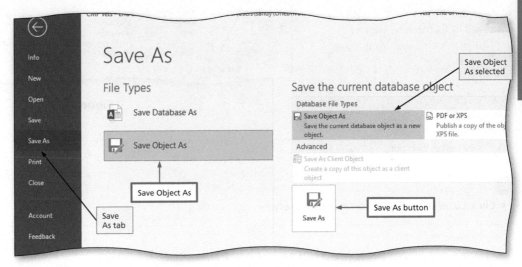

Figure 2–13

Can I just click the Save button on the Quick Access Toolbar as I did when saving the previous query?

If you clicked the Save button, you would replace the previous query with the version you just created. Because you want to save both the previous query and the new one, you need to save the new version with a different name. To do so, you must use Save Object As, which is available through the Backstage view.

❹

- With Save Object As selected in the File Types gallery, click the Save As button to display the Save As dialog box.
- Erase the name of the current query and type `m02q02` as the name for the saved query (Figure 2–14).

Q&A The current entry in the As text box is Query. Could I save the query as some other type of object?

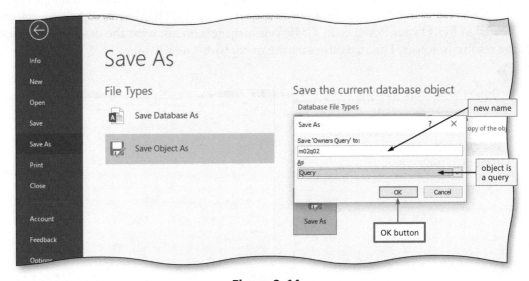

Figure 2–14

Although you usually would want to save the query as another query, you can also save it as a form or report by changing the entry in the As text box. If you do, Access would create either a simple form or a simple report for the query.

- Click OK (Save As dialog box) to save the query with the new name and close the Backstage view (Figure 2–15).

Q&A How can I tell that the query was saved with the new name?
The new name will appear on the tab.

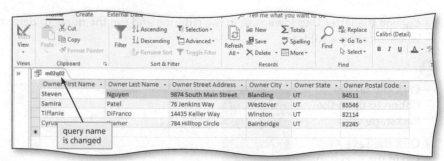

Figure 2–15

Other Ways

1. Click Design View button on status bar

- Click Close for m02q02 to close the query.

To Use Criteria for a Field Not Included in the Results

In some cases, you might require criteria for a particular field that should not appear in the results of the query. For example, you may want to see the Mobile Phone number for all Owners located in the 813 Owners Postal code in an Owners Query. The criteria involve the Owners Postal field, but you do not want to include the Owners Postal Code field in the results since this information is sensitive and you do not want everyone viewing the query to see this information.

To enter a criterion for the Owner Postal Code field, it must be included in the design grid. Normally, it would then appear in the results. To prevent this from happening, remove the check mark from its check box in the Show row of the grid. **Why?** *A check mark in the Show check box instructs Access to show the field in the result. If you remove the check mark, you can use the field in the query without displaying it in the query results.*

The following steps modify a previous query so that CMF Vets managers can select only those customers located in 813 Owner Postal code. CMF Vets managers do not want the owner postal code field to appear in the results, however. The steps also save the query with a new name.

- Open the Owners Query in Design view.

- Type `813*` as the criterion for the Owner Postal Code field (Figure 2–16).

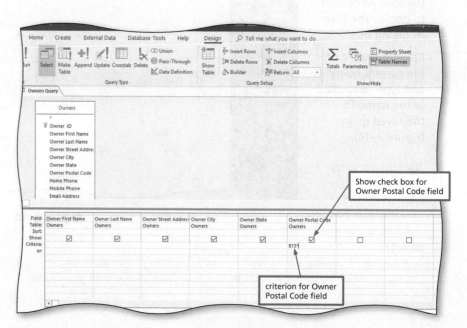

Figure 2–16

2

- Click the Show check box for the Owner Postal Code field to remove the check mark (Figure 2–17).

Q&A
Could I have removed the check mark before entering the criterion?
Yes. The order in which you perform the two operations does not matter.

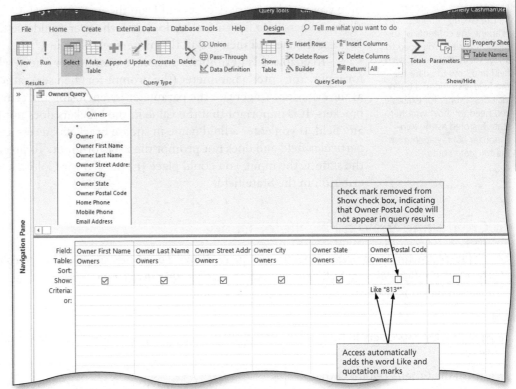

Figure 2–17

3

- Run the query (Figure 2–18).

🔍 **Experiment**

- Click the View button to return to Design view, enter a different Postal Code, such as 821*, as the criterion, and run the query. Repeat this process with additional Postal Codes, including at least one Postal Code

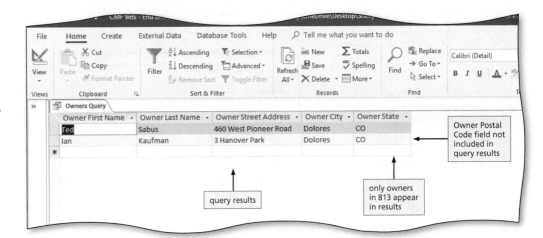

Figure 2–18

that is not in the database. When finished, remove the Owner Postal Code Criteria field and then close the query without saving the changes.

Creating a Parameter Query

If you wanted to find owners that lived in Colorado or Utah, you would either have to create a new query or modify the existing query by replacing CO with UT as the criterion. Rather than giving a specific criterion when you first create the query, occasionally you may want to be able to enter part of the criterion when you run the query and then have the appropriate results appear. For example, you might want a

BTW
Designing Queries
Before creating queries,
examine the contents of the
tables involved. You need to
know the data type for each
field and how the data for
the field is stored. If a query
includes a state, for example,
you need to know whether
state is stored as the two-
character abbreviation or as
the full state name.

query to return the owners and their associated states, specifying a different state each time you run the query. A user could run the query, enter CO as the state, and then see all the owners who live in Colorado. Later, the user could use the same query but enter UT as the state and then see all the owners who live in Utah.

To enable this flexibility, you create a parameter query, which prompts the user for input. You enter a parameter (the prompt for the user) rather than a specific value as the criterion. You create the parameter by enclosing the criterion value in square brackets. It is important that the value in the brackets does not match the name of any field. If you enter a field name in square brackets, Access assumes you want that particular field and does not prompt the user for input. To prompt the user to enter the state as the input, you could place [Enter CO for Colorado or UT for Utah] as the criterion in the State field.

To Create and View a Parameter Query

The following steps create a parameter query. ***Why?*** *The parameter query will give managers at CMF Vets the ability to enter a different state each time they run the query rather than having a specific state as part of the criterion in the query.* The steps also save the query with a new name.

- Open the Owners Query in Design view.

- Click in the Criteria cell for Owner State and enter [Enter CO for Colorado or UT for Utah] as the new criterion (Figure 2–19).

Q&A

What is the purpose of the square brackets?

The square brackets indicate that the text entered is not text that the value in the column must match. Without the brackets, Access would search for records in which the state is Enter CO for Colorado or UT for Utah.

What if I typed a field name in the square brackets?

Access would simply use the value in that field. To create a parameter query, you must not use a field name in the square brackets.

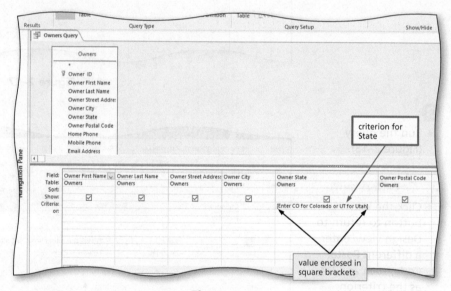

Figure 2–19

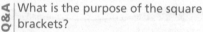

- Click the Run button (Query Tools Design tab | Results group) to display the Enter Parameter Value dialog box (Figure 2–20).

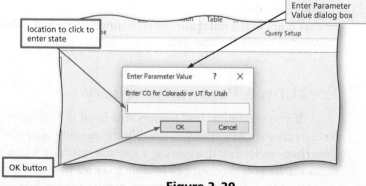

Figure 2–20

- Type CO as the parameter value in the Enter Parameter Value text box, and then click OK (Enter Parameter Value dialog box) to close the dialog box and view the query (Figure 2–20).

Experiment

- Try using other characters between the square brackets. In each case, run the query. When finished, change the characters between the square brackets back to Enter CO for Colorado or UT for Utah.

4

- Click File on the ribbon to open the Backstage view.

- Click the Save As tab in the Backstage view to display the Save As gallery.

- Click 'Save Object As' in the File Types area.

- With Save Object As selected in the File Types area, click the Save As button to display the Save As dialog box.

only accounts from Colorado are included

Figure 2–21

- Type Owner-State Query as the name for the saved query.

- Click OK (Save As dialog box) to save the query with the new name and close the Backstage view (Figure 2–21).

5

- Click Close for the Owner-State Query to close the query.

Break Point: If you wish to take a break, this is a good place to do so. You can exit Access now. To resume later, start Access, open the database called CMF Vets, and continue following the steps from this location forward.

To Use a Parameter Query

You use a parameter query like any other saved query. You can open it or you can print the query results. In either case, Access prompts you to supply a value for the parameter each time you use the query. If changes have been made to the data since the last time you ran the query, the results of the query may be different, even if you enter the same value for the parameter. *Why? In addition to the ability to enter different field values each time the parameter query is run, the query always uses the data that is currently in the table.* The following steps use the parameter query named Owner-State Query.

- Open the Navigation Pane.

- Right-click the Owner-State Query to produce a shortcut menu.

- Click Open on the shortcut menu to open the query and display the Enter Parameter Value dialog box (Figure 2–22).

Q&A

The title bar for my Navigation Pane contains Tables and Related Views rather than All Access Objects as it did previously. What should I do?
Click the Navigation Pane arrow and then click 'All Access Objects'.

I do not have the Search bar at the top of the Navigation Pane that I had previously. What should I do?
Right-click the Navigation Pane title bar arrow to display a shortcut menu, and then click Search Bar.

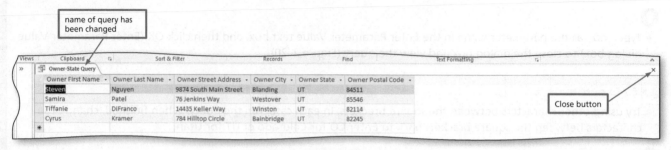

Figure 2–22

- Type   UT   in the Enter CO for Colorado or UT for Utah text box, and then click OK (Enter Parameter Value dialog box) to display the results, as shown in Figure 2–22.
- Close the query.

To Use a Number in a Criterion

To enter a number in a criterion, type the number without any dollar signs or commas. *Why? If you enter a dollar sign, Access assumes you are entering text. If you enter a comma, Access considers the criterion invalid.* The following steps create a query that CMF Vets managers might use to display all treatments whose current price is $25. The steps also save the query with a new name.

- Close the Navigation Pane.
- Click Create on the ribbon to display the Create tab.
- Click the Query Design button (Create tab | Queries group) to create a new query.
- If necessary, click the Treatment Cost table (Show Table dialog box) to select the table.
- Click the Add button to add the selected table to the query.
- Click Close to remove the dialog box from the screen.
- Drag the lower edge of the field list down far enough so all fields in the list are displayed.

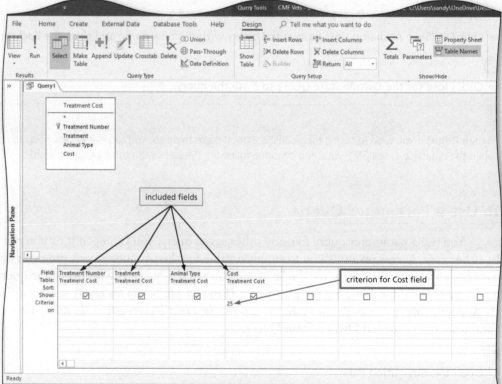

Figure 2–23

- Include the Treatment Number, Treatment, Animal Type, and Cost fields in the query.
- Type   25   as the criterion for the Cost field (Figure 2–23).

Q&A   Do I need to enter a dollar sign and decimal point?
No. Access will interpret 25 as $25 because the data type for the Cost field is currency.

- Run the query (Figure 2–24).

Q&A Why did Access display the results as $25.00 when I only entered 25?
Access uses the format for the field to determine how to display the result. In this case, the format indicated that Access should include the dollar sign, decimal point, and two decimal places.

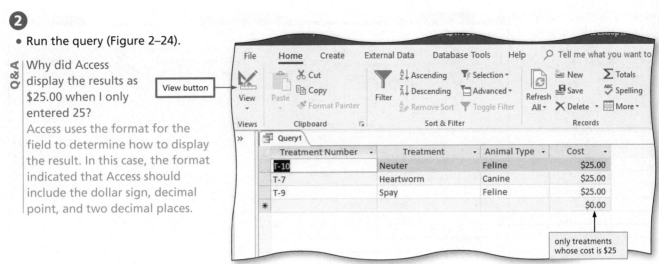

Figure 2–24

- Save the query as m02q03.

Q&A How do I know when to use the Save button to save a query or use the Backstage view to perform a Save As?
If you are saving a new query, the simplest way is to use the Save button on the Quick Access Toolbar. If you are saving changes to a previously saved query but do not want to change the name, use the Save button. If you want to save a previously saved query with a new name, you must use the Backstage view and perform a Save Object As.

- Close the query.

Comparison Operators

Unless you specify otherwise, Access assumes that the criteria you enter involves equality (exact matches). In the last query, for example, you were requesting those treatments that cost $25. In other situations, you might want to find a range of results; for example, you could request appointments whose appointment date is greater than 06/30/2021. If you want a query to return something other than an exact match, you must enter the appropriate **comparison operator**. The comparison operators are > (greater than), < (less than), >= (greater than or equal to), <= (less than or equal to), and NOT (not equal to).

To Use a Comparison Operator in a Criterion

The following steps use the > operator to create a query that CMF Vets managers might use to find all appointments whose appointment date is after 6/30/2021. *Why? A date greater than 6/30/2021 means the date comes after 7/1/2021 when both veterinarians are scheduled for vacations.* The steps also save the query with a new name.

1

- Start a new query using the Appointments table.

- Include the Appointment Date, Appointment Time, Treatment Number, Veterinarian, and Patient ID fields.

- Type >6/30/2021 as the criterion for the Appointment Date field (Figure 2–25).

Q&A Why did I not have to type the leading zero in the Month portion of the date?
It is fine as you typed it. You also could have typed 06/30/2021. Some people often type the day using two digits even if the date is a single digit as the numbers 1 through 9. You also could have typed a leading zero for both the month and the day: 06/30/2021.

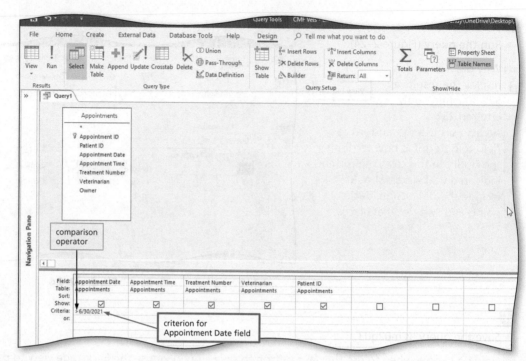

Figure 2–25

2

- Run the query (Figure 2–26).

🔍 **Experiment**

- Return to Design view. Try a different criterion involving a comparison operator in the Appointment Date field and run the query. When finished, return to Design view, enter the original criterion (>6/30/2021) in the Start Date field, and run the query.

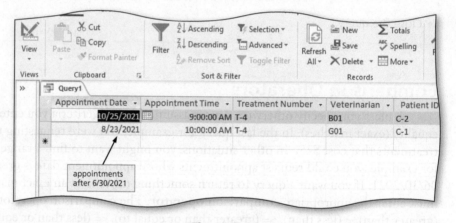

Figure 2–26

Q&A I returned to Design view and noticed that Access changed >6/30/2021 to >#6/30/2021#. Why does the date now have number signs around it?
This is the date format in Access. You usually do not have to enter the number signs because in most cases Access will insert them automatically.

My records are in a different order. Is this a problem?
No. The important thing is which records are included in the results. You will see later in this module how you can specify the specific order you want for cases when the order is important.

Can I use the same comparison operators with text data?
Yes. Comparison operators function the same whether you use them with number fields, currency fields, date fields, or text fields. With a text field, comparison operators use alphabetical order in making the determination.

 3

- Save the query as m02q04.
- Close the query.

Using Compound Criteria

Often your search data must satisfy more than one criterion. This type of criterion is called a **compound criterion** and is created using the words AND or OR.

In an **AND criterion**, each individual criterion must be true in order for the compound criterion to be true. For example, an AND criterion would allow you to find appointments after 6/30/2021 that are treated by Veterinarian B01.

An **OR criterion** is true if either individual criterion is true. An OR criterion would allow you to find appointments after 6/30/2021 or appointments that have Veterinarian B0l . In this case, any appointment after 6/30/2021 or whose Veterinarian is B01 will both be displayed.

BTW
**Queries:
Query-by-Example**
Query-By-Example, often referred to as QBE, was a query language first proposed in the mid-1970s. In this approach, users asked questions by filling in a table on the screen. The Access approach to queries is based on Query-by-Example.

To Use a Compound Criterion Involving AND

To combine criteria with AND, place the criteria on the same row of the design grid. *Why? Placing the criteria in the same row indicates that both criteria must be true in Access.* It is important to note that sometimes when you view the results of a query, there are no records that meet the criterion entered. At this point, you might want to check to be certain the criterion was entered correctly. And, if the criterion is entered correctly, it becomes easier to trust the results even though you might have expected another result. The following steps use an AND criterion to enable CMF Vets managers to find those appointments with an appointment date after 06/30/2021 and the Veterinarian B01. The steps also save the query.

- Start a new query using the Appointments table.
- Include the Appointment Date, Appointment Time, Treatment Number, Veterinarian, and Owner fields. ·
- Type >06/30/2021 as the criterion for the Appointment Date field.
- Type B01 as the criterion for the Veterinarian field (Figure 2–27).

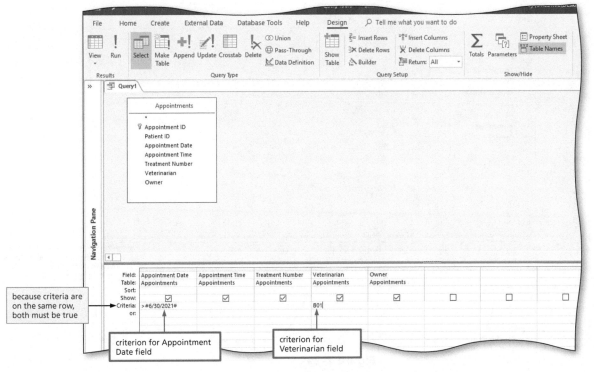

Figure 2–27

- Run the query (Figure 2–28) and Notice that Veterinarian B01 does have an appointment after 6/30/2021.

- Save the query as m02q05.

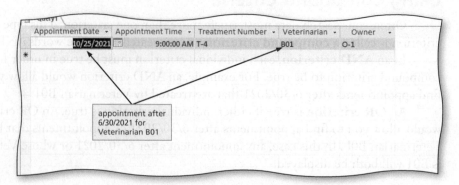

Figure 2–28

To Use a Compound Criterion Involving OR

To combine criteria with OR, each criterion must go on separate rows in the Criteria area of the grid. *Why? Placing criteria on separate rows indicates at least one criterion must be true in Access and also shows true if both criterion are true.* The following steps use an OR criterion to enable CMF Vets managers to find those Appointments who have an Appointment Date greater than 6/30/2021 or Appointments for B01. The steps also save the query with a new name.

- Return to Design view.
- If necessary, click the Criteria entry for the Veterinarian field and delete any existing text.
- Click the or row (the row below the Criteria row) for the Veterinarian field, delete any existing text if necessary, and then enter B01 as the entry (Figure 2–29).

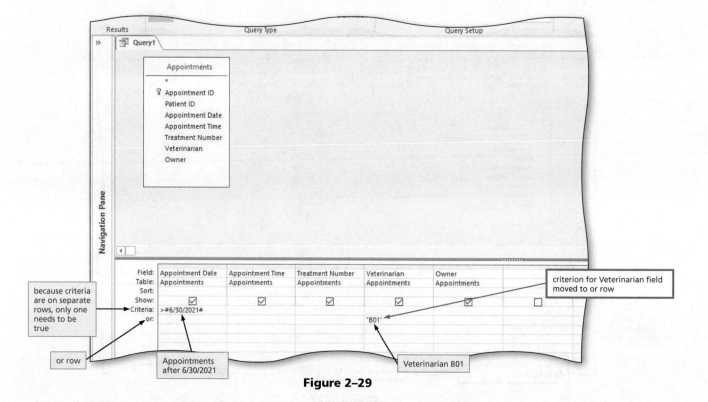

Figure 2–29

• Run the query (Figure 2–30).

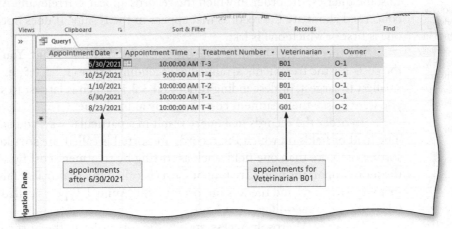

Figure 2–30

• Use Save As to save the query as m02q06.

Special Criteria

You can use three special criteria in queries:

1. If you want to create a criterion involving a range of values in a single field, you can use the **AND operator**. You place the word AND between the individual conditions. For example, if you wanted to find all Treatments whose cost is greater than or equal to $20 and less than or equal to $35, you would enter >= 20 AND <= 35 as the criterion in the Treatment Cost column.

2. You can select values in a given range by using the **BETWEEN operator**. This is often an alternative to the AND operator. For example, to find all appointments between 1/10/2021 and 10/25/2021, inclusive, you would enter BETWEEN 1/10/2021 AND 10/25/2021 as the criterion in the Appointment Date column. This is equivalent to entering >=1/10/2021 and <=10/25/2021.

3. You can select a list of values by using the **IN operator**. You follow the word IN with the list of values in parentheses. For example, to find the owners that live in Colorado (CO) **or** Utah (UT) you would enter IN ('CO', 'UT'). Unlike when you enter a simple criterion, you must enclose text values in quotation marks. The IN operator is like the OR operator, but it returns multiple values.

BTW
Rearranging Fields in a Query
To move a field in the design grid, click the column selector for the field to select the field and drag it to the appropriate location.

How would you find owners who live in Colorado or Utah without using the IN operator?
Place the text CO in the Criteria row of the State column. Place the text UT in the or row of the State column.

CONSIDER THIS

Sorting

In some queries, the order in which the records appear is irrelevant. All you need to be concerned about are the records that appear in the results. It does not matter which one is first or which one is last.

In other queries, however, the order can be very important. You may want to see the costs for the treatments arranged in ascending order (1,2,3,4,5,on so on), which is smallest to largest, or descending order (5,4,3,2,1, which is largest to smallest. Perhaps you want to see the treatment costs listed by animal type.

To order the records in a query result in a particular way, you **sort** the records. The field or fields on which the records are sorted is called the **sort key**. If you are sorting on more than one field (such as sorting by treatment cost by animal type), the more important field (Treatment Cost) is called the **major key** (also called the **primary sort key**) and the less important field (Animal Type) is called the **minor key** (also called the **secondary sort key**).

To sort in Microsoft Access, specify the sort order in the Sort row of the design grid below the field that is the sort key. If you specify more than one sort key, the sort key on the left will be the major sort key, and the one on the right will be the minor key.

To Clear the Design Grid

Why? *If the fields you want to include in the next query are different from those in the previous query, it is usually simpler to start with a clear grid, that is, one with no fields already in the design grid.* You always can clear the entries in the design grid by closing the query and then starting over. A simpler approach to clearing the entries is to select all the entries and then press the DELETE key. The following steps return to Design view and clear the design grid.

- If necessary, click the Design View button to display m02q06 in Design view.

- Click just above the Appointment Date column heading in the grid to select the column.

Q&A
I clicked above the column heading, but the column is not selected. What should I do?
You did not point to the correct location. Be sure the pointer changes into a down-pointing arrow, and then click again.

- Press and hold SHIFT and click just above the Owner column heading to select all the columns (Figure 2–31).

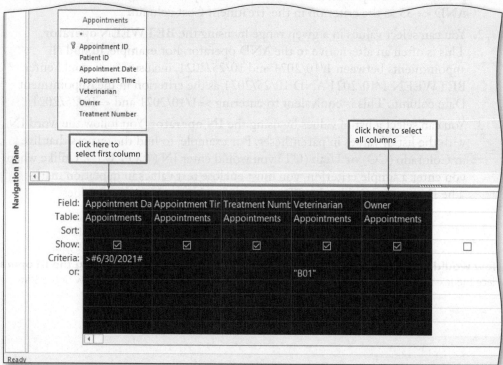

Figure 2–31

2

• Press DELETE to clear the design grid.

3

• Close the query without saving these changes.

To Import a Table

CMF Vets requires additional data to be able to run some of its required queries. As you learned previously, you can import data from external sources. The following steps import the Veterinary Vendors table from the CMF Vets Extra Tables database.

1 Open the Support_AC_CMF_Vets Extra Tables database from the Data Files on your hard drive, OneDrive, or other storage location, and then click the External Data tab. You should now have both databases open in Access.

2 With the CMF Vets database already open, click the 'New Data Source button' (External Data tab | Import & Link group).

3 Click From Database in the New Data Source menu, and then click Access to display the Get External Data - Access Database dialog box.

4 Click the Browse button and navigate to your storage location for the file, Support_AC_CMF_Vets Extra Tables.

5 Select Support_AC_CMF_Vets Extra Tables, and then click the Open button to select it as the data source.

6 If necessary, click the 'Import tables, queries, forms, reports, macros, and modules Into the current database' option button to indicate how and where to store the data in the current database

7 Click OK to display the Import Objects dialog box.

8 Select the Veterinary Vendors table to indicate the file to import, and then click OK to import the table.

9 Close the Get External Data – Access Database dialog box without saving the import steps.

10 Click Close and confirm that the Veterinary Vendors table is listed as a table object in the Navigation Pane.

To Sort Data in a Query

If you determine that the query results should be sorted, you will need to specify the sort key. The following steps sort the costs in the Treatment Cost table by indicating that the Cost field is to be sorted. The steps specify Ascending sort order. *Why? When sorting numerical data, Ascending sort order arranges the results in ascending order.*

• Create a new query based on the Treatment Cost table.

• Include the Treatment and Cost fields in the design grid.

• Click the Sort row in the Cost field column, and then click the Sort arrow to display a menu of possible sort orders (Figure 2–32).

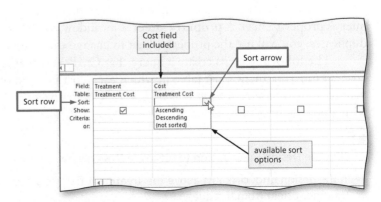

Figure 2–32

2

- Click Ascending to select the sort order (Figure 2–33).

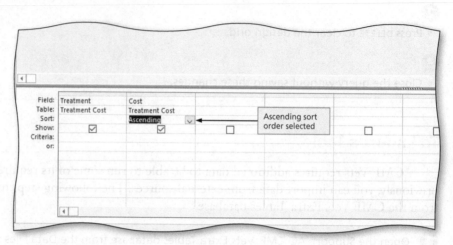

Ascending sort order selected

Figure 2–33

3

- Run the query (Figure 2–34) to display the treatment costs sorted in ascending order (lowest to highest).

- Save the query as m02q07.

Experiment

- Return to Design view and change the sort order to Descending. Run the query. Return to Design view and change the sort order back to Ascending. Run the query.

Q&A
Why do some costs appear more than once?
The same cost is associated with various treatments for felines and canines.

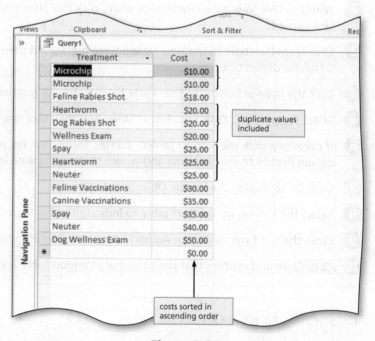

duplicate values included

costs sorted in ascending order

Figure 2–34

To Omit Duplicates

When you sort data, duplicates normally are included. In the query shown in Figure 2–34, for example, $20 appears more than once. Several other costs appear multiple times as well. You eliminate duplicates using the query's property sheet. A **property sheet** is a window containing the various properties of the object. To omit duplicates, you will use the property sheet to change the Unique Values property from No to Yes.

The following steps create a query that CMF Vets managers might use to obtain a sorted list of the costs in the Treatment Cost table in which each cost is listed only once. *Why? Unless you wanted to know how many costs are in the Treatment Cost table, the duplicates typically do not add any value.* The steps also save the query with a new name.

1

- Click the Design View button to return to Design view.

- In the design grid, click just above the Treatment field to select the field and then click DELETE to remove the Treatment field from the query.

- Click the second field (the empty field to the right of Cost) in the design grid to produce an insertion point.

- If necessary, click Design on the ribbon to display the Design tab.

- Click the Property Sheet button (Query Tools Design tab | Show/Hide group) to display the property sheet (Figure 2–35).

Q&A My property sheet looks different. What should I do?

If your sheet looks different, close the property sheet and repeat this step.

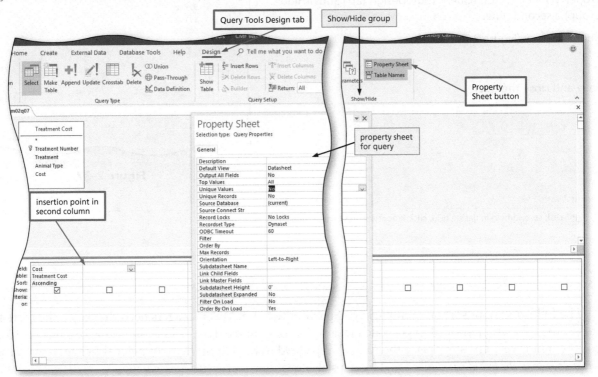

Figure 2–35

2

- Click the Unique Values property box, and then click the Unique Values arrow to display a list of available choices (Figure 2–36).

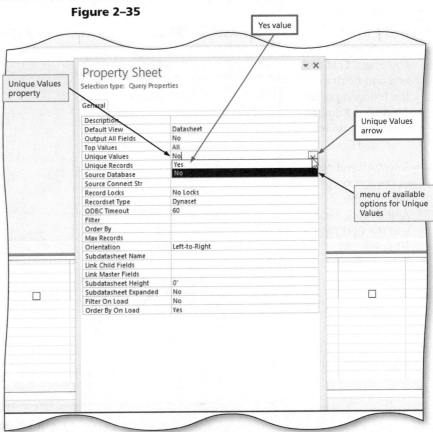

Figure 2–36

- Click Yes to indicate that the query will return unique values, which means that each value will appear only once in the query results.

- Close the Query Properties property sheet by clicking the Property Sheet button (Query Tools Design tab | Show/Hide group) a second time.

- Run the query (Figure 2–37).

- Save and close the query.

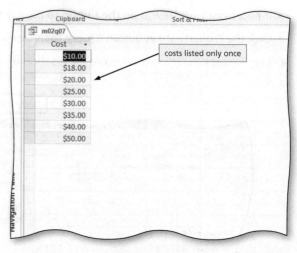

Figure 2–37

Other Ways

1. Right-click second field in design grid, click Properties on shortcut menu

To Sort on Multiple Keys

The following steps sort on multiple keys. Specifically, CMF Vets managers need the data to be sorted by Cost (low to high) within Animal Type, which means that the Animal Type field is the major key and the Cost field is the minor key. The steps place the Animal Type field to the left of the Cost field. *Why? In Access, the major key must appear to the left of the minor key.* The steps also save the query with a new name.

- Create a new query based on the Treatment Cost table and add fields in the following order: Treatment Number, Treatment, Animal Type, and Cost.

- Select Ascending as the sort order for both the Animal Type field and the Cost field (Figure 2–38).

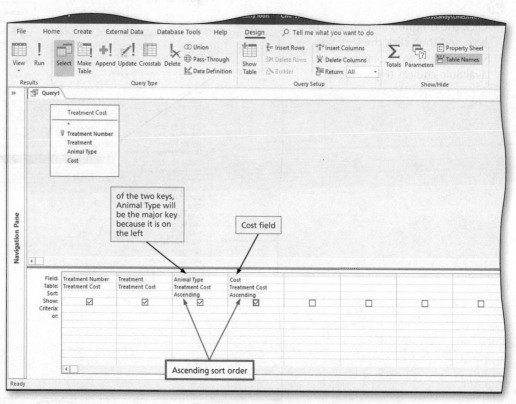

Figure 2–38

2

- Run the query (Figure 2–39) to display the treatment costs sorted first by animal type and then by cost.

 Experiment

- Return to Design view and try other sort combinations for the Animal Type and Cost fields, such as Descending for Animal Type and Ascending for Cost. In each case, run the query to see the effect of the changes. When finished, select Ascending as the sort order for both fields.

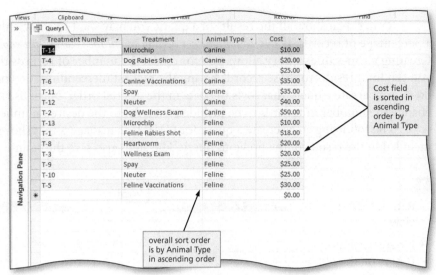

Figure 2–39

Q&A What if the Cost field is to the left of the Animal Type field?
It is important to remember that the major sort key must appear to the left of the minor sort key in the design grid. If you attempted to sort by Cost within Animal Type but placed the Cost field to the left of the Animal Type field, your results would not accurately represent the intended sort.

3

- Save the query as m02q08.

Is there any way to sort the records in this same order, but have the Cost field appear to the left of the Animal Type field in the query results?
Yes. Remove the check mark from the Animal Type field, and then add an additional Animal Type field at the end of the query. The first Animal Type field will be used for sorting but will not appear in the results. The second will appear in the results but will not be involved in the sorting process.

How do you approach the creation of a query that might involve sorting?
Examine the query or request to see if it contains words such as *order* or *sort*. Such words imply that the order of the query results is important. If so, you need to sort the query.

- If sorting is required, identify the field or fields on which the results are to be sorted. In the request, look for language such as *ordered by* or *sort the results by*, both of which would indicate that the specified field is a sort key.

- If using multiple sort keys, determine the major and minor keys. If you are using two sort keys, determine which one is the more important, or the major key. Look for language such as *view treatment costs within each animal type*, which implies that the overall order is by animal type. In this case, the Animal Type field would be the major sort key and the Cost field would be the minor sort key.

- Determine sort order. Words such as *increasing*, *ascending*, or *low-to-high* imply Ascending order. Words such as *decreasing*, *descending*, or *high-to-low* imply Descending order. Sorting in *alphabetical order* implies Ascending order. If there were no words to imply a particular order, you would typically use Ascending.

- Examine the query or request to see if there are any special restrictions. One common restriction is to exclude duplicates. Another common restriction is to list only a certain number of records, such as the first five records.

CONSIDER THIS

CONSIDER THIS

To Create a Top-Values Query

Rather than show all the results of a query, you may want to show only a specified number of records or a percentage of records. ***Why?*** *You might not need to see all the records, just enough to get a general idea of the results.* Creating a **top-values query** allows you to restrict the number of records that appear. When you sort records, you can limit results to those records having the highest (descending sort) or lowest (ascending sort) values. To do so, first create a query that sorts the data in the desired order. Next, use the Return box on the Design tab to change the number of records to be included from All to the desired number or percentage.

The following steps create a query for CMF Vets managers that shows only the first five records that were included in the results of the previous query. The steps also save the resulting query with a new name.

1

- Return to Design view.

- If necessary, click Design on the ribbon to display the Design tab.

- Click the Return arrow (Query Tools Design tab | Query Setup group) to display the Return menu (Figure 2–40).

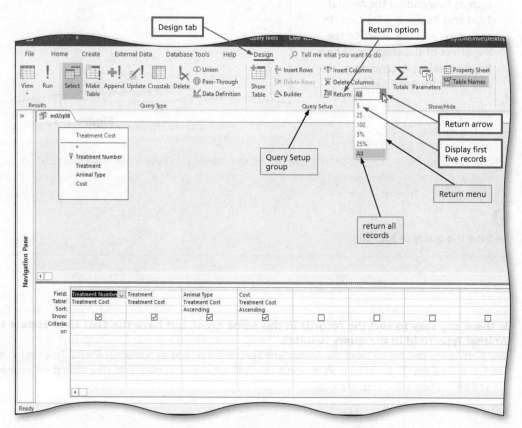

Figure 2–40

2

- Click 5 in the Return menu to specify that the query results should contain the first five rows.

Q&A Could I have typed the 5? What about other numbers that do not appear in the list?
Yes, you could have typed the 5. For numbers not appearing in the list, you must type the number.

- Run the query (Figure 2–41) to display only the first five records.

Figure 2–41

- Save the query as m02q09.

- Close the query.

Do I need to close the query before creating my next query?
Not necessarily. When you use a top-values query, however, it is important to change the value in the Return box back to All. If you do not change the Return value back to All, the previous value will remain in effect. Consequently, you might not get all the records you should in the next query. A good practice whenever you use a top-values query is to close the query as soon as you are done. That way, you will begin your next query from scratch, which ensures that the value is reset to All.

Joining Tables

In designing a query, you need to determine whether more than one table is required. For example, if the question being asked involves data from both the Appointments and Treatment Cost tables, then both tables are required for the query. For example, you might want a query that shows the appointment dates (from the Appointments table) along with the cost of the treatment and animal type (from the Treatment Cost table). Both the Appointments and Treatment Cost tables are required for this query. You need to **join** the tables to find records in the two tables that have identical values in matching fields (Figure 2–42). In this example, you need to find records in the Appointments table that have the same value in the Treatment Cost fields.

BTW
Ad Hoc Relationships
When you join tables in a query, you are creating an ad hoc relationship, that is, a relationship between tables created for a specific purpose and not a permanent change. To create general-purpose relationships, you use the Relationships window.

BTW
Join Types
The type of join that finds records from both tables that have identical values in matching fields is called an inner join. An inner join is the default join in Access. Outer joins are used to show all the records in one table as well as the common records; that is, the records that share the same value in the join field. In a left outer join, all rows from the table on the left are included. In a right outer join, all rows from the table on the right are included.

Appointments Table

Appointment ID	Patient ID	Appointment Date	Appointment Time	Treatment Number	Veterinarian	Owner
1	F-1	6/30/2021	10:00 AM	T-3	B01	O-1
2	C-2	10/25/2021	9:00 AM	T-4	B01	O-1
3	C-2	1/10/2021	10:00 AM	T-2	B01	O-1
4	F-1	6/30/2021	10:00 AM	T-1	B01	O-1
5	C-1	8/23/2021	10:00 AM	T-4	G01	O-2

for each appointment date, give the Treatment, Animal Type, and Cost

Treatment Cost Table

Treatment Number	Treatment	Animal Type	Cost
T-1	Feline Rabies Shot	Feline	$18
T-10	Neuter	Feline	$25
T-11	Spay	Canine	$35
T-12	Neuter	Canine	$40
T-13	Microchip	Feline	$10
T-14	Microchip	Canine	$10
T-2	Dog Wellness Exam	Canine	$50
T-3	Wellness	Feline	$20
T-4	Dog Rabies Shot	Canine	$20
T-5	Feline Vaccinations	Feline	$30
T-6	Canine Vaccinations	Canine	$35
T-7	Heartworm	Canine	$25
T-8	Heartworm	Feline	$20
T-9	Spay	Feline	$25

Figure 2–42

To Join Tables

If you have determined that you need to join tables, you first will bring field lists for both tables to the upper pane of the query window while working in Design view. Access will draw a line, called a **join line**, between matching fields in the two tables, indicating that the tables are related. You then can select fields from either table. Access joins the tables automatically.

The first step is to create a new query and add the Appointments table to the query. Then, add the Treatment Cost table to the query. A join line should appear, connecting the Treatment Number fields in the two field lists. ***Why might the join line not appear?*** *If the names of the matching fields differ from one table to the other, Access will not insert the line. You can insert it manually, however, by clicking one of the two matching fields and dragging the pointer to the other matching field.*

The following steps create a query to display information from both the Appointments table and the Treatment Cost table.

- Click the Query Design button (Create tab | Queries group) to create a new query.
- If necessary, click the Appointments table (Show Table dialog box) to select the table.
- Click the Add button (Show Table dialog box) to add a field list for the Appointments Table to the query (Figure 2–43).

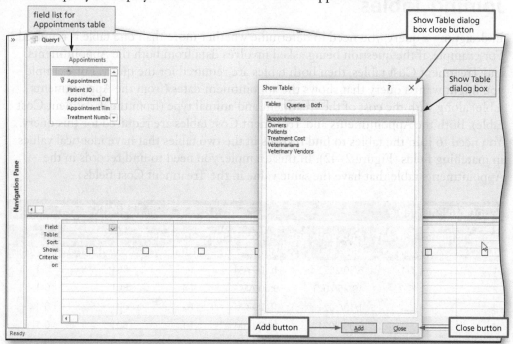

Figure 2–43

- Click the Treatment Cost table (Show Table dialog box).
- Click the Add button (Show Table dialog box) to add a field list for the Treatment Cost table.
- Close the Show Table dialog box by clicking its Close button.
- Expand the size of the two field lists so all the fields in the Appointments and Treatment Cost tables appear (Figure 2–44).

Q&A I did not get a join line. What should I do?
Ensure that the names of the matching fields are the same, the data types are the same, and the matching field is the primary key in one of the two tables. If all of these factors are true and you still do not have a join line, you can produce one by pointing to a matching field and dragging to the other matching field.

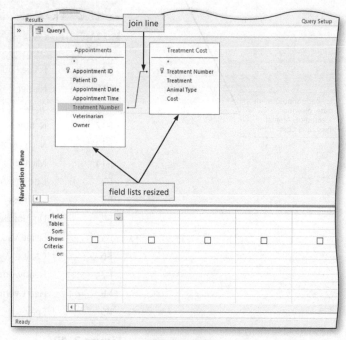

Figure 2–44

3

• In the design grid, include the Appointment Date field from the Appointments Table as well as the Treatment, Animal Type, and Cost fields from the Treatment Cost Table.

• Select Ascending as the sort order for both the Appointment Date field and the Treatment field (Figure 2–45).

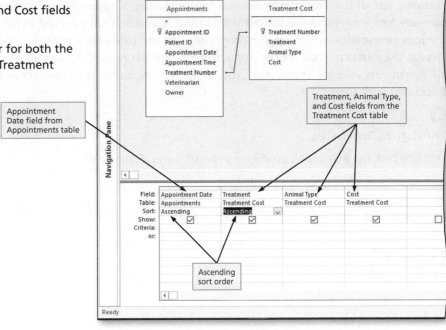

Figure 2–45

4

• Run the query (Figure 2–46).

5

• Click the Save button on the Quick Access Toolbar to display the Save As dialog box.

• Enter `Appointments and Treatments` as the query name.

• Click OK (Save As dialog box) to save the query.

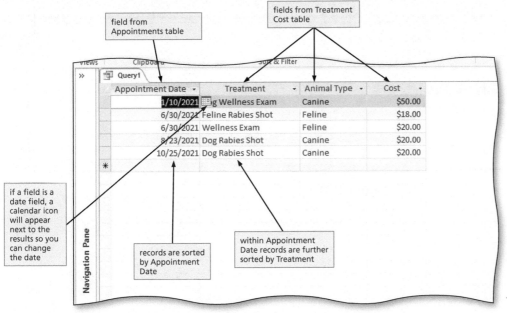

Figure 2–46

BTW

Join Line
If you do not get a join line automatically, there might be a problem with one of your table designs. Open each table in Design view and make sure that the data types are the same for the matching field in both tables and that one of the matching fields is the primary key in a table. If not, correct these errors and create the query again.

To Change Join Properties

Normally, records that do not match the query conditions do not appear in the results of a join query. For example, not all the Treatments, Animal Types, and Costs appear in the results. *Why? Not all of the treatments currently have an appointment associated with them.* To cause such a record to be displayed, you need to change the **join properties**, which are the properties that indicate which records appear in a join. The following steps change the join properties of the Appointments and Treatments Query so that CMF Vets managers can include all Treatments, Animal Types, and Costs in the results, rather than only those fields that have Appointments associated with them.

- Return to Design view.

- Right-click the join line to produce a shortcut menu (Figure 2–47).

Q&A I do not see Join Properties on my shortcut menu. What should I do?
If Join Properties does not appear on your shortcut menu, you did not point to the appropriate portion of the join line. You will need to point to the correct (middle) portion and right-click again.

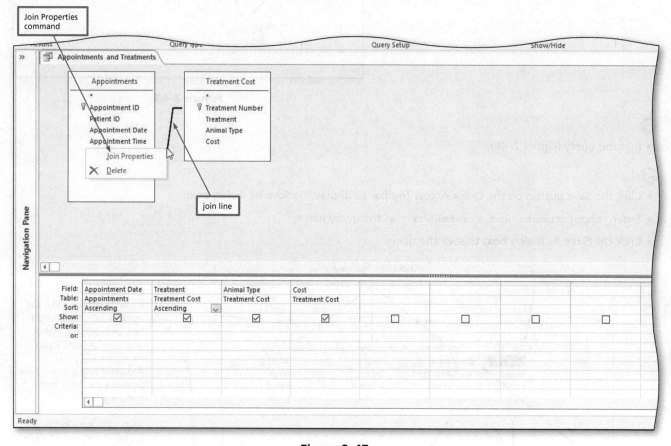

Figure 2–47

2

- Click Join Properties on the shortcut menu to display the Join Properties dialog box (Figure 2–48).

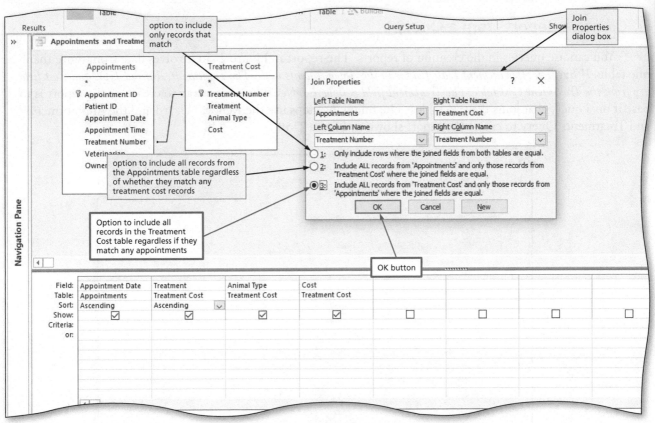

Figure 2–48

3

- Click option button 3 (Join Properties dialog box) to include all records from the Treatment Cost Table regardless of whether they match any appointments.

- Click OK (Join Properties dialog box) to modify the join properties and close the Join Properties dialog box.

- Run the query (Figure 2–49).

 Experiment

- Return to Design view, change the Join properties, and select option button 2. Run the query to see the effect of this option. When done, return to Design view, change the join properties, and once again select option button 3.

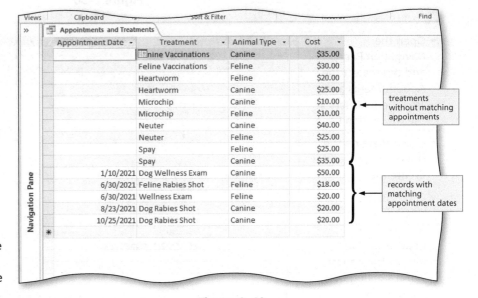

Figure 2–49

4

- Click the Save button on the Quick Access Toolbar to save the changes to the query.

- Close the Appointments and Treatments Query.

I see a dialog box that asks if I want to save the query. What should I do?
Click OK to save the query.

To Create a Report from a Query

You can use queries in the creation of reports. The report in Figure 2–50 involves data from more than one table. *Why? The Appointment Date field is in the Appointments table. The Treatment, Animal Type, and Cost fields are from the Treatment Cost table. The Treatment field is in both tables.* The easiest way to create such a report is to base it on a query that joins the two tables. The following steps use the Report Wizard and the Appointments and Treatments Query to create the report shown in Figure 2–50.

Figure 2–50

1

- Open the Navigation Pane, and then select the Appointments and Treatments Query in the Navigation Pane.

- Click Create on the ribbon to display the Create tab.

- Click the Report Wizard button (Create tab | Reports group) to display the Report Wizard dialog box (Figure 2–51).

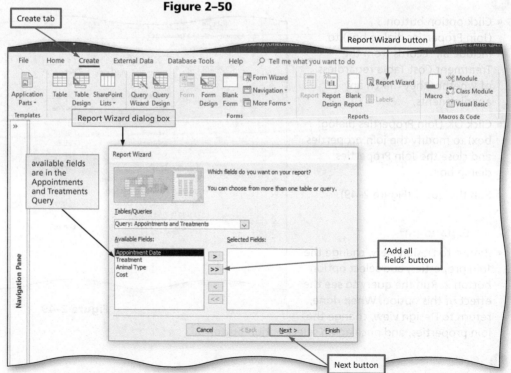

Figure 2–51

- Click the 'Add All Fields' button (Report Wizard dialog box) to add all the fields in the Appointments and Treatments Query.
- Click Next to display the next Report Wizard screen (Figure 2–52).

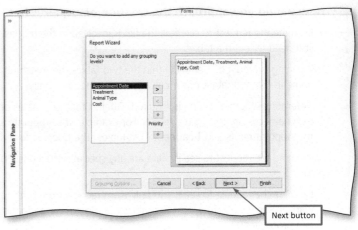

Figure 2–52

- Because you will not specify any grouping, click Next again to display the next Report Wizard screen.
- Because you already specified the sort order in the query, click Next again to display the next Report Wizard screen.
- Make sure that Tabular is selected as the Layout and Portrait is selected as the Orientation.
- Click Next to display the next Report Wizard screen.
- If necessary, erase the current title, and then type `Appointments and Treatments Report` as the new title.
- Click the Finish button to produce the report (Figure 2–53).

Figure 2–53

Q&A My report is very small and does not look like the one in the figure. What should I do?
Click the pointer, which should look like a magnifying glass, anywhere in the report to magnify the report.

- Close the Appointments and Treatments Report.

To Print a Report

Often, users will need to distribute database information in a printed format. CMF Vets would like to share the Appointments and Treatments reports with stakeholders who prefer a hard copy. The following steps print a hard copy of the report.

1 With the Appointments and Treatments Report selected in the Navigation Pane, click File on the ribbon to open the Backstage view.

2 Click the Print tab in the Backstage view to display the Print gallery.

3 Click the Quick Print button to print the report.

CONSIDER THIS

How would you approach the creation of a query that might involve multiple tables?

• Examine the request to see if all the fields involved in the request are in one table. If the fields are in two (or more) tables, you need to join the tables.

• If joining is required, identify within the two tables the matching fields that have identical values. Look for the same column name in the two tables or for column names that are similar.

• Determine whether sorting is required. Queries that join tables often are used as the basis for a report. If this is the case, it may be necessary to sort the results. For example, the Appointments and Treatments Report is based on a query that joins the Appointments and Treatment Cost tables. The query is sorted by Appointment Date and Treatment.

• Examine the request to see if there are any special restrictions. For example, the user may only want treatment costs higher than $20.

• Examine the request to see if you only want records from both tables that have identical values in matching fields. If you want to see records in one of the tables that do not have identical values in the other table, then you need to change the join properties.

Creating a Form for a Query

You have already learned how to create a form for a table. You can also create a form for a query. Recall that a form in a database is a formatted document with fields that contain data. Forms allow you to view and maintain data.

To Create a Form for a Query

The following steps create a form, then save the form. *Why? The form will be available for future use in viewing the data in the query.*

1

• If necessary, select the Appointments and Treatments Query in the Navigation Pane.

• Click Create on the ribbon to display the Create tab (Figure 2–54).

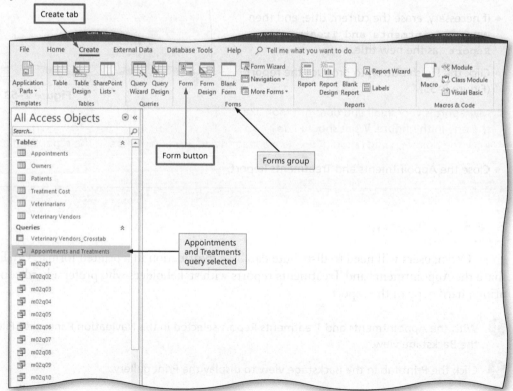

Figure 2–54

2

- Click the Form button (Create tab | Forms group) to create a simple form (Figure 2–55).

Q&A I see a field list also. What should I do? Click Close for the Field List.

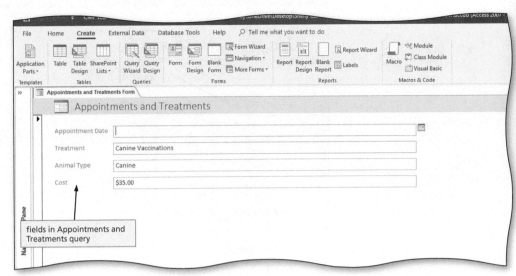

fields in Appointments and Treatments query

Figure 2–55

3

- Click the Save button on the Quick Access Toolbar to display the Save As dialog box.
- Enter **Form** at the end of the Appointments and Treatments name so that Appointments and Treatments Form appears as the complete name.
- Click OK to save the form.
- Click Close for the form to close the form.

Using a Form

After you have saved a form, you can use it at any time by right-clicking the form in the Navigation Pane and then clicking Open on the shortcut menu. If you plan to use the form to enter data, you must ensure you are viewing the form in Form view.

Break Point: If you wish to take a break, this is a good place to do so. You can exit Access now. To resume later, start Access, open the database called CMF Vets, and continue following the steps from this location forward.

Exporting Data from Access to Other Applications

You can **export**, or copy, tables or queries from an Access database so that another application (for example, Excel or Word) can use the data. The application that will receive the data determines the export process to be used. You can export to text files in a variety of formats. For applications to which you cannot directly export data, you often can export an appropriately formatted text file that the other application can import. Figure 2–56 shows the workbook produced by exporting the Appointments and Treatments Query to Excel. The columns in the workbook have been resized to best fit the data.

BTW
Exporting Data
You frequently need to export data so that it can be used in other applications and by other users in an organization. For example, the Accounting department might require financial data in an Excel format to perform certain financial functions. Marketing might require a list of owner names and addresses in Word or RTF format for marketing campaigns.

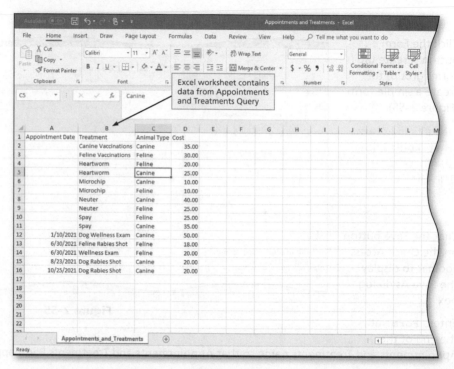

Figure 2–56

To Export Data to Excel

For CMF Vets managers to make the Appointments and Treatments Query available to Excel users, they need to export the data. To export data to Excel, select the table or query to be exported and then click the Excel button in the Export group on the External Data tab. The following steps export the Appointments and Treatments Query to Excel and save the export steps. *Why save the export steps? By saving the export steps, you could easily repeat the export process whenever you like without going through all the steps.* You would use the saved steps to export data in the future by clicking the Saved Exports button (External Data tab | Export group) and then selecting the steps you saved.

- If necessary, click the Appointments and Treatments Query in the Navigation Pane to select it.

- Click External Data on the ribbon to display the External Data tab (Figure 2–57).

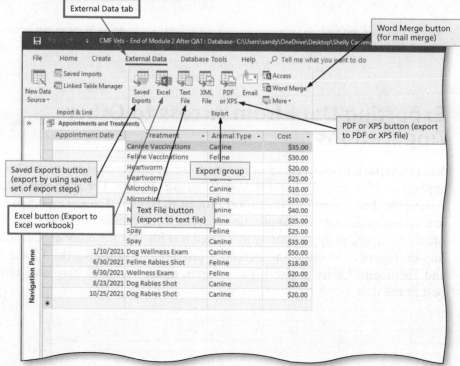

Figure 2–57

2

- Click the Excel button (External Data tab | Export group) to display the Export-Excel Spreadsheet dialog box.

- Click the Browse button (Export-Excel Spreadsheet dialog box), and then navigate to the location where you want to export the query (your hard drive, OneDrive, or other storage location).

- Confirm that the file format is Excel Workbook (*.xlsx), and the file name is Appointments and Treatments as the query name and then

click the Save button (File Save dialog box) to select the file name and location (Figure 2–58).

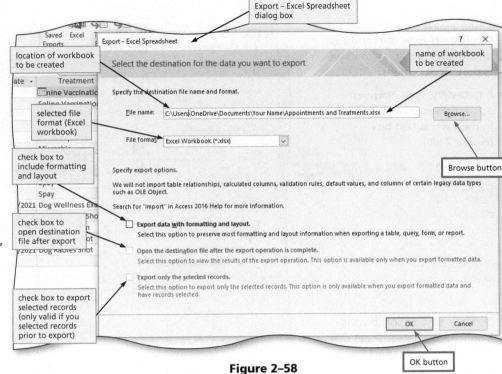

Figure 2–58

Q&A

Did I need to browse?
No. You could type the appropriate file location.

Could I change the name of the file?
You could change it. Simply replace the current file name with the one you want.

What if the file I want to export already exists?
Access will indicate that the file already exists and ask if you want to replace it. If you click Yes, the file you export will replace the old file. If you click No, you must either change the name of the export file or cancel the process.

3

- Click OK (Export-Excel Spreadsheet dialog box) to export the data (Figure 2–59).

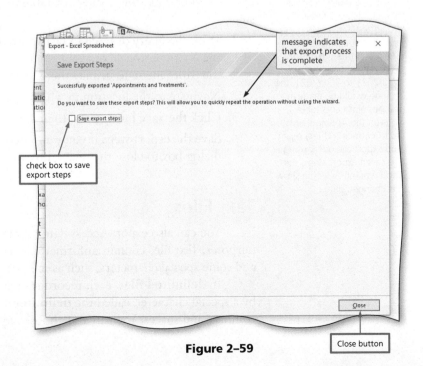

Figure 2–59

4

- Click the 'Save export steps' check box (Export-Excel Spreadsheet dialog box) to display the Save Export Steps options.

- If necessary, type **Export-Appointments and Treatments** in the Save as text box (Figure 2–60).

How could I reuse the export steps?
You can use these steps to export data in the future by clicking the Saved Exports button (External Data tab | Export group) and then selecting the steps you saved.

5

- Click the Save Export button (Export-Excel Spreadsheet dialog box) to save the export steps.

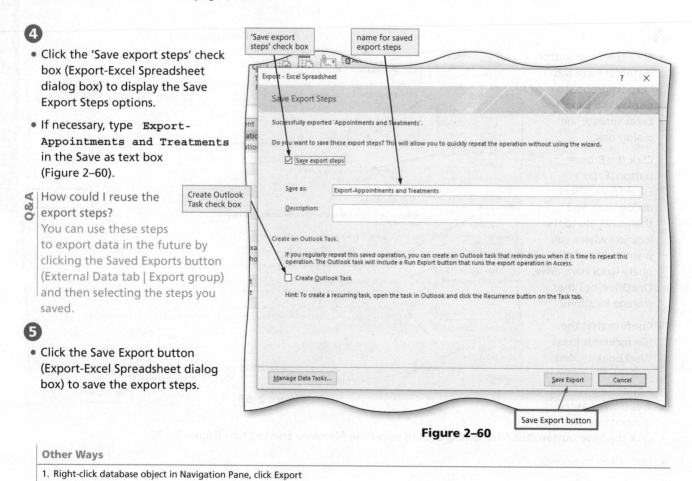

Figure 2–60

Other Ways

1. Right-click database object in Navigation Pane, click Export

---

Saving Export Steps
Because query results are based on the data in the underlying tables, a change to an underlying table would result in a new query answer. For example, if the appointment date for a patient changed from 8/23/2021 to 8/30/2021, the change would be made in the Appointments table. If you run the Appointments and Treatments Query again and export the query using the saved export steps, the Excel workbook would show the changed date.

TO EXPORT DATA TO WORD

It is not possible to export data from Access to the standard Word format. It is possible, however, to export the data as a rich text format (RTF) file, which Word can use. To export data from a query or table to an RTF file, you would use the following steps.

1. With the query or table to be exported selected in the Navigation Pane, click the More button (External Data tab | Export group) and then click Word on the More menu to display the Export-RTF File dialog box.

2. Navigate to the location in which to save the file and assign a file name.

3. Click the Save button, and then click OK to export the data.

4. Save the export steps if you want, or simply click Close in the Export-RTF File dialog box to close the dialog box without saving the export steps.

Text Files

You can also export Access data to text files, which can be used for a variety of purposes. Text files contain unformatted characters, including alphanumeric characters, and some special characters, such as tabs, carriage returns, and line feeds.

In **delimited files**, each record is on a separate line and the fields are separated by a special character, called the **delimiter**. Common delimiters are tabs, semicolons, commas, and spaces. You can also choose any other value that does not appear within the field contents as the delimiter. The comma-separated values (CSV) file often used in Excel is an example of a delimited file.

In **fixed-width files**, the width of any field is the same on every record. For example, if the width of the first field on the first record is 12 characters, the width of the first field on every other record must also be 12 characters.

TO EXPORT DATA TO A TEXT FILE

When exporting data to a text file, you can choose to export the data with formatting and layout. This option preserves much of the formatting and layout in tables, queries, forms, and reports. For forms and reports, this is the only option for exporting to a text file.

If you do not need to preserve the formatting, you can choose either delimited or fixed-width as the format for the exported file. The most common option, especially if formatting is not an issue, is delimited. You can choose the delimiter. You can also choose whether to include field names on the first row. In many cases, delimiting with a comma and including the field names is a good choice.

To export data from a table or query to a comma-delimited file in which the first row contains the column headings, you would use the following steps.

1. With the query or table to be exported selected in the Navigation Pane, click the Text File button (External Data tab | Export group) to display the Export-Text File dialog box.
2. Select the name and location for the file to be created.
3. If you need to preserve formatting and layout, be sure the 'Export data with formatting and layout' check box is checked. If you do not need to preserve formatting and layout, make sure the check box is not checked. Once you have made your selection, click OK in the Export-Text File dialog box.
4. To create a delimited file, be sure the Delimited option button is selected in the Export Text Wizard dialog box. To create a fixed-width file, be sure the Fixed Width option button is selected. Once you have made your selection, click the Next button.
5. a. If you are exporting to a delimited file, choose the delimiter that you want to separate your fields, such as a comma. Decide whether to include field names on the first row and, if so, click the 'Include Field Names on First Row' check box. If you want to select a text qualifier, select it in the Text Qualifier list. When you have made your selections, click the Next button.

   b. If you are exporting to a fixed-width file, review the position of the vertical lines that separate your fields. If any lines are not positioned correctly, follow the directions on the screen to reposition them. When you have finished, click the Next button.
6. Click the Finish button to export the data.
7. Save the export steps if you want, or simply click Close in the Export-Text File dialog box to close the dialog box without saving the export steps.

BTW
Distributing a Document
Instead of printing and distributing a hard copy of a document, you can distribute the document electronically. Options include sending the document via email; posting it on cloud storage (such as OneDrive) and sharing the file with others; posting it on social media, a blog, or other website; and sharing a link associated with an online location of the document. You also can create and share a PDF or XPS image of the document, so that users can view the file in Acrobat Reader or XPS Viewer instead of in Access.

Adding Criteria to a Join Query

Sometimes you will want to join tables, but you will not want to include all possible records. For example, you would like to create a report showing only those treatments whose cost is greater than $10.00. In this case, you would relate the tables and include fields just as you did before. You will also include criteria. To include only those treatments whose amount cost is more than $10.00, you will include >10 as a criterion for the Cost field.

To Restrict the Records in a Join

The following steps modify the Appointments and Treatments Query so that the results for CMF Vets managers include a criterion. *Why? CMF Vets managers want to include only those treatments whose cost is more than $10.*

- Open the Navigation Pane, if necessary, and then right-click the Appointments and Treatments Query to produce a shortcut menu.

- Click Design View on the shortcut menu to open the Appointments and Treatments Query in Design view.

- Close the Navigation Pane.

- Type >10 as the criterion for the Cost field (Figure 2–61).

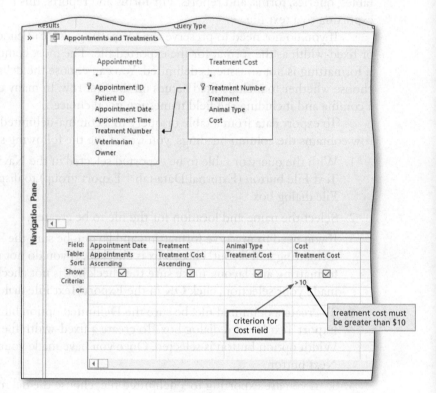

Figure 2–61

- Run the query (Figure 2–62).

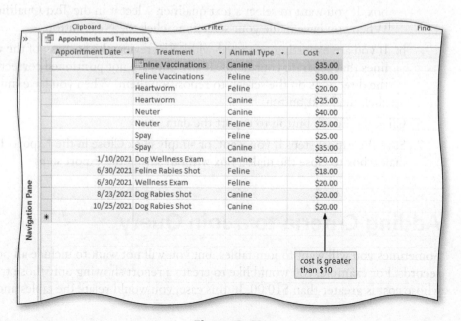

Figure 2–62

- Close the query.

- When asked if you want to save your changes, click No.

Q&A What would happen if I saved the changes?
The next time you used this query, you would only see treatments whose cost is more than $10.

Calculations

If a special calculation is required for a query, you need to determine whether the calculation is an **individual record calculation** (for example, adding the values in two fields for one record) or a **group calculation** (for example, finding the total of the values in a particular field on all the records).

CMF Vets managers might want to know the total cost of their inventory in the Veterinary Vendors table (quantity and cost) for each veterinary supply. This would seem to pose a problem because the table does not include a field for total cost. You can calculate it, however, because the total amount is equal to the quantity times the cost. A field that can be computed from other fields is called a **calculated field** or a **computed field** and is not usually included in the table. Including it introduces the possibility for errors in the table. If the value in the field does not happen to match the results of the calculation, the data is inconsistent. A calculated field is an individual record calculation because each calculation only involves fields in a single record.

CMF Vets managers might also want to calculate the average amount paid for the veterinary supplies of each vendor. That is, they may want the average paid for supplies from Duncan Veterinary Supplies, the average paid for supplies of Gaines Vet Supplies, and so on. This type of calculation is called a **group calculation** because each calculation involves groups of records. In this example, the supplies of Duncan Veterinary Supplies would form one group, the supplies of Gaines Vet Supplies would be a second group, and the supplies of Mayes Supplies Corporation would form a third group.

BTW
Expression Builder
Access includes a tool to help you create complex expressions. If you click Build on the shortcut menu (see Figure 2–63), Access displays the Expression Builder dialog box, which includes an expression box, operator buttons, and expression elements. You can type parts of the expression directly and paste operator buttons and expression elements into the box. You also can use functions in expressions.

To Use a Calculated Field in a Query

If you need a calculated field in a query, you enter a name, or alias, for the calculated field, a colon, and then the calculation in one of the columns in the Field row of the design grid for the query. Any fields included in the expression must be enclosed in square brackets ([ ]). For example, for the total amount, you will type Total Cost:[Quantity]*[Cost] as the expression.

You can type the expression directly into the Field row in Design view. The preferred method, however, is to select the column in the Field row and then use the Zoom command on its shortcut menu. When Access displays the Zoom dialog box, you can enter the expression. *Why use the Zoom command? You will not be able to see the entire entry in the Field row, because the space available is not large enough.*

You can use addition (+), subtraction (-), multiplication (*), or division (/) in calculations. If you have multiple calculations in an expression, you can include parentheses to indicate which calculations should be done first.

The following steps create a query that CMF Vets managers might use to obtain financial information on its inventory, including the total cost (quantity * cost), which is a calculated field.

- Create a query with a field list for the Veterinary Vendors table.

- Add the Vendor Name, State, Veterinary Supply, Quantity, and Cost fields to the query.

- Right-click the Field row in the first open column in the design grid to display a shortcut menu (Figure 2–63).

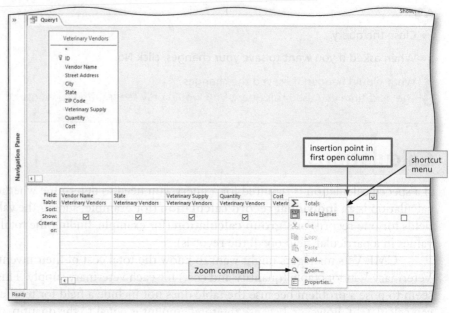

Figure 2–63

2

- Click Zoom on the shortcut menu to display the Zoom dialog box.

- Type `Total Cost:[Quantity]*` `[Cost]` in the Zoom dialog box (Figure 2–64) to enter the expression.

 Do I always need to put square brackets around field names?

If the field name does not contain spaces, square brackets are technically not required. It is a good practice, however, to get in the habit of using the brackets in field calculations.

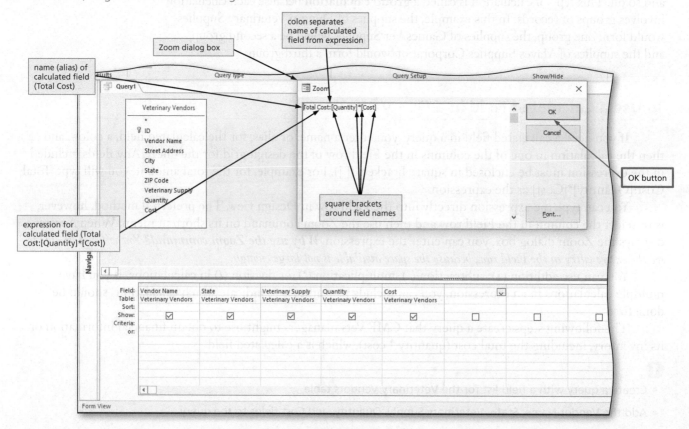

Figure 2–64

3

- Click OK (Zoom dialog box) to complete the expression (Figure 2–65) and close the dialog box.

- Widen the column if necessary to view the entire expression.

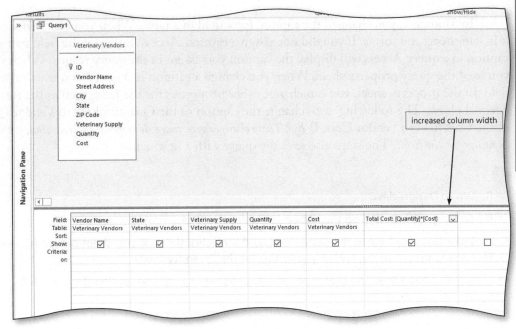

Figure 2–65

4

- Run the query (Figure 2–66) to see the calculated results for the new Total Cost field.

🔍 **Experiment**

- Return to Design view and try other expressions. In at least one case, omit the Total Cost and the colon. In at least one case, intentionally misspell a field name. In each case, run the query to see the effect of your changes. When finished, re-enter the original expression.

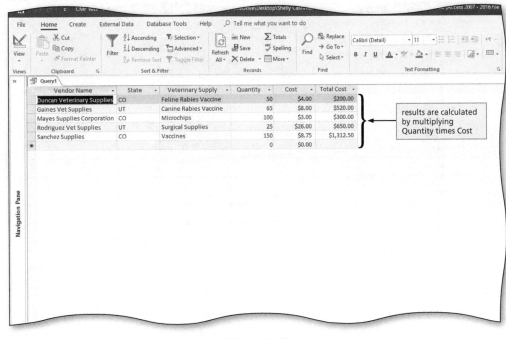

Figure 2–66

Q&A

Does the Total Cost field now exist as a field in the Vendors table?

When a field is created in Table Design View as a new calculated field in the table, it will appear as a field in the table.

Other Ways

1. Press SHIFT+F2

To Change a Caption

In Module 1, you changed the caption for a field in a table. When you assigned a caption, Access displayed it in datasheets and forms. If you did not assign a caption, Access displayed the field name. You can also change a caption in a query. Access will display the caption you assign in the query results. When you omitted duplicates, you used the query property sheet. When you change a caption in a query, you use the property sheet for the field. In the property sheet, you can change other properties for the field, such as the format and number of decimal places. The following steps change the caption of the Quantity field to Vendor Quantity and the caption of the Cost field to Vendor Cost. *Why? These changes give more descriptive information, yet very readable, column headings for the fields.* The steps also save the query with a new name.

- Return to Design view.

- If necessary, click Design on the ribbon to display the Query Tools Design tab.

- Click the Quantity field in the design grid, and then click the Property Sheet button (Query Tools Design tab | Show/Hide group) to display the properties for the Quantity field.

- Click the Caption box, and then type `Vendor Quantity` as the caption (Figure 2–67).

Q&A My property sheet looks different. What should I do?
Close the property sheet and repeat this step.

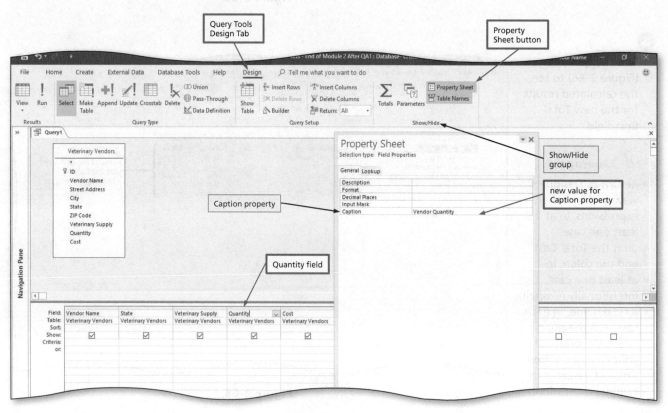

Figure 2–67

2

- Click the Cost field in the design grid to view its properties in the Property Sheet.
- Click the Caption box, and then type `Vendor Cost` as the caption.
- Close the Property Sheet by clicking the Property Sheet button a second time.
- Run the query (Figure 2–68).

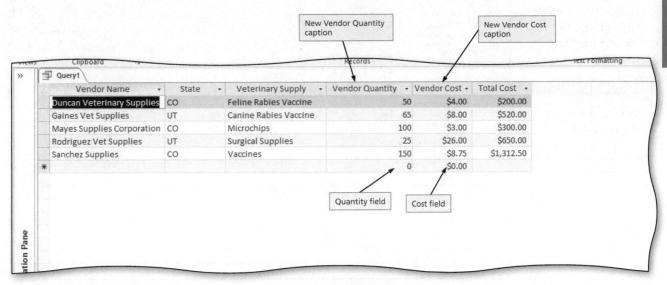

Figure 2–68

3

- Save the query as m02q10.
- Close the query.

Other Ways

1. Right-click field in design grid, click Properties on shortcut menu

To Calculate Statistics

For group calculations, Microsoft Access supports several built-in statistics: COUNT (count of the number of records), SUM (total), AVG (average), MAX (largest value), MIN (smallest value), STDEV (standard deviation), VAR (variance), FIRST (first value), and LAST (last value). These statistics are called aggregate functions. An **aggregate function** is a function that performs some mathematical function against a group of records. To use an aggregate function in a query, you include it in the Total row in the design grid. In order to do so, you must first include the Total row by clicking the Totals button on the Design tab. *Why? The Total row usually does not appear in the grid. Statistical calculations are performed regularly in Access queries by some, but not all learners. So, the process for these calculations requires extra steps.*

The following steps create a new query for the Veterinary Vendors table. The steps include the Total row in the design grid, and then calculate the average cost for all veterinary supplies.

1

- Create a new query with a field list for the Veterinary Vendors table.

- Click the Totals button (Query Tools Design tab | Show/Hide group) to include the Total row in the design grid.

- Add the Cost field to the query (Figure 2–69).

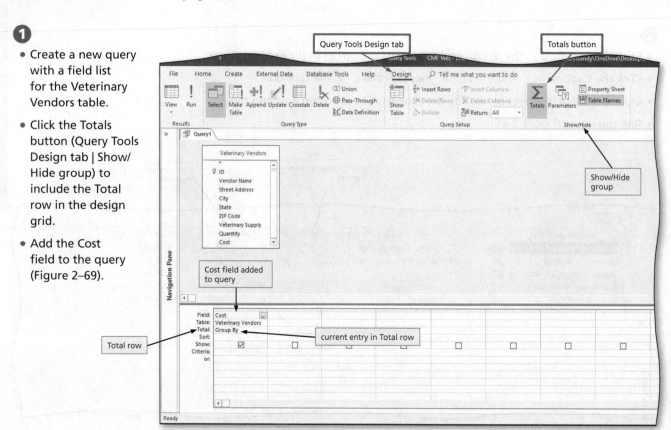

Figure 2–69

2

- Click the Total row in the Cost column to display the Total arrow.

- Click the Total arrow to display the Total list (Figure 2–70).

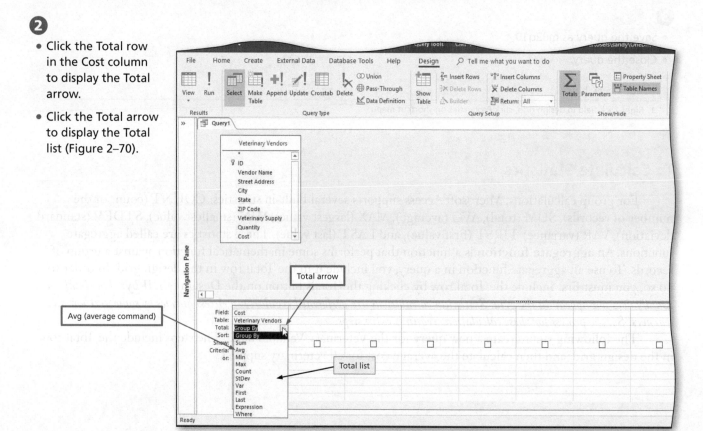

Figure 2–70

3

- Click Avg to select the calculation that Access is to perform (Figure 2–71).

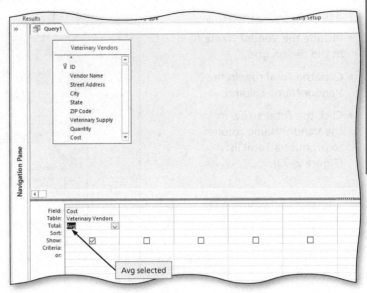

Figure 2–71

4

- Run the query (Figure 2–72).

Experiment

- Return to Design view and try other aggregate functions. In each case, run the query to see the effect of your selection. When finished, select Avg once again.

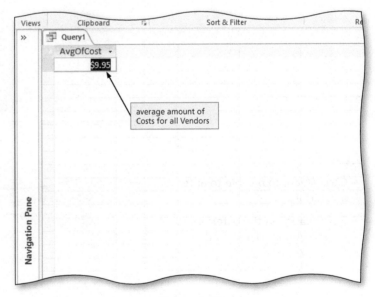

Figure 2–72

To Use Criteria in Calculating Statistics

Why? *Sometimes calculating statistics for all the records in the table is appropriate. In other cases, however, you will need to calculate the statistics for only those records that satisfy certain criteria.* To enter a criterion in a field, first you select Where as the entry in the Total row for the field, and then enter the criterion in the Criteria row. Access uses the word, Where, to indicate that you will enter a criterion. The following steps use this technique to calculate the average costs for purchases from Sanchez Supplies. The steps also save the query with a new name.

- Return to Design view.

- Include the Vendor Name field in the design grid.

- Click the Total row in the Vendor Name column.

- Click the Total arrow in the Vendor Name column to produce a Total list (Figure 2–73).

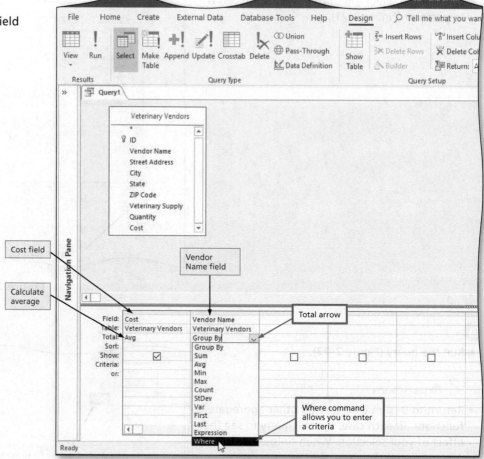

Figure 2–73

- Click Where to be able to enter a criterion.

- Type **San*** as the criterion for the Vendor Name field (Figure 2–74).

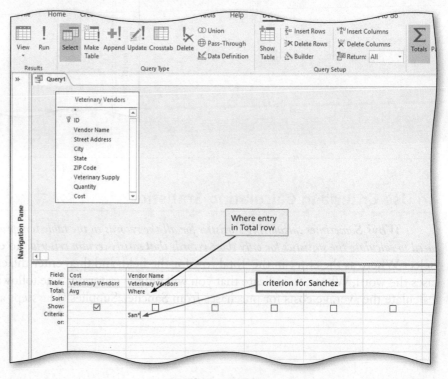

Figure 2–74

❸

- Run the query (Figure 2–75) and display the average cost of supplies for Sanchez Supplies.

❹

- Save the query as m02q11.

BTW
Criterion for Where
Access treats the criterion for the Where object just as it would for any criterion in a field. Therefore, if you want to use a wildcard rather than spelling out the entire criterion, such as Rod* for the Rod Supplies, Access recognizes and utilizes the wildcard to find the desired result.

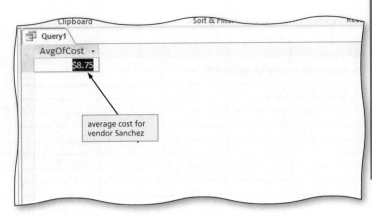

Figure 2–75

To Use Grouping

Why? Statistics are often used in combination with grouping; that is, statistics are calculated for groups of records. For example, CMF Vets managers could calculate the average amount paid for each veterinary supplier, which would require the average for the vendor specified in the criteria. **Grouping** means creating groups of records that share some common characteristic. In grouping by Veterinary Vendor, for example, the costs of Duncan Veterinary Supplies would form one group, the costs of Gaines Vet Supplies would form a second, and the costs of Mayes Supplies Corporation would form a third group. The calculations are then made for each group. To indicate grouping in Access, select Group By as the entry in the Total row for the field to be used for grouping. Even though the entry indicates Group By, the vendors will appear individually. Access needs to know the field that you want to review the averages on, and it indicates this by the text Group By. Group By does not mean that it will group together all the vendors, just refers to looking at that particular group.

The following steps create a query that calculates the average amount paid for each vendor supplier account at CMF Vets. The steps also save the query with a new name.

❶

- Return to Design view and clear the design grid.
- Include the Vendor Name field in the query.
- Include the Cost field in the query.
- Select Avg as the calculation in the Total row for the Cost field (Figure 2–76).

Q&A Why was it not necessary to change the entry in the Total row for the Vendor Name field?
Group By, which is the initial entry in the Total row when you add a field, is correct. Thus, you did not need to change the entry.

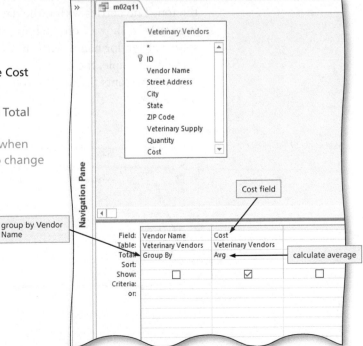

Figure 2–76

2

- Run the query (Figure 2–77).

3

- Save the query as m02q12.
- Close the query.

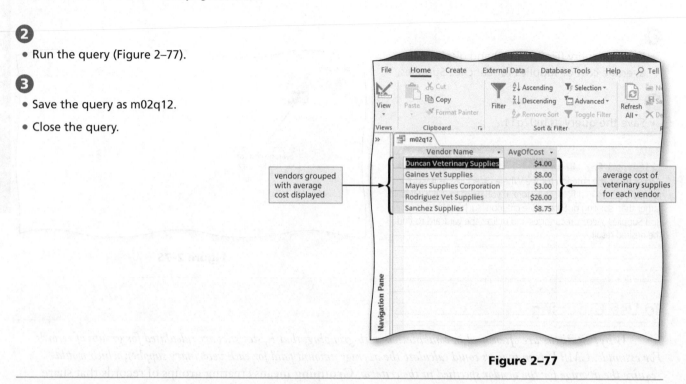

vendors grouped with average cost displayed

average cost of veterinary supplies for each vendor

Figure 2–77

Crosstab Queries

A **crosstab query**, or simply, crosstab, calculates a statistic (for example, sum, average, or count) for data that is grouped by two different types of information. One of the types will appear down the side of the resulting datasheet, and the other will appear across the top. Crosstab queries are useful for summarizing data by category or group.

For example, if a query must summarize the sum of the current costs grouped by both state and vendor name, you could have states as the row headings, that is, down the side. You could have vendor names as the column headings, that is, across the top. The entries within the datasheet represent the total of the cost amounts. Figure 2–78 shows a crosstab in which the total of cost amounts is grouped by both state and vendor name, with states down the left side and vendor name across the top. For example, the entry in the row labeled CO and in the column labelled Vendor Name represents the total of the current cost amounts by all vendors who are located in Colorado.

row headings (states)

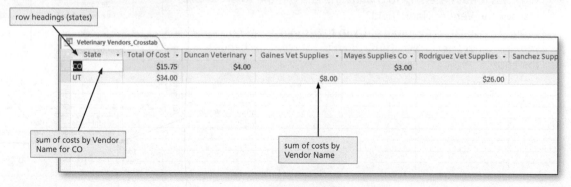

sum of costs by Vendor Name for CO

sum of costs by Vendor Name

Figure 2–78

How do you know when to use a crosstab query?

If data is to be grouped by two different types of information, you can use a crosstab query. You will need to identify the two types of information. One of the types will form the row headings and the other will form the column headings in the query results.

To Create a Crosstab Query

The following steps use the Crosstab Query Wizard to create a crosstab query. *Why? CMF Vets managers want to group data on cost by two types of information: state and vendor name.*

- Click Create on the ribbon to display the Create tab.
- Click the Query Wizard button (Create tab | Queries group) to display the New Query dialog box (Figure 2–79).

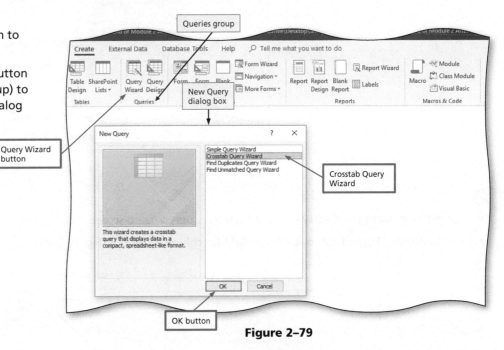

Figure 2–79

- Click Crosstab Query Wizard (New Query dialog box).
- Click OK to display the Crosstab Query Wizard dialog box (Figure 2–80).

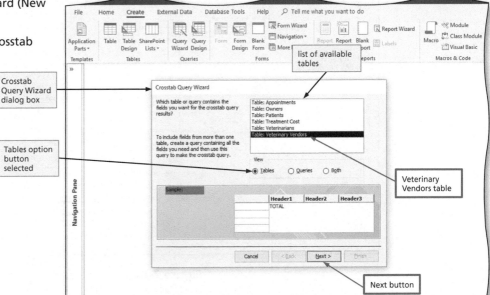

Figure 2–80

• With the Tables option button selected, click Table: Veterinary Vendors to select the Veterinary Vendors table, and then click the Next button to display the next Crosstab Query Wizard screen.

• Click the State field, and then click the Add Field button to select the State field for row headings (Figure 2–81).

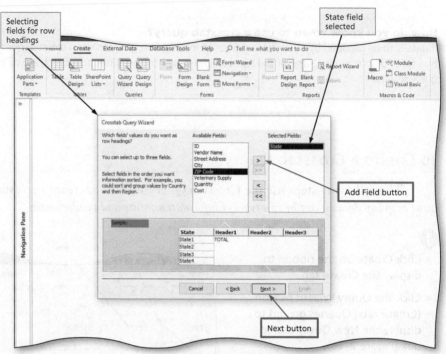

Figure 2–81

• Click the Next button to display the next Crosstab Query Wizard screen.

• Click the Vendor Name field to select the field for column headings (Figure 2–82).

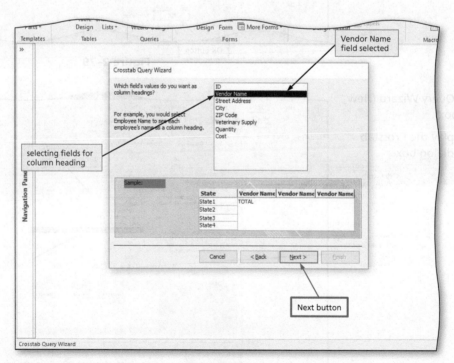

Figure 2–82

5

- Click Next to display the next Crosstab Query Wizard screen.
- Click the Cost field to select the field for calculations.

🔍 **Experiment**

- Click other fields. For each field, examine the list of calculations that are available. When finished, click the Cost field again.
- Click Sum to select the calculation to be performed (Figure 2–83).

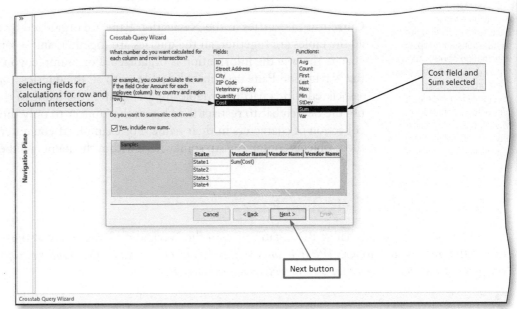

Figure 2–83

Q&A My list of functions is different. What did I do wrong?
Either you clicked the wrong field, or the Cost field has the wrong data type. For example, if you mistakenly assigned it the Short Text data type, you would not see Sum in the list of available calculations.

6

- Click Next to display the next Crosstab Query Wizard screen.
- If necessary, erase the text in the name text box and type `Veterinary Vendors_Crosstab` as the name of the query (Figure 2–84).

7

- If requested to do so by your instructor, name the crosstab query as FirstName LastName Crosstab where FirstName and LastName are your first and last names.
- Click the Finish button to produce the crosstab shown in Figure 2–78.
- Close the query.

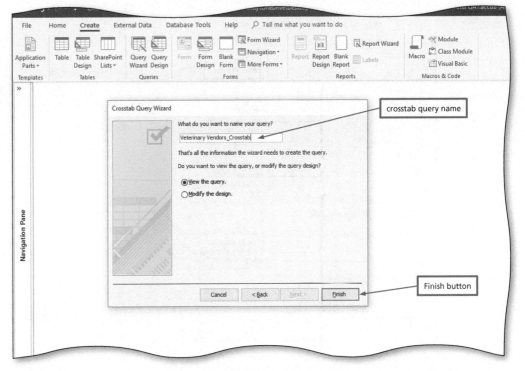

Figure 2–84

BTW
Access Help
At any time while using Access, you can find answers to questions and display information about various topics through Access Help. Used properly, this form of assistance can increase your productivity and reduce your frustrations by minimizing the time you spend learning how to use Access.

Customizing the Navigation Pane

Currently, the entries in the Navigation Pane are organized by object type. That is, all the tables are together, all the queries are together, and so on. You might want to change the way the information is organized. For example, you might want to have the Navigation Pane organized by table, with all the queries, forms, and reports associated with a particular table appearing after the name of the table. You can also use the Search bar to restrict the objects that appear to only those that have a certain collection of characters in their name. For example, if you entered the letters, Ap, only those objects containing Ap somewhere within the name will be included.

To Customize the Navigation Pane

The following steps change the organization of the Navigation Pane. They also use the Search bar to restrict the objects that appear. **Why?** *Using the Search bar, you can reduce the number of objects that appear in the Navigation Pane and just show the ones in which you are interested.*

- If necessary, click the 'Shutter Bar Open/Close Button' to open the Navigation Pane.

- Click the Navigation Pane arrow to produce the Navigation Pane menu and then click 'Tables and Related Views' to organize the Navigation Pane by table rather than by the type of object (Figure 2–85).

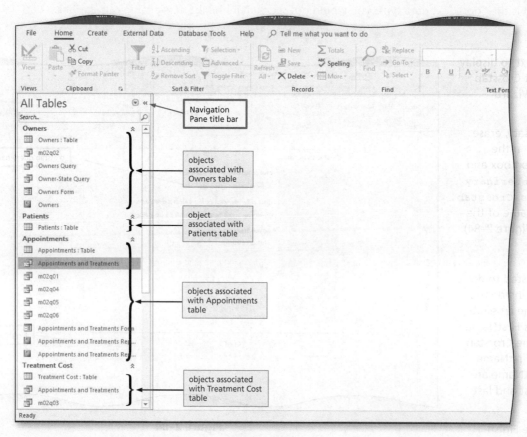

Figure 2–85

2

- Click the Navigation Pane arrow to produce the Navigation Pane menu.
- Click Object Type to once again organize the Navigation Pane by object type.

🔍 **Experiment**

- Select different Navigate To Category options to see the effect of the option. With each option you select, select different Filter By Group options to see the effect of the filtering. When you have finished experimenting, select the 'Object Type Navigate To Category' option and the 'All Access Objects Filter By Group' option.

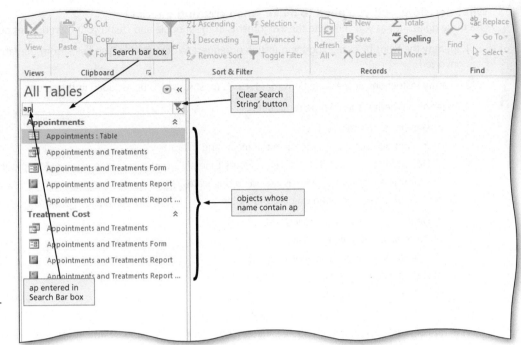

Figure 2–86

- If the Search bar does not appear, right-click the Navigation Pane and click Search Bar on the shortcut menu.

- Click in the Search box to produce an insertion point.

- Type **ap** as the search string to restrict the objects displayed to only those containing the desired string (Figure 2–86).

3

- Click the 'Clear Search String' button to remove the search string and redisplay all objects.

Q&A

Did I have to click the button to redisplay all objects? Could I simply have erased the current string to achieve the same result?
You did not have to click the button. You could have used the DELETE or BACKSPACE keys to erase the current search string.

- If desired, sign out of your Microsoft account.

- **sam** ⬆ Exit Access.

Summary

In this module you have learned to create queries, enter fields, enter criteria, use text and numeric data in queries, use wildcards, use compound criteria, create parameter queries, sort data in queries, join tables in queries, perform calculations in queries, and create crosstab queries. You also learned to create a report and a form that used a query, to export a query, and to customize the Navigation Pane.

What decisions will you need to make when creating queries?

Use these guidelines as you complete the assignments in this module and create your own queries outside of this class.

1. Identify the fields by examining the question or request to determine which fields from the tables in the database are involved.

2. Identify restrictions or the conditions that records must satisfy to be included in the results.

3. Determine whether special order is required.

    a) Determine the sort key(s).

    b) If using two sort keys, determine the major and minor key.

    c) Determine sort order. If there are no words to imply a particular order, you would typically use Ascending sort order.

    d) Determine restrictions, such as excluding duplicates.

4. Determine whether more than one table is required.

    a) Determine which tables to include.

    b) Determine the matching fields.

    c) Determine whether sorting is required.

    d) Determine restrictions.

    e) Determine join properties.

5. Determine whether calculations are required.

    a) For individual record calculations, determine the calculation and a name for the calculated field.

    b) For group calculations, determine the calculation as well as the field to be used for grouping.

6. If data is to be summarized and the data is to be grouped by two different types of information, create a crosstab query.

How should you submit solutions to questions in the assignments identified with a symbol?

Every assignment in this book contains one or more questions identified with a symbol. These questions require you to think beyond the assigned database. Present your solutions to the questions in the format required by your instructor. Possible formats may include one or more of these options: write the answer; create a document that contains the answer; present your answer to the class; discuss your answer in a group; record the answer as audio or video using a webcam, smartphone, or portable media player; or post answers on a blog, wiki, or website.

Apply Your Knowledge

Reinforce the skills and apply the concepts you learned in this module.

Using Wildcards in a Query, Creating a Parameter Query, Joining Tables, and Creating a Report

Instructions: Start Access. Open the Support_AC_Financial Services database from the Data Files. (If you did not previously complete the exercise, see your instructor for a copy of the modified database.)

Perform the following tasks:

1. Import the Accounting table from the Support_AC Financial Services – Extra Tables database.

2. Create a query for the Accounting table and add the CL #, Client Name, Amount Paid, and AU# fields to the design grid. Sort the records in descending order by Amount Paid. Add a criterion for the AU# field that allows the user to enter a different advisor each time the query is run. Run the query and enter 114 as the advisor to test the query. Save the query as Apply 2 Step 2 Query.

3. Create a query for the Accounting table and add the CL #, Client Name, and Current Due fields to the design grid. Add a criterion to find all clients whose current due amount is less than $500. Run the query and then save it as Apply 2 Step 3 Query.

4. Create a query that joins the Advisor and Client tables. Add the Advisor Number, Last Name, and First Name fields from the Advisor table and the Client Number and Client Name fields from the Client table to the design grid. Sort the records in ascending order by Client Number within Advisor. Run the query and save it as Advisor-Client Query. Note: if any error messages appear, check the field types of the fields in the query tables and make changes as necessary.

5. Create the report shown in Figure 2–87. The report uses the Advisor-Client Query.

Advisor-Client

AU#	Last Name	First Name	CL #	Client Name
103	Estevez	Enrique	AT13	Alton Repart
110	Hillsdale	Rachel	AZ01	Amanda Zito
110	Hillsdale	Rachel	BB35	Barbara Black
120	Short	Chris	BS24	Bob Schwartz
114	Liu	Chou	CC25	Carly Cohen
110	Hillsdale	Rachel	CJ45	Carl Jones
103	Estevez	Enrique	CP03	Cindy Platt
103	Estevez	Enrique	HC17	Heidi Croft
110	Hillsdale	Rachel	HN23	Henry Niemer
120	Short	Chris	KC12	Katy Cline
103	Estevez	Enrique	KD15	Kirk D'Elia
114	Liu	Chou	MM01	Moss Manni
110	Hillsdale	Rachel	PL03	Paul Loon
114	Liu	Chou	PS67	Patricia Singer

Figure 2–87

Continued >

STUDENT ASSIGNMENTS

Apply Your Knowledge *continued*

6. If requested to do so by your instructor, rename the Advisor-Client Report in the Navigation Pane as LastName-Client Report where LastName is your last name.

7. Submit the revised database in the format specified by your instructor.

8. ✳ What criteria would you enter in the Street field if you wanted to find all clients whose businesses were on Beard?

Extend Your Knowledge

Extend the skills you learned in this module and experiment with new skills. You may need to use Help to complete the assignment.

Creating Queries Using Criteria and Exporting a Query

Note: To complete this assignment, you will be required to use the Data Files. Please contact your instructor for information about accessing the Data Files.

Instructions: Start Access. Open the Students database, which you created from a template. The Students database provides a database structure for students and their guardians. The data will be entered next semester as new students register for classes.

1. Enter the student information shown in Figure 2–88 into the Student List that appears as the database is opened.

Open	First Name	Last Name	E-mail Address	Student ID	Level	Room	Special Circumstances
Open	Susan	Gomez	gomez@newmail.com	155	Senior	HS 449	
Open	Turner	Lewis	turner@newmail.com	203	Senior	HS 623	
Open	Bryan	Littleton	bryan@newmail.com	206	Senior	HS 623	
Open	Lebron	Mayes	Lebron@newmail.com	219	Senior	HS 450	
* (New)							

Figure 2–88

2. Create a query to find all Students located in room HS 623. Save the query as Extend 2-1 Step 2 Query.

3. Enter information for Tyron Black into the Guardian Details form, as shown in Figure 2–89.

4. Open the All Students Report and delete the date from the upper-left corner of the report.

5. Export the report as a Word file with the name All Students List.rtf and save the export steps.

6. Save the database and the exported RTF file in the format specified by your instructor.

7. ✳ How would you create the query in Step 1 that shows students who are not in room HS 623?

Figure 2–89

Expand Your World

Create a solution, which uses cloud and web technologies, by learning and investigating on your own from general guidance.

Problem: You are taking a general science course and the instructor would like you to gather some statistics and query the statistics on the dietary intake from community gardens.

Instructions:

1. Examine a website that contains research data on how individuals and families participate in growing their own food. Select data from both small and large cities near your current location.

2. Create a database containing one table that contains the following fields: Five-year increase in percentage of households gardening, percentage increase in low-income family gardening participants, and percentage increase in home gardens.

3. Create queries that do the following:
   a. return the largest quantity of increases in gardening.
   b. Calculate the difference between the largest gardening percentage increase and the lowest gardening percentage increase.

4. Submit the database in the format specified by your instructor.

5. Use an Internet search engine to find the most successful community garden near your location.

6. ✳ Which websites did you use to gather data and search for statistical information? How did the query result in Step 3 differ from historical averages? Do you think these statistics are significant? Why or why not?

In the Lab

Design, create, modify, and/or use a database following the guidelines, concepts, and skills presented in this module. This lab requires you to apply your creative thinking and problem-solving skills to design and implement a solution.

Lab: **Querying the Lancaster College Database**

Instructions: Open the Support_Access_Lancaster College database. If you do not have this database, contact your instructor for information about accessing the required files.

Part 1: Use the concepts and techniques presented in this module to create queries for the following. Save each query.

a) Create a new query that joins the Team and Field tables and shows the availability of the fields for the teams and sports. Include SeasonAvailable, Team ID, Sport Name, and Captain ID in the query. Sort in Ascending order by SeasonAvailable.

b) Find the CoachID, FirstName, LastName, and Office for coaches who work in offices that begin with SM.

c) Find all the students participating in pool activities. Include the StudentID and SportName fields.

d) Find all the students who are academically qualified to participate in sports. Include their ID, first and last names, and academic status. The result should appear as shown in Figure 2–90.

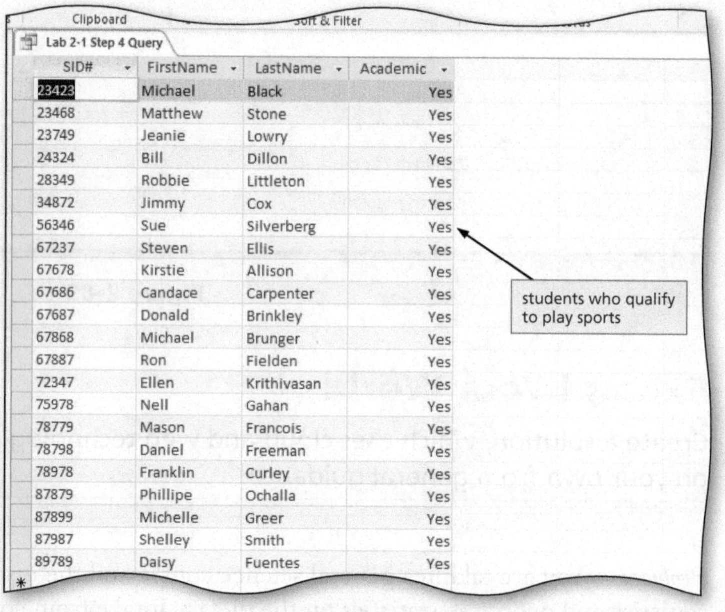

SID#	FirstName	LastName	Academic
23423	Michael	Black	Yes
23468	Matthew	Stone	Yes
23749	Jeanie	Lowry	Yes
24324	Bill	Dillon	Yes
28349	Robbie	Littleton	Yes
34872	Jimmy	Cox	Yes
56346	Sue	Silverberg	Yes
67237	Steven	Ellis	Yes
67678	Kirstie	Allison	Yes
67686	Candace	Carpenter	Yes
67687	Donald	Brinkley	Yes
67868	Michael	Brunger	Yes
67887	Ron	Fielden	Yes
72347	Ellen	Krithivasan	Yes
75978	Nell	Gahan	Yes
78779	Mason	Francois	Yes
78798	Daniel	Freeman	Yes
78978	Franklin	Curley	Yes
87879	Phillipe	Ochalla	Yes
87899	Michelle	Greer	Yes
87987	Shelley	Smith	Yes
89789	Daisy	Fuentes	Yes

students who qualify to play sports

Lab 2-1 Step 4 Query

Figure 2–90

Submit your assignment in the format specified by your instructor.

Part 2: You made several decisions while creating the queries in this assignment. What was the rationale behind your decisions? How would you modify the query in Step d to include students who already have waivers? How would you further modify the query to show the percentage of students that have waivers?

3 | Maintaining a Database

Objectives

You will have mastered the material in this module when you can:

- Add, change, and delete records
- Search for records
- Filter records
- Update a table design
- Use action queries to update records
- Use delete queries to delete records
- Specify validation rules, default values, and formats
- Create and use single-value lookup fields
- Create and use multivalued lookup fields
- Format a datasheet
- Specify referential integrity
- Use a subdatasheet
- Sort records

Introduction

Once you have created a database and loaded it with data, you must maintain it. **Maintaining the database** means modifying the data to keep it up to date by adding new records, changing the data for existing records, and deleting records. Updating can include mass updates or mass deletions (i.e., updates to, or deletions of, many records at the same time).

Maintenance of a database can also involve the need to **restructure the database** periodically. Restructuring can include adding new fields to a table, changing the characteristics of existing fields, and removing existing fields. Restructuring also includes the creation of validation rules and referential integrity. Validation rules ensure the validity of the data in the database, whereas referential integrity ensures the validity of the relationships between entities. Maintaining a database can also include filtering records, a process that ensures that only the records that satisfy some criterion appear when viewing and updating the data in a table. Changing the appearance of a datasheet is also a maintenance activity.

BTW
Organizing Files and Folders
You should organize and store files in folders so that you easily can find the files later. For example, if you are taking an introductory computer class called CIS 101, a good practice would be to save all Access files in an Access folder in a CIS 101 folder.

Project — Maintaining a Database

The CMF Veterinarian practice faces the task of keeping its database up to date. As the practice takes on new vendors, it will need to add new records, make changes to existing records, and delete records. CMF believes that it can serve its vendors better by changing the structure of the database to categorize the vendors by type of product they supply. The company will do this by adding a Product Type field to the Veterinary Vendors table. Additionally, the practice manager has realized that pet appointments need to be streamlined. Because appointments might involve more than one treatment, the appointment field will be a multivalued field, which is a field that can store multiple values or entries. Along with these changes, CMF wants to change the appearance of a datasheet when displaying data.

CMF would like the ability to make mass updates, that is, to update or delete many records in a single operation. It wants rules that limit users to entering only valid, or appropriate, data into the database. CMF also wants to ensure that the database cannot contain the name of a patient that is not associated with a specific owner.

Figure 3–1 summarizes some of the various types of activities involved in maintaining the CMF database.

Figure 3–1

Updating Records

BTW
The Ribbon and Screen Resolution
Access may change how the groups and buttons within the groups appear on the ribbon, depending on the computer or mobile device's screen resolution. Thus, your ribbon may look different from the ones in this book if you are using a screen resolution other than 1366 x 768.

Keeping the data in a database current requires updating records in three ways: adding new records, changing the data in existing records, and deleting existing records. You can add records to a database using Datasheet view and as you add records, the records appear on the screen in a datasheet. The data looks like a table. When you need to add additional records, you can use the same techniques.

You can use a simple form to view records. You can also use a **split form**, a form that allows you to simultaneously view both simple form and Datasheet views of the data. You can use either portion of a split form to add or update records. To add new records, change existing records, or delete records, you use the same techniques you used in Datasheet view.

To Create a Split Form

The following steps create a split form. **Why?** *With a split form, you have the advantage of seeing a single record in a form while simultaneously viewing several records in a datasheet.*

1

• **sam**⁊ ⬇ Start Access and open the database named CMF Vets from your hard disk, OneDrive, or other storage location.

• Open the Navigation Pane if it is currently closed.

• If necessary, click the Veterinary Vendors table in the Navigation Pane to select it.

• Click Create on the ribbon to display the Create tab.

• Click the More Forms button (Create tab | Forms group) to display the More Forms menu (Figure 3–2).

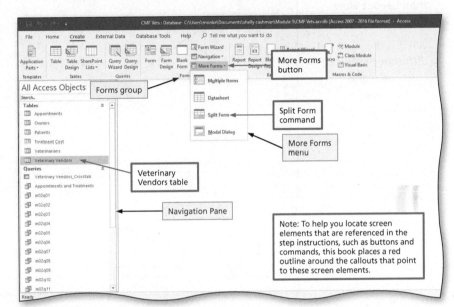

Figure 3–2

2

• Click Split Form to create a split form based on the Veterinary Vendors table.

• Close the Navigation Pane (Figure 3–3).

Q&A Is the form automatically saved? No. You will take specific actions later to save the form.

A field list appeared when I created the form. What should I do? Click the 'Add Existing Fields' button (Design tab | Tools group) to remove the field list.

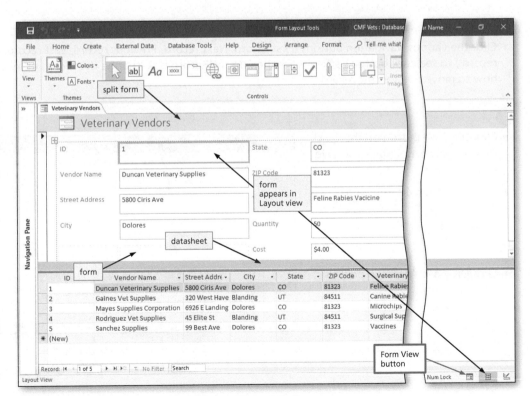

Figure 3–3

3

- Click the Form View button on the Access status bar to display the form in Form view rather than Layout view (Figure 3–4).

Q&A

What is the difference between Form view and Layout view?

Form view is the view you use to view, enter, and update data. Layout view is the view you use to make design changes to the form. It shows you the form with data in it so you can immediately see the effects of any design changes you make, but it is not intended to be used to enter and update data.

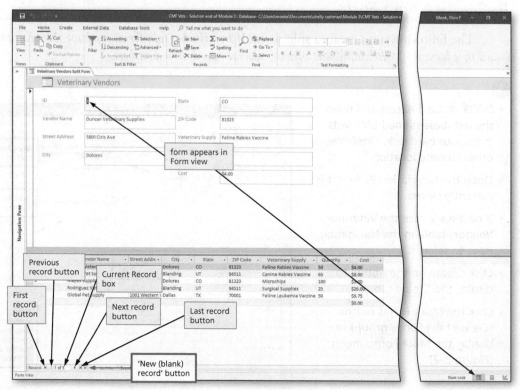

Figure 3–4

Experiment

- Click the various Navigation buttons (First record, Next record, Previous record, Last record, and 'New (blank) record') to see each button's effect. Click the Current Record box, change the record number, and press ENTER to see how to move to a specific record.

4

- Click the Save button on the Quick Access Toolbar to display the Save As dialog box.

- Save the form with the name **Veterinary Vendors Split Form** (Figure 3–5).

5

- Click OK (Save As dialog box) to save the form.

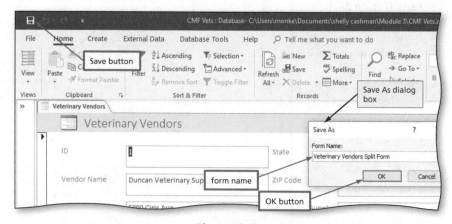

Figure 3–5

Other Ways

1. Right-click tab for form, click Form View on shortcut menu

To Use a Form to Add Records

Once a form or split form is open in Form view, you can add records using the same techniques you used to add records in Datasheet view. In a split form, the changes you make on the form are automatically made on the datasheet. You do not need to take any special action. The following steps use the split form that you just created to add records. *Why? With a split form, as you add a record, you can immediately see the effect of the addition on the datasheet.*

- Click the 'New (blank) record' button on the Navigation bar to enter a new record, and then type the data for the new record, as shown in Figure 3–6, keeping in mind that the ID field is an autonumber and will appear automatically when typing in a new record. Press TAB after typing the data in each field, except after typing the data for the final field (Cost).

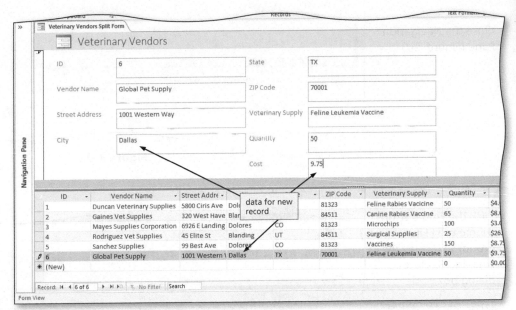

Figure 3–6

- Press TAB to complete the entry of the record.

- Close the form.

Other Ways

1. Click New button (Home tab | Records group)   2. Press CTRL+PLUS SIGN (+)

To Search for a Record

In the database environment, **searching** means looking for records that satisfy some criterion. Looking for the veterinary vendor that sells microchips is an example of searching. Running a query is another way of searching. In a query, Access has to locate those records that satisfied the criteria.

You can perform a search in Form view or Datasheet view without creating a query. The following steps search for the vendor that sells microchips. *Why? You want to locate the record quickly so you can update this vendor's record.*

- Open the Navigation Pane.

- Scroll down in the Navigation Pane, if necessary, so that Veterinary Vendors Split Form appears on your screen, right-click Veterinary Vendors Split Form to display a shortcut menu, and then click Open on the shortcut menu to open the form in Form view.

- Click the Veterinary Supply field.

Q&A Which command on the shortcut menu gives me Form view? I see both Layout view and Design view, but no option for Form view.

The Open command opens the form in Form view.

• Close the Navigation Pane (Figure 3–7).

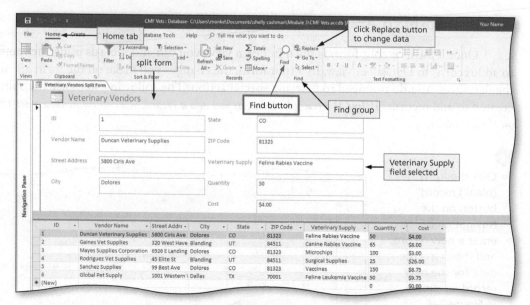

Figure 3–7

2

• Click the Find button (Home tab | Find group) to display the Find and Replace dialog box.

• Type `Microchips` in the Find What text box (Find and Replace dialog box), and then click the Find Next button to find veterinary supply microchips and display the record in the form (Figure 3–8).

Q&A Can I find records using this method in both Datasheet view and Form view?

Yes. You use the same process to find (and replace) records whether you are viewing the data with a split form, in Datasheet view, or in Form view.

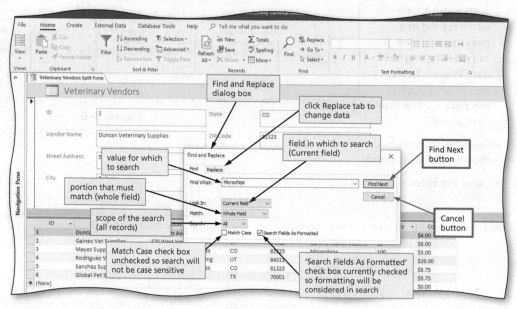

Figure 3–8

3

• Click Cancel (Find and Replace dialog box) to remove the dialog box from the screen.

Q&A Why does the button in the dialog box read Find Next, rather than simply Find?

In some cases, after locating a record that satisfies a criterion, you might need to find the next record that satisfies the same criterion. For example, if you just found the first supplier of microchips, you might then want to find the second supplier, then the third, and so on. To do so, click the Find Next button. You will not need to retype the value each time.

Other Ways

1. Press CTRL+F

Can you replace one value with another using the Find and Replace dialog box?
Yes. Either click the Replace button (Home tab | Find group) or click the Replace tab in the Find and Replace dialog box. You can then enter both the value to find and the new value.

To Update the Contents of a Record

The following step uses Form view to change the name of Veterinary Vendor ID 3 from Mayes Supplies Corporation to Mayes Supplies LLC. **Why?** *CMF determined that this supplier's name was incorrect and must be changed.* After locating the record to be changed, select the field to be changed by clicking the field. You can also press TAB repeatedly until the desired field is selected. Then make the appropriate changes. (Clicking the field automatically produces an insertion point. If you use TAB, you will need to press F2 to produce an insertion point.)

- Click in the Vendor Name field in the form for ID 3 immediately to the right of the "n" in Corporation.

- Backspace and replace the word Corporation with LLC.

- Press TAB to complete the change and move to the next field (Figure 3–9).

Q&A Could I have changed the contents of the field in the datasheet portion of the split form?
Yes. You first need to ensure the record to be changed appears in the datasheet. You then can change the value just as in the form.

Do I need to save my change?
No. Once you move to another record or close this form, the change to the name becomes permanent.

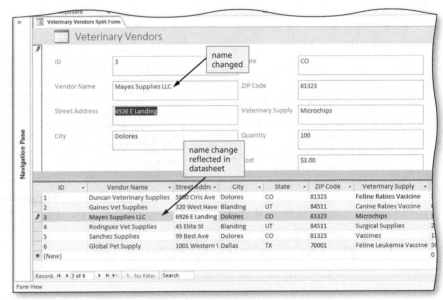

Figure 3–9

To Delete a Record

When records are no longer needed, you should delete them (remove them) from the table. The following steps delete ID 5, Sanchez Supplies. **Why?** *Sanchez has been providing an inferior product and CMF no longer wants to use them as a supplier, so the record can be deleted.*

- With the Veterinary Vendors Split Form open, click the record selector in the datasheet for ID 5, Vendor Name Sanchez Supplies, to select the record (Figure 3–10).

Q&A

That technique works in the datasheet portion. How do I select the record in the form portion?
With the desired record appearing in the form, click the record selector (the triangle in front of the record) to select the entire record.

What do I do if the record I want to delete does not appear on the screen?
First search for the record you want to delete using the Find and Replace dialog box.

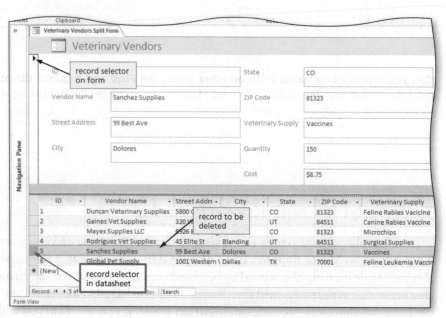

Figure 3–10

- Press DELETE to delete the record (Figure 3–11).

- Click Yes to complete the deletion.
- Close the Veterinary Vendors Split Form.

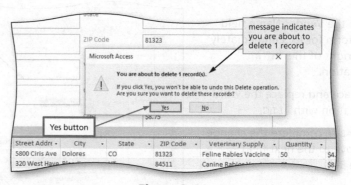

Figure 3–11

Other Ways

1. Click Delete arrow (Home tab | Records group), click Delete Record on Delete menu

Filtering Records

You can use the Find button in either Datasheet view or Form view to locate a record quickly that satisfies some criterion (for example, the ID 2). However, using these approaches returns all records, not just the record or records that satisfy the criterion. To have only the record or records that satisfy the criterion appear, use a **filter**. Four types of filters are available: Filter By Selection, Common Filters, Filter By Form, and Advanced Filter/Sort. You can use a filter in either Datasheet view or Form view.

To Use Filter By Selection

To use Filter By Selection, you give Access an example of the data you want by selecting the data within the table. You then choose the option you want on the Selection menu. The following steps use Filter By Selection in Datasheet view to display only the records for vendors in Blanding. *Why? Filter By Selection is appropriate for displaying these records and is the simplest type of filter.*

- Open the Navigation Pane.
- Open the Veterinary Vendors table, and then close the Navigation Pane.
- Click the City field on the second record to specify Blanding as the city (Figure 3–12).

Q&A Could I have selected the City field on another record where the city is also Blanding to select the same city?
Yes. It does not matter which record you select, as long as the city is Blanding.

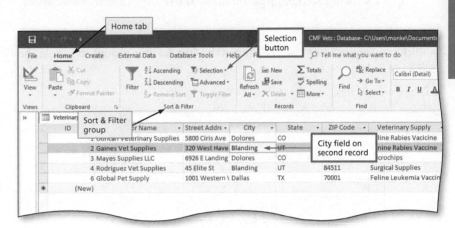

Figure 3–12

- Click the Selection button (Home tab | Sort & Filter group) to display the Selection menu (Figure 3–13).

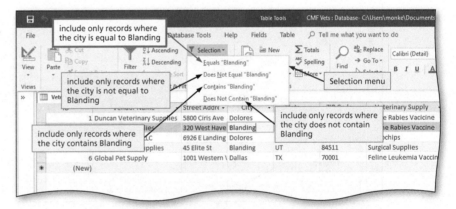

Figure 3–13

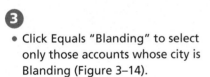

- Click Equals "Blanding" to select only those accounts whose city is Blanding (Figure 3–14).

Q&A Can I also filter in Form view?
Yes. Filtering works the same whether you are viewing the data with a split form, in Datasheet view, or in Form view.

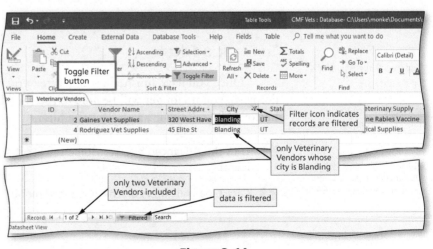

Figure 3–14

To Toggle a Filter

The Toggle Filter button switches between filtered and unfiltered displays of the records in the table. That is, if only filtered records currently appear, clicking the Toggle Filter button will redisplay all records. If all records are currently displayed and there is a filter that is in effect, clicking the Toggle Filter button will display only the filtered records. If no filter is active, the Toggle Filter button will be dimmed, so clicking it would have no effect.

The following step toggles the filter. *Why? CMF wants to once again view all the records.*

- Click the Toggle Filter button (Home tab | Sort & Filter group) to toggle the filter and redisplay all records (Figure 3–15).

Q&A Does that action clear the filter?

No. The filter is still in place. If you click the Toggle Filter button a second time, you will again see only the filtered records.

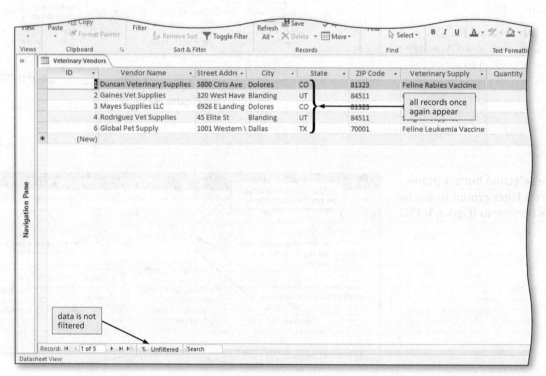

Figure 3–15

BTW
Access Screen
Resolution
If you are using a computer or mobile device to step through the project in this module and you want your screens to match the figures in this book, you should change your screen's resolution to 1366 x 768.

To Clear a Filter

Once you have finished using a filter, you can clear (remove) the filter. After doing so, you no longer will be able to use the filter by clicking the Toggle Filter button. The following steps clear the filter.

1. Click the Advanced button (Home tab | Sort & Filter group) to display the Advanced menu.

2. Click Clear All Filters on the Advanced menu.

To Use a Common Filter

If you have determined you want to include those accounts whose city begins with B, Filter By Selection would not be appropriate. *Why? None of the options within Filter By Selection would support this type of criterion.* You can filter individual fields by clicking the arrow to the right of the field name and using one of the **common filters** that are available for the field. Access includes a collection of filters that perform common filtering tasks; you can modify a common filter by customizing it for the specific field. The following steps customize a common filter to include only those accounts whose city begins with B.

1

• Click the City arrow to display the common filter menu.

• Point to the Text Filters command to display the custom text filters (Figure 3–16).

Q&A I selected the City field and then clicked the Filter button on the Home tab | Sort & Filter group. My screen looks the same. Is this right?
Yes. That is another way to display the common filter menu.

If I wanted certain cities included, could I use the check boxes?
Yes. Be sure the cities you want are the only ones checked.

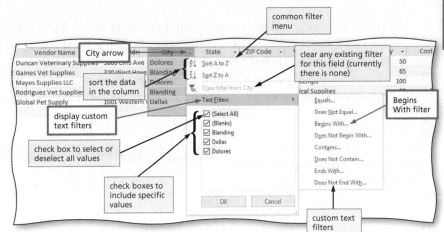

Figure 3–16

2

• Click Begins With to display the Custom Filter dialog box.

• Type **B** as the City begins with value (Figure 3–17).

Experiment

• Try other options in the common filter menu to see their effects. When done, once again select those accounts whose city begins with B.

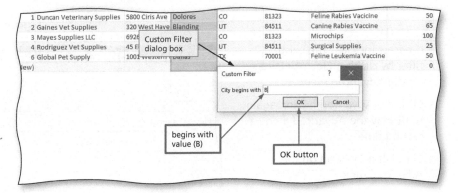

Figure 3–17

3

• Click the OK button to filter the records (Figure 3–18).

Q&A Can I use the same technique in Form view?
In Form view, you would need to click the field and then click the Filter button to display the Common Filter menu. The rest of the process is the same.

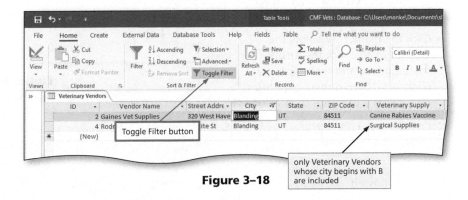

Figure 3–18

- Click the Toggle Filter button (Home tab | Sort & Filter group) to toggle the filter and redisplay all records.

Other Ways
1. Right-click field, click Text Filters on shortcut menu

To Use Filter By Form

Filter By Selection and the common filters method you just used are quick and easy ways to filter by the value in a single field. For filters that involve multiple fields, however, these methods are not appropriate, so you would use Filter By Form. ***Why?*** *Filter By Form allows you to filter based on multiple fields and criteria.* For example, Filter By Form would allow you to find only those vendors in Colorado whose quantity ordered is greater than 75. The following steps use Filter By Form to restrict the records that appear.

- Click the Advanced button (Home tab | Sort & Filter group) to display the Advanced menu (Figure 3–19).

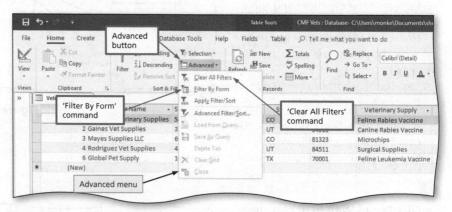

Figure 3–19

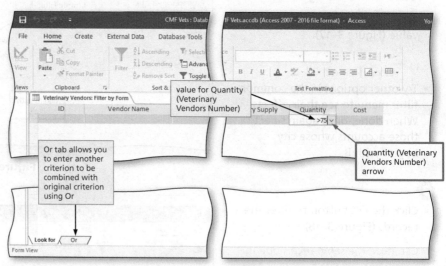

- If necessary, clear the existing filter by clicking Clear All Filters on the Advanced menu.
- Click the Advanced button again to display the Advanced menu a second time.
- Click Filter By Form on the Advanced menu.
- Click the blank row in the State field, and then choose CO from the menu to enter a criterion for the State field.
- Click the blank row below the Quantity field, click the arrow that appears, and then type >75 (Figure 3–20) to display quantities of supplies with more than 75 units from vendors in Colorado.

Figure 3–20

Q&A
Could I have clicked the arrow in the Quantity field and then made a selection, rather than typing a criterion?
No. Because your criterion involves something other than equality, you need to type the criterion rather than selecting from a list.

Is there any difference in the process if I am viewing a table in Form view rather than in Datasheet view?
In Form view, you will make your entries in a form rather than a datasheet. Otherwise, the process is the same.

3

- Click the Toggle Filter button (Home tab | Sort & Filter group) to apply the filter (Figure 3–21).

 Experiment

- Select Filter By Form again and enter different criteria. In each case, toggle the filter to see the effect of your selection. When done, once again select those vendors whose State is CO and whose Quantity is >75.

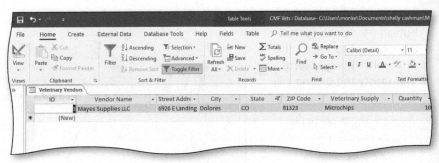

Figure 3–21

Other Ways

1. Click the Advanced button (Home tab | Sort & Filter group), click Apply Filter/Sort on Advanced menu

To Use Advanced Filter/Sort

In some cases, your criteria will be too complex even for Filter By Form. You might decide you want to include any vendor in Colorado whose Quantity is greater than 75. Additionally, you might want to include any account whose quantity is lower than 40, no matter which state the account is in. Further, you might want to have the results sorted by account name. The following steps use Advanced Filter/Sort to accomplish this task. *Why? Advanced Filter/Sort supports complex criteria as well as the ability to sort the results.*

1

- Click the Advanced button (Home tab | Sort & Filter group) to display the Advanced menu, and then click Clear All Filters on the Advanced menu to clear the existing filter.

- Click the Advanced button to display the Advanced menu a second time.

- Click Advanced Filter/Sort on the Advanced menu.

- Expand the size of the field list so all the fields in the Veterinary Vendors table appear.

- Add the Vendor Name field and select Ascending as the sort order to specify the order in which the filtered records will appear.

- Include the State field and enter CO as the criterion to limit the search to vendors in Colorado.

- Include the Quantity field and enter >75 as the criterion in the Criteria row and <40 as the criterion in the or row (Figure 3–22) to limit the search to vendors whose quantities are less than 40 or greater than 75.

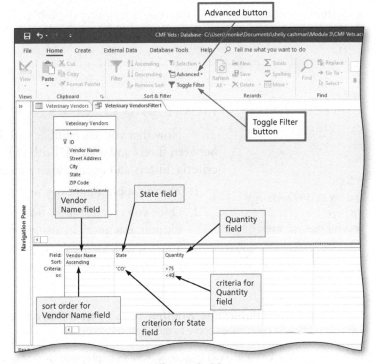

Figure 3–22

2

• Click the Toggle Filter button (Home tab | Sort & Filter group) to toggle the filter so that only records that satisfy the criteria will appear (Figure 3–23).

 Why are those particular records included?

The third and fourth records are included because the State is Colorado and the quantity is greater than 75. The other record is included because the quantity is less than 40.

 Experiment

• Select Advanced Filter/Sort again, and enter different sorting options and criteria. In each case, toggle the filter to see the effect of your selection. When done, change back to the sorting options and criteria you entered in Step 1.

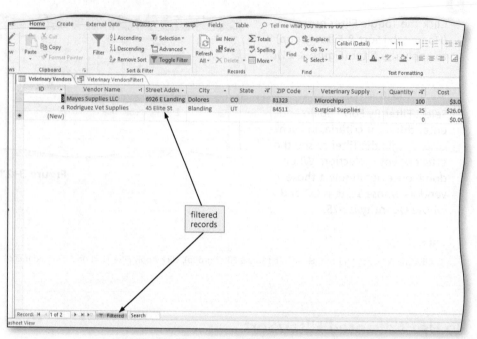

filtered records

Figure 3–23

3

• Close the Veterinary Vendors table. When asked if you want to save your changes, click the No button.

 Should I not have cleared all filters before closing the table?

If you are closing a table and not saving the changes, it is not necessary to clear the filter. No filter will be active when you next open the table.

Filters and Queries

Now that you are familiar with how filters work, you might notice similarities between filters and queries. Both objects are used to locate data that meets specific criteria. Filters and queries are related in three ways.

1. You can apply a filter to the results of a query just as you can apply a filter to a table.

2. Once you create a filter using Advanced Filter/Sort, you can save the filter settings as a query by using the Save as Query command on the Advanced menu.

3. You can restore filter settings that you previously saved in a query by using the Load from Query command on the Advanced menu.

BTW

Using Wildcards in Filters
Both the question mark(?) and the asterisk (*) wildcards can be used in filters created using Advanced Filter/Sort.

CONSIDER THIS

How do you determine whether to use a query or a filter?
The following guidelines apply to this decision.

• If you think that you will frequently want to display records that satisfy this exact criterion, you should consider creating a query whose results only contain the records that satisfy the criterion. To display those records in the future, simply open the query.

• If you are viewing data in a datasheet or form and decide you want to restrict the records to be included, it is easier to create a filter than a query. You can create and use the filter while you are viewing the data.

• If you have created a filter that you would like to be able to use again, you can save the filter as a query.

Once you have decided to use a filter, how do you determine which type of filter to use?

- If your criterion for filtering is that the value in a particular field matches or does not match a certain specific value, you can use Filter By Selection.

- If your criterion only involves a single field but is more complex (for example, the criterion specifies that the value in the field begins with a certain collection of letters), you can use a common filter.

- If your criterion involves more than one field, use Filter By Form.

- If your criterion involves more than a single And or Or, or if it involves sorting, you will probably find it simpler to use Advanced Filter/Sort.

Break Point: If you wish to take a break, this is a good place to do so. You can quit Access now. To resume at a later time, run Access, open the database called CMF Vets, and continue following the steps from this location forward.

Changing the Database Structure

When you initially create a database, you define its **structure**; that is, you assign names and types to all the fields. In many cases, the structure you first define will not continue to be appropriate as you use the database.

Perhaps a field currently in the table is no longer necessary. If no one ever uses a particular field, it is not needed in the table. Because it is occupying space and serving no useful purpose, you should remove it from the table. You would also need to delete the field from any forms, reports, or queries that include it.

More commonly, an organization will find that it needs to add data that was not anticipated at the time the database was first designed. The organization's own requirements may have changed. In addition, outside regulations that the organization must satisfy may change as well. Either case requires the addition of fields to an existing table.

Although you can make some changes to the database structure in Datasheet view, it is usually easier and better to make these changes in Design view.

TO CHANGE A FIELD'S DATA TYPE, PROPERTIES, AND PRIMARY KEY

A field in one of your tables might need a change of its data type and properties; for example, the data type might have been set that prevents the users from making calculations with the field. To make a change to the data type and properties of a field, you would use the following steps.

1. Open the table in Design view.
2. Next to the field name, click the box under Data Type.
3. Choose the correct data type from the menu.
4. A description of the field may be added under the column Description.
5. If necessary, change the field size in the Field Properties General tab below.
6. To change the key field, select the new key field by clicking in the grey box to the left of the field name. Choose Design tab | Tools Group click Primary Key.
7. When you close the table, you will be prompted to save the changes. Select Yes.

BTW
Using the Find Button
You can use the Find button (Home tab | Find group) to search for records in datasheets, forms, query results, and reports.

BTW
Changing Data Types
It is possible to change the data type for a field that already contains data. Before doing so, you should consider the effect on other database objects, such as forms, queries, and reports. For example, you could convert a Short Text field to a Long Text field if you find that you do not have enough space to store the data that you need. You also could convert a Number field to a Currency field or vice versa.

TO CHANGE A FIELD'S PROPERTIES IN DATASHEET VIEW

Alternatively, some of these changes may be done in Datasheet view. To use Datasheet view to change a field's name, caption, or data type, you would use the following steps.

1. Open the table in Datasheet view.
2. Select the desired field and Click the Fields tab | Properties Group.
3. Click Name and Caption, set a caption and description for the field.
4. In the Formatting group, you can set a data type.

TO DELETE A FIELD IN DESIGN VIEW

If a field in one of your tables is no longer needed, you should delete the field; for example, it might not serve a useful purpose, or it might have been included by mistake. To delete a field, you would use the following steps.

1. Open the table in Design view.
2. Click the row selector for the field to be deleted.
3. Press DELETE.
4. When Access displays the dialog box requesting confirmation that you want to delete the field, click Yes.

TO DELETE A FIELD IN DATASHEET VIEW

1. In Datasheet view, right-click the field and then click Delete Field.

TO MOVE A FIELD IN DESIGN VIEW

If you decide you would rather have a field in one of your tables in a different position in the table, you can move it. To move a field, you would use the following steps.

1. Open the table in Design view.
2. Click the row selector for the field to be deleted.
3. Drag the field to the desired position.
4. Release the mouse button to place the field in the new position.

TO MOVE A FIELD IN DATASHEET VIEW

If you are working in Datasheet view and want to move a field, you would use the following steps.

1. In Datasheet view, select the field and then hold down the mouse button. A dark line will appear on the left side of the column.
2. Drag the field to the desired position.
3. Release the mouse button to place the field in the new position.

To Change a Number Field Size in Design View

Most field size changes can be made in either Datasheet view or Design view. However, changing the field size for Number fields, such as the Quantity field, can only be done in Design view. Because the values in the Quantity field could have decimal places, such as a vendor product sold in bulk such as pounds or ounces, only Single, Double, or Decimal are possible choices for the field size. The difference between these choices concerns the amount of accuracy, that is, the number of decimal places to which the number is accurate. Double is more accurate than Single, for example, but requires more storage space. Because the quantity could only be two decimal places, Single is an acceptable choice.

The following steps change the field size of the Quantity field to Single, the format to Fixed, and the number of decimal places to 2, along with extending those changes to any form or report that uses this field. ***Why change the format and number of decimal places?*** *Changing the format and number ensures that each value will appear with precisely two decimal places.*

1

- Open the Navigation Pane, open the Veterinary Vendors table in Design view, and then close the Navigation Pane.

- If necessary, click the vertical scroll bar to display the Quantity field, and then click the row selector for the Quantity field to select the field (Figure 3–24).

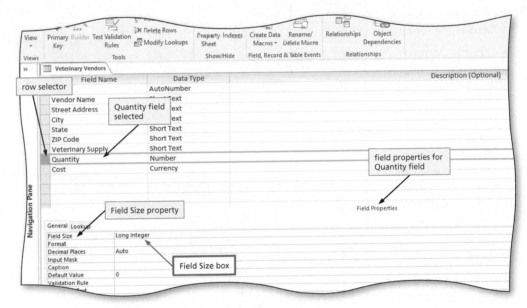

Figure 3–24

2

- Click the Field Size box to display the Field Size arrow.

- Click the Field Size arrow to display the Field Size menu (Figure 3–25).

Q&A What would happen if I left the field size set to Long Integer?
If the field size is

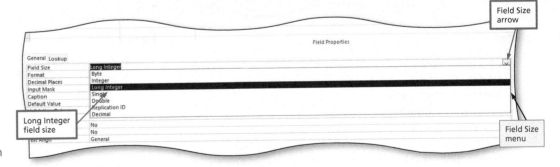

Figure 3–25

Long Integer, Integer, or Byte, no decimal places can be stored. For example, a value of .10 would be stored as 0. If you enter rates and the values all appear as 0, chances are you did not change the field size property.

3

- Click Single to select single precision as the field size.

- Click the Format box to display the Format arrow (Figure 3–26).

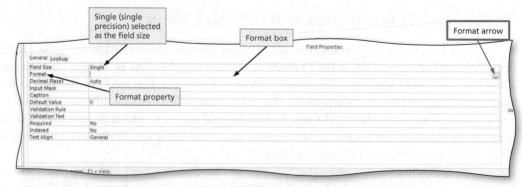

Figure 3–26

4

- Click the Format arrow to display the Format menu.

- Click Fixed to select fixed as the format.

- Click the Decimal Places box to display the Decimal Places arrow.

- Click the Decimal Places arrow to display the list of options so you can specify the number of decimal places.

- Click 2 to assign the number of decimal places.

- Click the Save button to save your changes (Figure 3–27).

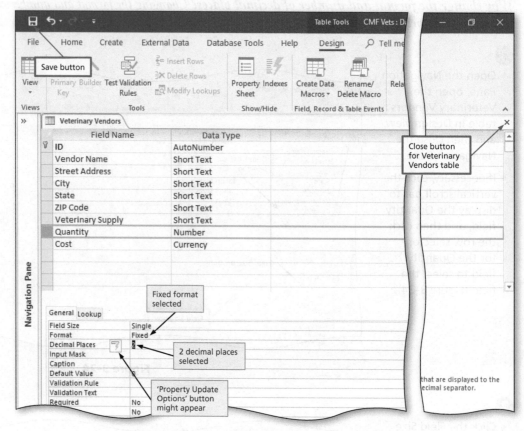

Figure 3–27

5

- Click the 'Property Update Options' button to display the options for updating the property of this field to any form or report that uses this field (Figure 3–28).

- Click Update Decimal Places everywhere Quantity is used to display the Update Properties dialog box (Figure 3–28).

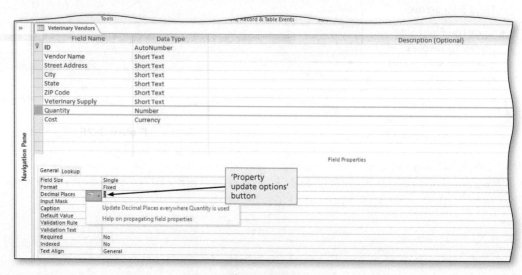

Figure 3–28

6

- In the Update Properties dialog box, ensure that Form: Veterinary Vendors Split Form is selected, and then click Yes to update that form to include the new decimal places for the Quantity field. (Figure 3–29).

Q&A Why did the 'Property Update Options' button appear?
You changed the number of decimal places. The 'Property Update Options' button offers a quick way of making the same change everywhere Quantity appears

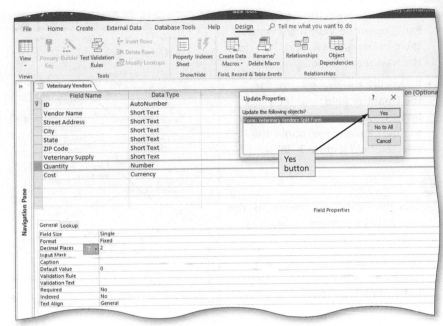

Figure 3–29

TO CHANGE THE FORMAT OF A NUMBER FIELD IN DATASHEET

Although the field size of number formatted fields cannot be changed in Datasheet view, the format of a number field can be changed in the datasheet. The number format can be General Number, Currency, Euro, Fixed, Standard, Percent, or Scientific. To change the format of a number field in the datasheet, you would use the following steps.

1. Open the table in Datasheet view.
2. Select the field that you want to change.
3. Click the Data Type arrow (Fields tab | Formatting Group) to display the Data Type menu, and then select the desired number format.

To Add a New Field

You can add fields to a table in a database. The following steps add the Product Type field to the Veterinary Vendors table immediately after the Veterinary Supply field. *Why? CMF has decided that it needs to categorize its suppliers by adding an additional field, Product Type. The possible values for Product Type are VAC (which indicates the vendor supplies vaccines), MC (which indicates the vendor supplies microchips), or SUP (which indicates the vendor sells surgical supplies).*

1

- If necessary, open the Navigation Pane, open the Veterinary Vendors table in Design view, and then close the Navigation Pane.

- Right-click the row selector for the Quantity field, and then click Insert Rows on the shortcut menu to insert a blank row above the selected field (Figure 3–30).

2

- Click the Field Name column for the new field to produce an insertion point.

- Type **Product Type** as the field name and then press TAB to move to the data type space.

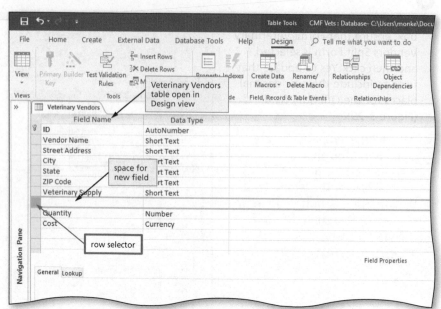

Figure 3–30

Other Ways

1. Click Insert Rows button (Table Tools Design tab | Tools group)

To Create a Lookup Field

A **lookup field** allows the user to select from a list of values when updating the contents of the field. The following steps make the Product Type field a lookup field. *Why? The Product Type field has only three possible values, making it an appropriate lookup field.*

1

- If necessary, click the Data Type column for the Product Type field, and then click the Data Type arrow to display the menu of available data types (Figure 3–31).

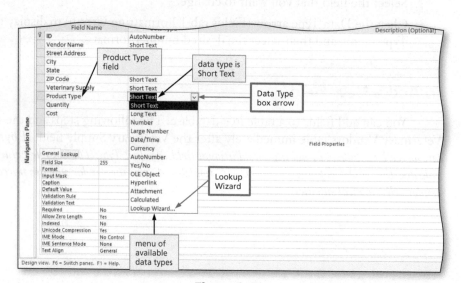

Figure 3–31

- Click Lookup Wizard, and then click the 'I will type in the values that I want.' option button (Lookup Wizard dialog box) to indicate that you will type in the values (Figure 3–32).

Q&A When would I use the other option button?
You would use the other option button if the data to be entered in this field were found in another table or query.

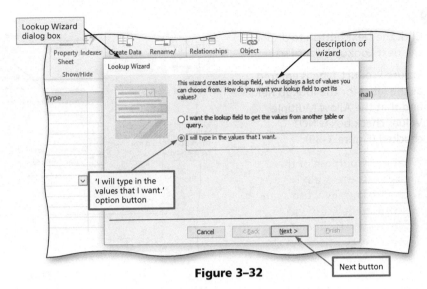

Figure 3–32

- Click the Next button to display the next Lookup Wizard screen (Figure 3–33).

Q&A Why did I not change the field size for the Product Type field?
You could have changed the field size to 3, but it is not necessary. When you create a lookup field and indicate specific values for the field, you automatically restrict the field size.

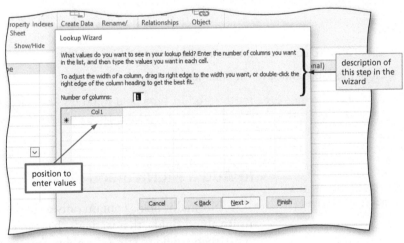

Figure 3–33

4

- Click the first row of the table (below Col1), and then type `VAC` as the value in the first row.

- Press the DOWN ARROW key, and then type `MC` as the value in the second row.

- Press the DOWN ARROW key, and then type `SUP` as the value in the third row (Figure 3–34).

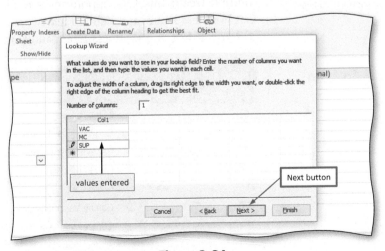

Figure 3–34

5

- Click the Next button to display the next Lookup Wizard screen.

- Ensure Product Type is entered as the label for the lookup field and that the Allow Multiple Values check box is NOT checked (Figure 3–35).

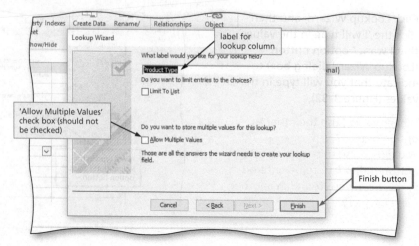

Figure 3–35

Q&A What is the purpose of the Limit To List check box?
With a lookup field, users can select from the list of values, in which case they can only select items in the list. They can also type their entry, in which case they are not necessarily limited to items in the list. If you check the Limit To List check box, users would be limited to items in the list, even if they type their entry. You will accomplish this same restriction later in this module with a validation rule, so you do not need to check this box.

6

- Click Finish to complete the definition of the lookup field.

- Close the table and save the changes.

Q&A Why does the data type for the Product Type field still show Short Text?
The data type is still Short Text because the values entered in the wizard were entered as text.

BTW
Multivalued Fields
Do not use multivalued fields if you plan to move your data to another relational database management system, such as SQL Server, at a later date. SQL Server and other relational DBMSs do not support multivalued fields.

To Add a Multivalued Field

Normally, fields contain only a single value. In Access, it is possible to have **multivalued fields**, that is, fields that can contain more than one value. CMF wants to use such a field to store the abbreviations of the various treatments done during appointments (see Table 3–1 for the treatment abbreviations and descriptions). Unlike the Product Type, where each product had only one type, appointments can require multiple treatments. One appointment might need T-1, T-3, and T-8 (Feline Rabies, Cat Wellness Exam, and Feline Heartworm). Another appointment might only need T-2 and T-12 (Dog Wellness Exam and Canine Neuter).

Table 3–1 Service Abbreviations and Descriptions			
Service Abbreviation	**Description**	**Service Abbreviation**	**Description**
T-1	Feline Rabies	T-8	Feline Heartworm
T-2	Dog Wellness Exam	T-9	Feline Spay
T-3	Cat Wellness Exam	T-10	Feline Neuter
T-4	Dog Rabies Shot	T-11	Canine Spay
T-5	Feline Vaccinations	T-12	Canine Neuter
T-6	Canine Vaccinations	T-13	Feline Microchip
T-7	Canine Heartworm	T-14	Canine Microchip

Creating a multivalued field uses the same process as creating a lookup field, with the exception that you check the Allow Multiple Values check box. The following steps create a multivalued field.

1. Open the Appointments table in Design view.

2. Click the row selector for the Treatment Number.

3. Click the Data Type arrow to display the menu of available data types for the Treatment Number field, and then click Lookup Wizard in the menu of available data types to start the Lookup Wizard.

4. Click the 'I will type in the values that I want.' option button to indicate that you will type in the values.

5. Click the Next button to display the next Lookup Wizard screen.

6. Click the first row of the table (below Col1), and then type T-1 as the value in the first row.

7. Enter the remaining values from the first column in Table 3–1. Before typing each value, press the DOWN ARROW to move to a new row.

8. Click the Next button to display the next Lookup Wizard screen.

9. Ensure that Treatment Number is entered as the label for the lookup field.

10. Click the Allow Multiple Values check box to allow the user to enter multiple values.

11. Click the Finish button to complete the definition of the Lookup Wizard field.

12. You will see a warning that says, You have changed the Treatment Number lookup column to store multiple values. You will not be able to undo this change once you save the table. Do you want to change Treatment Number to store multiple values? Click the Yes button.

13. Close the table and save the changes.

BTW
Modifying Table Properties
You can change the properties of a table by opening the table in Design view and then clicking the Property Sheet button. To display the records in a table in an order other than primary key (the default sort order), use the Order By property. For example, to display the Appointments table automatically in Patient ID order, change the Order By property setting to Appointments.Patient ID in the property box, close the property sheet, and save the change to the table design. When you open the Appointments table in Datasheet view, the records will be sorted in Patient ID order.

TO MODIFY SINGLE VALUED OR MULTIVALUED LOOKUP FIELDS

At some point you might want to change the list of choices in a lookup field. If you needed to modify a single value or multivalued lookup field, you would use the following steps.

1. Open the table in Design view and select the field to be modified.
2. Click the Lookup tab in the Field Properties pane.
3. Change the list in the Row Source property to the desired list of values.

To Add a Calculated Field

A field that can be computed from other fields is called a **calculated field** or a **computed field**. You can create a calculated field in a query. In Access 2019 it is also possible to include a calculated field in a table. Users will not be able to update this field. *Why? Access will automatically perform the necessary calculation and display the correct value whenever you display or use this field in any way.* The following steps add to the Veterinary Vendors table a field that calculates the product of the Quantity and Cost fields.

- Open the Veterinary Vendors table in Design view.
- Click in the blank row under Cost field.
- Type **Total Amount** as the field name, and then press the TAB key.
- Click the Data Type arrow to display the menu of available data types (Figure 3–36).

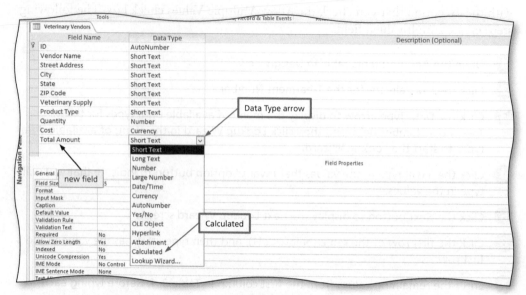

Figure 3–36

2

- Click Calculated to select the Calculated data type and display the Expression Builder dialog box (Figure 3–37).

Q&A I do not have the list of fields in the Expression Categories area. What should I do? Click Veterinary Vendors in the Expression Elements area.

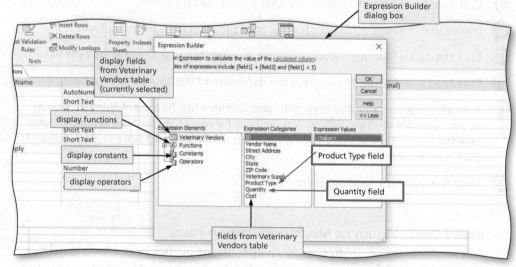

Figure 3–37

3

- Double-click the Quantity field in the Expression Categories area (Expression Builder dialog box) to add the field to the expression.
- Type a multiplication sign (*).

Q&A Could I select the multiplication sign from a list rather than typing it? Yes. Click Operators in the Expression Elements area to display available operators, and then double-click the multiplication sign.

- Double-click the Cost field in the Expression Categories area (Expression Builder dialog box) to add the field to the expression (Figure 3–38).

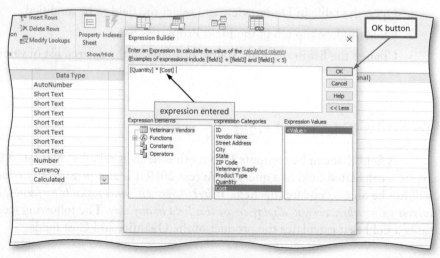

Figure 3–38

4

- Click OK (Expression Builder dialog box) to enter the expression in the Expression property of the Total Amount (Figure 3–39).

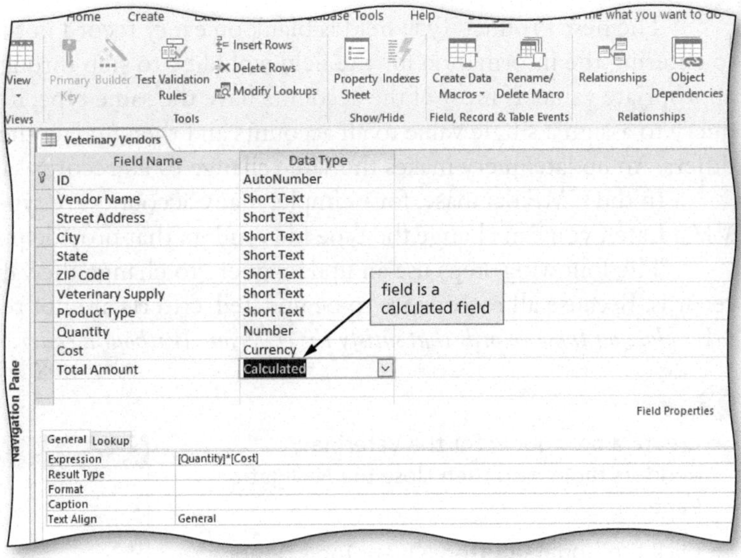

Q&A Could I have typed the expression in the Expression Builder dialog box rather than selecting the fields from a list?
Yes. You can use whichever technique you find more convenient.

When I entered a calculated field in a query, I typed the expression in the Zoom dialog box. Could I have used the Expression Builder instead?
Yes. To do so, you would click Build rather than Zoom on the shortcut menu.

Could I make a calculated field in Datasheet view of a table?
Yes, to do so, open the table in Datasheet view, click the Click to Add arrow in rightmost blank field space, select Calculated Field, and then indicate the type of data you want in that calculated field. Access displays the Expression Builder, where you can complete the calculated field.

Can I modify the calculated field in Design view?
Yes, in Design view, select the calculated field. In the property sheet for the selected field, click the General tab, if necessary, and click to the right of the Expression property. Click the small box with three dots the Expression Builder dialog box.

Figure 3–39

To Save the Changes and Close the Table

The following steps save the changes; that is, they save the addition of the new field and close the table.

1 Click the Save button on the Quick Access Toolbar to save the changes.

2 Close the Veterinary Vendors table.

Mass Changes

In some cases, rather than making individual changes to records, you will want to make mass changes. That is, you will want to add, change, or delete many records in a single operation. You can do this with action queries. Unlike select queries, which simply present data in specific ways, an **action query** adds, deletes, or changes data in a table. An **update query** allows you to make the same change to all records satisfying some criterion. If you omit the criterion, you will make the same changes to all records in the table. A **delete query** allows you to delete all the records satisfying some criterion. You can add the results of a query to an existing table by using an **append query**. You also can add the query results to a new table by using a **make-table query**.

BTW
Database Backup
If you are doing mass changes to a database, be sure to back up the database prior to doing the updates.

To Use an Update Query

The new Product Type field is blank on every record in the Veterinary Vendors table. One approach to entering the information for the field would be to step through the entire table, assigning each record its appropriate value. If most of the accounts have the same type, it would be more convenient to use an update query to assign a single value to all accounts and then update the Product Type for those accounts whose type differs. An update query makes the same change to all records satisfying a criterion.

In the CMF database, for example, many accounts are type VAC. Initially, you can set all the values to VAC. Later, you can change the type for vendors that provide products other than vaccines.

The following steps use an update query to change the value in the Product Type field to VAC for all the records. Because all records are to be updated, criteria are not required. ***Why?*** *If there is a criterion, the update only takes place on those records that satisfy the criterion. Without a criterion, the update applies to all records.*

- Create a new query for the Veterinary Vendors table, and then close the Navigation Pane.

- Click the Update button (Query Tools Design tab | Query Type group) to specify an update query, double-click the Product Type field to select the field, click the Update To row in the first column of the design grid, and then type **VAC** as the new value (Figure 3–40).

Q&A If I change my mind and do not want an update query, how can I change the query back to a select query?
Click the Select button (Query Tools Design tab | Query Type group).

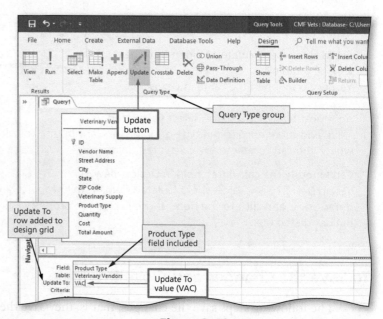

Figure 3–40

- Click the Run button (Query Tools Design tab | Results group) to run the query and update the records (Figure 3–41).

Q&A The dialog box did not appear on my screen when I ran the query. What happened?
If the dialog box did not appear, it means that you did not click the Enable Content button when you first opened the database. Close the database, open it again, and enable the content. Then, create and run the query again.

- Click the Yes button to make the changes.

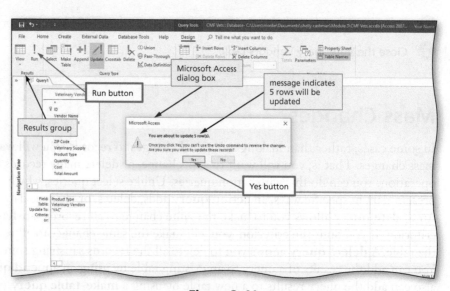

Figure 3–41

Experiment

- Create an update query to change the account type to MC. Enter a criterion to restrict the records to be updated, and then run the query. Open the table to view your changes. When finished, create and run an update query to change the account type to VAC on all records.
- Close the query. Because you do not need to use this update query again, do not save the query.

Other Ways

1. Right-click any open area in upper pane, point to Query Type on shortcut menu, click Update Query on Query Type submenu

TO USE A DELETE QUERY

In some cases, you might need to delete several records at a time. If, for example, CMF no longer dealt with any vendors in Texas (TX), the vendors with this value in the State field can be deleted from the CMF database. Instead of deleting these accounts individually, which could be very time-consuming in a large database, you can delete them in one operation by using a delete query, which is a query that deletes all the records satisfying the criteria entered in the query. To create a delete query, you would use the following steps.

1. Create a query for the table containing the records to be deleted.
2. In Design view, indicate the fields and criteria that will specify the records to delete.
3. Click the Delete button (Query Tools Design tab | Query Type group).
4. Run the query by clicking the Run button (Query Tools Design tab | Results group).
5. When Access indicates the number of records to be deleted, click the Yes button.

TO USE AN APPEND QUERY

An append query adds a group of records from one table, called the Source table, to the end of another table, called the Destination table. For example, suppose that CMF acquires some new vendors; these new vendors are accompanied by a related database. To avoid entering all this information manually, you can append it to the Veterinary Vendors table in the CMF database using the append query. To create an append query, you would use the following steps.

1. Create a query for the Source table.
2. In Design view, indicate the fields to include, and then enter any necessary criteria.
3. View the query results to be sure you have specified the correct data, and then return to Design view.
4. Click the Append button (Query Tools Design tab | Query Type group).
5. When Access displays the Append dialog box, specify the name of the Destination table and its location. Run the query by clicking the Run button (Query Tools Design tab | Results group).
6. When Access indicates the number of records to be appended, click the OK button.

BTW

Viewing Records before Updating
You can view records affected by an update query before running the query. To do so, use the Select button to convert the query to a select query, add any additional fields that would help you identify the records, and then view the results. Make any necessary corrections to the query in Design view. When you are satisfied, use the Update button to once again convert the query to an update query.

BTW

Delete Queries
If you do not specify any criteria in a delete query, Access will delete all the records in the table.

TO USE A MAKE-TABLE QUERY

In some cases, you might want to create a new table that contains only records from an existing table. If so, use a make-table query to add the records to a new table. To create a make-table query, you would use the following steps.

1. Create a query for the Source table.
2. In Design view, indicate the fields to include, and then enter any necessary criteria.
3. View the query results to be sure you have specified the correct data, and then return to Design view.
4. Click the Make Table button (Query Tools Design tab | Query Type group).
5. When Access displays the Make Table dialog box, specify the name of the Destination table and its location. Run the query by clicking the Run button (Query Tools Design tab | Results group).
6. When Access indicates the number of records to be inserted, click the OK button.

Break Point: If you wish to take a break, this is a good place to do so. You can quit Access now. To resume at a later time, start Access, open the database called CMF, and continue following the steps from this location forward.

Validation Rules

You now have created, loaded, queried, and updated a database. Nothing you have done so far, however, restricts users to entering only valid data, that is, data that follows the rules established for data in the database. An example of such a rule would be that product types can only be VAC, MC, or SUP. To ensure the entry of valid data, you create **validation rules**, or rules that a user must follow when entering the data. When the database contains validation rules, Access prevents users from entering data that does not follow the rules. You can also specify **validation text**, which is the message that appears if a user attempts to violate the validation rule.

Validation rules can indicate a **required field**, a field in which the user *must* enter data; failing to enter data into a required field generates an error. Validation rules can also restrict a user's entry to a certain **range of values**; for example, the values in the Quantity field must be between 0 and 1,000. Alternatively, rules can specify a **default value**, that is, a value that Access will display on the screen in a particular field before the user begins adding a record. To make data entry of account numbers more convenient for the user, you can also have lowercase letters appear automatically as uppercase letters. Finally, validation rules can specify a collection of acceptable values.

To Change a Field Size

The Field Size property for text fields represents the maximum number of characters a user can enter in the field. Because the field size for the ZIP Code field in the Veterinary Vendors table is the default 255, but a user would never enter a ZIP code that long. Conversely, if the field had been set to be only 5 spaces, then the ZIP code plus four would not fit into that field. Occasionally, you will find that the field size that seemed appropriate when you first created a table is no longer appropriate. In the Veterinary Vendors table, the ZIP code needs to be adjusted to fit 20 characters, in the case that there is a foreign postal code that is longer than the ZIP code plus four. To allow this longer postal code in the table, you need to change the field size for the

ZIP Code field to a Short Text that is smaller so it doesn't take up excess storage. The following step changes the field size for the ZIP code field from 255 to 20.

1 Open the Veterinary Vendors table in Design view and close the Navigation Pane.

2 Select the ZIP Code field by clicking its row selector.

3 Click the Field Size property to select it, delete the current entry (255), and then type 20 as the new field size.

To Specify a Required Field

To specify that a field is to be required, change the value for the Required property from No to Yes. The following step specifies that the Vendor Name field is a required field. *Why? Users will not be able to leave the Vendor Name field blank when entering or editing records.*

- Select the Vendor Name field by clicking its row selector.
- Click the Required property box in the Field Properties pane, and then click the arrow that appears.
- Click Yes in the list to make Vendor Name a required field (Figure 3–42).

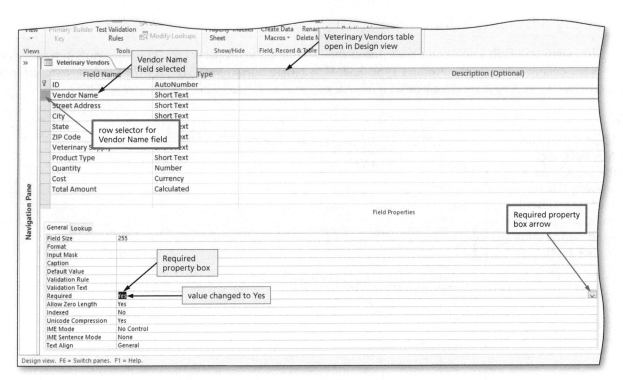

Figure 3–42

To Specify a Range

The following step specifies that entries in the Quantity field must greater than 0 and less than or equal to 1,000. To indicate this range, the criterion specifies that the Quantity amount must be both > 0 (greater than) and <= 1000 (less than or equal to 1,000). *Why? Combining these two criteria with the word, and, is logically equivalent to being between 0.00 and 1,001.00.*

- Select the Quantity field by clicking its row selector, click the Validation Rule property box to produce an insertion point, and then type >0 and <=1000 as the rule.

- Click the Validation Text property box to produce an insertion point, and then type Must be greater than 0.00 and at most 1,000.00 as the text (Figure 3–43).

Q&A What is the effect of this change?
Users will now be prohibited from entering a Quantity amount that is either less than or equal to 0.00 or greater than 1,000.00 when they add records or change the value in the Quantity field.

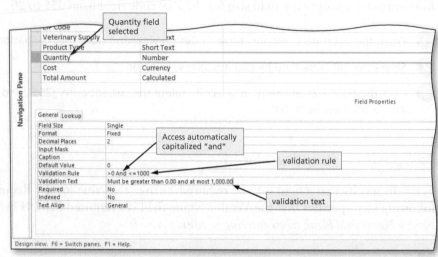

Figure 3–43

To Specify a Default Value

To specify a default value, enter the value in the Default Value property box. The following step specifies VAC as the default value for the Product Type field. *Why? More vendors for CMF have the type VAC than either of the other types. By making it the default value, if users do not enter an Product Type, the type will be VAC.*

- Select the Product Type field, click the Default Value property box to produce an insertion point, and then type =VAC as the value (Figure 3–44).

Q&A Do I need to type the equal (=) sign?
No. You could enter just VAC as the default value.

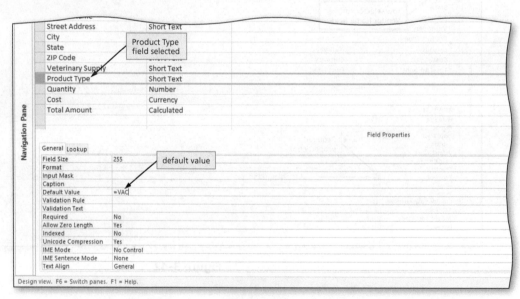

Figure 3–44

To Specify a Collection of Legal Values

The only **legal values**, or **allowable values**, for the Product Type field are VAC, MC, and SUP. The following step creates a validation rule to specify these as the only legal values for the Account Type field. *Why? The validation rule prohibits users from entering any other value in the Product Type field.*

1

- With the Product Type field selected, click the Validation Rule property box to produce an insertion point and then type `=VAC or =MC or =SUP` as the validation rule.

- Click the Validation Text property box, and then type `Must be VAC, MC, or SUP` as the validation text (Figure 3–45).

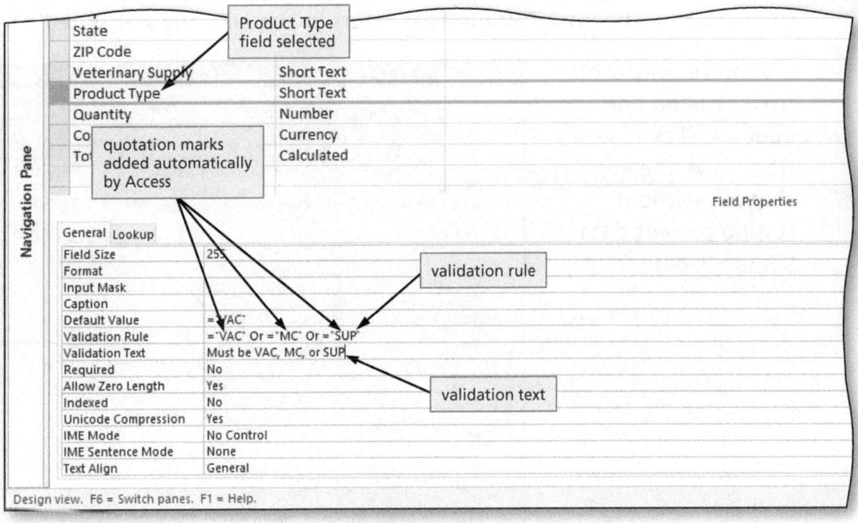

Q&A What is the effect of this change?
Users will now only be allowed to enter VAC, MC, or SUP in the Product Type field when they add records or make changes to this field.

Do I have to put quotation marks around VAC, MC and SUP?
No, you can just type in =VAC or =MC or =SUP. Access automatically will put quotation marks around the product types.

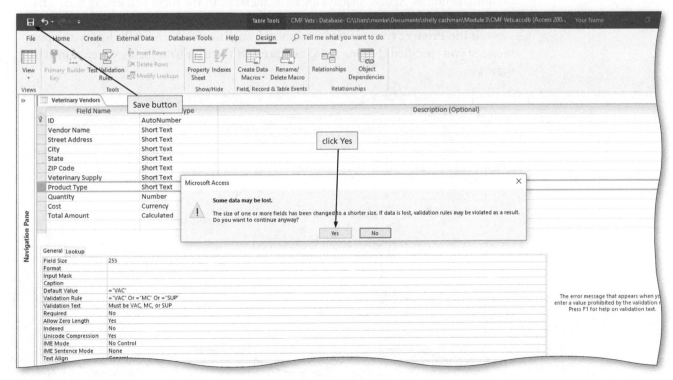

Figure 3–45

To Save the Validation Rules, Default Values, and Formats

The following steps save the validation rules, default values, and formats.

1 Click the Save button on the Quick Access Toolbar to save the changes (Figure 3–46).

Figure 3–46

2   Click the Yes button (Microsoft Access dialog box) to save the changes, even though the message warns that some data will be lost. This message refers to the ZIP code shortened length.

3   If a second Microsoft Access dialog box appears, click No to save the changes without testing current data (Figure 3–47).

Q&A   When would you want to test current data?
If you have any doubts about the validity of the current data, you should be sure to test the current data.

4   Close the Veterinary Vendors table.

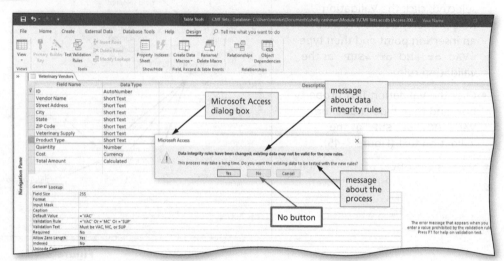

Figure 3–47

Q&A   Can I set validation rules, validation text, and properties in Datasheet view?
Yes, in Datasheet view, select the field and display the Fields. In the Properties group, you can also modify lookups. In the Field Validation group, you can set validation.

Updating a Table That Contains Validation Rules

Now that the CMF database contains validation rules, Access restricts the user to entering data that is valid and is formatted correctly. If a user enters a number that is out of the required range, for example, or enters a value that is not one of the permitted choices, Access displays an error message in the form of a dialog box. The user cannot update the database until the error is corrected.

If the Product type entered is not valid, such as xxx, Access will display the text message you specified (Figure 3–48) and prevent the data from being entered into the database.

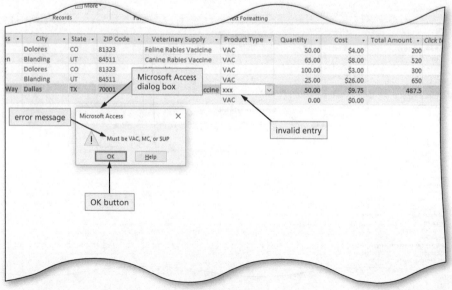

Figure 3–48

If the Current Due amount entered is not valid, such as 5000, which is too large, Access also displays the appropriate message (Figure 3–49) and refuses to accept the data.

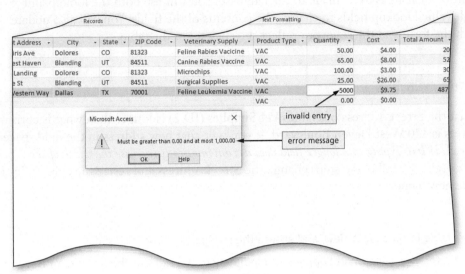

Figure 3–49

If a required field contains no data, Access indicates this by displaying an error message as soon as you attempt to leave the record (Figure 3–50). The field must contain a valid entry before Access will move to a different record, even if you did not specify validation text.

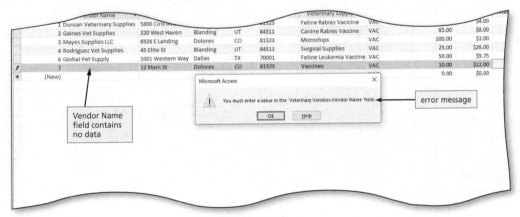

Figure 3–50

When entering invalid data into a field with a validation rule, is it possible that you could not enter the data correctly? What would cause this? If it happens, what should you do?

If you cannot remember the validation rule you created or if you created the rule incorrectly, you might not be able to enter the data. In such a case, you will be unable to leave the field or close the table because you have entered data into a field that violates the validation rule.

If this happens, first try again to type an acceptable entry. If this does not work, repeatedly press BACKSPACE to erase the contents of the field, and then try to leave the field. If you are unsuccessful using this procedure, press ESC until the record is removed from the screen. The record will not be added to the database.

Should the need arise to take this drastic action, you probably have a faulty validation rule. Use the techniques of the previous sections to correct the existing validation rules for the field.

CONSIDER THIS

Making Additional Changes to the Database

Now that you have changed the structure and created validation rules, there are additional changes to be made to the database. You will use both the lookup and multivalued lookup fields to change the contents of the fields. You will also update both the form and the report to reflect the changes in the table.

To Change the Contents of a Field

Perhaps you realized that the Street Address of Gaines Vet Supplies (ID 2) is longer than what is currently in the table. The correct address is 320 West Haven Boulevard. If you type that new address in the field space, the full address will be obscured. **Why?** *Typing in a longer field does not automatically increase the width of the corresponding column in the datasheet.* The following steps change the Street Address and resize the column in the datasheet to accommodate the new name.

- Open the Veterinary Vendors table in Datasheet view, and ensure the Navigation Pane is closed.

- Click in the Street Address field for ID 2, Gaines Vet Supplies, immediately to the right of the letter n, of Haven to produce an insertion point.

- Press SPACEBAR to enter a space.

- Enter the word `Boulevard,` and then press TAB to update the address.

Q&A I cannot add the extra characters. Whatever I type replaces what is currently in the cell. What happened and what should I do? You are typing in Overtype mode, not Insert mode. Press INSERT and correct the entry.

- Resize the Street Address column to best fit the new data by double-clicking the right boundary of the field selector for the Street Address field, that is, the column heading (Figure 3–51).

- Save the changes to the layout by clicking the Save button on the Quick Access Toolbar.

- Close the Veterinary Vendors table.

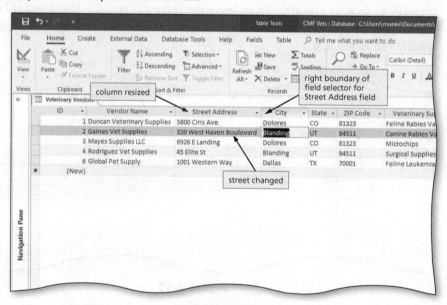

Figure 3–51

To Use a Lookup Field

Earlier, you changed all the entries in the Product Type field to VAC. You have created a rule that will ensure that only legitimate values (VAC, MC, or SUP) can be entered in the field. You also made Product Type a lookup field. **Why?** *You can make changes to a lookup field for individual records by simply clicking the field to be changed, clicking the arrow that appears in the field, and then selecting the desired value from the list.* The following steps change the incorrect Product Type values to the correct values.

- Open the Veterinary Vendors table in Datasheet view and ensure the Navigation Pane is closed.

- Click in the Product Type field on the third record (ID 3) to display an arrow.

- Click the arrow to display the drop-down list of available choices for the Product Type field (Figure 3–52).

Q&A
I got the drop-down list as soon as I clicked. I did not need to click the arrow. What happened?
If you click in the position where the arrow would appear, you will get the drop-down list. If you click anywhere else, you would need to click the arrow.

Could I type the value instead of selecting it from the list?
Yes. Once you have either deleted the previous value or selected the entire previous value, you can begin typing. You do not have to type the full entry. When you begin with the letter, M, for example, Access will automatically add the C.

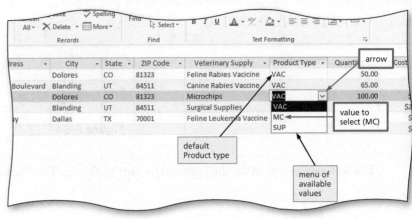

Figure 3–52

- Click MC to change the value.

- In a similar fashion, change the values on the other record to match that shown in Figure 3–53.

- Close the table.

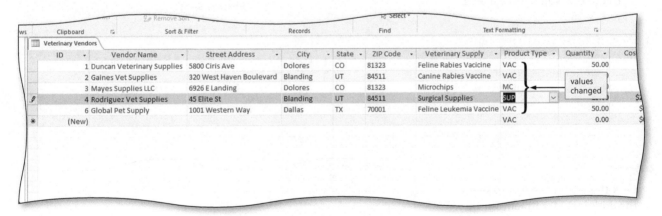

Figure 3–53

To Use a Multivalued Lookup Field

Using a multivalued lookup field is similar to using a regular lookup field. The difference is that when you display the list, the entries are all preceded by check boxes. *Why? Having the check boxes allows you to make multiple selections. You check all the entries that you want.* The appropriate entries are shown for the Appointments table in Figure 3–54. As indicated in the figure, most animals come into the CMF Veterinary office for more than one treatment.

Appointment ID	Patient ID	Appointment Date	Treatment Number	Veterinarian	Owner
1	P-3	6/30/2021	T-3, T-10	B01	O-6
2	P-7	10/25/2021	T-4, T-7, T-14	B01	O-8
3	P-2	1/10/2021	T-2	B01	O-5
4	P-4	6/30/2021	T-1, T-8	B01	O-1
5	P-5	8/23/2021	T-4, T-7	G01	O-4

Figure 3–54

The following steps make the appropriate entries for the Treatment Number field in the Appointments table.

- Open the Appointments table.

- Since the Patient IDs were changed in the Patients table in an earlier module, there need to be some corrections to the Appointments table. Before entering the Treatment Numbers in this section, change the data in the Appointments table's Patient ID and Owner ID fields to match those in Figure 3–54.

- Click the Treatment Number field on the first record to display the arrow.

- Click the arrow to display the list of Treatment Numbers available (Figure 3–55).

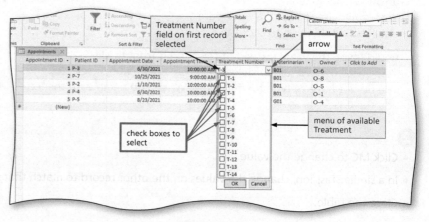

Figure 3–55

Q&A
What if there were too many treatments to fit?
Access would automatically include a scroll bar that you could use to scroll through all the choices.

- Click the T-10 check box to select the additional treatment for the first appointment; T-3 treatment has already been selected (Figure 3–56).

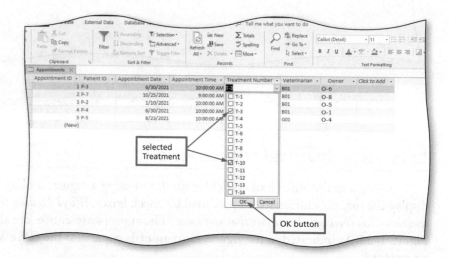

Figure 3–56

- Click the OK button to complete the selection.

- Using the same technique, enter the services given in Figure 3–54 for the remaining accounts.

- Double-click the right boundary of the field selector for the Treatment Number field to resize the field so that it best fits the data (Figure 3–57).

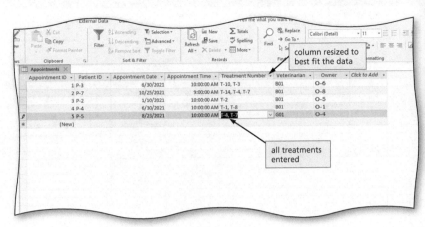

Figure 3–57

- Save the changes to the layout by clicking the Save button on the Quick Access Toolbar.

- Close the Appointments table.

Changing the Appearance of a Datasheet

You can change the appearance of a datasheet in a variety of ways. You can include totals in the datasheet. You can also change the appearance of gridlines or the text colors and font.

To Include Totals in a Datasheet

The following steps first include an extra row, called the Total row, in the datasheet for the Veterinary Vendors table. Note that this is not a calculated field. *Why? It is possible to include totals and other statistics at the bottom of a datasheet in the Total row.* The steps then display the total amount of money spent on all vendors.

- Open the Veterinary Vendors table in Datasheet view and close the Navigation Pane.

- Click the Totals button (Home tab | Records group) to include the Total row in the datasheet. Note that a blank row will appear above the Totals row.

- Click the Total row in the Total Amount column to display an arrow.

- Click the arrow to display a menu of available calculations (Figure 3–58).

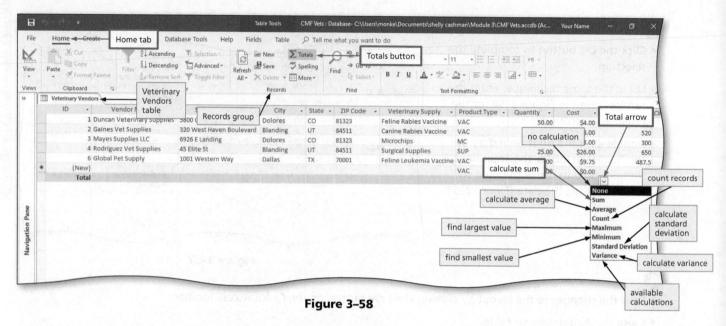

Figure 3–58

Q&A

Can I also create a totals row in a query?

Yes, you can create a totals row in the Datasheet view of a query just like you did in the Datasheet view of the table.

Will I always get the same list?

No. You will only get the items that are applicable to the type of data in the column. You cannot calculate the sum of text data, for example.

- Click Sum to calculate the total of the total amounts.

- Resize the Total Amount column to best fit the total amount (Figure 3–59), if necessary.

Experiment

- Experiment with other statistics. When finished, once again select the sum.

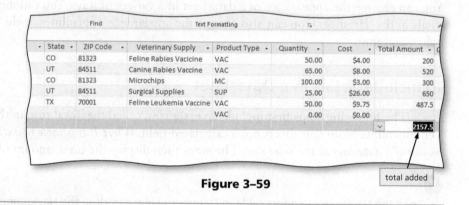

Figure 3–59

To Remove Totals from a Datasheet

If you no longer want the totals to appear as part of the datasheet, you can remove the Total row. The following step removes the Total row.

1 Click the Totals button (Home tab | Records group), which is shown in Figure 3–58, to remove the Total row from the datasheet.

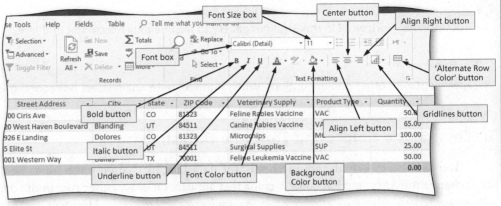

Figure 3–60

Figure 3–60 shows the various buttons, located in the Text Formatting group on the Home tab, that are available to change the datasheet appearance. The changes to the datasheet will be reflected not only on the screen, but also when you print or preview the datasheet.

To Change Gridlines in a Datasheet

The following steps change the datasheet so that only horizontal gridlines are included. *Why? You might prefer the appearance of the datasheet with only horizontal gridlines.*

1

- Open the Veterinary Vendors table in Datasheet view, if it is not already open.
- If necessary, close the Navigation Pane.
- Click the datasheet selector, the box in the upper-left corner of the datasheet, to select the entire datasheet (Figure 3–61).

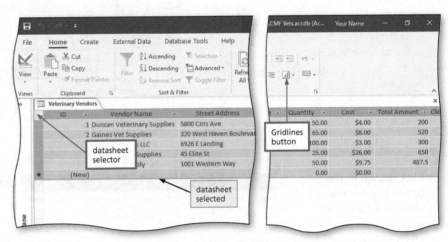

Figure 3–61

2

- Click the Gridlines button (Home tab | Text Formatting group) to display the Gridlines gallery (Figure 3–62).

Q&A Does it matter whether I click the button or the arrow?
In this case, it does not matter. Either action will display the gallery.

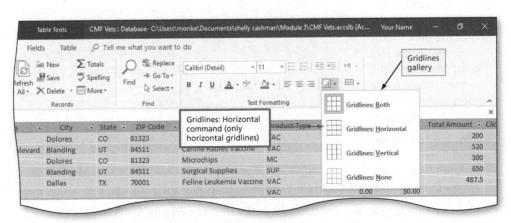

Figure 3–62

- Click Gridlines: Horizontal in the Gridlines gallery to include only horizontal gridlines.

 Experiment

- Experiment with other gridline options. When finished, once again select horizontal gridlines.

To Change the Colors and Font in a Datasheet

You can also modify the appearance of the datasheet by changing the colors and the font. The following steps change the Alternate Fill color, a color that appears on every other row in the datasheet. *Why? Having rows appear in alternate colors is an attractive way to visually separate the rows.* The steps also change the font color, the font, and the font size.

1

- With the datasheet for the Veterinary Vendors table selected, click the Alternate Row Color button arrow (Home tab | Text Formatting group) to display the color palette (Figure 3–63).

Q&A
Does it matter whether I click the button or the arrow?
Yes. Clicking the arrow produces a color palette. Clicking the button applies the currently selected color. When in doubt, you should click the arrow.

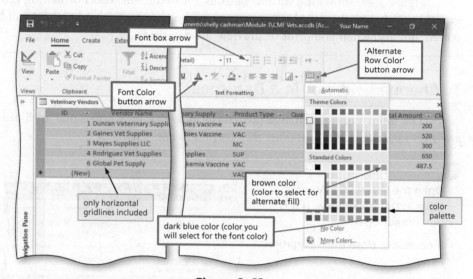

Figure 3–63

2

- Click Brown in the upper-right corner of Standard Colors to select brown as the alternate color.

- Click the Font Color button arrow, and then click the dark blue color that is the second color from the right in the bottom row in the Standard Colors to select the font color.

- Click the Font arrow, scroll down in the list until Bodoni MT appears, and then select Bodoni MT as the font. (If it is not available, select any font of your choice.)

- Click the Font Size arrow and select 10 as the font size (Figure 3–64).

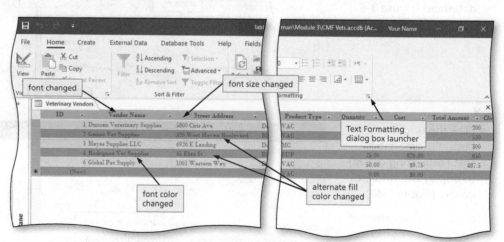

Figure 3–64

Q&A Does the order in which I make these selections make a difference?
No. You could have made these selections in any order.

Experiment

- Experiment with other colors, fonts, and font sizes. When finished, return to the options selected in these steps.

Using the Datasheet Formatting Dialog Box

As an alternative to using the individual buttons, you can click the Datasheet Formatting dialog box launcher, which is the arrow at the lower-right of the Text Formatting group, to display the Datasheet Formatting dialog box (Figure 3–65). You can use the various options within the dialog box to make changes to the datasheet format. Once you are finished, click the OK button to apply your changes.

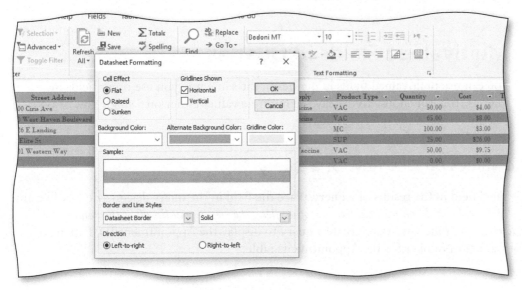

Figure 3–65

Q&A Can I also format my datasheet in other ways?
There are many other formatting options for your table in Datasheet view. You can select all the records as shown in Figure 3–61 by clicking the datasheet selector. Then you can bold, underline, or italicize your font in the Home tab | Text formatting group. Additionally, you can set the background color and align the data.

To Close the Datasheet without Saving the Format Changes

The following steps close the datasheet without saving the changes to the format. Because the changes are not saved, the next time you open the Account Manager table in Datasheet view it will appear in the original format. If you had saved the changes, the changes would be reflected in its appearance.

1 Close the Veterinary Vendors table.

2 Click the No button in the Microsoft Access dialog box when asked if you want to save your changes.

What kind of decisions should I make in determining whether to change the format of a datasheet?

• Would totals or other calculations be useful in the datasheet? If so, include the Total row and select the appropriate computations.

• Would another gridline style make the datasheet more useful? If so, change to the desired gridlines.

• Would alternating colors in the rows make them easier to read? If so, change the alternate fill color.

• Would a different font and/or font color make the text stand out better? If so, change the font color and/or the font.

• Is the font size appropriate? Can you see enough data at one time on the screen and yet have the data be readable? If not, change the font size to an appropriate value.

• Is the column spacing appropriate? Are some columns wider than they need to be? Do some columns not display all the data? Change the column sizes as necessary.

As a general guideline, once you have decided on a particular look for a datasheet, all datasheets in the database should have the same look, unless there is a compelling reason for a datasheet to differ.

Multivalued Fields in Queries

You can use multivalued fields in queries in the same way you use other fields in queries. You can choose to display the multiple values either on a single row or on multiple rows in the query results.

To Include Multiple Values on One Row of a Query

To include a multivalued field in the results of a query, place the field in the query design grid just like any other field. **Why?** *When you treat the multivalued field like any other field, the results will list all of the values for the multivalued field on a single row.* The following steps create a query to display the Appointment ID, Patient ID, Appointment Date, and Treatment Number for the Appointments table.

1

• Create a query for the Appointments table and close the Navigation Pane.

• Include the Appointment ID, Patient ID, Appointment Date, and Treatment Number fields in the query (Figure 3–66).

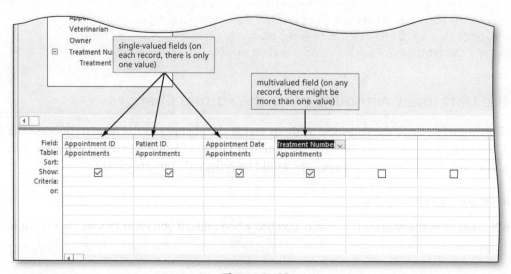

Figure 3–66

2

- Run the query and view the results (Figure 3–67).

Q&A Can I include criteria for the multivalued field?
Yes. You can include criteria for the multivalued field.

- Save the query as m03q01.

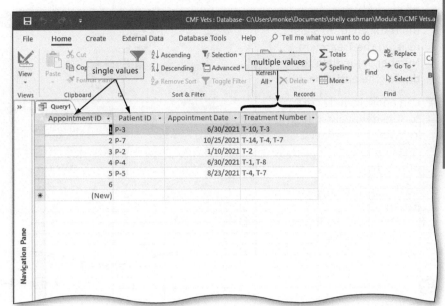

Figure 3–67

To Include Multiple Values on Multiple Rows of a Query

You might want to see the multiple treatment numbers needed for an appointment on separate rows rather than a single row. *Why? Each row in the results will focus on one specific treatment that is needed.* To do so, you need to use the Value property of the Treatment ID field by following the name of the field with a period and then the word, Value. The following steps use the Value property to display each service on a separate row.

- Switch to Design view and ensure that the Appointment ID, Patient ID, Appointment Date, and Treatment Number fields are included in the design grid.

- Click the Treatment Number field to produce an insertion point, press the RIGHT ARROW as necessary to move the insertion point to the end of the field name, and then type a period.

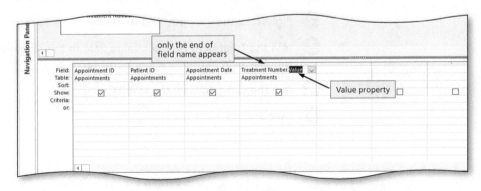

Figure 3–68

- If the word, Value, does not automatically appear after the period, type the word `Value` after the period following the word, Number, to use the Value property (Figure 3–68).

Q&A I do not see the word, Value. Did I do something wrong?
No. There is not enough room to display the entire name. If you wanted to see it, you could point to the right boundary of the column selector and then either drag or double-click.

I see Treatment Number.Value as a field in the field list. Could I have deleted the Treatment Number field and added the Treatment Number.Value field?
Yes. Either approach is fine.

- Run the query and view the results (Figure 3–69), resizing the Treatment Number.Value field to display the entire heading.

Q&A

Can I now include criteria for the multivalued field?
Yes. You could enter a criterion just like in any other query.

Could I sort the rows by Patient ID?
Yes. Select Ascending as the sort order just as you have done in other queries.

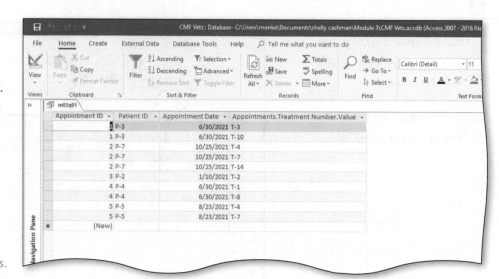

Figure 3–69

- Save the query as a new object in the database named m03q02.

- Close the query.

To Test an Existing Query with a Multivalued Field

Because the current join does not connect the common individual fields since it was changed to multivalued, you need to modify the join. The following steps change the join on an existing query that uses a multivalued field.

1. Open the Appointments and Treatments query in Design view.

2. Right click the join line, and then click DELETE to remove the join.

3. Join the Treatment Number.Value field in the Appointments table to the Treatment Number field in the Treatment Cost table.

4. Run the query to view the results.

5. Save and close the query.

Break Point: If you wish to take a break, this is a good place to do so. You can quit Access now. To resume at a later time, start Access, open the database called CMF Vets, and continue following the steps from this location forward.

BTW
Using Criteria with Multivalued Fields
To enter criteria in a multivalued field, simply enter the criteria in the Criteria row. For example, to find all patients who need feline rabies shots in the Appointments table, enter T-1 in the Criteria row under Treatment Number.

Referential Integrity

When you have two related tables in a database, it is essential that the data in the common fields match. There should not be a patient in the Patients table whose owner ID is O-2, for example, unless there is a record in the Owners table whose Owner ID is O-2. This restriction is enforced through **referential integrity**, which is the property that ensures that the value in a foreign key must match that of another table's primary key.

A **foreign key** is a field in one table whose values are required to match the *primary key* of another table. In the Patients table, the Owner ID field is a foreign key that must match the primary key of the Owners table; that is, the Owner ID for any patient must exist as an Owner ID currently in the Owners table. A patient whose Owner ID is O-9, for example, should not be stored in the Patients table because no such owner exists in the Owners table.

In Access, to specify referential integrity, you must explicitly define a relationship between the tables by using the Relationships button. As part of the process of defining a relationship, you indicate that Access is to enforce referential integrity. Access then prohibits any updates to the database that would violate the referential integrity.

The type of relationship between two tables specified by the Relationships command is referred to as a **one-to-many relationship**. This means that *one* record in the first table is related to, or matches, *many* records in the second table, but each record in the second table is related to only *one* record in the first. In the CMF Vets database, for example, a one-to-many relationship exists between the Owners table and the Patients table. *One* owner is associated with *many* patients, but each patient is associated with only a single owner. In general, the table containing the foreign key will be the *many* part of the relationship.

When specifying referential integrity, what special issues do you need to address?

You need to decide how to handle deletions of fields. In the relationship between owners and patients, for example, deletion of an owner for whom patients exist, such as Patient ID C-2, would violate referential integrity. The owner for Patient ID C-2 would no longer relate to any owner in the Owners table in the database. You can handle this in two ways. For each relationship, you need to decide which of the approaches is appropriate.

The normal way to avoid this problem is to prohibit such a deletion. The other option is to **cascade the delete**. This means that Access would allow the deletion but then delete all related records. For example, it would allow the deletion of the patient from the Patients table but then automatically delete any owners related to the deleted patient. In this example, cascading the delete would obviously not be appropriate.

You also need to decide how to handle the update of the primary key. In the relationship between owners and patients, for example, changing the Owner ID in the Owners table from C-2 to C-9 would cause a problem because some accounts in the Patients table have Owner ID C-2. These patients no longer would relate to any owner. You can handle this in two ways. For each relationship, you need to decide which of the approaches is appropriate.

The normal way to avoid this problem is to prohibit this type of update. The other option is to **cascade the update**. This means to allow the change, but make the corresponding change in the foreign key on all related records. In the relationship between owners and patients, for example, Access would allow the update but then automatically make the corresponding change for any account whose Owner ID is C-2. It will now be C-9.

CONSIDER THIS

To Specify Referential Integrity

The following steps use the Relationships button on the Database Tools tab to specify referential integrity by explicitly indicating a relationship between the Owners and Patients tables. The steps also ensure that updates will cascade, but that deletes will not. *Why? By indicating a relationship between tables, and specifying that updates will cascade, it will be possible to change the Owner ID for an owner, and the same change will automatically be made for all pets of that owner. By not specifying that deletes will cascade, it will not be possible to delete and owner who has patients (pets).*

1

- Click Database Tools on the ribbon to display the Database Tools tab. (Figure 3–70).

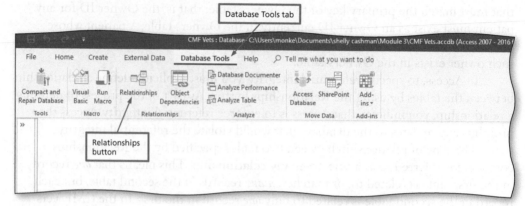

Figure 3–70

2

- Click the Relationships button (Database Tools tab | Relationships group) to open the Relationships window and display the Show Table dialog box (Figure 3–71).

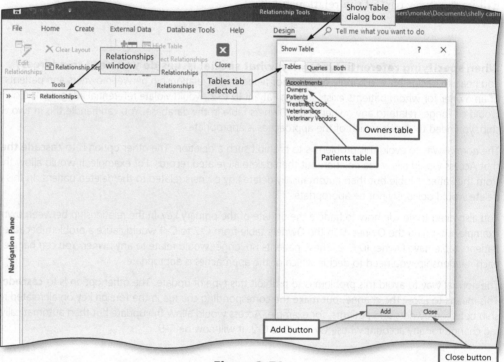

Figure 3–71

3

- Click the Owners table (Show Table dialog box), and then click the Add button to add a field list for the Owners table to the Relationships window.

- Click the Patients table (Show Table dialog box), and then click the Add button to add a field list for the Patients table to the Relationships window.

- Click the Close button (Show Table dialog box) to close the dialog box.

- Resize the field lists that appear so all fields are visible (Figure 3–72).

Q&A Do I need to resize the field lists?
No. You can use the scroll bars to view the fields. Before completing the next step, however, you would need to make sure the Owner ID fields in both tables appear on the screen.

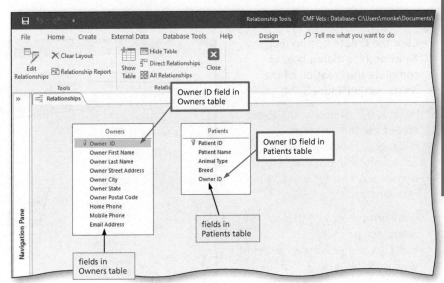

Figure 3–72

4

- Drag the Owner ID field in the Owners table field list to the Owner ID field in the Patients table field list to display the Edit Relationships dialog box and create a relationship.

Q&A Do I actually move the field from the Owners table to the Patients table?
No. The pointer will change shape to indicate you are in the process of dragging, but the field does not move.

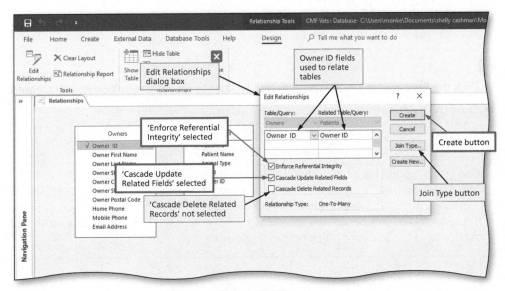

Figure 3–73

- Click the 'Enforce Referential Integrity' check box (Edit Relationships dialog box).

- Click the Cascade Update Related Fields check box (Figure 3–73).

Q&A The Cascade check boxes were dim until I clicked the Enforce Referential Integrity check box. Is that correct?
Yes. Until you have chosen to enforce referential integrity, the cascade options are not applicable.

5

- Click the Create button (Edit Relationships dialog box) to complete the creation of the relationship (Figure 3–74).

Q&A

What is the symbol at the lower end of the join line?
It is the mathematical symbol for infinity. It is used here to denote the "many" end of the relationship.

Can I print a copy of the relationship?
Yes. Click the Relationship Report button (Relationship Tools Design tab | Tools group) to produce a report of the relationship. You can print the report. You can also save it as a report in the database for future use. If you do not want to save it, close the report after you have printed it and do not save the changes.

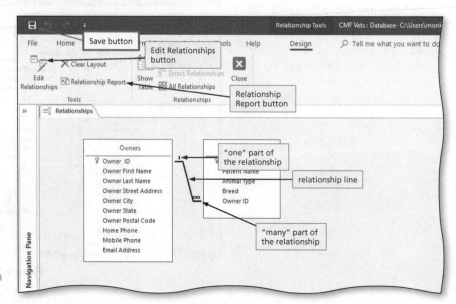

Figure 3–74

6

- Click the Save button on the Quick Access Toolbar to save the relationship you created.
- Close the Relationships window.

Q&A

What is the purpose of saving the relationship?
The relationship ensures that the data has referential integrity.

Can I later modify the relationship if I want to change it in some way?
Yes. Click Database Tools on the ribbon to display the Database Tools tab, and then click the Relationships button (Database Tools tab | Relationships group) to open the Relationships window. To add another table, click the Show Table button on the Design tab. To remove a table, click the Hide Table button. To edit a relationship, select the relationship and click the Edit Relationships button.

CONSIDER THIS

Can I change the join type as I can in queries?
Yes. Click the Join Type button in the Edit Relationships dialog box. Click option button 1 to create an INNER join, that is, a join in which only records with matching values in the join fields appear in the result. Click option button 2 to create a LEFT join, that is, a join that includes all records from the left-hand table, but only records from the right-hand table that have matching values in the join fields. Click option button 3 to create a RIGHT join, that is, a join that includes all records from the right-hand table, but only records from the left-hand table that have matching values in the join fields.

Effect of Referential Integrity

Referential integrity now exists between the Owners and the Patients tables. Access now will reject any number in the Owner ID field in the Patients table that does not match an Owner ID in the Owners table. Attempting to change the Owner ID for a patient to one that does not match any Owner ID in the Owner table would result in the error message shown in Figure 3–75. Similarly, attempting to add a patient whose Owner ID does not match would produce the same error message.

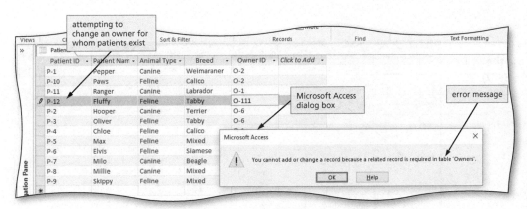

Figure 3–75

BTW
Relationships
You also can use the Relationships window to specify a one-to-one relationship. In a one-to-one relationship, the matching fields are both primary keys. If CMF maintained a mobile veterinary pet van for each veterinarian, the data concerning the van might be kept in a Van table, in which the primary key is Veterinarian ID — the same primary key as the Veterinarians table. Thus, there would be a one-to-one relationship between veterinarians and vans.

BTW
Exporting a Relationship Report
You also can export a relationship report. To export a report as a PDF or XPS file, right-click the report in the Navigation Pane, click Export on the shortcut menu, and then click PDF or XPS as the file type.

Access also will reject the deletion of an Owner ID for whom related accounts exist. Attempting to delete Owner ID O-2 from the Owners table, for example, would result in the message shown in Figure 3–76.

Access would, however, allow the change of an Owner ID in the Owners table. It would then automatically make the corresponding change to the Owner ID for all the patients that belong to that owner. For example, if you changed the Owner ID in the Owner table from O-2 to O-3, the Owner ID O-3 would appear in the Owner ID field for patients whose Owner ID had been O-2.

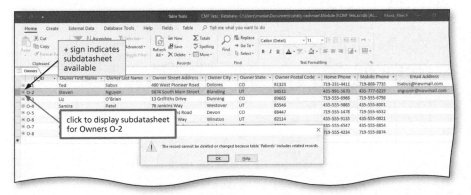

Figure 3–76

To Use a Subdatasheet

One consequence of the tables being explicitly related is that the patients for an owner can appear below the Owner ID in a **subdatasheet**. Because the two tables are joined by a common field, the data for the patient belonging to the owner can be embedded within that particular owner. *Why is a subdatasheet useful? A subdatasheet is useful when you want to review or edit data in joined or related tables.* The availability of such a subdatasheet is indicated by a plus sign that appears in front of the rows in the Owners table. The following steps display the subdatasheet for Owner O-1.

● Open the Owners table in Datasheet view and close the Navigation Pane (Figure 3–77).

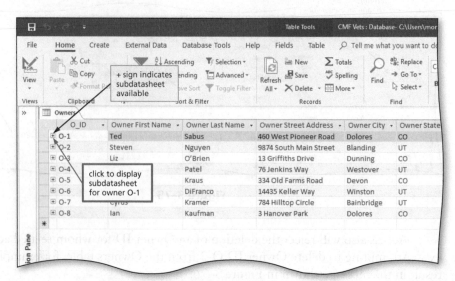

Figure 3–77

● Click the plus sign in front of the row for Owner ID O-1 to display the subdatasheet (Figure 3–78).

Q&A How do I hide the subdatasheet when I no longer want it to appear?
When you clicked the plus sign, it changed to a minus sign. Click the minus sign.

How do I remove a subdatasheet?
Open the table with the subdatasheet closed and click the More button (Home tab | Records Group) to display a menu. Select Subdatasheet, Remove.

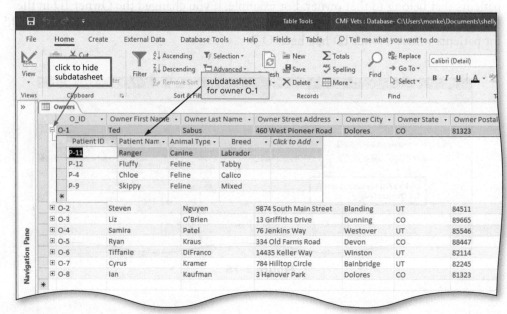

Figure 3–78

Experiment

● Display subdatasheets for other owners. Display more than one subdatasheet at a time. Remove the subdatasheets from the screen.

● If requested by your instructor, replace the city and state for Owner ID O-1 with your city and state.

● Close the Owners table.

Handling Data Inconsistency

In many organizations, databases evolve and change over time. One department might create a database for its own internal use. Employees in another department may decide they need their own database containing much of the same information. For example, the Purchasing department of an organization might create a database of products that it buys and the Receiving department may create a database of products that it receives. Each department is keeping track of the same products. When the organization eventually merges the databases, they might discover inconsistencies and duplication. The Find Duplicates Query Wizard and the Find Unmatched Query Wizard can assist in clearing the resulting database of duplication and errors.

BTW
Database Design:
Validation
In most organizations, decisions about what is valid and what is invalid data are made during the requirements gathering process and the database design process.

TO FIND DUPLICATE RECORDS

One reason to include a primary key for a table is to eliminate duplicate records. A possibility still exists, however, that duplicate records can get into your database. You would use the following steps to find duplicate records using the Find Duplicates Query Wizard.

1. Click Create on the ribbon, and then click the Query Wizard button (Create tab | Queries group).
2. When Access displays the New Query dialog box, click Find Duplicates Query Wizard and then click the OK button.
3. Identify the table and field or fields that might contain duplicate information.
4. Indicate any other fields you want displayed.
5. Finish the wizard to see any duplicate records.

TO FIND UNMATCHED RECORDS

Occasionally, you might need to find records in one table that have no matching records in another table. For example, you might want to determine which owners currently have no patients. You would use the following steps to find unmatched records using the Find Unmatched Query Wizard.

1. Click Create on the ribbon, and then click the Query Wizard button (Create tab | Queries group).
2. When Access displays the New Query dialog box, click Find Unmatched Query Wizard and then click the OK button.
3. Identify the table that might contain unmatched records, and then identify the related table.
4. Indicate the fields you want displayed.
5. Finish the wizard to see any unmatched records.

Ordering Records

Normally, Access sequences the records in the Owners table by Owner ID whenever listing them because the Owner ID field is the primary key. You can change this order, if desired.

To Use the Ascending Button to Order Records

To change the order in which records appear, use the Ascending or Descending buttons. Either button reorders the records based on the field in which the insertion point is located. The following steps order the records by city using the Ascending button. **Why?** *Using the Ascending button is the quickest and easiest way to order records.*

- Open the Owners table in Datasheet view.

- Click the Owner City field on the first record to select the field (Figure 3–79).

Q&A Did I have to click the field on the first record?
No. Any other record would have worked as well.

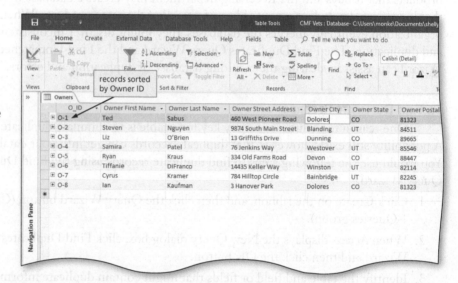

Figure 3–79

- Click the Ascending button (Home tab | Sort & Filter group) to sort the records by City (Figure 3–80).

- Close the Owners table.

- Click the No button (Microsoft Access dialog box) when asked if you want to save your changes.

Q&A What if I saved the changes?
The next time you open the table the records will be sorted by city.

- If desired, sign out of your Microsoft account.

- **sam** ↑ Exit Access.

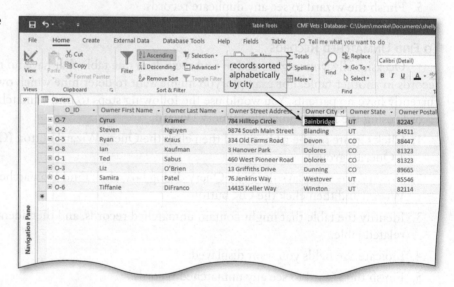

Figure 3–80

Other Ways

1. Right-click field name, click Sort A to Z (for ascending) or Sort Z to A (for descending)

2. Click field selector arrow, click Sort A to Z or Sort Z to A

To Use the Ascending Button to Order Records on Multiple Fields

Just as you are able to sort the answer to a query on multiple fields, you can also sort the data that appears in a datasheet on multiple fields. To do so, the major and minor keys must be next to each other in the datasheet with the major key on the left. If this is not the case, you can drag the columns into the correct position. Instead of dragging, however, usually it will be easier to use a query that has the data sorted in the desired order.

BTW
Access Help
At any time while using Access, you can find answers to questions and display information about various topics through Access Help. Used properly, this form of assistance can increase your productivity and reduce your frustrations by minimizing the time you spend learning how to use Access.

To sort on a combination of fields where the major key is just to the left of the minor key, you would use the following steps.

1. Click the field selector at the top of the major key column to select the entire column.
2. Hold down SHIFT and then click the field selector for the minor key column to select both columns.
3. Click the Ascending button to sort the records.

Summary

In this module you have learned how to use a form to add records to a table, search for records, delete records, filter records, change the database structure, create and use lookup fields, create calculated fields, create and use multivalued fields, make mass changes, create validation rules, change the appearance of a datasheet, specify referential integrity, and use subdatasheets.

CONSIDER THIS

What decisions will you need to make when maintaining your own databases?
Use these guidelines as you complete the assignments in this module and maintain your own databases outside of this class.

1. Determine when it is necessary to add, change, or delete records in a database.

2. Determine whether you should filter records.

    a) If your criterion for filtering is that the value in a particular field matches or does not match a certain specific value, use Filter By Selection.

    b) If your criterion only involves a single field but is more complex, use a common filter.

    c) If your criterion involves more than one field, use Filter By Form.

    d) If your criterion involves more than a single And or Or, or if it involves sorting, use Advanced Filter/Sort.

3. Determine whether additional fields are necessary or whether existing fields should be deleted.

4. Determine whether validation rules, default values, and formats are necessary.

    a) Can you improve the accuracy of the data entry process by enforcing data validation?

    b) What values are allowed for a particular field?

    c) Are there some fields in which one particular value is used more than another?

    d) Should some fields be required for each record?

    e) Are there some fields for which special formats would be appropriate?

5. Determine whether changes to the format of a datasheet are desirable.

    a) Would totals or other calculations be useful in the datasheet?

    b) Would different gridlines make the datasheet easier to read?

    c) Would alternating colors in the rows make them easier to read?

    d) Would a different font and/or font color make the text stand out better?

    e) Is the font size appropriate?

    f) Is the column spacing appropriate?

6. Identify related tables in order to implement relationships between the tables.

    a) Is there a one-to-many relationship between the tables?

    b) If so, which table is the one table?

    c) Which table is the many table?

7. When specifying referential integrity, address deletion and update policies.

    a) Decide how to handle deletions. Should deletion be prohibited or should the delete cascade?

    b) Decide how to handle the update of the primary key. Should the update be prohibited or should the update cascade?

CONSIDER THIS

How should you submit solutions to questions in the assignments identified with a symbol?
Every assignment in this book contains one or more questions identified with a symbol. These questions require you to think beyond the assigned database. Present your solutions to the questions in the format required by your instructor. Possible formats may include one or more of these options: write the answer; create a document that contains the answer; present your answer to the class; discuss your answer in a group; record the answer as audio or video using a webcam, smartphone, or portable media player; or post answers on a blog, wiki, or website.

Apply Your Knowledge

Reinforce the skills and apply the concepts you learned in this module.

Adding Lookup Fields, Specifying Validation Rules, Updating Records, Updating Reports, and Creating Relationships

Instructions: Run Access. Open the Support_AC_Financial Services database (If you do not have the database, see your instructor for a copy of the modified database.)

Perform the following tasks:

1. Open the Client table in Design view.
2. Add a Lookup field called Client Type to the Client table. The field should be inserted after the Advisor Number field. The field will contain data on the type of client. The client types are TRT (trust), INV (invest), and RET (retirement). Save the changes to the Client table.
3. Create the following validation rules for the Client table.
   a. Specify the legal values TRT, INV, and RET for the Client Type field. Enter **Must be TRT, INV, or RET** as the validation text.
   b. Make the Client Name field a required field.
4. Save the changes and close the table. You do not need to test the current data.
5. Create an update query for the Client table. Change all the entries in the Client Type field to INV. Run the query and save it as Client Type Update Query.
6. Open the Client table in Datasheet view, update the following records, and then close the table:
   a. Change the client type for clients BB35, CC25, CJ45, and CP03 to RET.
   b. Change the client type for clients MM01 and PS67 to TRT.
7. Create a split form for the Client table. Save the form as Client Split Form.
8. Open the Client Split Form in Form view, find client HN23, and change the client name from Henry Niemer to Henry Neimer. Close the form.
9. Establish referential integrity between the Advisor table (the one table) and the Client table (the many table). Cascade the update but not the delete. Save the relationship.
10. If requested to do so by your instructor, rename the Client Split Form as Split Form for First Name Last Name where First Name Last Name is your name.
11. Submit the revised database in the format specified by your instructor.
12. ✳ The values in the Client Type field are currently in the order TRT, INV, and RET. How would you reorder the values to INV, RET, and TRT in the Client Type list?

Extend Your Knowledge

Extend the skills you learned in this module and experiment with new skills. You may need to use Help to complete the assignment.

Creating Action Queries, Changing Table Properties, and Adding Totals to a Datasheet

Note: To complete this assignment, you will be required to use the Data Files. Please contact your instructor for information about accessing the Data Files.

Instructions: Healthy Pets is a small veterinary practice in Lebanon, Colorado that is run by a veterinarian that would like to retire. CMF Vets has been approached about buying the Healthy Pets practice. Healthy Pets needs to do some database maintenance by finding duplicate records and finding unmatched records.

Perform the following tasks:

1. Run Access and open the Support_AC Healthy Vets database. Create a make-table query to create the Potential Clients table in the Healthy Vets database shown in Figure 3–81. Run the query and save it as Make Table Query.

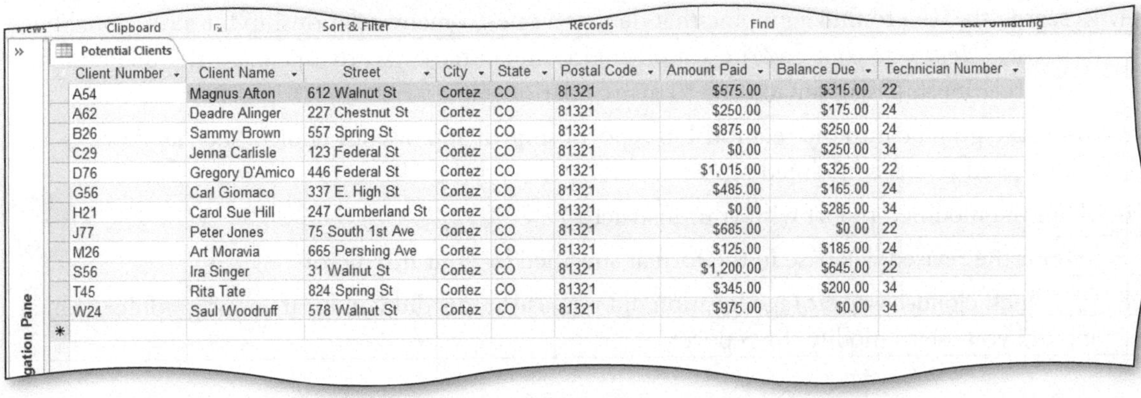

Figure 3–81

2. Open the Potential Clients table and change the font to Arial with a font size of 10. Resize the columns to best fit the data. Save the changes to the table and close the table.

3. Open the Technician table and add the Totals row to the table. Calculate the average hourly rate and the total Earnings YTD. Save the changes to the table layout and close the table.

4. Use the Find Duplicates Query Wizard to find duplicate information in the City field of the Client table. Include the Client Name in the query. Save the query as City Duplicates Query and close the query.

5. Use the Find Unmatched Query Wizard to find all records in the Technician table that do not match records in the Client table. Technician Number is the common field in both tables. Include the Technician Number, Last Name, and First Name in the query. Save the query as Technician Unmatched Query and close the query.

6. If requested to do so by your instructor, change the client name in the Client table for client number S56 to First Name Last Name where First Name Last Name is your name. If your name is longer than the space allowed, simply enter as much as you can.

7. Submit the revised database in the format specified by your instructor.

8. ✸ What differences, if any, are there between the Client table and the Potential Clients table you created with the make-table query?

Expand Your World

Create a solution, which uses cloud and web technologies, by learning and investigating on your own from general guidance.

Problem: The Physical Therapy clinic wants to ensure that all Clients are matched with Therapists. The database needs a relationship created to ensure this matching. Your boss wants a copy of the report of this relationship.

Perform the following tasks:
Run Access and open the Support_AC_Physical Therapy database. (If you do not have the database, see your instructor for a copy of the modified database.)

1. Create a relationship between the Client table and the Therapist table on the Therapist Number field. Enforce referential integrity and Cascade Update Related Fields.

2. Create a relationship report for the relationship and save the report as First Name Last Name Relationship Report where First Name Last Name is your name.

3. Export the relationship as an RTF/Word document to a cloud-based storage location of your choice. Do not save the export steps.

4. Research the web to find a graphic that depicts a one-to-many relationship for a relational database. (*Hint:* Use your favorite search engine and enter keywords such as ERD diagram, entity-relationship diagram, or one to many relationship.)

5. Insert the graphic into the relationship report using an app of your choice, such as Word Online, and save the modified report.

6. Share the modified report with your instructor.

7. Submit the revised database in the format specified by your instructor.

8. ☀ Which cloud-based storage location did you use? How did you locate your graphic? Which app did you use to modify the report?

In the Labs

Design, create, modify, and/or use a database following the guidelines, concepts, and skills presented in this module.

Lab: Maintaining the Lancaster College Database

Instructions: Open the Support_AC_Lancaster College database (If you do not have the database, see your instructor for a copy of the modified database.)

Part 1:   Use the concepts and techniques presented in this module to modify the database according to the following requirements:

1. Import the table Students Payments Extra table from your data files.

2. The coaches are concerned that there is no backup activity if they are ill. They would like an additional multivalued lookup field, Alternative SportsName, added to the Coach table. Table 3–2 lists the SportsName abbreviations that coaches would like.

Table 3–2 Alternative SportsName Abbreviations and Descriptions

SportsName Abbreviations	SportsName
TRK	Track
TEN	Tennis
WRS	Wrestling
FTB	Football
STB	Softball
POL	Pool
PING	PingPong
SWIM	Swimming
SOC	Soccer
BKB	Basketball

3. The accountant in charge of the student payments has asked for a calculated field that will figure the addition of the amount that the students have paid already plus their balance due. Add that calculated field to the appropriate table.

4. Create the following rule for the Coach table and save the changes: Make Coach First Name and Last Name required fields.

5. Using Filter By Form, delete all the records in the Student Payments table where any student's amount paid is zero and the balance due is greater than zero.

6. Add the data shown in Figure 3–82 to the Coach table for the Alternative SportsName field. Resize the field to best fit.

Coach ID	First Name	Last Name	SN	Alternative SportsName
17893	Lakisha	Black	Track	SOC
18797	Bill	Brinkly	Tennis	
18798	Tom	Smith	Wrestling	
18990	William	Gutierez	Football	STB, WRS
18999	Sharon	Stone	Softball	
78978	Frank	Terranova	Pool	
78979	Gail	French	Ping Pong	
79798	Daniel	Costner	Swimming	POL
79879	Gary	Faulkner	Soccer	
82374	Jean	Epperson	Basketball	SOC, TEN, TRK

Figure 3–82

7. Change the field size for the Alternative SportsName to 50.

8. In the Team table, find the record for CaptainID 78978, and change the CaptainID to 78797.

9. If requested to do so by your instructor, in the Student table, change the last name for Student ID 34872 to your last name. If your last name is longer than 15 characters, simply enter as much as you can.

Continued >

In the Labs *continued*

10. In the Participation table change the Student ID field to Short Text 20.

11. Establish referential integrity between the Student table (the one table) and the Participation table (the many table). Cascade the update but not the delete.

Submit the revised database in the format specified by your instructor.

Part 2:   ✸ The Alternative SportsName field currently has 10 values. If Lancaster College picked up another sport, such as fencing, how would you add FEN to the Alternative SportsName field list? You added a calculated field in the Student Payments table. Does the calculated field actually exist in the database? Are there any issues that you need to consider when you create a calculated field?

4 | Creating Reports and Forms

Objectives

You will have mastered the material in this module when you can:

- Create reports and forms using wizards
- Modify reports and forms in Layout view
- Group and sort data in a report
- Add totals and subtotals to a report
- Conditionally format controls
- Resize columns
- Filter records in reports and forms

- Print reports and forms
- Apply themes
- Add a field to a report or form
- Add a date
- Change the format of a control
- Move controls
- Create and print mailing labels

Introduction

One of the advantages to maintaining data in a database is the ability to present the data in attractive reports and forms that highlight certain information. Reports present data in an organized format that is usually printed. The data can come from one or more tables. On the other hand, you usually view forms on the screen, although you can print them. In addition to viewing data, you can also use forms to update data. That is, you can use forms to add records, delete records, or change records. Like reports, the data in the form can come from one or more tables. This module shows how to create reports and forms by creating two reports and a form. There are several ways to create both reports and forms. One approach is to use the Report or Form Wizard. You can also use either Layout view or Design view to create or modify a report or form. In this module, you will use Layout view for this purpose. In later modules, you will learn how to use Design view. You will also use the Label Wizard to produce mailing labels.

Project — Reports and Forms

CMF Vets is now able to better keep track of its customer information and to target the needs of the practice by using its database. CMF Vets hopes to improve its decision-making capability further by using custom reports that meet the practice's specific needs. Figure 4–1 shows the Appointments and Treatments report, which is a modified version of an existing report. The report features grouping. The report shown in

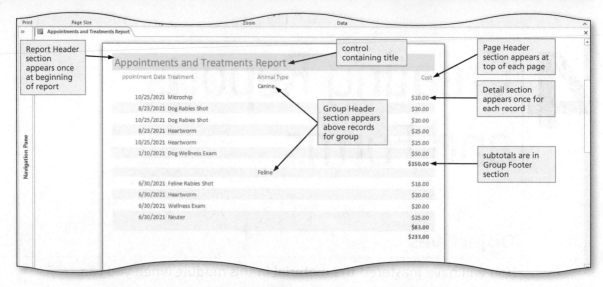

Figure 4–1a Top Portion of Appointments and Treatments Report

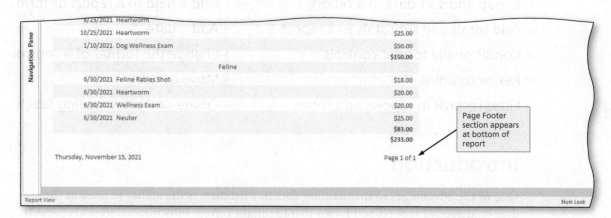

Figure 4–1b Bottom Portion of Appointments and Treatments Report

BTW
Consider Your Audience
Always design reports and forms with your audience in mind. Make your reports and forms accessible to individuals who may have problems with colorblindness or reduced vision.

Figure 4–1 groups records by Animal Type. There are two separate groups, one each for the two animal types, Canine and Feline. The appropriate type appears above each group. The totals of the Cost field for the animal types in the group (called a **subtotal**) appear after the group. At the end of the report is the grand total of the same field.

Figure 4–2 shows the second report. This report encompasses data from both the Appointments and Treatment Costs tables. Like the report in Figure 4–1, the data is grouped, and it is also grouped by animal type. Not only does the treatment appear in each group, but its cost appears as well. This report contains conditional formatting.

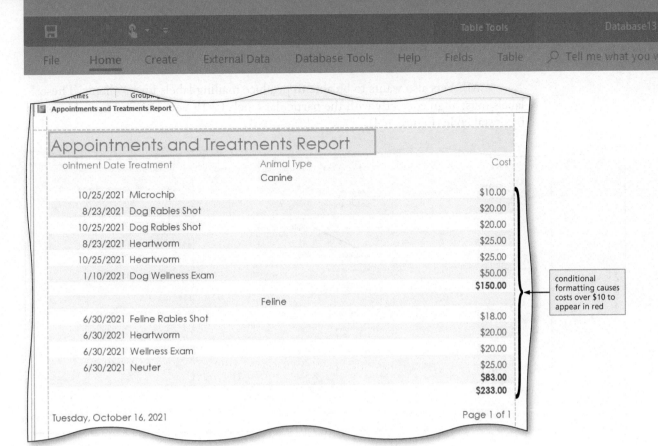

Figure 4–2

CMF Vets also wants to improve the process of updating data by using a custom form, as shown in Figure 4–3. The form has a title, but unlike the form you can create by clicking the Form button, this form does not contain all the fields in the Appointments table. In addition, the fields are in a different order than in the table. For this form, CMF Vets likes the appearance of including the fields in a stacked layout.

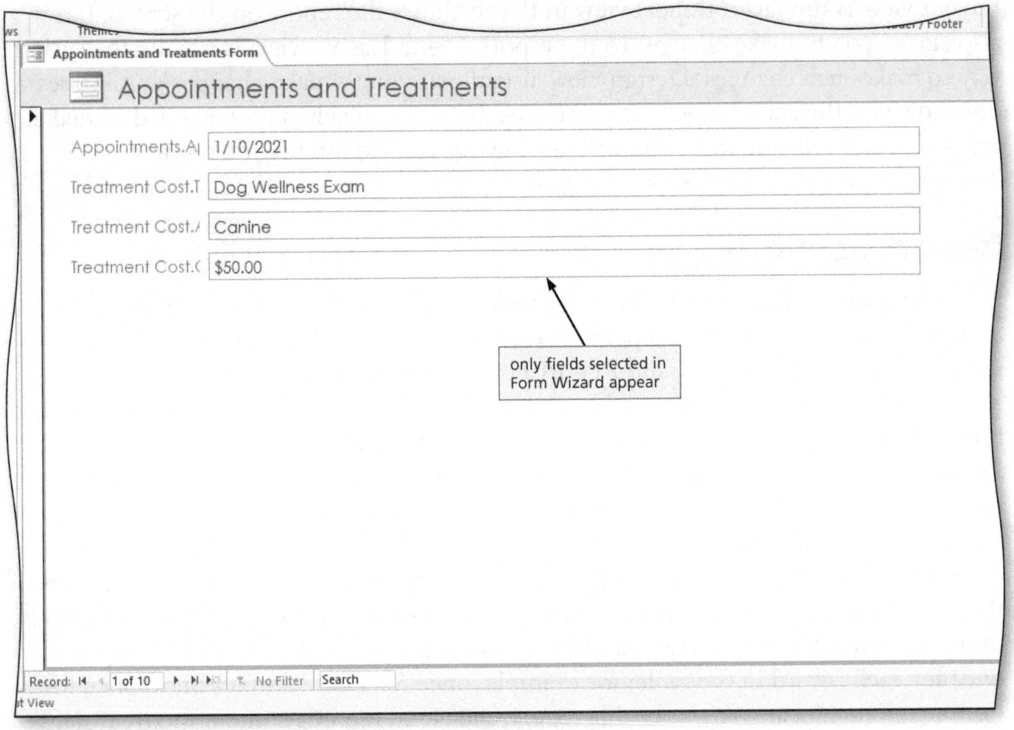

Figure 4–3

CMF Vets also wants to be able to produce mailing labels for its clients. These labels must align correctly with the particular labels CMF Vets uses and must be sorted by postal code (Figure 4–4).

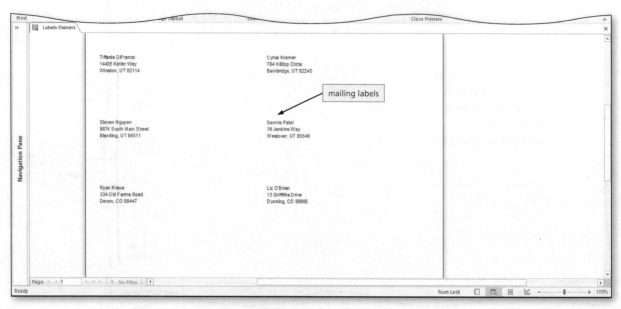

Figure 4–4

Report Creation

When working with a report in Access, there are four different ways to view the report: Report view, Print Preview, Layout view, and Design view. Report view shows the report on the screen. Print Preview shows the report as it will appear when printed. Layout view is similar to Report view in that it shows the report on the screen, but it also allows you to make changes to the report. Using Layout view is usually the easiest way to make such changes. Design view also allows you to make changes, but it does not show you the actual report. It is most useful when the changes you need to make are complex. In this module, you will use Layout view to modify the report.

Report Sections

A report is divided into various sections to help clarify the presentation of data. A typical report consists of a Report Header section, Page Header section, Detail section, Page Footer section, and Report Footer section (Figure 4–1).

The contents of the Report Header section appear once at the beginning of the report. In the Appointments and Treatments Report, the report title is in the Report Header section. The contents of the Report Footer section appear once at the end of the report. In the Appointments and Treatments Report, the Report Footer section contains the grand totals of Costs. The contents of the Page Header section appear once at the top of each page and typically contain the column headers. The contents of the Page Footer section appear once at the bottom of each page; Page Footer sections often contain a date and a page number. The contents of the Detail section appear once for each record in the table; for example, once for Feline Rabies Shot, once for Canine microchip, and so on. In this report, the detail records contain the treatments for canines and felines and the cost for the treatments.

When the data in a report is grouped, there are two additional sections. The contents of the Group Header section are printed above the records in a particular group, and the contents of the Group Footer section are printed below the group. In the Appointments and Treatments Report shown in Figure 4–1, the Group Header section contains the Animal Type, and the Group Footer section contains the subtotals of costs for the treatments.

To Group and Sort in a Report

In Layout view of the report, you can specify both grouping and sorting by using the Group & Sort button on the Design tab. The following steps open the Appointments and Treatments Report in Layout view and then specify both grouping and sorting in the report. *Why? CMF Vets managers have determined that the records in the report should be grouped by animal type. That is, all the costs of a given animal type should appear together immediately after the type. Within the given animal types, costs are to be ordered from lowest to highest cost.*

1

- **sam** ↓ Because the field Treatment Number in the Appointments table is now a multivalued field, you need to adjust the join line in the Appointments and Treatments query to reflect the changed field. Open the Appointments and Treatments query in Design View, click the join line, press Delete, then rejoin the fields from the Treatment Number.Value field in the Appointments table to the Treatment Number field in the Treatment Cost table. Save and close the query.

- Right-click the Appointments and Treatments Report in the Navigation Pane to produce a shortcut menu.

- Click Layout View on the shortcut menu to open the report in Layout view. Scroll through the report to view the subtotal or total fields that are already in the report.

- Close the Navigation Pane.

- If a field list appears, close the field list by clicking the 'Add Existing Fields' button (Report Layout Tools Design tab | Tools group).

- Click the Group & Sort button (Report Layout Tools Design tab | Grouping & Totals group) to display the Group, Sort, and Total pane (Figure 4–5).

Q&A My report is in a different order. Do I need to change it?
No. You will change the order of the records in the following steps.

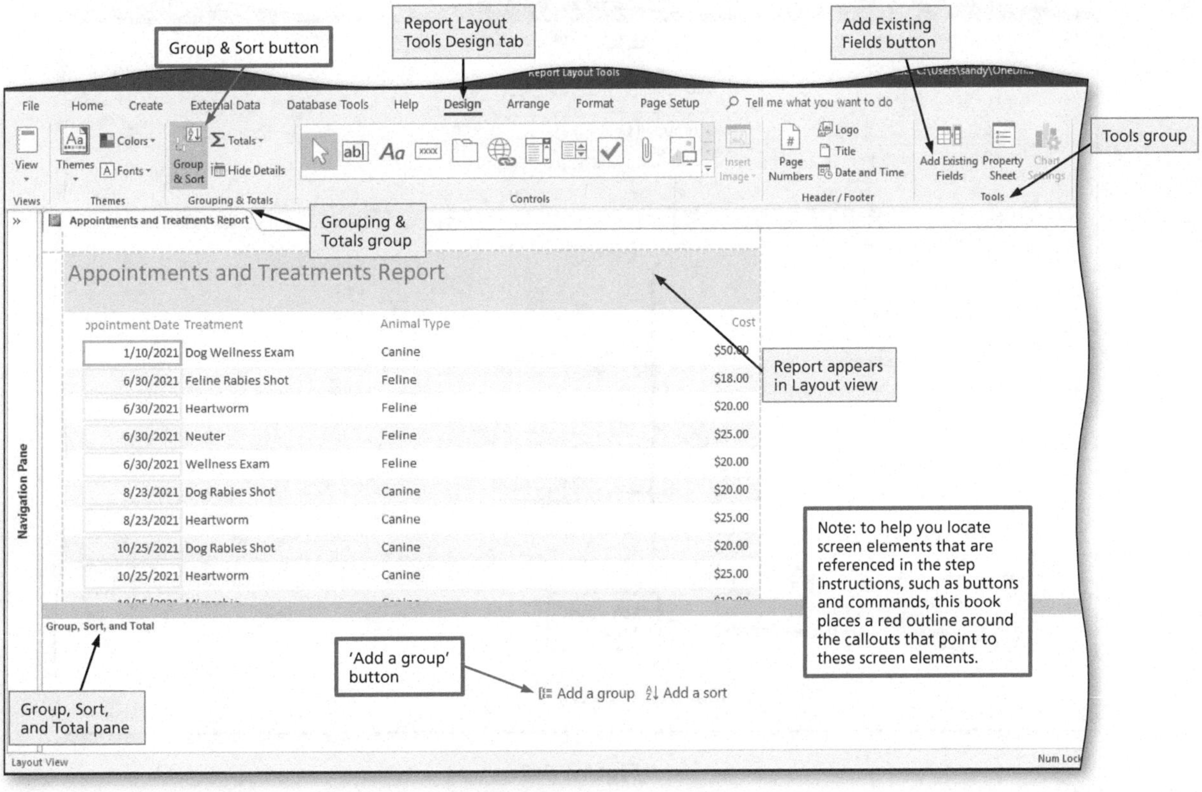

Figure 4–5

2

• Click the 'Add a group' button to add a group (Figure 4–6) and display a field list.

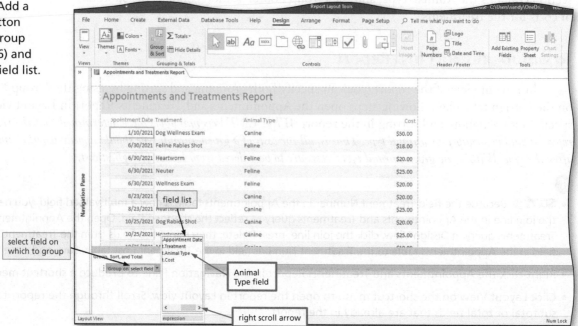

Figure 4–6

3

• Click the Treatment Cost.Animal Type field in the field list to select a field for grouping and group the records on the selected field (Figure 4–7).

Q&A

Does the field on which I group have to be the first field?

No. If you select a field other than the first field, Access will move the field you select into the first position.

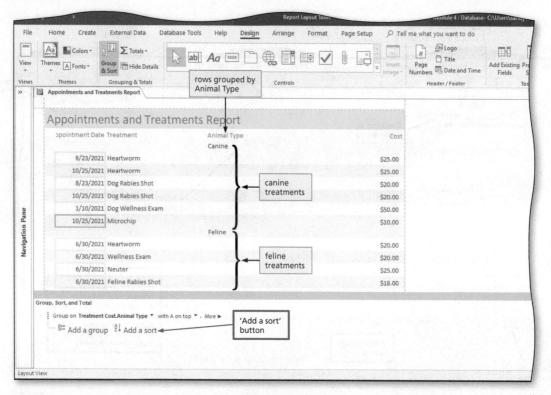

Figure 4–7

4

- Click the 'Add a sort' button to add a sort (Figure 4–8).

Q&A

The formatting in my file does not match these screenshots, did I do something wrong? The formatting in your data file may change if the file is closed and re-opened. You will not be penalized for this if you followed the steps correctly.

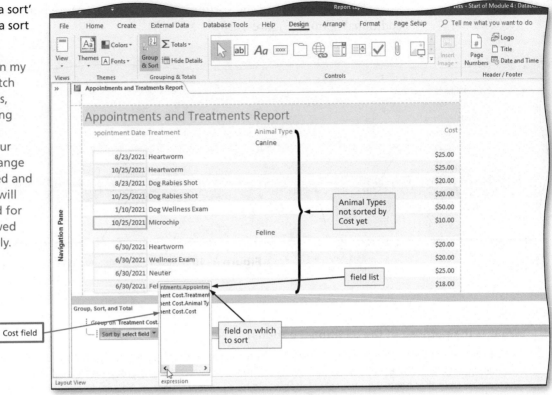

Figure 4–8

5

- Click the Treatment Cost. Cost field in the field list to specify the field on which the records in each group will be sorted (Figure 4–9).

Q&A

I thought the report would be sorted by Animal Type, because I chose to group on that field. What is the effect of choosing to sort by Cost?
This sort takes place within groups. You are specifying that within the list of the same Animal Types, the rows will be ordered by Cost.

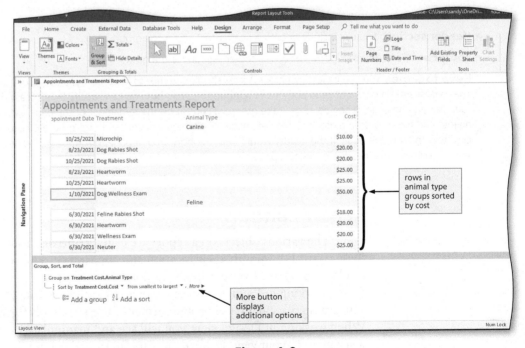

Figure 4–9

Grouping and Sorting Options

For both grouping and sorting, you can click the More button to specify additional options (Figure 4–10).

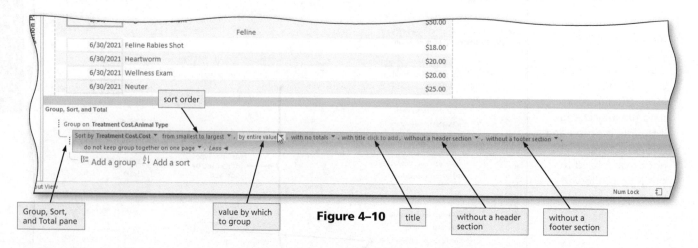

Figure 4–10

CONSIDER THIS

What is the purpose of the additional options?

- **Value.** You can choose the number of characters of the value on which to group. Typically, you would group by the entire value, for example, the entire city name. You could choose, however, to only group on the first character, in which case all accounts in cities that begin with the same letter would be considered a group. You could also group by the first two characters or by a custom number of characters.

- **Totals.** You can choose the values to be totaled. You can specify whether the totals are to appear in the group header or in the group footer and whether to include a grand total. You can also choose whether to show group totals as a percentage of the grand total.

- **Title.** You can customize the group title.

- **Header section.** You can include or omit a header section for the group.

- **Footer section.** You can include or omit a footer section for the group.

- **Keep together.** You can indicate whether Access should attempt to keep portions of a group together on the same page. The default setting does not keep portions of a group together, but you can specify that Access should keep a whole group together on one page, when possible. If the group will not fit on the remainder of the page, Access will move the group header and the records in a group to the next page. Finally, you can choose to have Access keep the header and the first record together on one page. If the header would fit at the bottom of a page, but there would not be room for the first record, Access will move the header to the next page.

BTW
Grouping
You should allow sufficient white space between groups. If you feel the amount is insufficient, you can add more space by enlarging the group header or group footer.

Report Controls

The various objects on a report are called **controls**. You can manipulate these controls to modify their location and appearance. The report title, column headers, contents of various fields, subtotals, and so on are all contained in controls. When working in Layout view, as you will do in this module, Access handles details concerning placement, sizing, and format of these controls for you automatically. When working in Design view, you will see and manipulate the controls. Even when working in Layout view, however, it is useful to understand the concepts of controls.

The report shown in Figure 4–1 has a control containing the title, Appointments and Treatments Report. The report also includes controls containing each column header (Appointment Date, Treatment, Animal Type, and Cost). A control in the Group Header section displays the animal type.

There are two controls in the Group Footer section: One control displays the subtotal of Cost and a second displays the subtotal of Costs for all the groups. The Detail section has controls containing the appointment date, treatment, animal type, and cost.

Access has three types of controls: bound controls, unbound controls, and calculated controls. **Bound controls** are used to display data that comes from the database, such as the account number and name. **Unbound controls** are not associated with data from the database and are used to display such things as the report's title. Finally, **calculated controls** are used to display data that is calculated from other data, such as a total.

BTW
Report Design Considerations
The purpose of any report is to present specific information. Make sure that the meaning of the row and column headings is clear. You can use different fonts and sizes by changing the appropriate properties, but do not overuse them. Finally, be consistent when creating reports. Once you decide on a general report style or theme, stick with it throughout your database.

To Add Totals and Subtotals

To add totals or other statistics, use the Totals button on the Design tab. You then select from a menu of aggregate functions, which are functions that perform some mathematical function against a group of records. The available aggregate functions, or calculations, are Sum (total), Average, Count Records, Count Values, Max (largest value), Min (smallest value), Standard Deviation, and Variance. Because the report is grouped, each group will have a **subtotal**, that is, a total for just the records in the group. At the end of the report, there will be a **grand total**, that is, a total for all records.

The following steps specify totals for the Cost field. *Why? Along with determining to group data in this report, CMF Vets managers have also determined that subtotals and a grand total of the Cost field should be included.*

- Click any record in the Cost field, and then click the Totals button (Report Layout Tools Design tab | Grouping & Totals group) to display the list of available calculations (Figure 4–11).

Q&A Can I click the column header?
Yes, you can try to click the column header, but if you are unable to select the field, click the Cost field on any record. If you click the column header and the Totals button does not become available, you will need to click a Cost field in a record.

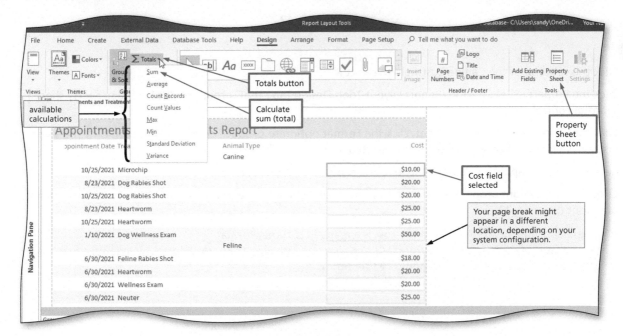

Figure 4–11

2

- Click Sum to calculate the sum of the Cost values.

- If the subtotal does not appear completely, click the subtotal and then drag the lower boundary of the control for the subtotal to the approximate position shown in Figure 4–12.

Q&A

I moved the control rather than resizing it. What did I do wrong?

You dragged the control rather than dragging its lower boundary. Click the Undo button on the Quick Access Toolbar to undo your change and then drag again, making sure you are pointing to the lower boundary.

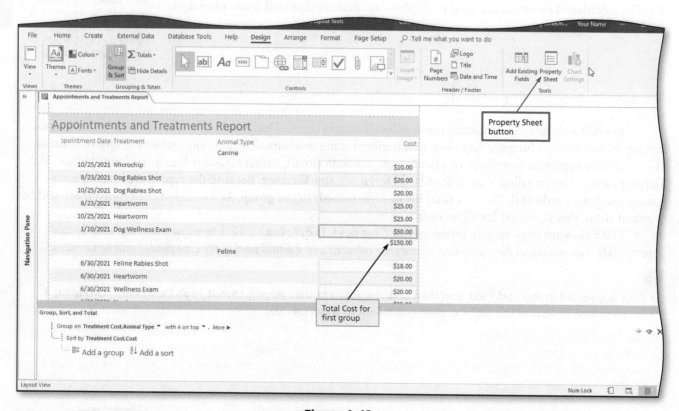

Figure 4–12

3

- Click the subtotal of the Canine Cost field to select it.

- Click the Property Sheet button (Report Layout Tools Design tab | Tools group) to display the property sheet for the subtotal control.

- Click the All tab in the Property Sheet, click the Format option to produce an arrow, and then click the arrow to display available currency formats for the selected item.

- Click Currency to apply the Currency style to the subtotal of the Cost field.

- Click the Font Weight property to produce an arrow, click the arrow, and then click Bold to format the Cost with bold font (Figure 4–13)

Q&A

Why am I applying a currency style if the cost is already in currency format?

Access contains many options for currency. Confirming and applying the correct format will ensure that the format is correct even if you make other changes to the report.

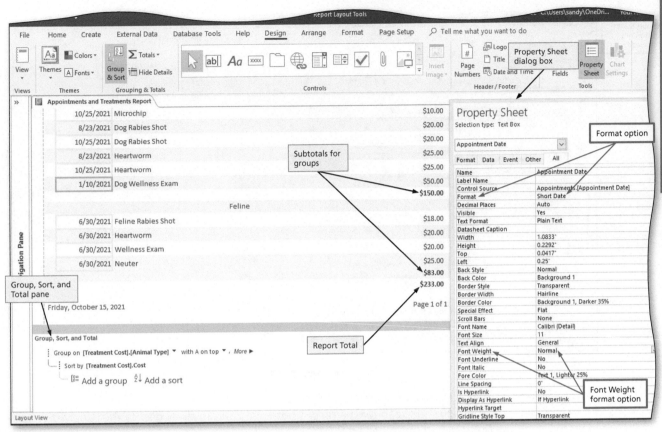

Figure 4–13

- Click the Property Sheet button (Report Layout Tools Design tab | Tools group) to close the property sheet.

- Scroll to the bottom of the report and use the same technique to change the format for the grand total of Cost to Currency and Bold.

- If necessary, drag the lower boundaries of the controls for the grand total so that the numbers appear completely.

- Click Save to save the report.

Other Ways

1. Right-click column header for field on which to group, click Group On (field name)

To Remove the Group, Sort, and Total Pane

The following step removes the Group, Sort, and Total pane from the screen. *Why? Because you have specified the required grouping and sorting for the report, you no longer need to use the Group, Sort, and Total pane.*

- Click the Group & Sort button (Report Layout Tools Design tab | Grouping & Totals group) to remove the Group, Sort, and Total pane (Figure 4–14).

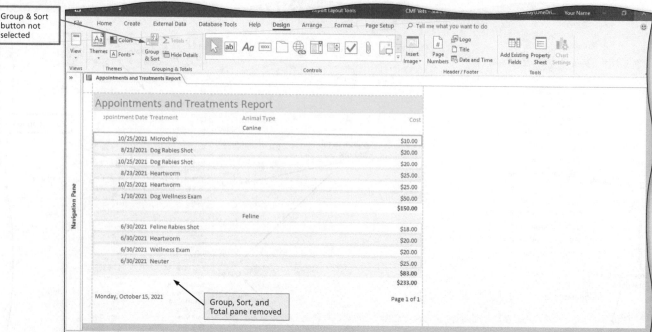

Figure 4–14

Q&A Do I need to remove the Group, Sort, and Total pane?

No. Doing so provides more room on the screen for the report, however. You can easily display the pane whenever you need it by clicking the Group & Sort button again.

Other Ways
1. Click 'Close Grouping Dialog Box' button

CONSIDER THIS

How do you determine the organization of the report or form?
Determine various details concerning how the data in your report or form is to be organized.

Determine sort order. Is there a special order in which the records should appear?

Determine grouping. Should the records be grouped in some fashion? If so, what should appear before the records in a group? If, for example, records are grouped by city, the name of the city should probably appear before the group. What should appear after the group? For example, does the report include some fields for which subtotals should be calculated? If so, the subtotals would come after the group. Determine whether you need multiple levels of grouping.

To Conditionally Format Controls

Conditional formatting is special formatting that is applied to values that satisfy some criterion. CMF Vets management has decided to apply conditional formatting to the Cost field. *Why? They would like to emphasize values in the Cost field that are greater than or equal to $20.00 by changing the font color to red.* By emphasizing the treatments equal to or higher in cost than $20, they can review the higher treatment costs that may be affected by price increases from vendors. The following steps conditionally format the Cost field by specifying a **rule** that states that if the values in the field are greater than or equal to $20.00, such values will be formatted in red.

1

• Confirm that you are still in Layout View and scroll to the top of the report.

• Click Format on the ribbon to display the Report Layout Tools Format tab.

- Click the Cost field on the first record to select the field (Figure 4–15).

Q&A Does it have to be the first record?
No. You could click the field on any record.

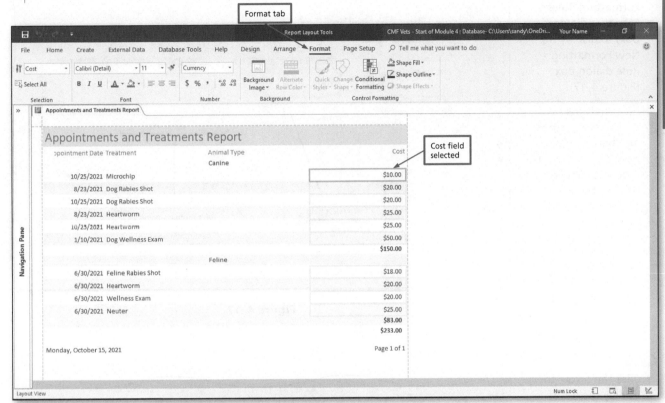

Figure 4–15

2

- Click the Conditional Formatting button (Report Layout Tools Format tab | Control Formatting group) to display the Conditional Formatting Rules Manager dialog box (Figure 4–16).

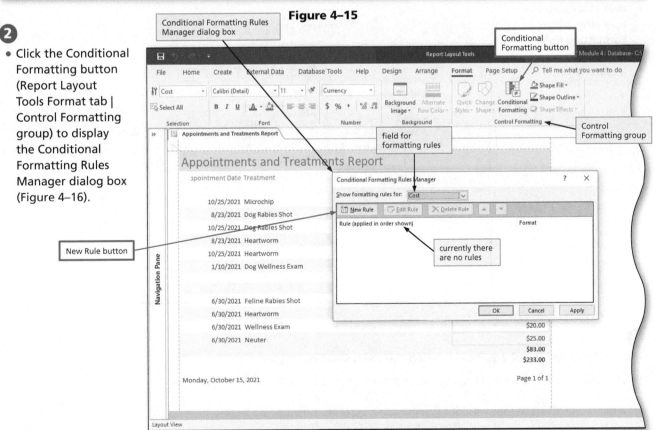

Figure 4–16

● Click the New Rule
button (Conditional
Formatting Rules
Manager dialog
box) to display the
New Formatting
Rule dialog box
(Figure 4–17).

Q&A I see that there are
two boxes to enter
numbers. I only
have one number to
enter, 20. Am I on
the right screen?
Yes. Next, you
will change the
comparison operator
from "between"
to "greater than or
equal to." Once you
have done so, Access
will only display one
box for entering a number.

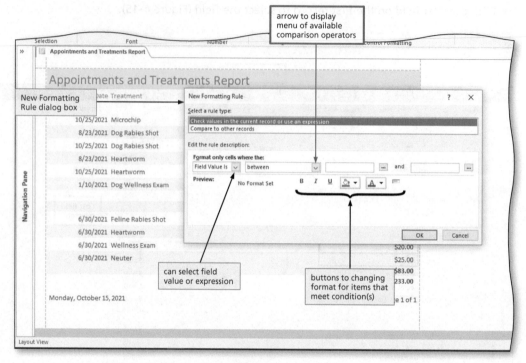

Figure 4–17

● Click the arrow to
display the list of
available comparison
operators (New
Formatting Rule
dialog box)
(Figure 4–18).

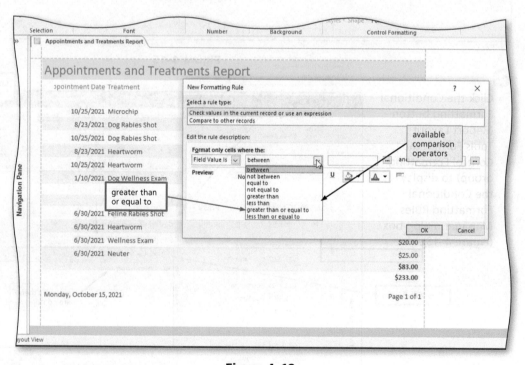

Figure 4–18

● Click "greater than or equal to" to select the comparison operator.

● Click the box for the comparison value, and then type   20   as the comparison value.

Q&A What is the effect of selecting this comparison operator and entering this number?
Values in the field that are greater than or equal to 20 satisfy this rule. Any formatting that you now specify will
apply to those values and no others.

- Click the Font
Color arrow
(New Formatting
Rule dialog
box) to display
a color palette
(Figure 4–19).

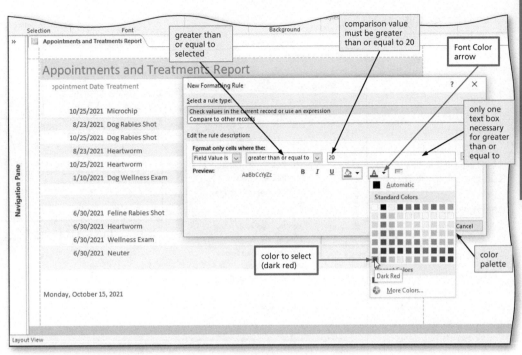

Figure 4–19

- Click the dark red
color in the lower-
left corner of the
color palette to
select the color
(Figure 4–20).

Q&A What other
changes could I
specify for those
values that satisfy
the rule?
You could specify
that the value is
bold, italic, and/
or underlined. You
could also specify
a background
color.

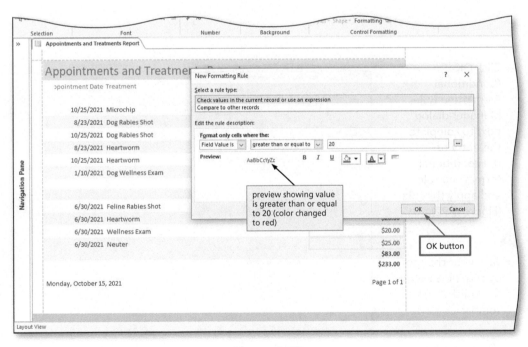

Figure 4–20

- Click OK (New Formatting Rule dialog box) to enter the rule (Figure 4–21).

Q&A What if I have more than one rule?
The rules are applied in the order in which they appear in the dialog box. If a value satisfies the first rule, the
specified formatting will apply, and no further rules will be tested. If not, the value will be tested against the
second rule. If it satisfies the rule, the formatting for the second rule would apply. If not, the value would be tested
against the third rule, and so on.

Can I change this conditional formatting later?

Yes. Select the field for which you had applied conditional formatting on any record, click the Conditional Formatting button (Report Layout Tools Format tab | Control Formatting group), click the rule you want to change, click the Edit Rule button, and then make the necessary changes. You can also delete the selected rule by clicking the Delete Rule button, or move the selected rule by clicking the Move Up or Move Down buttons.

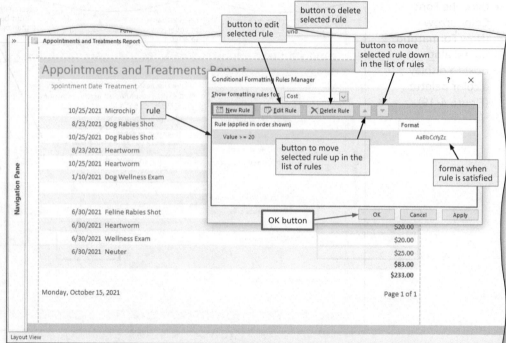

Figure 4–21

8

● Click OK (Conditional Formatting Rules Manager dialog box) to complete the entry of the conditional formatting rules and apply the rule (Figure 4–22).

9

● Save your changes by clicking Save on the Quick Access Toolbar.

 Experiment

● After saving your changes, experiment with different rules. Add a second rule that changes the format for any current

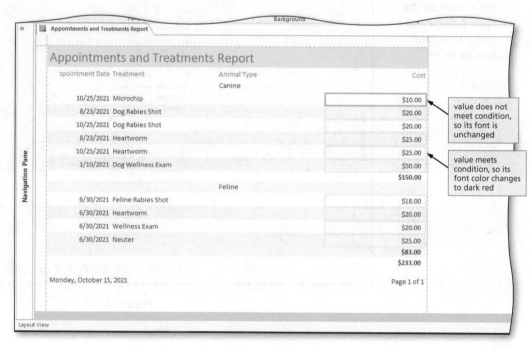

Figure 4–22

due amount that is greater than or equal to $25 to a different color to see the effect of multiple rules. Change the order of rules to see the effect of a different order. When you have finished, delete any additional rules you have added so that the report contains only the one rule that you created earlier.

To Filter Records in a Report

You sometimes might want to filter records in a report. *Why? You may want to include in a report only those records that satisfy some criterion and be able to change that criterion easily.* To filter records in a report, you can use the filter buttons in the Sort & Filter group on the Home tab. If the filter involves only one field, however, right-clicking the field provides a simple way to filter. The following steps filter the records in the report to include only those records on which the cost amount is not $25.

1

• While still in Layout View, right-click the Cost field on the first record where Cost is 25 to display the shortcut menu (Figure 4–23).

Q&A Did I have to pick the first record where the value is $25.00?
No. You could pick any record on which the Cost value is $25.00.

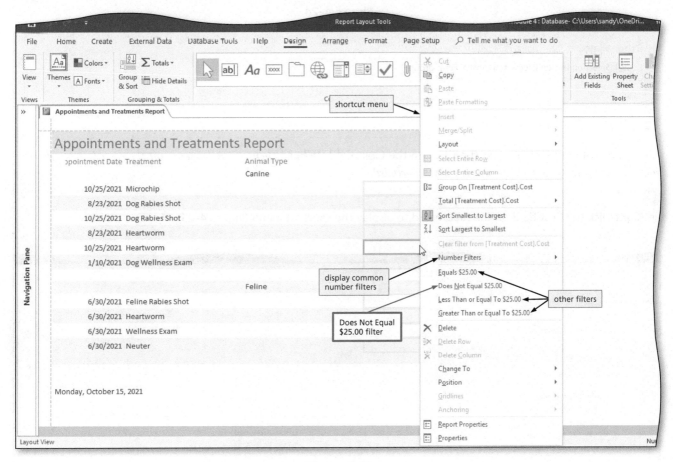

Figure 4–23

2

• Click 'Does Not Equal $25.00' on the shortcut menu to restrict the records in the report to those on which the Cost value is not $25.00 (Figure 4–24).

Q&A When would you use Number Filters?
You would use Number Filters if you need filters that are not on the main shortcut menu or if you need the ability to enter specific values other than the ones shown on the shortcut menu. If those filters are insufficient for your needs, you can use Advanced Filter/Sort, which is accessible through the Advanced button (Home tab | Sort & Filter group).

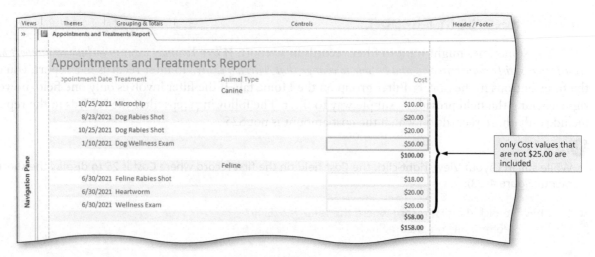

Figure 4–24

Other Ways

1. Click Selection button (Home tab | Sort & Filter group)

To Clear a Report Filter

The following steps clear the filter on the Cost field. *Why? When you no longer want the records to be filtered, you clear the filter so that all records are again included.*

- Right-click the Cost field on the first record to display the shortcut menu (Figure 4–25).

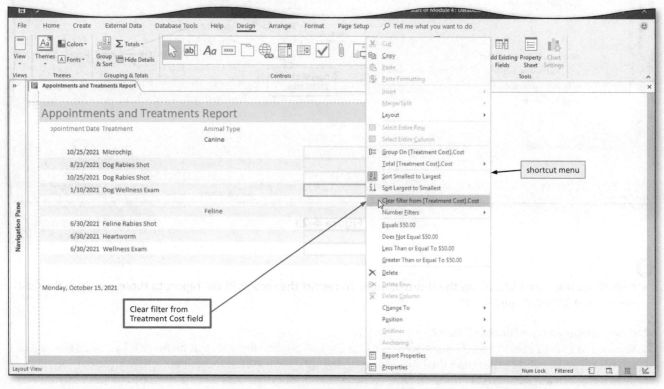

Figure 4–25

Q&A | Did I have to pick the first record?
No. You could pick the Cost field on any record.

- Click Clear filter from [Treatment Cost]. Cost on the shortcut menu to clear the filter and redisplay all records.

Experiment

- Try other filters on the shortcut menu for the Cost field to see their effect. When you are done with each, clear the filter.

- Save your work.

- Close the Appointments and Treatments Report.

Other Ways

1. Click Advanced button (Home tab | Sort & Filter group)

The Arrange and Page Setup Tabs

When working on a report in Layout view, you can make additional layout changes by using the Report Layout Tools Arrange and/or Page Setup tabs. The Arrange tab is shown in Figure 4–26. Table 4–1 shows the buttons on the Arrange tab along with the Enhanced ScreenTips that describe their function.

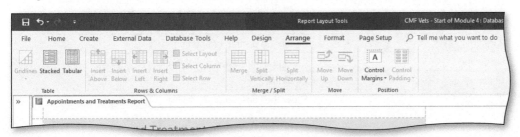

Figure 4–26

Table 4–1 Arrange Tab	
Button	**Enhanced ScreenTip**
Gridlines	Gridlines.
Stacked	Create a layout similar to a paper form, with labels to the left of each field.
Tabular	Create a layout similar to a spreadsheet, with labels across the top and data in columns below the labels.
Insert Above	Insert above.
Insert Below	Insert below.
Insert Left	Insert left.
Insert Right	Insert right.
Select Layout	Select layout.
Select Column	Select column.
Select Row	Select row.
Merge	Merge cells.
Split Vertically	Split the selected control into two rows.
Split Horizontally	Split the selected control into two columns.
Move Up	Move up.
Move Down	Move down.
Control Margins	Specify the location of information displayed within the control.
Control Padding	Set the amount of spacing between controls and the gridlines of a layout.

BTW
Using the Arrange Tab
Because the commands located on the Arrange tab are actions associated with previously selected controls, be sure to select the desired control or controls first.

BTW
Searching for Records in a Report
You can use the Find button to search for records in a report. To do so, open the report in Report view or Layout view and select the field in the report on which to search. Click the Find button (Home tab | Find group) to display the Find and Replace dialog box. Type the desired value on which to search in the Find What text box (Find and Replace dialog box), and then click the Find Next button.

The Report Layout Tools Page Setup tab is shown in Figure 4–27. Table 4–2 shows the buttons on the Page Setup tab along with the Enhanced ScreenTips that describe their function.

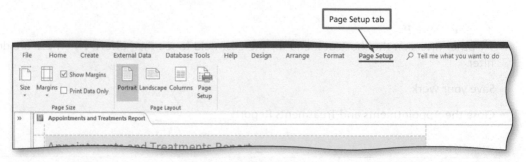

Figure 4–27

Table 4–2 Page Setup Tab	
Button	**Enhanced ScreenTip**
Size	Choose a paper size for the current document.
Margins	Select the margin sizes for the entire document or the current section.
Show Margins	Show margins.
Print Data Only	Print data only.
Portrait	Change to portrait orientation.
Landscape	Change to landscape orientation.
Columns	Columns.
Page Setup	Show the Page Setup dialog box.

BTW
Distributing a Document
Instead of printing and distributing a hard copy of a document, you can distribute the document electronically. Options include sending the document via email; posting it on cloud storage (such as OneDrive) and sharing the file with others; posting it on a social networking site, blog, or other website; and sharing a link associated with an online location of the document. You can also create and share a PDF or XPS image of the document, so that users can view the file in Acrobat Reader or XPS Viewer instead of in Access.

TO PRINT A REPORT

If you want to print your report, you would use the following steps.

1. With the report selected in the Navigation Pane, click File on the ribbon to open the Backstage view.
2. Click the Print tab in the Backstage view to display the Print gallery.
3. Click the Quick Print button to print the report.

Q&A How can I print multiple copies of my report?
Click File on the ribbon to open the Backstage view. Click the Print tab, click Print in the Print gallery to display the Print dialog box, increase the number in the Number of Copies box, and then click OK (Print dialog box).

Break Point: If you wish to take a break, this is a good place to do so. You can quit Access now. To resume at a later time, start Access, open the database called CMF Vets, and continue following the steps from this location forward.

Multiple-Table Reports

Sometimes you will create reports that require data from more than one table. You can use the Report Wizard to create a report based on multiple tables just as you can use it to create reports based on single tables or queries. The following steps use the Report Wizard to create a report that includes fields from the Appointments, Treatment Cost, and Owners tables.

To Create a Report that Involves Multiple Tables

Currently, the Owners and the Patients tables are the only tables with an existing relationship that was created previously. In order to produce the report currently needed by the managers, you will need to add the Appointments and Treatment Cost tables. *Why? CMF Vets managers need a report that shows detailed appointment information that includes the Appointment Date, Treatment Number, Treatment Cost, Treatment Name, and Owner Last Name information from existing tables.*

Before starting to create reports from multiple tables, it is always a good idea to check the current relationships between tables and add any necessary tables to the relationship. The Appointments table will be the basis for much of the information in the report requested by CMF Vets managers. The following steps review the existing relationships and add the necessary tables. You previously created the relationship between the Owners and Patients tables.

1

- Click the Database Tools tab, and then click the Relationships button (Database Tools tab | Relationships group) (Figure 4–28).

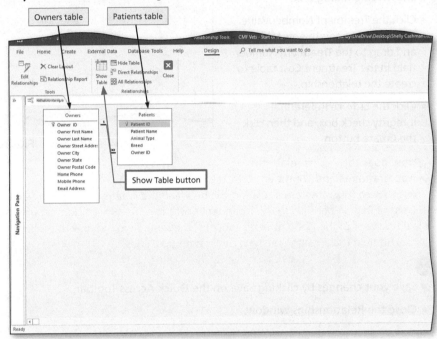

Figure 4–28

2

- Click the Show Table button to view available tables.

- Click the Appointments table and then click the Add button to add this table to the Relationships window (Figure 4–29).

- Close the Show Table dialog box.

- Click the Owner ID field in the Owners table and drag to the Owner field in the Appointments table to create the relationship.

 What are the lines that appear between the tables in the Relationships window?
The lines depict the relationships between tables. The relationship between the Patients and Appointments tables is based on the Patient ID field. A relationship exists between the Owners ID field in the Owners table and the Owners field in the Appointments table.

- Click the Enforce Referential Integrity check box, and then click the Create button.

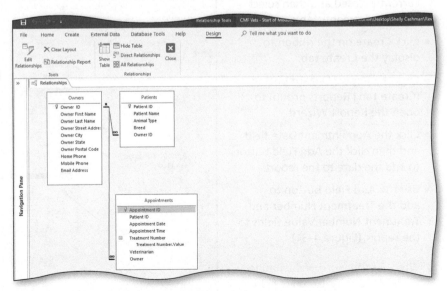

Figure 4–29

- Next, you will add the Treatment Cost table, so you can view the cost of the appointment. Click the Show Table button.

- Click the Treatment Cost table in the Show Table dialog box and click the Add button to add the table to the Relationship window (Figure 4–30), and then close the Show Table dialog box.

- Click the Treatment Number.Value field in the Appointments table and drag to the Treatment Number field in the Treatment Cost table to create the relationship.

- Click the Enforce Referential Integrity check box, and then click the Create button.

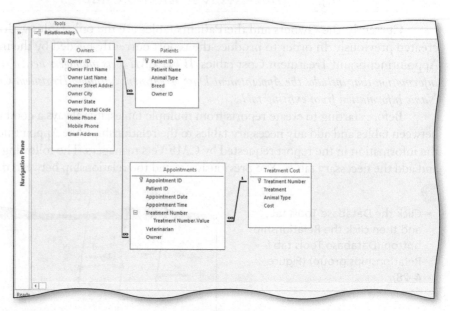

Figure 4–30

Q&A How does the Access relate the Appointments and Treatment Cost tables?
Access recognizes there is a relationship between the Treatment Number.Value field in the Appointments table and the Treatment Number field in the Treatment Cost table. Treatment Number and Treatment Number.Value are displayed on two lines in the Appointments table for the same field because this field was previously updated to a multivalued lookup field that displays the field on two multiple lines.

- Save your changes by clicking Save on the Quick Access Toolbar.

- Close the Relationships window.

- Open the Navigation Pane if it is currently closed and then select the Appointments table.

- Click Create on the ribbon to display the Create tab.

- Click the Report Wizard button (Create tab | Reports group) to open the Report Wizard.

- Click the Appointment Date field and then click the Add Field button to add the date to the report.

- Use the Add Field button to add the Treatment Number and Treatment Number.Value fields to the report (Figure 4–31).

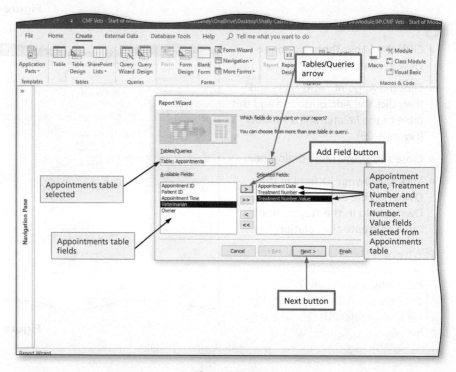

Q&A Why was the word, Value, added to the Treatment Number field name?
Access changes the field name automatically when it is a multivalued lookup field.

Figure 4–31

- Click the Tables/
Queries arrow to
display available
tables and then click
the Treatment Cost
table.

- Click the Cost field
and then click the
Add Field button.

- Click the Treatment
field and then click
the Add Field button
(Figure 4–32).

- Click the Tables/
Queries arrow to
display available
tables and then click
the Owners table to
select it as the data
source.

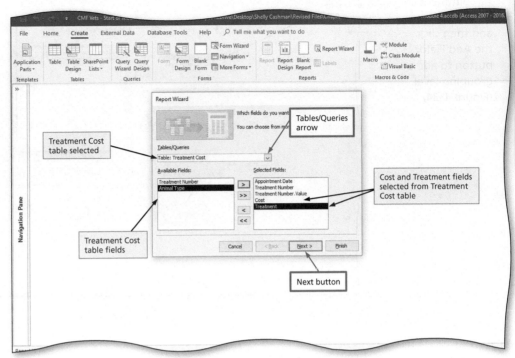

Figure 4–32

- Click the Owner Last
Name field and then
click the Add Field
button to add the
Owner Last Name
field to the report
(Figure 4–33).

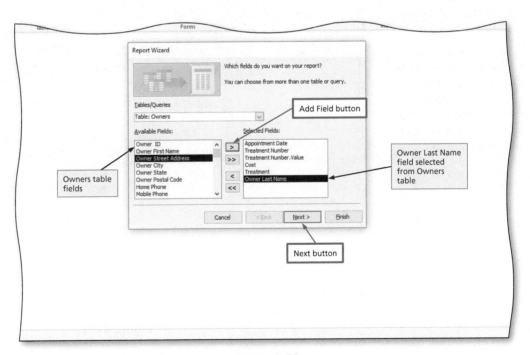

Figure 4–33

- Now that all the fields have been added, click Next.

- Because the report is to be based on the Appointments table and that table already is selected, click Next.

- Click the Appointment Date field and then click the Add Field button to add a grouping level (Figure 4–34)

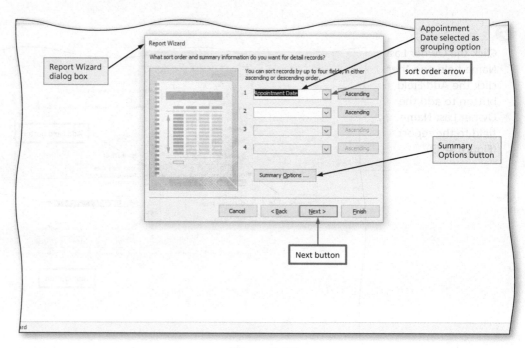

Figure 4–34

 9

- Click Next to move to the next Report Wizard screen.
- To sort by Appointment Date, click the arrow to select sort order, and then click the Appointment Date (Figure 4–35).

Figure 4–35

 10

- Click the Summary Options button to display the Summary Options dialog box.
- Click the Sum check box to calculate the sum of Cost.

- If necessary, click the Detail and Summary option button to select it (Figure 4–36).

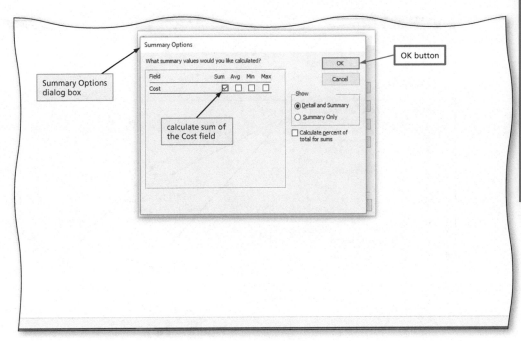

Figure 4–36

11

- Click OK (Summary Options dialog box) to close the Summary Options dialog box.

- Click Next to move to the next screen in the wizard, confirm that Stepped layout is selected, and then click the Landscape option button to select the orientation.

- Click Next to move to the next screen

- Click the text box for the title, delete any existing text, and then type **Owner Appointment Cost** as the title (Figure 4–37).

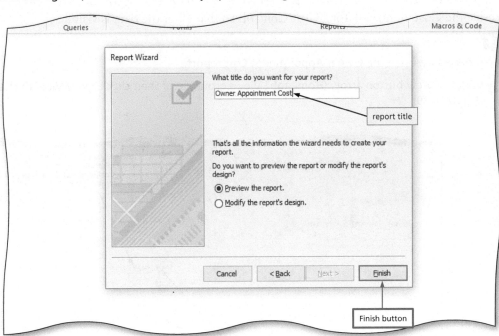

Figure 4–37

12

- Click Finish to produce the report (Figure 4–38).

- Save the report as Owner Appointment Cost. Click the Close Print Preview Button (Print Preview tab | Close Preview group).

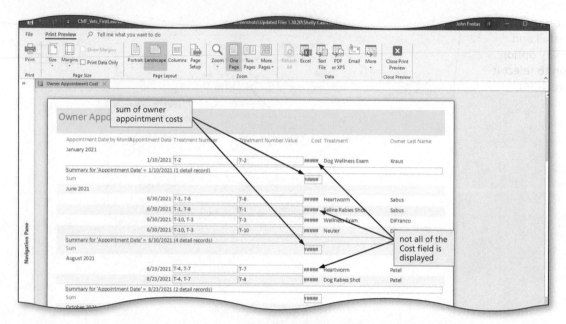

Figure 4–38

To Modify the Report

CMF Vets needs to change the sizes of some of the objects that appear in the Owner Appointment Cost report. *Why? The size of the controls does not allow all of the data to appear in some of the controls.* The following steps resize the Cost, Sum, and Total Cost Controls so that all of the data is visible.

- If necessary, open the Owner Appointment Cost report.
- Click the View button arrow (Home tab | Views group), and then click Layout View to change the view (Figure 4–39).

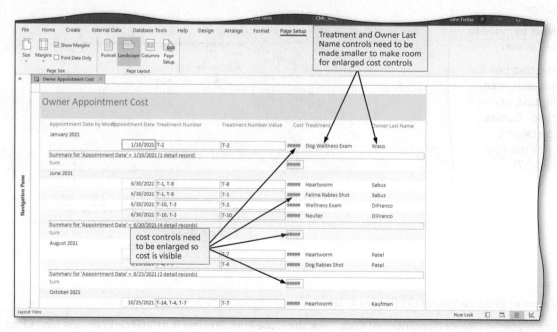

Figure 4–39

- Click the Owner Last Name control under the Owner Last Name heading to select it.

- Point to the left border of the Owner Last Name control until the pointer becomes double-headed arrow (Figure 4–40). Then, drag the pointer to the right to make the control smaller.

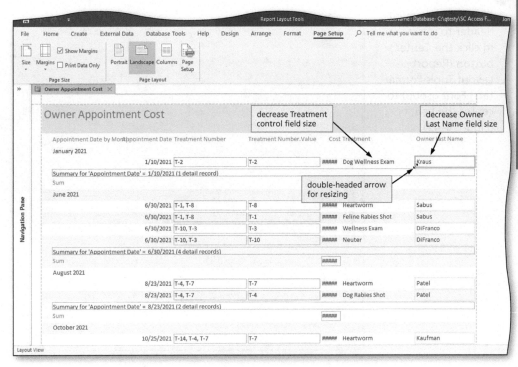

Figure 4–40

- Using the process you followed in Step 2, decrease the size of the Treatment Control.

- Click the Cost control and point to the right border of the selection handle, and then drag the border to the right to increase size of the control until all of the cost is displayed (see Figure 4–41).

- Increase the size of the Sum control so that it resembles Figure 4–41.

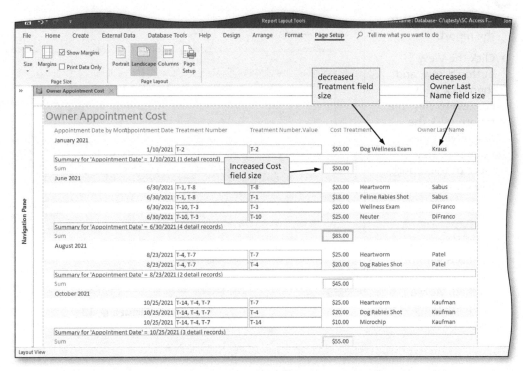

Figure 4–41

- Using the same technique, resize is the Grand Total Cost control at the end of the report. You will have to scroll to the bottom of the report to display the control.

- Click the Treatment header to select it, click the Center button (Report Layout Tools Format tab | Font group) to center the header (Figure 4–42).

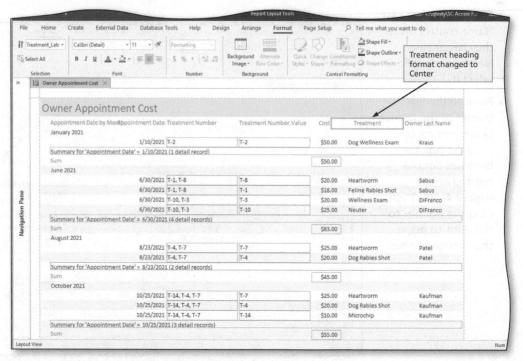

Figure 4–42

- Save the changes to the report.

- Click the View button arrow, and then click Print Preview to view the report. Click the magnifying glass pointer to view more of the report (Figure 4–43).

 **Experiment**

- Zoom in on various positions within the report. When finished, view a complete page of the report.

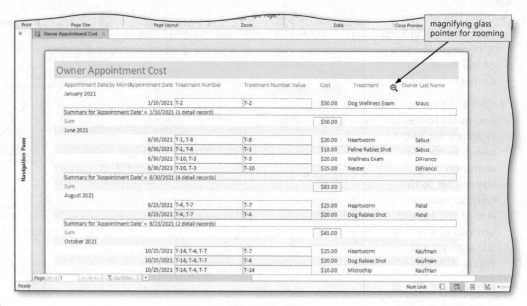

Figure 4–43

- Click the 'Close Print Preview' button (Print Preview tab | Close Preview group) to close Print Preview.

Q&A What is the purpose of the dashed vertical line near the right edge of the screen?
The line shows the right border of the amount of the report that will print on one page. If any portion of the report extends beyond the line, the report may not print correctly.

- If necessary, drag the right border of a control to the approximate position to resize the control so that no portion of the control extends beyond the dashed vertical line. Close the field list, if necessary.

Q&A Do I have to resize all the controls that begin with Summary individually?

No. When you resize one of them, the others will all be resized the same amount automatically.

- Ensure that the control for the Page Number is visible, click the Page number to select it, and then drag it to the left, if necessary, so that no portion of the control extends beyond the dashed line.

- Save your work.

- Click the Close button for the report to close the report and remove it from the screen.

Q&A When would I use the Summary Options button?

You would use the Summary Options button if you want to specify subtotals or other calculations for the report while using the wizard. You can also use it to produce a summary report by selecting Summary Only, which will omit all detail records from the report.

CONSIDER THIS

How do you determine the tables and fields that contain the data needed for the report?
First, you need to know the requirements for the report. Precisely what data is the report intended to convey? Once you understand those requirements, follow these guidelines:

Examine the requirements for the report to determine the tables. Do the requirements only relate to data in a single table, or does the data come from multiple tables? What is the relationship between the tables?

Examine the requirements for the report to determine the fields necessary. Look for all the data items specified for the report. Each should correspond to a field in a table or be able to be computed from fields in a table. This information gives you the list of fields to include.

Determine the order of the fields. Examine the requirements to determine the order in which the fields should appear. Be logical and consistent in your ordering. For example, in an address, the city should come before the state and the state should come before the postal code, unless there is some compelling reason for another order.

Creating a Report in Layout View

You can use the Report button initially to create a report containing all the fields in a table. You can then delete the unwanted fields so that the resulting report contains only the desired fields. At that point, you can use Layout view to modify the report and produce the report you want.

You can also use Layout view to create single- or multiple-table reports from scratch. To do so, you first create a blank report and display a field list for the table containing the first fields you want to include on the report.

There are times when you might want to create a report that has multiple columns. For example, a telephone list with employee name and phone number could print in multiple columns. To do so, create the report using Layout view or Design view and then click the Page Setup tab, click the Columns button, enter the number of columns, select the desired column layout, and then click OK.

You then would drag any fields you want from the table onto the report in the order you want them to appear. You would then change the size of the controls as you did previously by clicking the control, pointing to the edge of the selected control, and dragging to the desired size.

If the report involves a second table, you display the fields from the second table in the field list and then drag the fields from the second table onto the report in the desired order.

When you create a report in Layout view, the report does not automatically contain a title, but you can add one by clicking the Title button (Report Layout Tools Design tab | Header/Footer group).

Once you have added the title, you can type whatever title you want for the report.

BTW

Adding a Second Table to a Report
If the report involves a second table, be sure the fields in the second table appear, and then drag the fields from the second table onto the report in the desired order. (If the field list covers the portion of the report where you want to drag the fields, move the field list to a different position by dragging its title bar.)

To Create a Report in Layout View by Creating a Blank Report

CMF Vets needs an additional report that shows information related to treatments and their costs. Managers at the practice want to create the report in Layout view. *Why? Layout view works best when you need to change the look and feel of a report because you can rearrange fields and change their sizes.* The following steps create a report in Layout view.

1

- Click Create on the ribbon to display the Create tab.
- Click the Blank Report button (Create tab | Reports group) to create a blank report.
- If a field list does not appear, display it by clicking the 'Add Existing Fields' button (Report Layout Tools Design tab | Tools group) (Figure 4–44).

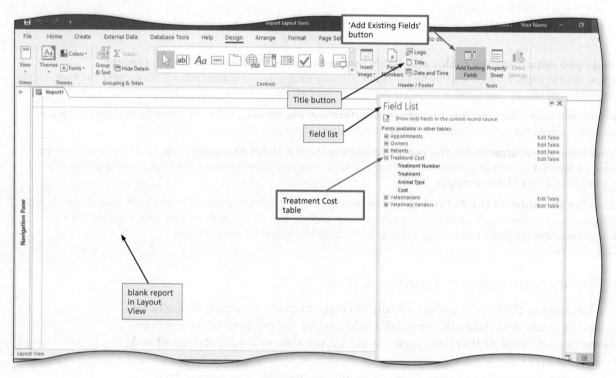

Figure 4–44

2

- If the tables do not appear in the field list, click 'Show all tables.'
- Click the plus sign next to the Treatment Cost table to display its fields in the field list.

Q&A I do not see the fields for the Treatment Cost table.
If the fields in the table do not appear, click the plus sign in front of the name of the table.

- Drag the Treatment Number, Treatment, Animal Type, and Cost fields from the field list to the report, positioning the fields as shown in Figure 4–45.

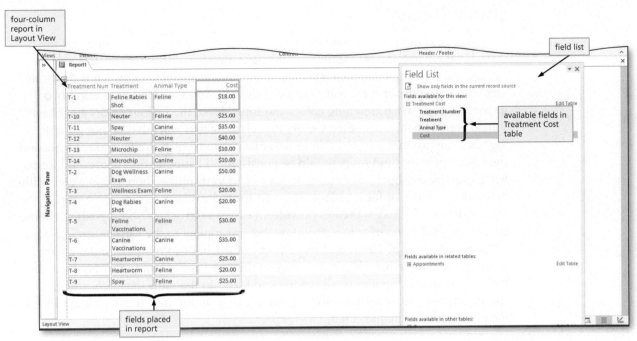

Figure 4–45

③

- To add a title, click the Title button (Report Layout Tools Design tab | Header/Footer group) and then type **Treatment Cost Report** (Figure 4–46).

- Save the report as Treatment Cost Report.

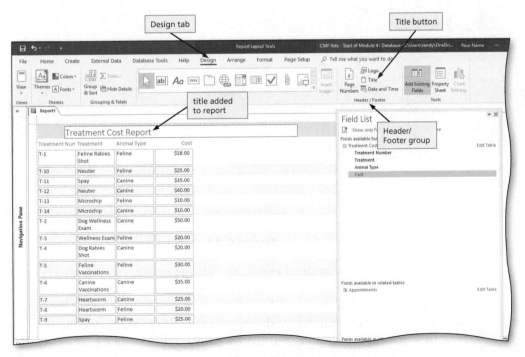

Figure 4–46

Using Themes

The most important characteristic of a report or form is that it presents the desired data in a useful arrangement. Another important characteristic, however, is the general appearance of the form. The colors and fonts that you use in the various sections of a report or form contribute to this look. You should keep in mind two important goals when assigning colors and fonts. First, the various colors and fonts should complement each other. Colors that clash or two fonts that do not go well together can produce a report that looks unprofessional or is difficult to read. Second, the choice of colors and fonts should be consistent. That is, all the reports and forms within a database should use the same colors and fonts unless there is some compelling reason for a report or form to look different from the others.

Fortunately, Access themes provide an easy way to achieve both goals. A **theme** consists of a selection of colors and fonts that are applied to the various sections in a report or form. The colors and fonts in any of the built-in themes are designed to complement each other. When you assign a theme to any object in the database, the theme immediately applies to all reports and forms in the same database, unless you specifically indicate otherwise. To assign a theme, you use the Theme picker, which is a menu of available themes (Figure 4–47).

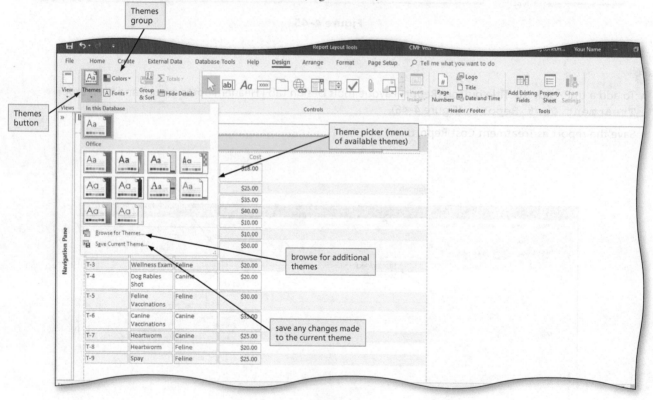

Figure 4–47

If you point to any theme in the Theme picker, you will see a ScreenTip giving the name of the theme. When you select a theme, the colors and fonts represented by that theme will immediately be applied to all reports and forms. If you later decide that you would prefer a different theme, you can change the theme for all of the objects in the database by repeating the process with a different theme.

You can also use the Browse for Themes command to browse for themes that are not listed as part of a standard Access installation, but which are available for download. You can also create your own customized theme by specifying a combination of fonts and colors and using the Save Current Theme command to save your combination. If, after selecting a theme using the Themes button, you do not like

BTW

Using Themes
Office themes are designed to enhance an organization's brand identity. Many organizations consistently use themes, styles, and color schemes to visually assist in identifying their products and/or services.

the colors in the current theme, you can change the theme's colors. Click the Colors button (Report Layout Tools Design tab | Themes group) (Figure 4–48), and then select an alternative color scheme.

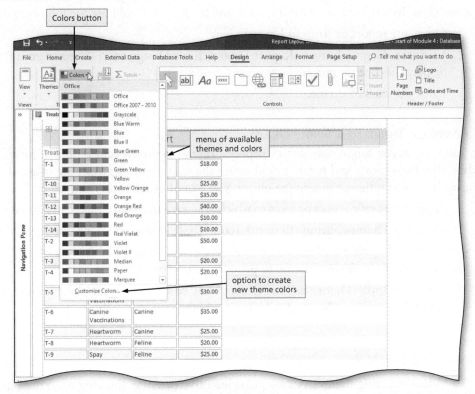

Figure 4–48

Similarly, if you do not like the fonts in the current theme, you can click the Fonts button (Report Layout Tools Design tab | Themes group) (Figure 4–49). You can then select an alternative font for the theme.

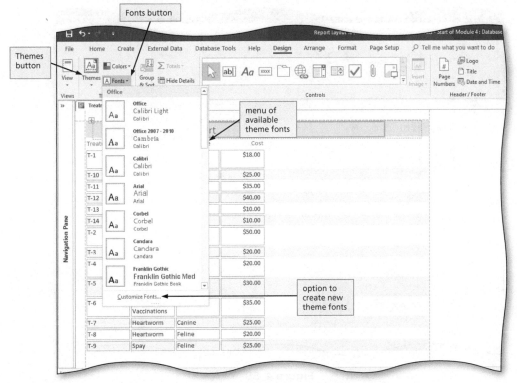

Figure 4–49

TO ASSIGN A THEME TO ALL OBJECTS

To assign a theme, it is easiest to use Layout view. You can use Design view as well, but it is easier to see the result of picking a theme when you are viewing the report or form in Layout view. To assign a theme to all reports and forms, you would use the following steps.

1. Open any report or form in Layout view.
2. Click the Themes button (Report Layout Tools Design tab | Themes group) to display the Theme picker.
3. Click the desired theme.

TO ASSIGN A THEME TO A SINGLE OBJECT

In some cases, you might only want to apply a theme to the current report or form, while all other reports and forms would retain the characteristics from the original theme. To assign a theme to a single object, you would use the following steps.

1. Open the specific report or form to which you want to assign a theme in Layout view.
2. Click the Themes button (Report Layout Tools Design tab | Themes group) to display the Theme picker.
3. Right-click the desired theme to produce a shortcut menu.
4. Click the Apply Theme to This Object Only command on the shortcut menu to apply the theme to the single object on which you are working.

Live Preview for Themes

When selecting themes, Access provides a **live preview** showing what the report or form will look like with the theme before you actually select and apply the theme. The report or form will appear as it would in the theme to which you are currently pointing (Figure 4–50). If you like that theme, you then can select the theme by clicking the left mouse button.

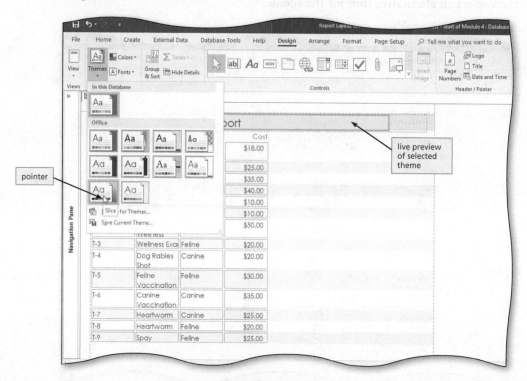

Figure 4–50

To Create a Summary Report

A report that includes group calculations such as subtotals, but does not include the individual detail lines, is called a **summary report**. *Why? You might need a report that only shows the overall group calculations, but not all the records.* The following steps hide the detail lines in the Appointments and Treatments report, thus creating a summary report.

1

- Open the Treatment Cost Report in Layout view. Apply the Slice theme to the report. Save your changes and close the report.
- Open the Appointments and Treatments report in Layout view and close the Navigation Pane.
- Click the Hide Details button (Report Layout Tools Design tab | Grouping & Totals group) to hide the details in the report (Figure 4–51).

Q&A | How can I see the details once I have hidden them?
Click the Hide Details button a second time.

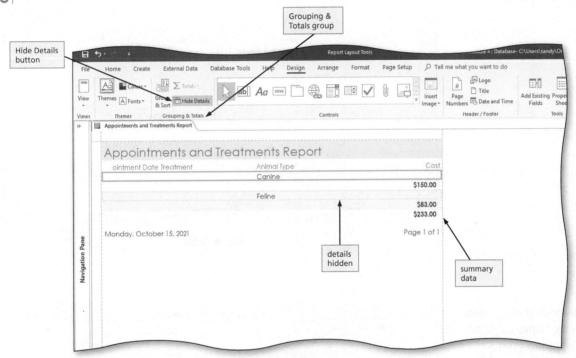

Figure 4–51

- Close the report without saving your changes.

Q&A | What would happen if I saved the report?
The next time you view the report, the details would still be hidden. If that happened and you wanted to show all the details, just click the Hide Details button a second time.

Break Point: If you wish to take a break, this is a good place to do so. You can quit Access now. To resume at a later time, start Access, open the database called CMF Vets, and continue following the steps from this location forward.

Form Creation

You can create a simple form consisting of all the fields in the Appointments table using the Form button (Create tab | Forms group). To create more customized forms, you can use the Form Wizard. Once you have used the Form Wizard to create a form, you can modify that form in either Layout view or Design view.

BTW
Summary Reports
You can create a summary report in either Layout view or Design view.

To Use the Form Wizard to Create a Form

The following steps use the Form Wizard to create an initial version of the Veterinary Vendors Form. *Why? Using the Form Wizard is the easiest way to create this form.* The initial version will contain the Vendor Name, Street Address, City, State, ZIP Code, Veterinary Supply, Product Type, Quantity, Cost, and Total Amount fields.

- Open the Navigation Pane and select the Veterinary Vendors table.

- Click Create on the ribbon to display the Create tab.

- Click the Form Wizard button (Create tab | Forms group) to start the Form Wizard (Figure 4–52).

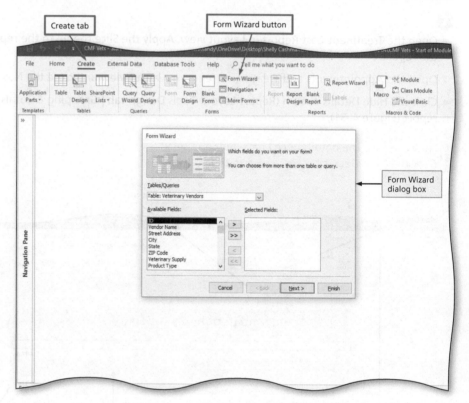

Figure 4–52

- Add the Vendor Name, Street Address, City, State, ZIP Code, Veterinary Supply, Product Type, Quantity, Cost, and Total Amount fields to the form (Figure 4–53).

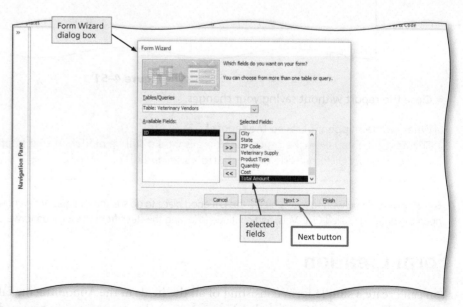

Figure 4–53

- Click Next to display the next Form Wizard screen (Figure 4–54).

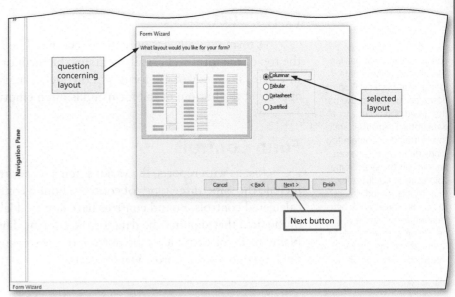

Figure 4–54

- Be sure the Columnar layout is selected, and then click Next to display the next Form Wizard screen.

- Click in the Title text box and delete existing text. Type **Veterinary Vendors Form** for the title (Figure 4–55).

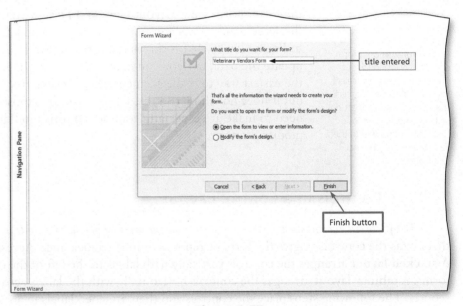

Figure 4–55

- Click Finish to complete and display the form (Figure 4–56).

- Click the form's Close button to close the Veterinary Vendors Form.

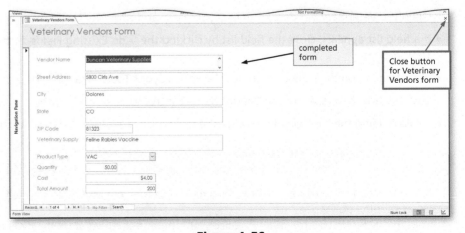

Figure 4–56

BTW
Form Design Considerations
Forms should be appealing visually and present data logically and clearly. Properly designed forms improve both the speed and accuracy of data entry. Forms that are too cluttered or contain too many different effects can be hard on the eyes. Some colors are more difficult than others for individuals to see. Be consistent when creating forms. Once you decide on a general style or theme for forms, stick with it throughout your database.

BTW
Conditional Formatting
Conditional formatting is available for forms as well as reports. To conditionally format controls on a form, open the Form in Layout view or Design view, select the control to format, click the Conditional Formatting button, and then follow the steps found within the To Conditionally Format Controls section.

Form Sections

A form typically has only three sections. The Form Header section appears at the top of the form and usually contains the form title. It may also contain a logo and/or a date. The body of the form is in the Detail section. The Form Footer section appears at the bottom of the form and is often empty.

Form Controls

Just as with reports, the various items on a form are called controls. Forms include the same three types of controls: bound controls, unbound controls, and calculated controls. Bound controls have attached labels that typically display the name of the field that supplies the data for the control. The **attached label** for the Vendor Name field, for example, is the portion of the screen immediately to the left of the field. It contains the words, Vendor Name.

Views Available for Forms

When working with a form in Access, there are three different ways to view the form: Form view, Layout view, and Design view. Form view shows the form on the screen and allows you to use the form to update data. Layout view is similar to Form view in that it shows the form on the screen. In Layout view, you cannot update the data, but you can make changes to the layout of the form, and it is usually the easiest way to make such changes. Design view also allows you to make changes, but it does not show you the actual form. It is most useful when the changes you need to make are especially complex. In this module, you will use Layout view to modify the form.

To Place Controls in a Control Layout

Why? *To use Layout view with a form, the controls must be placed in a control layout.* A **control layout** is a guide that aligns the controls to give the form or report a uniform appearance. Access has two types of control layouts. A **stacked layout** arranges the controls vertically with labels to the left of the control and is commonly used in forms. A **tabular layout** arranges the controls horizontally with the labels across the top and is typically used in reports. The following steps place the controls and their attached labels in a stacked control layout.

- Open the Veterinary Vendors Form in Layout view and close the Navigation Pane.

- If a field list appears, close the field list by clicking the 'Add Existing Fields' button (Report Layout Tools Design tab | Tools group).

- Click Arrange on the ribbon to display the Form Layout Tools Arrange tab.

- Click the attached label for the Vendor Name control to select the control.

- While holding the SHIFT key down, click the remaining attached labels and all the controls (Figure 4–57).

Q&A Did I have to select the attached labels and controls in that order?
No. As long as you select all of them, the order in which you selected them does not matter.

When I clicked some of the controls, they moved so they are no longer aligned as well as they are in the figure. What should I do?
You do not have to worry about it. Once you complete the next step, they will once again be aligned properly.

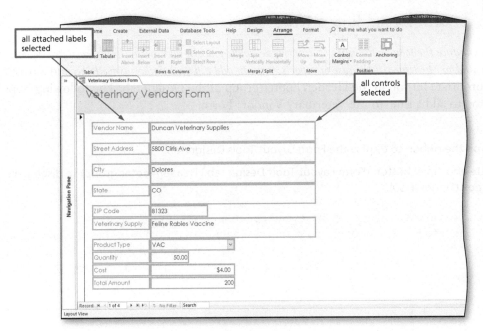

Figure 4–57

2

* Click the Stacked button (Form Layout Tools Arrange tab | Table group) to place the controls in a stacked layout (Figure 4–58).

Q&A

How can I tell whether the controls are in a control layout?
Look for the Control Layout indicator in the upper-left corner of the control layout.

What is the difference between stacked layout and tabular layout?
In a stacked layout, which is more often used in forms, the controls are placed vertically with the labels to the left of the controls. In a tabular layout, which is more often used in reports, the controls are placed horizontally with the labels above the controls.

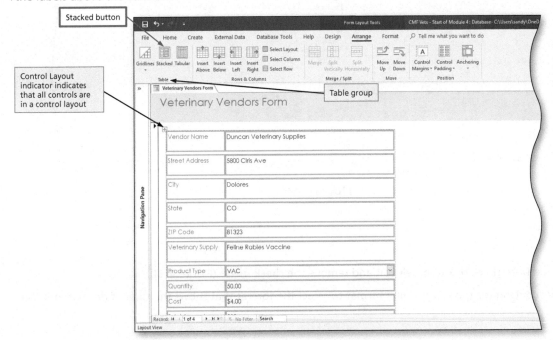

Figure 4–58

To Enhance a Form by Adding a Time

Why? *To enhance the look or usability of a report or form, you can add special items, such as a logo or title. You can also add the date and/or the time. In the case of reports, you can add a page number as well.* To add any of these items, you use the appropriate button in the Header/Footer group of the Design tab. The following steps use the 'Date and Time' button to add a time to the Veterinary Vendors Form.

- Click Design on the ribbon to display the Form Layout Tools Design tab.

- Click the 'Date and Time' button (Form Layout Tools Design tab | Header/Footer group) to display the Date and Time dialog box (Figure 4–59).

Q&A What is the purpose of the various check boxes and option buttons?
If the Include Date check box is checked, you must pick a date format from the three option buttons underneath the check box. If it is not checked, the option buttons will be dimmed. If the Include Time check box is checked, you must pick a time format from the three option buttons underneath the check box. If it is not checked, the option buttons will be dimmed.

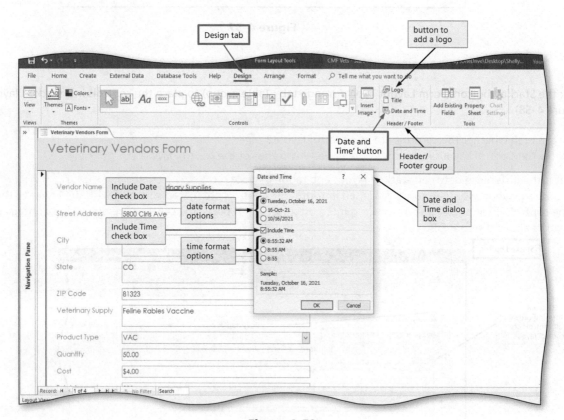

Figure 4–59

- Click the Include Date check box to deselect it and remove the check mark (Figure 4–60).

- Click the option button for the second Time format to select the format that shows the time of day without the seconds.

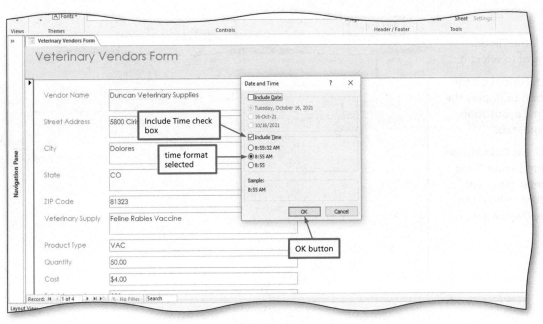

Figure 4–60

❸
- Click OK (Date and Time dialog box) to add the time to the form (Figure 4–61).

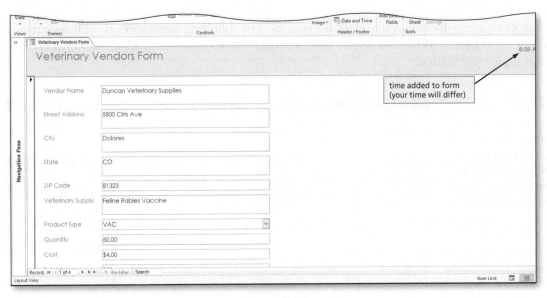

Figure 4–61

To Change the Format of a Control

You can change the format of a control by clicking the control and then clicking the appropriate button on the Format tab. The following step uses this technique to bold the time. ***Why?*** *Formatting controls on a form lets you visually emphasize certain controls.*

- Click the Time control to select it.

- Click Format on the ribbon to display the Form Layout Tools Format tab.

- Click the Bold button (Form Layout Tools Format tab | Font group) to bold the time (Figure 4–62).

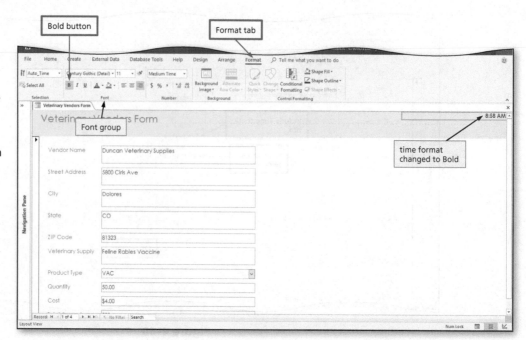

Figure 4–62

To Move a Control

You can move a control by dragging the control. The following step moves the Time control to the lower edge of the form header. **Why?** *The default location of some controls might not be ideal; moving controls lets you adjust the design to your specifications.*

- Point to the Time control so that the pointer changes to a four-headed arrow, and then drag the Time control to the lower boundary of the form header in the approximate position shown in Figure 4–63.

Q&A

I moved my pointer a little bit and it became a two-headed arrow. Can I still drag the pointer?

If you drag when the pointer is a two-headed arrow, you will resize the control. To move the control, it must be a four-headed arrow.

Could I drag other objects as well? For example, could I drag the title to the center of the form header?

Yes. Just be sure you are pointing at the object and the pointer is a four-headed arrow. You can then drag the object to the desired location.

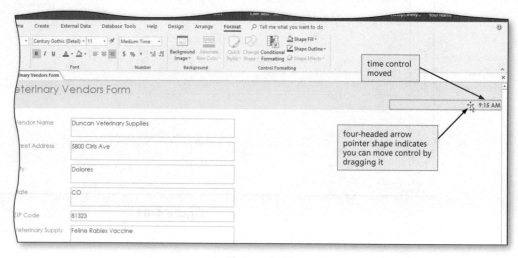

Figure 4–63

To Move Controls in a Control Layout

Just as you moved the Time control in the previous section, you can move any control within a control layout by dragging the control to the location you want. As you move it, a line will indicate the position where the control will be placed when you release the mouse button or your finger. You can move more than one control in the same operation by selecting multiple controls prior to moving them.

The following steps move controls in the Owners form. These steps will move the Home Phone and Mobile Phone fields so that they follow the Owner Last Name field. *Why? The home phone and mobile phone fields are the primary fields used to contact the owners, and these fields would be easier to access while viewing the Owner's Last Name.*

- Save changes to the Veterinary Vendors Form and then close the form.
- Open the Owners Form in Layout View.
- Click the label for the Home Phone field to select it.

- Hold the SHIFT key down and click the control for the Home Phone field, then click the label and the control for the Mobile Phone field to select both fields and their labels (Figure 4–64).

Q&A Why did I have to hold the SHIFT key down when I clicked the remaining controls?
If you did not hold the SHIFT key down, you would only select the control for the Home Phone field (the last control selected). The other controls no longer would be selected.

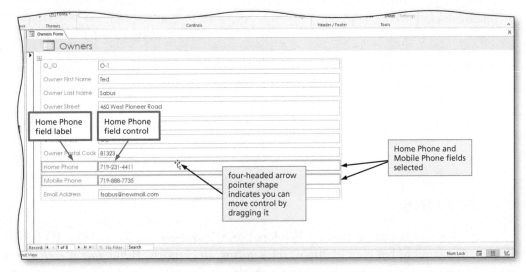

Figure 4–64

- Drag the fields straight up to the position shown in Figure 4–65; you will see a line as you move the fields to their new location

Q&A What is the purpose of the line by the pointer?
It shows you where the fields will be positioned.

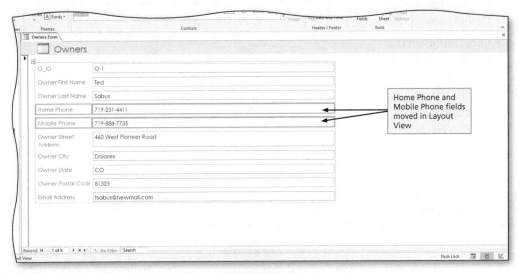

Figure 4–65

- Release the mouse button to complete the movement of the fields (Figure 4–66).

- Save and Close the Owners Form.

Q&A
I inadvertently had the line under the label rather than the data when I released the mouse button. The data that I moved is now under the field names. How do I fix this?

You can try to move it back where it was, but that can be tricky. The easiest way is to use the Undo button on the Quick Access Toolbar to undo your change.

I inadvertently moved my pointer so that the line became vertical and was located between a label and the corresponding data when I released the mouse button. It seemed to split the form. The data I moved appears right where the line was. It is between a label and the corresponding data. How do I fix this?

Use the Undo button on the Quick Access Toolbar to undo your change.

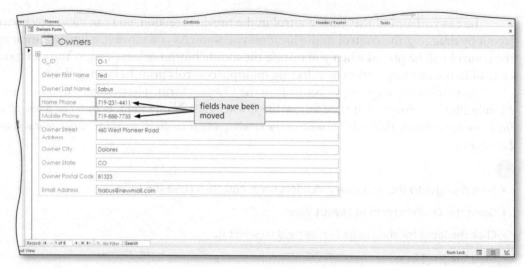

Figure 4–66

To Add a Field

After reviewing the Veterinary Vendors Form, management decided that ID fields would help keep information straight between multiple tables, forms, and reports. *Why? Just as with a report, once you have created an initial form, you might decide that the form should contain an additional field.* The following steps use a field list to add the ID field to the Veterinary Vendors Form.

- Open the Veterinary Vendors Form in Design view.

- Click Design on the ribbon to display the Form Design Tools Design tab.

- Click the 'Add Existing Fields' button (Form Design Tools Design tab | Tools group) to display a field list (Figure 4–67).

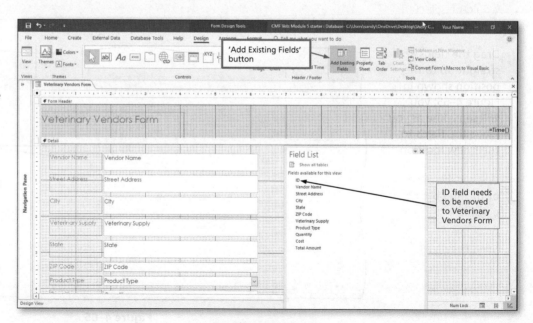

Figure 4–67

2

- Point to the ID field in the field list, and then drag the pointer to the position shown in Figure 4–68 (at approximately 0.5 on the vertical ruler and 7.5 on the horizontal ruler). For illustration purposes do not release the mouse button yet.

Q&A Does it have to be exact?
The exact position is not critical at this time as long the pointer is in the general position shown in the figure.

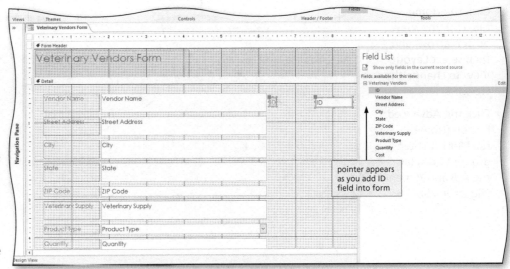

Figure 4–68

3

- Release the mouse button to place the field (Figure 4–69).

Q&A What if I make a mistake?
Just as when you are modifying a report, you can delete the field by clicking the field and then pressing DELETE. You can move the field by dragging it to the correct position.

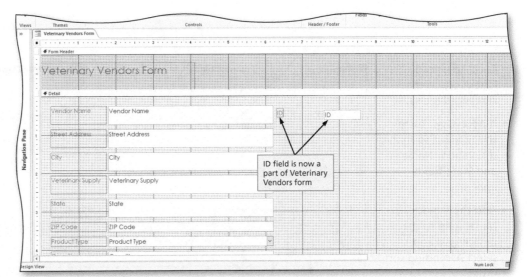

Figure 4–69

4

- Click the 'Add Existing Fields' button (Form Design Tools Design tab | Tools group) to remove the field list.

- Switch between Layout view and Form view to confirm that the form resembles the figure; adjust the field placement as necessary.

- Save your work.

To Filter and Sort Using a Form

Why? *Just as in a datasheet, you often need to filter and sort data when using a form.* You can do so using Advanced Filter/Sort, which is a command on the Advanced menu. The following steps use Advanced Filter/Sort to filter the records to records whose state begins with the letter C. The effect of this filter and sort is that you use the form to view only view those vendors whose state begins with C. In addition, you will see the order of the vendors you will need to set up with appointments.

- Click the Home tab, click the View button arrow, and then select Layout View to change the view.

- Click the Advanced button (Home tab | Sort & Filter group) to display the Advanced menu (Figure 4–70).

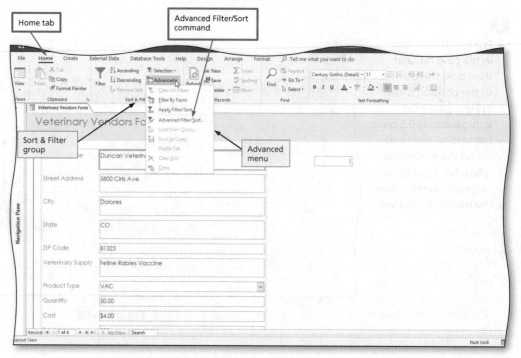

Figure 4–70

- Click Advanced Filter/Sort on the Advanced menu.

- If necessary, resize the field list so that the Vendor Name and State fields appear.

- Add the Vendor Name field to the design grid and select Ascending sort order.

- Add the State field and type C* as the criterion for the State field (Figure 4–71).

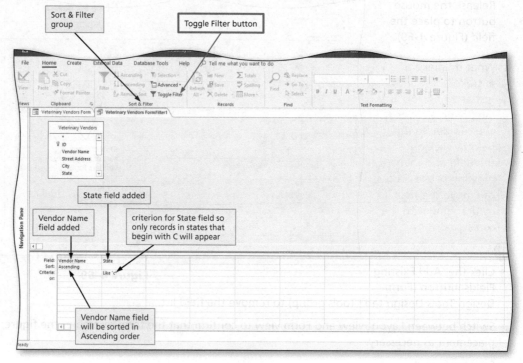

Figure 4–71

- Click the Toggle Filter button (Home tab | Sort & Filter group) to filter the records (Figure 4–72).

Q&A
I can only see one record at a time in the form. How can I see which records are included?
You need to scroll through the records using the arrows in the Navigation bar.

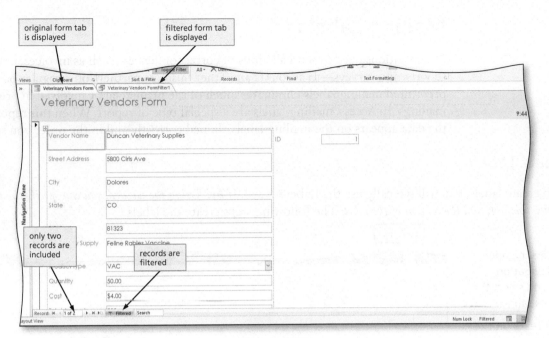

Figure 4–72

To Clear a Form Filter

When you no longer want the records to be filtered, you clear the filter. The following steps clear the current filter for the Veterinary Vendors Form.

1 Click the Advanced button (Home tab | Sort & Filter group) to display the Advanced menu.

2 Click Clear All Filters on the Advanced menu to clear the filter.

3 Save your work.

4 Close the form.

BTW
Printing Forms
To change the page setup and page layout options, such as adjusting margins and changing the orientation, for a form, use the Print Preview window. To open the Print Preview window for a form, click File on the ribbon, click Print, and then click Print Preview.

To PRINT A FORM

You can print all records, a range of records, or a selected record of a form by selecting the appropriate print range. To print the selected record, the form must be open. To print all records or a range of records, you can simply highlight the form in the Navigation Pane. To print a specific record in a form, you would use the following steps.

1. Be sure the desired form is open and the desired record is selected.
2. Click File on the ribbon to open the Backstage view.
3. Click the Print tab in the Backstage view to display the Print gallery.
4. Click the Print button to display the Print dialog box.
5. Click the Selected Record(s) option button in the Print Range section, and then click OK.

The Arrange Tab

Forms, like reports, have an Arrange tab that you can use to modify the form's layout. However, the Page Setup tab is not available for forms. The buttons on the Arrange tab and the functions of those buttons are just like the ones described in Table 4–1.

Mailing Labels

Organizations need to send all kinds of correspondence—such as invoices, letters, reports, and surveys—to accounts and other business partners on a regular basis. Using preprinted mailing labels eliminates much of the manual labor involved in preparing mailings. In Access, mailing labels are a special type of report. When this report prints, the data appears on the mailing labels aligned correctly and in the order you specify.

To Create Labels

To create labels, you will typically use the Label wizard. *Why? Using the wizard, you can specify the type and dimensions, the font, and the content of the label.* The following steps create the labels.

- If necessary, open the Navigation Pane and select the Owners table.

- Click Create on the ribbon to display the Create tab.

- Click the Labels button (Create tab | Reports group) to display the Label Wizard dialog box.

- Ensure that English is selected as the Unit of Measure and that Avery is selected in the Filter by manufacturer box.

- If necessary, scroll through the product numbers until C2163 appears, and then click C2163 in the Product number list to select the specific type of labels (Figure 4–73).

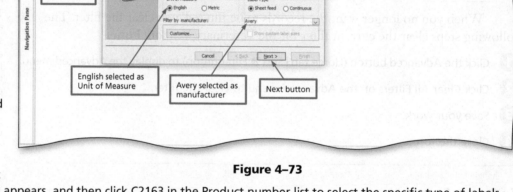

Figure 4–73

- Click Next (Figure 4–74).

Q&A

What font characteristics could I change with this screen?

You could change the font, the font size, the font weight, and/or the font color. You could also specify italic or underline.

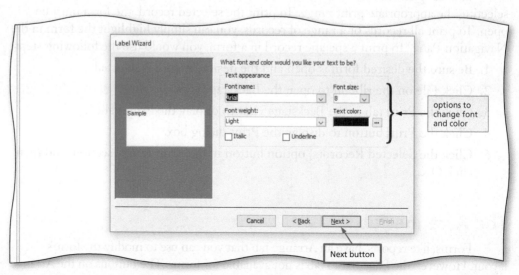

Figure 4–74

- Click Next to accept the default font and color settings.
- Click the Owner First Name field, and then click the Add Field button (Figure 4–75).

Q&A What should I do if I make a mistake?
You can erase the contents of any line in the label by clicking in the line to produce an insertion point and then using DELETE or BACKSPACE to erase the current contents. You then can add the correct field by clicking the field and then clicking the Add Field button.

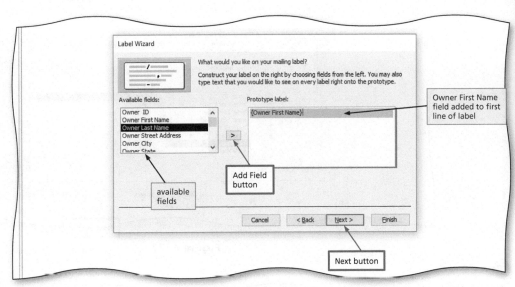

Figure 4–75

- Press the SPACEBAR, add the Owner Last Name field.
- Click the second line of the label, and then add the Owner Street Address field.
- Click the third line of the label.
- Add the Owner City field, type , (a comma), press the SPACEBAR, add the Owner State field, press the SPACEBAR, and then add the Owner Postal Code field (Figure 4–76).

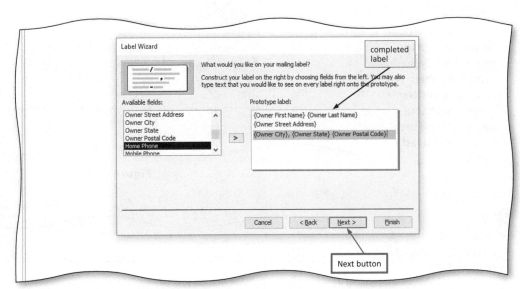

Figure 4–76

5

- Because you have now added all the necessary fields to the label, click Next.
- Select the Owner Postal Code field as the field to sort by, and then click the Add Field button (Figure 4–77).

Q&A Why am I sorting by postal code?
When you need to do a bulk mailing, that is, send a large number of items using a special postage rate, businesses that provide mailing services often require that the mail be sorted in postal code order.

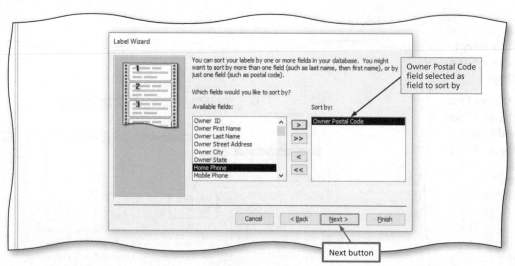

Figure 4-77

6

- Click Next.

- Ensure the name for the report (that is, the labels) is Labels Owners (Figure 4-78).

- If requested to do so by your instructor, name the labels report as Labels FirstName LastName where FirstName and LastName are your first and last names.

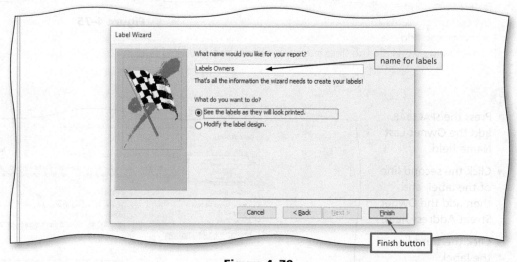

Figure 4-78

7

- Click Finish to complete the labels (Figure 4-79).

8

- Close the Labels Owners report.

- If desired, sign out of your Microsoft account.

- **sam** ↑ Exit Access.

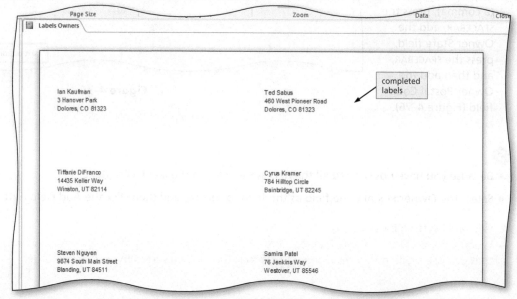

Figure 4-79

To Print Labels

You print labels just as you print a report. The only difference is that you must load the labels in the printer before printing. If you want to print labels, you would use the following steps once you have loaded the labels in your printer.

1. With the labels you wish to print selected in the Navigation Pane, click File on the ribbon to open the Backstage view.

2. Click the Print tab in the Backstage view to display the Print gallery.

3. Click the Quick Print button to print the report.

Q&A I want to load the correct number of labels. How do I know how many pages of labels will print?

If you are unsure how many pages of labels will print, open the label report in Print Preview first. Use the Navigation buttons in the status bar of the Print Preview window to determine how many pages of labels will print.

BTW
Customizing Mailing Labels
Once you create mailing labels, you can customize them just as you can customize other reports. In Design view, you can add a picture to the label, change the font size, adjust the spacing between controls, or make any other desired changes.

Summary

In this module you have learned to use wizards to create reports and forms, modify the layout of reports and forms using Layout view, group and sort in a report, add totals to a report, conditionally format controls, filter records in reports and forms, resize and move controls, add fields to reports and forms, create a stacked layout for a form, add a date/time, move controls in a control layout, apply themes, and create mailing labels.

CONSIDER THIS

What decisions will you need to make when creating your own reports and forms?

Use these guidelines as you complete the assignments in this module and create your own reports and forms outside of this class.

1. Determine whether the data should be presented in a report or a form.

   a. Do you intend to print the data? If so, a report would be the appropriate choice.

   b. Do you intend to view the data on the screen, or will the user update data? If so, a form would be the appropriate choice.

2. Determine the intended audience for the report or form.

   a. Who will use the report or form?

   b. Will the report or form be used by individuals external to the organization? For example, many government agencies require reports from organizations. If so, government regulations will dictate the report requirements. If the report is for internal use, the user will have specific requirements based on the intended use.

   c. Adding unnecessary data to a report or form can make the form or report unreadable. Include only data necessary for the intended use.

   d. What level of detail should the report or form contain? Reports used in day-to-day operations need more detail than weekly or monthly reports requested by management.

3. Determine the tables that contain the data needed for the report or form.

   a. Is all the data found in a single table?

   b. Does the data come from multiple related tables?

4. Determine the fields that should appear on the report or form.

5. Determine the organization of the report or form.

   a. In what order should the fields appear?

   b. How should they be arranged?

   c. Should the records in a report be grouped in some way?

   d. Are any calculations required?

e. Should the report be used to simply summarize data?

f. Should the data for the report or form be filtered in some way?

6. Determine the format of the report or form.

a. What information should be in the report or form header?

b. Do you want a title and date?

c. Do you want a logo?

d. What information should be in the body of the report or form?

e. Is any conditional formatting required?

f. What style should be applied to the report or form? In other words, determine the visual characteristics that the various portions of the report or form should have.

g. Is it appropriate to apply a theme to the reports, forms, and other objects in the database?

7. Review the report or form after it has been in operation to determine whether any changes are necessary.

a. Is the order of the fields still appropriate?

b. Are any additional fields required?

8. For mailing labels, determine the contents, order, and type of label.

a. What fields should appear on the label?

b. How should the fields be arranged?

c. Is there a certain order (for example, by postal code) in which the labels should be printed?

d. Who is the manufacturer of the labels and what is the style number for the labels?

e. What are the dimensions for each label?

f. How many labels print across a page?

How should you submit solutions to questions in the assignments identified with a symbol?

Every assignment in this book contains one or more questions identified with a symbol. These questions require you to think beyond the assigned database. Present your solutions to the questions in the format required by your instructor. Possible formats may include one or more of these options: write the answer; create a document that contains the answer; present your answer to the class; discuss your answer in a group; record the answer as audio or video using a webcam, smartphone, or portable media player; or post answers on a blog, wiki, or website.

CONSIDER THIS

Apply Your Knowledge

Reinforce the skills and apply the concepts you learned in this module.

Creating Two Reports and a Form

Instructions: Start Access. Open the Support_AC_Financial Services database (If you do not have the database, see your instructor for a copy of the modified database.)

Perform the following tasks:

1. Create a report from the Accounting table that shows clients who owe money to Financial Services. Group the report by Client number and sort the report by Current Due in Ascending order. Add subtotals and a total to the Current Due field. Save the report as Clients with Current Due Amounts. Your finished report should look like Figure 4–80.

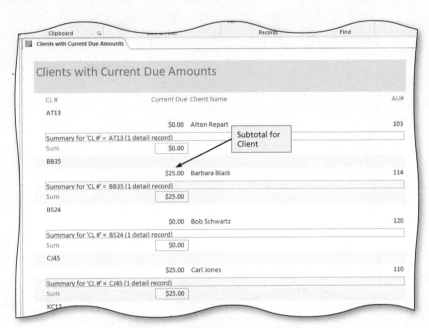

Figure 4–80

2. Create a report that counts the number of clients for each Advisor. Group the report by Advisor and use the title Count of Clients by Advisor Report. Save the report. Your finished report should look like Figure 4–81.

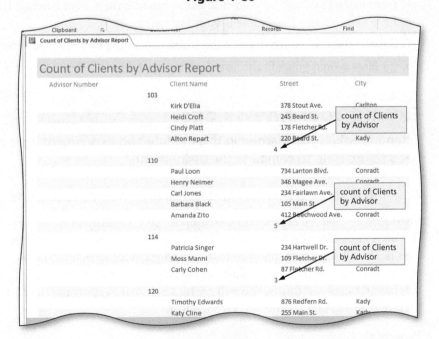

Figure 4–81

Continued >

Apply Your Knowledge *continued*

3. Create the Current Due by Client Form shown in Figure 4–82. The form has a columnar layout and includes the current date. Bold the date control and change the Alignment to Left-Align. Include the Client's Current Due amount. Decrease the size of the CL# and Client Name controls so they reflect the appropriate size for these fields. Use Figure 4–82 for reference. Save the form.

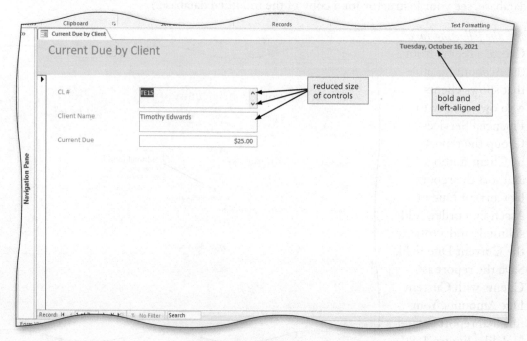

Figure 4–82

4. If requested to do so by your instructor, rename the Client Advisor Report as Clients by LastName where LastName is your last name.

5. Submit the revised database in the format specified by your instructor.

6. ✳ How would you add the City field to the Advisor-Client Report so that the field appears below the Client Name field?

Extend Your Knowledge

Extend the skills you learned in this module and experiment with new skills. You may need to use Help to complete the assignment.

Creating a Summary Report and Assigning Themes to Reports and Forms

Instructions: Start Access. Open the Support_AC_Healthy Pets database from the Data Files (If you do not have the database, see your instructor for a copy of the modified database.). Healthy Pets is a small veterinary practice that is run by a veterinarian who would like to retire. CMF Vets has been approached about buying the Healthy Pets practice. Healthy Pets needs to update its database reports and forms. You will create a summary report for the Healthy Pets database, assign a theme to an existing report, and create a form.

Perform the following tasks:

1. Use the Report Wizard to create the summary report shown in Figure 4–83. Apply the Slice theme. Group the report by Client ID Number and sort by Client Name. Sum the Balance Due field for the Summary option. Save your report as Client Amount Due Summary Report.

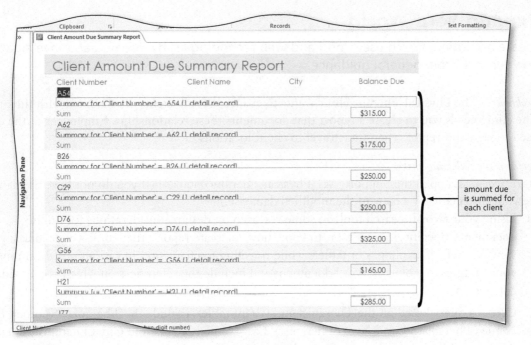

Figure 4–83

2. Create the Technician Form shown in Figure 4–84. The form has a Columnar control layout. Save the changes to the form.

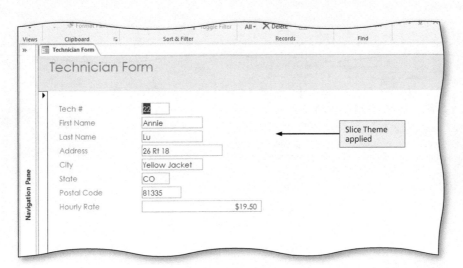

Figure 4–84

3. If requested to do so by your instructor, open the Technician Form in Form view and change the first name and last name for Tech# 22 to your first and last names.

4. Submit the revised database in the format specified by your instructor.

5. ✳ How would you change the theme font for the Technician Form to Arial?

Expand Your World

Create a solution, which uses cloud and web technologies, by learning and investigating on your own from general guidance.

Problem: The Physical Therapy clinic wants to ensure that all clients are matched with therapists. The clinic needs you to create a report that documents these relationships. Employees of the clinic need to view this report when they travel to client locations.

Perform the following tasks:
Start Access and open the Support_AC_Physical Therapy database (If you do not have the database, see your instructor for a copy of the modified database.)

1. Using your favorite search tool, do some research on design considerations for online documents. Specifically, you want to know how to create reports that employees can easily view on their smartphones or tablets while traveling to client sites in various cities. Summarize your findings in a blog or Word document and include the references on which you based your conclusions.

2. Create a query based on the Therapist and Client tables. Include the Therapist Number, First Name (Therapist), Last Name (Therapist), Last Name (Client), and City (Therapist) in either the cities of Portage or Empeer. Save the query as Therapist Serving Empeer or Portage.

3. Create a report based on the Therapist Serving Empeer or Portage query so that therapists and managers can easily view each of the clients and their associated therapists.

4. Group the report by Therapist Number and sort the report by Client Last Name using a Stepped Layout in Portrait orientation. Increase the size of the Report Title control so that the entire report name is displayed. Save the report as Clients Served by Therapists as shown in Figure 4–85.

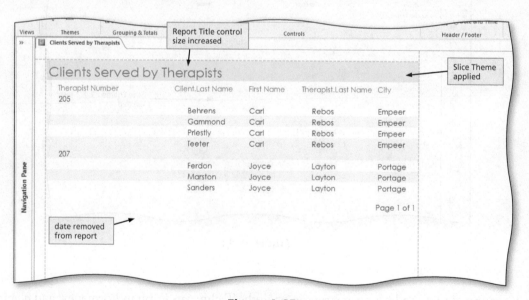

Figure 4–85

5. Add the Slice theme to the Clients Served by Therapists report. Remove the Date fields from the report and save the revised report with the new theme.

6. After completing the report, submit the revised database and update the blog Word document you created in Step 1. Submit the files in the format specified by your instructor.

7. Physical Therapy clinic managers want to know available options for an online network other than SharePoint, which is cost prohibitive at this time. Discuss the creation of an Access app and how Microsoft simplifies this process in Microsoft Access. Post your findings to the blog or document in the format specified by your instructor.

8. ✵ Should all reports and forms for a particular company use the same basic design and themes? Why or why not?

In the Labs

Design, create, modify, and/or use a database following the guidelines, concepts, and skills presented in this module.

Lab: Updating Reports and Forms in the Lancaster College Database

Instructions: Open the Support_AC_Lancaster College database (If you do not have the database, see your instructor for a copy of the modified database.)

Part 1: Use the concepts and techniques presented in this module to create reports and forms so that the data is easily viewed and understood.

a. The athletic director wants to see student ID numbers for all students, and she wants to be able to quickly see which students, and how many of them, have waivers. Using a Tabular layout, create a report that does not contain grouping. Include sorting, formatting, and a calculation that will produce a report similar to that shown in Figure 4–86.

Figure 4–86

Continued >

STUDENT ASSIGNMENTS

b. Create a one-page report that includes all fields in the Team table. Apply grouping and sorting as shown in Figure 4–87. Adjust the size of the controls and the layout as necessary

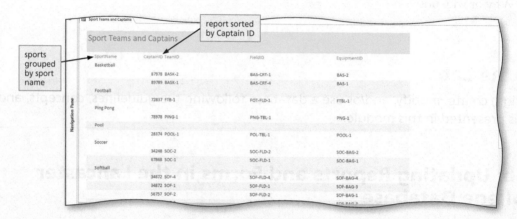

Figure 4–87

c. Create a form for the Student table that includes each student's name, ID, phone numbers, and waiver status. Filter the form to display all students who need a waiver and sort the results in descending order by last name. Save the form as Filtered Student Form.

d. Submit your assignment in the format specified by your instructor.

Part 2: You made several decisions while creating these reports and forms, including conditionally formatting values. What was the rationale behind your decisions? Which formatting option did you choose for the conditional formatting? Why? What other options are available?

5 | Multiple-Table Forms

Objectives

You will have mastered the material in this module when you can:

- Add Yes/No, Long Text, and Attachment fields
- Use the Input Mask Wizard
- Update fields and enter data
- Change row and column size
- Create a form with a subform in Design view
- Modify a subform and form design

- Enhance the form title
- Change tab stops and tab order
- Use the form to view data and attachments
- View object dependencies
- Use Date/Time, Long Text, and Yes/No fields in a query
- Create a form with a datasheet

Introduction

This module adds to the CMF Vets database several new fields that require special data types. It then creates a form incorporating data from two tables. Recall that the two tables, Veterinarians and Appointments, contain information about the veterinarians in the practice and the appointments those veterinarians have. These two tables should be related in a one-to-many relationship, with one veterinarian being related to many appointments, but each appointment being related to only one veterinarian. The form that you create will show one veterinarian at a time, but also will include the many appointments of that veterinarian. This module also creates queries that use the added fields.

Project — Multiple-Table Forms

CMF Vets uses its database to keep records about veterinarians and appointments. The practice is in the process of hiring some specialty veterinarians to cover complicated cases. The increase in personnel means that CMF Vets needs to maintain additional data on its veterinarians. The practice wants to promote the newly hired specialty veterinarians and their status as board-certified professionals. They also want to include each veterinarian's specialty as well as the veterinarian's picture. Additionally, CMF Vets wants to connect the new clinicians' online resources, such as a Linked In profile. These files are separate from the database; some are maintained in Word and

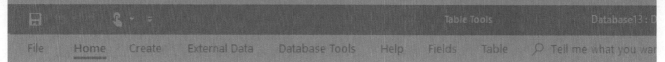

others as PDFs. CMF Vets would like a way to attach these files to the corresponding veterinarian's record in the database. Finally, CMF Vets wants to adjust the Phone Numbers fields in the Veterinarians table. Users should type only the digits in the telephone number and then have Access format the number appropriately. If the user enters 8255553455, for example, Access will format the number as (825) 555–3455.

After the proposed fields have been added to the database, CMF Vets want users to be able to use a form that incorporates the Veterinarians and Appointments tables and includes the newly added fields as well as some of the existing fields in the Veterinarians table. The form should also include the veterinarian ID, the first and last name of the veterinarian, and their office phone and cell phone. CMF Vets would like to see multiple appointments for each veterinarian on the screen at the same time (Figure 5–1). The database should allow users to scroll through all the appointments and see the patient ID, date and time of the appointment and the treatment requested. At any time, the veterinarian's resume can be opened for viewing. Finally, CMF Vets will need queries that use the board-certified, Start Date, and Specialty fields.

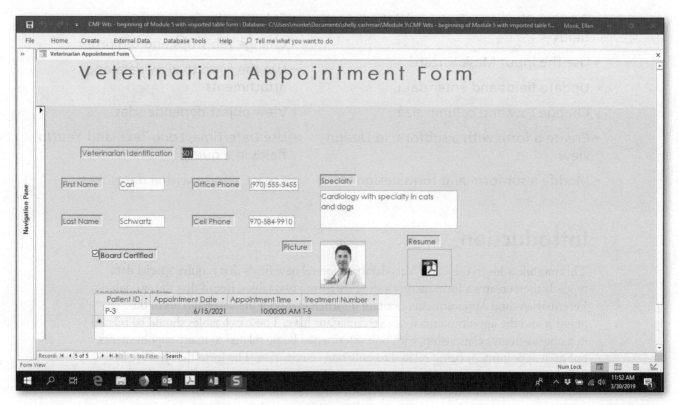

Figure 5–1

Adding Special Fields

Having analyzed its requirements, the management of CMF has identified a need for some new fields for the Veterinarians table. They need a Board-certified field, which uses a value of Yes or No to indicate whether a specialist veterinarian has attained the Board certification; this field's data type will be Yes/No. They need a Specialty field that identifies each veterinarian's unique abilities, which will be a Long Text field.

The Resume field, which must be able to contain multiple attachments for each veterinarian, will be an Attachment field. The Picture field is the only field whose data type is uncertain — it could be either OLE Object, which can contain objects created by a variety of applications, or Attachment. CMF Vets has decided to attach the pictures in order to store the picture data more efficiently. An OLE Object, which stands for Object Linking and Embedding, creates a bitmap of the picture file, which can be very large.

The office wants to assist users in entering the correct format for a phone number, so the field will use an input mask. An **input mask** specifies how data is to be entered and how it will appear. For example, an input mask can indicate that a phone number has parentheses around the first three digits and a hyphen between the sixth and seventh digits.

The form shown in Figure 5–1 contains two attachment fields, the Picture field and the Resume field. When viewed as a table, these both appear as paper clips, not as the actual attachment. However, when the table's attachment fields are displayed in a form, you can view the picture itself and an icon of the document, in this case, a PDF file.

To Add Fields with New Data Types to a Table

You add the new fields to the Veterinarians table by modifying the design of the table and inserting the fields at the appropriate position in the table structure. The following steps add the Board Certification, Specialty, Picture, and Resume fields to the Veterinarian table. *Why? CMF has determined that they need these fields added to the table.*

- Start Access and open the database named CMF Vets from your hard disk, OneDrive, or other storage location. If you do not have the CMF Vets database, contact your instructor for the required file.

- If necessary, enable the content and open the Navigation Pane.

- Right-click the Veterinarians table to display a shortcut menu (Figure 5–2).

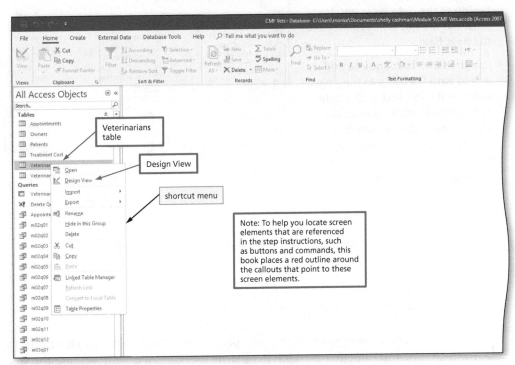

Figure 5–2

- Click Design View on the shortcut menu to open the table in Design view (Figure 5–3).

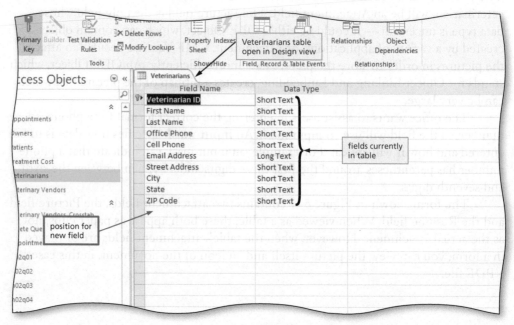

Figure 5–3

- Click the first open field to select the position for the first additional field.
- Type **Board Certified** as the field name, press the TAB key, click the Data Type arrow, select Yes/No as the data type, and then press the TAB key twice to move to the next field.
- Use the same technique to add a field with Specialty as the field name and Long Text as the data type, a field with Picture as the field name and Attachment as the data type, and a field with Resume as the field name and Attachment as the data type (Figure 5–4).

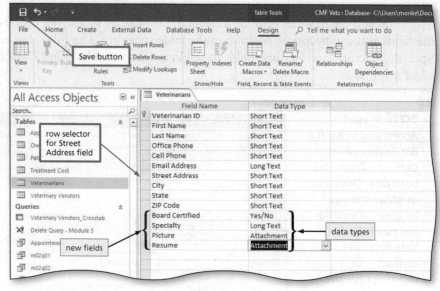

Figure 5–4

- Click the Save button on the Quick Access Toolbar to save your changes.

To Use the Input Mask Wizard

As mentioned previously, an input mask specifies how data, such as a phone number, is to be entered and how it will appear. You can enter an input mask directly, but you usually will use the Input Mask Wizard. *Why?* *The wizard assists you in the creation of the input mask by allowing you to select from a list of the most frequently used input masks.*

To use the Input Mask Wizard, select the Input Mask property in the field's property sheet and then select the Build button. The following steps specify how both telephone numbers, office and cell, are to appear by using the Input Mask Wizard.

1

- Click the Office Phone field.

- Click the Input Mask property box (Figure 5–5).

Q&A Do I need to change the data type?
No. Short Text is the appropriate data type for the Phone Number field.

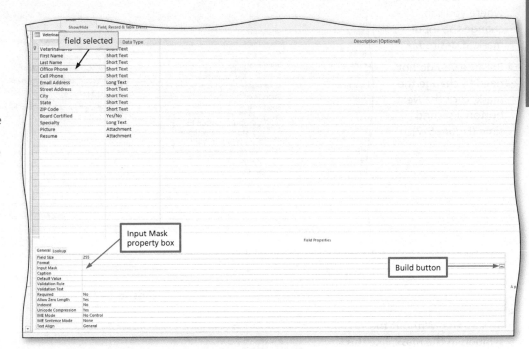

Figure 5–5

2

- Click the Build button to use a wizard to enter the input mask.

- If a dialog box appears asking you to save the table, click Yes. (If a dialog box displays a message that the Input Mask Wizard is not installed, check with your instructor before proceeding with the following steps.)

- Ensure that Phone Number is selected (Figure 5–6).

Experiment

- Click different input masks and enter data in the Try It text box to see the effect of the input mask. When you are done, click the Phone Number input mask.

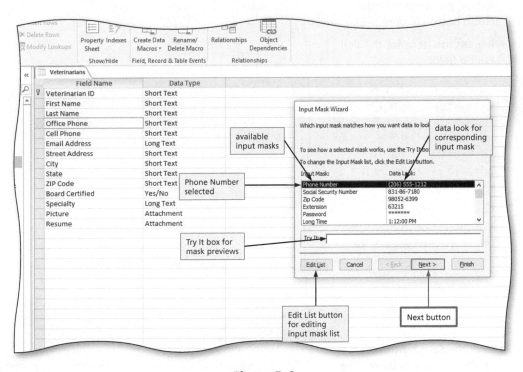

Figure 5–6

- Click the Next button to move to the next Input Mask Wizard screen, where you can change the input mask, if desired.

- Because you do not need to change the mask, click the Next button a second time (Figure 5–7).

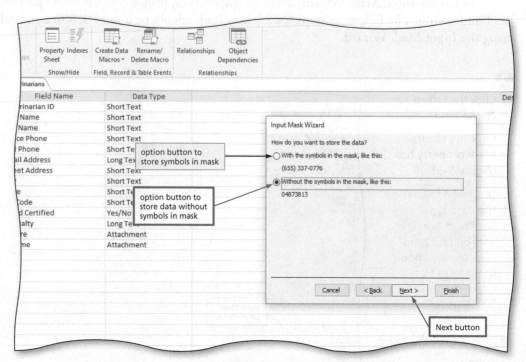

Figure 5–7

- Be sure the 'Without the symbols in the mask, like this:' option button is selected, click the Next button to move to the next Input Mask Wizard screen, and then click the Finish button (Figure 5–8).

- Repeat the steps for the Cell Phone field.

Q&A Why does the data type not change to Input Mask?
The data type of the Phone Number field is still Short Text. The only thing that changed is one of the field properties, the Input Mask property.

Could I have typed the value in the Input Mask property myself, rather than using the wizard?
Yes. Input masks can be complex, however, so it is usually easier and safer to use the wizard.

- Click the Save button on the Quick Access Toolbar to save your changes.

- Close the Veterinarians table.

Figure 5–8

Adding Fields in Datasheet View

Previously you added fields to a table using Design view. You can also add fields in Datasheet view. One way to do so is to use the Add & Delete group on the Table Tools Fields tab (Figure 5–9). Select the field that precedes the position where you want to add the new field, and then click the appropriate button. You can click the Short Text button to add a Short Text field, the Number button to add a Number field, the Currency button to add a Currency field, and so on. Alternatively, you can click the More Fields button as shown in the figure to display the Data Type gallery. You then can click a data type in the gallery to add a field with that type.

The gallery provides more options for ways to display various types of data. For example, if you click the Check Box version of a Yes/No field, the field will be displayed as a check box, which is the common way to display such a field. If instead you click the Yes/No version of a Yes/No field, the value in the field will be displayed as either the word, Yes, or the word, No.

If you scroll down in the Data Type gallery, you will find a Quick Start section. The commands in this section give you quick ways of adding some common types of fields. For example, clicking Address in the Quick Start section immediately adds several fields: Address, City, State Province, Zip Postal, and Country Region. Clicking Start and End Dates immediately adds both a Start Date field and an End Date field.

BTW

Input Mask Characters

When you create an input mask, Access adds several characters. These characters control the literal values that appear when you enter data. For example, the first backslash in the input mask in Figure 5–8 displays the opening parenthesis. The double quotations marks force Access to display the closing parenthesis and a space. The second backslash forces Access to display the hyphen that separates the first and second part of the phone number.

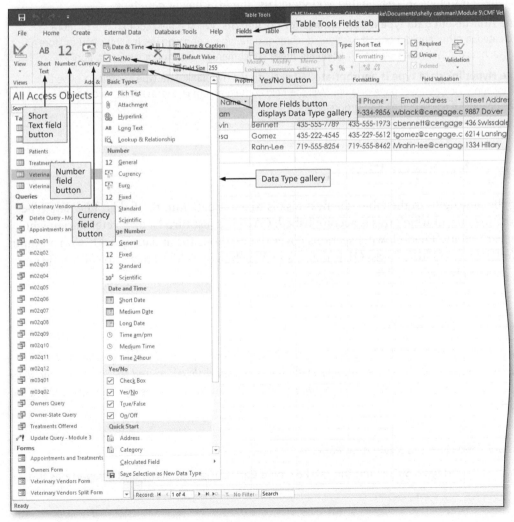

Figure 5–9

In Datasheet view, you can rename fields by right-clicking the field name, clicking Rename Field on the shortcut menu, and then typing the new name. Delete a field by clicking the field and then clicking the Delete button (Table Tools Fields tab | Add & Delete group). Move a field from one location to another by dragging the field.

CONSIDER THIS

How do you determine if fields need special data types or an input mask?

Determine whether an input mask is appropriate. Sometimes the data in the field should be displayed in a special way, for example, with parentheses and a hyphen like a phone number, or separated into three groups of digits, like a Social Security number. If so, should Access assist the user in entering the data in the right format? For example, by including an input mask in a field, Access can automatically insert the parentheses and a hyphen when a user enters phone number digits.

Determine whether the Yes/No data type is appropriate. A field is a good candidate for the Yes/No data type if the only possible field values are Yes or No, True or False, or On or Off.

Determine whether the Long Text data type is appropriate. A field that contains text that is variable in length and potentially very long is an appropriate use of the Long Text data type. If you want to use special text effects, such as bold and italic, you can assign the field the Long Text data type and change the value of the field's Text Format property from Plain Text to Rich Text. You can also collect history on the changes to a Long Text field by changing the value of the field's Append Only property from No to Yes. If you do so, when you right-click the field and click Show Column History on the shortcut menu, you will see a record of all changes made to the field.

Determine whether the Attachment data type or the OLE Object data type is appropriate for a picture. Does the field contain a picture? Does it contain an object created by other applications that support **OLE (Object Linking and Embedding)**? Is your storage space limited? If storage space is limited, you should use the Attachment data type.

Determine whether the Attachment data type is appropriate for documents. Will the field contain one or more attachments that were created in other applications? If so, the Attachment data type is appropriate. It allows you to store multiple attachments on each record. You can view and manipulate these attachments in their original application.

Determine whether the Hyperlink data type is appropriate. A field with the hyperlink data type contains a hyperlink, that is, a link to another location such as a webpage or a file. Will the field contain an email address, links to other Office documents, or links to webpages? If so, Hyperlink is appropriate.

Updating the New Fields

After adding the new fields to the table, the next task is to enter data into the fields. The data type determines the manner in which this is accomplished. CMF has just hired a new veterinarian who specializes in cardiology. The following sections cover the methods for updating fields with an input mask, Yes/No fields, Long Text fields, OLE fields, and Attachment fields. They also show how you would enter data in Hyperlink fields.

To Enter Data Using an Input Mask

Why? *When you are entering data in a field that has an input mask, Access will insert the appropriate special characters in the proper positions. This means Access will automatically insert the parentheses around the area code, the space following the second parenthesis, and the hyphen in the Phone Number field.* The following steps use the input mask to add the telephone numbers.

- Open the Veterinarians table and close the Navigation Pane.

- Click on a blank Veterinarian ID and type, S01. Using the tab key, type Carl as the first name and Schwartz as the last name.

- Click at the beginning of the Office Phone field on the first record to display an insertion point in the field (Figure 5–10).

Q&A I do not see the parentheses and hyphen as shown in the figure. Did I do something wrong?

Depending on exactly where you click, you might not see the symbols. Regardless, as soon as you start typing in the field, the symbols should appear.

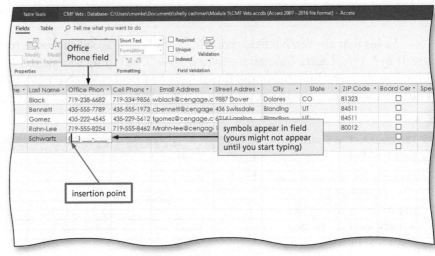

Figure 5–10

2

- Type 9705553455 as the telephone number (Figure 5–11).

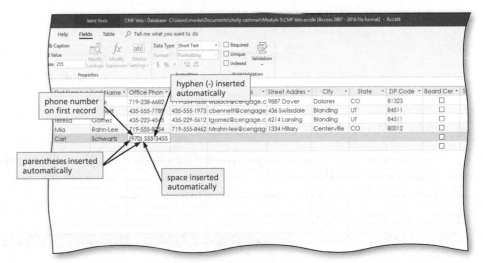

Figure 5–11

3

- Use the same technique to enter the Cell Phone, and the rest of the data for the record, as shown in Figure 5–12.

Q&A Do I need to click at the beginning of the field for the phone numbers?

Yes. If you do not, the data will not be entered correctly.

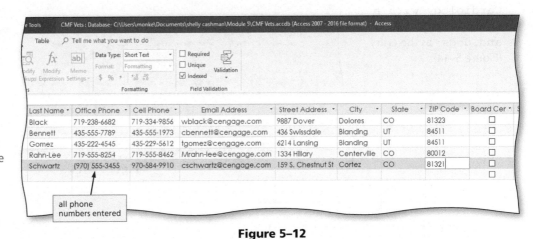

Figure 5–12

BTW

Input Mask on New Records
When you place an input mask on a field with existing data, only the new records added will adhere to that input mask.

To Enter Data in Yes/No Fields

Fields that are Yes/No fields contain check boxes. To set the value to Yes, place a check mark in the check box. *Why? A check mark indicates the value is Yes or True.* To set a value to No, leave the check box blank. The following step sets the value of the Board Certified field, a Yes/No field, to Yes for the new specialty veterinarian. The other veterinarians do not yet have board certification.

- Tab over to the Board Certified field.

- Click the check box in the Board Certified field for this new record to place a check mark in the box (Figure 5–13).

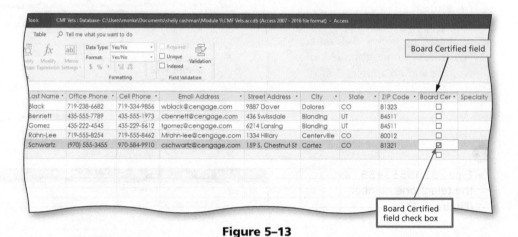

Figure 5–13

To Enter Data in Long Text Fields

To update a long text field, simply type the data in the field. You will later change the spacing to allow more room for the text. *Why? With the current row and column spacing on the screen, only a small portion of the text will appear.* The following steps enter each veterinarian's specialty.

- Tab over to the Specialty field.

- For the new record type **Cardiology with a specialty in cats and dogs** as the entry (Figure 5–14).

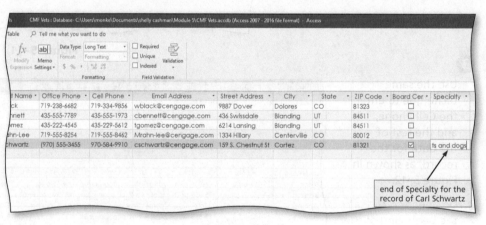

Figure 5–14

To Change the Row and Column Size

Only a small portion of the special skills data appears in the datasheet. To allow more of the information to appear, you can expand the size of the rows and the columns. You can change the size of a column by using the field selector. The **field selector** is the bar containing the field name. To change the size of a row, you use a record's record selector.

The following steps resize the column containing the Specialty field and the rows of the table. *Why? Resizing the column and the rows allows the entire Specialty field text to appear.*

1

- If your screen does not display all the fields, use the right scroll arrow to scroll the fields to the position shown in Figure 5–15, and then drag the right edge of the field selector for the Specialty field to the right to resize the Specialty column to the approximate size shown in the figure.

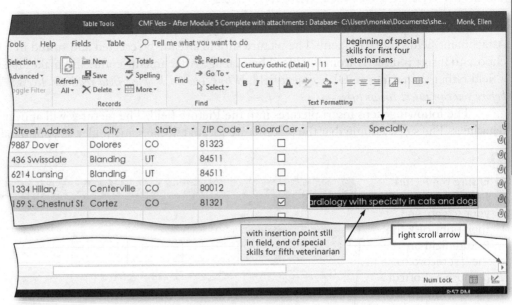

Figure 5–15

2

- Drag the lower edge of the record selector to approximately the position shown in Figure 5–16.

Q&A | Can rows be different sizes?
No. Access formats all rows to be the same size.

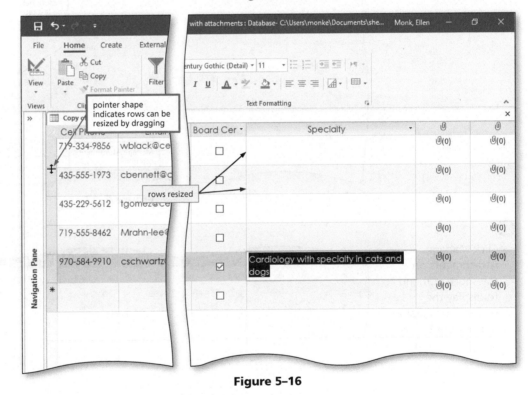

Figure 5–16

Other Ways

1. Right-click record selector, click Row Height to change row spacing
2. Right-click field selector, click Field Width to change column size

Undoing Changes to Row Height and Column Width

If you later find that the changes you made to the row height or the column width are no longer appropriate, you can undo them. To undo changes to the row height, right-click the row selector, click Row Height on the shortcut menu, and then click the Standard Height check box in the Row Height dialog box. To undo changes to the column width, right-click the field selector, click Field Width on the shortcut menu, and then click the Standard Width check box in the Column Width dialog box.

BTW

Entering Data in Long Text Fields
You also can enter data in a long text field using the Zoom dialog box. To do so, click the long text field and then press SHIFT+F2 to open the Zoom dialog box.

To Enter Images in Attachment Fields

To insert a picture into an Attachment field, you use the Manage Attachments command on the Attachment field's shortcut menu. The picture should already be created and stored in a file, and then you could choose to insert it directly from the file. The Manage Attachments command makes it easy to attach a picture to a field rather than using an OLE object field. **Why?** *The OLE object field requires Access to open the Paint application before you can insert the picture.*

The following steps insert pictures into the Picture field. The pictures will appear as paper clips in the datasheet. The steps assume that the pictures are located in the same folder as your database.

* Ensure the Picture field appears on your screen, and then right-click the Picture field on the last record to produce a shortcut menu (Figure 5–17).

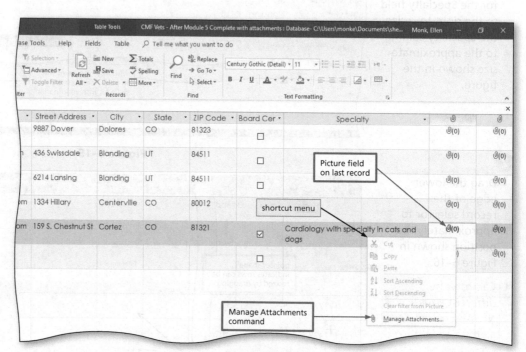

Figure 5–17

* Click Manage Attachments on the shortcut menu to display the Attachments dialog box (Figure 5–18).

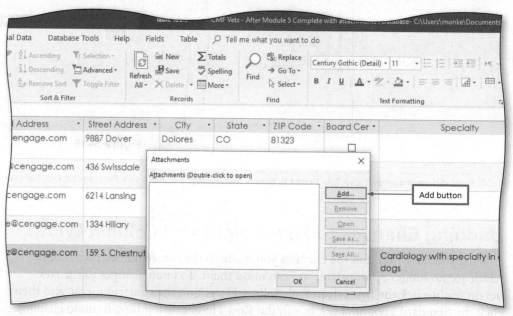

Figure 5–18

3

• Click the Add button

Q&A Unlike the figure, my window is maximized. Does that make a difference? No. The same steps will work in either case.

• Navigate to the image file for Carl Schwartz, click to select it, and then click Open (Figure 5–19).

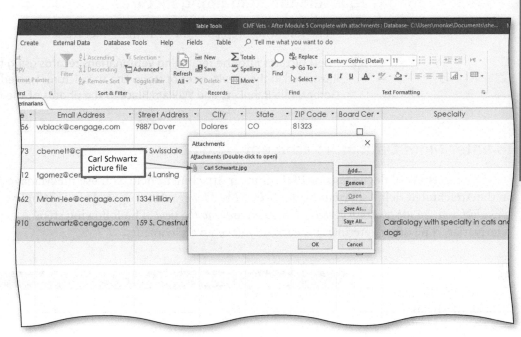

Figure 5–19

4

• Click the OK button to attach the picture (Figure 5–20).

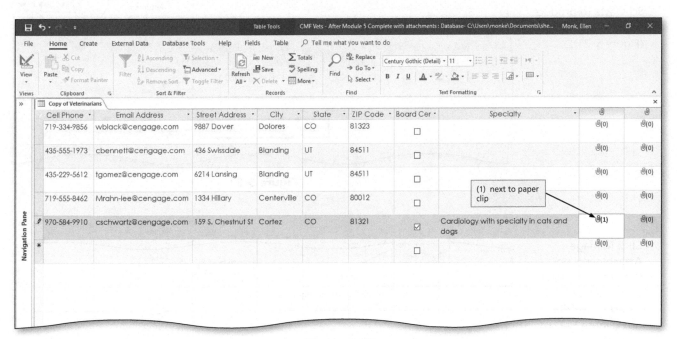

Figure 5–20

Q&A I do not see the picture. I just see the paper clip. Is that correct? Yes. You will see the actual picture when you use this field in a form.

To Insert the Remaining Pictures

The following step adds the remaining pictures.

 Insert pictures into the remaining veterinarians records using the techniques illustrated in the previous set of steps. Use the pictures named Calvin Bennet, Teresa Gomez, Mia RahnLee, and William Black as the photos of the veterinarians.

To Enter More Data in Attachment Fields

To insert Word documents or PDFs into an Attachment field, you use the Manage Attachments command on the Attachment field's shortcut menu. *Why? The Manage Attachments command displays the Attachments dialog box, which you can use to attach as many files as necessary to the field.* The following steps attach two files to the fifth veterinarian. The other veterinarians currently have no attachments.

- Ensure the Resume field, which has a paper clip in the field selector, appears on your screen, and then right-click the Resume field on the record of Carl Schwartz to produce a shortcut menu (Figure 5–21).

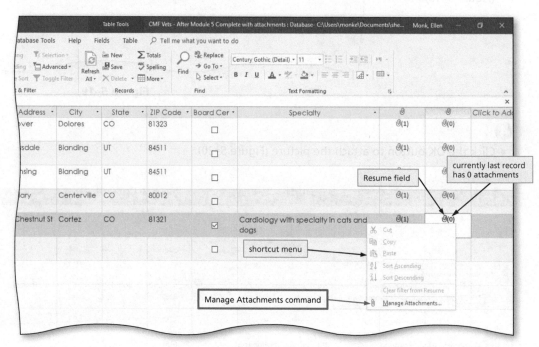

Figure 5–21

- Click Manage Attachments on the shortcut menu to display the Attachments dialog box (Figure 5–22).

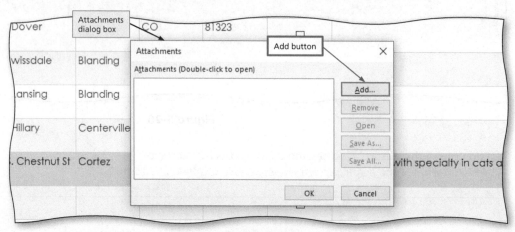

Figure 5–22

3

- Click Add (Attachments dialog box) to display the Choose File dialog box, where you can add an attachment.
- Navigate to the location containing your attachment files.
- Click Resume Carl Schwartz, a Word file, and then click the Open button (Choose File dialog box) to attach the file.
- Click Add (Attachments dialog box).
- Click Innovations in Cat Cardiology by C Schwartz, a PDF file, and then click Open to attach the second file (Figure 5–23).

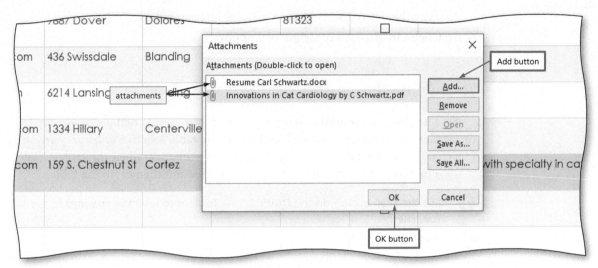

Figure 5–23

4

- Click OK (Attachments dialog box) to close the Attachments dialog box (Figure 5–24). The other records have no attachments.

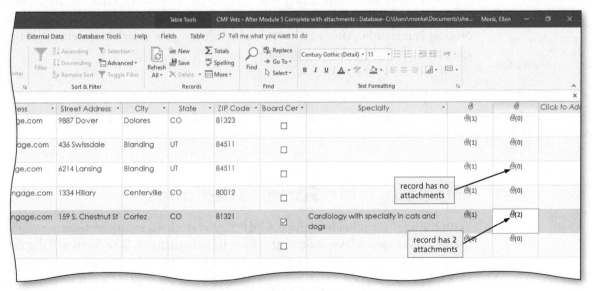

Figure 5–24

BTW
Hyperlink Fields
Hyperlink fields are used
to store web or other
Internet addresses and email
addresses. Hyperlinks can
find webpages, intranet
servers, database objects
(reports, forms, and such),
and even documents on
your computer or another
networked mobile device.

TO ENTER DATA IN HYPERLINK FIELDS

If your database contained a Hyperlink field, you would insert data using the following steps.

1. Right-click the Hyperlink field in which you want to enter data to display a shortcut menu.
2. Point to Hyperlink on the shortcut menu to display the Hyperlink submenu.
3. Click Edit Hyperlink on the Hyperlink submenu to display the Insert Hyperlink dialog box.
4. Type the desired web address in the Address text box.
5. Click OK (Insert Hyperlink dialog box).

To Save the Properties

The row and column spacing are table properties. When changing any table properties, the changes apply only as long as the table is active *unless they are saved*. Once you have saved them, they will apply every time you open the table.

The following steps first save the properties and then close the table.

1 Click the Save button on the Quick Access Toolbar to save the changes to the table properties.

2 Close the table.

BTW
**Viewing
Attachments of
Documents**
To view attachments of
documents, such as a Word
document or a PDF, you must
have the application that
created the attachment file
installed on your computer.

Viewing Document Attachments in Datasheet View

You can view the attachments in the Resume field by right-clicking the field and then clicking Manage Attachments on the shortcut menu. The attachments then appear in the Attachments dialog box. To view an attachment, click the attachment and then click the Open button (Attachments dialog box). The attachment will appear in its original application. After you have finished viewing the attachment, close the original application and close the dialog box.

Break Point: If you wish to stop working through the module at this point, you can resume the project at a later time by starting Access, opening the database called CMF Vets, and continuing to follow the steps from this location forward.

Multiple-Table Form Techniques

With the additional fields in place, CMF Vets is ready to incorporate data from both the Veterinarians and Appointments tables in a single form. The form will display data concerning one veterinarian at a time. It will also display data concerning the many appointments assigned to the veterinarian. The relationship between veterinarians and appointments is a one-to-many relationship in which the Veterinarians table is the "one" table and the Appointments table is the "many" table.

To include the data for the many appointments of a veterinarian on the form, the appointments will appear in a **subform**, which is a form that is contained within another form. The form in which the subform is contained is called the **main form**. Thus, the main form will contain veterinarian data, and the subform will contain appointment.

When a form includes data from multiple tables, how do you relate the tables?
Once you determine that you need data from more than one table, you need to determine the main table and its relationship to any other table.

Determine the main table the form is intended to view and/or update. You need to identify the purpose of the form and the table it is really intended to show, which is the *main* table.

Determine how the additional table should fit into the form. If the additional table is the "many" part of the relationship, the data should probably be in a subform or datasheet. If the additional table is the "one" part of the relationship, the data should probably simply appear as fields on the form.

To Create a Form in Design View

You can create a form in Design view. ***Why?*** *Design view gives you increased flexibility in laying out a form by using a blank design on which you place objects in the precise locations you want.* The following steps create a form in Design view. Before you create this form, you must form a relationship between the Veterinarians table and the Appointments table.

- CMF Vets staff have decided to replace the Appointments table to eliminate the Multivalued property of the Treatment Number field. Delete the Appointments table (delete its relationships when prompted), then import the updated Appointments table from the Support_AC_CMF_Vets_Mod 5 Extra Table data file without saving import steps.
- Click the Relationships button (Database Tools tab | Relationships group) to display the Relationships window.
- Click the Show Table button to display the Show Table dialog box. Click Veterinarians table, click the Add button, and then click Close to add the Veterinarians table to the relationship.
- Drag the cursor from Veterinarian ID in the Veterinarians table to Veterinarian in the Appointments table.
- Click the 'Enforce Referential Integrity' check box to check it. Click Create. Repeat to create a relationship from the Treatment Number field in the Treatment Cost table to the Treatment Number field in the Appointments table. Repeat to create a relationship from the Patient ID field in the Patients table to the Patient ID field in the Appointments table.
- Close the Relationships window and save the changes.
- If necessary, open the Navigation Pane and be sure the Veterinarians table is selected.
- Click Create on the ribbon to display the Create tab (Figure 5–25).

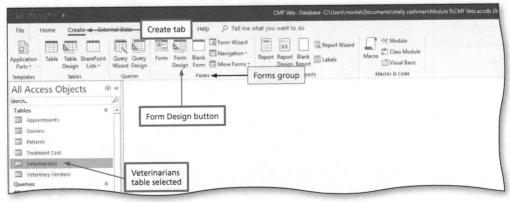

Figure 5–25

2

- Click the Form Design button (Create tab | Forms group) to create a new form in Design view.
- Close the Navigation Pane.
- If a field list does not appear, click the 'Add Existing Fields' button (Form Design Tools Design tab | Tools group) to display a field list (Figure 5–26). If you do not see the tables listed, click 'Show all tables'. (Your list might show all fields in the Veterinarians table.)

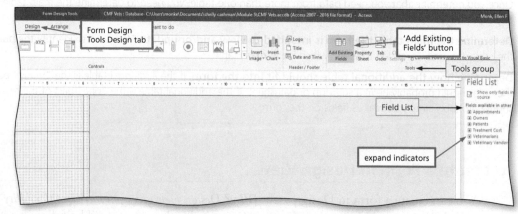

Figure 5–26

 Q&A Can I join tables on common fields even though the names of the fields are different?
Yes, you can join tables on fields with different names as long as the data and the data types are the same for both fields.

To Add a Control for a Field to the Form

To place a control for a field on a form, drag the field from the field list to the desired position. The following steps place the Veterinarian ID field on the form. *Why? Dragging is the easiest way to place a field on a form.*

1

- If necessary, click the expand indicator for the Veterinarians table to display the fields in the table. Drag the Veterinarian ID field in the field list for the Veterinarians table to the approximate position shown in Figure 5–27. (For illustration purposes, do not release the mouse button yet.)

Q&A Do I have to be exact?
No. Just be sure you are in the same general location.

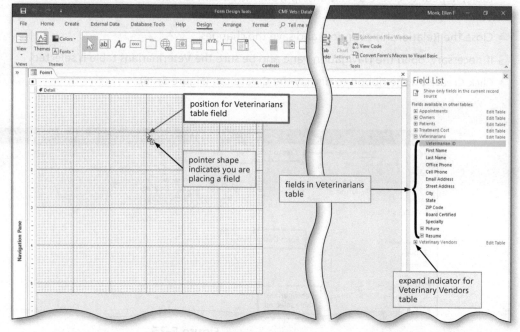

Figure 5–27

- Release the mouse button to place a control for the field (Figure 5–28).

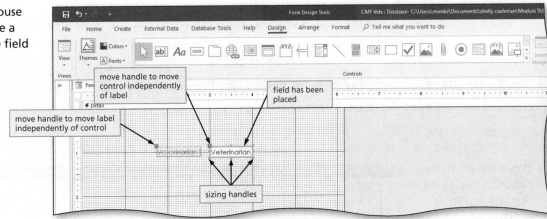

Figure 5–28

To Add Controls for Additional Fields

The following step places controls for the First Name, Last Name, Office Phone, and Cell Phone fields on the form by dragging the fields from the field list. *Why? These fields all need to be included in the form.*

- Drag the First Name, Last Name, Office Phone, and Cell Phone fields and their labels to the approximate positions shown in Figure 5–29.

Q&A

Do I have to align them precisely?
You can, but you do not need to. In the next steps, you will instruct Access to align the fields properly.

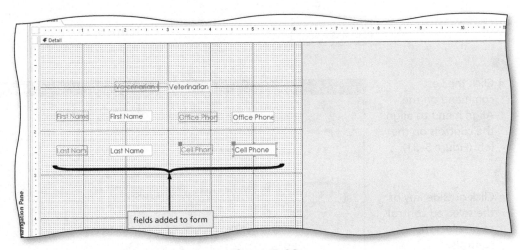

Figure 5–29

What if I drag the wrong field from the field list? Can I delete the control?
Yes. With the control selected, press DELETE.

To Align Controls on the Left

Why? Often, you will want form controls to be aligned in some fashion. For example, the controls might be aligned so their right edges are even with each other. In another case, controls might be aligned so their top edges are even. To ensure that a group of controls is aligned properly with each other, select all of the affected controls, and then use the appropriate alignment button on the Form Design Tools Arrange tab.

You can use one of two methods to select multiple controls. One way is to use a ruler. If you click a position on the horizontal ruler, you will select all the controls for which a portion of the control is under that position on the ruler. Similarly, if you click a position on the vertical ruler, you will select all the controls for which a portion of the control is to the right of that position on the ruler.

The second way to select multiple controls is to select the first control by clicking it. Then, select all the other controls by holding down SHIFT while clicking the control.

The following steps select the First Name and Last Name controls and then align them so their left edges line up.

- Click the First Name control (the white space, not the label) to select the control.

- Press and hold SHIFT and click the Last Name control to select an additional control.

Q&A I selected the wrong collection of fields. How can I start over?
Simply begin the process again, making sure you do not hold the SHIFT key down when you select the first field.

- Click Arrange on the ribbon to display the Form Design Tools Arrange tab.

- Click the Align button (Form Design Tools Arrange tab | Sizing & Ordering group) to display the Align menu (Figure 5–30).

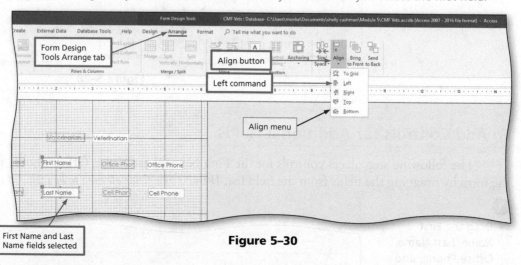

Figure 5–30

- Click the Left command on the Align menu to align the controls on the left (Figure 5–31).

- Click outside any of the selected controls to deselect the controls.

- Using the same technique, if necessary, align the labels for the First Name and Last Name fields on the left.

- Using the same technique, align the Office Phone and Cell Phone fields on the left.

- If necessary, align the labels for the Office Phone and Cell Phone fields on the left.

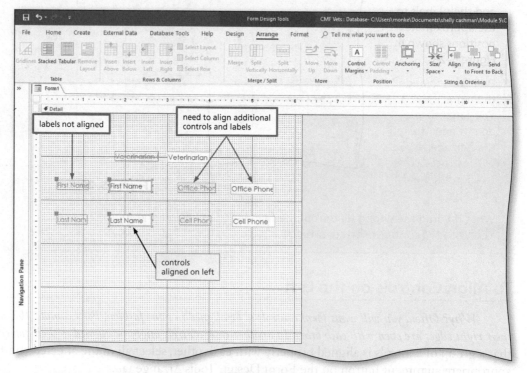

Figure 5–31

Other Ways

1. Right-click selected controls, point to Align

To Align Controls on the Top and Adjust Vertical Spacing

Why? *Aligning the top edges of controls improves the neatness and appearance of a form. In addition, you might want the vertical spacing between controls to be the same.* The following steps align the First Name and Office Phone controls so that they are aligned on the top. Once these controls are aligned, you adjust the vertical spacing so that the same amount of space separates each row of controls.

- Select the label for the First Name control, the First Name control, the label for the Office Phone control, and the Office Phone control.

- Click the Align button (Form Design Tools Arrange tab | Sizing & Ordering group) to display the Align menu (Figure 5–32).

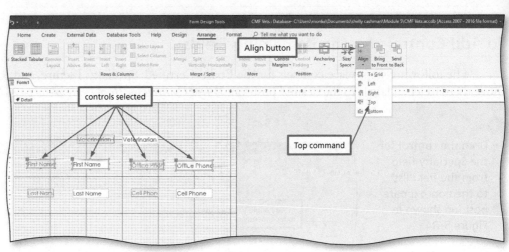

Figure 5–32

- Click the Top command on the Align menu to align the controls on the top.

- Select the Last Name and Cell Phone fields and their labels and align the controls to the top.

- Click outside any of the selected controls to deselect the controls.

- Select the four fields.

- Click the Size/Space button (Form Design Tools Arrange tab | Sizing & Ordering group) to display the Size/Space menu (Figure 5–33).

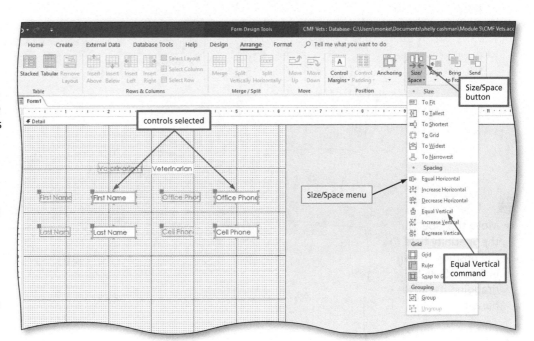

Figure 5–33

Q&A Do I need to select the labels too?

No. If you select the control, its label also is selected.

- Click Equal Vertical on the Size/Space menu to specify the spacing.

Q&A What is the purpose of the other commands on the Size/Space menu?

You can adjust the spacing to fit the available space. You can adjust the space to match the tallest, shortest, widest, or narrowest section. You can adjust the space to match the closest grid points. You can specify equal horizontal spacing. Finally, you can increase or decrease either the vertical or the horizontal spacing.

Q&A What do you do if the field list obscures part of the form, making it difficult to place fields in the desired locations?
You can move the field list to a different location by dragging its title bar. You can also resize the field list by pointing to the border of the field list so that the pointer changes to a double-headed arrow. You then can drag to adjust the size.

- Because it is a good idea to save the form before continuing, click the Save button on the Quick Access Toolbar.
- Type **Veterinarian Appointment Form** as the name of the form, and then click OK to save the form.

To Add Controls for the Remaining Fields

The following steps place controls for the Board Certified, Specialty, Picture, and Resume fields and also move their attached labels to the desired position. *Why? Controls for these fields are to be included in the completed form.*

❶

- Drag the control for the Specialty field from the field list to the approximate position shown in Figure 5–34.

Q&A Is there enough space on the form to add the Specialty field?
Yes. The size of the form will expand as you drag the field to the form.

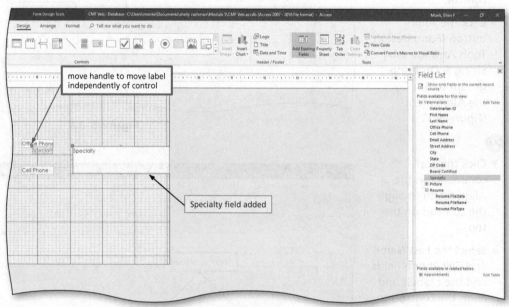

Figure 5–34

❷

- Move the label for the Specialty field to the position shown in Figure 5–35 by dragging its move handle.

Q&A I started to move the label and the control moved along with it. What did I do?
You were not pointing at the handle to move the label independently of the control. Make sure you are pointing to the little box in the upper-left corner of the label.

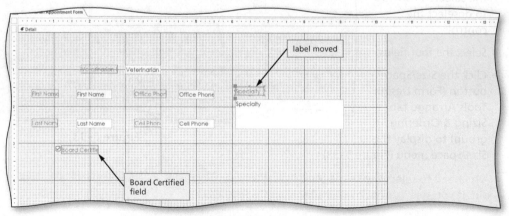

Figure 5–35

- Drag the Board Certified field to the position shown in Figure 5–35.

3

• Using the same techniques, move the control for the Picture field to the approximate position shown in Figure 5–36 and move its label to the position shown in the figure.

Q&A
My picture label is next to the field, not above it as shown in the figure. Is that a problem?
This is fine. You will rearrange the labels later in the module.

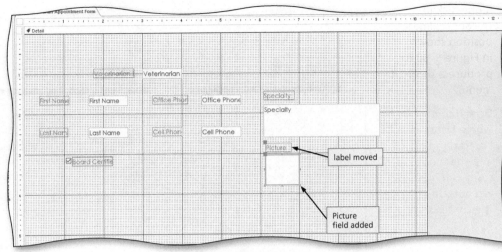

Figure 5–36

4

• Click the control for the Picture field and drag the lower-right corner to the approximate position shown in Figure 5–37 to resize the control.

• Add the control for the Resume field in the position shown in the figure and move its attached label to the position shown in the figure.

• Click the control for the Resume field and drag the lower-right corner to the approximate position shown in Figure 5–37 to resize the control.

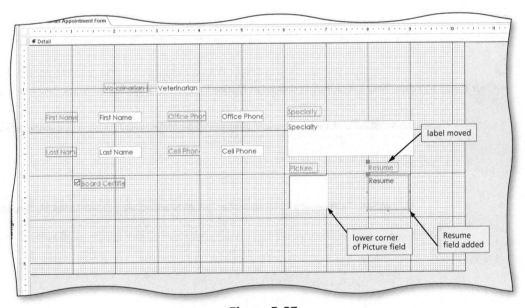

Figure 5–37

To Use a Shortcut Menu to Change the Fill/Back Color

You can use the Background Color button on the Form Design Tools Format tab to change the background color of a form. You can also use a shortcut menu. The following steps use a shortcut menu to change the background color of the form to gray. **Why?** *Using a shortcut menu is a simple way to change the background color.*

1

- Right-click in
  the approximate
  position shown
  in Figure 5–38 to
  produce a shortcut
  menu.

Q&A Does it matter
where I right-click?
You can right-click
anywhere on the
form as long as you
are outside of all
the controls.

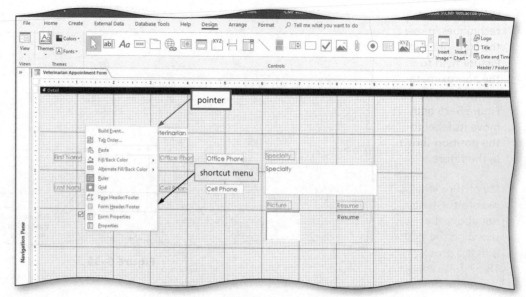

Figure 5–38

2

- Point to the Fill/Back Color arrow on the shortcut menu to display a color palette (Figure 5–39).

3

- Click the gray color (row 3, column 1) shown in Figure 5–39 to change the fill/back color to gray.

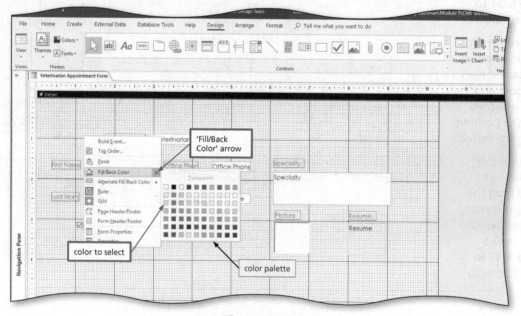

Figure 5–39

To Add a Title

A form should have a descriptive title. **Why?** *The title gives a concise visual description of the purpose of the form.*
The following step adds a title to the form.

1

- Click Design on the ribbon to select the Form Design Tools Design tab.

- Click the Title button (Form Design Tools Design tab | Header/ Footer group) to add a title to the form (Figure 5–40).

 Could I change this title if I want something different?
Yes. Change it just like you change any other text.

Why is there a new section?
The form title belongs in the Form Header section. When you clicked the Title button, Access added the Form Header section automatically and placed the title in it.

Could I add a Form Header section without having to click the Title button?
Yes. Right-click anywhere on the form background and click Form Header/Footer on the shortcut menu.

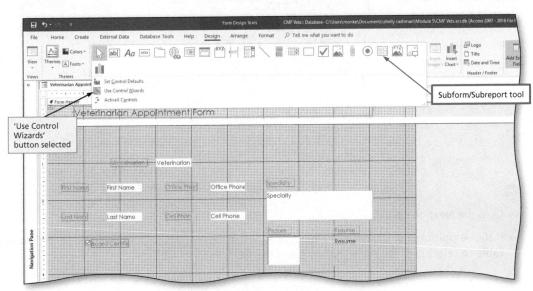

Figure 5–40

To Place a Subform

The Controls group on the Form Design Tools Design tab contains buttons called tools that you use to place a variety of types of controls on a form. To place a subform on a form, you use the Subform/Subreport tool. Before doing so, however, you should ensure that the 'Use Control Wizards' button is selected. *Why? If the 'Use Control Wizards' button is selected, a wizard will guide you through the process of adding the subform.* The following steps use the SubForm Wizard to place a subform.

1

- Click the More button (Form Design Tools Design tab | Controls group) (shown in Figure 5–40) to display a gallery of available tools (Figure 5–41).

Figure 5–41

2

- Be sure the 'Use Control Wizards' button is selected, click the Subform/Subreport tool on the Form Design Tools Design tab, and then move the pointer to the approximate position shown in Figure 5–42.

Q&A How can I tell whether the 'Use Control Wizards' button is selected? The icon for the 'Use Control Wizards' button will be highlighted, as shown in Figure 5–41. If it is not, click the 'Use Control Wizards' button to select it, click the More button, and then click the Subform/Subreport tool.

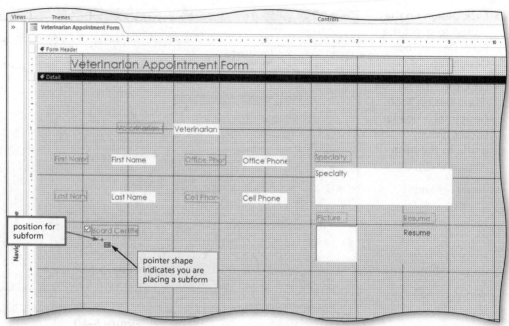

Figure 5–42

3

- Click the position shown in Figure 5–42 and then ensure the 'Use existing Tables and Queries' option button is selected (SubForm Wizard dialog box) (Figure 5–43).

Q&A My control is placed on the screen, but no wizard appeared. What should I do? Press the DELETE key to delete the control you placed. Ensure that the 'Use Control Wizards' button is selected, as described previously.

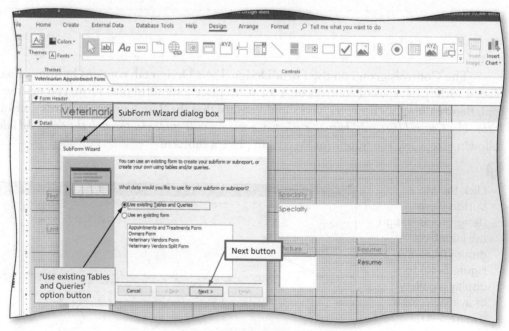

Figure 5–43

4

- Click the Next button.

- If the Appointments table is not already selected, click the Tables/Queries arrow, and then click the Appointments table to select it as the table that contains the fields for the subform.

• Add the Patient ID, Appointment Date, Appointment Time, and Treatment Number fields by clicking the field, and then clicking the Add Field button (SubForm Wizard dialog box) (Figure 5–44).

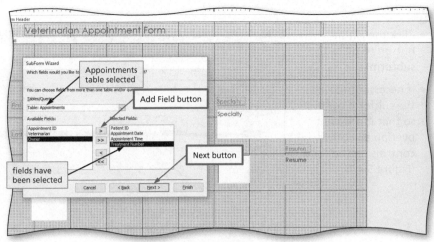

Figure 5–44

• Click Next to move to the next SubForm Wizard dialog box.

• Be sure the 'Choose from a list.' option button is selected (Figure 5–45).

Q&A | Why do I use this option?
Most of the time, Access will have determined the appropriate fields to link the subform and the main form and placed an entry specifying those fields in the list. By choosing from the list, you can take advantage of the information that Access has created for you. The other option is to define your own, in which case you would need to specify the appropriate fields.

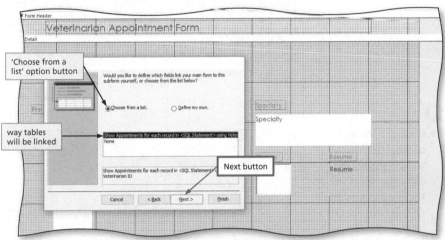

Figure 5–45

• Click the Next button.

• Type **Appointments subform** as the name of the subform (Figure 5–46).

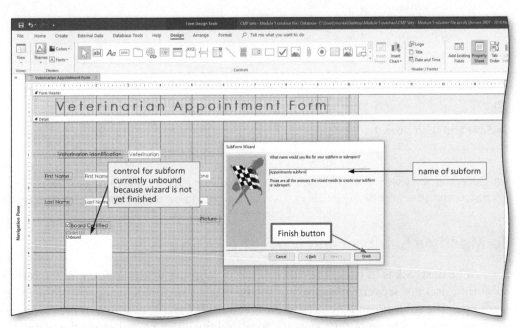

Figure 5–46

- Click the Finish button to place the subform.

- If necessary, move the subform control so that it does not overlap any other controls on the form (Figure 5–47).

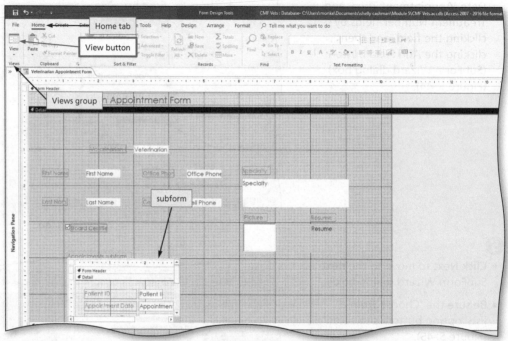

Figure 5–47

- Click the View button (Home tab | Views group) to view the form in Form view and scroll to the fifth record (Figure 5–48).

Q&A
Everything looks good except the subform. I do not see all the fields I should see. What should I do?
You need to modify the subform, which you will do in the upcoming steps.

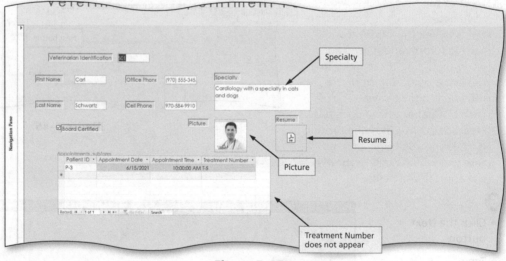

Figure 5–48

- Save and then close the form.

Break Point: If you wish to stop working through the module at this point, you can resume the project at a later time by starting Access, opening the database called CMF Vets, and continuing to follow the steps from this location forward.

To Modify a Subform and Move the Picture

The next task is to resize the columns in the subform, which appears on the form in Datasheet view. The subform exists as a separate object in the database; it is stored independently of the main form. The following steps open the subform and then resize the columns. *Why? The column sizes need to be adjusted so that the data is displayed correctly.* The steps then view the form and finally move and resize the picture.

1

- Open the Navigation Pane.
- Right-click the Appointments subform to produce a shortcut menu.
- Click Open on the shortcut menu to open the form.
- If a field list appears, click the 'Add Existing Fields' button (Form Tools Datasheet tab | Tools group) to remove the field list.
- Resize the columns to best fit the data by double-clicking the right boundaries of the field selectors (Figure 5–49).

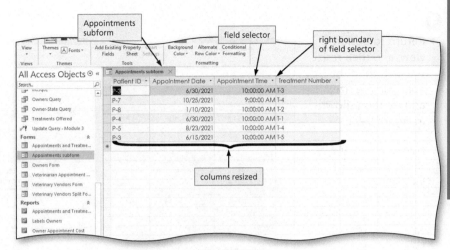

Figure 5–49

2

- Save your changes, and then close the subform.
- Open the Veterinarian Appointment Form in Design view, and then close the Navigation Pane.
- Click the boundary of the subform to select it.
- Adjust the approximate size and position of your subform to match the one shown in Figure 5–50.

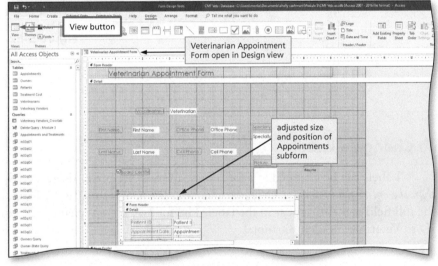

Figure 5–50

3

- Adjust the size of any labels in the main form whose names are obscured.
- Click the View button (Form Design Tools Design tab | Views group) to view the form in Form view (Figure 5–51).

 Q&A

Could I have clicked the View arrow and then clicked Form View?
Yes. You can always use the arrow. If the icon for the view you want appears on the face of the View button, however, you can just click the button.

The picture seems to be a slightly different size from the one in Figure 5–51. How do I fix this?
You can move and also resize the picture, which you will do in the next step.

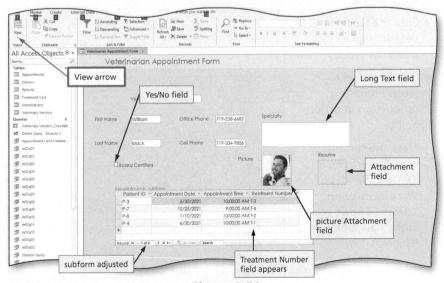

Figure 5–51

4

- Return to Design view, and then resize the picture to the approximate size and location shown in Figure 5–52.

Q&A How can I tell if the new size and location is correct? View the form. If you are not satisfied with the size or location, return to Design view and make the necessary adjustments. Repeat the process until you are satisfied. You may have to allow a small amount of white on one of the borders of the picture. You will learn about some options you can use to adjust the specific look of the picture later in this module.

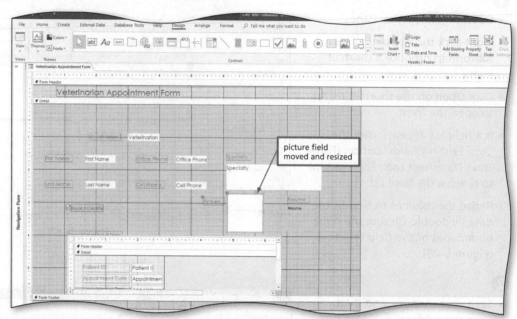

Figure 5–52

To Change a Label

Labels can be changed in a form to be more descriptive. *Why? The form has enough room to display more than the entire field name, so adding extra information adds clarity.* In the form, there is plenty of room for more than the full field name to appear in the label. The following steps change the contents of the label from Veterinarian ID to Veterinarian Identification.

1

- If necessary, return to Design view.
- Click the label for the Veterinarian ID to select the label.
- Click the label a second time to produce an insertion point.
- Erase the current label (Veterinarian ID), and then type **Veterinarian Identification** as the new label (Figure 5–53).

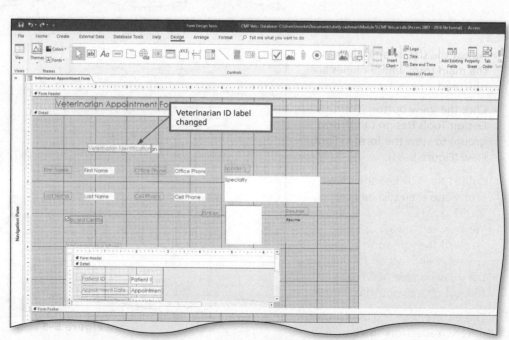

Figure 5–53

- Click outside the label to deselect it.

- Click the label to select it.

Why did I need to deselect the label and then select it again?
With the insertion point appearing in the label, you could not move the label. By deselecting it and then selecting it again, the label will be selected, but there will be no insertion point.

- Drag the move handle in the upper-left corner to move the label to the approximate position shown in Figure 5–54.

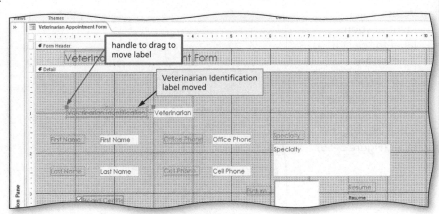

Figure 5–54

3

- Save your changes.

Is there any way to determine the way pictures fit within the control?
Yes. Access determines the portion of a picture that appears as well as the way it appears using the **size mode** property. The three size modes are as follows:

Clip: This size mode displays only a portion of the picture that will fit in the space allocated to it.

Stretch: This size mode expands or shrinks the picture to fit the precise space allocated on the screen. For photographs, usually this is not a good choice because fitting a photograph to the allocated space can distort the picture, giving it a stretched appearance.

Zoom: This size mode does the best job of fitting the picture to the allocated space without changing the look of the picture. The entire picture will appear and be proportioned correctly. Some white space may be visible either above or to the right of the picture, however.

To Change the Size Mode

Currently, the size mode for the picture should be Zoom, which is appropriate. If it were not and you wanted to change it, you would use the following steps.

1. Click the control containing the picture, and then click the Property Sheet button (Form Design Tools Design tab | Tools group) to display the control's property sheet.

2. Click the Picture Size Mode property, and then click the Picture Size Mode property arrow.

3. Click Zoom, and then close the property sheet by clicking its Close button.

To Change Label Effects and Colors

Access allows you to change many of the characteristics of the labels in the form. You can change the border style and color, the background color, the font, and the font size. You can also apply special label effects, such as raised or sunken. The following steps change the font color of the labels and add special effects. *Why?* *Modifying the appearance of the labels improves the appearance of the form.*

• Click the Veterinarian Identification label to select it, if necessary.

• Select each of the remaining labels by holding down SHIFT while clicking the label (Figure 5–55).

Q&A Does the order in which I select the labels make a difference?
No. The only thing that is important is that they are all selected when you are done.

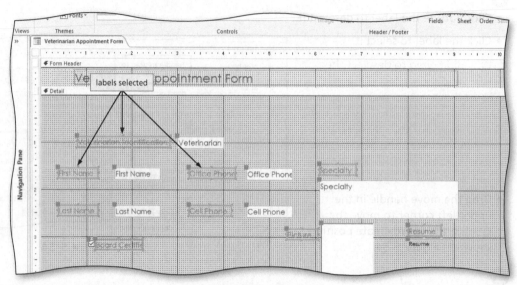

Figure 5–55

• Display the Form Design Tools Format tab.

• Click the Font Color arrow (Form Design Tools Format tab | Font group) to display a color palette (Figure 5–56).

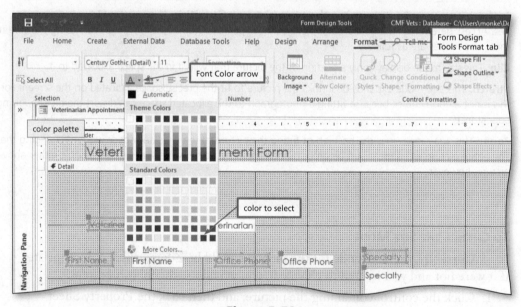

Figure 5–56

• Click the dark blue color in the second position from the right in the bottom row of Standard Colors to change the font color for the labels.

Experiment

• Try other colors by clicking the Font Color arrow and then clicking the other color to see which colors you think would be good choices for the font. View the form to see the effect of your choice, and then return to Design view. When done, select the blue color.

• Display the Form Design Tools Design tab.

• Click the Property Sheet button (Form Design Tools Design tab | Tools group) to produce the property sheet for the selected labels. If your property sheet appears on the left side of the screen, drag it to the right. Make sure the All tab is selected.

- Click the Border Style property box to display the Border Style property arrow, and then click the arrow to display a menu of border styles (Figure 5–57).

Q&A The property sheet is too small to display the property arrow. Can I change the size of the property sheet?
Yes. Point to the border of the property sheet so that the pointer changes to a two-headed arrow. You then can drag to adjust the size.

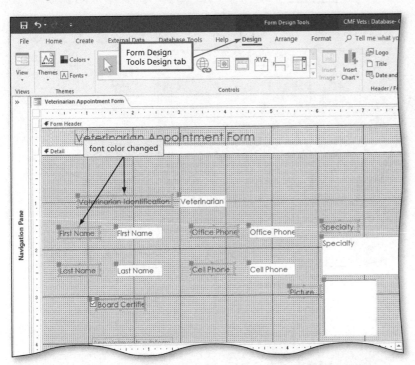
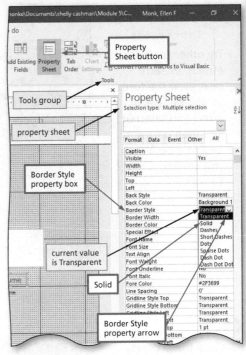

Figure 5–57

4

- Click Solid in the menu of border styles to select a border style.

- Click the Border Width property box to display the Border Width property arrow, and then click the arrow to display a menu of border widths.

- Click 3 pt to change the border width to 3 pt.

- Click the Special Effect property box to display the Special Effect property arrow, and then click the arrow to display a menu of special effects (Figure 5–58).

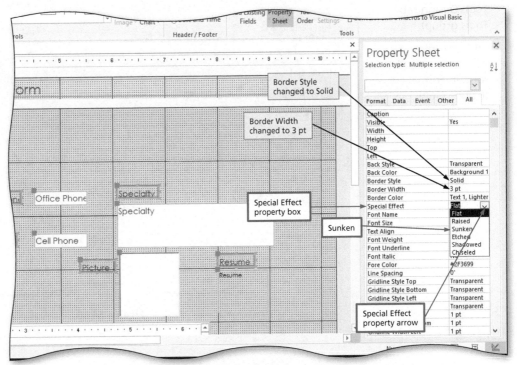

Figure 5–58

5

- Click Sunken in the menu of special effects to select a special effect (Figure 5–59).

 Experiment

- Try other special effects. In each case, view the form to see the special effect you selected and then return to Design view. When you are done, select Sunken.

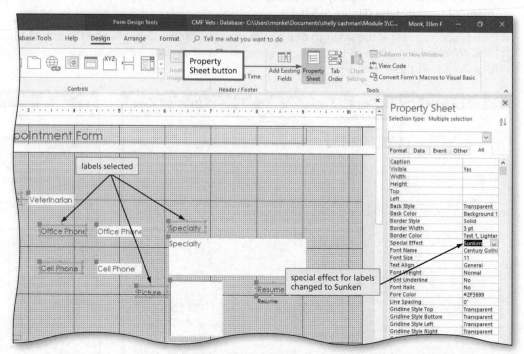

Figure 5–59

6

- Close the property sheet by clicking the Property Sheet button (Form Design Tools Design tab | Tools group).

- Click the View button to view the form in Form view (Figure 5–60).

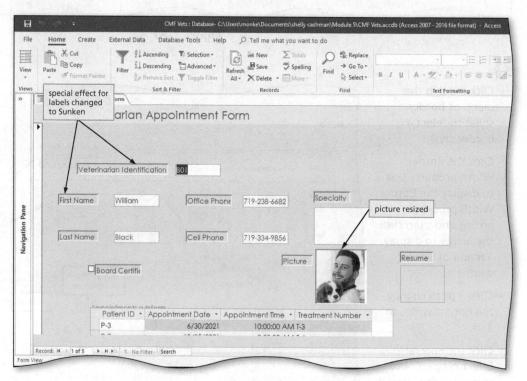

Figure 5–60

To Modify the Appearance of a Form Title

Why? *You can enhance the title in a variety of ways by changing its appearance. These options include moving it, resizing it, changing the font size, changing the font weight, and changing the alignment.* The following steps enhance the form title.

1

- Return to Design view.

- Resize the Form Header section by dragging down the lower boundary of the section to the approximate position shown in Figure 5–61.

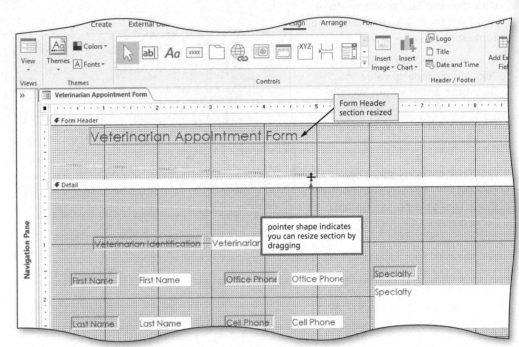

Figure 5–61

2

- Click the control containing the form title to select the control.

- Drag the lower-right sizing handle to resize the control to the approximate size shown in Figure 5–62.

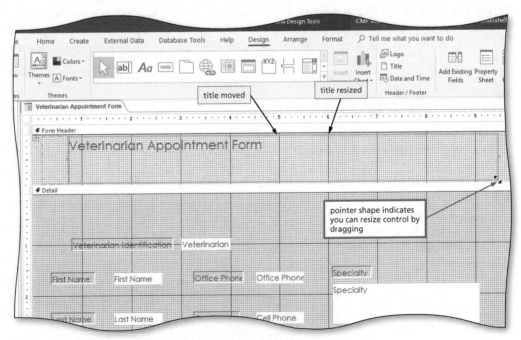

Figure 5–62

- Click the Property Sheet button (Form Design Tools Design tab | Tools group) to display the control's property sheet.

- Click the Font Size property box, click the Font Size property arrow, and then type 28 to change the font size.

- In a similar fashion, change the Text Align property value to Distribute and the Font Weight property value to Semi-bold (Figure 5–63).

- Close the property sheet by clicking the Property Sheet button (Form Design Tools Design tab | Tools group).

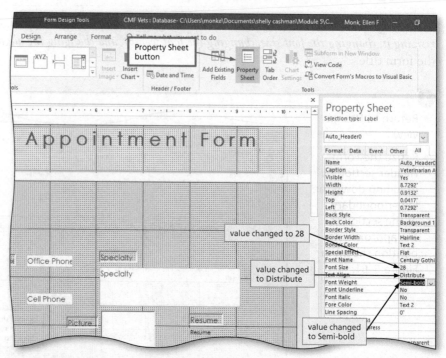

Figure 5–63

Other Ways
1. Enter font size value in Font Size box

To Change a Tab Stop

Users can repeatedly press the TAB key to move through the controls on the form; however, they should bypass the Picture and Resume controls because users do not enter data into these fields. To omit these controls from the tab stop sequence, the following steps change the value of the Tab Stop property for the controls from Yes to No. **Why?** *Changing the Tab Stop property for these fields to No removes them from the Tab Stop sequence.*

- Click the Picture control to select it.

- Hold down SHIFT while clicking the Resume control to select it as well (Figure 5–64).

- Click the Property Sheet button (Form Design Tools Design tab | Tools group) to display the property sheet.

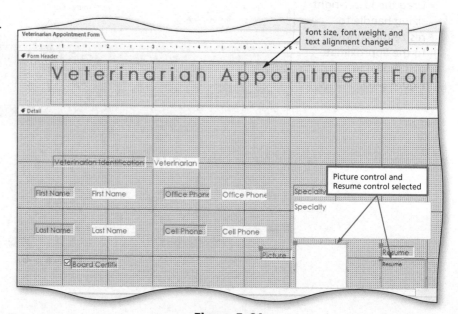

Figure 5–64

- Make sure the All tab (Property Sheet) is selected, click the down scroll arrow until the Tab Stop property appears, click the Tab Stop property, click the Tab Stop property arrow, and then click No to instruct Access to skip the Picture and Resume fields in the tab sequence.

- Close the property sheet.

Q&A I do not see the Tab Stop property. What did I do wrong?
You clicked the labels for the controls, not the controls.

- Save your changes.

- Click the View button to view the form in Form view. It should look like the form shown in Figure 5–1.

- Close the form.

Break Point: If you wish to stop working through the module at this point, you can resume the project at a later time by starting Access, opening the database called CMF Vets, and continuing to follow the steps from this location forward.

Changing the Tab Order

Users can repeatedly press the TAB key to move through the fields on a form. Access determines the order in which the fields are encountered in this process. If you prefer a different order, you can change the order by clicking the Tab Order button (Form Design Tools Design tab | Tools group). You then can use the Tab Order dialog box (Figure 5–65) to change the order by dragging rows (fields) to their desired order as indicated in the dialog box.

BTW

Auto Order Button
If you click the Auto Order button in the Tab Order dialog box, Access will create a top-to-bottom and left- to-right tab order.

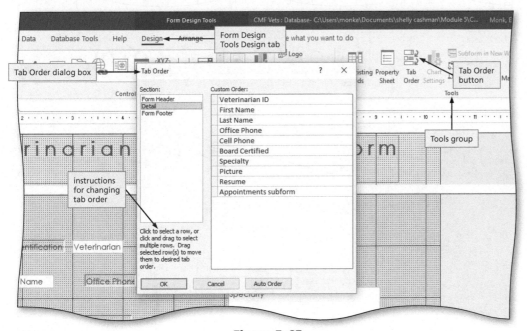

Figure 5–65

To Use the Form

The form gives you flexibility in selecting both veterinarians and the appointments. *Why? You can use the Navigation buttons at the bottom of the screen to move among veterinarians. You can use the Navigation buttons in the subform to move among the appointments currently shown on the screen.* The following steps use the form to display desired data.

1

- Open the Navigation Pane if it is currently closed.

- Right-click the Veterinarian Appointment Form, and then click Open on the shortcut menu.

- Scroll to the fifth record, Carl Schwartz.

- Close the Navigation Pane.

- Right-click the Resume field to display a shortcut menu (Figure 5–66).

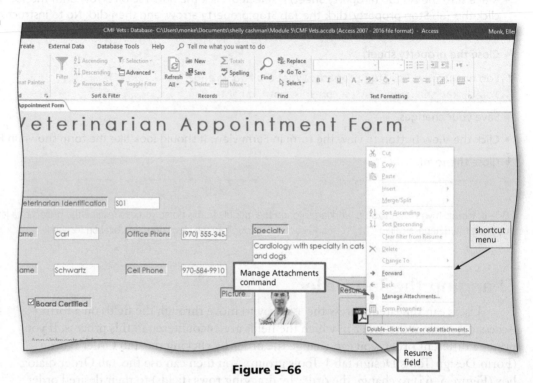

Figure 5–66

2

- Click the Manage Attachments command on the shortcut menu to display the Attachments dialog box (Figure 5–67).

Q&A How do I use this dialog box? Select an attachment and click the Open button to view the attachment in its original application. Click the Add button to add a new attachment or the Remove button to remove the selected attachment. By clicking the Save As button, you can save the selected attachment as a file in whatever location you specify. You can save all attachments at once by clicking the Save All button.

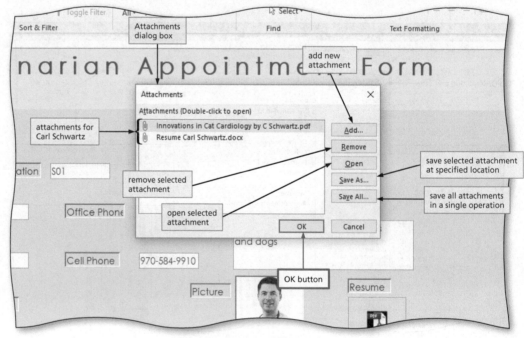

Figure 5–67

Experiment

- Open both attachments to see how they look in the original applications. When finished, close each original application.

3

- Click the OK button to close the Attachments dialog box.

- Click the form's Previous record button four times to record number 1 to display the data for William Black (Figure 5–68).

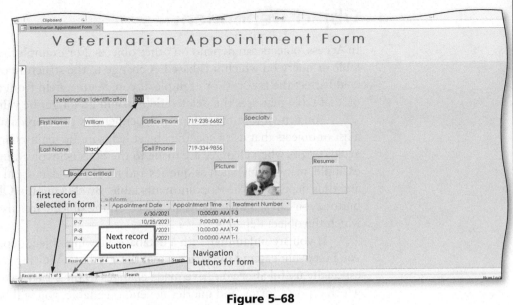

Figure 5–68

4

- Click the subform's Next record button once to highlight the veterinarian's appointment on 10/25/2021. (Figure 5–69).

5

- Close the form.

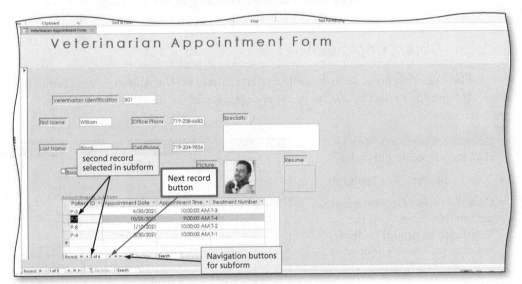

Figure 5–69

Navigation in the Form

BTW
Navigation
To go to a specific record in the main form, enter the record number in the Current Record box for the main form. To go to a specific record in the subform, enter the record number in the Current Record box for the subform.

The previous steps illustrated the way you work with a main form and subform. Clicking the Navigation buttons for the main form moves to a different veterinarian. Clicking the Navigation buttons for the subform moves to different appointments of the veterinarian who appears in the main form. The following are other actions you can take within the form:

1. To move from the last field in the main form to the first field in the subform, press TAB. To move back to the last field in the main form, press SHIFT+TAB.

2. To move from any field in the subform to the first field in the next record's main form, press CTRL+TAB.

3. To switch from the main form to the subform using touch or the mouse, click anywhere in the subform. To switch back to the main form, click any control in the main form. Clicking the background of the main form will not cause the switch to occur.

Object Dependencies

In Access, objects can depend on other objects. For example, a report depends on the table or query on which it is based. A change to the structure of the table or query could affect the report. For example, if you delete a field from a table, any report based on that table that uses the deleted field would no longer be valid.

You can view information on dependencies between database objects. Viewing a list of objects that use a specific object helps in the maintenance of a database and avoids errors when changes are made to the objects involved in the dependency. For example, many items, such as queries and forms, use data from the Appointments table and thus depend on the Appointments table. By clicking the Object Dependencies button, you can see what items are based on the object. You also can see the items on which the object depends.

If you are unfamiliar with a database, viewing object dependencies can help you better understand the structure of the database. Viewing object dependencies is especially useful after you have made changes to the structure of tables. If you know which reports, forms, and queries depend on a table, you will be better able to make changes to a table without negatively affecting the related database objects.

To View Object Dependencies

The following steps view the objects that depend on the Appointments table. *Why? The objects that depend on the Appointments might be affected by any change you make to the Appointments table.*

- Open the Navigation Pane and click the Appointments table.

- Display the Database Tools tab.

- Click the Object Dependencies button (Database Tools tab | Relationships group) to display the Object Dependencies pane.

- If necessary, click the 'Objects that depend on me' option button to select it (Figure 5–70).

🔎 Experiment

- Click the 'Objects that I depend on' option button to see the objects on which the Appointments table depends. Then try both options for other objects in the database.

- Close the Object Dependencies pane by clicking the Object Dependencies button (Database Tools tab | Relationships group) a second time.

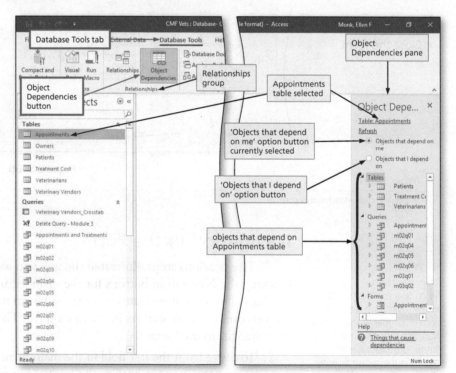

Figure 5–70

Date/Time, Long Text, and Yes/No Fields in Queries

By specifying appointment dates using Date/Time fields, CMF Vets can run queries to find veterinarians' appointments before or after a certain date. Similarly, management of the practice can search for veterinarians with specific qualifications by adding Long Text and Yes/No fields.

To use Date/Time fields in queries, you simply type the dates, including the slashes. To search for records with a specific date, you must type the date. You can also use comparison operators. To find all the appointments whose date is after June 1, 2021, for example, you type >6/1/2021 as the criterion.

You can also use Long Text fields in queries by searching for records that contain a specific word or phrase in the Long Text field. To do so, you use wildcards. For example, to find all the veterinarians who have the word, cardiology, somewhere in the Specialty field, you type *cardiology* as the criterion. The asterisk at the beginning indicates that any characters can appear before the word, cardiology. The asterisk at the end indicates that any characters can appear after the word, cardiology.

To use Yes/No fields in queries, type the word, Yes, or the word, No, as the criterion. The following steps create and run queries that use Date/Time, Long Text, and Yes/No fields.

BTW
Long Text Fields in Queries
When you query long text fields, consider alternative spellings and phrases. For example, Computer Science also can be referenced as CS.

BTW
Date Fields in Queries
To test for the current date in a query, type Date() in the Criteria row of the appropriate column. Typing Date() in the Criteria row for the Appointment Date, for example, finds those veterinarians who are scheduled for appointments today.

To Use Date/Time, Long Text, and Yes/No Fields in a Query

The following steps use Date/Time, Long Text, and Yes/No fields in queries to search for veterinarians and appointments that meet specific criteria. *Why? CMF wants to find veterinarian appointments after 6/1/2021 and who have the word, cardiology, in their speciality field and who have met their board certification.*

- Create a query for the Veterinarians and Appointments tables and include the Veterinarian's First Name, Last Name Appointment Date, Specialty, and Board Certified fields in the query (Figure 5–71).

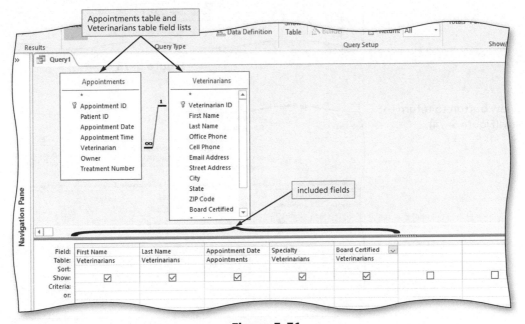

Figure 5–71

2

- Click the Criteria row under the Appointment Date field, and then type >6/1/2021 as the criterion.

- Click the Criteria row under the Specialty field, and then type *cardiology* as the criterion (Figure 5–72).

Q&A

Why does the date have number signs (#) around it?
This is the date format in Access. Access reformatted the date appropriately as soon as you selected the Criteria row for the Specialty field.

Are wildcard searches in long text fields case-sensitive?
No.

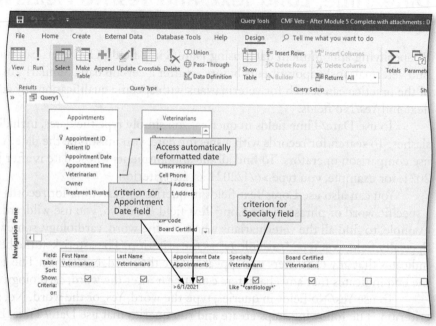

Figure 5–72

3

- View the results (Figure 5–73). Expand the Specialty field to display the entire record, if necessary.

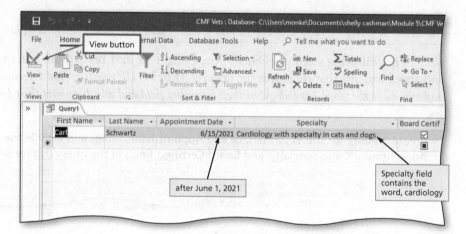

Figure 5–73

4

- Click the View button to return to Design view (Figure 5–74).

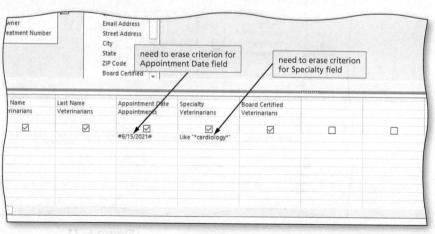

Figure 5–74

5

- Erase the criteria in the Appointment Date and Specialty fields.

- Click the Criteria row under the Board Certified field, and then type **Yes** as the criterion (Figure 5–75).

Q&A Do I have to type Yes?
You could also type True.

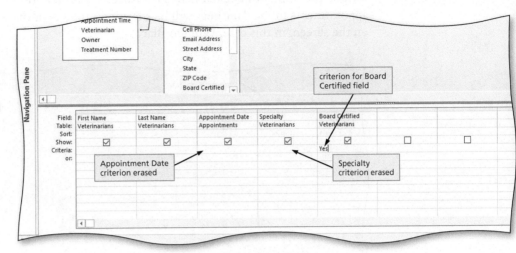

Figure 5–75

6

- View the results (Figure 5–76).

Experiment

- Try other combinations of values in the Appointment Date field, the Specialty field, and/or the Board Certified field. In each case, view the results.

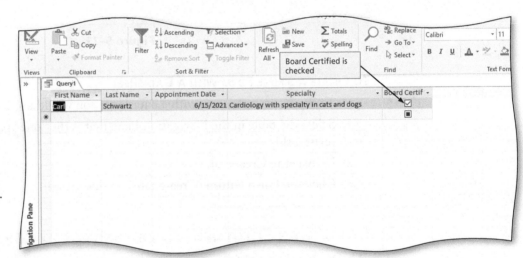

Figure 5–76

7

- Close the query without saving the results.

- If desired, sign out of your Microsoft account.

- Exit Access.

BTW
Date Formats
To change the date format for a date in a query, change the format property for the field using the field's property sheet. To change the date format for a field in a table, open the table in Design view and change the format property for the field.

Datasheets in Forms

Subforms are not available in forms created in Layout view, but you can achieve similar functionality to subforms by including datasheets. Like subforms, the datasheets contain data for the "many" table in the relationship.

Creating a Simple Form with a Datasheet

If you create a simple form for a table that is the "one" table in a one-to-many relationship, Access automatically includes the "many" table in a datasheet within the form. If you create a simple form for the Veterinarians table, for example, Access will include the Appointments table in a datasheet within the form, as in Figure 5–77. The appointments in the datasheet will be the appointments of the veterinarian currently on the screen, in this case, William Black.

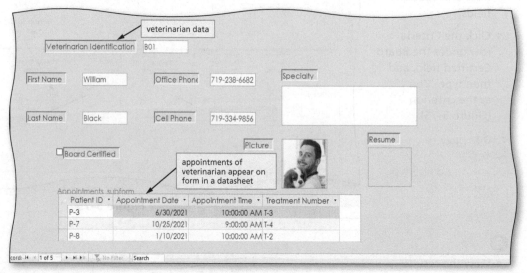

Figure 5–77

To Create a Simple Form with a Datasheet

To create a simple form with a datasheet, you would use the following steps.

1. Select the table in the Navigation Pane that is the "one" part of a one-to-many relationship.
2. Display the Create tab.
3. Click the Form button (Create tab | Forms group).

Creating a Form with a Datasheet in Layout View

You can create a form with a datasheet in Layout view. To create a form based on the Veterinarians table that includes the appointments, which is stored in the Appointments table, you would first use the field list to add the required fields from the "one" table. In Figure 5–78, fields from the Veterinarians table have been added to the form.

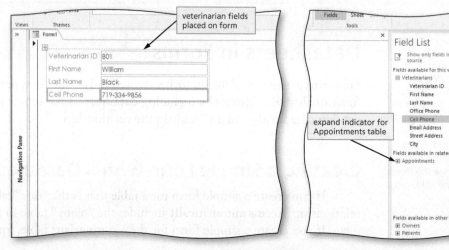

Figure 5–78

Next, you would use the field list to add a single field from the "many" table, as shown in Figure 5–79, in which the Appointment Date field has been added. Access will automatically create a datasheet containing this field.

BTW
Placing Fields on a Datasheet
Be sure to select the datasheet before adding additional fields to the datasheet. When dragging a field from the field list to the datasheet, drag the field to the right boundary of the previous field. The pointer will change to show that you are placing a control and you will see a vertical line.

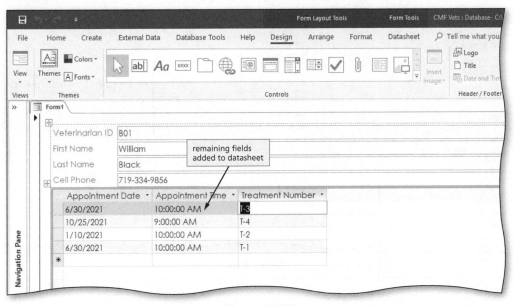

Figure 5–79

Finally, you would click the datasheet to select it and then use the field list to add the other fields from the "many" table that you want to include in the form, as shown in Figure 5–80.

Figure 5–80

Can you modify the form so that the complete labels for the veterinarian fields appear?
Yes. Click any of the labels for the account manager fields to select the label, and then click the Select Column button (Arrange tab | Rows & Columns group) to select all the labels. You can then drag the right boundary of any of the labels to resize all the labels simultaneously.

CONSIDER THIS

TO CREATE A FORM WITH A DATASHEET IN LAYOUT VIEW

Specifically, to create a form with a datasheet in Layout view, you would use the following steps.

1. Display the Create tab.
2. Click the Blank Form button (Create tab | Forms group) to create a form in Layout view.
3. If a field list does not appear, click the 'Add Existing Fields' button (Form Layout Tools Design tab | Tools group) to display a field list.
4. If necessary, click 'Show all tables' to display the available tables.
5. Click the expand indicator (the plus sign) for the "one" table to display the fields in the table, and then drag the fields to the desired positions.
6. Click the expand indicator for the "many" table and drag the first field for the datasheet onto the form to create the datasheet.
7. Select the datasheet and drag the remaining fields for the datasheet from the field list to the desired locations in the datasheet.

Creating a Multiple-Table Form Based on the Many Table

All the forms discussed so far in this module were based on the "one" table, in this case, the Veterinarians table. The records from the "many" table were included in a subform. You can also create a multiple-table form based on the "many" table, in this case, the Appointments table. Such a form is shown in Figure 5–81.

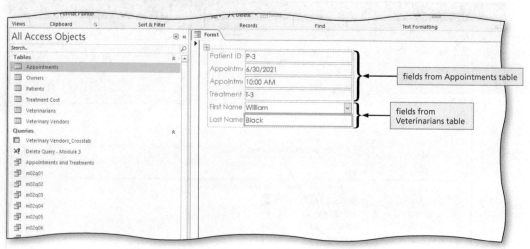

Figure 5–81

In this form, the Patient ID, Appointment Date, Appointment Time, and Treatment Number fields are in the Veterinarians table. The First Name and Last Name fields are found in the Veterinarians table and are included in the form to help to identify the veterinarian whose appointment is appearing in the upper fields.

To Create a Multiple-Table Form Based on the Many Table

To create a multiple-table form based on the "many" table, you would use the following steps.

1. Click the Blank Form button (Create tab | Forms group) to create a form in Layout view.
2. If a field list does not appear, click the 'Add Existing Fields' button on the Design tab to display a field list.
3. Drag the fields for the "many" table to the desired positions.
4. **sam↑** Drag the fields for the "one" table to the desired positions.

BTW
Distributing a Document
Instead of printing and distributing a hard copy of a document, you can distribute the document electronically. Options include sending the document via email; posting it on cloud storage (such as OneDrive) and sharing the file with others; posting it on a social networking site, blog, or other website; and sharing a link associated with an online location of the document. You also can create and share a PDF or XPS image of the document, so that users can view the file in Acrobat Reader or XPS Viewer instead of in Access.

Summary

In this module you have learned to use Yes/No, Long Text, and Attachment data types; create and use an input mask; create a form and add a subform; enhance the look of the controls on a form; change tab order and stops; use a form with a subform; create queries involving Yes/No, Date/Time, and Long Text fields; view object dependencies; and create forms containing datasheets in Layout view.

CONSIDER THIS

What decisions will you need to make when creating your own forms?

Use these guidelines as you complete the assignments in this module and create your own forms outside of this class.

1. Determine the purpose of the fields to see if they need special data types.
    a. If the field only contains values such as Yes and No or True and False, it should have Yes/No as the data type.
    b. If the field contains an extended description, it should have Long Text as the data type.
    c. If the field contains a picture and you need to conserve storage space, its data type should be Attachment.
    d. If the field contains attachments, its data type should be Attachment.
2. Determine whether the form requires data from more than one table.
3. If the form requires data from more than one table, determine the relationship between the tables.
    a. Identify one-to-many relationships.
    b. For each relationship, identify the "one" table and the "many" table.
4. If the form requires data from more than one table, determine on which of the tables the form is to be based.
    a. Which table contains data that is the focus of the form, that is, which table is the main table?
5. Determine the fields from each table that need to be on the form.
    a. Decide exactly how the form will be used, and identify the fields that are necessary to support this use.
    b. Determine whether there are any additional fields that, while not strictly necessary, would make the form more functional.
6. When changing the structure of a table or query, examine object dependencies to see if any report or form might be impacted by the change.
7. Determine the tab order for form controls.
    a. Change the tab order if the form requires a certain progression from one control to the next.
    b. Remove tab stops for those controls for which form navigation is not required.
8. Review the form to determine whether any changes are necessary.
    a. Are there visual changes, such as different colors or a larger font, that would make the form easier to use?
    b. Does the form have a similar look to other forms in the database?
    c. Does the form conform to the organization's standards?

How should you submit solutions to questions in the assignments identified with a symbol?

Every assignment in this book contains one or more questions identified with a symbol. These questions require you to think beyond the assigned database. Present your solutions to the questions in the format required by your instructor. Possible formats may include one or more of these options: write the answer; create a document that contains the answer; present your answer to the class; discuss your answer in a group; record the answer as audio or video using a webcam, smartphone, or -portable media player; or post answers on a blog, wiki, or website.

Apply Your Knowledge

Reinforce the skills and apply the concepts you learned in this module.

Adding Phone Number, Yes/No, Long Text, and Picture Attachment Fields, Using an Input Mask Wizard, and Querying Long Text Fields

Note: To complete this assignment, you will be required to use the Data Files. Please contact your instructor for information about accessing the Data Files.

Instructions: Start Access, and then open the Support_AC_Financial Services database (If you do not have the database, see your instructor for a copy of the modified database.)

Perform the following tasks:

1. Open the Advisor table in Design view.
2. Add the Phone Number, CFA Certification, Other Skills, and Picture fields to the Advisor table structure, as shown in Figure 5–82. Create an input mask for the new Phone Number field. Store the phone number data without symbols. CFA Certification is a field that indicates whether the advisor has completed all the exams for a chartered financial analyst.

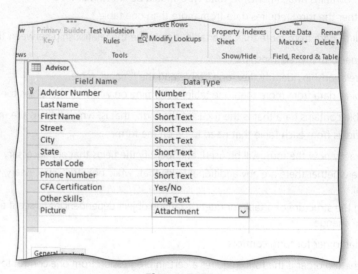

Figure 5–82

3. Add the data shown in Table 5–1 to the Advisor table. Adjust the row and column spacing to best fit the data. Save the changes to the layout of the table.

Table 5–1 Data for Advisor Table				
Advisor Number	Phone Number	CFA Certification	Other Skills	Picture
103	615-555-2222	Yes	Worked 10 years in the financial industry.	Pict1.jpg
110	931-555-4433	Yes	Has a master's degree in computational finance.	Pict2.jpg
114	423-555-8877	No	Worked as an accountant for 20 years.	Pict3.jpg
120	931-555-5498	No	Working on a master's degree in finance.	Pict4.jpg

4. If requested to do so by your instructor, change the phone number for advisor number 103 to your phone number.

5. Query the Advisor table to find all supervisors who have CFA Certification. Include the Advisor Number, Last Name, First Name, and Phone Number fields in the query result. Save the query as Apply 5 Step 5 Query.

6. Query the Advisor table to find all advisors with a master's degree or pursuing a master's degree who have completed the CFA Certification. Include the Advisor Number, Last Name, First Name, and Other Skills fields in the query result. Save the query as Apply 5 Step 6 Query.

7. Submit the revised database in the format specified by your instructor.

8. ✹ What value did you enter in the criteria row for the CFA Certification field in the query in Step 6 above? Could you have entered the criteria differently? If yes, then how would you enter the criteria?

Extend Your Knowledge

Extend the skills you learned in this module and experiment with new skills. You may need to use Help to complete the assignment.

Adding Hyperlink Fields and Creating Multiple-Table Forms Using Layout View

Note: To complete this assignment, you will be required to use the Data Files. Please contact your instructor for information about accessing the Data Files. Start Access, and then open the Support_AC_Healthy Pets database (If you do not have the database, see your instructor for a copy of the modified database.)

Instructions: Healthy Pets is a veterinarian practice that is being closed due to retirements. CMF is thinking of buying the practice to expand its client base. Before the management makes any decisions on this, they need more information about the technicians who work at Healthy Pets. Each technician has a webpage about their qualifications. You will add a Hyperlink field to the Technician table. You will also create the form shown in Figure 5–83.

Continued >

Extend Your Knowledge *continued*

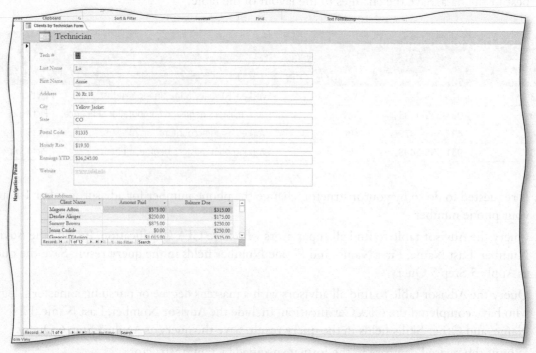

Figure 5–83

Perform the following tasks:

1. Open the Technician table in Design view and add a field with the Hyperlink data type. Insert the field after the Earnings YTD field. Use Website as the name of the field.

2. Switch to Datasheet view and add data for the Website field to the first record. Use your school website as the URL. If necessary, resize the column so the complete URL is displayed.

3. If requested to do so by your instructor, enter your name as the technician name for the first record of the Technician table.

4. Use Layout view to create the multiple-table form shown in Figure 5–83. The Client table appears as a subform in the form. The Technician table is the "one" table in the form. Use Clients by Technician Form as the form name.

5. Submit the revised database in the format specified by your instructor.

6. ✱ How would you add a field for an email address to the Technician table?

Expand Your World

Create a solution, which uses cloud and web technologies, by learning and investigating on your own from general guidance.

Problem: Support_AC_Physical Therapy is a database of clients and therapists. You will add Attachment fields to the Clients table. Then, you will insert images that you download from the Internet. Finally, you will create a multiple-table form for the database.

Note: To complete this assignment, you will be required to use the Data Files. Please contact your instructor for information about accessing the Data Files. Start Access, and then open the Physical Therapy database (If you do not have the database, see your instructor for a copy of the modified database.)

Instructions: Perform the following tasks:

1. Access any website containing royalty-free images and search the images to find four different pictures of parts of the body that might require physical therapy. As a suggestion, you might choose knee, shoulder, back, and foot.

2. Save these images to a storage location of your choice.

3. Open the Client table in Design view. Add a Body Part Image field with an Attachment data type. Add a Picture field with an Attachment data type. Assign the caption, Picture, to the Picture field. The fields should appear after the Therapist Number field.

4. Use the techniques shown in the module to add the images to the Body Part Image field. Reuse the 4 images as needed throughout the records. Add pictures of yourself, your friends, or family members as attachments to the Picture field.

5. Create a multiple-table form based on the Client table. Include the Client Number, First Name, Last Name, and Therapist Number fields from the Client table. Include the therapist's first and last name on the form from the Therapist table.

6. Include a title for the form and the current date. Save the form as Client Therapist Form, and then open the form in Design view.

7. Add the Body Part Image field and the Picture field to the form. If necessary, use the size mode property to adjust your images in the Body Part Image field so that they appear appropriately.

8. Submit the revised database in the format specified by your instructor.

In the Labs

Design, create, modify, and/or use a database following the guidelines, concepts, and skills presented in this module.

Lab: Adding Fields and Creating Multiple-Table Forms for the Lancaster College Database

Instructions: Open the Support_AC_Lancaster College database (If you do not have the database, see your instructor for a copy of the modified database.)

Part 1: The sports department of Lancaster College would like you to add some fields to the Coach table. They would also like to create a form for the Sport table that shows the details of each coach. Use the concepts and techniques presented in this module to perform each of the following tasks:

a. For the Coach table, delete the Alternative SportsName field, then add a picture field and a notes field.

b. For the coach pictures, use your own photos. For the Notes field, add the notes shown in Table 5–2. Make sure all data appears in the datasheet.

Continued >

In the Lab *continued*

Table 5–2 Data for Coach Table	
Coach ID	**Notes**
17893	Runner up for national Olympics team
18797	Competed in the Australian Open 2012
18798	Wrestling coach at Lancaster for 25 years
18990	Experience in NFL
18999	All-star softball championship, 2015
78978	Junior Olympian Freestyle
78979	Ping Pong Coach at Lancaster for 20 years
79798	State Champion, Butterfly
79879	Played in Premier League, 1998
82374	Played semi-professionally in 1995

c. First change the Coach ID in both the Sport table and the Coach table to Short text with a field size of 10. Form a relationship between the two tables on the Coach ID.

d. Create a Coach Sport Master Form for the Coach table that is similar in design to the form shown in Figure 5–1. Include the Coach ID, First Name, Last Name, Picture, and Notes fields from the Coach table on the form. The subform should display the SportName, Coach ID, Min Players, Max Players, and Begin Date fields from the Sport table. Customize the form by adding special effects to controls and labels and by changing the background color of the form. Add a title and the current date to the form header.

e. Create a query that finds all sports with a minimum players of at least 5 and whose coach played in the NFL.

Submit your assignment in the format specified by your instructor.

Part 2: You made several decisions while adding the fields and creating the form for this assignment. What was the rationale behind your decisions? Would you add any additional fields to the Coach table?

6 | Advanced Report Techniques

Objectives

You will have mastered the material in this module when you can:

- Create and relate additional tables
- Create queries for reports
- Create reports in Design view
- Add fields and text boxes to a report
- Format report controls
- Group and ungroup report controls
- Update multiple report controls

- Add and modify a subreport
- Modify section properties
- Add a title, page number, and date to a report
- Preview, print, and publish a report
- Add totals and subtotals to a report
- Include a conditional value in a report

Introduction

Previously you created forms in Design view. In this module, you will create two reports in Design view. Both reports feature grouping and sorting. The first report contains a subreport, which is a report that is contained within another report. The subreport contains data from a query and is related to data in the main report. The second report uses aggregate functions to calculate subtotals and totals. It also uses a function to calculate a value where the actual calculation will vary from record to record depending on whether a given criterion is true.

Project — Creating Detailed Reports

CMF Vets managers want a master list of owners and the veterinarian assigned to each owner. This list should be available as an Access report and will have the name Owners and Account Information Master List. For each owner, the report will include full details for all the owners assigned to the veterinarian. In addition to offering its veterinarian services, CMF Vets offers workshops designed to educate owners on various aspects of pet products, health trends, and new health procedures. Data on workshop participation is stored in the database. For veterinarians who are participating in workshops, the report should list the specific workshops being offered to the owners and the pets assigned to the owners.

The Owners and Account Information Master List report is shown in Figure 6–1a. The report is organized by Owner ID, with the data for each Owner ID beginning on a new page. For each veterinarian, the report lists the Veterinarian ID number; the report then lists data for each owner served by that veterinarian. The owner data includes the Owner ID, owner first name, owner last name, veterinarian, appointment dates, treatment numbers, and cost of those treatments. For each workshop the owner is taking, the report lists the workshop code, description, total hours the workshop requires, hours already spent, and hours remaining.

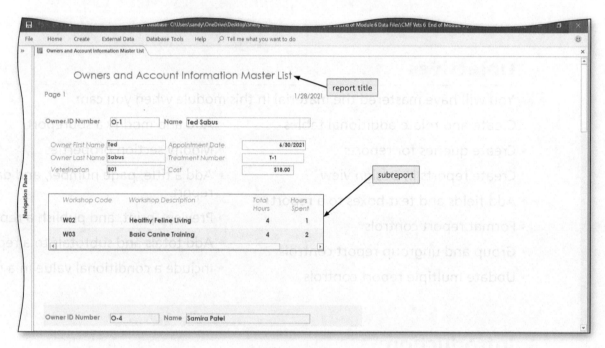

Figure 6–1a

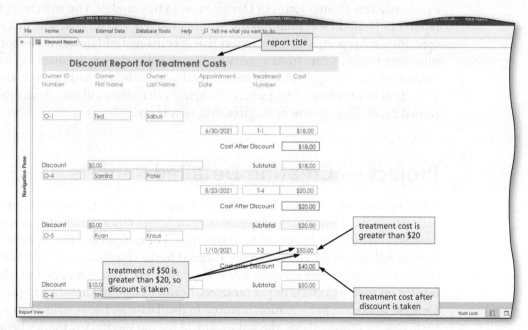

Figure 6–1b

To attract new clients and reward current clients, some companies offer discounts. CMF Vets managers are considering offering a discount on the treatment costs over $20 to their current clients. The exact amount of the discount depends on how much the treatment costs. If treatment cost is more than $20, the discount will be 20 percent of the treatment cost amount. If the treatment cost is $20 or less, then no discount will be given. To assist in determining the discount, CMF Vets managers need a report like the one shown in Figure 6–1b. The report groups clients by appointments. It includes a subtotal of the treatment costs for the appointment. In addition, the report includes a discounted cost for the treatment, if the treatment cost is more than $20. Finally, it shows the cost of the treatment less the discount amount.

Additional Tables

CMF Vets veterinarians are frequently asked to present workshops on various aspects of canine and feline health tips, canine training classes, and latest canine and feline health news. CMF Vets would like to incorporate the workshop data into the CMF Vets database.

Before creating the reports, you need to create two additional tables for the CMF Vets database. The first table, Workshop, is shown in Table 6–1a. As described in Table 6–1a, each workshop has a code and a description. The table also includes the total hours for which the workshop is usually offered and its increments; that is, the standard time blocks in which the workshop is usually offered. Table 6–1b contains the specific workshops that the veterinarians at CMF Vets offer to their clients. The first row, for example, indicates that workshop W01 is called Healthy Canine Living. It is typically offered in two-hour increments for a total of four hours.

BTW

The Ribbon and Screen Resolution
Access may change how the groups and buttons within the groups appear on the ribbon, depending on the computer's screen resolution. Thus, your ribbon may look different from the ones in this book if you are using a screen resolution other than 1366 x 768.

BTW

Touch Screen Differences
The Office and Windows interfaces may vary if you are using a touch screen. For this reason, you might notice that the function or appearance of your touch screen differs slightly from this module's presentation.

BTW

Touch and Pointers
Remember that if you are using your finger on a touch screen, you will not see the pointer.

Table 6–1a Structure of Workshop Table

Field Name	Data Type	Field Size	Description
Workshop Code	Short Text	3	Primary Key
Workshop Description	Short Text	50	
Hours	Number	Integer	
Increments	Number	Integer	

Table 6–1b Workshop Table

Workshop Code	Workshop Description	Hours	Increments
W01	Healthy Canine Living	4	2
W02	Healthy Feline Living	4	2
W03	Basic Canine Training	3	1
W04	Intermediate Canine Training	3	1
W05	Advanced Canine Training	3	1

BTW
Enabling the Content
For each of the databases
you use in this module,
you will need to enable the
content.

BTW
**AutoNumber Field
as Primary Key**
When you create a table
in Datasheet view, Access
automatically creates an ID
field with the AutoNumber
data type as the primary
key field. As you add
records to the table, Access
increments the ID field so
that each record will have
a unique value in the field.
AutoNumber fields are useful
when there is no data field
in a table that is a suitable
primary key.

BTW
**Copying the
Structure of a Table**
If you want to create a table
that has a structure similar
to an existing table, you can
copy the structure of the
table only. Select the table in
the Navigation Pane and click
Copy, then click Paste. In the
Paste Table As dialog box,
type the new table name and
click the Structure Only option
button. Then, click the OK
button. To modify the new
table, open it in Design view.

The second table, Workshop Offerings, is described in Table 6–2a and contains an owner ID, a workshop code, the total number of hours that the workshop is scheduled for the owner, and the number of hours already spent by the owner in the workshop. The primary key of the Workshop Offerings table is a combination of the Owner ID and Workshop Code fields.

Table 6–2a Structure of Workshop Offerings Table			
Field Name	**Data Type**	**Field Size**	**Description**
Owner ID	Short Text	5	Part of Primary Key
Workshop Code	Short Text	3	Part of Primary Key
Total Hours	Number	Integer	
Hours Spent	Number	Integer	

Table 6–2b gives the data for the Workshop Offerings table. For example, the first record shows that Owner ID O-1 currently has scheduled workshop W03 (Basic Canine Training). The workshop is scheduled for four hours, and the owner has so far spent two hours in class.

Table 6–2b Workshop Offerings Table			
Owner ID	**Workshop Code**	**Total Hours**	**Hours Spent**
O-1	W03	4	2
O-2	W01	4	1
O-5	W03	4	2
O-1	W02	4	1
O-6	W04	4	0
O-8	W03	4	0
O-3	W02	4	1

If you examine the data in Table 6–2b, you see that the Owner ID field cannot be the primary key for the Workshop Offerings table. The first and fourth records, for example, both have an Owner ID of O-1. The Workshop Code field also cannot be the primary key. The fourth and seventh records have the same workshop code.

To Create the New Tables

You will use Design view to create the new tables. The steps to create the new tables are similar to the steps you used previously to add fields to an existing table and to define primary keys. The only difference is the way you specify a primary key. **Why?** *In the Workshop Offerings table, the primary key consists of more than one field, which requires a slightly different process.* To specify a primary key containing more than one field, you must select both fields that make up the primary key by clicking the row selector for the first field, and then hold down the SHIFT key while clicking the row selector for the second field. Once the fields are selected, you can use the Primary Key button to indicate that the primary key consists of both fields. The following steps create the tables in Design view.

1

sam↓ Start
Access and open the
CMF Vets database
from your hard disk,
OneDrive, or other
storage location.

• If necessary, close
the Navigation Pane.

• Display the Create
tab (Figure 6–2).

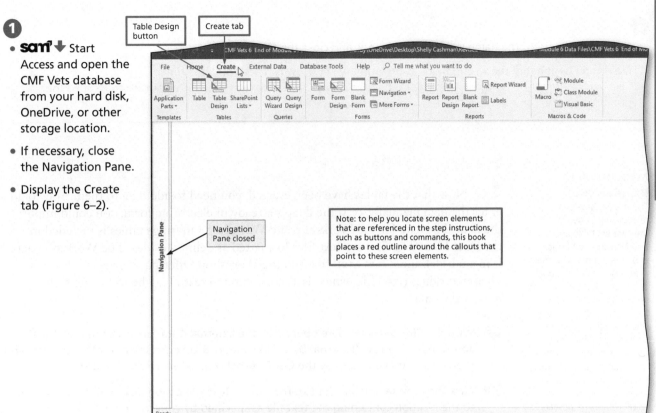

Figure 6–2

2

• Click the Table Design button (Create tab | Tables group) to create a table in Design view.

• Enter the information for the fields in the Workshop table as indicated in Table 6–1a, making Workshop Code the
primary key, and specifying the indicated field sizes.

• Save the table using the name **Workshop** and close the table.

• Display the Create tab and then
click the Table Design button
(Create tab | Tables group) to
create a second table in
Design view.

• Enter the information
for the fields in the
Workshop Offerings
table as indicated in
Table 6–2a.

• Click the row selector for the
Owner ID field.

• Hold down SHIFT and then click
the row selector for the Workshop
Code field so that both fields are
selected.

• Click the Primary Key button
(Table Tools Design tab | Tools
group) to select the combination
of the two fields as the primary
key (Figure 6–3).

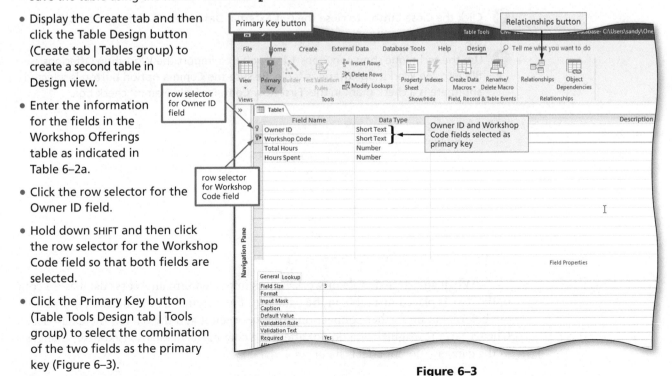

Figure 6–3

• Save the table using the name Workshop Offerings and close the table.

Q&A I realized I designated the wrong fields as the primary key. How can I correct the primary key?
Click any field that currently participates in the primary key, and click the Primary Key button to remove the primary key. You can then specify the correct primary key.

BTW
Many-to-Many Relationships
There is a many-to-many relationship between the Owners table and the Workshop table. To implement a many-to-many relationship in a relational database management system such as Access, you create a third table, often called a junction or intersection table, that has as its primary key the combination of the primary keys of each of the tables involved in the many-to-many relationship. The primary key of the Workshop Offerings table is the combination of the Owner ID and the Workshop Code fields.

To Import the Data

Now that the tables have been created, you need to add data to them. You could enter the data manually, or if the data is already in electronic form, you could import the data. The data for the Workshop and Workshop Offerings tables is included in the Data Files. The files are text files formatted as delimited files. The Workshop data is in a tab-delimited text (.txt) file, and the Workshop Offerings data is in a comma-separated values (.csv) file, which is also a delimited text file. The following steps import the data.

1 With the CMF Vets database open, click the External Data tab, click the New Data Source button arrow (External Data tab | Import & Link group), point to From File, and then click Text File to display the Get External Data – Text File dialog box.

2 Click the Browse button (Get External Data - Text File dialog box) and then navigate to the location containing the text file as specified by your instructor.

3 Click the Workshop file, then click Open.

4 If necessary, click the 'Append a copy of the records to the table' option button, and then select the Workshop table from the list. Click OK. With the Delimited option button selected, click Next.

5 With the Tab option button selected, click the 'First Row Contains Field Names' check box, click Next, and then click Finish.

6 Click the Close button to close the Get External Data - Text File dialog box without saving the import steps.

7 Use the technique shown in Steps 1 through 6 to import the Workshop Offerings.csv file into the Workshop Offerings table. Be sure the Comma option button is selected and there is a check mark in the 'First Row Contains Field Names' check box.

Q&A I got an error message after I clicked the Finish button that indicated there were errors. The data was not imported. What should I do?
First, click the Cancel button to terminate the process. Then, review the structure of the table in Design view to ensure that the field names are all spelled correctly and that the data types are correct. Correct any errors you find, save your work, and then redo the steps to import the data.

Linking versus Importing

When an external table or worksheet is imported into an Access database, a copy of the data is placed in a table in the database. The original data still exists, just as it did before, but no further connection exists between it and the data in the database. Changes to the original data do not affect the data in the database. Likewise, changes in the database do not affect the original data.

It is also possible to link data stored in a variety of formats to Access databases. To do so, you would select the 'Link to the data source by creating a linked table' option button when importing data, rather than the 'Import the source data into a new table in the current database' or 'Append a copy of the records to the table' option buttons. With linking, the connection is maintained; changes made to the data in the external table or worksheet affect the Access table.

To identify that a table is linked to other data, Access displays an arrow in front of the table in the Navigation Pane. In addition, an icon is displayed in front of the name that indicates the type of file to which the data is linked. For example, an Excel icon in front of the name indicates that the table is linked to an Excel worksheet.

TO MODIFY LINKED TABLES

After you link tables between a worksheet and a database or between two databases, you can modify many of the linked table's features. To rename the linked table, set view properties, and set links between tables in queries, you would use the following steps.

1. Click the 'Linked Table Manager' button (External Data tab | Import & Link group) to update the links.

2. Select the linked table for which you want to update the links.

3. Click the OK button.

BTW
Linking
Two of the primary reasons to link data from another program to Access are to use the query and report features of Access. When you link an Access database to data in another program, all changes to the data must be made in the source program. For example, if you link an Excel workbook to an Access database, you cannot edit the linked table in Access. You must make all changes to the data in Excel.

To Relate the New Tables

The following steps relate, or create a relationship between, the tables. *Why? The new tables need to be related to the existing tables in the CMF Vets database. The Owners and Workshop Offerings tables are related through the Owner ID field that exists in both tables. The Workshop and Workshop Offerings tables are related through the Workshop Code fields in both tables.*

1

- If necessary, close any open datasheet on the screen by clicking its Close button, and then display the Database Tools tab.

- Click the Relationships button (Database Tools tab | Relationships group), shown in Figure 6–3, to open the Relationships window (Figure 6–4).

Q&A I only see one table; did I do something wrong?
Click the All Relationships button to display all the tables in relationships.

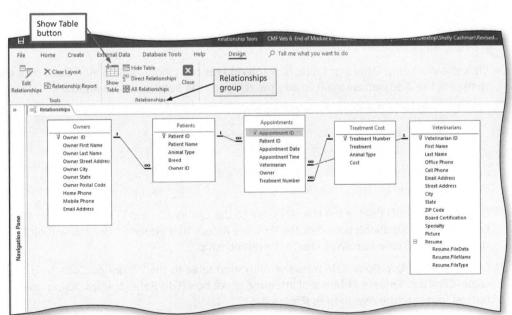

Figure 6–4

- Click the Show Table button (Relationship Tools Design tab | Relationships group) to display the Show Table dialog box (Figure 6–5).

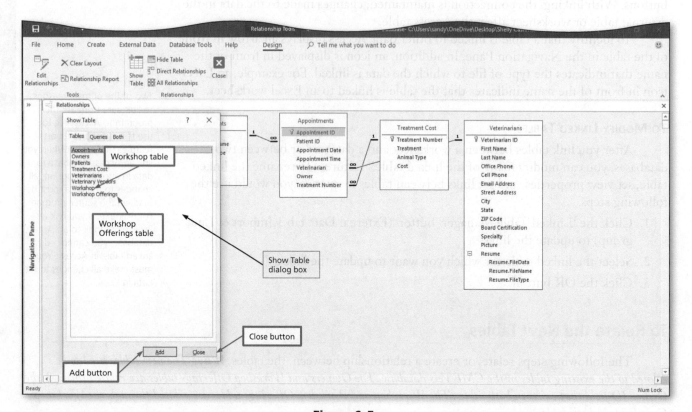

Figure 6–5

- Click the Workshop Offerings table, click the Add button (Show Table dialog box), click the Workshop table, and then click the Add button again to add the tables to the Relationships window.

- Click Close to close the Show Table dialog box.

◁ I cannot see all of the tables; some are obscured.
Q&A Drag the tables to another location in the Relationship window for easier viewing.

I cannot see the Workshop Offerings table. Should I repeat the step?
If you cannot see the table, it is behind the dialog box. You do not need to repeat the step.

- Drag the Owner ID field in the Owners table to the Owner ID field in the Workshop Offerings table to display the Edit Relationships dialog box. Click the 'Enforce Referential Integrity' check box (Edit Relationships dialog box) and then click the Create button to create the relationship.

- Drag the Workshop Code field from the Workshop table to the Workshop Code field in the Workshop Offerings table. Click the 'Enforce Referential Integrity' check box (Edit Relationships dialog box) and then click the Create button to create the relationship (Figure 6–6).

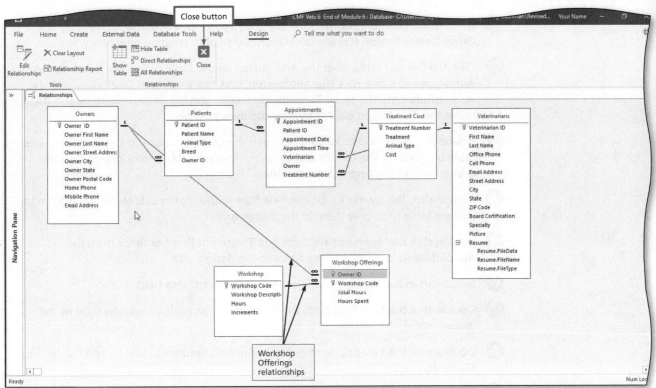

Figure 6–6

4
• Save the changes and then click the Close button (Relationship Tools Design tab | Relationships group).

Creating Reports in Design View

Previously, you have used both Layout view and the Report Wizard to create reports. However, you can simply create the report in Design view. You can also use Design view to modify a report you previously created. If you create a report in Design view, you must place all the fields in the desired locations. You must also specify any sorting or grouping that is required.

Whether you use the wizard or simply use Design view to create a report, you must determine on which table or query to base the report. If you decide to base the report on a query, you must first create the query, unless it already exists.

To Create a Query for the Report

CMF Vets management requirements for the reports specify that it would be convenient to use two queries. These queries do not yet exist, so you will need to create them. The first query relates owners and their account information. The owner account information consists of appointments, treatments scheduled, and expected treatment costs for the owner's pets. The second query relates workshops and workshop offerings. The following steps create the Owners and Account Information query.

BTW
Invalid Relationships
If Access will not allow you to create a relationship and enforce referential integrity, it could be because the two matching fields do not have the same data type. Open the tables in Design view and check the data types and field sizes. You should also check to be sure you do not have a foreign key value in the many table that does not match the primary key value in the one table. Create a Find Unmatched Query using the Query Wizard to find the unmatched records in the many table.

1 If necessary, close the Navigation Pane, display the Create tab, and then click the Query Design button (Create tab | Queries group) to create a new query.

2 Click the Owners table, click the Add button (Show Table dialog box), click the Appointments table, click the Add button, click the Treatment Cost table, click the Add button, close the Show Table dialog box by clicking its Close button, and then resize the field lists to display as many fields as possible.

3 If necessary, create a relationship between the Owners table and the Appointments table by selecting the Owner ID field in the Owners table and dragging it to the Owner field in the Appointments table.

4 Double-click the Owner ID, Owner First Name, and Owner Last Name fields from the Owners table to display them in the design grid.

5 Double-click the Appointment Date and Treatment Number fields from the Appointments table to add the fields to the design grid.

6 Select Sort in Ascending Order on the Appointment Date field.

7 Double-click the Cost field from the Treatment Cost table to add the field to the design grid.

8 Double-click the Veterinarian field from the Appointments table to add the field to the design grid.

9 Run the query to view the results and scroll through the fields to make sure you have included all the necessary fields. If you have omitted a field, return to Design view and add it (Figure 6–7).

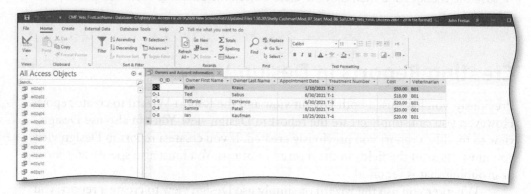

Figure 6–7

10 Click the Save button on the Quick Access Toolbar to save the query, type `Owners and Account Information` as the name of the query, and then click OK.

11 Close the query.

To Create an Additional Query for the Report Using Expression Builder

The following steps create the Workshop Offerings and Workshops query, which includes a calculated field for hours remaining, that is, the total number of hours minus the hours spent. *Why? CMF Vets managers need to include in the Owners and Account Information Master List the number of hours that remain in a workshop offering.*

1

- Display the Create tab and then click the Query Design button (Create tab | Queries group) to create a new query.
- Click the Workshop table, click the Add button (Show Table dialog box), click the Workshop Offerings table, click the Add button, and then click Close to close the Show Table dialog box.
- Double-click the Owner ID and Workshop Code fields from the Workshop Offerings table to add the fields to the design grid.
- Double-click the Workshop Description field from the Workshop table.
- Double-click the Total Hours and Hours Spent fields from the Workshop Offerings table to add the fields to the design grid.
- Click in the top cell in the Field row of the first open column in the design grid to select it.
- Click the Builder button (Query Tools Design tab | Query Setup group) to display the Expression Builder dialog box (Figure 6–8).

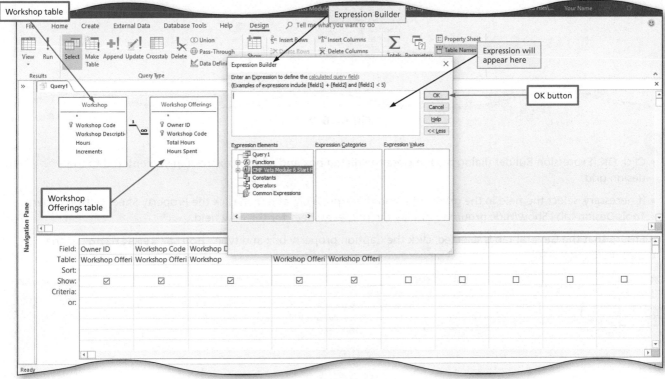

Figure 6–8

2

- Double-click CMF Vets in the Expression Elements section to display the categories of objects within the CMF Vets database, and then double-click Tables to display a list of tables.
- Click the Workshop Offerings table to select it.
- Double-click the Total Hours field to add it to the expression.
- Type a minus sign (–) to add it to the expression.
- Double-click the Hours Spent field to add it to the expression (Figure 6–9).

Q&A Why are the fields preceded by a table name and an exclamation point?
This notation qualifies the field; that is, it indicates to which table the field belongs.

Could I type the expression instead of using the Expression Builder?
Yes. You could type it directly into the design grid. You could also right-click the column and click Zoom to allow you to type the expression in the Zoom dialog box. Finally, you could use the Expression Builder, but simply type the expression rather than clicking any buttons. Use whichever method you find most convenient.

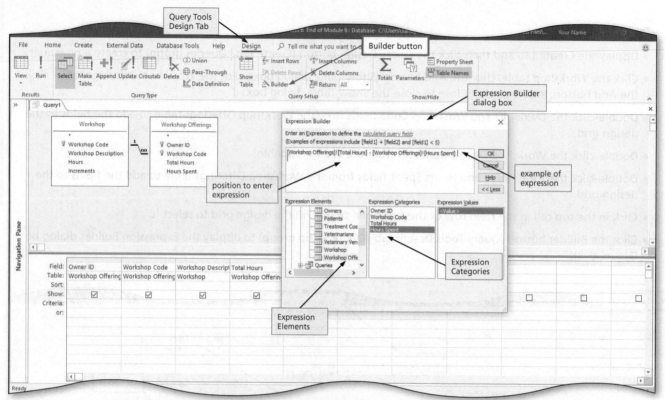

Figure 6–9

3

- Click OK (Expression Builder dialog box) to close the dialog box and add the expression you entered to the design grid.

- If necessary, select the field in the grid containing the expression, and then click the Property Sheet button (Query Tools Design tab | Show/Hide group) to display the property sheet for the new field.

- Ensure that the General tab is selected, click the Caption property box and type **Hours Remaining** as the caption (Figure 6–10).

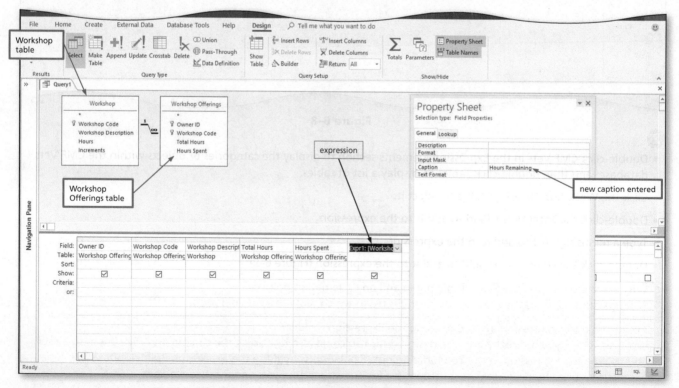

Figure 6–10

Q&A I do not have a Caption property in my property sheet. What went wrong? What should I do?
You either inadvertently clicked a different location in the grid, or you have not yet completed entering the expression. The easiest way to ensure you have done both is to click any other column in the grid and then click the column with the expression.

4
- Close the property sheet and then view the query (Figure 6–11). (Your results might be in a different order.)

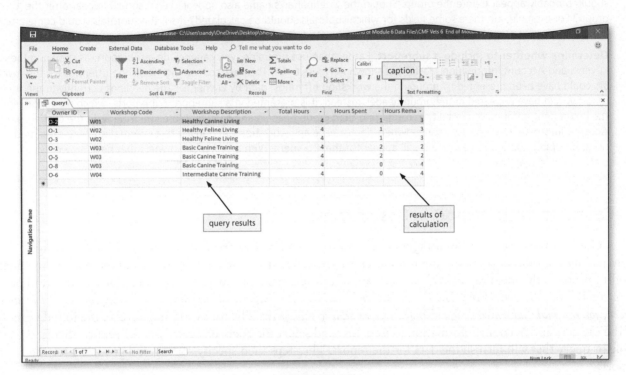

Figure 6–11

5
- Increase the width of the fields in the Design Grid to view the entire field name, and then verify that your query results match those in the figure. If not, return to Design view and make the necessary corrections.
- Click the Save button on the Quick Access Toolbar, type **Workshop Offerings and Workshops** as the name of the query, and then click the OK button to save the query.
- Close the query.

Other Ways

1. Right-click field in grid, click Build

How do you determine the tables and fields for the report?
If you determine that data should be presented as a report, you need to then determine what tables and fields contain the data for the report.

Examine the requirements for the report in general to determine the tables. Do the requirements only relate to data in a single table, or does the data come from multiple tables? Is the data in a query, or could you create a query that contains some or all of the fields necessary for the report?

Examine the specific requirements for the report to determine the fields necessary. Look for all the data items that are specified for the report. Each item should correspond to a field in a table, or it should be able to be computed from a field or fields in a table. This information gives you the list of fields to include in the query.

CONSIDER THIS

Determine the order of the fields. Examine the requirements to determine the order in which the fields should appear. Be logical and consistent in your ordering. For example, in an address, the city should come before the state, and the state should come before the postal code, unless there is some compelling reason for another order.

What decisions do you make in determining the organization of the report?
Determine sort order. Is there a special order in which the records should appear?

Determine grouping. Should the records be grouped in some fashion? If so, what information should appear before the records in a group? If, for example, owners are grouped by veterinarian ID number, the ID number of the veterinarian should probably appear before the group. Should the veterinarian's name also appear? What should appear after the group? For example, are there some fields for which subtotals should be calculated? If so, the subtotals would come after the group.

Determine whether to include a subreport. Rather than use grouping, you can include a subreport, as shown in the Owners and Account Information Master List shown in Figure 6–1a. The data concerning workshop offerings for the owners could have been presented by grouping the workshop offerings' data by Owner ID. The headings currently in the subreport would have appeared in the group header. Instead, it is presented in a subreport. Subreports, which are reports in their own right, offer more flexibility in formatting than group headers and footers. More importantly, in the Owners and Account Information Master List, some owners do not have any workshop offerings. If this information were presented using grouping, the group header will still appear for these owners. With a subreport, owners that have no workshop offerings do not appear.

To Create an Initial Report in Design View

Creating the report shown in Figure 6–1a from scratch involves creating the initial report in Design view, adding the subreport, modifying the subreport separately from the main report, and then making the final modifications to the main report. When you want to create a report from scratch, you use Design view rather than the Report Wizard. *Why? The Report Wizard is suitable for simple, customized reports. Using the Report Design screen, you can make advanced design changes, such as adding subreports.* The following steps create the initial version of the Owners and Account Information Master List and select the **record source** for the report; that is, the table or query that will furnish the data for the report. The steps then specify sorting and grouping for the report.

- Display the Create tab.
- Click the Report Design button (Create tab | Reports group) to create a report in Design view.
- Ensure the selector for the entire report, the box in the upper-left corner of the report, contains a small black square, which indicates that the report is selected.
- Click the Property Sheet button (Report Design Tools Design tab | Tools group) to display a property sheet.

Q&A Can I make the property sheet box wider so I can see more of the items in the Record Source list?
Yes, you can make the property sheet wider by dragging its left or right border.

- Drag the left border, if necessary, to increase the width of the property sheet.
- With the All tab (Property Sheet) selected, click the Record Source property box arrow to display the list of available tables and queries (Figure 6–12).

Q&A Can I move the property sheet?
Yes, you can move the property sheet by dragging its title bar.

Can I increase the size of the Record Source list?
You cannot change the width of the Record Source list, because it is determined by the dialog box, but you can scroll down in the list to view additional record sources.

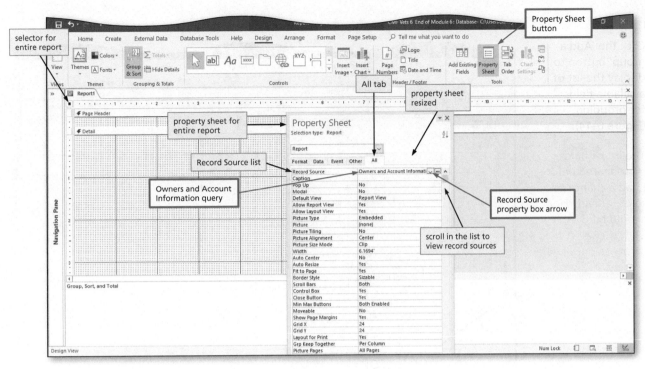

Figure 6–12

2

- Click the Owners and Account Information query to select the query as the record source for the report.

- Close the property sheet by clicking the Property Sheet button (Report Design Tools Design tab | Tools group).

To Group and Sort

In Design view of the report, you can specify both grouping and sorting by using the Group & Sort button on the Design tab, just as you did in Layout view. The following steps specify both grouping and sorting in the report. *Why? CMF Vets managers have determined that the records in the report should be grouped by Owner ID. That is, all the information of a given owner should appear together. Within the account information of a given owner, they have determined that appointments are to be ordered by appointment date.*

- Click the Group & Sort button (Report Design Tools Design tab | Grouping & Totals group) to display the Group, Sort, and Total pane (Figure 6–13).

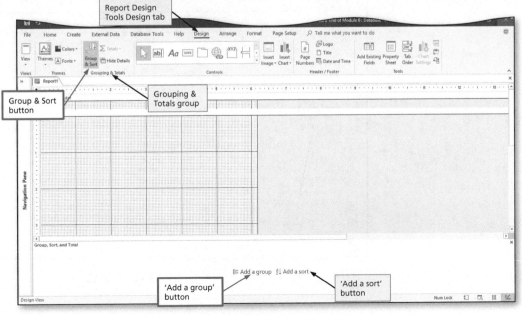

Figure 6–13

2

- Click the 'Add a group' button to display the list of available fields for grouping (Figure 6–14).

Q&A The list of fields disappeared before I had a chance to select a field. What should I do?
Click the select field arrow to once again display the list of fields.

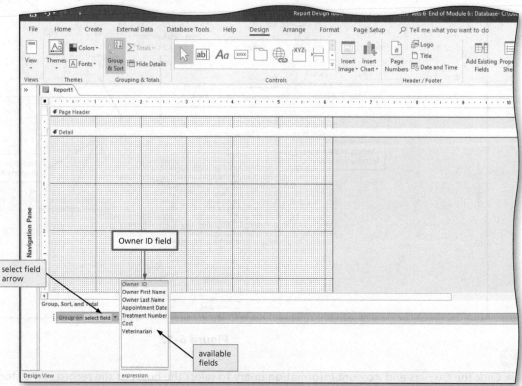

Figure 6–14

3

- Click the Owner ID field to group by owner ID number (Figure 6–15).

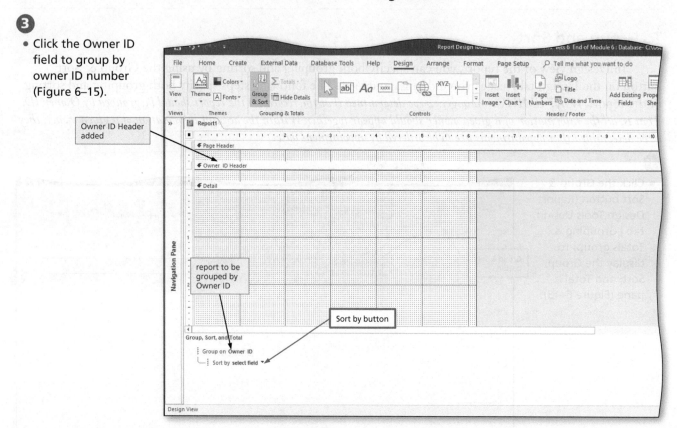

Figure 6–15

4

- Click the Sort by button to display the list of available fields for sorting (Figure 6–16). If the Sort by button does not appear for you, click the 'Add a sort' button.

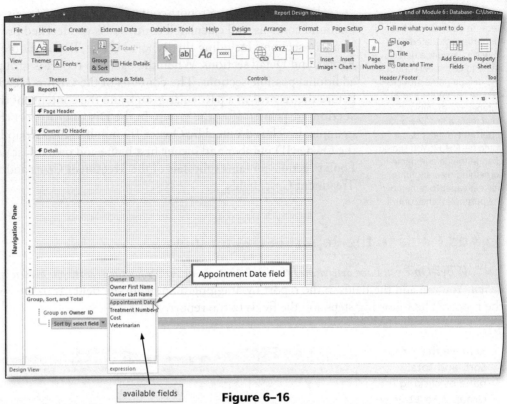

Figure 6–16

5

- Click the Appointment Date field to sort appointments by date of the appointment (Figure 6–17).

- Save the report, using Owners and Account Information Master List as the report name.

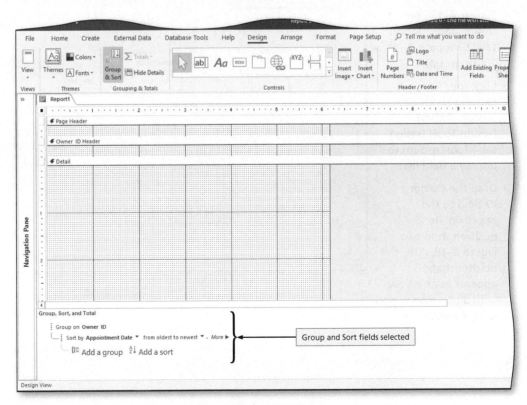

Figure 6–17

Other Ways

1. Right-click any open area of report, click Sorting & Grouping

Controls and Sections

Recall earlier that a report contains three types of controls: bound controls, unbound controls, and calculated controls. As you learned previously, reports contain standard sections, including the Report Header, Report Footer, Page Header, Page Footer, and Detail sections. When the data in a report is grouped, there are two additional possible sections. The contents of the **Group Header section** are printed before the records in a particular group, and the contents of the **Group Footer section** are printed after the group. In the Discount Report (Figure 6–1b), for example, which is grouped by Owner ID number, the Group Header section contains the Owner ID number and owner first name and owner last name, and the Group Footer section contains subtotals of the Treatment Costs and the Discount Amount for Treatment Costs fields.

To Add Fields to the Report in Design View

Why? *Once you have determined the fields that are necessary for the report, you need to add them to the report design.* You can add the fields to the report by dragging them from the field list to the appropriate position on the report. The following steps add the fields to the report.

- Remove the 'Group, Sort, and Total' pane by clicking the Group & Sort button, which is shown in Figure 6–13 (Report Design Tools Design tab | Grouping & Totals group).

- Click the 'Add Existing Fields' button (Report Design Tools Design tab | Tools group) to display a field list.

- Drag the Owner ID field to the approximate position shown in Figure 6–18. (The pointer shape appears as an arrow with a plus sign as you drag a field.)

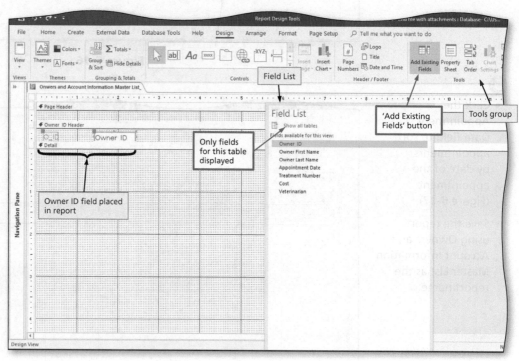

Figure 6–18

My field list does not look like the one in the figure. It has several tables listed, and at the top it has 'Show only fields in the current record source.' Yours has 'Show all tables.' What should I do?

Click the 'Show only fields in the current record source' link. Your field list should then match the one in the figure.

2

• Release the mouse button to place the field and then align the Owner ID field as shown (Figure 6–19).

• Place the remaining fields in the positions shown in Figure 6–19.

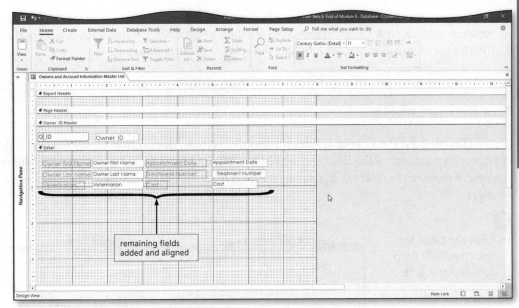

Figure 6–19

3

• Adjust the positions of the labels to those shown in the figure. If any field is not in the correct position, drag it to its correct location. To move the control or the attached label separately, drag the large handle in the upper-left corner of the control or label. You can align controls using the Align button (Report Design Tools Arrange tab | Sizing & Ordering group) or adjust spacing by using the Size/Space button (Report Design Tools Arrange tab | Sizing & Ordering group).

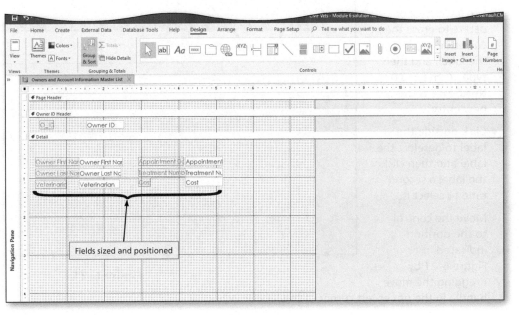

Figure 6–20

Q&A

Sometimes I find it hard to move a control a very small amount. Is there a simpler way to do this other than dragging it with a mouse?

Yes. Once you have selected the control, you can use the arrow keys to move the control a very small amount in the desired direction.

Could I drag several fields from the field list at once?

Yes. You can select multiple fields by selecting the first field, holding down the CTRL key and selecting the additional fields. Once you have selected multiple fields, you can drag them all at once. How you choose to select fields and drag them onto the report is a matter of personal preference.

 **Experiment**

- Select more than one control and then experiment with the Size/Space and the Align buttons (Report Design Tools Arrange tab | Sizing & Ordering group) to see their effects. After trying each one, click the Undo button to undo the change. If you used the Arrange tab, redisplay the Design tab.

To Change Labels

The label for the Owner ID field currently contains the caption O_ID for that field. The following step changes the contents of the label for the Owner ID field from O_ID to Owner ID Number. *Why? Because there is plenty of room on the report to display longer names for the field, you can make the report more descriptive by changing the label.*

- Click the label for the Owner ID field to select the label.

- Click the label for the O_ID field a second time to produce an insertion point.

- Use BACKSPACE or DELETE to erase the current entry in the label, and then type **Owner ID Number** as the new entry.

- Click outside the label to deselect the label and then click the label a second time to select it.

- Move the control to the position indicated in Figure 6–21 by dragging the move handle in the upper-left corner of the label.

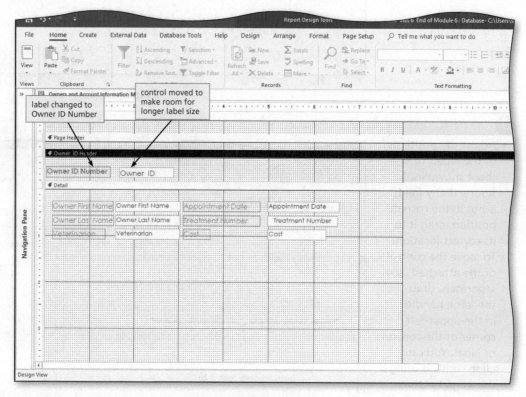

Figure 6–21

Using Other Tools in the Controls Group

Previously, you used the Subform/Subreport tool within the Controls group on the Design tab to place special controls on a form. The Controls group has additional tools available that can be used with forms and reports. A description of the additional tools appears in Table 6–3.

Table 6–3 Additional Tools in the Controls Group

Tool	Description
Select	Select to be able to size, move, or edit existing controls. If you click another tool and want to cancel the effect of the tool before using it, you can click the Select tool.
Text Box	Create a text box for entering, editing, and displaying data. You can also bind the text box to a field in the underlying table or query.
Label	Create a label, a box containing text that cannot be edited and is independent of other controls, such as a title.
Button	Create a command button.
Tab Control	Create a tab control, which contains a series of tabbed pages. Each tabbed page can contain its own controls.
Hyperlink	Inserts a hyperlink to an existing file, Web page, database object, or email address.
Option Group	Create an option group, which is a rectangle containing a collection of option buttons. To select an option, you click the corresponding option button.
Insert or Remove Page Break	Insert or remove a physical page break (typically in a report).
Combo Box	Create a combo box, which is a combination of a text box and a list box.
Chart	Create a chart.
Line	Draw a line on a form or report.
Toggle Button	Add a toggle button. With a toggle button, a user can make a Yes/No selection by clicking the button. The button either appears to be pressed (for Yes) or not pressed (for No).
List Box	Create a list box, a box that allows the user to select from a list of options.
Rectangle	Create a rectangle.
Check Box	Insert a check box. With a check box a user can make multiple Yes/No selections.
Unbound Object Frame	Insert an OLE object (for example, a graph, picture, sound file, or video) that is not contained in a field in a table within the database.
Attachment	Insert an Attachment field.
Option Button	Insert an option button. With an option button, a user can make a single Yes/No selection from among a collection of at least two choices.
Subform/ Subreport	Create a subform (a form contained within another form) or a subreport (a report contained within another report).
Bound Object Frame	Insert an OLE object (for example, a graph, picture, sound file, or video) that is contained in a field in a table within the database.
Image	Insert a frame into which you can insert a graphic. The graphic will be the same for all records.

To Add Text Boxes

You can place a text box in a report or form by using the Text Box tool in the Controls group on the Design tab. The text box consists of a control that is initially unbound and an attached label. The next step is to update the **control source**, which is the source of data for the control. You can do so by entering the expression in the text box or by updating the Control Source property in the property sheet with the expression.

Once you have updated the control source property with the expression, the control becomes a **calculated control**. If the expression is just a single field (for example, =[Cost]), the control would be a **bound control**. *Why? The control is bound (tied) to the corresponding field.* The process of converting an unbound control to a bound control is called **binding**. Expressions can also be arithmetic operations: for example, calculating the sum of Cost and current due. Many times, you need to **concatenate**, or combine, two or more text data items into a single expression; the process is called **concatenation**. To concatenate text data, you use the **ampersand (&)** operator. For example, =[Owner First Name] & ' ' & [Owner Last Name] indicates the concatenation of a first name, a single blank space, and a last name.

The following steps add text boxes and create calculated controls. Remember that controls can be resized by clicking the control to select it and then dragging the edge of the control to the desired size.

1

- Click the Text Box tool (Report Design Tools Design tab | Controls group) and move the pointer to the approximate position shown in Figure 6–22.

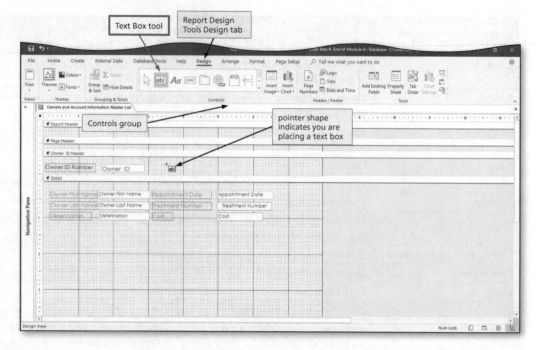

Figure 6–22

2

- Click the position shown in Figure 6–22 to place a text box on the report (Figure 6–23).

Q&A My text box overlapped an object already on the screen. Is that a problem?
No. You can always move and/or resize your text box to the desired location and size later.

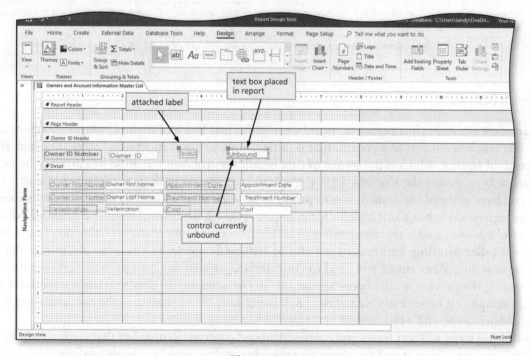

Figure 6–23

3

- Click in the text box to produce an insertion point (Figure 6–24).

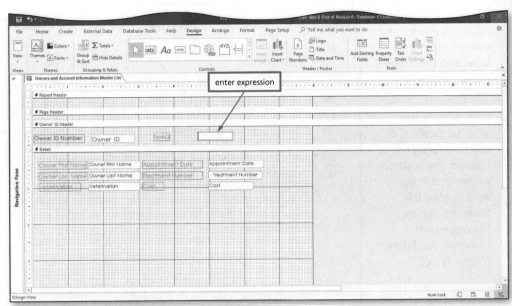

Q&A I inadvertently clicked somewhere else, so the text box was no longer selected. When I clicked the text box a second time, it was selected, but there was no insertion point. What should I do?
Simply click another time.

Figure 6–24

4

- In the text box, type `=[Owner First Name] & ' ' & [Owner Last Name]` to display the first name of the owner, followed by a space, and then the last name of the owner.

Q&A Could I use the Expression Builder instead of typing the expression?
Yes. Click the Property Sheet button and then click the Build button, which contains three dots, next to the Control Source property.

Do I need to use single quotes (')?
No. You could also use double quotes (").

- Click in the text box label to select the label and then click the label a second time to produce an insertion point (Figure 6–25).

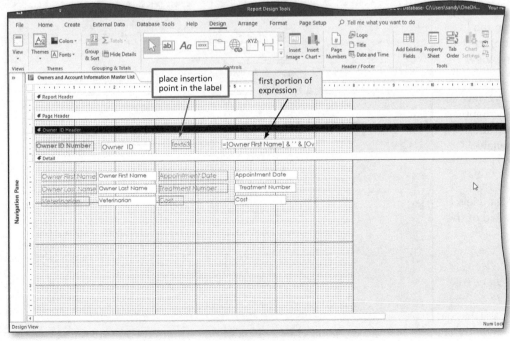

Figure 6–25

5

- Use BACKSPACE or DELETE to erase the current entry in the label and then type **Name** as the new entry.

- Click outside the label to deselect it and then drag the label to the position shown in the figure by dragging the Move handle in the upper-left corner of the label (Figure 6–26).

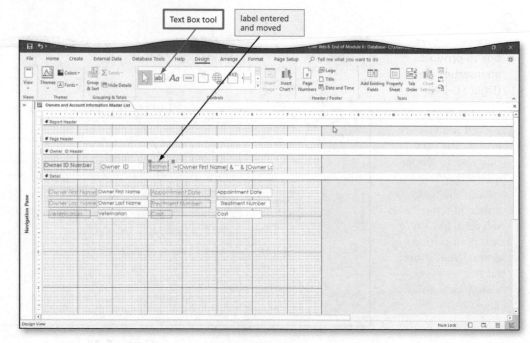

Figure 6–26

6

- Save the report.

Q&A My label is not in the correct position. What should I do?

Click outside the label to deselect it, click the label, and then drag it to the desired position.

To View the Report in Print Preview

The following steps view the report in Print Preview. *Why? As you are working on a report in Design view, it is useful to periodically view the report to gauge how it will look containing data. One way to do so is to use Print Preview.*

1

- Click the View button arrow (Report Design Tools Design tab | Views group) to produce the View menu.

- Click Print Preview on the View menu to view the report in Print Preview (Figure 6–27).

Q&A What would happen if I clicked the View button instead of the View button arrow?

The icon on the View button is the icon for Report View, so you would view the results in Report view. This is another useful way to view a report, but compared with Print Preview, Report View does not give as accurate a picture of how the final printed report will look.

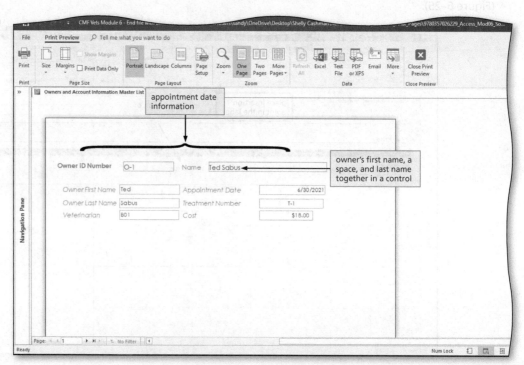

Figure 6–27

The treatment number field does not appear centered in the control. Also, the fields from the next appointment appear at the bottom of the report. How can I address these issues?

You will address these issues in the next sections.

2

- Click the 'Close Print Preview' button (Print Preview tab | Close Preview group) to return to Design view.

Other Ways
1. Click Print Preview button on status bar

To Format a Control

Why? *When you add controls to a report, you often need to format the control, for example, to add a bold or an alignment format.* You can use a control's property sheet to change the control's property. If a property does not appear on the screen, you have two choices. You can click the tab on which the property is located. For example, if it were a control related to data, you would click the Data tab to show only data-related properties. Many people, however, prefer to click the All tab, which shows all properties, and then simply scroll through the properties, if necessary, until locating the appropriate property. You can also increase or decrease the size of a control by clicking the control to select it and then dragging the edge of the control to the desired size. The following steps change the format of the Treatment Number control to Center by changing the Text Align of the Format property.

1

- If the field list is open, remove it by clicking the 'Add Existing Fields' button (Report Design Tools Design tab | Tools group).
- Click the control containing Treatment Number to select it, and then click the Property Sheet button (Report Design Tools Design tab | Tools group) to display the property sheet.
- If necessary, click the All tab (Figure 6–28).

 Experiment

- Click the other tabs in the property sheet to see the types of properties on each tab. When finished, once again click the All tab.

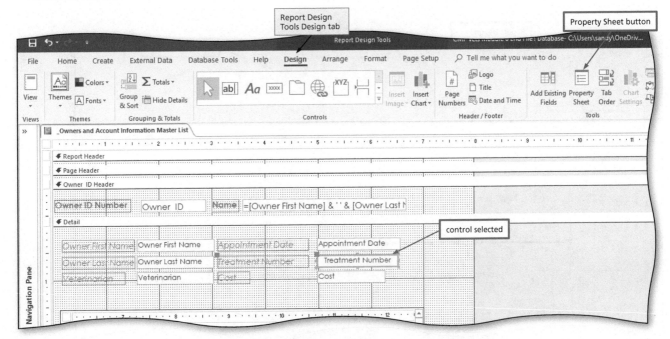

Figure 6–28

- If necessary, click the Text Align property box, click the arrow that appears, and then click Center to select Center as the control's alignment.
- Remove the property sheet by clicking the Property Sheet button (Report Design Tools Design tab | Tools group) a second time.
- Preview the report using Print Preview to see the effect of the property changes.
- Click the 'Close Print Preview' button (Print Preview tab | Close Preview group) to return to Design view.

Other Ways

1. Right-click control, click Properties

To Group Controls

The following steps group the controls within the Detail section. **Why?** *If your report contains a collection of controls that you will frequently want to format in the same way, you can simplify the process of selecting all the controls by grouping them. Once they are grouped, selecting any control in the group automatically selects all of the controls in the group. You can then apply the desired change to all the controls.*

- Click the Owner First Name control to select it.

Q&A Do I click the white space or the label?
Click the white space.

- While holding the SHIFT key down, click all the other controls in the Detail section to select them.

Q&A Does it matter in which order I select the other controls?
No. It is only important that you ultimately select all the controls.

- Release SHIFT.
- Display the Report Design Tools Arrange tab.
- Click the Size/Space button (Report Design Tools Arrange tab | Sizing & Ordering group) to display the Size/Space menu (Figure 6–29)

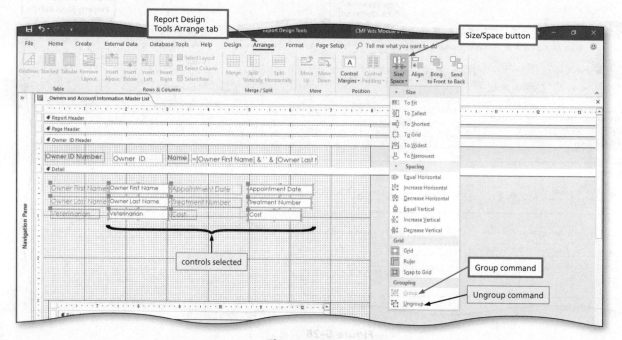

Figure 6–29

2

- Click Group on the Size/Space button menu to group the controls.

Q&A What if I make a mistake and group the wrong collection of controls?
Ungroup the controls using the following steps, and then group the correct collection of controls.

TO UNGROUP CONTROLS

If you no longer need to simultaneously modify all the controls you have placed in a group, you can ungroup the controls. To do so, you would use the following steps.

1. Click any of the controls in a group to select the entire group.
2. Display the Report Design Tools Arrange tab.
3. Click the Size/Space button (Report Design Tools Arrange tab | Sizing & Ordering group) to display the Size/Space button menu.
4. Click the Ungroup button on the Size/Space button menu to ungroup the controls.

Can you group controls in forms?
Yes. The process is identical to the process of grouping controls in reports.

CONSIDER THIS

To Modify Grouped Controls

To modify grouped controls, click any control in the group to select the entire group. *Why? Any change you make then affects all controls in the group.* The following steps bold the controls in the group, resize them, and then change the border style.

1

- If necessary, click any one of the grouped controls to select the group.

- Display the Report Design Tools Format tab.

- Click the Bold button (Report Design Tools Format tab | Font group) to bold all the controls in the group (Figure 6–30).

- Click the Property Sheet button (Report Design Tools Design tab | Tools group) to display the property sheet for the grouped controls.

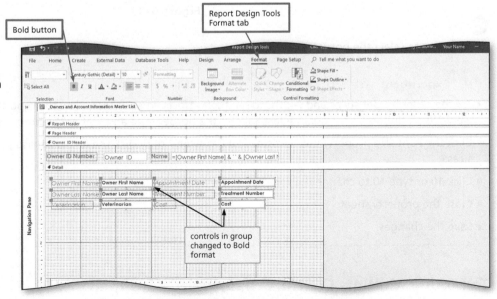

Figure 6–30

 Q&A How do I change only one control in the group?
Double-click the control to select just the one control and not the entire group. You then can make any change you want to that control.

Do I need to use the Owner First Name field or could I use another field?
Any field in the group will work.

- With the All tab (Property Sheet) selected, ensure the Border Style property is set to Solid. If it is not, click the Border Style property box to display an arrow, click the arrow to display the list of available border styles, and click Solid.

- Click the Border Width property box to display an arrow and then click the arrow to display the list of available border widths (Figure 6–31).

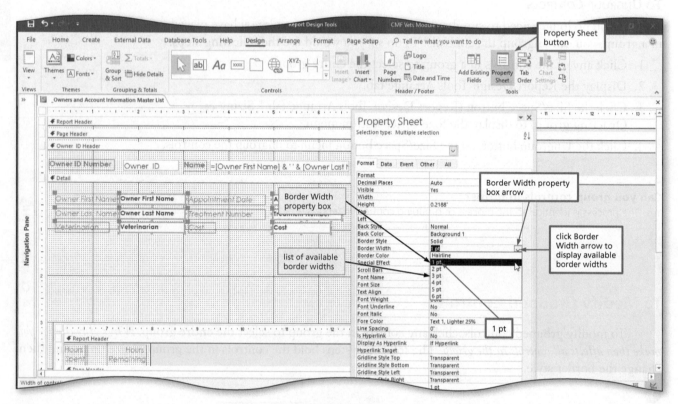

Figure 6–31

- Click 1 pt to select the border width.

 **Experiment**

- Try the other border styles and widths to see their effects. In each case, view the report and then return to Design view. When finished, once again select Solid as the border style and 1 pt as the border width.

- Click the Font Size property box to display an arrow and then click the arrow to display the list of available font sizes.

- Click 10 or type 10 to change the font size to 10.

- Close the property sheet.

- Save the changes.

To Modify Multiple Controls That Are Not Grouped

To modify multiple controls that are not grouped together, you must simultaneously select all the controls you want to modify. To do so, click one of the controls and then hold the SHIFT key down while selecting the others. The following steps italicize all the labels in the Detail section and then bold all the controls and labels in the Owner ID Header section. Finally, the steps increase the size of the Name control. *Why? With the current size, some names are not displayed completely.*

1

- Click the label for the Owner First Name control to select it.

- While holding the SHIFT key down, click the labels for all the other controls in the Detail section to select them.

- Release the SHIFT key.

- Display the Report Design Tools Format tab.

- Click the Italic button (Report Design Tools Format tab | Font group) to italicize the labels (Figure 6–32).

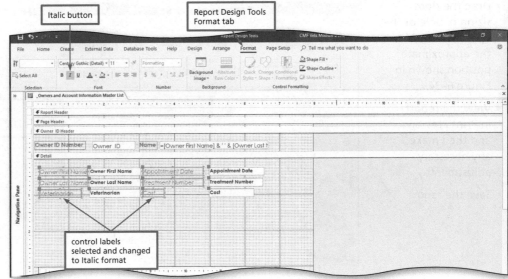

Figure 6–32

2

- Click in the vertical ruler to the left of the Owner ID control to select all the controls in the section.

Q&A | What exactly is selected when I click in the vertical ruler?
If you picture a horizontal line through the point you clicked, any control that intersects that horizontal line would be selected.

- Use the buttons on the Report Design Tools Arrange tab to align the controls on the top, if necessary.

- Display the Report Design Tools Format tab, if necessary, and then click the Bold button (Report Design Tools Format tab | Font group) to bold all the selected controls (Figure 6–33).

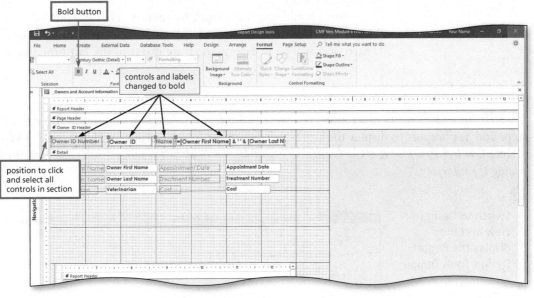

Figure 6–33

3

- Click outside the selected controls to deselect them. Click the control containing the expression for the owner's name to select it.

Q&A | Why do I have to deselect the controls and then select one of them a second time?
If you do not do so, any action you take would apply to all the selected controls rather than just the one you want.

- Drag the right sizing handle of the selected control to the approximate position shown in Figure 6–34.

- View the report in Print Preview and then make any necessary adjustments.

- Save the report.

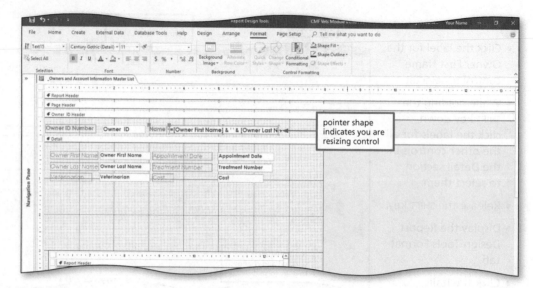

Figure 6–34

Undoing and Saving

Remember that if you make a mistake, you can often correct it by clicking the Undo button on the Quick Access Toolbar. Clicking the Undo button will reverse your most recent change. You can also click the Undo button more than once to reverse multiple changes.

You should save your work frequently. That way, if you have problems that the Undo button will not fix, you can close the report without saving it and open it again. The report will be in exactly the state it was in the last time you saved it.

To Add a Subreport

To add a subreport to a report, you use the Subform/Subreport tool on the Design tab. The following steps add a subreport to display the workshop data, after first ensuring the 'Use Control Wizards' button is selected. **Why?** *Provided the 'Use Control Wizards' button is selected, a wizard will guide you through the process of adding the subreport.*

- Switch to Design view and then display the Report Design Tools Design tab.

- Click the More button, which is shown in Figure 6–35a (Report Design Tools Design tab | Controls group), to display a gallery of available tools (Figure 6–35b).

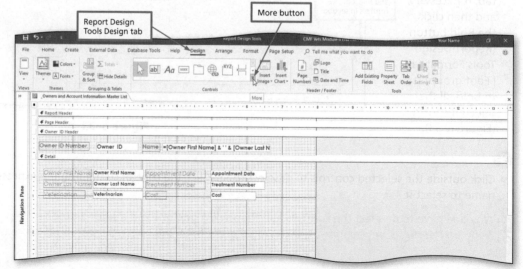

Figure 6–35a More Button

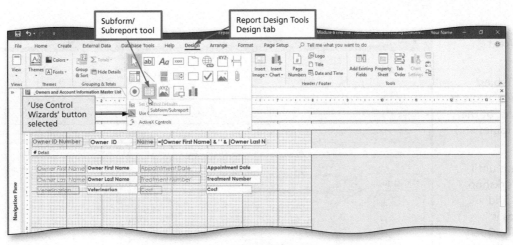

Figure 6–35b Design Tools Gallery

2

- Be sure the 'Use Control Wizards' button is selected, click the Subform/ Subreport tool, and then move the pointer, which has changed to a plus sign with a subreport, to the approximate position shown in Figure 6–36.

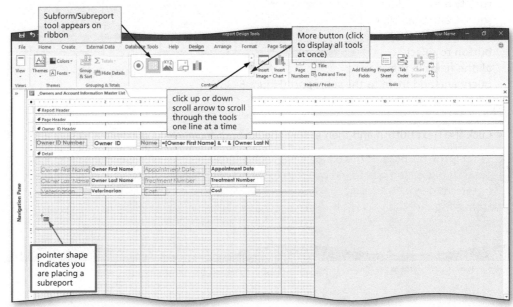

Figure 6–36

3

- Click the position shown in Figure 6–36 to place the subreport and display the SubReport Wizard dialog box. Be sure the 'Use existing Tables and Queries' option button is selected (Figure 6–37).

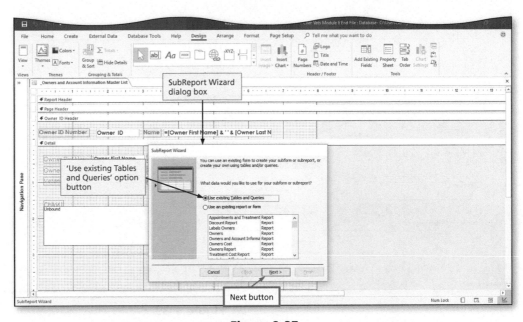

Figure 6–37

- Click the Next button.
- Click the Tables/ Queries box arrow to display a list of the available tables and queries.
- Scroll down until Query: Workshop Offerings and Workshops is visible, click Query: Workshop Offerings and Workshops to specify it as the data source, and then click the 'Add All Fields' button to select all the fields in the query and add them to the subreport (Figure 6–38).

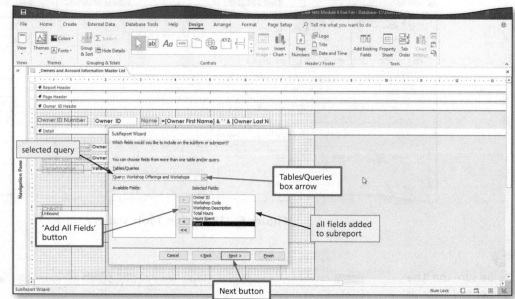

Figure 6–38

- Click the Next button and then ensure the 'Choose from a list.' option button is selected (Figure 6–39).

Q&A What is the purpose of this dialog box?
You use this dialog box to indicate the fields that link the main report (referred to as a "form") to the subreport (referred to as a "subform"). If the fields have the same name, as they often will, you can simply select 'Choose from a list' and then accept the selection Access already has made.

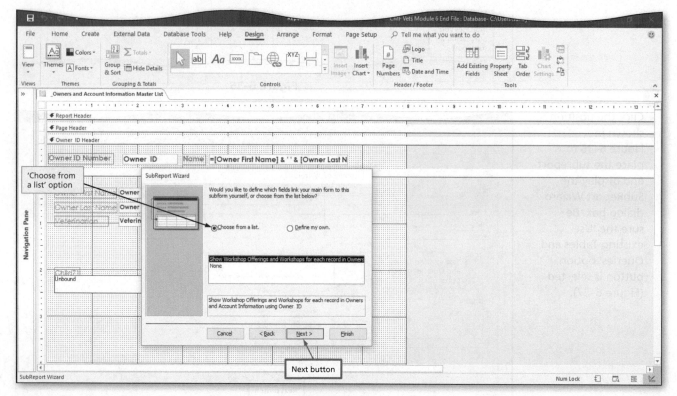

Figure 6–39

- Click the Next button, change the subreport name to **Workshop Offerings by Owner ID**, and then click the Finish button to add the subreport to the Owner and Account Information Master List report (Figure 6–40).

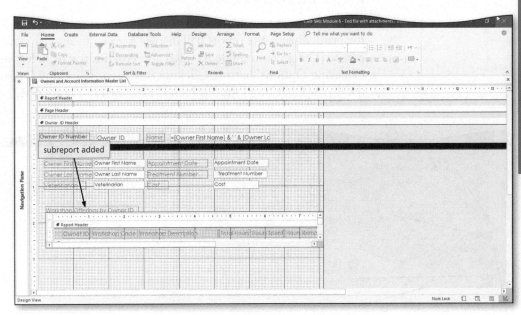

Figure 6–40

- Click outside the subreport to deselect the subreport.
- Save your changes.
- Close the report.

Break Point: If you wish to stop working through the module at this point, you can resume the project at a later time by starting Access, opening the database called CMF Vets, and continuing to follow the steps from this location forward.

To Open the Subreport in Design View

The following step opens the subreport in Design view so it can be modified. *Why? The subreport appears as a separate report in the Navigation Pane. You can modify it just as you modify any other report.*

1

- Open the Navigation Pane, scroll down so that the Workshop Offerings by Owner ID report appears, and then right-click the Workshop Offerings by Owner ID report to produce a shortcut menu.

- Click Design View on the shortcut menu to open the subreport in Design view (Figure 6–41). If necessary, increase

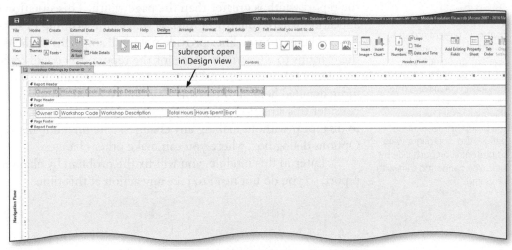

Figure 6–41

the size of the subreport by selecting it and dragging the border edges to the side.

Print Layout Issues

If there is a problem with your report, for example, a report that is too wide for the printed page, the report will display a green triangular symbol in the upper-left corner. The green triangle is called an **error indicator**. Clicking it displays an 'Error Checking Options' button. Clicking the 'Error Checking Options' button produces the 'Error Checking Options menu,' as shown in Figure 6–42.

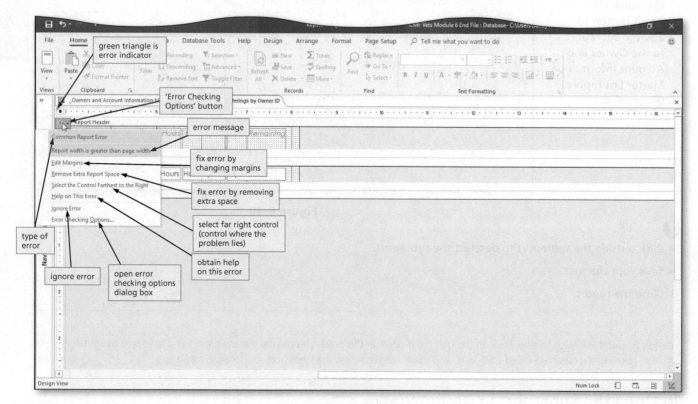

Figure 6–42

BTW
Subreports
Subreports provide more control in presenting data effectively than multiple levels of grouping can. Because grouping places headers in columns, it often can be difficult to determine the relationship between the group header and the detail. Also, you might want to present subreports side by side. You cannot do that with grouping.

The first line in the menu is simply a statement of the type of error that occurred. The second is a description of the specific error, in this case, the fact that the report width is greater than the page width. This situation could lead to data not appearing where you expect it to, as well as the printing of some blank pages.

The next three lines provide potential solutions to the error. You could change the margins to allow more space for the report. You could remove some extra space. You could select the control farthest to the right and move it. The fourth line gives more detailed help on the error. The Ignore Error command instructs Access to not consider this situation an error. Selecting Ignore Error would cause the error indicator to disappear without making any changes. The final line displays the Error Checking Options dialog box, where you can make other changes.

Later in this module, you will fix the problem by changing the width of the report, so you do not need to take any action at this time.

To Modify the Controls in the Subreport

The following step modifies the subreport by deleting the Owner ID control and revising the appearance of the column headings. ***Why?*** *Because the Owner ID appears in the main report, it does not need to be duplicated in the subreport.*

- Hide the Navigation Pane.

- Click the Owner ID control in the Detail section to select the control. Hold the SHIFT key down and click the Owner ID control in the Report Header section to select both controls.

- With both controls selected, press DELETE to delete the controls.

- Adjust the placement of the labels in the Report Header section to match those shown in Figure 6–43. The last three field headings are longer than the other headings; therefore, you might want to place the heading on two lines instead of just one line.

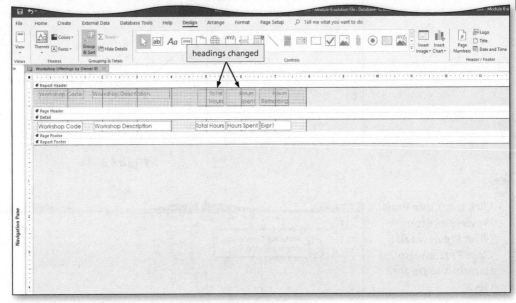

- Break the heading for the Total Hours column over two lines by clicking in front of the word, Hours, to produce an insertion point and then pressing SHIFT+ENTER to move the second word to a second line.

Figure 6–43

- Break the headings for the Hours Spent and Hours Remaining columns over two lines using the same technique.

- Change the sizes and positions of the controls to match those in the figure by selecting the controls and dragging the sizing handles.

Q&A | Why does Expr1 appear in the Detail section under the Hours Remaining label?
Expr1 indicates that Hours Remaining is a calculated control.

How can you adjust fields where some of the entries are too long to fit in the available space?
This problem can be addressed in several ways.

1. Move the controls to allow more space between controls. Then, drag the appropriate handles on the controls that need to be expanded to enlarge them.

2. Use the Font Size property to select a smaller font size. This will allow more data to fit in the same space.

3. Use the Can Grow property. By changing the value of this property from No to Yes, the data can be spread over two lines, thus allowing all the data to print. Access will split data at natural break points, such as commas, spaces, and hyphens.

CONSIDER THIS

To Change the Can Grow Property

The third approach to handling entries that are too long is the easiest to use and also produces a very readable report. The following steps change the Can Grow property for the Workshop Description field. ***Why?*** *Changing the Can Grow property allows Access to optimize the size of fields in reports.*

1

- Click the View button arrow and then click Print Preview to preview the report (Figure 6–44). If an error message appears, indicating the report is too wide, click OK.

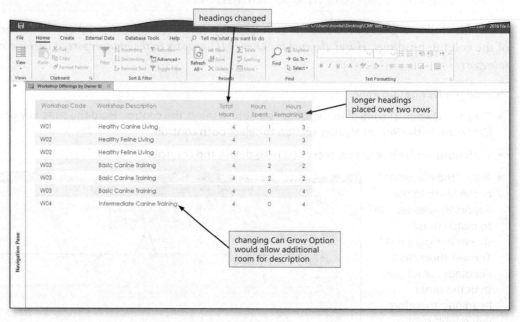

Figure 6–44

2

- Click the 'Close Print Preview' button (Print Preview tab | Close Preview group) to return to Design view.

- If necessary, click outside all of the selected controls to deselect the controls.

- Click the Workshop Description control in the Detail section to select it.

- Click the Property Sheet button (Report Design Tools Design tab | Tools group) to display the property sheet.

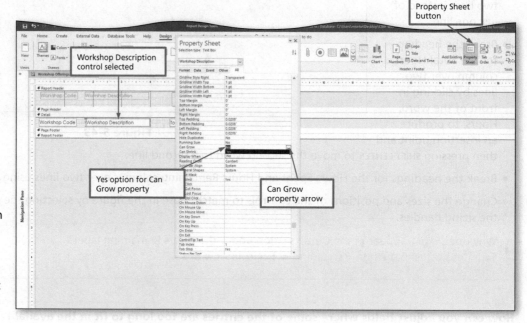

Figure 6–45

- With the All tab selected, scroll down until the Can Grow property appears, and then click the Can Grow property box arrow to display the list of possible values for the Can Grow property (Figure 6–45).

Q&A What is the effect of the Can Shrink property?

If the value of the Can Shrink property is set to Yes, Access will remove blank lines that occur when the field is empty.

3

- Click Yes in the list to allow the Workshop Description control to grow as needed.

- Close the property sheet.

To Change the Appearance of the Controls in the Subreport

Why? CMF Vets managers prefer certain formatting for the subreport controls. The following steps change the controls in the Detail section to bold. They also change the background color in the Report Header section to white.

- Drag the right boundary of the subreport to the approximate position shown in Figure 6–46.

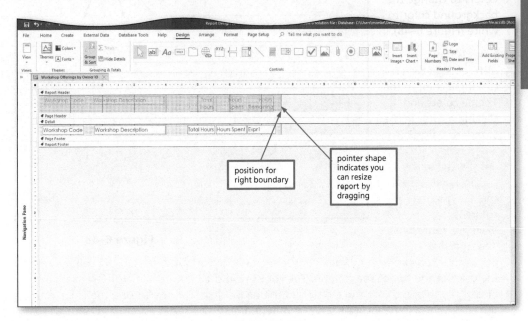

Figure 6–46

2
- Display the Report Design Tools Format tab.

- Click the ruler to the left of the controls in the Detail section to select the controls, and then click the Bold button (Report Design Tools Format tab | Font group) to bold the controls.

- Click the title bar for the Report Header to select the header without selecting any of the controls in the header.

- Click the Background Color button arrow (Report Design Tools Format tab | Font group) to display a color palette (Figure 6–47).

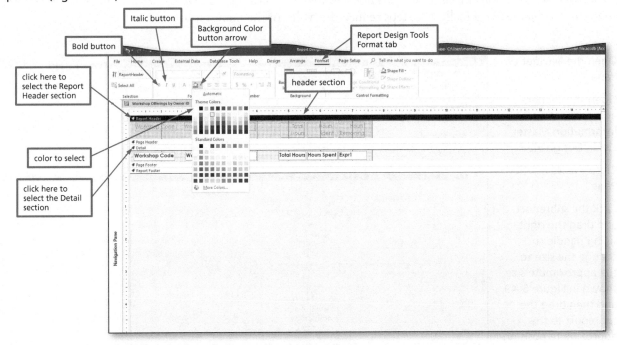

Figure 6–47

- Click White,
  Background 1 in the
  first row, first column
  of the Standard
  Colors to change the
  background color to
  white (Figure 6–48).

Q&A What is the
difference between
clicking a color in the
Theme colors and
clicking a color in the
Standard Colors?
The theme colors
are specific to the
currently selected
theme. The first
column, for
example, represents
"background 1," one

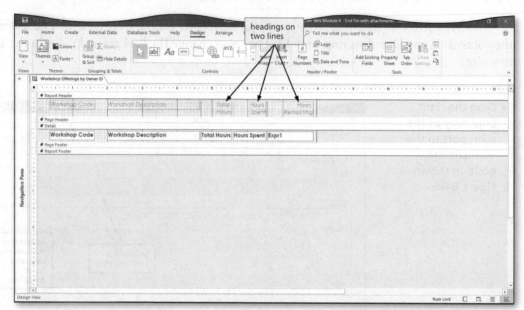

Figure 6–48

of the selected background colors in the theme. The various entries in the column represent different intensities of
the color at the top of the column. The colors would be different if a different theme were selected. If you select
one of the theme colors and a different theme is selected in the future, the color you selected would change to
the color in the same location. On the other hand, if you select a standard color, a change of theme would have no
effect on the color.

- Save the changes, and then close the subreport.

To Resize the Subreport and the Report in Design View

The following steps resize the subreport control in the main report. They then reduce the height of the
detail section. **Why?** *Any additional white space at the bottom of the detail section appears as extra space at the end of each
detail line in the final report.* Finally, the steps reduce the width of the main report.

- Open the Navigation
  Pane.

- Open the Owners
  and Account
  Information Master
  List in Design view.

- Close the Navigation
  Pane.

- Click the subreport
  and drag the right
  sizing handle to
  change the size to
  the approximate size
  shown in Figure 6–49,
  and then drag the
  subreport to the
  approximate position
  shown in the figure.

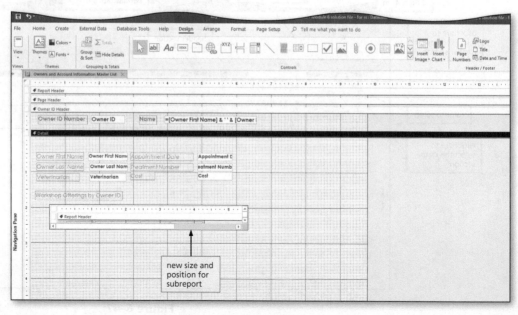

Figure 6–49

2

- Scroll down in the main report so that the lower boundary of the Detail section appears, and then drag the lower boundary of the detail section up to a position about one inch below the subreport.
- Switch to Report view; your report should resemble Figure 6–50. If necessary, return to Design view and adjust the boundaries.

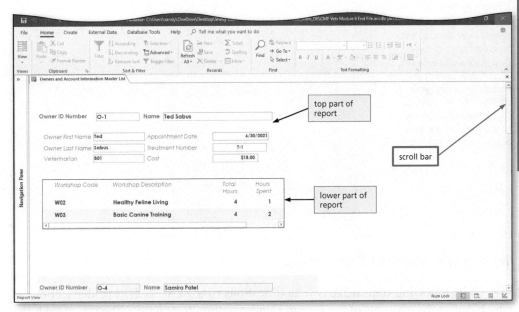

Figure 6–50

Q&A I scrolled down to see the lower boundary of the Detail section, and the controls are no longer on the screen. What is the easiest way to drag the boundary when the position to which I want to drag it is not visible?

You do not need to see the location to drag to it. As you get close to the top of the visible portion of the screen, Access will automatically scroll. You might find it easier, however, to drag the boundary near the top of the visible portion of the report, use the scroll bar to scroll up, and then drag some more. You might have to scroll more than once.

3

- If necessary, scroll back up to the top of the report, click the label for the subreport (the label that reads Workshop Offerings by Owner ID), and then press DELETE to delete the label.
- Resize the report by dragging its right border to the location shown in Figure 6–51.

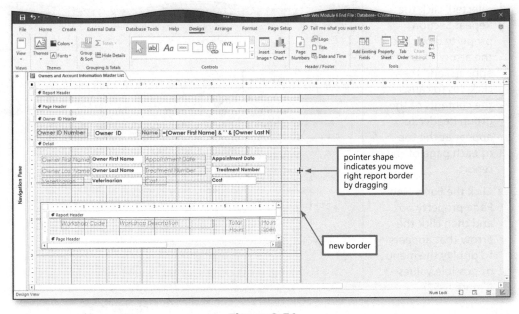

Figure 6–51

BTW
**Viewing Report
Modifications**
As you work through this
module, switch between
Design view and either
Report view or Print Preview
frequently to view your
changes. An easy way to
switch back and forth is
to use the different view
buttons on the status bar.

To Modify Section Properties

The following steps make two modifications to the Owner ID Header section. The first modification, which causes the contents of the Group Header section to appear at the top of each page, changes the Repeat Section property to Yes. *Why? Without this change, the Owner ID and name would only appear at the beginning of the group of accounts of that owner ID. If the list of accounts occupies more than one page, it would not be apparent on subsequent pages which owner ID is associated with those accounts.* The second modification changes the Force New Page property to Before Section, causing each section to begin at the top of a page.

- Click the Owner ID Header bar to select the header, and then click the Property Sheet button (Report Design Tools Design tab | Tools group) to display the property sheet.

- With the All tab selected, click the Repeat Section property box, click the arrow that appears, and then click Yes to cause the contents of the group header to appear at the top of each page of the report.

- Click the Force New Page property box, and then click the arrow that appears to display the menu of possible values (Figure 6–52).

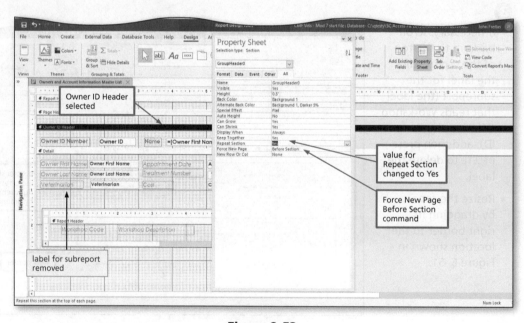

Figure 6–52

- Click Before Section to cause a new group to begin at the top of the next page.

- Close the property sheet.

To Add a Title, Page Number, and Date

You can add a title, page number, and date to a report using tools on the Design tab. The following steps add a title, page number, and date to the Owners and Account Information Master List report. The steps move the date to the page header by first cutting the date from its original position and then pasting it into the page header. *Why? The date is automatically added to the report header, which means it only would appear once at the beginning of the report. If it is in the page header, the date will appear at the top of each page.*

1

- Display the Report Design Tools Design tab, if necessary, and then click the Title button (Report Design Tools Design tab | Header/Footer group) to add a title.

The title is the same as the name of the report object. Can I change the report title without changing the name of the report object in the database?
Yes. The report title is a label, and you can change it using any of the techniques that you used for changing column headings and other labels.

- Click the Page Numbers button (Report Design Tools Design tab | Header/Footer group) to display the Page Numbers dialog box.

- Be sure the Page N and 'Top of Page [Header]' option buttons are selected.

- If necessary, click the Alignment arrow and select Left (Page Numbers dialog box) (Figure 6–53).

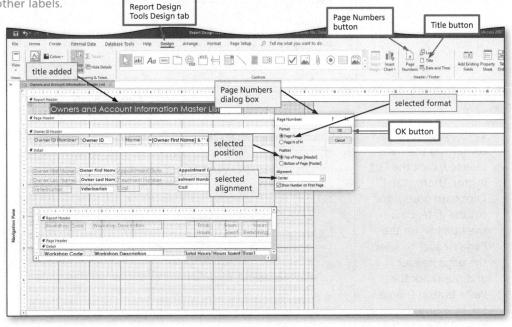

Figure 6–53

2

- Click OK (Page Numbers dialog box) to add the page number to the Report Header section.

- Click the 'Date and Time' button (Report Design Tools Design tab | Header/Footer group) to display the Date and Time dialog box.

- Click the option button for the third date format and click the Include Time check box to remove the check mark (Figure 6–54).

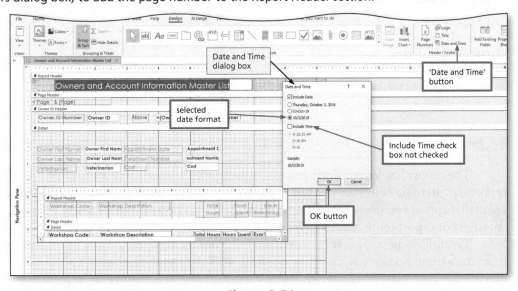

Figure 6–54

3

- Click the OK button (Date and Time dialog box) to add the date to the Report Header.

- Display the Home tab.

- If the Date control is no longer selected, click the Date control to select it (Figure 6–55).

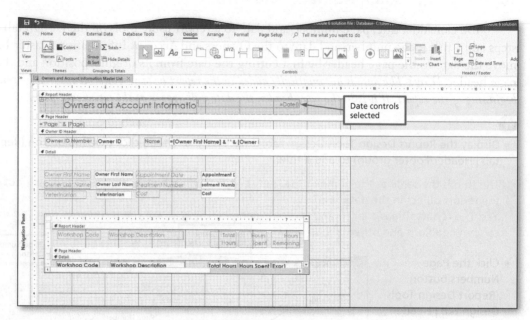

Figure 6–55

4

- With the control containing the date selected, click the Cut button (Home tab | Clipboard group) to cut the date, click the title bar for the Page Header to select the page header, and then click the Paste button (Home tab | Clipboard group) to paste the Date control at the beginning of the page header.

- Drag the Date control, which is currently sitting on top of the Page Number control, to the position shown in Figure 6–56.

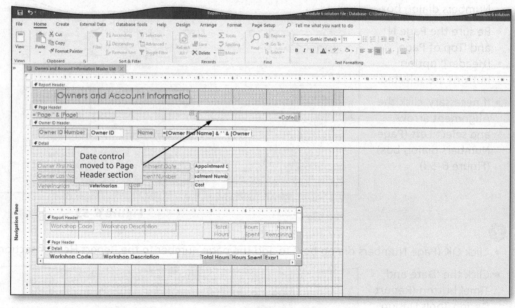

Figure 6–56

To Remove the Header Background Color and the Alternate Color

The report header currently has a blue background, which is not what CMF Vets wants. In addition, the report has alternate colors, as you saw in Figure 6–44. An **alternate color** is a color different from the main color that appears on every other line in a datasheet or report. Using alternate colors can sometimes make a datasheet or report more readable, but is not always desirable.

The following steps first remove the color from the report header. They then remove the alternate colors from the various sections in the report, starting with the Detail section. *Why? Access automatically assigns alternate colors within the report. In reports with multiple sections, the alternate colors can be confusing. If you do not want these alternate colors, you must remove them.*

1

- Right-click the title bar for the Report Header to select the header without selecting any of the controls in the header and produce a menu.

- Point to the 'Fill/Back Color' arrow to display a color palette (Figure 6–57).

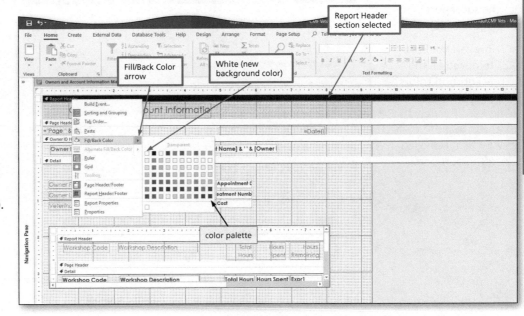

Figure 6–57

2

- Click White, Background 1 in the first row, first column of the color palette to change the background color for the header.

- Right-click a blank area of the Detail section to select the details section and produce a menu.

- Point to the 'Alternate Fill/Back Color' arrow to display a color palette (Figure 6–58).

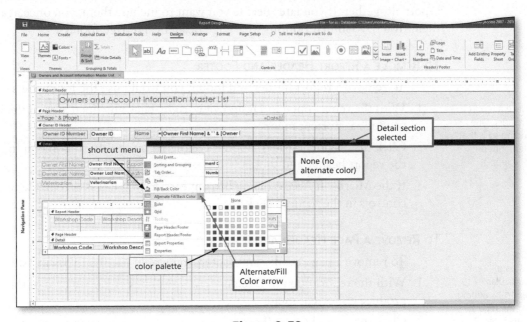

Figure 6–58

3

- Click None on the color palette to remove the alternate color for the Detail section.

- Save and then close the report. Open the subreport in Design view.

- Remove the header background color and the alternate color from the subreport, just as you removed them from the main report.

- Save and then close the subreport (Figure 6–59).

How can I be sure I removed all the background colors? Open the report in Print Preview to check that all color has been removed from the report.

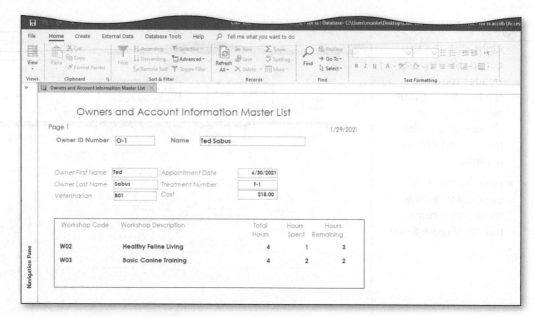

Figure 6–59

Headers and Footers

Access gives you some options for including or omitting headers and footers in your reports. They go together, so if you have a report header, you will also have a report footer. If you do not want one of the sections to appear, you can shrink its size so there is no room for any content, or you can remove the header or footer from your report altogether. If you later decide you want to include them, you once again can add them. You have similar options with page headers and page footers.

TO REMOVE A REPORT HEADER AND FOOTER

To remove a report header and footer, you would use the following steps.

1. With the report open in Design view, right-click any open area of the report to produce a shortcut menu.
2. Click the 'Report Header/Footer' command on the shortcut menu to remove the report header and footer.
3. If the Microsoft Access dialog box appears, asking if it is acceptable to delete any controls in the section, click Yes.

TO REMOVE A PAGE HEADER AND FOOTER

To remove a page header and footer, you would use the following steps.

1. With the report open in Design view, right-click any open area of the report to produce a shortcut menu.
2. Click the 'Page Header/Footer' command on the shortcut menu to remove the page header and footer.
3. If the Microsoft Access dialog box appears, asking if it is acceptable to delete any controls in the section, click Yes.

TO INSERT A REPORT HEADER AND FOOTER

To insert a report header and footer, you would use the following steps.

1. With the report open in Design view, right-click any open area of the report to produce a shortcut menu.
2. Click the 'Report Header/Footer' command on the shortcut menu to insert a report header and footer.

TO INSERT A PAGE HEADER AND FOOTER

To insert a page header and footer, you would use the following steps.

1. With the report open in Design view, right-click any open area of the report to produce a shortcut menu.
2. Click the 'Page Header/Footer' command on the shortcut menu to insert a page header and footer.

TO INCLUDE AN IMAGE IN A REPORT

You can include a picture (image) in a report. You can also use a picture (image) as the background on a report. To include an image in a report, you would use the following steps.

1. Open the report in Design view or Layout view.
2. Click the Insert Image button (Report Design Tools Design tab | Controls group), and then click the Browse command.
3. Select the desired image.
4. Click the desired location to add the image to the report.

TO USE AN IMAGE AS BACKGROUND FOR A REPORT

To include an image as a background for a report, you would use the following steps.

1. Open the report in Design view or Layout view.
2. Click anywhere in the report, click the Background Image button (Report Design Tools Format tab | Background group), and then click the Browse command.
3. Select the desired image for the background.

TO PUBLISH A REPORT

You can make a report available as an external document by publishing the report as either a PDF or XPS file. If you wanted to do so, you would use the following steps.

1. Select the report to be published in the Navigation Pane.
2. Display the External Data tab.
3. Click the PDF or XPS button (External Data tab | Export group) to display the Publish as PDF or XPS dialog box.
4. Select the appropriate Save as type (either PDF or XPS).
5. Select either 'Standard (publishing online and printing)' or 'Minimum size (publishing online).'
6. If you want to publish only a range of pages, click the Options button and select the desired range.

BTW
White Space
In page layout and report design, white space is the space on a printed page that is left unmarked. This includes margins, spacing between records, and space around graphics. Not enough white space can make a report look cluttered and can be difficult to read. Too much white space wastes paper. Thoughtful use of white space can make a report more visually appealing.

BTW
Distributing a Document
Instead of printing and distributing a hard copy of a document, you can distribute the document electronically. Options include sending the document via email; posting it on cloud storage (such as OneDrive) and sharing the file with others; posting it on a social networking site, blog, or other website; and sharing a link associated with an online location of the document. You also can create and share a PDF or XPS image of the document, so that users can view the file in Acrobat Reader or XPS Viewer instead of in Access.

7. Click the Publish button to publish the report in the desired format.

8. If you want to save the export steps, click the 'Save export steps' check box, then click the Save Export button. If not, click the Close button.

Break Point: If you wish to stop working through the module at this point, you can resume the project at a later time by starting Access, opening the database called CMF Vets, and continuing to follow the steps from this location forward.

Creating a Second Report

CMF Vets managers would also like a report that groups accounts by Owner ID and Treatment Costs. The report should include subtotals and a discount amount based on the cost of the treatments. Finally, it should show the cost of the treatment less the discount. The discount amount is based on the treatment cost. Accounts that have treatment costs more than $20 will receive a 20 percent discount, and accounts that have treatment costs $20 or less will not receive a discount.

BTW
Graphs
You can add graphs (charts) to a report using the Chart tool. To add a graph (chart) to a report, click the Chart tool, move the pointer to the desired location, and click the position to place the graph. Follow the directions in the Chart Wizard dialog box to specify the data source for the chart, the values for the chart, and the chart type.

To Create a Second Report

The following steps create the Discount Report, select the record source, and specify grouping and sorting options.

1 If necessary, close the Navigation Pane.

2 Display the Create tab and then click the Report Design button (Create tab | Reports group) to create a report in Design view.

3 Ensure the selector for the entire report, which is the box in the upper-left corner of the report, contains a small black square indicating it is selected, and then click the Property Sheet button (Report Design Tools Design tab | Tools group) to display a property sheet.

4 With the All tab selected, click the Record Source property box arrow, and then click the Owners and Account Information query to select the query as the record source for the report.

5 Close the property sheet.

6 Click the Group & Sort button (Report Design Tools Design tab | Grouping & Totals group) to display the 'Group, Sort, and Total' pane.

7 Click the 'Add a group' button to display the list of available fields for grouping, and then click the Owner ID field to group by Owner ID. When you add a group, a header will appear above each Owner ID.

8 Click the 'Add a sort' button to display the list of available fields for sorting, and then click the Appointment Date field to sort by appointment date.

9 Remove the 'Group, Sort, and Total' pane by clicking the Group & Sort button (Report Design Tools Design tab | Grouping & Totals group).

10 Click the Save button on the Quick Access Toolbar, type **Discount Report** as the report name, and click OK to save the report.

Q&A | Why save it at this point?
You do not have to save it at this point. It is a good idea to save it often, however. Doing so will give you a convenient point from which to restart if you have problems. If you have problems, you could close the report without saving it. When you reopen the report, it will be in the state it was in when you last saved it.

To Remove the Color from the Report Header

The following steps remove the color from the Report Header section by changing the background color for the header to white.

1 Click the View button arrow and then click Design View to return to Design view.

2 Right-click the report header to produce a menu.

3 Point to the 'Fill/Back Color' arrow on the shortcut menu to display a color palette.

4 Click White, Background 1 in the first row, first column to change the background color to white.

To Add and Move Fields in a Report

As with the previous reports, you can add a field to the report by dragging the field from the field list. After adding a field to a report, you can adjust the placement of the field's label, separating it from the control to which it is attached by dragging the move handle in its upper-left corner. This technique does not work, however, if you want to drag the attached label to a section different from the control's section. If you want the label to be in a different section, you must select the label, cut the label, select the section to which you want to move the label, and then paste the label. You then can move the label to the desired location.

The following steps add the Owner ID field to the Owner ID Header section and then moves the label to the Page Header section. *Why? The label should appear at the top of each page, rather than in the group header.*

1

- Click the 'Add Existing Fields' button (Report Design Tools Design tab | Tools group) to display a field list. (Figure 6–60).

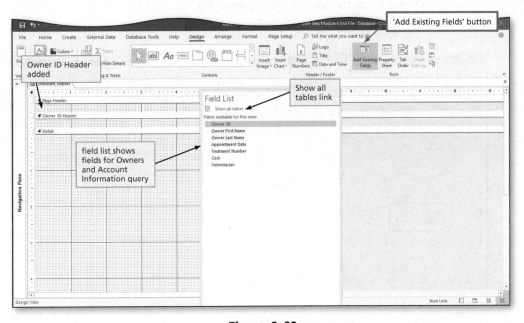

Figure 6–60

Q&A | My field list displays 'Show only fields in the current record source,' not 'Show all tables,' as in the figure. What should I do?
Click the 'Show only fields in the current record source' link at the top of the field list to display only those fields in the Owners and Account Information query.

• Drag the Owner ID field to the approximate position shown in Figure 6–61.

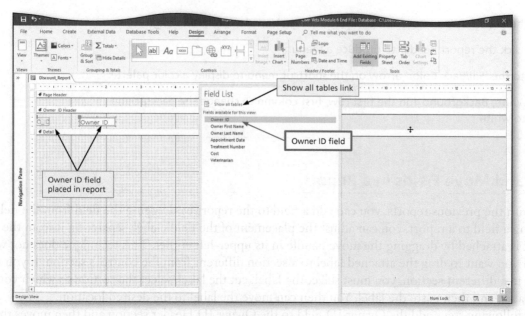

Figure 6–61

• Click the label for the Owner ID control to select it (Figure 6–62).

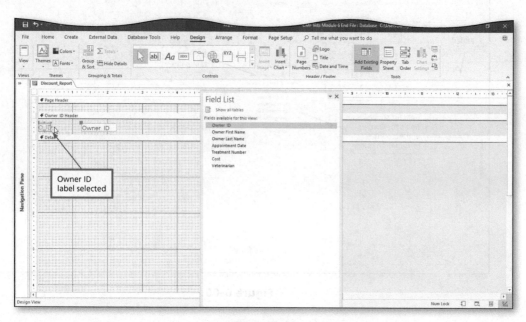

Figure 6–62

4

- Display the Home tab.
- Click the Cut button (Home tab | Clipboard group) to cut the label.
- Click the Page Header bar to select the page header (Figure 6–63).

Q&A Do I have to click the bar, or could I click somewhere else within the section?
You could also click within the section. Clicking the bar is usually safer, however. If you click in a section intending to select the section, but click within one of the controls in the section, you will select the control rather than the section. Clicking the bar always selects the section.

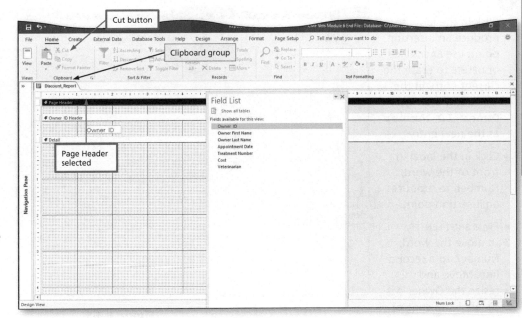

Figure 6–63

5

- Click the Paste button (Home tab | Clipboard group) to paste the label in the Page Header section (Figure 6–64).

Q&A When would I want to click the Paste button arrow rather than just the button?
Clicking the arrow displays the Paste button menu, which includes the Paste command and two additional commands. Paste Special allows you to paste data into different formats. Paste Append, which is available if you have cut or copied a record, allows you to paste the record to a table with a similar structure. If you want the simple Paste command, you can just click the button.

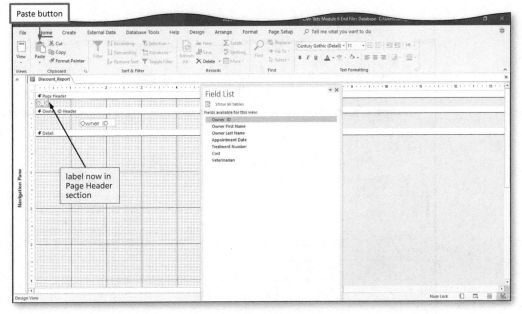

Figure 6–64

- Click in the label to produce an insertion point, use BACKSPACE or DELETE to erase the current entry in the label, and then type **Owner ID Number** as the new entry.

- Click in the label in front of the word, Number, to produce an insertion point.

- Press SHIFT+ENTER to move the word, Number, to a second line. Move and resize the Owner ID label and control as necessary to match Figure 6-65.

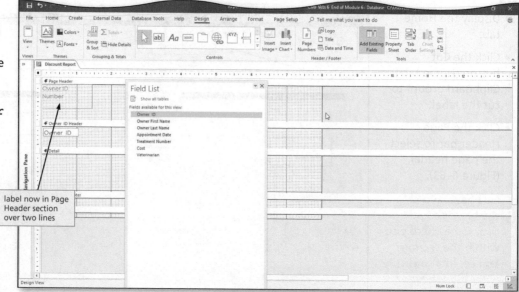

Figure 6–65

To Add the Remaining Fields

The following steps add all the remaining fields for the report by dragging them into the Detail section. **Why?** *Dragging them moves them onto the report, where you can now relocate the controls and labels individually to the desired locations.* The next steps move the labels into the Page Header section, and move the controls containing the fields to the appropriate locations.

- Select the Owner First Name, Owner Last Name, Appointment Date, Treatment Number, and Cost fields as shown in Figure 6–66.

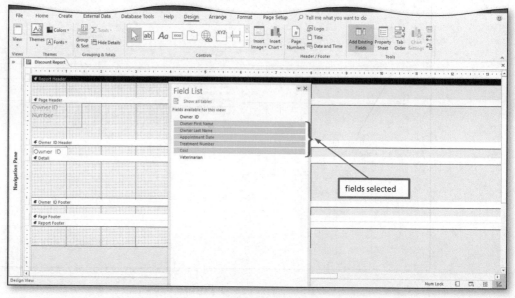

Figure 6–66

- Drag the Owner First Name, Owner Last Name, Appointment Date, Treatment Number, and Cost fields into the Detail section and close the field list as shown in Figure 6–67.

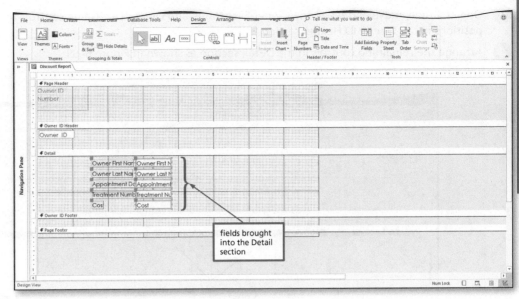

Figure 6–67

Could I drag them all at once?

Yes. You can select multiple fields by selecting the first field, holding down the SHIFT key, and then selecting other adjacent fields. To select fields that are not adjacent to each other, hold down the CTRL key and select the additional fields. Once you have selected multiple fields, you can drag them all at once. How you choose to select fields and drag them onto the report is a matter of personal preference.

When I paste the label, it is always placed at the left edge, superimposing the Owner ID control. Can I change where Access places it?

Unfortunately, when you paste to a different section, Access places the control at the left edge. You will need to drag each control to its proper location after pasting it into the Page Header section.

2 One at a time, move and resize the Owner First Name and Owner Last Name Appointment Date, Treatment Number, and Cost control labels to the Page Header section as shown in Figure 6–68.

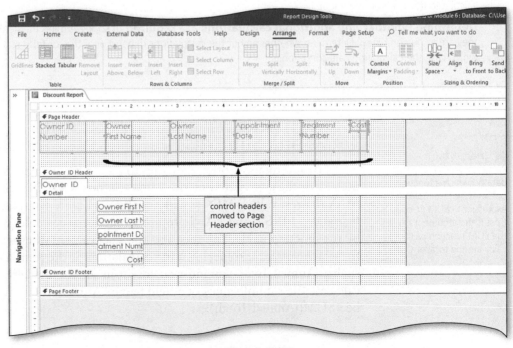

Figure 6–68

3 One at a time, move and resize the Owner First Name and Owner Last Name controls to the approximate positions in the Owner ID Header section.

4 Arrange the remaining controls in the Detail section as shown in Figure 6–69.

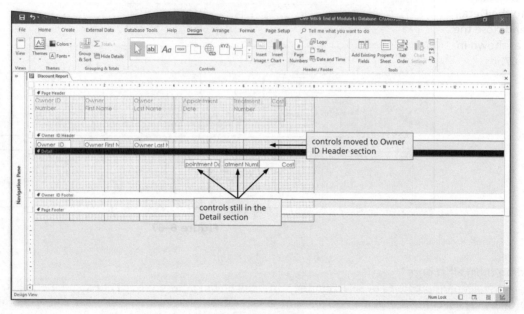

Figure 6–69

How will you incorporate calculations in the report?
Determine details concerning any calculations required for the report.

Determine whether to include calculations in the group and report footers. The group footers or report footers might require calculated data such as subtotals or totals. Determine whether the report needs other statistics that must be calculated (for example, average).

Determine whether any additional calculations are required. If so, determine the fields that are involved and how they are to be combined. Determine whether any of the calculations depend on a true or false statement for a criterion, in which case the calculations are conditional.

BTW
Arguments
An argument is a piece of data on which a function operates. For example, in the expression = SUM ([Cost]), Cost is the argument because the SUM function will calculate the total of Cost.

Totals and Subtotals

To add totals or other statistics to a footer, add a text box control. You can use any of the aggregate functions in a text box: COUNT, SUM, AVG (average), MAX (largest value), MIN (smallest value), STDEV (standard deviation), VAR (variance), FIRST, and LAST. To use a function, type an equal (=) sign, followed by the function name. You then include a set of parentheses containing the item for which you want to perform the calculation. If the item name contains spaces, such as Annual Total, you must enclose it in square brackets. For example, to calculate the sum of values of a field named Annual Total, the expression would be =SUM([Annual Total]).

Access will perform the calculation for the appropriate collection of records. If you enter the SUM expression in the Owner ID Footer section, Access will only calculate the subtotal for accounts with the given owner ID; that is, it will calculate the appropriate subtotal. If you enter the SUM expression in the Report Footer section, Access will calculate the total for all accounts.

1
- Use the Group and Sort pane to add an Owner ID footer.
- Click the Text Box tool (Report Design Tools Design tab | Controls group), and then point to the position shown in Figure 6–70.

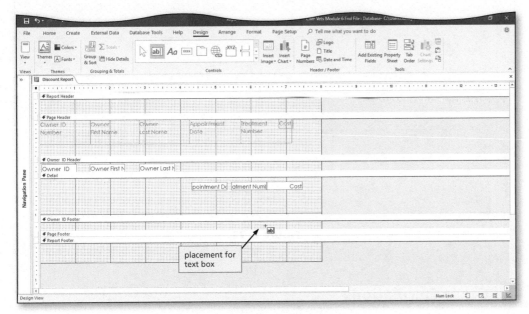

Figure 6–70

2
- Click the position shown in Figure 6–70 to place a text box (Figure 6–71).

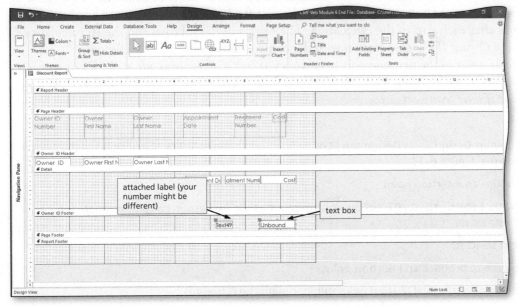

Figure 6–71

- Click the text box to produce an insertion point.

- Type **=Sum([Cost])** in the control to enter the expression calculation, and then press ENTER.

- Format the calculation to currency by clicking the Report Design Tools Format tab and clicking the 'Apply Currency Format' button.

- Click the text box label to select it.

- Click the label a second time to produce an insertion point.

- Use the DELETE or BACKSPACE key to delete the Text12 label (your number might be different).

- Type **Subtotal** as the label. Click outside the label to deselect it and then drag the label to the position shown in Figure 6–72.

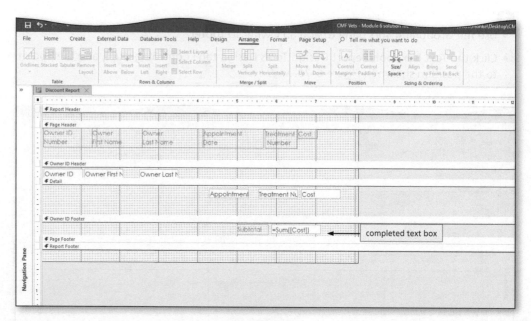

Figure 6–72

To Add Subtotals and Other Calculations

The following step creates a subtotal. The second calculation is a discount for treatment costs over $20. This discount is applied using the IIf (Immediate If) calculation. When using the IIf calculation, it first finds what you are looking for, which in this case are treatment costs over $20. Then, if a treatment cost is found to be over $20, you want to apply a 20 percent or (.20) discount to the treatment cost. But, if the treatment cost is $20 or less, then no discount is given. The IIf calculation for this example, would be entered manually in a control as follows: **=IIf([cost]>20,[cost]*0.2,0)**. Notice that the cost field needs to be in square brackets. Also, note that there are commas after each part of the calculation. The results of the subtotal and the IIf calculations will both be displayed in the Owner ID Footer section with the control labels Subtotal and Discount.

The steps change the format of the new controls to currency *Why?* *The requirements at CMF Vets managers indicate that the Discount Report should contain subtotals for the appointment costs and a discount for customers who are paying more than $20 for one of their treatment costs.*

- Click the Text Box tool (Report Design Tools Design tab | Controls group), and then click the position in the Owner ID Footer section, as shown in Figure 6–73.

- Click the text box to produce an insertion point.

- Type **=IIf([cost]>20,[cost]*0.2,0)** in the control to enter the expression calculation as shown in Figure 6–73, and then press ENTER.

- Click the text box label to select it.

- Click the label a second time to produce an insertion point.

- Use DELETE or BACKSPACE to delete the Text18 label (your number might be different).

- Type **Discount** as the label.

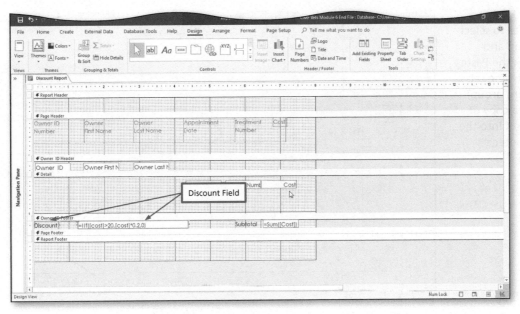

Figure 6–73

- Format the calculation to currency by clicking the Report Design Tools Format tab and clicking the 'Apply Currency Format' button.
- Switch between Design view and Layout view to review the results by clicking the (Report Design Tools) Design tab and selecting the View arrow.

To Add a Header and Footer to the Discount Report

Report titles are typically placed in a Report Header. You can also place in the footer section calculation fields that total controls for the entire report. *Why? CMF Vets wants to include a total on the report.* The following steps add a Report Header and Footer and place controls in them.

1
- Right-click any open area of the report to display a shortcut menu (Figure 6–74).
- Click 'Report Header/ Footer' to display the Report Header and Footer sections.
- Click the Subtotal control in the Owner ID Footer section to select the control.
- Display the Home tab.
- Click the Copy button (Home tab | Clipboard group) to copy the selected controls to the Clipboard.

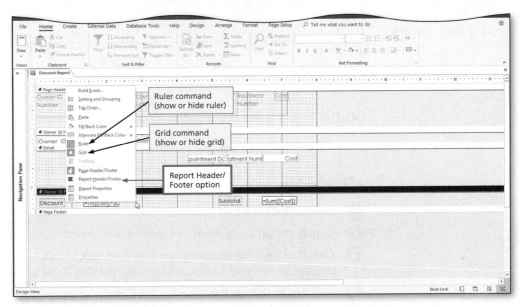

Figure 6–74

• Click the Report
Footer bar to select
the footer, and
then click the Paste
button (Home tab
| Clipboard group)
to paste a copy of
the control into the
report footer
(Figure 6–75).

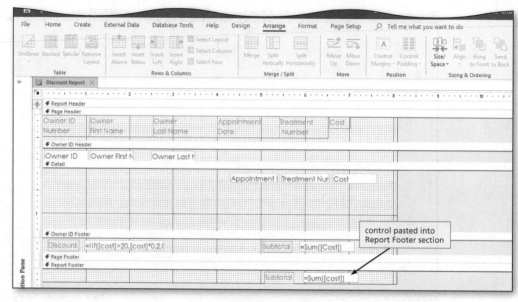

Figure 6–75

2

• Click the label in
the Report Footer
section to select the
label, and then click
a second time to
produce an insertion
point.

• Use the BACKSPACE
or DELETE key to
erase the current
contents, type
Total to change
the label, and then
move the label to
the position shown
in Figure 6–76.

• Save your changes.

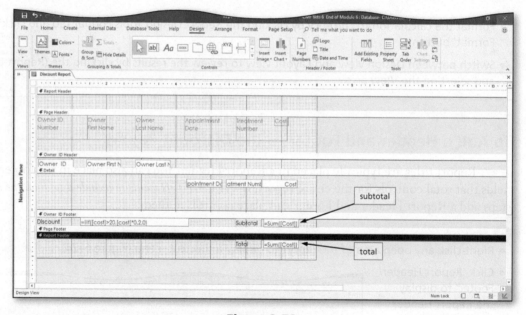

Figure 6–76

To Change the Can Grow Property

The following steps change the Can Grow property for the Owner Last Name
control so that names that are too long to fit in the available space will extend to
additional lines.

1 Select the Owner Last Name control.

2 Display the property sheet and scroll down until the Can Grow property appears.

3 Click the Can Grow property box and then click the Can Grow property box arrow to
display the menu of available values for the Can Grow property.

4 Click Yes to change the value for the Can Grow property.

5 Close the property sheet.

To View the Report

The following steps view the report in Report view, which is sometimes more convenient when you want to view the lower portion of the report.

1 Click the View button arrow on the Home tab to display the View button menu.

2 Click Report View on the View button menu to view the report in Report view.

3 Scroll down to the bottom of the report so that the total appears on the screen (Figure 6–77a top of report and Figure 6–77b bottom of report).

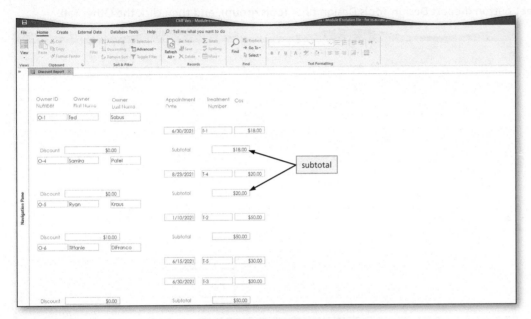

Figure 6–77a Top of Report

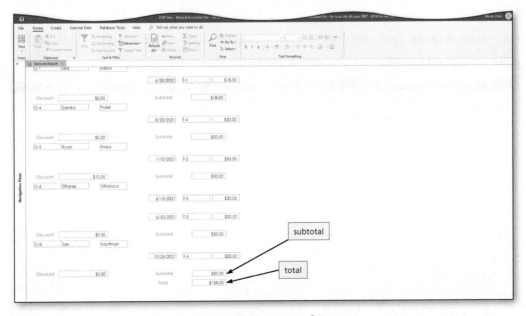

Figure 6–77b Bottom of Report

Other Ways

1. Click the Report View button on the status bar

To Use Expression Builder to Add a Calculation

The CMF Vets requirements for this report also involved showing the Cost subtotal less the Discount amount. Before entering the calculation into a control, you decide to change the Control name Text13 to Subtotal in the property sheet. By changing the control names to something meaningful, you will not need to remember their control name, such as Text13. These steps use Expression Builder change both expression name Text13 and Subtotal properties. *Why? Expression Builder is a convenient way to include a calculation.*

- With the Discount Report in Design view, click the Subtotal control in the Owner ID Footer to select it.
- Click the Property Sheet button (Report Design Tools Design tab | Tools group), and then click the Other tab.
- Click in the Name box, delete any existing text, if necessary, and then type **Subtotal** for the Name (Figure 6–78).

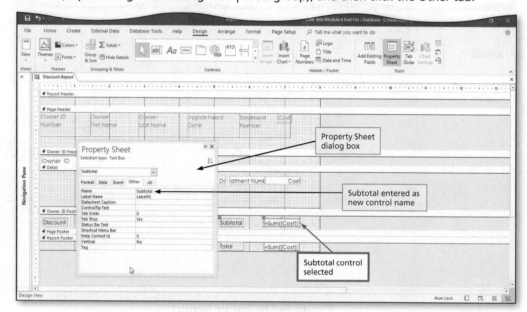

Figure 6–78

- If necessary, drag the property sheet to the right, and then click the IIf calculation control to select it.
- Click in the Name box in the Property Sheet Other tab and delete any existing text, if necessary.
- Type **Discount** for the Name (Figure 6–79) and then close the Property Sheet dialog box.

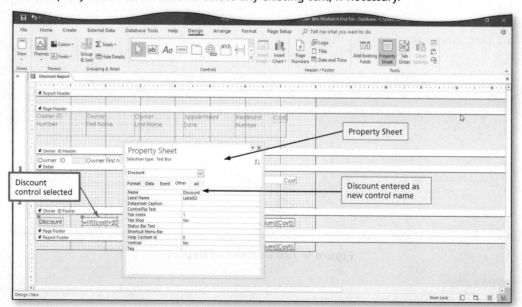

Figure 6–79

- Click the Text Box
tool (Report Design
Tools Design tab |
Controls group),
and then click in
the approximate
position in the
Detail section to
place the control
for the calculation
(Figure 6–80).

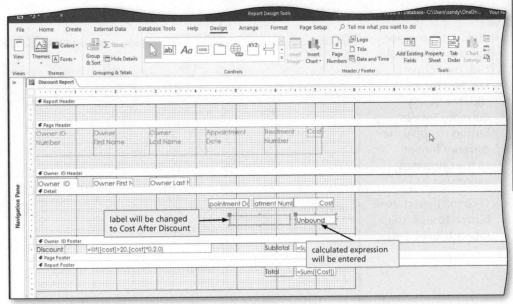

Figure 6–80

❸

- Click the text box control and then click the Property Sheet button.

- Click the All tab, click the Control Source property, and then click the Build button to display the Expression Builder dialog box.

- Click Discount Report in the Expression Elements category in the first column.

- Type an equal sign (=) in the Expression Builder box.

- Scroll down in the second column so that Subtotal appears, and then double-click the Subtotal control in the second column.

- Type a minus sign (–), scroll down in the second column so that Discount appears, and then double-click the Discount control to add it to the expression (Figure 6–81).

- Click OK to close the
Expression Builder
dialog box and then
close the Property
Sheet dialog box.

- Click the label for
the expression
field and then click
the label for the
expression field
a second time to
produce an insertion
point.

- Use BACKSPACE or
DELETE to erase the
current entry in
the label, and then
type **Cost After
Discount** as the
new entry.

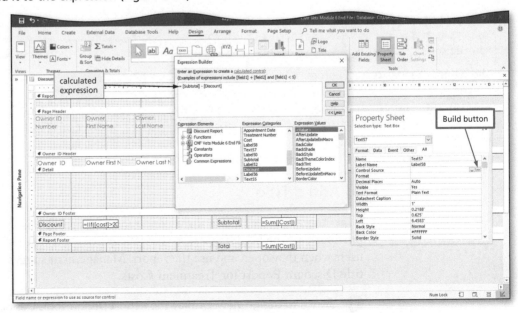

Figure 6–81

4

• Click the Expression Calculation control, click the Format tab, and then click the 'Apply Currency Format' button to apply the currency format to the calculated expression.

• Click the Report View button to view the report (Figure 6–82).

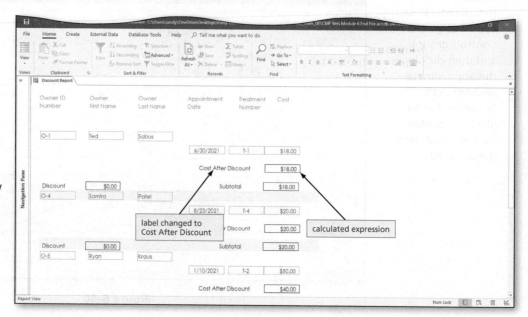

Figure 6–82

5

• Save your changes.

Q&A

Are there other ways I could enter the expression?
Yes. You could just type the whole expression. On the other hand, you could select the function just as in these steps, and, when entering each argument, you could select the fields from the list of fields and click the desired operators.

How can I place the control accurately when there are no gridlines?
When you click the position for the control, Access will automatically expand the grid. You can then adjust the control using the grid.

Can I automatically cause controls to be aligned to the grid?
Yes. Click the Size/Space button (Report Design Tools Arrange tab | Sizing & Ordering group) and then click Snap to Grid on the Size/Space menu. From that point on, any controls you add will be automatically aligned to the grid.

Why did I choose Control Source instead of Record Source?
You use Record Source to select the source of the records in a report, usually a table or a query. You use the Control Source property to specify the source of data for the control. This allows you to bind an expression or field to a control.

The report size was correct before. Why would I need to resize it?
When you move a control and a portion of the control extends into the area to the right of the right boundary of the report, the report will be resized. The new larger size will remain even if you move the control back to the left. Thus, it is possible that your report has a larger size than it did before. If this is the case, you need to drag the right boundary to resize the report.

To Add a Title

You can add a title to the second report using buttons on the Design tab, as you previously learned. Adding a title clearly identifies this report for management and users when they open and use the report. Management suggested this report have the title Discount Report for Treatment Costs.

1 Switch to Design view. Display the Report Design Tools Design tab, if necessary, and then click the Title button (Report Design Tools Design tab | Header/Footer group) to add a title.

2 Type `Discount Report for Treatment Costs` as the title.

3 Click outside the title to deselect the title.

4 Click the title again and then click the (Report Design Tools) Format tab.

5 Click the Bold button to format the title.

6 View the report in Print Preview (Figure 6–83).

7 Close Print Preview.

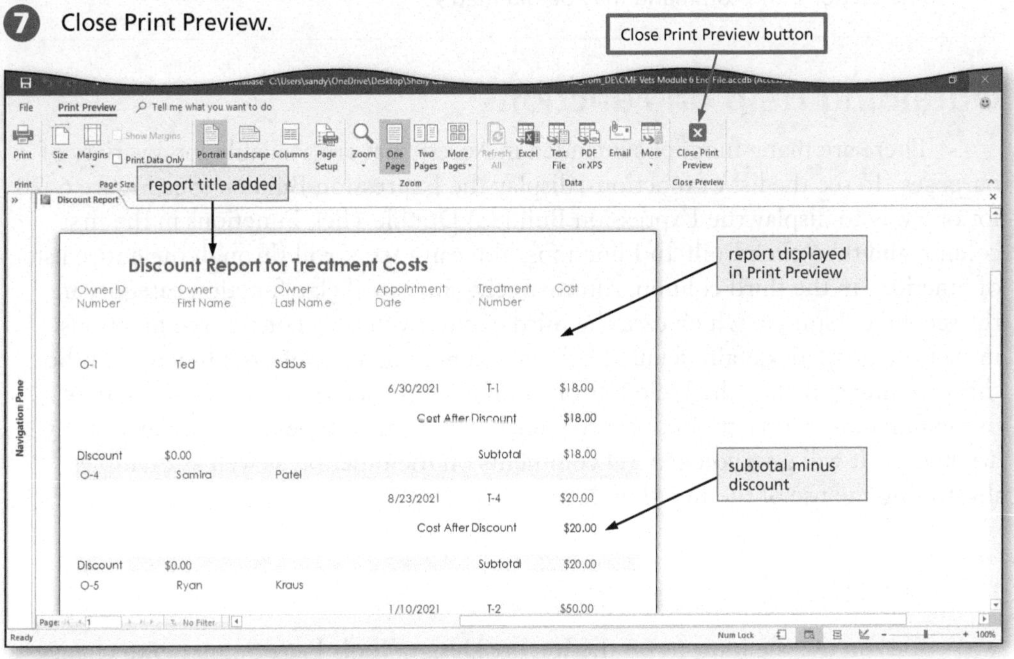

Figure 6–83

To Change the Border Style

If you print or preview the report, you will notice that all the controls have boxes around them. The box is the border, which you can select and modify if desired. You would use the following steps to remove the boxes around the controls by changing the border style to transparent.

1 Select all controls in the report besides the Title in the Report Header. You can click the first one, and then hold SHIFT while clicking all the others. Alternatively, you can click in the ruler to the left of the Page Header section and then hold SHIFT while clicking to the left of all the other remaining sections.

2 Display the Report Design Tools Design tab.

3 Click the Property Sheet button (Report Design Tools Design tab | Tools group) to display the property sheet.

4 Click the Border Style property box and then click the Border Style property box arrow to display the menu of available border styles.

5 Click Transparent to change the border style. Close the property sheet.

To Remove the Alternate Color

Just as with the Owner ID Master List, the Discount Report also has alternate colors that need to be removed. You would use the following steps to remove the alternate colors from the various sections in the report, starting with the Detail section.

1 Right-click the Detail section to produce a shortcut menu.

2 Point to the Alternate Fill/Back Color arrow to produce a color palette.

③ Click None on the color palette to specify that there is to be no alternate color for the selected section.

④ Using the same techniques, remove the alternate color from all other sections. (For some sections, the command may be dimmed.)

Obtaining Help on Functions

There are many functions included in Access that are available for a variety of purposes. To see the list of functions, display the Expression Builder. (See Figure 6–78 for one way to display the Expression Builder.) Double-click Functions in the first column and then click Built-In Functions. You can then scroll through the entire list of functions in the third column. Alternatively, you can click a function category in the second column, in which case the third column will only contain the functions in that category. To obtain detailed help on a function, highlight the function in the third column and click the Help button. The Help presented will show the syntax of the function, that is, the specific rule for how you must type the function and any arguments. It will give you general comments on the function as well as examples illustrating the use of the function.

Report Design Tools Page Setup Tab

You can use the buttons on the Report Design Tools Page Setup tab to change margins, orientation, and other page setup characteristics of the report (Figure 6–84a). If you click the Margins button, you can choose from among some predefined margins or set your own custom margins (Figure 6–84b). If you click the Columns button, you will see the Page Setup dialog box with the Columns tab selected (Figure 6–84c). You can use this tab to specify multiple columns in a report as well as the column spacing. You can specify orientation by clicking the Page tab (Figure 6–84d). You can also select paper size, paper source, and printer using this tab. If you click the Page Setup button, you will see the Page Setup dialog box with the Print Options tab selected (Figure 6–84e). You can use this tab to specify custom margins.

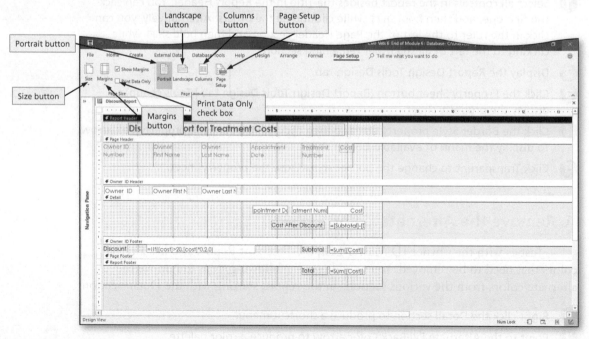

Figure 6–84a Page Setup Tab

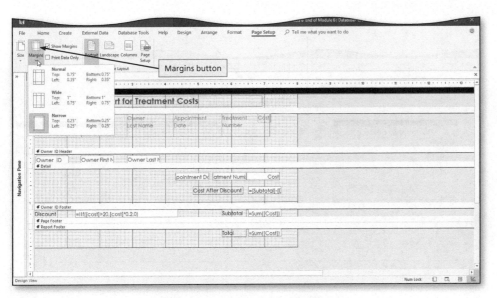

Figure 6–84b Margins Gallery

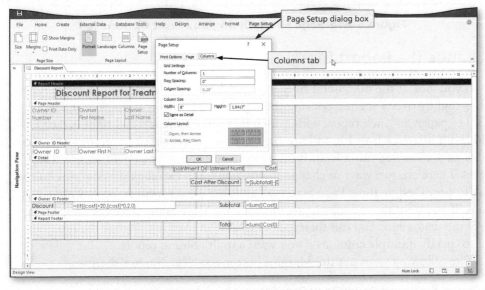

Figure 6–84c Page Setup Dialog Box Columns Tab

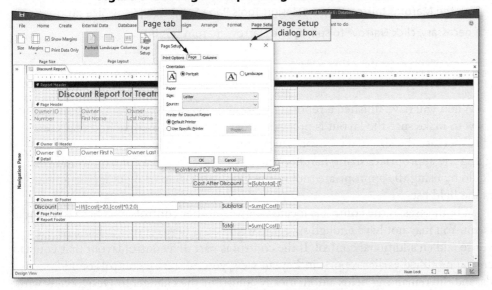

Figure 6–84d Page Setup Dialog Box Page Tab

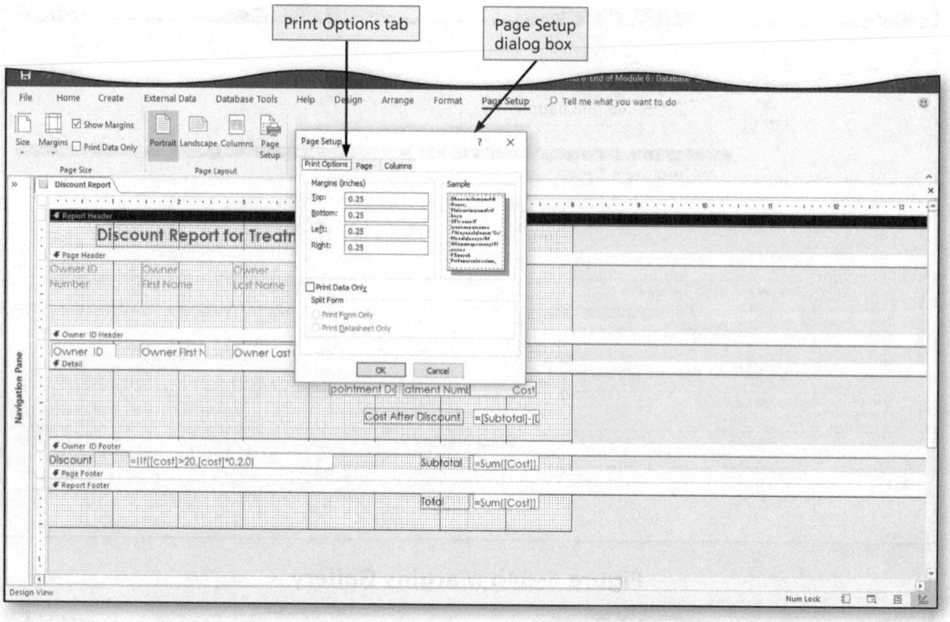

Figure 6–84e Page Setup Dialog Box Print Options Tab

To Change the Report Margins

If you look at the horizontal ruler in Figure 6–84, you will notice that the report width is slightly over 7 inches. Because the report will probably print on standard 8½" × 11" paper, a 7-inch report with 1-inch margins on the left and right, which would result in a 9-inch width, will not fit. To allow the report to fit on the page, you could change the orientation from Portrait to Landscape or you could reduce the margins. There are two ways to change the margins. You can click the Margins button on the Report Design Tools Page Setup tab and then select from some predefined options. If you want more control, you can click the Page Setup button to display the Page Setup dialog box. You can then specify your own margins, change the orientation, and also specify multiple columns if you want a multicolumn report.

The following steps use the Margins button to select Narrow margins.

1. Display the Report Design Tools Page Setup tab.
2. Click the Margins button (Report Design Tools Page Setup tab | Page Size group).
3. If necessary, click Narrow to specify the Narrow margin option.

BTW
Drop Down Controls
Drop down boxes can be combo boxes or list boxes. To add a combo box to a report, click the Combo Box tool, move the pointer to the desired location, and click the position to place the combo box. Follow the directions in the Combo Box Wizard dialog box to specify the options and values for the combo box. To add a list box to a report, click the List Box tool and follow the steps listed above for a combo box.

Fine-Tuning a Report

When you have finished a report, you should review several of its pages in Print Preview to make sure the layout is precisely what you want. You may find that you need to increase the size of a control, which you can do by selecting the control and dragging the appropriate sizing handle. You may decide to add a control, which you could do by using the appropriate tool in the Controls group or by dragging a field from the field list.

In both cases, if the control is located between other controls, you have a potential problem. You may not have enough space between the other controls to increase the size or to add an additional control. If the control is part of a control layout that you had when you modified earlier reports in Layout view, you can resize controls or add new fields, and the remaining fields automatically adjust for the change. In Design view with individual controls, you must make any necessary adjustments manually.

To Make Room For Resizing or Adding Controls

To make room for resizing a control or for adding controls, you would use the following steps.

1. Select all controls to the right of the control you want to resize, or to the right of the position where you want to add another control.
2. Drag any of the selected controls to the right to make room for the change.

To Save and Close a Report

Now that you have completed your work on your report, you should save the report and close it. The following steps first save your work on the report and then close the report.

1 If instructed to do so by your instructor, change the title of the Discount Report to LastName Report where LastName is your last name.

2 Click the Save button on the Quick Access Toolbar to save your work.

3 Close the Discount Report.

4 Preview and then print the report.

5 If desired, sign out of your Microsoft account.

6 **sam** Exit Access.

Summary

In this module you have learned to create and relate additional tables; create queries for a report; create reports in Design view; add fields and text boxes to a report; format controls; group and ungroup controls; modify multiple controls; add and modify a subreport; modify section properties; add a title, page number, and date; add subtotals; use a function in a text box; and publish a report.

CONSIDER THIS

What decisions will you need to make when creating your own reports?

Use these guidelines as you complete the assignments in this module and create your own reports outside of this class.

1. Determine the intended audience and purpose of the report.

   a. Identify the user or users of the report and determine how they will use it.

   b. Specify the necessary data and level of detail to include in the report.

2. Determine the source of data for the report.

   a. Determine whether all the data is in a single table or whether it comes from multiple related tables.

3. Determine whether the data is stored in a query.

   a. You might need to create multiple versions of a report for a query where the criterion for a field changes, in which case, you would use a parameter query and enter the criterion when you run the report.

   b. If the data comes from multiple related tables, you might want to create a query and use the query as a source of data.

4. Determine the fields that belong on the report.

   a. Identify the data items that are needed by the user of the report.

5. Determine the organization of the report.

   a. The report might be enhanced by displaying the fields in a particular order and arranged in a certain way.

   b. Should the records in the report be grouped in some way?

   c. Should the report contain any subreports?

6. Determine any calculations required for the report.

    a. Should the report contain totals or subtotals?

    b. Are there any special calculations?

    c. Are there any calculations that involve criteria?

7. Determine the format and style of the report.

    a. What information should be in the report heading?

    b. Do you want a title and date?

    c. Do you want special background colors or alternate colors?

    d. Should the report contain an image?

    e. What should be in the body of the report?

How should you submit solutions to questions in the assignments identified with a symbol?

Every assignment in this book contains one or more questions identified with a symbol. These questions require you to think beyond the assigned database. Present your solutions to the questions in the format required by your instructor. Possible formats may include one or more of these options: write the answer; create a document that contains the answer; present your answer to the class; discuss your answer in a group; record the answer as audio or video using a webcam, smartphone, or portable media player; or post answers on a blog, wiki, or website.

CONSIDER THIS

Apply Your Knowledge

Reinforce the skills and apply the concepts you learned in this module.

Adding a Table and Creating a Report with a Subreport

Note: To complete this assignment, you will be required to use the Data Files. Please contact your instructor for information about accessing the Data Files.

Instructions: Start Access and then open the Support_AC_Financial Services database that you modified previously. (If you did not complete the exercise, see your instructor for a copy of the modified database.)

Perform the following tasks:
1. Create a table in which to store data about financial services performed for clients. Use Services as the name of the table. The Services table has the structure shown in Table 6–4.

Table 6–4 Structure of Services Table			
Field Name	**Data Type**	**Field Size**	**Description**
Client Number	Short Text	4	Part of Primary Key
Service Date	Date/Time (Change Format property to Short Date)		Part of Primary Key
Hours Worked	Number (Change Format property to Fixed and Decimal Places to 2)	Single	

2. Import the Services.csv file into the Services table. The file is delimited by commas and the first row contains the field names. Do not save the import steps.

3. Create a one-to-many relationship (enforce referential integrity) between the Client table and the Services table. Save the relationship and close the Relationships window.

4. Create a query that joins the Advisor and Client tables. Include the Advisor Number, First Name, and Last Name fields from the Advisor table. Include all fields except the Client Type and Advisor Number fields from the Client table. Save the query as Advisors and Clients.

5. Create the report shown in Figure 6–85. The report uses the Advisors and Clients query as the basis for the main report and the Services table as the basis for the subreport. Use the name Advisors and Clients Master List for the report. The report title has a Text Align property value of Center.

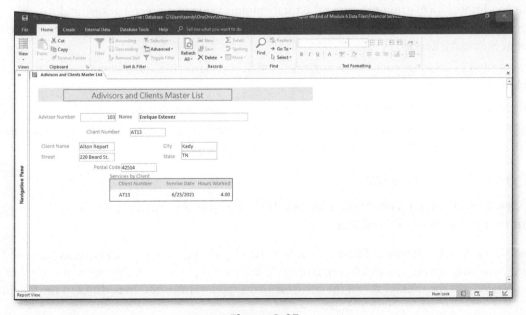

Continued >

Figure 6–85

Expand Your World *continued*

The Border Width property for the detail controls is 1 pt and the subreport name is Services by Client. The report is similar in style to the Owners and Account Information Master List shown in Figure 6–1a.

6. If requested to do so by your instructor, change the title for the report to First Name Last Name Master List where First Name and Last Name are your first and last names.

7. Submit the revised database in the format specified by your instructor.

8. ✸ How would you change the font weight of the report title to bold?

Extend Your Knowledge

Extend the skills you learned in this module and experiment with new skills. You may need to use Help to complete the assignment.

Modifying Reports

Note: To complete this assignment, you will be required to use the Data Files. Please contact your instructor for information about accessing the Data Files.

Instructions: Healthy Pets is a veterinarian practice that is being closed due to retirements. CMF is considering buying this practice to expand their client basis. Start Access and then open the Support_AC_Healthy Pets database.

Perform the following tasks:

1. Open the Client Amount Due Summary Report in Design view. Insert a date field and a page number field in the report header.

2. Format the date and page number so that they are aligned with the right edge of the report.

3. Change the report title to Revised Client Summary Report. Change the report header background to white. Change the font of the title text to Bookman Old Style with a font weight of semi-bold. Make sure the entire title is visible and the title is centered across the report.

4. Add a label to the report footer section. The label should contain text to indicate the end of the report, for example, End of Report or similar text.

5. Remove any extra white space in the Detail section of the report.

6. Use conditional formatting to format the total amount value in a green background for all records where the value is equal to or greater than $200.00. Save the altered report as Revised Client Summary Report.

7. If requested to do so by your instructor, open the Technician table and add your name to the table.

8. Submit the revised database in the format specified by your instructor.

9. ✸ Do you think the borders surrounding the controls enhance or detract from the appearance of the Client Amount Due Summary report? Explain your position.

Expand Your World

Create a solution, which uses cloud and web technologies, by learning and investigating on your own from general guidance.

Problem: Support_AC_Physical Therapy is a database containing therapists and clients (patients). To have access to additional research concerning their patient's physical challenges requiring therapy and procedures the therapists can use for treatments, you want to add hyperlinks in the Client table to websites such as WebMD, Health and Wellness Prevention, Health and Wellness, and Falls and Fall Prevention; these hyperlinks should link to content and articles related to health issues. Research how to add a hyperlink in an Access table. The therapists want specific websites for specific patients; this information is shown in Table 6–5. After placing these hyperlinks in the Support_AC_Physical Therapy Client table, add the hyperlink to the Client Therapist Report.

Perform the following tasks:

1. Start Access and open the Support_AC_Physical Therapy database from the Data Files.
2. Search the web to find how to add a hyperlink in an Access table and also in a report that was created previously.
3. Create a new field in the Client table and add the websites shown in Table 6–5 in the new field for the client indicated.

Table 6–5 Clients and Associated Hyperlinks	
Client Number	**Hyperlink**
AB10	https://www.webmd.com/fitness-exercise/video/office-exercises-in-5-minutes
GM52	https://www.betterhealth.vic.gov.au/health/videos/exercise-and-stretching-in-the-office
TR35	https://www.youtube.com/watch?v=vAsNz_BRgv8

4. Open the Client Therapist Report in Design view and delete any alternate background color in the report.
5. Add the hyperlink field to the Client Therapist Report.
6. Review the report in Report view and verify the accuracy of the website hyperlinks.
7. Save your changes.
8. Submit the revised database in the format specified by your instructor.
9. ✳ What steps did you select to create a hyperlink? What website did you use? Justify your selection.

In the Labs

Design, create, modify, and/or use a database following the guidelines, concepts, and skills presented in this module

Lab: Adding a Table and Creating Reports for the Lancaster College Database

Problem: From time to time, equipment needs to be updated or replaced. Team managers, coaches, and administrators want to keep track of the changes as part of the database.

Instructions: Perform the following tasks:

Part 1: The sports department of Lancaster College would like to create a table that tracks orders of new sports equipment.

1. Start Access and open the Lancaster College database you used previously. If you did not use this database, see your instructor about accessing the required files.
2. Create a table in which to store the item order information using the structure shown in Table 6–6. Use Orders as the name of the table.

Continued >

In the Labs *continued*

Table 6–6 Structure of Orders Table			
Field Name	**Data Type**	**Field Size**	**Description**
Equipment ID	Short Text	30	Part of Primary Key
Date Ordered	Date/Time (Use Short Date format)		Part of Primary Key
Number Ordered	Number	Integer	
Coach ID	Short Text	10	

3. Import the data from the Orders.xlsx workbook to the Orders table. Do not save the import steps.

4. Add the Orders table to the Relationships window and establish a one-to-many relationship between the Coach table and the Orders table. Save the relationship.

5. Create a query that joins the Coach table and the Orders table. Include the Equipment ID and Date Ordered from the Orders table. Include Coach ID, First Name, Last Name, Office, and Sport Name from the Coach table. Save the query as Coaches and Orders.

6. Create the report shown in Figure 6–86. The report uses the Coaches and Orders query as the basis for the main report and the Sport table as the basis for the subreport. Use the name Coaches and Orders Master List as the name for the report and the name Sports table as the name for the subreport. Change the Text Align property for the title to Center.

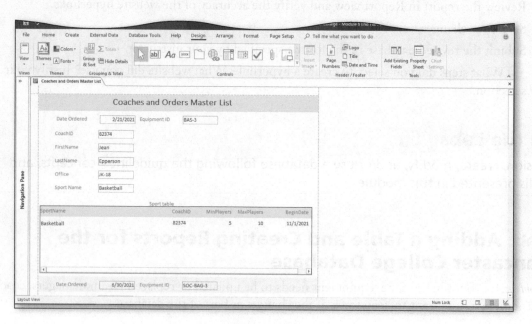

Figure 6–86

7. The page number and current date appear in the report footer section. Change the Can Grow property for the Last Name field to Yes.

8. If instructed to do so by your instructor, add a label to the report footer with your first and last name.

9. Submit the revised database in the format specified by your instructor.

10. ✹ Adding a subreport can provide quick reference to other database information. What are your thoughts about using the Sport table for the subreport? Do you think it is helpful or would you use another table in the subreport?

Submit your assignment in the format specified by instructor.

Part 2: You made several decisions, such as adding new relationships, creating and modifying a report, and adding a subreport control. What was the rationale behind your decisions? Would you add any additional fields to this table?

7 | Advanced Form Techniques

Objectives

You will have mastered the material in this module when you can:

- Add combo boxes that include selection lists
- Add combo boxes for searching
- Format and resize controls
- Apply formatting characteristics with the Format Painter
- Add command buttons
- Modify buttons and combo boxes

- Add a calculated field
- Use tab controls to create a multipage form
- Add and modify a subform
- Insert charts
- Modify a chart type
- Format a chart

Introduction

In other modules, you created basic forms using the Form Wizard, and you created more complex forms using Design view. In this module, you will create two new forms that feature more advanced form elements. The first form contains two combo boxes, one for selecting data from a related table and one for finding a record on the form. It also contains command buttons to accomplish various tasks.

The second form you will create is a **multipage form**, a form that contains more than one page of information. The form contains a tab control that allows you to access two different pages. Clicking the first tab displays a page containing a subform. Clicking the second tab displays a page containing two charts.

Project — Advanced Form Techniques

CMF Vets wants two additional forms to use with its Veterinarians and Appointments tables. The first form, Appointment View and Update Form (Figure 7–1a), contains the fields in the Appointments table. The form has five command buttons: Next Record, Previous Record, Add Record, Delete Record, and Close Form. Clicking any of these buttons causes the action indicated on the button to occur.

The form also contains a combo box for the Veterinarian, Owner, and Patient fields, which assists users in viewing who is involved in the appointment (Figure 7–1b).

To assist users in finding an account when they know the appointment number, the form also includes a combo box they can use for this purpose (Figure 7–1c). After displaying the list of appointments by clicking the arrow, the user can simply select the

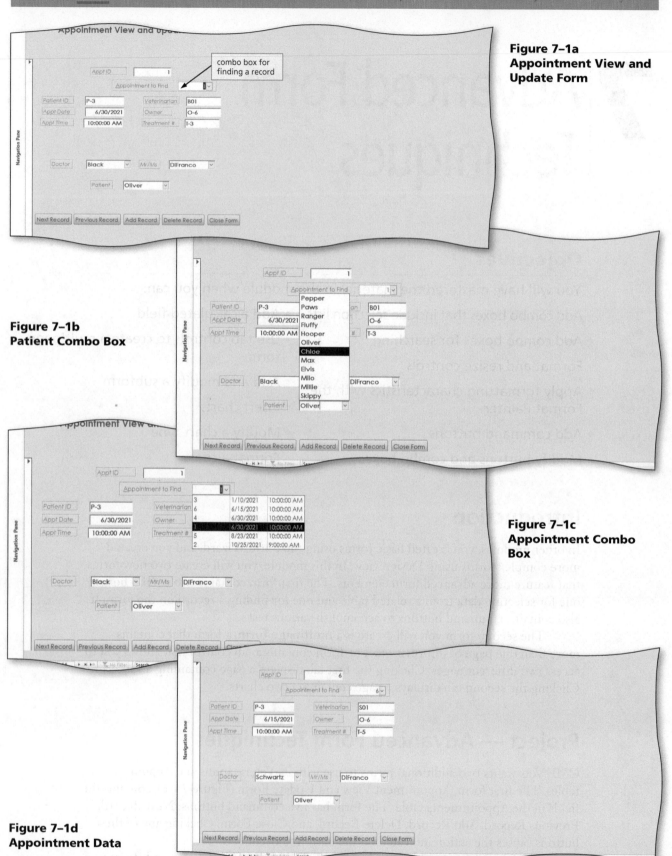

Figure 7–1a
Appointment View and Update Form

combo box for finding a record

Figure 7–1b
Patient Combo Box

Figure 7–1c
Appointment Combo Box

Figure 7–1d
Appointment Data

appointment they want to find; Access will then locate the account and display that appointment's data in the form (Figure 7–1d).

For the second new form, CMF Vets needs a multipage form that lists the emergency hours and on call hours of each veterinarian. Each of the two pages that make up the form is displayed in its own tab page. Selecting the first tab, the one labeled Datasheet, displays a subform listing information about the on call and emergency hours for each veterinarian (Figure 7–2a).

Selecting the other tab, the one labeled Charts, displays two charts that illustrate the on call and emergency hours spent by each veterinarian (Figure 7–2b). In both charts, the slices of the pie represent the various hours. They are color-coded, and the legend at the bottom indicates the meaning of the various colors. The size of the pie slice gives a visual representation of the portion of the hours spent on call or in emergencies for a specific veterinarian. The chart also includes specific percentages. If you look at the purple slice in the Emergency Hours by Vet chart, for example, you see that the color represents March for Dr. William Black. It signifies 33 percent of the total. Thus, out of the 6 months, Dr. Black has spent 33 percent of his emergency hours during the month of March.

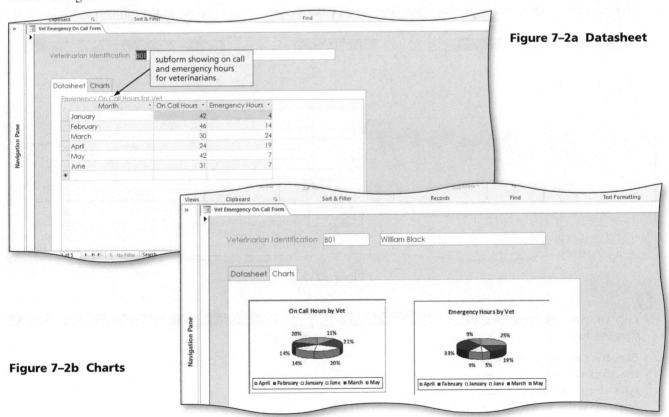

Figure 7–2a Datasheet

Figure 7–2b Charts

Creating a Form with Combo Boxes and Command Buttons

After planning a form, you might decide that including features such as combo boxes and command buttons will make the form easier to use. You can include such items while modifying the form in Design view.

BTW
Enabling the Content
For each of the databases you use in this module, you will need to enable the content.

To Create a Form in Design View

As you have previously learned, Access provides several different ways to create a form, including tools such as the Form Wizard and the Form button. The following steps create a form in Design view. *Why? Creating a form in Design view gives you the most flexibility in laying out the form. You will be presented with a blank design on which to place objects.*

1
- **sam** ↓ Start Access and open the database named CMF Vets from your hard disk, OneDrive, or other storage location.
- Display the Create tab.
- Click the Form Design button (Create tab | Forms group) to create a new form in Design view.
- If necessary, close the Navigation Pane.
- Ensure the form selector for the entire form, the box in the upper-left corner of the form, is selected.
- If necessary, click the Property Sheet button (Form Design Tools Design tab | Tools group) to display a property sheet.
- With the All tab selected, click the Record Source arrow, and then click the Appointments table to select the Appointments table as the record source.
- Click Save on the Quick Access Toolbar, then type `Appointments Master Form` as the form name (Figure 7–3).

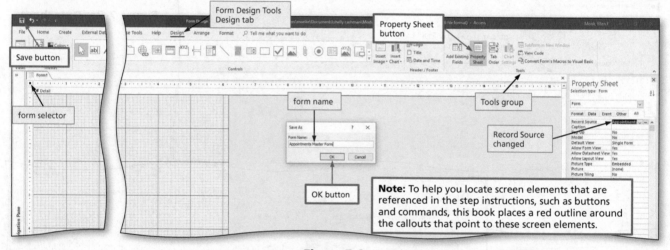

Figure 7–3

2
- Click OK (Save As dialog box) to save the form.
- Click the Caption property in the property sheet, and then type `Appointment View and Update Form` as the new caption.
- Close the property sheet by clicking the Property Sheet button on the Form Design Tools Design tab.
- Click the 'Add Existing Fields' button (Form Design Tools Design tab | Tools group) to display the field list (Figure 7–4).

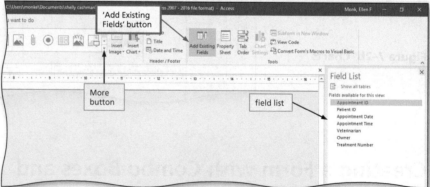

Figure 7–4

Q&A Why does the name on the tab not change to the new caption, Appointment View and Update Form?
The name on the tab will change to the new caption in Form view. In Design view, you still see the name of the form object.

To Add Fields to the Form Design

After deciding which fields to add to the Appointment View and Update Form, you can place them on the form by dragging the fields from the field list to the desired position. The following steps first display only the fields in the Appointments table in the field list, and then place the appropriate fields on the form.

1 If necessary, click the 'Show only fields in the current record source' link at the top of the field list to change the link to 'Show all tables' and display only the fields in the Appointments table.

2 Drag the Appointment ID field from the field list to the top-center area of the form.

3 Click the label once to select it and then click it a second time to produce an insertion point, use BACKSPACE or DELETE as necessary to erase the current entry (Appointment ID), and then type `Appt ID` as the new label.

4 Click outside the label to deselect it, click the label to select it a second time, and then drag the sizing handle on the right side to make the label narrower and, if necessary, move the label to the approximate position shown Figure 7–5.

Q&A Why am I changing the label for Appointment ID?
In these forms, you can be creative in the layout and labeling of fields. You might make the name or label for a long field shorter or a short field longer, depending on the design.

5 Click the Patient ID field in the field list.

6 While holding the SHIFT key down, click the Appointment Date field and the Appointment Time field in the field list to select multiple fields, drag the selected fields to the approximate position shown in Figure 7–5, and then release the mouse button.

7 Select the Veterinarian through Treatment Number fields and then drag the selected fields to the approximate position shown in the figure.

Q&A I added a field twice by mistake. Can I delete the control?
Yes, select the control and press the DELETE key.

8 Change the labels for Appointment Date and Appointment Time fields to `Appt Date` and `Appt Time`, respectively. Change the label for Treatment Number to `Treatment #`. Adjust the sizing, placement, and alignment of the controls to approximately match those in the figure. If controls for any of the fields are not aligned properly, align them by dragging them to the desired location or by using the alignment buttons on the Form Design Tools Arrange tab.

9 Close the field list.

BTW

The Ribbon and Screen Resolution
Access may change how the groups and buttons within the groups appear on the ribbon, depending on the computer's screen resolution. Thus, your ribbon may look different from the ones in this book if you are using a screen resolution other than 1366 x 768.

BTW

Touch Screen Differences
The Office and Windows interfaces may vary if you are using a touch screen. For this reason, you might notice that the function or appearance of your touch screen differs slightly from this module's presentation.

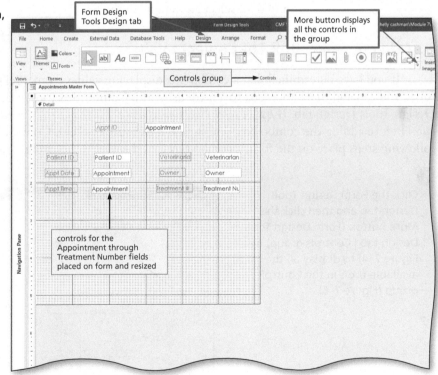

Figure 7–5

How do you decide on the contents of a form?

To design and create forms, follow these general guidelines:

Determine the fields that belong on the form. If you determine that data should be presented as a form, you then need to determine what tables and fields contain the data for the form.

Examine the requirements for the form in general to determine the tables. Do the requirements only relate to data in a single table, or does the data come from multiple tables? How are the tables related?

Examine the specific requirements for the form to determine the fields necessary. Look for all the data items that are specified for the form. Each item should correspond to a field in a table or be able to be computed from a field in a table. This information gives you the list of fields.

Determine whether there are any special calculations required, such as adding the values in two fields or combining the contents of two text fields. If special calculations are needed, what are they? What fields are involved and how are they to be combined?

Combo Boxes

BTW
Combo Boxes
You also can create combo boxes for reports.

When entering data for a Veterinarian, the value must match the number of a veterinarian ID currently in the Veterinarians table. To assist users in entering this data, the form will contain a combo box. A **combo box** combines the properties of a **text box**, which is a box into which you can type an entry, and a **list box**, which is a box you can use to display a list from which to select a value. With a combo box, the user can either type the data or click the combo box arrow to display a list of possible values and then select an item from the list.

To Add a Combo Box That Selects Values

If you have determined that a combo box displaying values from a related table would be useful on your form, you can add the combo box to a form using the Combo Box tool in the Controls group on the Form Design Tools Design tab. *Why? A combo box that allows the user to select a value from a list is a convenient way to enter data.* Before adding the combo box, you should make sure the 'Use Control Wizards' button is selected. The following steps place on the form a combo box that displays values from a related table for the Veterinarian field.

1
• Click the Form Design Tools Design tab and then click the More button (Form Design Tools Design tab | Controls group) (see Figure 7–4) to display all the available tools in the Controls group (Figure 7–6).

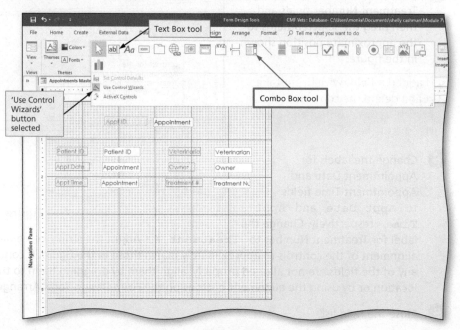

Figure 7–6

2

- With the 'Use Control Wizards' button in the Controls group on the Form Design Tools Design tab selected, click the Combo Box tool (Form Design Tools Design tab | Controls group), and then move the pointer, whose shape has changed to a small plus symbol accompanied by a combo box, to the position shown in Figure 7–7.

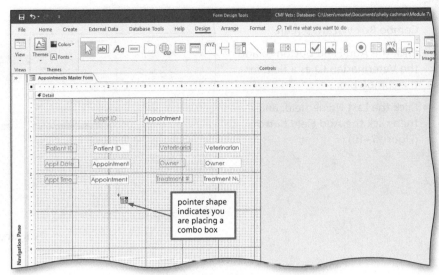

Figure 7–7

3

- Click the position shown in Figure 7–7 to place a combo box and display the Combo Box Wizard dialog box.

- If necessary, in the Combo Box Wizard dialog box, click the 'I want the combo box to get the values from another table or query.' option button (Figure 7–8).

 Q&A Why did I receive a security warning when I placed a combo box in the form?
Depending on your security settings, you may receive a warning when creating a combo box. Choosing the Open button will allow the Combo Box Wizard to initiate.

What is the purpose of the other options?
Use the second option if you want to type a list from which the user will choose. Use the third option if you want to use the combo box to search for a record.

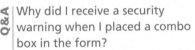

Figure 7–8

4

- Click Next, and then, with the Tables option button selected in the View area, click Table: Veterinarians (Figure 7–9) in the list of tables to specify that the combo box values will come from the Veterinarians table.

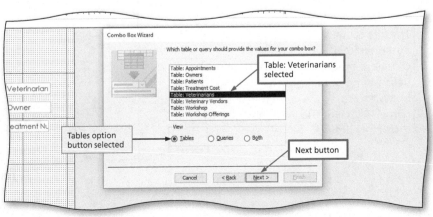

Figure 7–9

- Click Next to display the next Combo Box Wizard screen.
- Click the Add Field button to add the Veterinarian ID as a field in the combo box.
- Click the Last Name field, and then click the Add Field button (Figure 7–10).

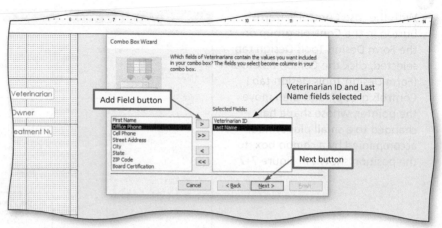

Figure 7–10

- Click Next to display the next Combo Box Wizard screen.
- Click the arrow in the first text box, and then select the Veterinarian ID field to sort the data by Veterinarian ID (Figure 7–11).

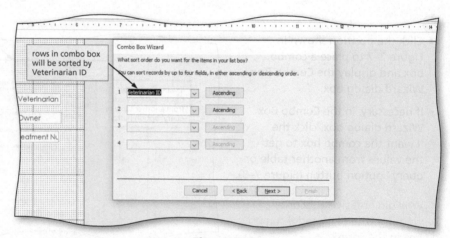

Figure 7–11

- Click Next to display the next Combo Box Wizard screen (Figure 7–12).

Q&A What is the key column? Do I want to hide it?
The key column would be the Veterinarian ID, which is the column that identifies a last name. Because the purpose of this combo box is to display the veterinarian's name, you want the Veterinarian IDs to be hidden.

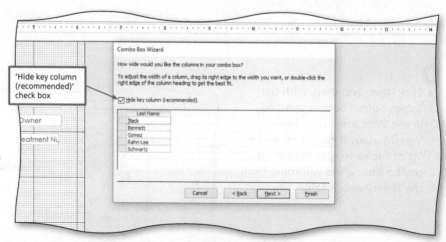

Figure 7–12

8

- Click Next to display the next Combo Box Wizard screen.
- Click the 'Store that value in this field:' button.
- Because you want the value that the user selects to be stored in the Veterinarian field in the Appointments table, click the 'Store that value in this field:' box arrow, and then click Veterinarian (Figure 7–13).

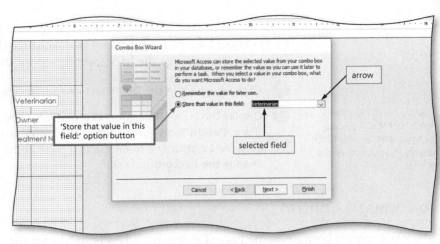

Figure 7–13

9

- Click Next to display the next Combo Box Wizard screen.
- Type **Doctor** as the label for the combo box, and then click the Finish button to place the combo box.

Q&A Could I change the label to something else?
Yes. If you prefer a different label, you could change it.

- Move the Doctor label by dragging its Move handle to the position shown in Figure 7–14. Resize the label, if necessary, to match the figure.

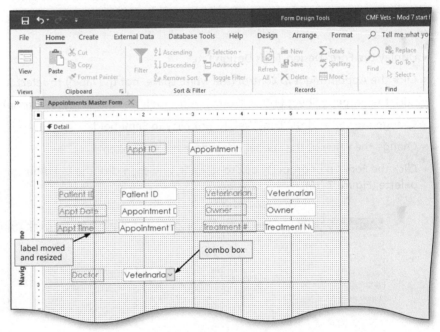

Figure 7–14

10

- Repeat steps 1-9 for Owner Last Name from the Owners table and the Patient Name from the Patients table. Type **Mr/Ms** as the label for the Owner Last Name combo box and **Patient** as the label for the Patient Name combo box.
- Move the combo boxes and labels by dragging their move handles to the positions shown in Figure 7–15. Resize the labels, if necessary, to match the figure.
- Save your changes to the form.

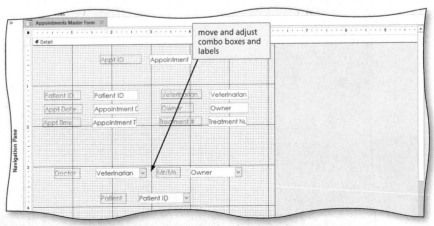

Figure 7–15

To Use the Background Color Button

As you learned in another module, you can use the Background Color button on the Form Design Tools Format tab to change the background color of a form. The following steps change the background color of the form to a light gray.

① Click anywhere in the Detail section but outside all the controls to select the section.

BTW
Touch and Pointers
Remember that if you are using your finger on a touch screen, you will not see the pointer.

② Display the Form Design Tools Format tab, click the Background Color button arrow (Form Design Tools Format tab | Font group) to display a color palette, and then click the Light Gray 2 color, the first color in the third row under Standard Colors, to change the background color.

To Format a Control

You can use buttons on the Form Design Tools Design tab to format a control in a variety of ways. The following steps use the property sheet, however, to make a variety of changes to the format of the Appointment ID control. **Why?** *Using the property sheet gives you more choices over the types of changes you can make to the form controls than you have with simply using the buttons.*

- Display the Form Design Tools Design tab.
- Click the Appointment ID control (the white space, not the label) to select it.
- Click the Property Sheet button (Form Design Tools Design tab | Tools group) to display the property sheet.
- Change the value of the Font Weight property to Semi-bold.
- Change the value of the Special Effect property to Sunken.
- Click the Fore Color property box to select it, and then click the Build button (the three dots) to display a color palette (Figure 7–16).

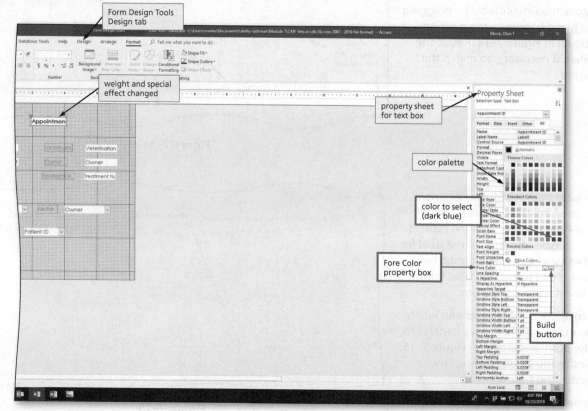

Figure 7–16

2

- Click the Dark Blue color (the second color from the right in the bottom row under Standard Colors) to select it as the fore color, which is the font color.

- Click the label for the Appt ID field to select it.

- Change the value of the Font Italic property to Yes.

- Change the Special Effect property to Etched (Figure 7–17).

3

- Close the property sheet.

Q&A Should I not have closed the property sheet before selecting a different control?
You could have, but it is not necessary. The property sheet displayed on the screen always applies to the currently selected control or group of controls.

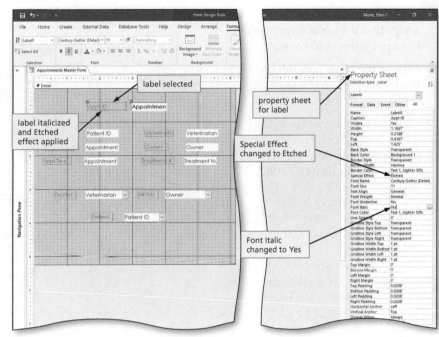

Figure 7–17

To Use the Format Painter

Once you have formatted a control and its label the way you want, you can format other controls in exactly the same way by using the Format Painter. *Why? If you click the control whose format you want to copy, click the Format Painter button on the Format tab, and then click another control, Access will automatically apply the characteristics of the first control to the second one.* If you want to copy the format to more than one other control, double-click the Format Painter button instead of simply clicking the button, and then click each of the controls that you want to change. The following steps copy the formatting of the Appointment ID control and label to the other controls.

1

- Display the Form Design Tools Format tab.

- Click the Appointment ID control to select it, and then double-click the Format Painter button (Form Design Tools Format tab | Font group) to select the Format Painter.

- Point to the Patient ID control (Figure 7–18).

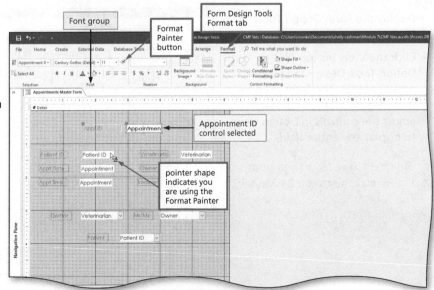

Figure 7–18

2

- Click the Patient ID control to assign to it the same formatting as the Appointment ID control.

- Click all the other controls on the form to assign the same formatting to them.

- Click the Format Painter button (Form Design Tools Format tab | Font group) to deselect the Format Painter (Figure 7–19).

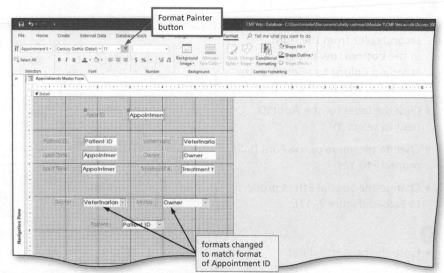

Figure 7–19

Q&A Do I always have to click the Format Painter button when I have finished copying the formatting?
If you double-clicked the Format Painter button to enable you to copy the formatting to multiple controls, you need to click the Format Painter button again to turn off the copying. If you single-clicked the Format Painter button to enable you to copy the formatting to a single control, you do not need to click the button again. As soon as you copy the formatting to the single control, the copying will be turned off.

Does the order in which I click the other controls matter?
No. The only thing that is important is that you ultimately click all the controls whose formatting you want to change.

3

- Save your changes to the form.

To View the Form

The following steps view the form in Form view and then return to Design view. *Why? As you are working on the design of a form, it is a good idea to periodically view the form in Form view to see the effects of your changes.*

1

- Display the Form Design Tools Design tab.

- Click the View button (Form Design Tools Design tab | Views group) to view the form in Form view (Figure 7–20). If necessary, adjust the controls in Design view to display the entire field.

Q&A Why did I have to change from the Format tab to the Design tab?
The Format tab does not have a View button.

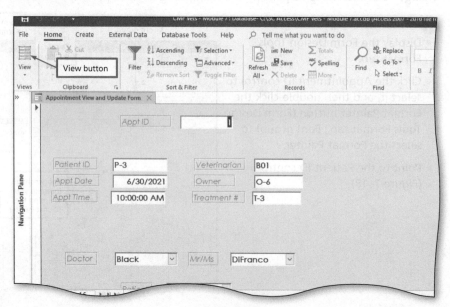

Figure 7–20

2

- Click the View button arrow (Home tab | Views group) to produce the View button menu.
- Click Design View on the View menu to return to Design view.

Q&A Could I simply click the View button?
No. The icon on the View button is the one for Layout view. Clicking the button would show you the form in Layout view, but you are working on the form in Design view.

Other Ways

1. Click Form View button on status bar

2. Click Design View button on status bar

To Add a Title and Expand the Form Header Section

The following steps insert the Form Header and Form Footer sections, and then add a title to the Form Header section. They also expand the Form Header section.

1 Click the Title button (Form Design Tools Design tab | Header/Footer group) to add a Form Header section and to add a control for the title to the Form Header section.

2 Drag the lower boundary of the Form Header section down to the approximate position shown in Figure 7–21.

3 Select the title control, display the Form Design Tools Format tab, and then click the Bold button (Form Design Tools Format tab | Font group) to make the title bold.

4 Drag the right sizing handle to the approximate position shown in the figure to resize the control to the appropriate size for the title.

BTW
Font versus Foreground Color
The font color also is called the foreground color. When you change the font color using the ribbon, you click the Font Color button. If you use the property sheet to change the color, you click the Fore Color property, click the Build button, and then click the desired color.

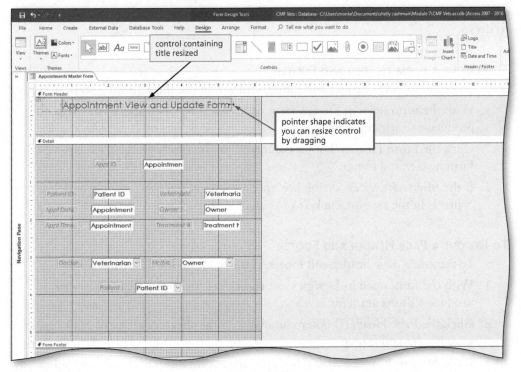

Figure 7–21

To Change the Background Color of the Form Header

The background color of the form header in the form in Figure 7–1 is the same as the rest of the form. The following steps change the background color of the form header appropriately.

1 Click anywhere in the Form Header section but outside the control to select the section.

2 If necessary, display the Form Design Tools Format tab.

3 Click the Background Color button arrow (Form Design Tools Format tab | Font group) to display a color palette.

4 Click the Light Gray 2 color, the first color in the third row under Standard Colors, to change the background color.

5 Save your changes to the form.

Headers and Footers

Just like with reports, you have control over whether your forms contain a form header and footer. They go together, so if you have a form header, you will also have a form footer. If you do not want the header and footer sections to appear, you can shrink the size so there is no room for any content. You can also remove the sections from your form altogether. If you later decide you want to include them, you can once again add them. You have similar options with page headers and page footers, although typically page headers and page footers are only used with reports. If you had a very long form that spanned several pages on the screen, you might choose to use page headers and footers, but it is not common to do so.

TO REMOVE A FORM HEADER AND FOOTER

To remove a form header and footer, you would use the following steps.

1. With the form open in Design view, right-click any open area of the form to produce a shortcut menu.
2. Click the Form Header/Footer command on the shortcut menu to remove the form header and footer.
3. If the Microsoft Access dialog box appears, asking if it is acceptable to delete any controls in the section, click Yes.

TO REMOVE A PAGE HEADER AND FOOTER

To remove a page header and footer, you would use the following steps.

1. With the form open in Design view, right-click any open area of the form to produce a shortcut menu.
2. Click the Page Header/Footer command on the shortcut menu to remove the page header and footer.
3. If the Microsoft Access dialog box appears, asking if it is acceptable to delete any controls in the section, click Yes.

To Insert a Form Header and Footer

To insert a form header and footer, you would use the following steps.

1. With the form open in Design view, right-click any open area of the form to produce a shortcut menu.
2. Click the Form Header/Footer command on the shortcut menu to insert a form header and footer.

To Insert a Page Header and Footer

To insert a page header and footer, you would use the following steps.

1. With the form open in Design view, right-click any open area of the form to produce a shortcut menu.
2. Click the Page Header/Footer command on the shortcut menu to insert a page header and footer.

Images

You can include a picture (image) in a form. You can also use a picture (image) as the background for a form.

To Include an Image in a Form

To include an image in a form, you would use the following steps.

1. Open the form in Design view or Layout view.
2. Click the Insert Image button (Form Design Tools Design tab | Controls group) and then click the Browse command.
3. Select the desired image.
4. Click the desired location to add the image to the form.

To Use an Image as Background for a Form

To include an image as background for a form, you would use the following steps.

1. Open the form in Design view or Layout view.
2. Click anywhere in the form, click the Background Image button (Form Design Tools Format tab | Background group), and then click the Browse command.
3. Select the desired image for the background.

Break Point: If you wish to stop working through the module at this point, you can quit Access now. You can resume the project later by starting Access, opening the database called CMF Vets, opening the Appointments Master Form in Design view, and continuing to follow the steps from this location forward.

Command Buttons

Command buttons are buttons placed on a form that users can click to carry out specific actions. To add command buttons, you use the Button tool in the Controls group on the Form Design Tools Design tab. When using the series of Command Button Wizard dialog boxes, you indicate the action that should be taken when the command button is clicked, for example, go to the next record. Within the Command Button Wizard, Access includes several categories of commonly used actions.

BTW
Record Order
When you use the Next Record button to move through the records, recall that the records are in order by Appointment ID, which is the primary key, and not alphabetical order.

When would you include command buttons in your form?
You can make certain actions more convenient for users by including command buttons. Buttons can carry out record navigation actions (for example, go to the next record), record operation actions (for example, add a record), form operation actions (for example, close a form), report operation actions (for example, print a report), application actions (for example, quit application), and some miscellaneous actions (for example, run a macro).

To Add Command Buttons to a Form

You might find that you can improve the functionality of your form by adding command buttons. *Why?* *Command buttons enable users to accomplish tasks with a single click.* Before adding the buttons, you should make sure the 'Use Control Wizards' button is selected.

In the Record Navigation action category, you will select the Go To Next Record action for one of the command buttons. From the same category, you will select the Go To Previous Record action for another. Other buttons will use the Add New Record and the Delete Record actions from the Record Operations category. The Close Form button will use the Close Form action from the Form Operations category.

The following steps add command buttons to move to the next record, move to the previous record, add a record, delete a record, and close the form.

 1

- Display the Form Design Tools Design tab, click the More button in the control gallery, and then ensure the 'Use Control Wizards' button is selected.

- Click the Button tool (Form Design Tools Design tab | Controls group) and then move the pointer to the approximate position shown in Figure 7–22.

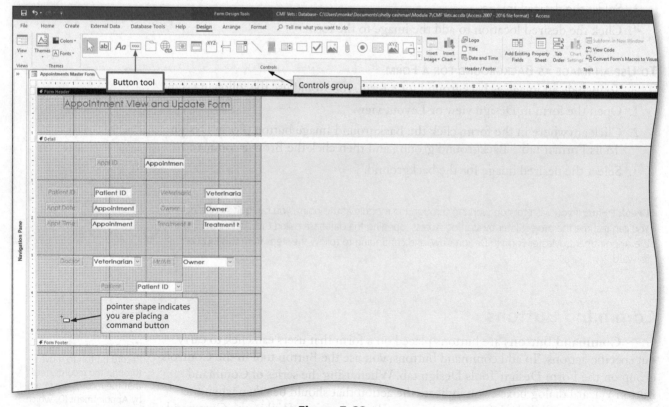

Figure 7–22

2

- Click the position shown in Figure 7–22 to display the Command Button Wizard dialog box.

- With Record Navigation selected in the Categories box, click Go To Next Record in the Actions box (Figure 7–23).

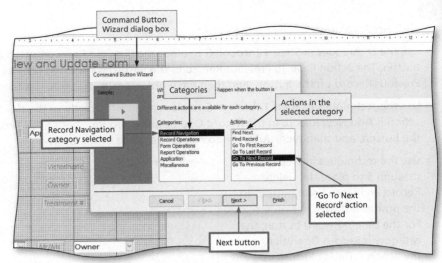

Figure 7–23

3

- Click Next to display the next Command Button Wizard screen.

- Click the Text option button (Figure 7–24).

Q&A What is the purpose of these option buttons?

Choose the first option button to place text on the button. You then can specify the text to be included or accept the default choice. Choose the second option button to place a picture on the button. You can then select a picture.

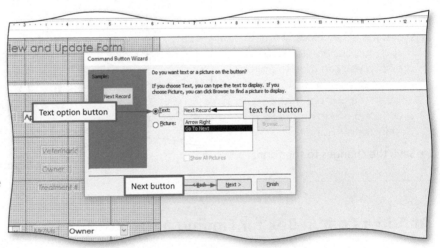

Figure 7–24

4

- Because Next Record is the desired text and does not need to be changed, click Next.

- Type **Next Record** as the name of the button (Figure 7–25).

Q&A Does the name of the button have to be the same as the text that appears on the face of the button?

No. The text is what will appear on the screen. You use the name when you need to refer to the specific button. They can be different, but this can lead to confusion. Thus, many people will typically make them the same.

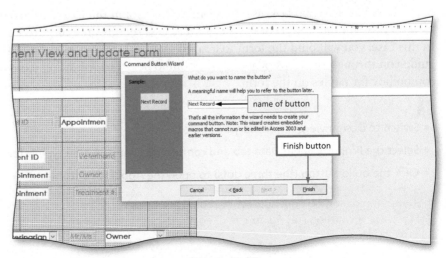

Figure 7–25

- Click Finish to finish specifying the button.

- Use the techniques in Steps 1 through 5 to place the Previous Record button directly to the right of the Next Record button. The action is Go To Previous Record in the Record Navigation category. Choose the Text option button and Previous Record on the button, and then type `Previous Record` as the name of the button.

- Use the techniques in Steps 1 through 5 to place a button directly to the right of the Previous Record button. The action is Add New Record in the Record Operations category. Choose the Text option button and Add Record on the button, and then type `Add Record` as the name of the button.

- Use the techniques in Steps 1 through 5 to place the Delete Record and Close Form buttons in the positions shown in Figure 7–26. For the Delete Record button, the category is Record Operations and the action is Delete Record. For the Close Form button, the category is Form Operations and the action is Close Form.

Q&A My buttons are not aligned like yours are. What should I do?
If your buttons are not aligned properly, you can drag them to the correct positions. You can also use the buttons in the Sizing & Ordering group on the Form Design Tools Arrange tab.

- Save the changes to the form.

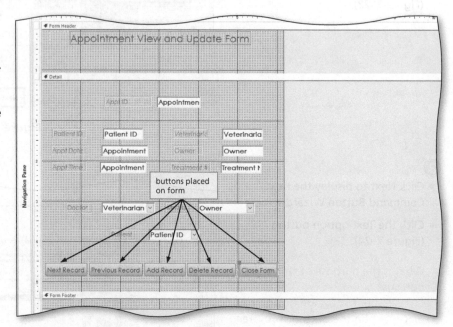

Figure 7–26

To Add a Combo Box for Finding a Record

Although you can use the Find button (Home tab | Find group) to locate records on a form or a report, it is often more convenient to use a combo box. ***Why?*** *You can click the combo box arrow to display a list and then select the desired entry from the list.*

To create a combo box, use the Combo Box tool in the Controls group on the Design tab. Before the Combo Box will find the records, Microsoft Access requires the form to be bound to an existing table or query. In this case, you will bind the form to a saved query. Once that is accomplished, the Combo Box Wizard will guide you through the steps of adding the combo box. The following steps create the query and then place a combo box for names on the form.

- Switch to Design view, if necessary.

- Select the Property Sheet Data tab and confirm that the selection type is form.

- Click the build button (the three dots) to open the Appointments Master Form: Query Builder.

Q&A A warning dialog box opened. What should I do?
If you see a warning stating You Invoked the Query Builder on a Table, do you want to create a query based on the table? click Yes.

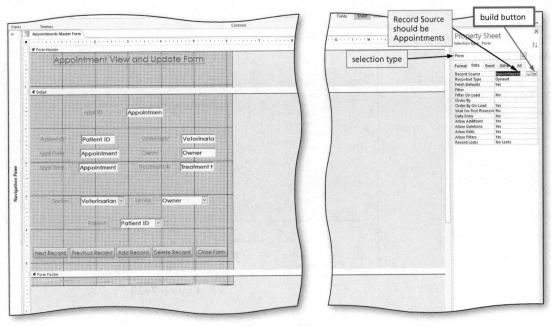

Figure 7–27

2
• Create the query as shown in Figure 7–28. Recall that to add tables to the query, you must click the Show Table button (Design tab | Query Setup group).

• Use the Save As button (Query Tools Design tab | Close Group) to save the query, as shown in Figure 7–28.

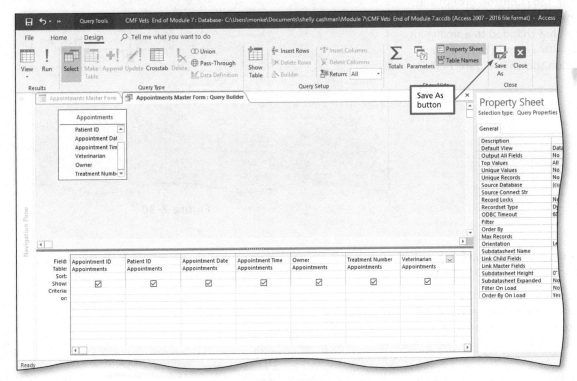

Figure 7–28

● Save Query1 as Queryform and
click OK as shown in Figure 7–29.

● Close the query builder and save
any changes.

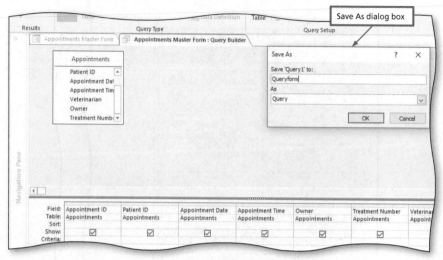

Figure 7–29

● Click the More button (Form
Design Tools Design tab | Controls
group) to display all the controls.

● With the 'Use Control Wizards'
button selected, click the Combo
Box tool (Form Design Tools
Design tab | Controls group) and
then move the pointer, whose
shape has changed to a small plus
sign with a combo box, to the
position shown in Figure 7–30.

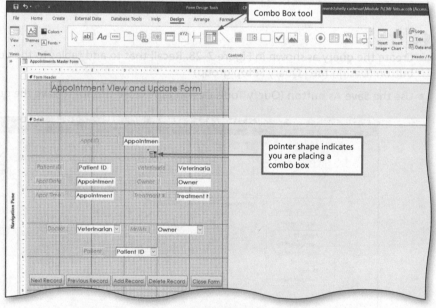

Figure 7–30

● Click the position shown in Figure 7–30
to display the Combo Box Wizard.

● Click the 'Find a record on my form
based on the value I selected in
my combo box.' option button to
specify that the user will select from
a list of values.

● Click Next, click the Appointment ID
field, and then click the Add Field
button to select the Appointment
ID for the combo box (Figure 7–31).
Repeat these steps for the
Appointment Date field and the
Appointment Time field.

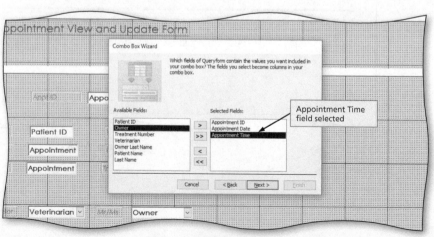

Figure 7–31

6
- Click Next.
- If necessary, adjust any column width shown in Figure 7–32.

Q&A Can I also resize the column to best fit the data by double-clicking the right boundary of the column heading?
Yes.

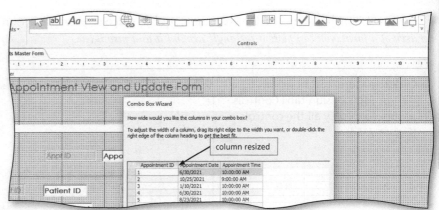

Figure 7–32

7
- Click Next and then type **&Appointment to Find** as the label for the combo box.

Q&A What is the purpose of the ampersand in front of the letter, A?
The ampersand (&) in front of the letter, A, indicates that users can select the combo box by pressing ALT+A

- Click Finish, and, if necessary, position and resize as necessary the control and label in the approximate position so that your screen resembles Figure 7–33.

Q&A Why is the letter, A, underlined?
The underlined letter, A, in the word, Appointment, indicates that you can press ALT+A to select the combo box. It is underlined because you preceded the letter, A, with the ampersand.

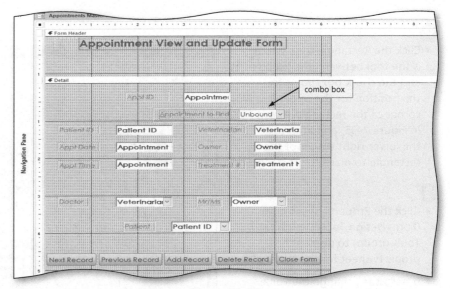

Figure 7–33

When would you include a combo box in your form?
A combo box is a combination of a text box, where users can type data, and a list box, where users can click an arrow to display a list. Would a combo box improve the functionality of the form? Is there a place where it would be convenient for users to enter data by selecting the data from a list, either a list of predefined items or a list of values from a related table? If users need to search for records, including a combo box can assist in the process.

To Place a Rectangle

The following steps use the Rectangle tool to place a rectangle around the combo box. *Why? To emphasize an area of a form, you can place a rectangle around it as a visual cue.*

1

- Click the More button (Form Design Tools Design tab | Controls group) to display all the controls (Figure 7–34).

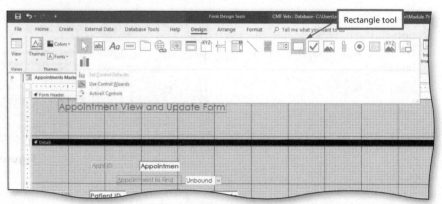

Figure 7–34

2

- Click the Rectangle tool, which is the tool between the list box and the check box, point to the position for the upper-left corner of the rectangle shown in Figure 7–35, and drag to the lower-right corner of the rectangle to place the rectangle.

3

- Click the Property Sheet button (Form Design Tools Design tab | Tools group) to display the property sheet for the rectangle.

- If necessary, change the value of the Special Effect property to Etched.

- Make sure the value of the Back Style property is Transparent, so the combo box will appear within the rectangle.

- Adjust any widths to make all labels visible.

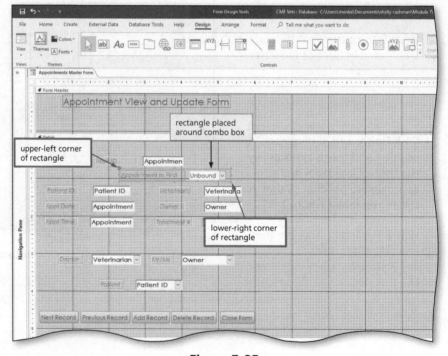

Figure 7–35

 What if the value is not Transparent?

If the value is not Transparent, the rectangle will cover the combo box completely and the combo box will not be visible.

- Close the property sheet.

- Save and then close the form.

To Open the Appointment View and Update Form

BTW
VBA
Visual Basic for Applications (VBA) is a programming language that can be used with Access. As with other programming languages, programs in VBA consist of code; that is, a collection of statements, also called commands, which are instructions that will cause actions to take place when the program executes. VBA is included with all Microsoft Office apps.

Once you have created the form, you can use it at any time by opening it. The following steps open the Appointment View and Update Form.

1 Open the Navigation Pane, and then right-click the Appointments Master Form to display the shortcut menu.

2 Click Open on the shortcut menu to open the form.

3 Close the Navigation Pane (Figure 7–36).

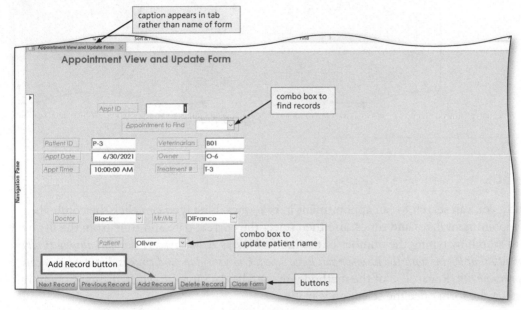

Figure 7–36

Using the Buttons

BTW
Converting Macros to VBA Code
You can convert macros that are attached to forms to VBA (Visual Basic for Applications) code. To do so, open the form in Design view and click the 'Convert Form's Macros to Visual Basic' button. You also can convert macros that are attached to reports.

To move from record to record on the form, you can use the buttons to perform the actions you specify. To move forward to the next record, click the Next Record button. Click the Previous Record button to move back to the previous record. Clicking the Delete Record button will delete the record currently on the screen. Access will display a message requesting that you verify the deletion before the record is actually deleted. Clicking the Close Form button will remove the form from the screen.

To Test the Add Record Button

The following step uses the Add Record button. **Why?** *Clicking the Add Record button will clear the contents of the form so you can add a new record.*

1
- Click the Add Record button (Figure 7–37).

There is no insertion point in the Patient ID field. How would I begin entering a new record?
To begin entering a record, you would have to click the Patient ID field before you can start typing.

Why does new appear in the Appointment ID field?
The value new refers to the autonumber type field, which will automatically assign a new Appointment ID as you begin to fill in the form.

Experiment

- Try each of the other buttons to see their effects. Do not delete any records. After clicking the Close Form button, open the form once again and close the Navigation Pane.

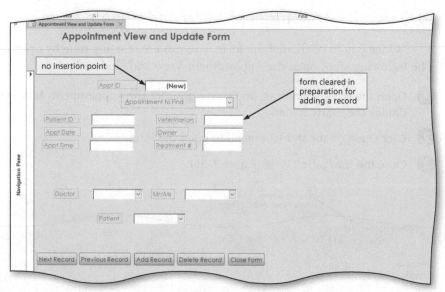

Figure 7–37

To Use the Combo Box

Using the combo box, you can search for an appointment in two ways. First, you can click the combo box arrow to display a list of appointment dates and times, and then select the correct date and time from the list by clicking it. It is also easy to search by typing the number of the month. *Why? As you type, Access will automatically display the number of the month that begins with the number you have typed. Once the date and time is displayed, you can select the date and time by pressing TAB.* Regardless of the method you use, the data for the selected appointment on that date and time appears on the form once the selection is made.

The following steps first locate the appointment whose month is 8 and then use the Next Record button to move to the next appointment.

- Click the 'Appointment to Find' arrow to display a list of appointment dates and times (Figure 7–38).

Q&A Does the list always appear in numerical order? Can I make it in chronological order (by date)? No, not always. You will change the combo box later so that the records will always be in chronological order.

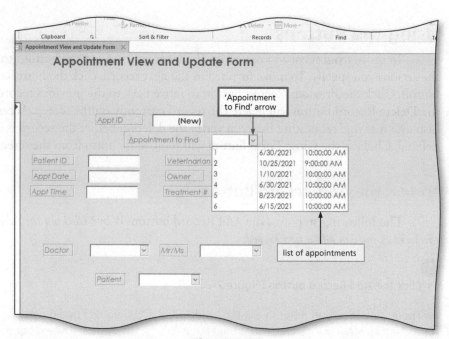

Figure 7–38

2
- Click 3 to display the data for 1/10/2021 in the form (Figure 7–39).

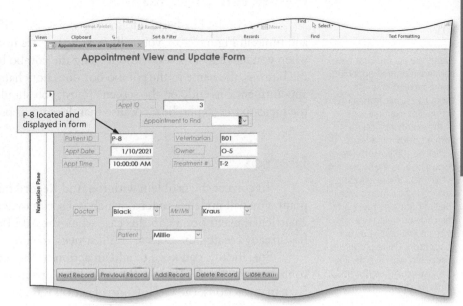

Figure 7–39

3
- Click the Next Record button to display the next record (Figure 7–40).

Q&A Why does the combo box still contain Appointment 3, rather than the correct Appointment? This is a problem with the combo box. You will address this issue later.

🔍 **Experiment**
- Select the entry in the combo box, delete and enter the number, 5, to find the appointment on 8/23/2021.

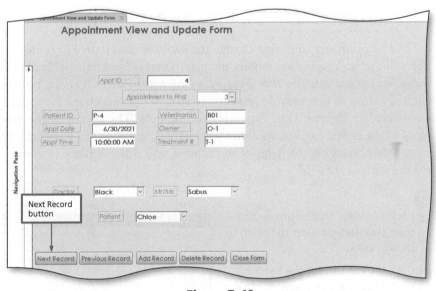

Figure 7–40

Issues with the Add Record Button

Although clicking the Add Record button does erase the contents of the form in preparation for adding a new record, there is a problem with it. After clicking the Add Record button, there should be an insertion point in the control for the first field you need to type into — the Patient ID field — but there is not. To display an insertion point automatically when you click the Add Record button, you need to change the focus. A control is said to have the **focus** when it becomes active; that is, when it becomes able to receive user input through mouse, touch, or keyboard actions. At any point in time, only one item on the form has the focus. In addition to adding a new record, clicking the Add Record button needs to update the focus to the Patient ID field.

BTW
Focus
Sometimes it is difficult to determine which object on the screen has the focus. If a field has the focus, an insertion point appears in the field. If a button has the focus, a small rectangle appears inside the button.

Issues with the Combo Box

BTW

Events
Events are actions that have happened or are happening at the present time. An event can result from a user action. For example, one of the events associated with a button on a form is clicking the button. The corresponding event property is On Click. If you associate VBA code or a macro with the On Click event property, the code or macro will execute any time you click the button. Using properties associated with events, you can instruct Access to run a macro, call a Visual Basic function, or run an event procedure in response to an event.

The combo box has the following issues. First, if you examine the list of dates and times in Figure 7–38, you will see that they are not in chronological order. Second, when you move to a record without using the combo box, such as when navigating using the buttons, the name in the combo box does not change to reflect the name of the appointment currently on the screen. Third, you should not be able to use TAB to change the focus to the combo box, because that does not represent a field to be updated.

Macros

To correct the problem with the Add Record button not displaying an insertion point, you will update a **macro**, which is a series of actions that Access performs when a particular event occurs, in this case when the Add Record button is clicked. Access has already created the macro; you just need to add a single action to it.

Specifically, you need to add an action to the macro that will move the focus to the control for the Patient ID field. The appropriate action is GoToControl. Like many actions, the GoToControl action requires additional information, called arguments. The argument for the GoToControl action is the name of the control, in this case, the Patient ID control.

To Modify the Macro for the Add Record Button

The following steps first change the name of the control to remove spaces (a requirement in VBA, which you will use later) and then modify the macro that is associated with the Add Record button. *Why? Modifying the macro lets you add an action that changes the focus to the Patient ID field.* You can use different methods of changing control names so that they do not contain spaces. One approach is to simply remove the space. This approach would change Patient ID to PatientID, for example. The approach you will use is to insert an underscore (_) in place of the space. For example, you will change Patient ID to Patient_ID.

After changing the name of the control, you will complete an action that changes the focus to the control for the Patient ID field.

- Click the View button arrow and then click Design View to return to Design view.

- Click the control for the Patient ID field (the white space, not the label), and then click the Property Sheet button (Form Design Tools Design tab | Tools group) to display the property sheet.

- If necessary, click the All tab. Ensure the Name property is selected, click immediately following the word, Patient, press DELETE to delete the space, and then type an underscore (_) to change the name to Patient_ID (Figure 7–41).

- Click the control for Appointment ID field and on the property sheet repeat the previous steps and rename the field Appointment_ID.

- Click the control for the Appointment to Find combo box and on the property sheet repeat the previous steps and rename the combo box Appointment_to_Find.

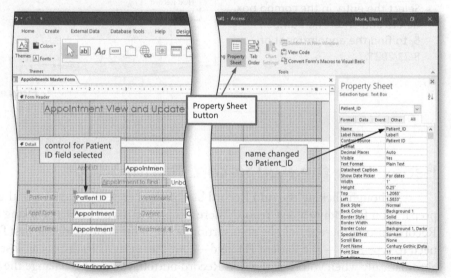

Figure 7–41

Q&A Could I just erase the old name and type Patient ID?
Yes. Use whichever method you find most convenient.

● Close the property sheet, and then right-click the Add Record button to display a shortcut menu (Figure 7–42).

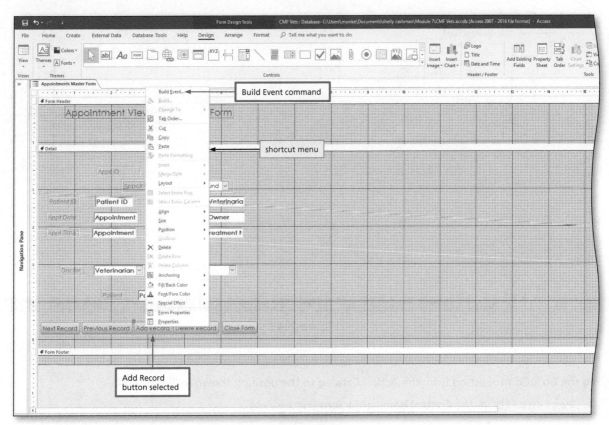

Figure 7–42

2
● Click Build Event on the shortcut menu to display the macro associated with the On Click event that Access created automatically.

● If the Action Catalog, the catalog that lists all of the available actions, does not appear, click the Action Catalog button (Macro Tools Design tab | Show/Hide group) to display the Action Catalog.

● In the Action Catalog, if the expand indicator is an open triangle in front of Actions, click the triangle to display all actions.

● If the expand indicator in front of Database Objects is an open triangle, click the expand indicator to display all actions associated with Database Objects (Figure 7–43).

Q&A How can I recognize actions? How can I recognize the arguments of the actions?
The actions are in bold. The arguments for the action follow the action and are not bold. The value for an argument appears to the right of the argument. The value for the 'Go to' argument of the OnError action is Next, for example.

What is the purpose of the actions currently in the macro?
The first action indicates that, if there is an error, Access should proceed to the next action in the macro rather than immediately stopping the macro. The second action causes Access to go to the record indicated by the values in the arguments. The value, New, indicates that Access should to go to a new record. Because the final action has a condition, the action will be executed only if the condition is true, that is, the error code contains a value other than 0. In that case, the MsgBox action will display a description of the error.

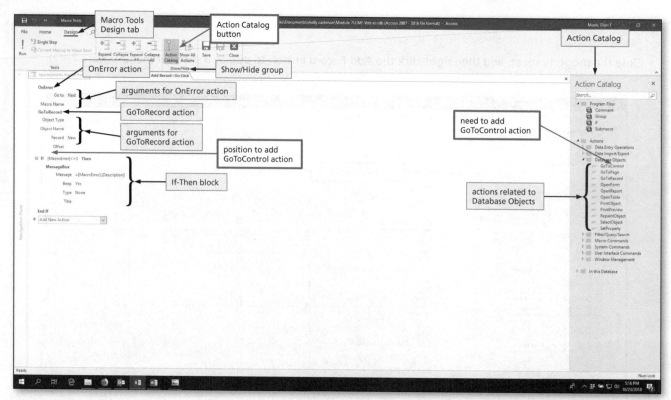

Figure 7–43

3

• Drag the GoToControl action from the Action Catalog to the position shown in Figure 7–44.

• Type **Patient_ID** as the Control Name argument (Figure 7–44).

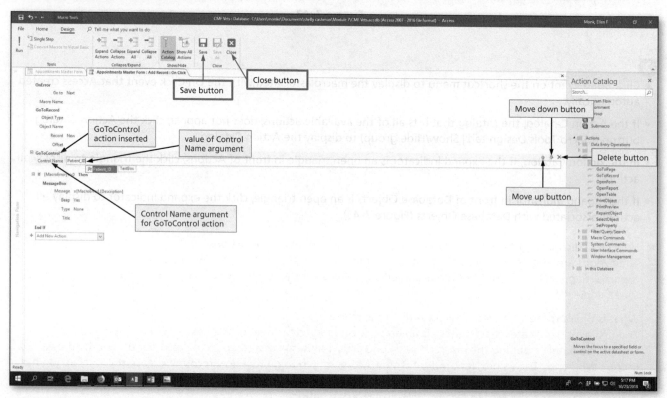

Figure 7–44

Q&A

What is the effect of the GoToControl action?
When Access executes this action, the focus will move to the control indicated in the Control Name argument, in this case, the Patient_ID control.

I added the GoToControl action to the wrong place in the macro. How do I move it?
To move it up in the list, click the Move up button. To move it down, click the Move down button.

I added the wrong action. What should I do?
Click the Delete button to delete the action you added, and then add the GoToControl action. If you decide you would rather start over instead, click Close (Macro Tools Design tab | Close group) and then click the No button when asked if you want to save your changes. You can then begin again from Step 2.

- Click Save (Macro Tools Design tab | Close group) to save your changes.

- Click Close (Macro Tools Design tab | Close group) to close the macro and return to the form design.

To Modify the Combo Box

The combo box might not display dates in chronological order. To ensure the data is always sorted in the correct order, you need to modify the query that Access has created for the combo box so the data is sorted by Appointment Date. The following steps modify the query.

- Click the Appointment to Find combo box (the white space, not the label), display the Form Design Tools Design tab, and then click the Property Sheet button (Form Design Tools Design tab | Tools group).

- Scroll down in the property sheet so that the Row Source property appears, click the Row Source property, and then click the Build button (the three dots) to display the Query Builder.

- Click the Sort row in the Appointment Date field, click the arrow that appears, and then click Ascending to change the order to ensure the Appointment Dates are always in chronological order in the combo box (Figure 7–45).

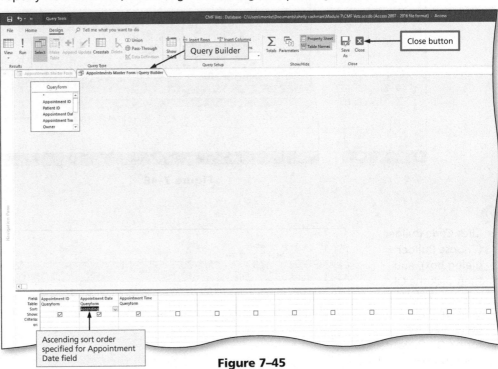

Figure 7–45

- Click Save on the Quick Access Toolbar to save your changes.

- Close the Query Builder window by clicking Close (Query Tools Design tab | Close group).

To Correct Issues with the Combo Box

The form does not update the Appointment Date and Time in the combo box to reflect the appointment currently on the screen unless the Appointment to Find is chosen. The following steps modify the query and then the code associated with the On Current event property appropriately. *Why? Modifying the VBA code lets you update the form actions appropriately.* The final step changes the Tab Stop property for the combo box from Yes to No.

- Click the form selector (the box in the upper-left corner of the form) to select the form.
- If necessary, Click the Property Sheet button (Form Design Tools Design tab | Tools group), scroll down until the On Current property appears, and then click the On Current property.
- Click the Build button (the three dots) to display the Choose Builder dialog box (Figure 7–46).

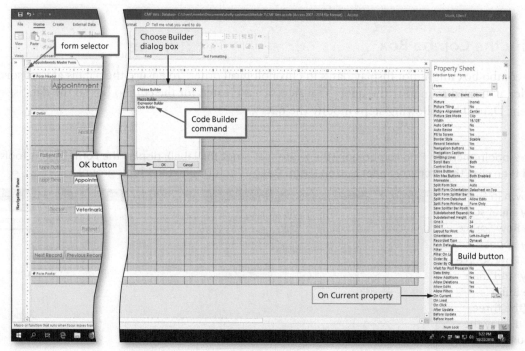

Figure 7–46

- Click Code Builder (Choose Builder dialog box), and then click the OK button to display the VBA code generated for the form's On Current event property (Figure 7–47).

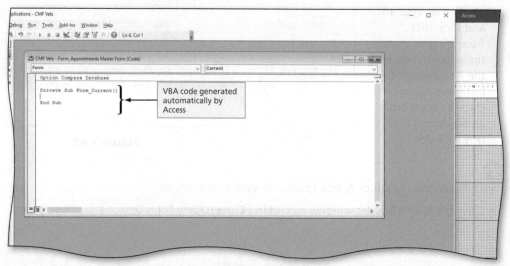

Figure 7–47

3

- Press TAB and then type `Appointment_to_Find = Appointment_ID ' Update the combo box` as shown in Figure 7–48, to create the command and a comment that describes the effect of the command.

Q&A How would I construct a command like this in my own form?
Begin with the name you assigned to the combo box, followed by an equal sign, and then the name of the control containing the primary key of the table. The portion of the statement following the single quotation mark is a comment describing the purpose of the command. You could simply type the same thing that you see in this command.

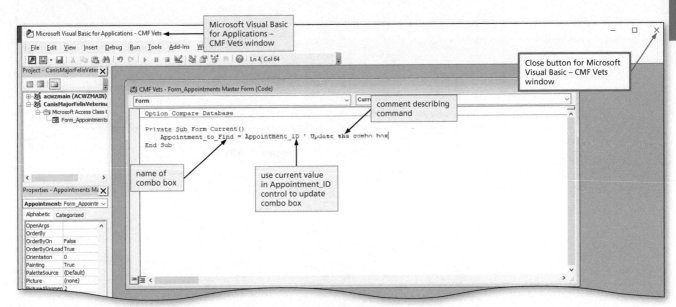

Figure 7–48

4

- Click Close for the Microsoft Visual Basic for Applications - CMF Vets window.

- Click the Appointment to Find combo box.

- In the property sheet, scroll down until the Tab Stop property appears, click the Tab Stop property, and then click the Tab Stop property box arrow.

- Click No to change the value of the Tab Stop property, which skips over the combo box in the tab sequence, and then close the property sheet.

- Save your changes and then close the form.

Using the Modified Form

The problems with the Add Record button and the combo box are now corrected. When you click the Add Record button, an insertion point appears in the Patient ID field (Figure 7–49a). When you click the Appointment to Find box arrow, the list of dates are in chronological order (Figure 7–49b). After using the Appointment to Find box to find an appointment (Figure 7–49c) and clicking the Next Record button, the Appointment to Find box is updated with the correct date and time (Figure 7–49d).

BTW
Comments in Macros
You can use the Comment action in the Action Catalog to place comments in macros.

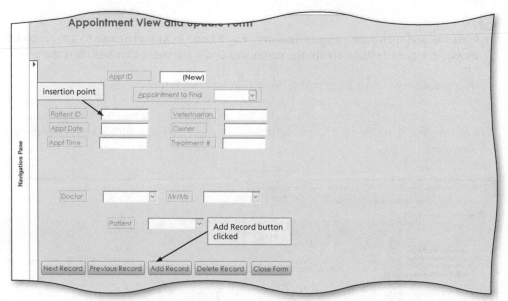

Figure 7–49a

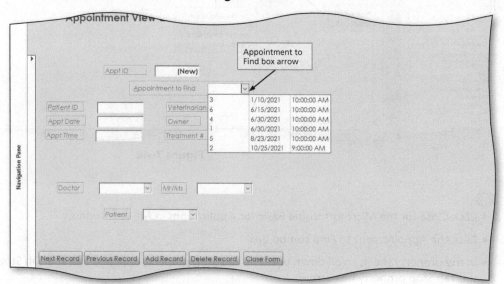

Figure 7–49b

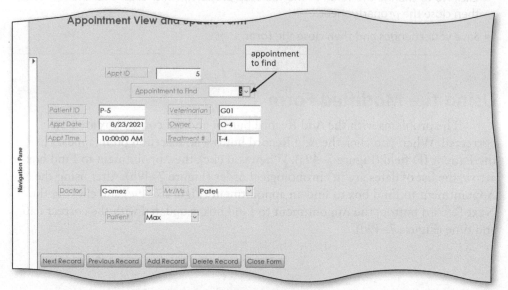

Figure 7–49c

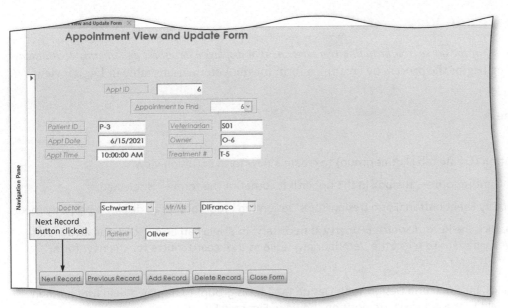

Figure 7–49d

Break Point: If you wish to stop working through the module at this point, you can quit Access now. You can resume the project later by starting Access, opening the database called CMF Vets, and continuing to follow the steps from this location forward.

Creating a Multipage Form

If you have determined that you have more data than will fit conveniently on one screen, you can create a **multipage form**, a form that includes more than a single page. There are two ways to create a multipage form. One way is to insert a page break at the desired location or locations. An alternative approach, which produces a nice-looking and easy-to-use multipage form, is to insert a tab control. The multiple pages, called tabbed pages, are all contained within the tab control. To move from one page in the tab control to another, a user simply clicks the desired tab. The tab control shown in Figure 7–2, for example, has a tab labeled Datasheet that contains a datasheet showing the relevant data. It has a second tab, labeled Charts, that displays the relevant data in two charts.

To Import a Table

The management at CMF Vets would like to track the emergency hours and the on call hours of their veterinarians. This information is stored in a table named Emergency On Call Hours. You will need to import the table to create the form.

1. Click the New Data Source arrow (External Data tab | Import & Link group) to display the options for importing data.
2. Point to From Database, and then click Access to display the Get External Data – Access Database dialog box.
3. Navigate to the location containing your data files (if you do not have the required files, see your instructor), select the Emergency On Call Extra Table, and then select the only table available, Emergency on Call Hours.

To Create a Form in Design View

Why? *The form will contain the tab control including two tabs: one that displays a datasheet and another that displays two charts.* The following step begins the process by creating a form for the Veterinarians table in Design view.

- Close the Navigation Pane.
- Display the Create tab.
- Click the Form Design button (Create tab | Forms group) to create a new form in Design view.
- Ensure the selector for the entire form — the box in the upper-left corner of the form — is selected.
- If necessary, click the Property Sheet button (Form Design Tools Design tab | Tools group) to display a property sheet.
- With the All tab selected, click the Record Source property, if necessary, to display an arrow, click the arrow that appears, and then click Veterinarians to select the Veterinarians table as the record source for the new form.
- Close the property sheet.
- Click the 'Add Existing Fields' button (Form Design Tools Design tab | Tools group) to display a field list and then drag the Veterinarian ID field to the approximate position shown in Figure 7–50.
- Change the label for the Veterinarian ID field from Veterinarian ID to Veterinarian Identification. Resize and move the label to the position shown in the figure.

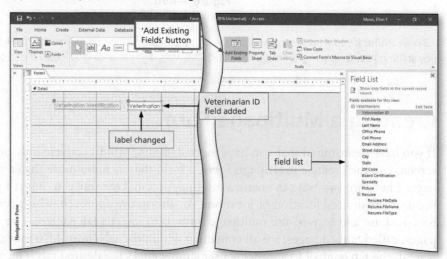

Figure 7–50

To Use the Text Box Tool with Concatenation

Why? *If you have determined that* **concatenation,** *which simply means combining objects in a series, is appropriate for a form, you can create a concatenated field by using the Text Box tool in the Controls group on the Design tab and then indicating the concatenation that is to be performed.* The following steps add a concatenated field, involving two text fields, First Name and Last Name. Specifically, you will concatenate the first name, a single space, and the last name.

- Click the Text Box tool (Form Design Tools Design tab | Controls group) and then move the pointer, whose shape has changed to a small plus symbol accompanied by a text box, to the position shown in Figure 7–51.

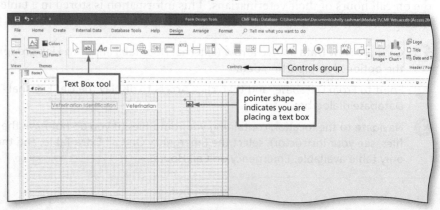

Figure 7–51

2

- Click the position shown in Figure 7–51 to place a text box on the report.

- Click in the text box to produce an insertion point.

- Type `=[First Name]&' '&[Last Name]` as the entry in the text box.

- Click the attached label to select it (Figure 7–52).

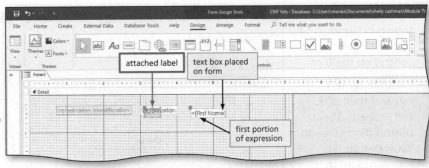

Figure 7–52

3

- Press DELETE to delete the attached label.

- Resize the Veterinarian ID control to the approximate size shown in Figure 7–53.

- Click the text box to select it, drag it to the position shown in Figure 7–53, and then drag the right sizing handle to the approximate position shown in the figure.

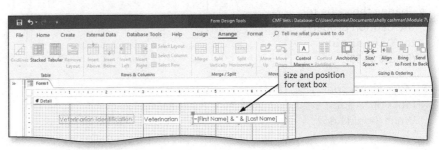

Figure 7–53

BTW
Concatenation is often used in computing to combine or merge two things. For example, if you have two separate fields such as first name and last name, you can concatenate them to show a full name.

4

- Close the field list by clicking the 'Add Existing Fields' button (Form Design Tools Design tab | Tools group).

- Save the form using the name, Vet Emergency On Call Form.

To Use Tab Controls to Create a Multipage Form

Why? *To use tabs on a form, you need to insert a tab control.* The following steps insert a tab control with two tabs: Datasheet and Charts. Users will be able to click the Datasheet tab in the completed form to view On Call and Emergency Hours in Datasheet view. Clicking the Charts tab will display two charts representing the same hour data as in the Datasheet tab.

1

- Click the Tab Control tool (Form Design Tools Design Tab | Controls group) and move the pointer to the approximate location shown in Figure 7–54.

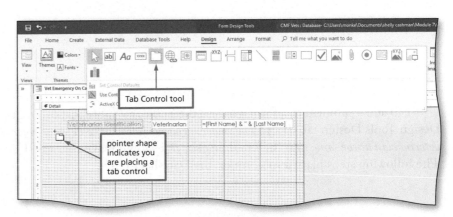

Figure 7–54

2

- Click the position shown in Figure 7–54 to place a tab control on the form.

- Click the far left tab and then click the Property Sheet button (Form Design Tools Design tab | Tools group) to display a property sheet.

- Change the value for the Caption property to **Datasheet** (Figure 7–55).

My property sheet looks different. What should I do?
Be sure you clicked the far left tab before displaying the property sheet. The highlight should be within the border of the tab, as shown in the figure.

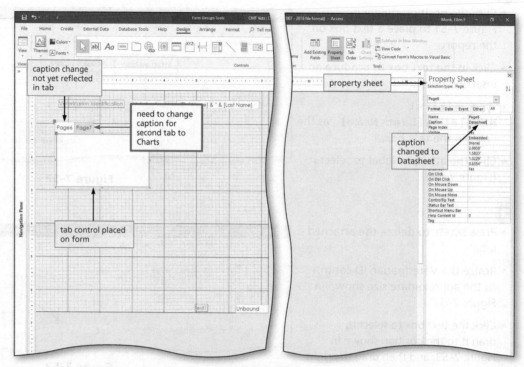

Figure 7–55

3

- Click the second tab without closing the property sheet.
- Change the value for the Caption property to **Charts**.
- Close the property sheet.

CONSIDER THIS

When would you include a tab control in your form?
If the form contains more information than will conveniently fit on the screen at a time, consider adding a tab control. With a tab control, you can organize the information within a collection of tabbed pages. To access any of the tabbed pages, users need only click the corresponding tab.

To Add a Subform

To add a subform to a form, you use the Subform/Subreport tool in the Controls group on the Form Design Tools Design tab. **Why?** *The subform enables you to show data for emergency and on call hours for a given veterinarian at the same time.* Before doing so, you should make sure the 'Use Control Wizards' button is selected. The following steps place a subform on the Datasheet tab.

1

- Click the Datasheet tab.

- Resize the tab control to the approximate size shown in Figure 7–56 by dragging the appropriate sizing handles.

Q&A Why do I need to resize the tab control?
Because there needs to be enough room in the form to display all the datasheet columns and the two charts, you will need to make the tab control larger.

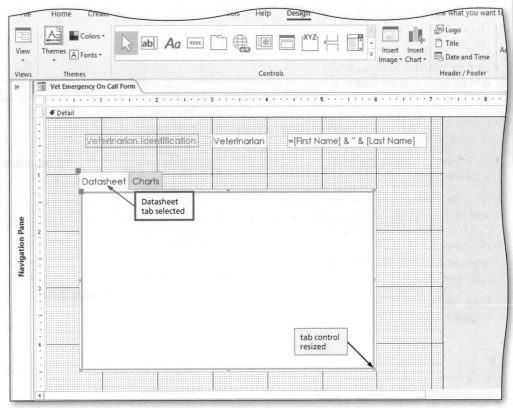

Figure 7–56

2

- Click the More button (Form Design Tools Design tab | Controls group).

- With the 'Use Control Wizards' button selected, click the Subform/ Subreport tool (Form Design Tools Design tab | Controls group) and then move the pointer to the approximate position shown in Figure 7–57.

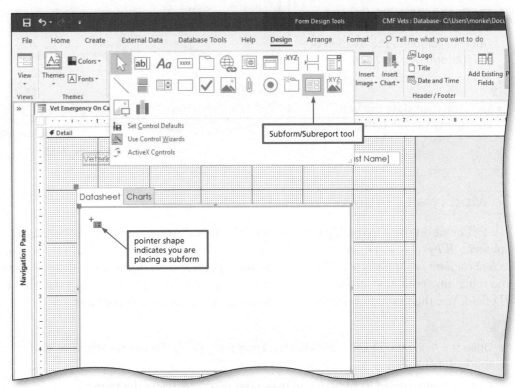

Figure 7–57

- Click the position shown in Figure 7–57 to open the SubForm Wizard.
- Be sure the 'Use existing Tables and Queries' option button is selected.
- If necessary, click Open to close the security warning.
- Click Next to display the next SubForm Wizard screen.
- Click the Tables/Queries arrow, and then click the Emergency On Call Hours table to indicate that the fields for the subform will be selected from the Emergency On Call Hours table.
- Click the 'Add All Fields' button (Figure 7–58).

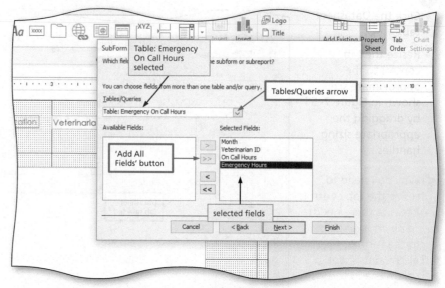

Figure 7–58

- Click Next.
- Be sure the 'Choose from a list' option button is selected.
- Click Next.
- Change the name of the subform to **Emergency On Call Hours for Vet**, and then click Finish to complete the creation of the subform (Figure 7–59).

- Save and then close the Vet Emergency On Call form.

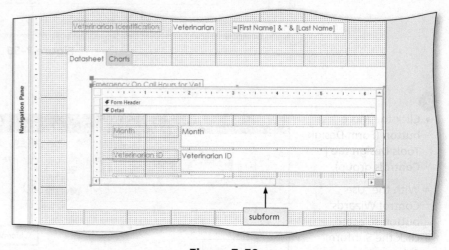

Figure 7–59

To Modify a Subform

The next task is to modify the subform. The first step is to remove the Veterinarian ID field from the subform. *Why? The Veterinarian ID field needed to be included initially in the subform because it is the field that is used to link the data in the subform to the data in the main form. It is not supposed to appear in the form, however.* In addition, the remaining columns need to be resized to appropriate sizes. The following step first removes the Veterinarian ID field. You then switch to Datasheet view to resize the remaining columns.

- Open the Navigation Pane, right-click the Emergency On Call Hours for Vet form, and then click Design View on the shortcut menu.
- Click the Veterinarian ID control, and then press DELETE to delete the control.

- Save the subform and close it.

- Right-click the Emergency On Call Hours for Vet subform in the Navigation Pane and click Open on the shortcut menu.

- Resize each column to best fit the data by double-clicking the right boundary of the column's field selector (Figure 7–60).

- Save the subform and then close it.

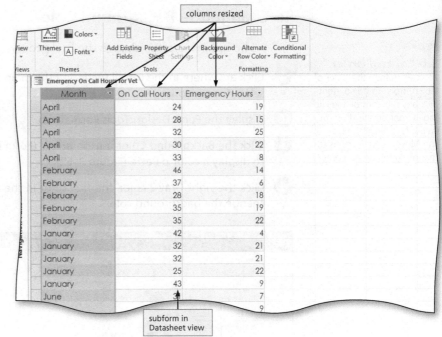

Figure 7–60

To Resize the Subform

The following step resizes the subform. *Why? The size should enable the user to clearly view all the data.*

- If necessary, open the Navigation Pane, right-click the Vet Emergency On Call form and then click Design View on the shortcut menu.

- Close the Navigation Pane.

- Resize the subform to the size shown in Figure 7–61 by dragging the right sizing handle.

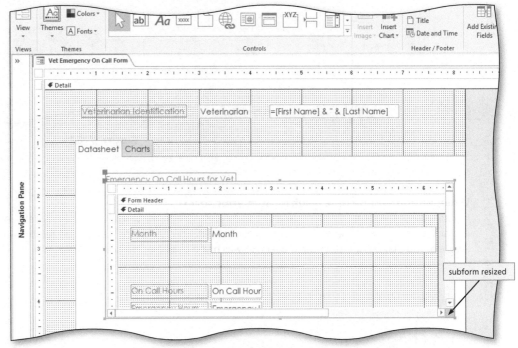

Figure 7–61

To Change the Background Color

The following steps change the background color of the form to a light gray.

1 Click anywhere in the Detail section in the main form but outside all the controls to select the section.

2 Display the Form Design Tools Format tab.

3 Click the Background Color button arrow (Form Design Tools Format tab | Font group) to display a color palette (Figure 7–62).

4 Click the Light Gray 2 color, the first color in the third row under Standard Colors, to change the background color.

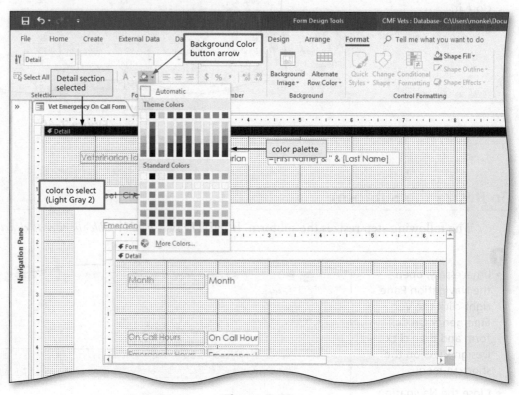

Figure 7–62

When would you include a subform in your form?
If the fields for the form come from exactly two tables, a one-to-many relationship exists between the two tables, and the form is based on the "one" table, you will often place the data for the "many" table in a subform. If there are more than two tables involved, you may be able to create a query on which you can base the subform.

CONSIDER THIS

To Insert Charts

Why? *To visually represent data in a table or query, you can create a chart.* To insert a chart, use the Chart tool on the Form Design Tools Design tab. The Chart Wizard will then ask you to indicate the fields to be included on the chart and the type of chart you want to insert. The following steps insert a chart that visually represents the amount of time spend in on call and emergency hours.

1

- Display the Form Design Tools Design tab.

- Click the Charts tab on the tab control to switch to that tab.

- Click the More button (Form Design Tools Design tab | Controls group) to display the design tools.

- Click the Chart tool, and then move the pointer to the approximate position shown in Figure 7–63.

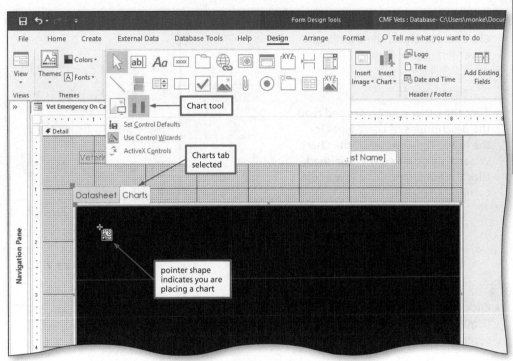

Figure 7–63

2

- Click the position shown in Figure 7–63 to display the Chart Wizard dialog box.

- The Chart Wizard dialog box indicates that the data will come from a table, scroll down so that the Emergency On Call Hours table appears, and then click the Emergency On Call Hours table to indicate the specific table containing the desired fields.

- Click Next.

- Select the Month and On Call Hours fields by clicking them and then clicking the Add Field button (Figure 7–64).

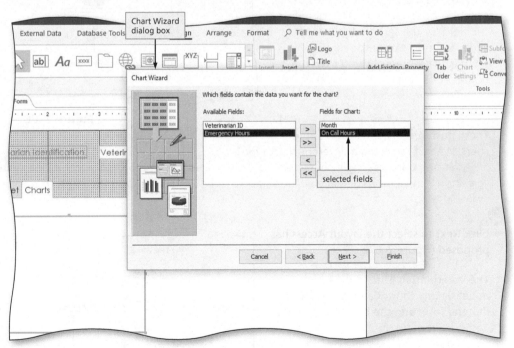

Figure 7–64

3

- Click Next.

- Click the Pie Chart, the chart in the lower-left corner (Figure 7–65).

🔍 **Experiment**

- Click the other chart types and read the descriptions of chart types in the lower-right corner of the Chart Wizard dialog box. When finished, click the Pie Chart in the lower-left corner.

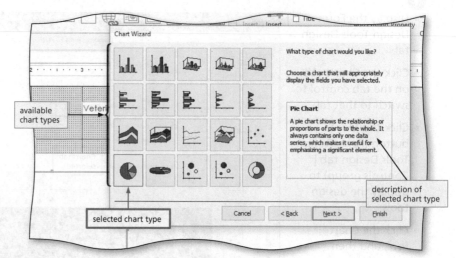

Figure 7–65

4

- Click Next to create the chart (Figure 7–66). Your screen might take several seconds to refresh.

Q&A What do these positions represent? Can I change them?
The field under the chart represents the data that will be summarized by slices of the pie. The other field is used to indicate the series. In this example, the field for the series is the workshop code, and the sizes of the slices of the pie will represent the sum of the number of hours spent. You can change these by dragging the fields to the desired locations.

These positions make sense for a pie chart. What if I selected a different chart type?
The items on this screen will be relevant to the particular chart type you select. Just as with the pie chart, the correct fields will often be selected automatically. If not, you can drag the fields to the correct locations.

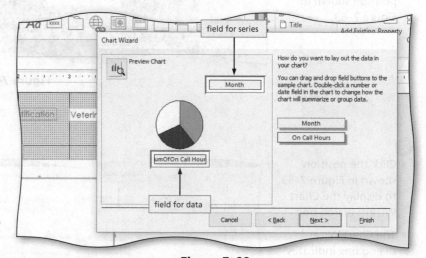

Figure 7–66

5

- Click Next to select the layout Access has proposed (Figure 7–67).

Q&A The Veterinarian ID field does not appear in my chart. Can I still use it to link the form and the chart?
Yes. Even though the Veterinarian ID does not appear, it is still included in the query on which the chart is based. In fact, it is essential that it is included so that you can link the document (that is, the form) and the chart. Linking the document and the chart ensures that the chart will accurately reflect the data for the correct veterinarian, that is, the veterinarian who currently appears in the form.

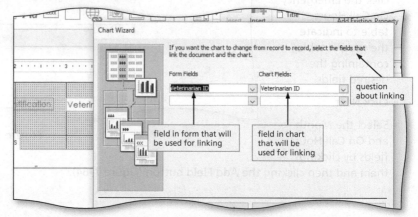

Figure 7–67

6

- Click Next, type **On Call Hours by Vet** as the title, and then click the Finish button (Figure 7–68).

Q&A
The data does not look right. What is wrong and what do I need to do to fix it?

The data in your chart might be fictitious, as in Figure 7–68. In that case, the data simply represents the general way the chart will look. When you view the actual form, the data represented in the chart should be correct.

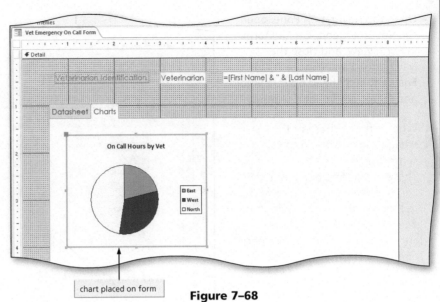

chart placed on form

Figure 7–68

7

- Use the techniques shown in Steps 1 through 6 to add a second chart at the position shown in Figure 7–69. In this chart, which is also based on the Emergency On Call Hours table, select Emergency Hours instead of On Call Hours and type **Emergency Hours by Vet** as the title of the chart instead of On Call Hours by Vet.

- Resize the two charts to the size shown in the figure, if necessary, by clicking the chart and then dragging an appropriate sizing handle.

- If requested to do so by your instructor, add a title with your first and last name to the form.

- Save your changes and close the form.

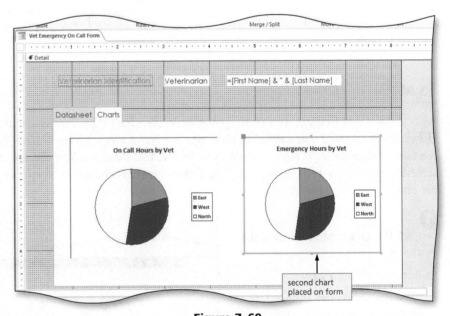

second chart placed on form

Figure 7–69

To Use the Form

You use this form just like the other forms you have created and used. When using the form, it is easy to move from one tabbed page to another. ***Why?*** *All you have to do is to click the tab for the desired tabbed page.* The following step uses the form to view the on call and emergency data.

1

- Open the Navigation Pane, open the Vet Emergency On Call form in Form view, and close the Navigation Pane (Figure 7–70). Ensure that all headings are visible and adjust any column widths.

Q&A

What is the purpose of the navigation buttons in the subform?

These navigation buttons allow you to move within the records in the subform, that is, within the emergency and on call hours for the veterinarian whose number and name appear at the top of the form.

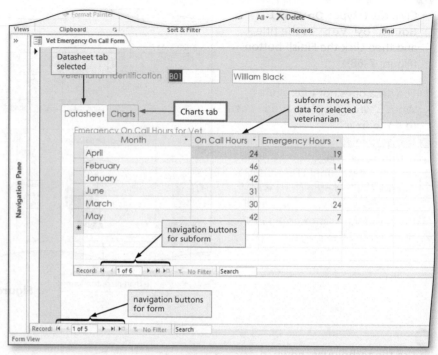

Figure 7–70

To Modify a Chart Type

When you first create a chart, you specify the chart type. You sometimes will later want to change the type. *Why? You might find that a different chart type is a better way to represent data. In addition, you have more options when you later change the chart type than when you first created the chart.* You change the type by editing the chart and selecting the Chart Type command. The following steps change the chart type by selecting a different style of pie chart.

- Click the Charts tab to display the charts.
- Return to Design view.
- Click the Charts tab, if necessary, to display the charts in Design view (Figure 7–71).

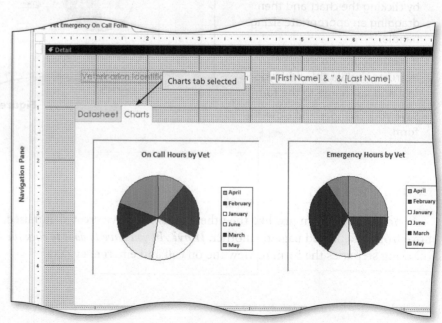

Figure 7–71

2

- Click the On Call Hours by Vet chart to select it, and then right-click the chart to display a shortcut menu (Figure 7–72).

Q&A

Does it matter where I right-click?
You should right-click within the rectangle but outside any of the items within the rectangle, in other words, in the white space.

My shortcut menu is very different. What should I do?
Click the View button arrow, then click Design View to ensure that you are viewing the form in Design view, and then try again.

- Point to Chart Object on the shortcut menu to display the Chart Object submenu (Figure 7–72).

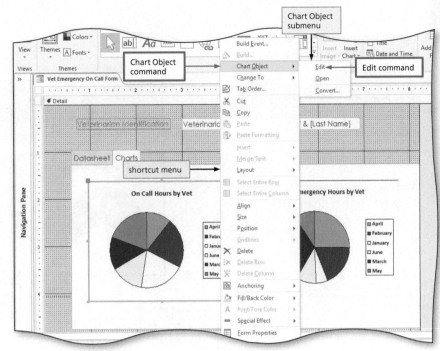

Figure 7–72

3

- Click Edit on the Chart Object submenu to edit the chart. Access will automatically display the underlying chart data in Datasheet view (Figure 7–73).

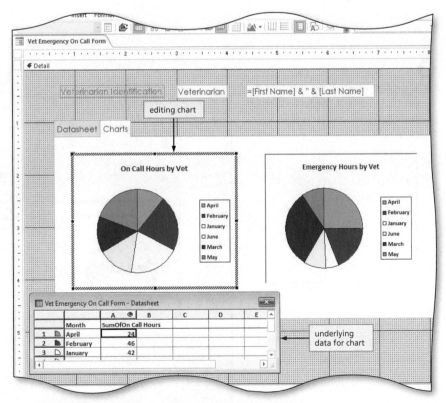

Figure 7–73

4

● Right-click the chart to display
the shortcut menu for editing the
chart (Figure 7–74).

Q&A Does it matter where I right-click?
You should right-click within the
rectangle but outside any of the
items within the rectangle, in
other words, in the white space.

What types of changes can I make
if I select Format Chart Area?
You can change things such as
border style, color, fill effects, and
fonts.

How do I make other changes?
By clicking Chart Options on the
shortcut menu, you can change
titles, legends, and labels. For 3-D
charts, by clicking 3-D View on the
shortcut menu, you can change
the elevation and rotation of the
chart. You can also format specific
items on the chart, as you will see
in the next section.

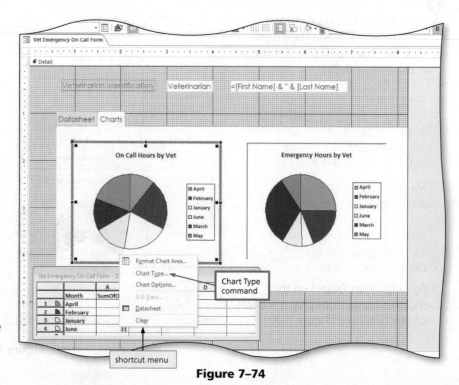

Figure 7–74

5

● Click the Chart Type command
on the shortcut menu to display
the Chart Type dialog box
(Figure 7–75).

Q&A What is the relationship
between the Chart type and the
Chart sub-type?
You can think of Chart types
as categories of charts. There
are column charts, bar charts,
line charts, and so on. Once you
have selected a category, the
chart sub-types are those charts
in that category. If you have
selected the Pie chart category,
for example, the charts within
the category are the ones
shown in the list of chart sub-
types in Figure 7–75.

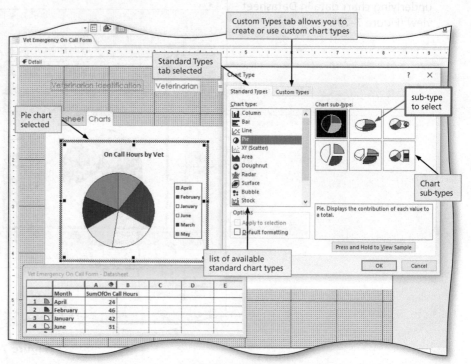

Figure 7–75

6 Click the chart sub-type in the middle of the first row of chart sub-types to select it as the chart sub-type.

🔎 **Experiment**

• Click each of the chart types and examine the chart sub-types associated with that chart type. When finished, select Pie as the chart type and the sub-type in the middle of the first row as the chart sub-type.

• Click the OK button to change the chart sub-type.

• Click outside the chart and the datasheet to deselect the chart.

• Make the same change to the other chart (Figure 7–76).

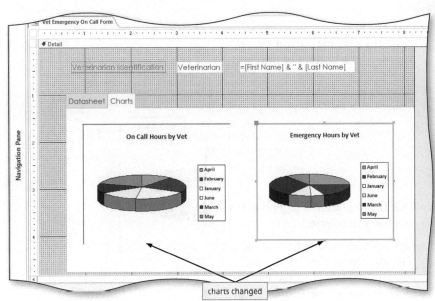

Figure 7–76

To Format a Chart

After right-clicking a chart, pointing to Chart Object, and then clicking Edit, you have many formatting options available. You can change the border style, color, fill effects, and fonts by using the Format Chart Area command. You can change titles, legends, and labels by using the Chart Options command. You can also format specific portions of a chart by right-clicking the portion you want to format and then clicking the appropriate command on the shortcut menu. The following steps use this technique to move the legend so that it is at the bottom of the chart. They also include percentages in the chart. ***Why?*** *Percentages provide valuable information in a pie chart.*

• Right-click the On Call Hours by Vet chart to display a shortcut menu, point to Chart Object on the shortcut menu to display the Chart Object submenu, and then click Edit on the Chart Object submenu.

• Right-click the legend to display a shortcut menu, and then click Format Legend on the shortcut menu to display the Format Legend dialog box.

• Click the Placement tab (Figure 7–77).

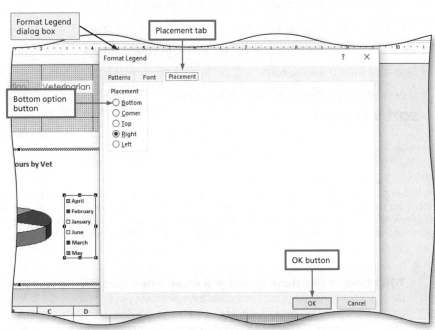

Figure 7–77

2

- Click the Bottom option button to specify that the legend should appear at the bottom of the chart.

Q&A What other types of changes can I make in this dialog box?
Click the Patterns tab to change such things as border style, color, and fill effects. Click the Font tab to change the font and/or font characteristics.

- Click OK to place the legend at the location you selected.

- Right-click the pie chart to display a shortcut menu, and then click Format Data Series on the shortcut menu to display the Format Data Series dialog box.

- Click the Data Labels tab.

- Click the Percentage check box to specify that percentages are to be included (Figure 7–78).

Q&A I see a Patterns tab just as with the legend, but how would I use the Options tab? Also, does the fact that these are check boxes rather than option buttons mean that I can select more than one?
Use the Options tab to indicate whether the color is to vary by slice and to specify the angle of the first slice in the pie. Because these are check boxes, you can select as many as you want. Selecting too many can clutter the chart, however.

These options make sense for a pie chart, but what about other chart types?
The options that you see will vary from one chart type to another. They will be relevant for the selected chart type.

3

- Click OK to include percentages on the chart.

- Click outside the chart and the datasheet to deselect the chart.

- Move the legend and add the percentages, to the other chart.

- View the form in Form view to see the effect of your changes.

- Save and then close the form.

- If desired, sign out of your Microsoft account.

- **sam** ↑ Exit Access.

Figure 7–78

BTW
Distributing a Document
Instead of printing and distributing a hard copy of a document, you can distribute the document electronically. Options include sending the document via email; posting it on cloud storage (such as OneDrive) and sharing the file with others; posting it on a social networking site, blog, or other website; and sharing a link associated with an online location of the document. You also can create and share a PDF or XPS image of the document, so that users can view the file in Acrobat Reader or XPS Viewer instead of in Access.

What type of decisions should you make when considering whether to use a chart?
Do you want to represent data in a visual manner? If so, you can include a chart. If you decide to use a chart, you must determine which type of chart would best represent the data. If you want to represent total amounts, for example, a bar chart may be appropriate. If instead you want to represent portions of the whole, a pie chart may be better.

CONSIDER THIS

Summary

In this module you have learned how to create a form in Design view, add a combo box that displays information from a related table as well as a combo box that is used to find records on a form, format controls and use the Format Painter, add command buttons to a form, modify a button and a combo box, add a calculated field to a form, use a tab control to create a multipage form, add and modify a subform, insert charts, change chart types, and format charts.

CONSIDER THIS

What decisions will you need to make when creating your own forms?
Use these guidelines as you complete the assignments in this module and create your own forms outside of this class.

1. Determine the intended audience and the purpose of the form.

   a. Who will use the form?

   b. How will they use it?

   c. What data do they need?

   d. What level of detail do they need?

2. Determine the source of data for the form.

   a. Determine whether data comes from a single table or from multiple related tables.

   b. Which table or tables contain the data?

3. Determine the fields that belong on the form.

   a. What data items are needed by the user of the form?

4. Determine any calculations required for the form.

   a. Decide whether the form should contain any special calculations, such as adding two fields.

   b. Determine whether the form should contain any calculations involving text fields, such as concatenating (combining) the fields.

5. Determine the organization of the form.

   a. In what order should the fields appear?

   b. How should they be arranged?

   c. Does the form need multiple pages?

6. Determine any additional controls that should be on the form.

   a. Should the form contain a subform?

   b. Should the form contain a chart?

   c. Should the form contain command buttons to assist the user in performing various functions?

   d. Should the form contain a combo box to assist the user in searching for a record?

7. Determine the format and style of the form.

   a. What should be in the form heading?

   b. Do you want a title?

   c. Do you want an image?

   d. What should be in the body of the form?

   e. What visual characteristics, such as background color and special effects, should the various portions of the form have?

CONSIDER THIS

How should you submit solutions to questions in the assignments identified with a symbol?
Every assignment in this book contains one or more questions identified with a symbol. These questions require you to think beyond the assigned database. Present your solutions to the questions in the format required by your instructor. Possible formats may include one or more of these options: write the answer; create a document that contains the answer; present your answer to the class; discuss your answer in a group; record the answer as audio or video using a webcam, smartphone, or portable media player; or post answers on a blog, wiki, or website.

Apply Your Knowledge

Reinforce the skills and apply the concepts you learned in this module.

Creating a Multipage Form for the Financial Services Database

Note: To complete this assignment, you will be required to use the Data Files. Please contact your instructor for information about using the Data Files.

Instructions: Start Access. Open the Support_AC_Financial Services database. (If you do not have this database, see your instructor for a copy of the modified database.)

Perform the following tasks:

1. Create the Amount Paid and Current Due form shown in Figure 7–79. Concatenate the first and last name of the advisor and change the background color to Light Gray 1 (the first color in row 2 of the Standard Colors.) The Datasheet tab displays a subform listing information about payments from clients of the advisor (Figure 7–79a). Data for the subform is based on the Accounting table. Data for the Chart tab is also based on the Accounting table and displays the amount paid by each client for the specified advisor, in this case, Number 110, Rachel Hillsdale (Figure 7–79b).

2. If requested to do so by your instructor, rename the Amount Paid and Current Due form as LastName Services Data where LastName is your last name.

3. Submit the revised database in the format specified by your instructor.

4. ✷ How can you add a title to the Amount Paid and Current Due form?

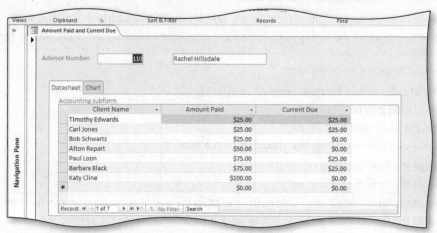

Figure 7–79a

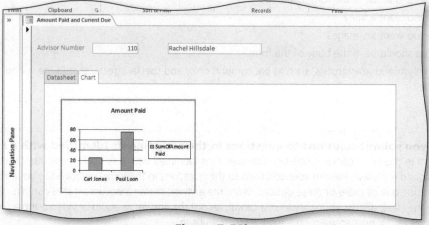

Figure 7–79b

Extend Your Knowledge

Extend the skills you learned in this module and experiment with new skills. You may need to use Help to complete the assignment.

Modifying Forms

Note: To complete this assignment, you will be required to use the Data Files. Please contact your instructor for information about accessing the Data Files.

Instructions: Start Access and then open the Support_AC_Healthy Pets database. (If you do not have the database, see your instructor for a copy of the modified database.)

Perform the following tasks:

1. Open the Technician form in Design view. Insert the current date in the form header. Bold the label for Technician Form.

2. Change the font color of the title to Dark Red (Standard colors).

3. Add a tab control to the form. Name the first tab Clients.

4. Add a subform to the Clients tab control. The Client table is the basis of the subform. Display the Client Name, Amount Paid and Balance Due fields in a datasheet on the subform. Name the subform Client subform1. Resize the datasheet so that all columns appear in the control.

5. Delete the other tab.

6. Add a command button to close the form and use the picture option to place a picture on the button.

7. Save the changes to the form.

8. If requested to do so by your instructor, open the Technician table in Datasheet view and change the first and last name of technician 22 to your first and last name.

9. Submit the revised database in the format specified by your instructor.

10. ✹ What chart would be appropriate to add to this form?

Expand Your World

Create a solution, which uses web technologies, by learning and investigating on your own from general guidance.

Problem: The Physical Therapy clinic needs a form to help them organize their therapists and clients. You will create a Master Form to include a hyperlink. You will also include a combo box to find a field and link that to the records displayed in the table by editing the VBA code.

Note: To complete this assignment, you will be required to use the Data Files. Please contact your instructor for information about accessing the Data Files. Start Access, and then open the Support_AC_Physical Therapy database. (If you do not have the database, see your instructor for a copy of the modified database.)

Perform the following tasks:

1. Create a form design and save it as Master Form.

2. At the top of the form, add the Therapist Number.

3. Add any other fields you think are necessary from the Clients table.

4. Add Client to Find combo box. Adjust the On Current VBA code so that the client changes to match the record when the records are advanced.

Continued >

Expand Your World *continued*

5. Access any website containing royalty-free images and search for an image suitable to use as a background image to the form.

6. Add a hyperlink for a local physical therapy clinic website to the top of the form.

7. Access any website containing royalty-free images and search for an image suitable to use on a Close Form command button; for example, a Stop sign or a door. Save the image to a storage location of your choice.

8. Add a Close Form command button to the form using the image you downloaded.

9. Save your changes to the Master Form.

10. Submit the revised database in the format specified by your instructor.

11. ✺ What image did you choose as the background for your form? What image did you choose for the command button? Why did you make those choices?

In the Labs

Design, create, modify, and/or use a database following the guidelines, concepts, and skills presented in this module

Lab: Applying Advanced Form Techniques to the Lancaster College Database

Part 1: The administrators at Lancaster College need a form to use to find and contact students. They also need a form to track seminar attendance by the coaches. Open the Support_AC_Lancaster College database from the Data Files. (If you do not have the database, see your instructor for a copy of the modified database.) Then, use the concepts and techniques presented in this module to perform each of the following tasks:

a. Modify the Coach Sport Master Form so that it is similar in style and appearance to the form shown in Figure 7–1a. The form should include a combo box to search for coaches by last name with first name included in the list. Include command buttons to go to the next record, go to the previous record, add records, delete records, and close the form. The user should not be able to tab to the combo box. When the Add Record button is clicked, the focus should be the First Name.

b. Import a table called Coach Training Hours.

c. Create a query that joins the Coach and Coach Training Hours tables. Include the Coach Id field from the Coach table, and the Seminar Code and Hours Spent fields from the Coach Training Hours table. Add a calculated field for Hours Remaining (Total Hours – Hours Spent). Save the query.

d. Create a form for the Coach table that is similar to the form shown in Figure 7–2a. The form should have two tabs, a Datasheet tab and a Charts tab. The Datasheet tab displays a subform listing information about seminars for coaches. Data for the subform is based on the query you created in Step c. The Charts tab includes two charts that represent the hours spent and hours remaining for coach seminars. Data for the Charts tab is also based on the query created in Step c.

Submit your assignment in the format specified by your instructor.

Part 2: You made several decisions while creating these two forms. What was the rationale behind your decisions? What chart style did you choose for the two charts? Why? What other chart styles could you use to represent the data?

8 | Macros, Navigation Forms, and Control Layouts

Objectives

You will have mastered the material in this module when you can:

- Create and modify macros and submacros
- Create a menu form with command buttons
- Create a menu form with an option group
- Create a macro for the option group
- Use an IF statement in a macro
- Create datasheet forms

- Create user interface (UI) macros
- Create navigation forms
- Add tabs to a navigation form
- Create data macros
- Create and remove control layouts
- Use the Arrange tab to modify control layouts on forms and reports

Introduction

In this module, you will learn how to create and test macros that open forms and that preview reports and export reports. You will create a menu form with command buttons as well as a menu form with an **option group**, which is an object that enables you to make a selection by choosing the option button corresponding to your choice. You will also create and use user interface (UI) macros in forms. CMF Vets requires a navigation form that will allow users to open forms and reports simply by clicking appropriate tabs and buttons. You will learn about the use of data macros for ensuring that updates to the database are valid. Finally, you will learn how to use control layouts on forms and reports.

Project—Macros, Navigation Forms, and Control Layouts

CMF Vets managers would like users to be able to access forms and reports simply by clicking tabs and buttons, rather than by using the Navigation Pane. A **navigation form** like the one shown in Figure 8–1a is a form that includes tabs to display forms and reports. CMF Vets plans to use the navigation form because they believe it will improve the user-friendliness of the database, thereby improving employee satisfaction and efficiency. This navigation form contains several useful features. With the

Veterinarians tab selected, you can click the Veterinarian ID on any row to see the data for the selected veterinarian displayed in the Datasheet view. (Figure 8–1b). The form does not appear in a tabbed sheet, the way tables, queries, forms, and reports normally do. Rather, it appears as a **pop-up form**, a form that stays on top of other open objects, even when another object is active.

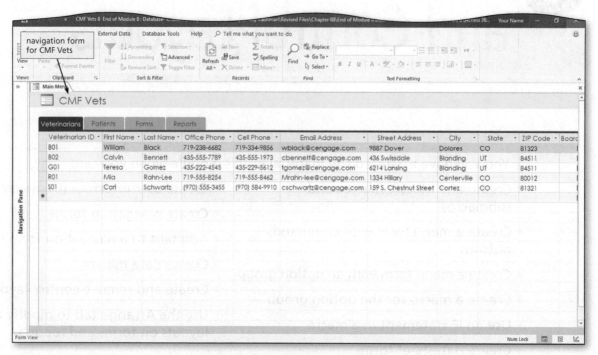

Figure 8–1a Navigation Form

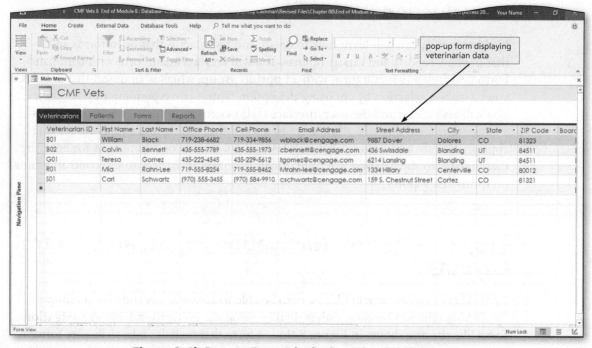

Figure 8–1b Pop-up Form Displaying Veterinarian Data

Clicking the Patients tab of the navigation form displays patient's data. As with veterinarians, clicking the patient number on any record displays data for that patient in a pop-up form.

Clicking the Forms tab in the CMF Vets navigation form displays buttons for each of the available forms (Figure 8–1c). You can open the desired form by clicking the appropriate button.

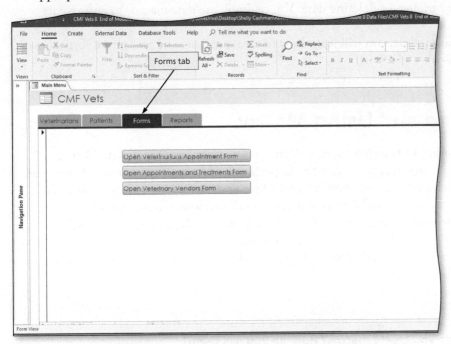

Figure 8–1c Buttons to Display Forms

Clicking the Reports tab displays an option group for displaying reports (Figure 8–1d). You can preview or export any of the reports one at a time by clicking the corresponding option button.

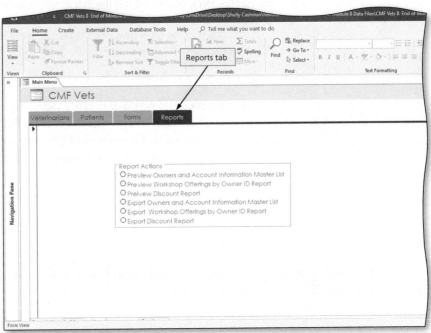

Figure 8–1d Option Buttons to Display Report Actions

Before creating the navigation form, CMF Vets managers will create **macros**, which are collections of actions designed to carry out specific tasks. To perform the actions in a macro, you run the macro. When you run a macro, Access will execute the various steps, called **actions**, in the order indicated by the macro. You run the navigation form macros by clicking certain buttons in the form.

CMF Vets managers will also create another type of macro, a data macro. A **data macro** is a special type of macro that enables you to add logic to table events such as adding, changing, or deleting data. You typically use data macros to ensure data validity.

In this module, you will learn how to create and use the navigation form shown in Figure 8–1.

Creating and Using Macros

Similar to other Office apps, Access allows you to create and use macros. A macro consists of a series of actions that Access performs when the macro is run. When you create a macro, you specify these actions. Once you have created a macro, you can simply run the macro, and Access will perform the various actions you specified. For example, the macro might open a form in read-only mode, a mode that prohibits changes to the data. Another macro might export a report as a PDF file. You can group related macros into a single macro, with the individual macros existing as submacros within the main macro.

CONSIDER THIS

How do you create macros? How do you use them?
You create a macro by entering a specific series of actions in a window called the Macro Builder window. Once a macro is created, it exists as an object in the database, and you can run it from the Navigation Pane by right-clicking the macro and then clicking Run on the shortcut menu. Macros can also be associated with buttons on forms. When you click the corresponding button on the form, Access will run the macro and complete the corresponding action. Whether a macro is run from the Navigation Pane or from a form, the effect is the same: Access will execute the actions in the order in which they occur in the macro.

In this module, you will create macros for a variety of purposes. Access provides a collection of standard actions in the Macro Builder; as you enter actions, you will select them from a list. The names of the actions are self-explanatory. The action to open a form, for example, is OpenForm. Thus, it is not necessary to memorize the specific actions that are available.

To Begin Creating a Macro

The following steps begin creating a macro. *Why? Once you have created the macro, you will be able to add the appropriate actions.*

1

• **sam¹** ↓ Start Access and open the database named CMF Vets from your hard drive, OneDrive, or other storage location.

• CMF Vets has decided to change the name of the Veterinarian Appointment Form to reflect practice growth. Rename this form to Veterinarians Appointment Form.

• The Appointments and Treatments query must be replaced for consistency with the change made to the Appointments table when the Treatment Number field was converted from a multi-valued field to a single-valued field.

• Delete the Appointments and Treatments query.

• Create a new query based on the Appointments and Treatment Cost tables. Include the Appointment Date field from the Appointments table and the Treatment, Animal Type, and Cost fields from the Treatment Cost table. Sort the Appointment Date and Treatment fields in Ascending order. Save the query as Appointments and Treatments.

• If necessary, close the Navigation Pane.

• Display the Create tab (Figure 8–2).

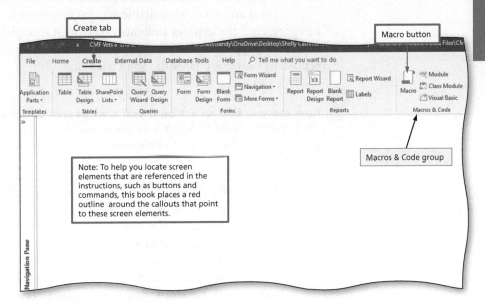

Note: To help you locate screen elements that are referenced in the instructions, such as buttons and commands, this book places a red outline around the callouts that point to these screen elements.

Figure 8–2

2

• Click the Macro button (Create tab | Macros & Code group) to create a new macro.

• Click the Action Catalog button (Macro Tools Design tab | Show/Hide group) if necessary to display the action catalog (Figure 8–3).

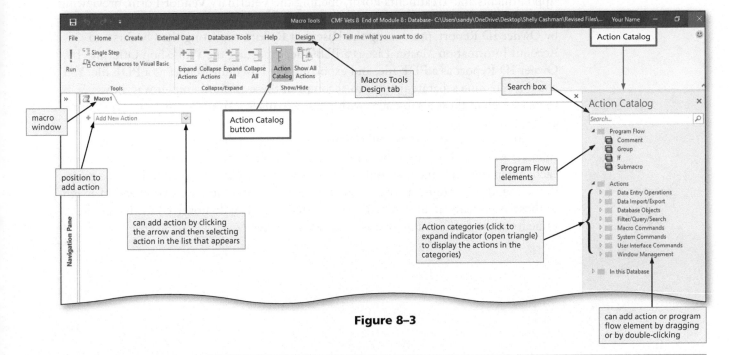

Figure 8–3

BTW
Macros
A macro is a series of commands used to automate repeated tasks. You can create macros in other Office apps, such as Word and Excel.

The Macro Builder Window

You create a macro by adding actions in the macro window, shown in Figure 8–3. You can add actions by clicking the Add New Action arrow and selecting the desired action from the list of possible actions. You can also use the Action Catalog, which is a list of macro actions organized by type. If the Action Catalog does not appear, click the Action Catalog button (Macro Tools Design tab | Show/Hide group) to display it. You can add an action by double-clicking the action in the Action Catalog or by dragging it.

Access arranges the available actions in categories. To see the actions in a category, click the **expand indicator** (the open triangle) in front of the category. The actions will appear and the expand indicator will change to a solid triangle. To hide the actions in a category, click the solid triangle.

CONSIDER THIS

How can you find an action if you are not sure which category contains the action?
You can search the list by typing in the Search box. Access will then reduce the list of actions displayed to only those actions whose names or descriptions contain the text you have typed.

Many actions require additional information, called the **arguments** of the action. For example, if the action is OpenForm, Access needs to know which form is to be opened. You indicate the form to be opened by setting the value of the Form Name argument to the desired form. If the value for the Form Name argument for the OpenForm action is Appointments and Treatments Form, then Access will open the Appointments and Treatments form when it executes this action.

Actions can have more than one argument. For example, in addition to the Form Name argument, the OpenForm action also has a Data Mode argument. If the value of the Data Mode argument is Read Only, then the form will be opened in read-only mode, which indicates users will be able to view but not change data. When you select an action, the arguments will appear along with the action, and you can make any necessary changes to them.

In the forms you will create later in this module, you need macros for opening the Veterinarians Appointment Form as read-only (to prevent updates), opening the Appointments and Treatments Form, opening the Veterinary Vendor Form, previewing the Owners and Account Information Master List, previewing the Workshop Offerings by Owner ID Report, previewing the Discount Report, exporting the Owners and Account Information Master List as a PDF file, exporting the Workshop Offerings by Owner ID Report as a PDF file, and exporting the Discount Report as a PDF file. You could create nine separate macros to accomplish these tasks. A simpler way, however, is to make each of these a submacro within a single macro. You can run a submacro just as you can run a macro.

You will create a macro called Forms and Reports that contains these nine submacros. Table 8–1 shows the submacros. Submacros can contain many actions, but each one in this table includes only a single action. For each submacro, the table gives the action, those arguments that need to be changed, and the values you need to assign to those arguments. If an argument is not listed, then you do not need to change the value from the default value that is assigned by Access.

BTW
Touch and Pointers
Remember that if you are using your finger on a touch screen, you will not see the pointer.

Table 8–1 Forms and Reports Macro		
Submacro	**Action**	**Arguments to be Changed**
Open Veterinarians Appointment Form		
	OpenForm	Form Name: Veterinarians Appointment Form
		Data Mode: Read Only
Open Appointments and Treatments Form		
	OpenForm	Form Name: Appointments and Treatments Form
Open Veterinary Vendors Form		
	OpenForm	Form Name: Veterinary Vendors Form
Preview Owners and Account Information Master List		
	OpenReport	Report Name: Owners and Account Information Master List View: Print Preview
Preview Workshop Offerings by Owner ID Report		
	OpenReport	Report Name: Workshop Offerings by Owner ID View: Print Preview
Preview Discount Report		
	OpenReport	Report Name: Discount Report View: Print Preview
Export Owners and Account Information Master List		
	ExportWithFormatting	Object Type: Report Object Name: Owners and Account Information Master List Output Format: PDF Format (*.pdf)
Export Workshop Offerings by Owner ID Report		
	ExportWithFormatting	Object Type: Report Object Name: Workshop Offerings by Owner ID Output Format: PDF Format (*.pdf)
Export Discount Report		
	ExportWithFormatting	Object Type: Report Object Name: Discount Report Output Format: PDF Format (*.pdf)

To Add an Action to a Macro

To continue creating the Forms and Reports macro, enter the actions in the Macro Builder. In these steps, you will enter actions by double-clicking the action in the Action Catalog. *Why? The actions in the Action Catalog are organized by function, making it easier to locate the action you want.* Access will add the action to the Add New Action box. If there is more than one Add New Action box, you need to ensure that the one where you want to add the action is selected before you double-click.

The following steps add the first action. They also make the necessary changes to any arguments. Finally, the steps save the macro.

1

● Double-click the Submacro element from the Program Flow section of the Action Catalog to add a submacro and then type `Open Veterinarians Appointment Form` as the name of the submacro (Figure 8–4).

Q&A How can I tell the purpose of the various actions?

If necessary, expand the category containing the action so that the action appears. Point to the action. An expanded ScreenTip will appear, giving you a description of the action.

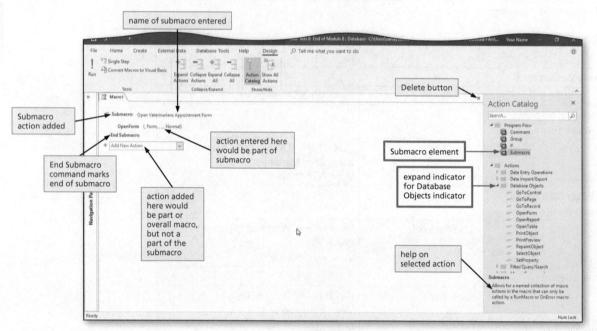

Figure 8–4

2

● Click the expand indicator for the Database Objects category of actions to display the actions within the category.

● Double-click the OpenForm action to add it to the submacro (Figure 8–5).

Q&A What should I do if I add an action in the wrong position? What should I do if I add the wrong action?

If you add an action in the wrong position, use the Move up or Move down buttons to move it to the correct position. If you added the wrong action, click the DELETE button to delete the action, and then fix the error by adding the correct action.

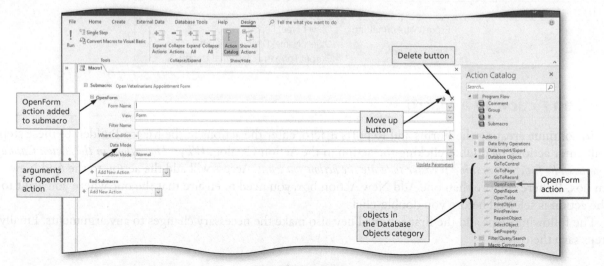

Figure 8–5

- Click the drop-down arrow for the Form Name argument and then select Veterinarians Appointment Form as the name of the form to be opened.

- Click the drop-down arrow for the Data Mode argument and then select Read Only to specify that users cannot change the data in the form (Figure 8–6).

Q&A What is the effect of the other Data Mode options?

Add allows viewing records and adding new records, but not updating records. Edit allows viewing records, adding new records, and updating existing records.

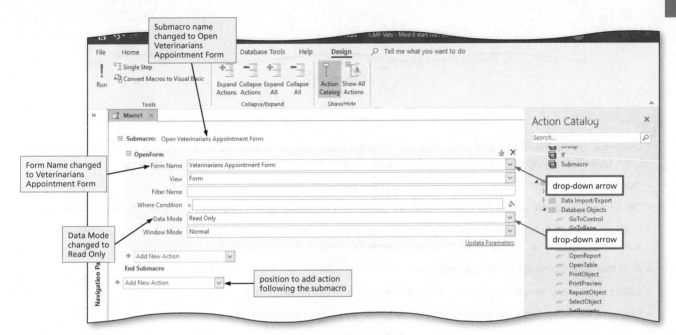

Figure 8–6

- Click the Save button on the Quick Access Toolbar, type **Forms and Reports** as the name of the macro, and then click OK to save the macro.

To Add More Actions to a Macro

To complete the macro, you need to add the additional actions shown in Table 8–1. You add the additional actions just as you added the first action. Initially, Access displays all the actions you have added with their arguments clearly visible. After you have added several actions, you might want to collapse some or all of the actions. *Why? Collapsing actions makes it easier to get an overall view of your macro.* You can always expand any action later to see details concerning the arguments. The following steps add additional actions to a macro, collapsing existing actions when necessary to provide a better view of the overall macro structure.

- Click the minus sign (–) in front of the OpenForm action to collapse the action (Figure 8–7).

Q&A Could I also use the buttons on the ribbon?

Yes, you can use the buttons in the Collapse/Expand group on the Macro Tools Design tab. Click the Expand Actions button to expand the selected action, or click the Collapse Actions button to collapse the selected action. You can expand all actions at once by clicking the Expand All button, or you can collapse all actions at once by clicking the Collapse All button.

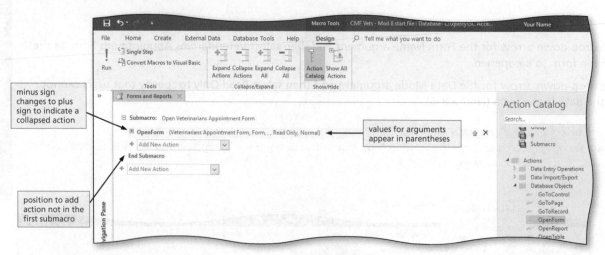

Figure 8–7

2

- Double-click the Submacro element from the Program Flow section of the Action Catalog to add a submacro, and then type `Open Appointments and Treatments Form` as the name of the submacro.

- Double-click the OpenForm action to add it to the submacro.

- Click the drop-down arrow for the Form Name argument and then select Appointments and Treatments Form.

- Double-click the Submacro element again to create a third submacro, and then type `Open Veterinary Vendors Form` as the name of the new submacro.

- Add the OpenForm action to the submacro.

- Select Veterinary Vendors Form as the value for the Form Name argument.

- Set Data Mode to Read Only and set Window Mode to Normal (Figure 8–8).

 Do I have to change the values of any of the other arguments?
No. The default values that Access sets are appropriate.

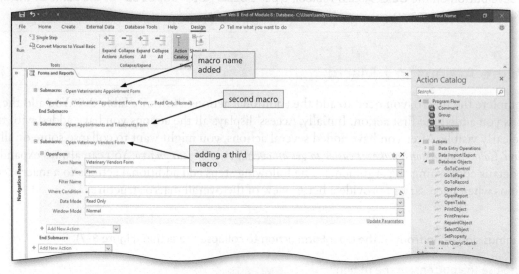

Figure 8–8

- For each of the submacros, click the minus sign in front of the submacro to collapse the submacro.
- Add a submacro named Preview Owners and Account Information Master List.
- Add the OpenReport action to the macro.
- Select Owners and Account Information Master List as the report name.
- Select Print Preview as the view (Figure 8–9).

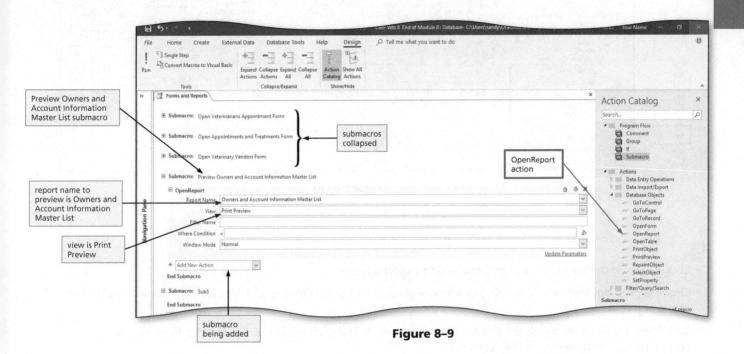

Figure 8–9

4

- Collapse the Preview Owners and Account Information Master List submacro.
- Add the Preview Workshop Offerings by Owner ID Report submacro. Include the action described in Table 8–1. The report name is Workshop Offerings by Owner ID Report and the view is Print Preview.
- Add the Preview Discount Report submacro. Include the action described in Table 8–1. The report name is Discount Report and the view is Print Preview.
- Collapse the Preview Workshop Offerings by Owner ID report and Preview Discount Report submacros.
- Click the triangle to the left of Database Objects in the Action Catalog to collapse the Database Objects category, and then expand the Data Import/Export category.
- Add a submacro called Export Owners and Account Information Master List.
- Add the ExportWithFormatting action, which will export and maintain any special formatting in the process.
- Click the drop-down arrow for the Object Type argument to display a list of possible object types (Figure 8–10).

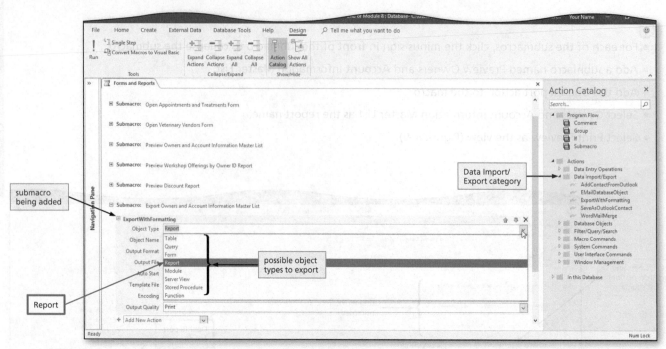

Figure 8–10

- Click Report in the list to indicate that Access is to export a report.
- Click the drop-down arrow for the Object Name argument and select Owners and Account Information Master List as the object name.
- Click the drop-down arrow for the Output Format argument and then select PDF Format (*.pdf) as the Output Format to export the report in PDF format.

6

- Add the Export Workshop Offerings by Owner ID Report submacro and the action from Table 8–1.
- Select Report as the Object Type and select Workshop Offerings by Owner ID as the report name.
- Select PDF Format (*.pdf) as the Output Format to export the report in PDF format.
- Add the Export Discount Report submacro and the action from Table 8–1.
- Select Report as the Object Type and Discount Report as the report name.
- Select PDF Format (*.pdf) as the Output Format to export the report in PDF format.
- Save the macro by clicking the Save button. The completed macro appears in Figure 8–11.
- Close the macro by clicking its Close button, shown in Figure 8–11.

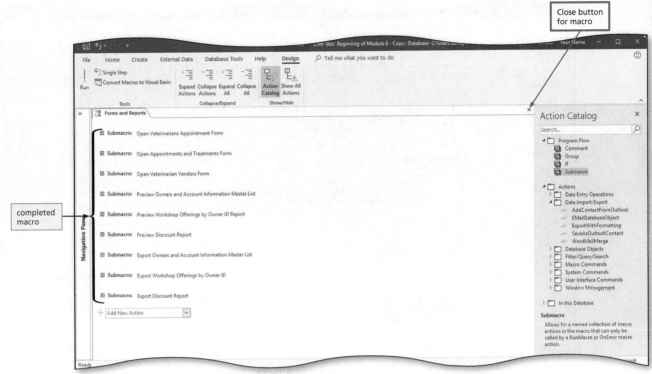

Figure 8–11

Opening Databases Containing Macros

It is possible that a macro stored in a database can contain a computer virus. By default, Access disables macros when it opens a database and displays a security warning. If the database comes from a trusted source and you are sure that it does not contain any macro viruses, click the Enable Content button. You can make adjustments to Access security settings by clicking File on the ribbon to open the Backstage view, and then clicking Options to display the Access Options dialog box, clicking Trust Center, clicking Trust Center Settings, and then clicking Macro Settings.

Errors in Macros

Macros can contain errors. The macro might open the wrong table or produce a wrong message. If you have problems with a macro, you can **single-step the macro**, that is, proceed through a macro a step at a time in Design view.

Figure 8–12 shows a macro open in Design view. This macro first has an action to open the Appointments table in Datasheet view in Read Only mode. It then changes the view to Print Preview. Next, it opens the Appointments table in Datasheet view, this time in Edit mode. Finally, it opens the Owners Query in Datasheet view in Edit mode. The macro in the figure is a common type of macro that opens several objects at once. To open all these objects, the user only has to run the macro. Unfortunately, this macro contains an error. The name of the Appointments table is written as "Appointment" in the second OpenTable action.

BTW

Converting a Macro to VBA Code
If you want to use many of the resources provided by Windows or communicate with another Windows app, you will need to convert any macros to VBA (Visual Basic for Applications) code. To convert a macro to VBA code, open the macro in Design view and click the 'Convert Macros to Visual Basic' button (Macro Tools Design tab | Tools group). When the Convert Macro dialog box appears, select the appropriate options, and then click Convert.

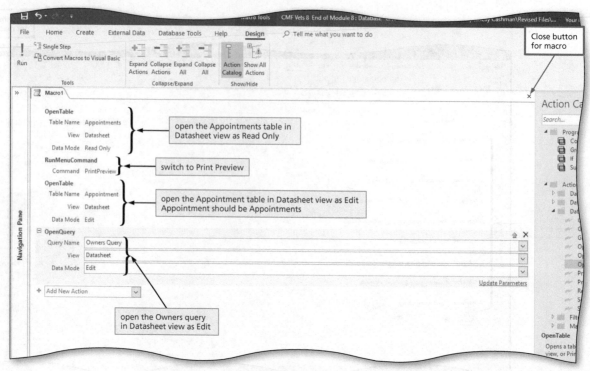

Figure 8–12

BTW

Saving a Macro as a VBA Module

You can save a macro as a VBA module using the Save Object As command in Backstage view. Open the macro in Design view, click File on the ribbon to open Backstage view, and then click Save As. When the Save As gallery appears, click 'Save Object As' in the File Types area, and then click the Save As button. When the Save As dialog box appears, click Module in the As text box and then click the OK button.

To run this macro in single-step mode, you would first click the Single Step button (Macro Tools Design tab | Tools group). You would next click the Run button (Macro Tools Design tab | Tools group) to run the macro. Because you clicked the Single Step button, Access would display the Macro Single Step dialog box (Figure 8–13). The dialog box shows the action to be executed and the values of the various arguments. You can click the Step button to proceed to the next step.

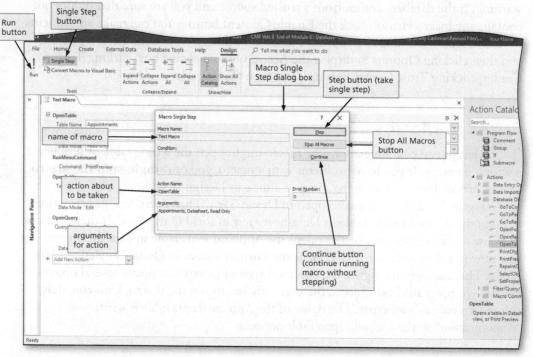

Figure 8–13

With this macro, after you clicked the Step button twice, you would arrive at the screen shown in Figure 8–14. Access is about to execute the OpenTable command. The arguments are Appointment, Datasheet, and Edit. At this point, you might spot the fact that "Appointment" is misspelled. It should be "Appointments." If so, you could click the 'Stop All Macros' button and then correct the object name.

BTW
**Program Flow
Actions**
Actions in the Program Flow category can change the order macro actions are executed or help structure a macro.

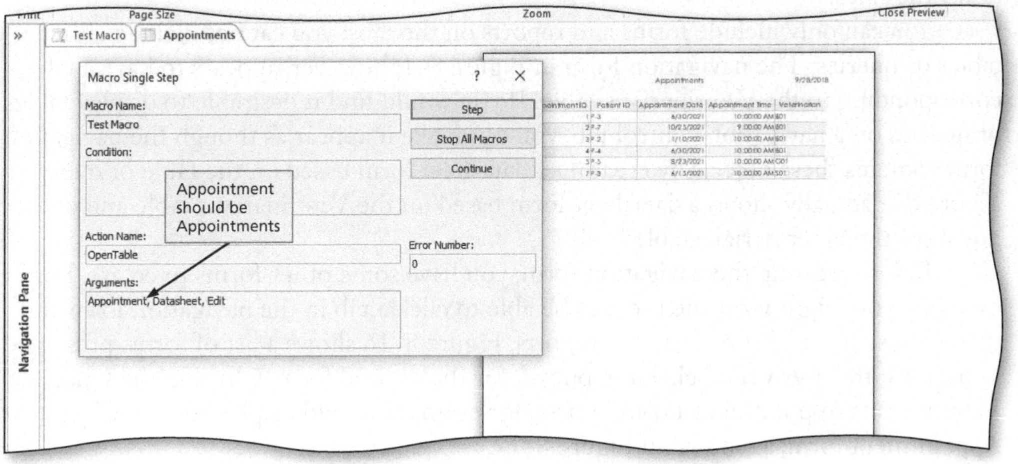

Figure 8–14

If you instead click the Step button, the misspelled name will cause the macro to terminate (abort). Access would display the appropriate error message in the Microsoft Access dialog box (Figure 8–15). This error indicates that Access could not find the object named Appointment. Armed with this knowledge, you can click the OK button, stop the macro, and then make the necessary change.

Figure 8–15

You do not need to step through a macro to discover the error. You can simply run the macro, either by clicking the Run button (Macro Tools Design tab | Tools group) with the macro open or by right-clicking the macro in the Navigation Pane and clicking Run. In either case, Access will run the macro until it encounters the error. When it does, it will display the same message shown in Figure 8–15. Just as with stepping through the macro, you would click the OK button, stop the macro, and then make the necessary change.

Once the macros are corrected, click the single-step button to turn off this feature. If this feature is not turned off, all macros will run in single-step mode.

Break Point: If you wish to stop working through the module at this point, you can resume the project later by running Access, opening the database called CMF Vets, and continuing to follow the steps from this location forward.

Creating and Using a Navigation Form

Figure 8–1a showed a navigation form for CMF Vets. A navigation form is a form that contains a **navigation control**, a control that can display a variety of forms and reports. Like the form in Figure 8–1, navigation controls contain tabs. Clicking the tab displays the corresponding form or report. The tabs can be arranged across the top and/or down the sides.

You can only include forms and reports on the tabs; you cannot include either tables or queries. The navigation form in Figure 8–1, however, appears to have a tab corresponding to the Veterinarians table. If you would find it desirable to display tables or queries on a navigation control tab, you can make it appear as though the navigation form contains these objects by creating a datasheet form based on the table or query. Figure 8–1 actually shows a datasheet form based on the Veterinarians table and does not show the Veterinarians table itself.

Before creating the navigation form, you have some other forms to create. For example, you might want the users to be able to click a tab in the navigation form and then choose from a list of forms or reports. Figure 8–16 shows a list of forms presented as buttons; the user would click the button for the desired form. Clicking the Open Veterinarians Appointment Form button, for example, would display the Veterinarians Appointment form, as shown in Figure 8–17.

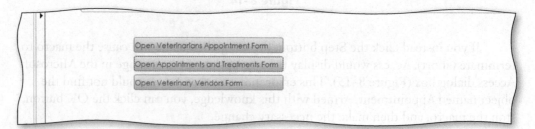

Figure 8–16

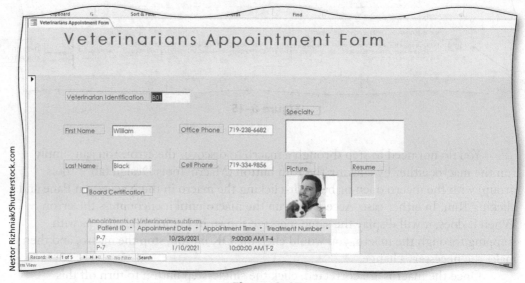

Figure 8–17

To implement options like these, you create blank forms and add either the command buttons or the option group. You then include the form you have created in the navigation form. When users click the corresponding tab, Access displays the form and users can then click the appropriate button.

To Create a Menu Form Containing Command Buttons

Why? *A menu form in which you make a selection by clicking the appropriate command button provides a convenient way to select a desired option.* You can create a menu form by adding command buttons to the form. The following steps use this technique to create a menu form with three buttons: Open Veterinarians Appointment Form, Open Appointments and Treatments Form, and Open Veterinary Vendors Form. The actions assigned to each button will run a macro that causes the desired action to occur. For example, the action for the Open Veterinarians Appointment Form button will run the Open Veterinarians Appointment Form submacro, which in turn will open the Veterinarians Appointment Form.

The following steps create a form in Design view and then add the necessary buttons.

1
- Display the Create tab.

- Click the Form Design button (Create tab | Forms group) to create a blank form in Design view.

- If a field list appears, click the 'Add Existing Fields' button (Form Design Tools Design tab | Tools group) to remove the field list.

- If a property sheet appears, click the Property Sheet button (Form Design Tools Design tab | Tools group) to remove the property sheet (Figure 8–18).

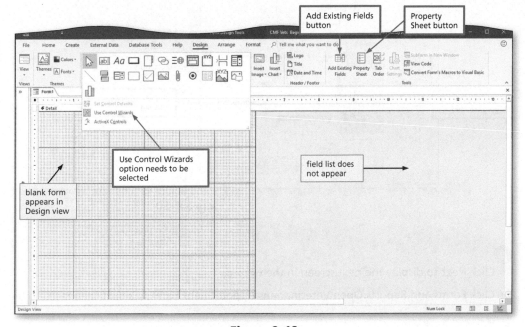

Figure 8–18

2
- If necessary, confirm that the 'Use Control Wizards' button is selected, by clicking the More button located in the Controls group.

- Click the Button tool (Form Design Tools Design tab | Controls group) and move the pointer to the approximate position shown in Figure 8–19.

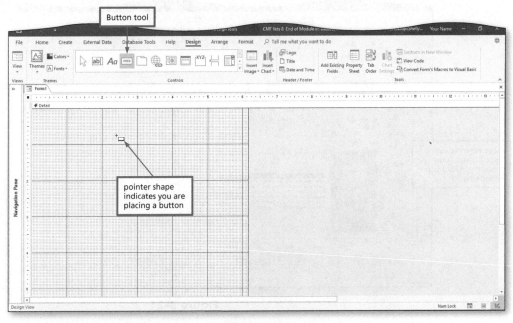

Figure 8–19

3

- Click the position shown in Figure 8–19 to display the Command Button Wizard dialog box.
- Click Miscellaneous in the Categories box, and then click Run Macro in the Actions box (Figure 8–20).

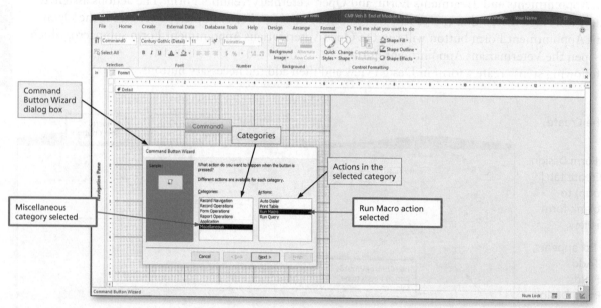

Figure 8–20

4

- Click Next to display the next screen in the wizard.
- Click Forms and Reports.Open Veterinarians Appointment Form to select the macro to be run (Figure 8–21).

Q&A | What does this notation mean?
The portion before the period is the macro and the portion after the period is the submacro. Thus, this notation means the Open Veterinarians Appointment Form submacro within the Forms and Reports macro.

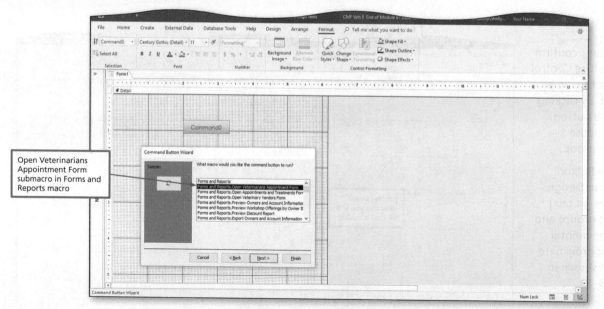

Figure 8–21

5

- Click Next to display the next Command Button Wizard screen.
- Click the Text option button to indicate that the button will display explanatory text rather than an image.

Q&A What is the purpose of these option buttons?
Choose the first option button to place text on the button. You can then specify the text to be included or accept the default choice. Choose the second option button to place a picture on the button. You can then select a picture.

- If necessary, delete the default text and then type **Open Veterinarians Appointment Form** as the text (Figure 8–22).

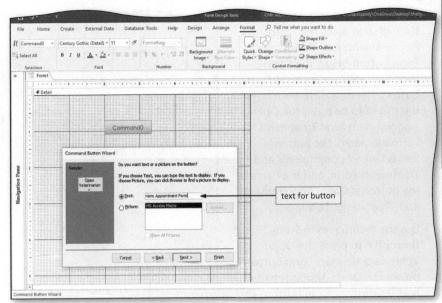

Figure 8–22

6

- Click the Next button.
- Type **Open_Veterinarians_Appointment_Form** as the name of the button (Figure 8–23).

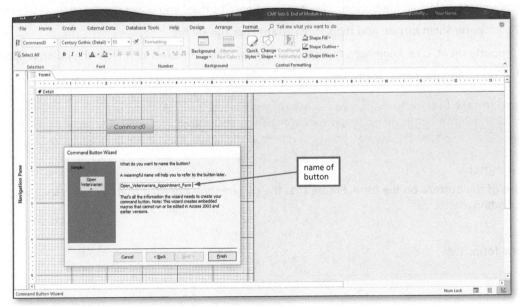

Figure 8–23

Q&A Why do you include the underscores in the name of the button?
If you are working with macros or VBA, you cannot have spaces in names. One way to avoid spaces and still make readable names is to include underscores where you would normally use spaces. Thus, Open Veterinarians Appointment Form becomes Open_Veterinarians_Appointment_Form.

- Click the Finish button to finish specifying the button.

- Use the techniques in Steps 2 through 6 to place the Open Appointments and Treatments Form button below the Open Veterinarians Appointment Form button. The only difference is that the macro to be run is the Open Appointments and Treatments Form submacro, the button text is Open Appointments and Treatments Form, and the name of the button is Open_Appointments_and_Treatments_Form.

- Use the techniques in Steps 2 through 6 to place the Open Veterinary Vendors Form button below the Open Appointments and Treatments Form button. The only difference is that the macro to be run is the Open Veterinary Vendors Form submacro, the text is Open Veterinary Vendors Form, and the name of the button is Open_Veterinary_Vendors_Form.

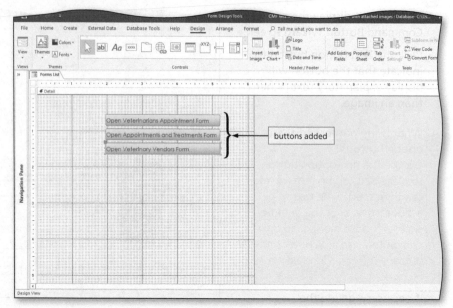

Figure 8–24

- Adjust the spacing of the buttons to approximately match those in Figure 8–24, using the tools on the Arrange tab.

- Move the buttons by selecting each one, pointing to its edge, and then dragging to move it.

- Resize each button by clicking the button to select it and then dragging the square handles that appear on the border of the control.

- For equal spacing, select all the buttons, click the Size/Space button, and select the Equal Vertical option.

- Click the Property Sheet button and then, if necessary, click the All tab.

- In the property sheet, click Alignment to display an arrow, and then select Left from the list that appears.

- Save the form using the name, Forms List.

Q&A

How can I test the buttons to make sure the macros work?

Right-click the Forms List form in the Navigation Pane and click Open. Click each of the buttons on the form. If there are errors in any of the macros, open the macro in the Macro Builder window and correct the errors.

 **Experiment**

- Test each of the buttons on the form. Ensure that the correct form opens. If there are errors, correct the corresponding macro.

- Close the form.

Option Groups

You might find it useful to allow users to make a selection from some predefined options by including an option group. An **option group** is a rectangle containing a collection of option buttons. To perform an action, you simply click the corresponding option button. Figure 8–25 shows a list of reports presented in an option group where the user would click the desired option button. Notice that the user could click an option button to preview a report. The user could click a different option button to export the report as a PDF file. Clicking the 'Preview Owners and Account Information Master List Report' option button, for example, would display a preview of the Owners and Account Information Master List (Figure 8–26). Clicking the Close Print Preview button would return you to the option group.

BTW

Viewing VBA Code
You can view VBA code that is attached to a form or report. To do so, open the form or report in Design view and click the View Code button (Report Design Tools Design tab | Tools group) for reports or (Form Design Tools Design tab | Tools group) for forms.

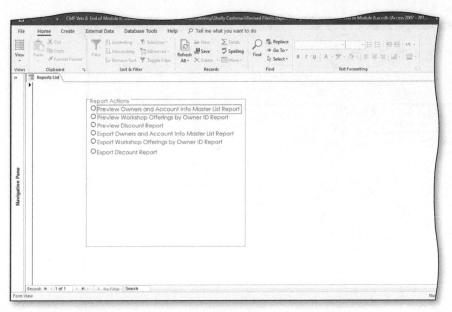

Figure 8–25

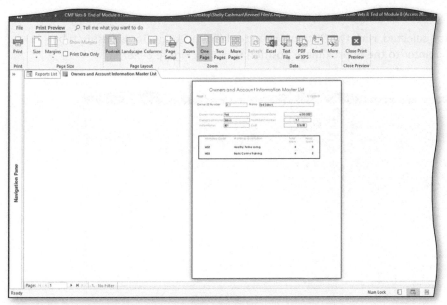

Figure 8–26

To Create a Menu Form Containing an Option Group

The form you are creating will contain an option group. *Why? The option group allows users to select an option button to indicate either a report to preview or a report to export.*

The following steps use the Option Group tool to create the option group named Report Actions.

- Display the Create tab.
- Click the Form Design button (Create tab | Forms group) to create a blank form in Design view.
- If a field list appears, click the 'Add Existing Fields' button (Form Design Tools Design tab | Tools group) to remove the field list (Figure 8–27).

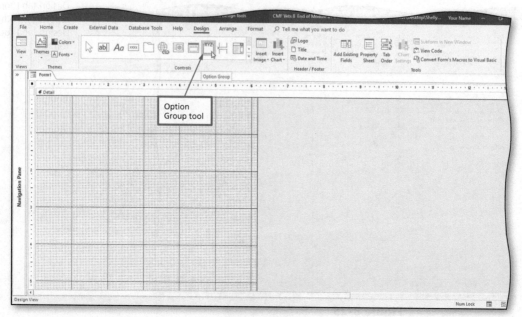

Figure 8–27

- With the 'Use Control Wizards' button selected, click the Option Group tool (Form Design Tools Design tab | Controls group) and then move the pointer to the approximate position shown in Figure 8–28.

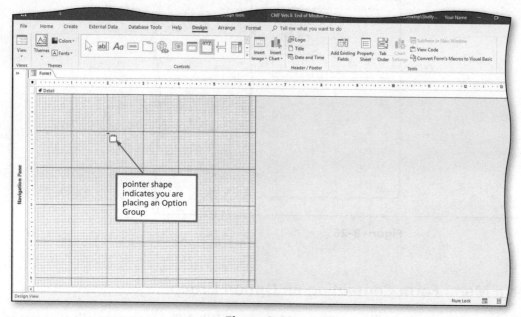

Figure 8–28

3
• Click the position shown in Figure 8–28 to place an option group and start the Option Group Wizard (Figure 8–29).

Q&A The Option Group Wizard did not start for me. What should I do?
You must not have had the 'Use Control Wizards' button selected. With the option group selected, press DELETE to delete the option group. Select the 'Use Control Wizards' button, and then add the option group a second time.

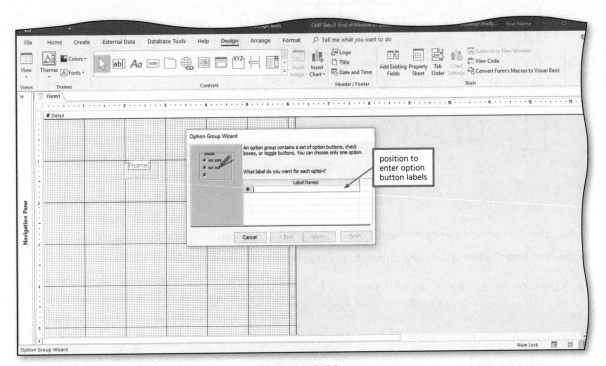

Figure 8–29

• Type **Preview Owners and Account Info Master List Report** in the first row of label names and press DOWN ARROW to specify the label for the first button in the group.

Q&A Why is the name of the form changed?
This form name is abbreviated from Information to Info here because there is not enough room for the entire name

• Type **Preview Workshop Offerings by Owner ID Report** in the second row of label names and press DOWN ARROW.

• Type **Preview Discount Report** in the third row of label names and press DOWN ARROW.

• Type **Export Owners and Account Info Master List Report** in the fourth row of label names and press DOWN ARROW.

• Type **Export Workshop Offerings by Owner ID Report** in the fifth row of label names and press DOWN ARROW.

• Type **Export Discount Report** in the sixth row of label names (Figure 8–30).

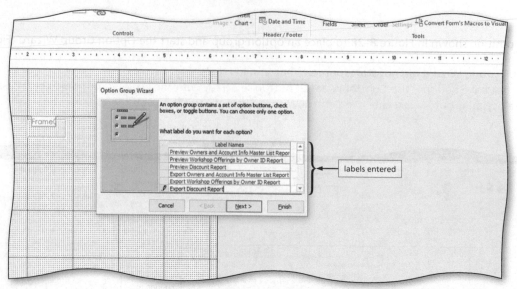

Figure 8–30

④

• Click the Next button to move to the next Option Group Wizard screen.

• Click the 'No, I don't want a default.' option button to select it (Figure 8–31).

Q&A | What is the effect of specifying one of the options as the default choice?
The default choice will initially be selected when you open the form. If there is no default choice, no option will be selected.

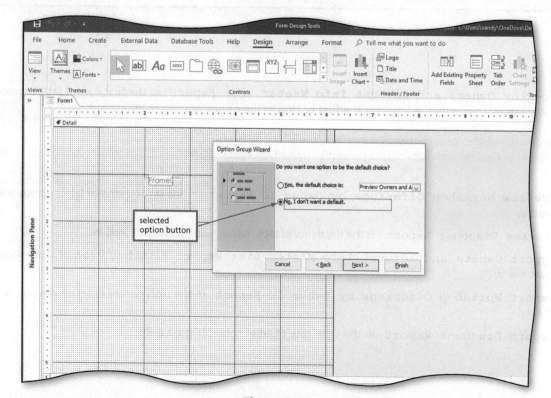

Figure 8–31

5

- Click Next to move to the next Option Group Wizard screen and then verify that the values assigned to the labels match those shown in Figure 8–32.

Q&A What is the purpose of the values that appear for each option?

You can use the values in macros or VBA. You will use them in a macro later in this module.

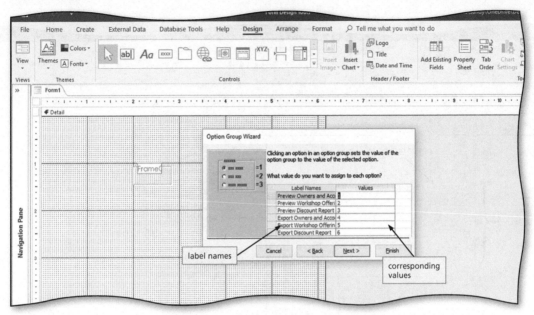

Figure 8–32

6

- Click Next to move to the next Option Group Wizard screen, and then ensure that Option buttons is selected as the type of control and Etched is selected as the style (Figure 8–33).

Experiment

- Click different combinations of types and styles to see the effects on the samples shown in the dialog box. When finished, select Option buttons as the type and Etched as the style.

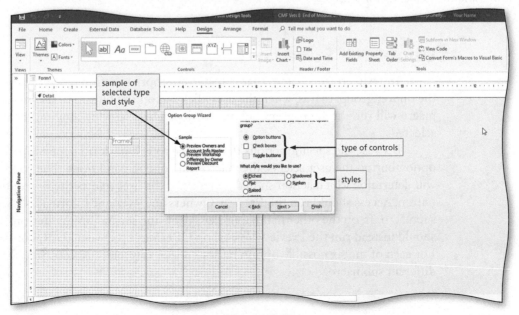

Figure 8–33

7

- Click Next to move to the next Option Group Wizard screen and then type `Report Actions` as the caption.
- Click Finish to complete the addition of the option group (Figure 8–34).

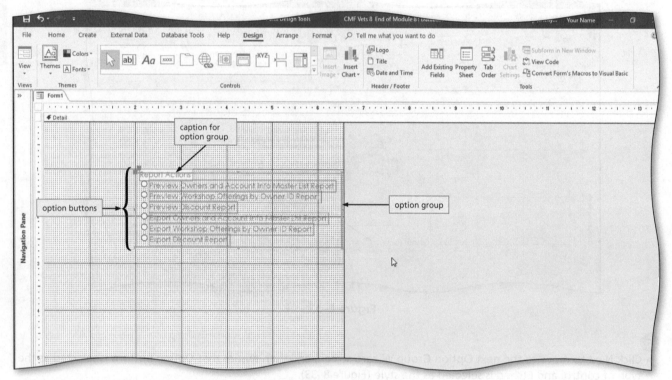

Figure 8–34

8

- Save the form using the name, Reports List.

Using an If Statement

You will create a macro that will take appropriate action when the user updates the option group, that is, when the user clicks an option button in the group. The macro will run the appropriate submacro, depending on which option the user has selected.

Because the specific actions that the macro will perform depends on the option button the user selects, the macro will contain conditions. The conditions will determine which action should be taken. If the user selects the first option button, Access should run the Preview Owners and Account Information Master List submacro. If, on the other hand, the user selects the second option button, Access should instead run the Preview Workshop Offerings by Owner ID Report submacro. For each of the six possible option buttons a user can select, Access should run a different submacro.

To instruct Access to perform different actions based on certain conditions, the macro will contain an If statement. The simplest form of an If statement is:

```
If condition Then
        action
End If
```

If the condition is true, Access will take the indicated action. If the condition is false, no action will be taken. For example, the condition could be that the user selects the first option button, and the action could be to run the Owners and Account Information Master List submacro. No action would be taken if the user selects any other button.

Another form of the If statement contains an Else clause. This form is:

```
If condition Then
        first action
Else
        second action
End If
```

If the condition is true, the first action is taken; if the condition is false, the second action is taken. For example, the condition could be that the user selects option button 1; the first action could be to run the Preview Owners and Account Information Master List submacro, and the second action could be to run the Preview Workshop Offerings by Owner ID submacro. If the user selects option button 1, Access would run the Preview Owners and Account Information List submacro. If the user selects any other option button, Access would run the Preview Workshop Offerings by Owner ID Report submacro. Because there are six option buttons, the macro needs to use an If statement with multiple Else Ifs to account for all of the options. This type of If statement has the form:

```
If first condition Then
        first action
Else If second condition Then
        second action
Else If third condition Then
        third action
...
End If
```

The first condition could be that the user selects the first option button; the second condition could be that the user selects the second option button; the third condition could be that the user selects the third option button, and so on. The first action could be that Access runs the first submacro; the second action could be that it runs the second submacro; and the third could be that it runs the third submacro. In this case, there are six option buttons and six submacros. For six conditions, as required in this macro, the If statement will contain five Else Ifs. The If statement along with the five Else Ifs will collectively contain six conditions: one to test if the user selected option 1, one for option 2, one for option 3, one for option 4, one for option 5, and one for option 6.

To Create a Macro with a Variable for the Option Group

The following steps begin creating the macro and add an action to set a variable to the desired value. *Why? The expression that contains the option number is [Forms]![Veterinarians Appointment Form]![Form_Options]. Because this expression is fairly lengthy, the macro will begin by setting a temporary variable to this expression. A variable is a named location in computer memory. You can use a variable to store a value that you can use later in the macro. You will assign the name Optno (short for option number) as the variable name for the expression. This location can contain a value, in this case, the option number on the form. In each of the conditions, you can then use Optno rather than the full expression.*

- If necessary, switch to Design view and select the option group. If the Property Sheet is not displayed, click the Property Sheet button.
- If necessary, click the All tab.
- Change the name of the option group to Form_Options (Figure 8–35).

Q&A

Why this name?

The name Form_Options reflects the fact that these are options that control the action that will be taken on this form. The underscore keeps the name from containing a space.

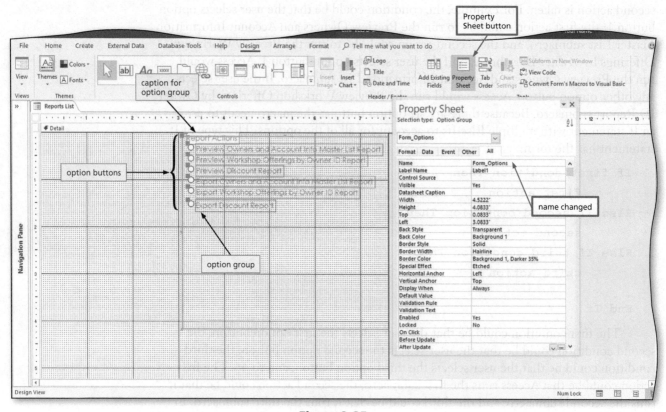

Figure 8–35

- Click the After Update property.
- Click the Build button to display the Choose Builder dialog box (Figure 8–36).

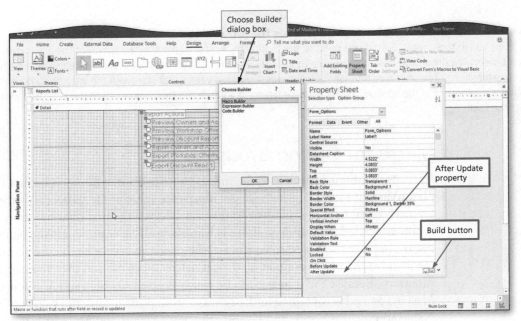

Figure 8–36

3

- With Macro Builder selected in the Choose Builder dialog box, click the OK button to create a macro.
- If necessary, click the Action Catalog button (Macro Tools Design tab | Show/Hide group) to display the Action Catalog.
- If necessary, collapse any category that is expanded.
- Expand the Macro Commands action category.
- Double-click the SetTempVar action in the Action Catalog to add the SetTempVar action to the macro.
- Type `Optno` as the value for the Name argument.
- Type `[Form_Options]` as the value for the Expression argument (Figure 8–37).

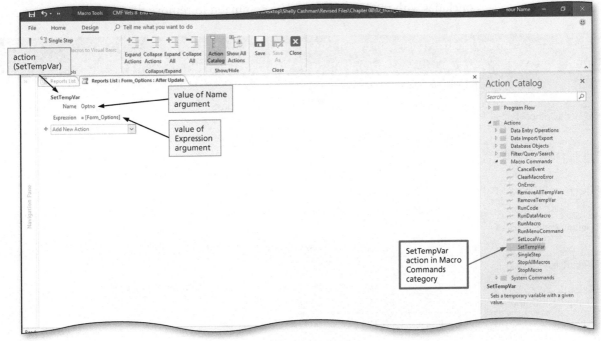

Figure 8–37

How does Access make it easier to enter values for arguments?
Access helps you in three ways. First, if you point to the argument, Access displays a description of the argument. Second, many arguments feature a drop-down List, where you can display the List and then select the desired value. Finally, if you begin typing an expression, a feature called IntelliSense will suggest possible values that start with the letters you have already typed and that are appropriate in the context of what you are typing. If you see the value you want in the List, you can simply click it to select the value.

Macro for Option Group

As mentioned previously, the macro contains six conditions. The first is [TempVars]! [Optno]=1, which simply means the value in the temporary variable Optno is equal to 1. In other words, the user selected the first option button. The action associated with this condition is RunMacro. The argument is the name of the macro. Because the macro to be run is a submacro, the name of the macro includes both the name of the macro containing the submacro, a period, and then the name of the submacro. Because the submacro to be run is Preview Owners and Account Information Master List and is contained in the Forms and Reports macro, the value of the Macro Name argument is Forms and Reports.Preview Owners and Account Info Master List. (This name needs to be shortened to fit in name space when creating the macro.)

The conditions and actions for options 2 through 6 are similar to the first submacro. The only difference is which submacro is associated with each option button. The conditions, actions, and arguments that you will change for the Form_Options macro are shown in Table 8–2. If the option number is 1, for example, the action is RunMacro. For the RunMacro action, you will change the Macro Name argument to Preview Owners and Account Info Master List submacro in the Forms and Reports macro. This name is shortened again to fit the space. On the other hand, if the option number is 2, for example, the action is again RunMacro. If the option number is 2, however, you will set the Macro Name argument to the Workshop Offerings by Owner ID submacro in the Forms and Reports macro. Similar actions take place for the other possible values for the Optno variable, that is, for option buttons 3-6. Because the temporary variable, Optno, is no longer needed at the end of the macro, the macro concludes with the RemoveTempVar command to remove this variable.

Table 8–2 Macro for After Update Property of the Option Group		
Condition	**Action**	**Arguments to be Changed**
	SetTempVar	Name: Optno Expression: [Form_Options]
If [TempVars]![Optno]=1		
	RunMacro	Macro Name: Forms and Reports.Preview Owners and Account Information Master List
Else If [TempVars]![Optno]=2		
	RunMacro	Macro Name: Forms and Reports.Preview Workshop Offerings by Owner ID Report
Else If [TempVars]![Optno]=3		
	RunMacro	Macro Name: Forms and Reports.Preview Discount Report
Else If [TempVars]![Optno]=4		
	RunMacro	Macro Name: Forms and Reports.Export Owners and Account Information Master List
Else If [TempVars]![Optno]=5		
	RunMacro	Macro Name: Forms and Reports.Export Workshop Offerings by Owner ID Report
Else If [TempVars]![Optno]=6		
	RunMacro	Macro Name: Forms and Reports.Export Discount Report
End If		
	RemoveTempVar	Name: Optno

To Add Actions to the Form Options Macro

The following steps add the conditions and actions to the Form_Options macro. *Why? The macro is not yet complete. Adding the conditions and actions will complete the macro.*

1

- Double-click the If element from the Program Flow section of the Action Catalog to add an If statement to the submacro and then type `[TempVars]![Optno]=1` as the condition in the If statement.

- With the Macro Commands category expanded, double-click RunMacro to add the RunMacro action.

- Click the drop-down arrow for the Macro Name argument and select the Preview Owners and Account Information Master List submacro within the Forms and Reports macro as the value for the argument (Figure 8–38).

Q&A What should I do if I add an action in the wrong position? What should I do if I add the wrong action?

If you add an action in the wrong position, use the Move up or Move down buttons to move it to the correct position. If you added the wrong action, click the Delete button to delete the action, and then fix the error by adding the correct action.

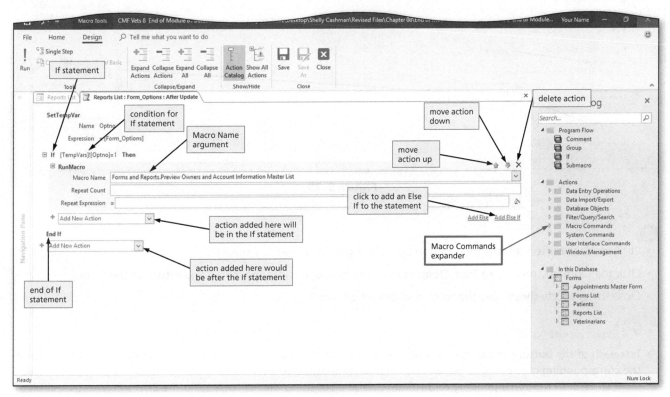

Figure 8–38

2

- Click 'Add Else If' to add an Else If clause to the If statement.

- Add the conditions and actions associated with options 2, 3, 4, 5, and 6 as described in Table 8–2, and specify the arguments for the actions. Click 'Add Else If' after adding each action except for the last one.

Q&A Do I have to enter all these actions? They seem to be very similar to the ones associated with option 1.

You can copy and paste the action for option 1. Right-click the action to select it and display a shortcut menu. Click Copy on the shortcut menu. Right-click the action just above where you want to insert the selected action and then click Paste. If the new action is not inserted in the correct position, select the new action and then click either the Move up or Move down buttons to move it to the correct location. Once the action is in the correct location, you can make any necessary changes to the arguments.

- Add the RemoveTempVar action and argument after the end of the If statement, as shown in Figure 8–39.
- Type **Optno** as the name of the TempVar to remove.

Q&A

Do I need to remove the temporary variable?

Technically, no. In fact, if you plan to use this temporary variable in another macro and want it to retain the value you assigned in this macro, you would definitely not remove it. If you do not plan to use it elsewhere, it is a good idea to remove it, however.

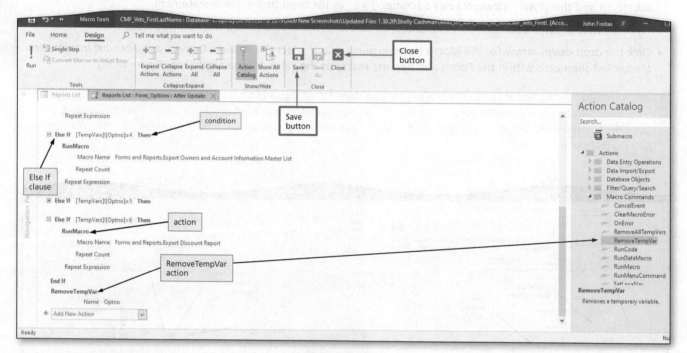

Figure 8–39

- Click the Save button (Macro Tools Design tab | Close group) to save the macro.
- Click the Close button (Macro Tools Design tab | Close group) to close the macro and return to the form.
- Close the property sheet, save the form, and close the form.

 **Experiment**

- Test each of the buttons in the option group. If you do not preview or export the correct report, correct the error in the corresponding macro. If you get an error indicating that the section width is greater than the page width, you have an error in the corresponding report. Correct the error using the instructions in the Errors in Macros section of this module.

Break Point: If you wish to stop working through the module at this point, you can resume the project at a later time by running Access, opening the database called CMF Vets, and continuing to follow the steps from this location forward.

User Interface (UI) Macros

A **user interface (UI) macro** is a macro that is attached to a user interface object, such as a command button, an option group, or a control on a form. The macro you just created for the option group is thus a UI macro, as were the macros you attached to command buttons. A common use for UI macros is to associate actions with the clicking of a control on a form. In the Veterinarians form shown in Figure 8–40, for example, if you click the Veterinarian ID on the row in the datasheet where the Veterinarian ID is B01, Access displays the data for that account in a pop-up form (Figure 8–41), that is, a form that stays on top of other open objects, even when another object is active.

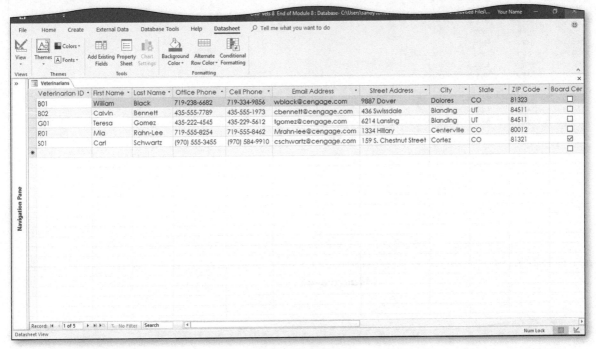

Figure 8–40

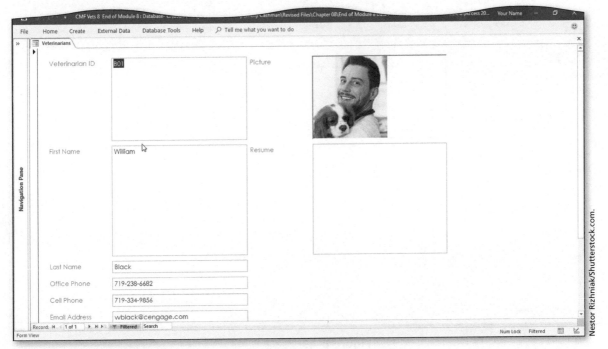

Figure 8–41

Similarly, in the Patients form shown in Figure 8–42, for example, if you click the patient number on the row in the datasheet where the patient number is P-1, Access displays the data for that patient in a pop-up form (Figure 8–43).

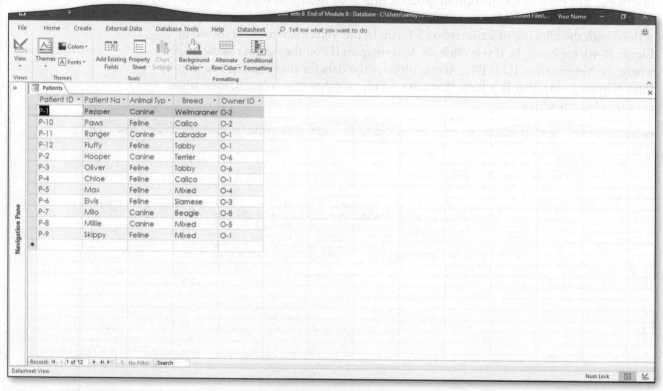

Figure 8–42

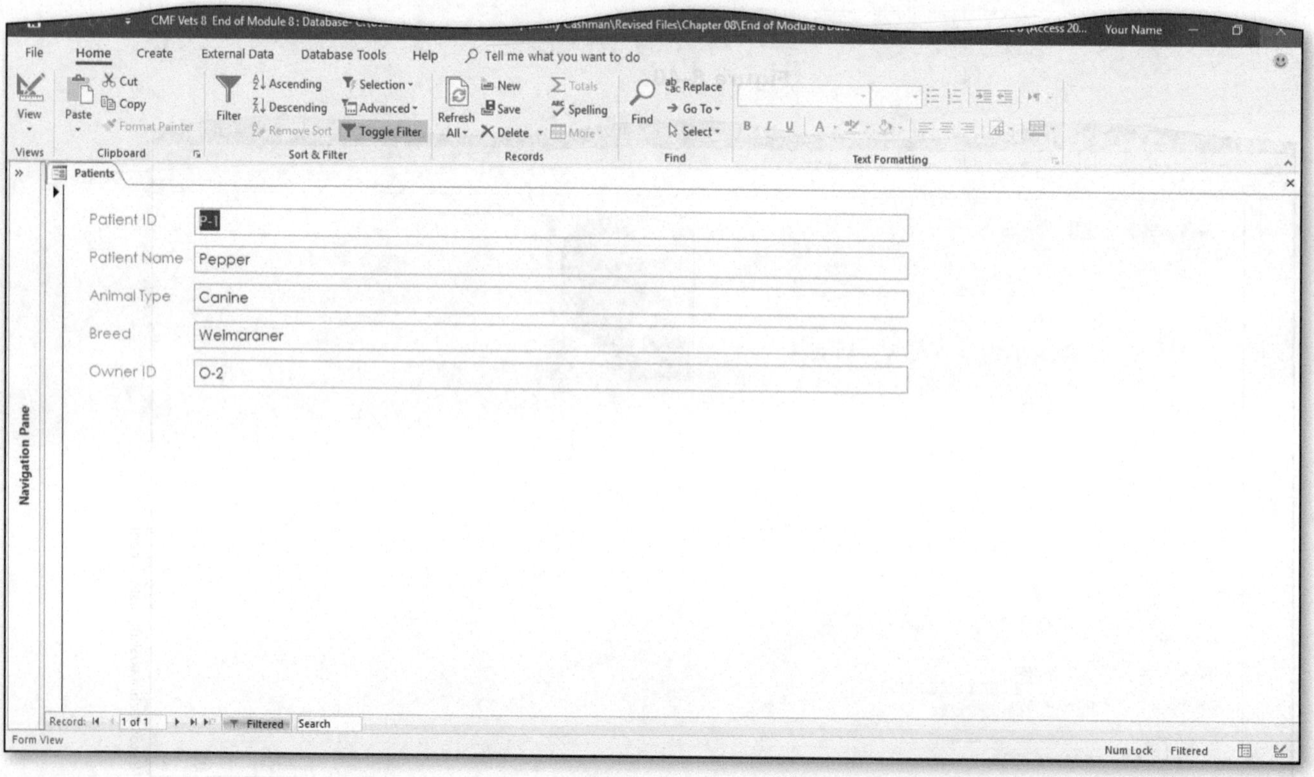

Figure 8–43

Recall that you can only use forms and reports for the tabs in a navigation form, yet the Veterinarian ID tab appears to display the Veterinarians table in Datasheet view. You can make it appear as though you are displaying the Veterinarians table in Datasheet view by creating a datasheet form that you will call Veterinarians. You will create a UI macro in this Veterinarians datasheet form. The UI macro that will be associated with the clicking of the Veterinarian ID on some record in the Veterinarians form will display the selected account in the Veterinarians Form.

To display the Veterinarians form, the UI macro will use the OpenForm action. You must set the Form Name argument of the OpenForm action to the actual name of the form to be opened, Veterinarians. (Account View and Update Form is just the form caption.) CMF Vets wants to prevent the user from updating data using this form, so the Data Mode argument is set to Read Only. The form should appear as a pop-up, which you accomplish by setting the value of the Window Mode argument to Dialog.

The form should display only the record that the user selected. If the user clicks Veterinarian ID B01 in the Veterinarian form, for example, the form should display only the data for account B01. To restrict the record that appears in the form, you include the Where Condition argument in the UI macro. The condition needs to indicate that the Veterinarian ID in the form to be opened, Veterinarians form, needs to be equal to the Veterinarian ID the user selected in the Veterinarians form.

In the Where Condition, you can simply refer to a control in the form to be opened by using its name. If the name has spaces, you must enclose it in square brackets. Thus, the name for the Veterinarian ID in the Veterinarians Form is simply [Veterinarian ID]. To reference a control that is part of any other form, the expression must include both the name of the form and the name of the control, separated by an exclamation point. Thus, the Veterinarian ID in the Veterinarians form would be [Veterinarians]![Veterinarian ID]. This declaration works correctly when you are programming a macro that simply opens the Veterinarians form. However, when you associate the Veterinarians datasheet with a tab in the navigation form, Veterinarians becomes a subform, which requires modification to the expression. This means that a form that works correctly when you open the form might not work correctly when the form is assigned to a tab in a navigation form. A safer approach avoids these issues by using a temporary variable.

Table 8–3 shows the UI macro for the Veterinarians form. It is associated with the On Click event for the Veterinarian ID control. When a user clicks a Veterinarian ID, the UI macro will display the data for the selected account in the Veterinarians Form. The main function of the macro is to open the appropriate form using the OpenForm action.

BTW

Distributing a Document
Instead of printing and distributing a hard copy of a document, you can distribute the document electronically. Options include sending the document via email; posting it on cloud storage (such as OneDrive) and sharing the file with others; posting it on a social networking site, blog, or other website; and sharing a link associated with an online location of the document. You also can create and share a PDF or XPS image of the document, so that users can view the file in Acrobat Reader or XPS Viewer instead of in Access.

Table 8–3 UI Macro Associated with On Click Event in the Veterinarians Form		
Condition	**Action**	**Arguments to Be Changed**
	SetTempVar	Name: VI Expression: [Veterinarian ID]
	OpenForm	Form Name: Veterinarians Where Condition: [Veterinarian ID]=[TempVars]![VI] Data Mode: Read Only Window Mode: Dialog
	RemoveTempVar	Name: VI

In the macro shown in Table 8–3, the first action, SetTempVar, assigns the temporary variable VI to the Veterinarian ID. The two arguments are Name, which is set to VI, and Expression, which is set to [Veterinarian ID]. The VI temporary variable refers to the Veterinarian ID in the Veterinarians form; recall that the completed macro will open the Veterinarians form. You then can use that temporary variable in the Where Condition argument. The expression is thus [Veterinarian ID]=[TempVars]![VI]. The [Veterinarian ID] portion refers to the Veterinarian ID in the Veterinarians form. The [TempVars]![VI] portion is the temporary variable that has been set equal to the Veterinarian ID in the Veterinarian form. The macro ends by removing the temporary variable.

Table 8–4 shows the macro for the Patients form, which is very similar to the macro for the Veterinarians form.

Table 8–4 UI Macro Associated with On Click Event in the Patients Form		
Condition	**Action**	**Arguments to Be Changed**
	SetTempVar	Name: PI Expression: [Patient ID]
	OpenForm	Form Name: Patients Where Condition: [Patient ID]=[TempVars]![PI] Data Mode: Read Only Window Mode: Dialog
	RemoveTempVar	Name: PI

To Create Datasheet Forms

The following steps create two datasheet forms, one for the Veterinarians table and one for the Patients table. *Why? The datasheet forms enable the Veterinarians and Patients tables to appear as if displayed in Datasheet view, despite the Access restriction that prevents tables from being used on tabs in a navigation form.*

- Open the Navigation Pane and select the Veterinarians table.
- Display the Create tab and then click the More Forms button (Create tab | Forms group) to display the More Forms gallery (Figure 8–44).

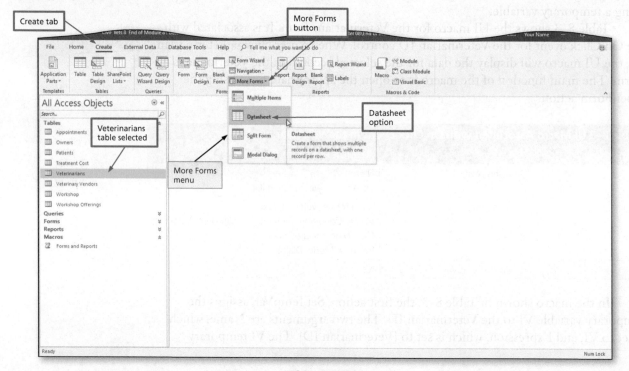

Figure 8–44

2

- Click Datasheet to create a datasheet form.
- Save the form using the name, Veterinarians.

Q&A Is it acceptable to use the same name for the form as for the table?
Yes. In this case, you want it to appear to the user that the Veterinarians table is open in Datasheet view. One way to emphasize this fact is to use the same name as the table.

What is the difference between this form, Veterinarians, and the form named Veterinarians Form?
The Veterinarians Form is a simple form that displays only one record at a time. The Veterinarians form you just created displays all of the veterinarian data in a datasheet.

- Use the same technique to create a datasheet form named Patients for the Patients table.
- Close both forms.

To Create UI Macros for the Datasheet Forms

The following steps create the UI macro shown in Table 8–3 for the Veterinarians datasheet form and the UI macro shown in Table 8–4 for the Patients datasheet form. *Why? The UI macros will display the appropriate pop-up forms as a result of clicking the appropriate position on the forms.*

1

- Open the Veterinarians form and then close the Navigation Pane.
- Click the Veterinarian ID heading to select the Veterinarian ID column in the datasheet.
- If necessary, click the Property Sheet button (Form Tools Datasheet tab | Tools group) to display a property sheet.
- Click the Event tab to display only event properties.

Q&A Why click the Event tab? Why not just use the All tab as we have before?
You can always use the All tab; however, if you know the category that contains the property in which you are interested, you can greatly reduce the number of properties that Access will display by clicking the tab for that category. That gives you fewer properties to search through to find the property you want. Whether you use the All tab or one of the other tabs is strictly a matter of personal preference.

- Click the On Click event and then click the Build button (the three dots) to display the Choose Builder dialog box (Figure 8–45).

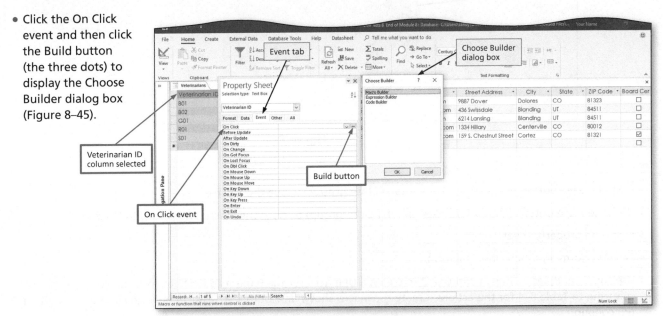

Figure 8–45

- Click the OK button (Choose Builder dialog box) to display the Macro Builder window.
- Add the SetTempVar action to the macro, enter `VI` (be sure to use a capital i and not a number 1) as the value for the Name argument, and enter `[Veterinarian ID]` as the value for the Expression argument.
- If necessary, click the Action Catalog button on the Design tab. Add the OpenForm action to the macro, select Veterinarians as the value for the Form Name argument, leave the value of the View argument set to Form, enter `[Veterinarian ID]=[TempVars]![VI]` as the value for the Where Condition argument, select Read Only as the value for the Data Mode argument, and select Dialog as the value for the Window Mode argument.

Q&A | What does this expression mean?

The portion before the equal sign, [Veterinarian ID], refers to the Veterinarian ID in the form just opened, that is, in the Veterinarians form. The portion to the right of the equal sign, [TempVars]![VI_ID], is the temporary variable that was set equal to the Veterinarian ID Number on the selected record in the Veterinarians Form. This Where Condition guarantees that the record displayed in the Veterinarians Form will be the record with the same Veterinarians ID as the one selected in the Veterinarians Form.

- Add the RemoveTempVar action to the macro and enter `VI` as the value for the Name argument (Figure 8–46).

Q&A | Why do you need to remove the temporary variable?

Technically, you do not. It has fulfilled its function, however, so it makes sense to remove it at this point.

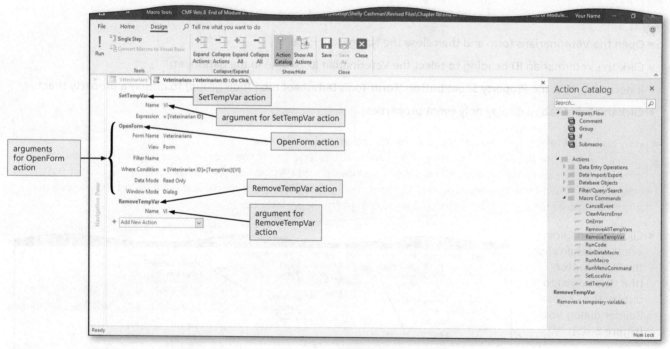

Figure 8–46

- Click the Save button (Macro Tools Design tab | Close group) to save the macro.
- Click the Close button (Macro Tools Design tab | Close group) to close the macro and return to the form.
- Close the property sheet.
- Save the form and then close the form.
- Use the techniques in Steps 1 through 3 to create a UI macro for the Patients datasheet form called Patients, referring to Table 8–4 for the actions. Create the macro shown in Figure 8–47 associated with clicking the Patient ID (PI) column.

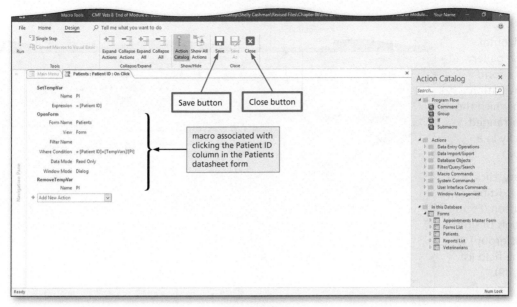

Figure 8–47

4

- Click the Save button (Macro Tools Design tab | Close group) to save the macro.

- Click the Close button (Macro Tools Design tab | Close group) to close the macro and return to the datasheet form.

- Close the property sheet.

- Save the form and then close the form.

To Create a Navigation Form

You now have all the forms you need to include in the navigation form. The following steps create the navigation form using horizontal tabs. ***Why?*** *Horizontal tabs are common on navigation forms and are easy to use.* The steps then save the form and change the title.

1

- If necessary, open the Navigation Pane.

- Click the Create tab and then click the Navigation button (Create tab | Forms group) to display the gallery of available navigation forms (Figure 8–48).

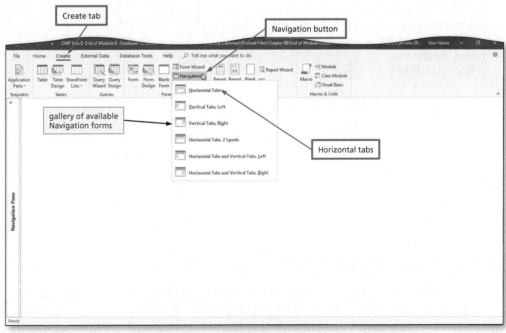

Figure 8–48

- Click Horizontal Tabs in the gallery to create a form with a navigation control in which the tabs are arranged horizontally in a single row.

- If necessary, click the 'Add Existing Fields' button (Form Layout Tools Design tab | Tools group) to display the field list (Figure 8–49).

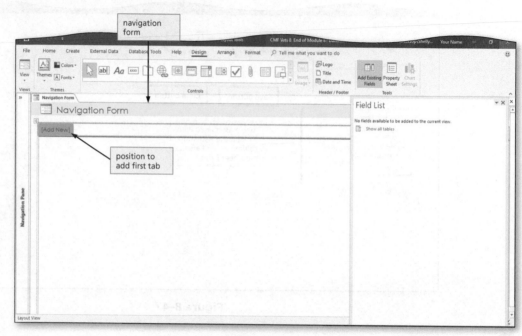

Figure 8–49

- Save the form using the name, Main Menu.

- Click the form title twice: once to select it and the second time to produce an insertion point.

- If necessary, switch to Design view. Erase the current title and then type **CMF Vets** as the new title (Figure 8–50).

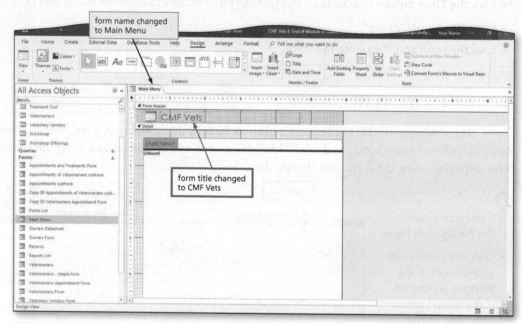

Figure 8–50

- Save the form.

To Add Tabs to a Navigation Form

To add a form or report to a tab in a navigation form, be sure the Navigation Pane is open, and then drag the form or report to the desired tab. As a result, users can display that form or report by clicking the tab. For the CMF Vets navigation form, you will drag four forms to the tabs. The Veterinarians datasheet form that appears to display the Veterinarians table open in Datasheet view. Similarly, the Patients form is a datasheet form that appears to display the Patients table open in Datasheet view. The Forms List form contains three buttons users can click to display the form of their choice. Finally, the Reports List form contains an option group that users can use to select a report to preview or export. The following steps add the tabs to the navigation form. They also change the name of the Forms List and Reports List tabs. *Why? The names of the tabs do not have to be the same as the name of the corresponding forms. By changing them, you can often make tabs more readable.*

1

- In Layout view, scroll down in the Navigation Pane so that the form named Veterinarians appears, and then drag the form to the position shown in the figure to add a new tab (Figure 8–51).

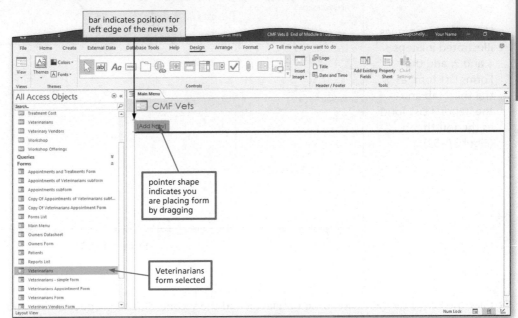

Figure 8–51

2

- Release the left mouse button to add the Veterinarians as the first tab.

- Drag the Patients form to the position shown in the figure to add a new tab (Figure 8–52).

Q&A

What should I do if I made a mistake and added a form or report to the wrong location?
You can rearrange the tabs by dragging them. Often, the simplest way to correct a mistake is to click the Undo button to reverse your most recent action, however. You can also choose to simply close the form without saving it and then start over.

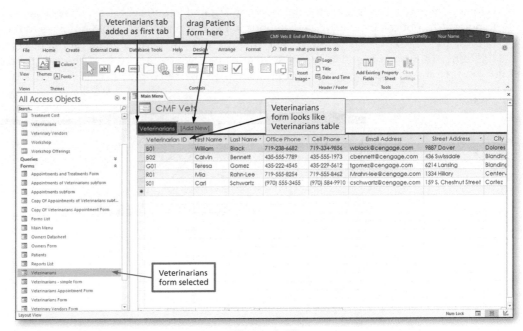

Figure 8–52

- Release the left mouse button to add the Patients form as the second tab.

- Using the techniques illustrated in Steps 1 and 2, add the Forms List form as the third tab and the Reports List form as the fourth tab (Figure 8–53).

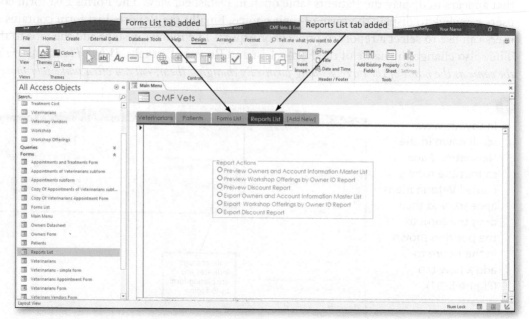

Figure 8–53

- Click the Forms List tab twice: once to select it and the second time to produce an insertion point.

- Change the name from Forms List to Forms.

- In a similar fashion, change the name of the Reports List tab from Reports List to Reports (Figure 8–54).

Q&A

I created these two forms using the names Forms List and Reports List. Now I have changed the names to Forms and Reports. Why not call them Forms and Reports in the first place, so I would not have to rename the tabs?
Because the words, forms and reports, have specific meaning in Access, you cannot use these names when creating the forms. Thus, you needed to use some other names, like Forms List and Reports List. Because tabs within forms are not database objects, you can rename them to be any name you want.

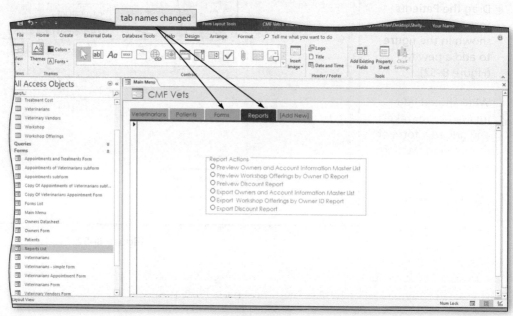

Figure 8–54

⑤
- Save the Main Menu form.
- Open the Main Menu in Form View and click on each tab to test it for accuracy.
- If requested to do so by your instructor, rename the Main Menu form as LastName Main Menu where LastName is your last name.
- Close the form.

Using a Navigation Form

The Main Menu navigation form is complete and ready for use. To use the navigation form, right-click the form in the Navigation Pane, and then click Open on the shortcut menu. The Main Menu form then will appear with the first tabbed object (see Figure 8–1). To display the other forms, simply click the appropriate tab.

How do you determine the organization of the navigation form?
Once you decide you want a navigation form, you need to decide how to organize the form.

- **Determine which tasks should be accomplished by having the user click tabs or buttons in the navigation form.** Which forms should be opened? Which reports should be opened? Are there any tables or queries that you need to be able to open in the navigation form? If so, you must create forms for the tables or queries.

- **Determine any special requirements for the way the tasks are to be performed.** When a form is opened, should a user be able to edit data, or should the form open as read-only? Should a report be exported or simply viewed on the screen?

- **Determine how to group the various tasks.** Should forms or reports simply be assigned to the tabs in the navigation form? Should they be grouped as buttons on a menu form? Should they be placed as options within an option group? (For consistency, you would usually decide on one of these approaches and use it throughout. In this module, one menu form uses command buttons, and the other uses an option group simply to illustrate both approaches.) As far as the navigation form is concerned, is a single set of horizontal tabs sufficient, or would you also like vertical tabs? Would you like two rows of horizontal tabs?

Data Macros

A data macro is a special type of macro that is associated with specific table-related events, such as updating a record in a table. The possible events are Before Change, Before Delete, After Insert, After Update, and After Delete. Data macros allow you to add logic to these events. For example, the data macro shown in Table 8–5 is associated with the Before Change event, an event that occurs after the user has changed the data but before the change is actually made in the database.

> **BTW**
> **Data Macros**
> Data macros are similar to SQL triggers. You attach logic to record or table events and any forms and code that update those events inherit the logic. Data macros are stored with the table.

Table 8–5 Data Macro for Before Change Event		
Condition	**Action**	**Arguments to Be Changed**
If [Hours Spent]>[Total Hours]		
	SetField	Name: [Hours Spent] Value: [Total Hours]
Else If [Hours Spent]<0		
	SetField	Name: [Hours Spent] Value: 0
End If		

This macro will examine the value in the Hours Spent field in the Workshop Offerings table. If the user's update would cause the value in the Hours Spent field to be greater than the value in the Total Hours field, the macro will change the value in the Hours Spent field so that it is equal to the value in the Total Hours field. Likewise, if the update would cause the value in the Hours Spent field to be less than zero, the macro will set the value in the Hours Spent field to 0. These changes take place after the user has made the change on the screen but before Access commits the change to the database, that is, before the data in the database is actually changed.

There are other events to which you can assign data macros. The actions in a data macro associated with the Before Delete event will take place after a user has indicated that he or she wants to delete a record, but before the record is actually removed from the database. The actions in a macro associated with the After Insert event will take place immediately after a record physically is added to the database. The actions in a macro associated with the After Update event will take place immediately after a record is physically changed in the database. The actions in a macro associated with the After Delete event will take place immediately after a record is physically removed from the database.

To Create a Data Macro

The following steps create the data macro in Table 8–5, a macro that will be run after a user makes a change to a record in the Workshop Offerings table, but before the record is updated in the database. *Why? CMF Vets management wants a way to prevent users from entering invalid data into the database.*

1

- Open the Workshop Offerings table in Datasheet view and close the Navigation Pane.

- Display the Table Tools Table tab (Figure 8–55).

Q&A

What is the meaning of the events in the Before Events and After Events groups? Actions in macros associated with the Before Events group will occur after the user has taken action to change or delete a record, but before the change or deletion is made permanent in the database. Actions in macros associated with the After Events group will occur after the corresponding update has been made permanent in the database.

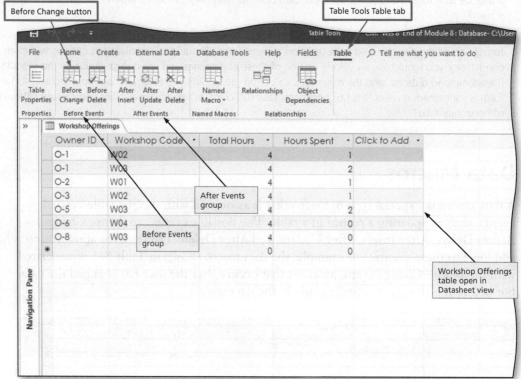

Figure 8–55

2

- Click the Before Change button (Table Tools Table tab | Before Events group).

- Double-click the IF element from the Program Flow section of the Action Catalog to add an IF statement to the macro and then type `[Hours Spent]>[Total Hours]` as the condition in the IF statement.

- Add the SetField action to the macro.

- Enter `[Hours Spent]` in the Name field and then enter `[Total Hours]` in the Value field.

- Add an Else If statement.

- Type `[Hours Spent]<0` for the Else If condition.

- Add the SetField action to the macro.

- Enter `[Hours Spent]` in the Name field and then enter `0` (zero) in the Value field.

- Confirm that your macro looks like one shown in Figure 8–56, and correct any errors if necessary.

Q&A | What happened to all the actions that were in the list? In the previous macros we created, there seemed to be many more actions available.
There are only certain actions that make sense in data macros. Only those actions appear. Therefore, the list of actions that appears is much smaller in a data macro than in other macros.

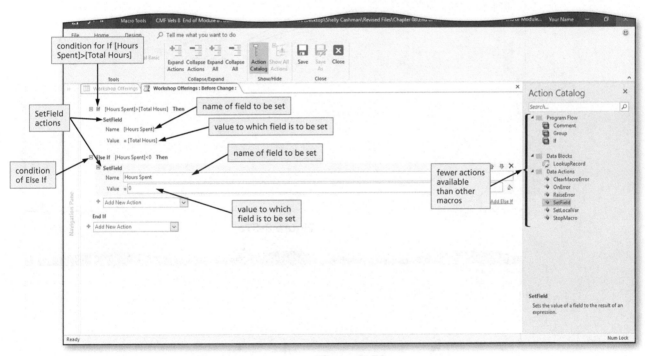

Figure 8–56

3

- Save and close the macro.

- Save and close the Workshop Offerings table.

- If desired, sign out of your Microsoft account.

- **sam**⬆ Exit Access.

Note: Unless your instructor indicates otherwise, you are encouraged to simply read the material in this module from this point on for understanding without carrying out any operations.

Using a Table That Contains a Data Macro

If you update a table that contains a data macro, the actions in the data macro will be executed whenever the corresponding event takes place. If the data macro corresponds to the Before Change event, the actions will be executed after the user has changed the data, but before the change is saved in the database. With the data macro you just created, for example, if a user attempts to change the data in such a way that the Hours Spent is greater than the Total Hours (Figure 8–57a), as soon as the user takes an action that would require saving the record, Access makes Hours Spent equal to Total Hours (Figure 8–57b). Likewise, if a user attempts to set Hours Spent to a negative number (Figure 8–58a), as soon as the user takes an action that would require saving the record, Access will set Hours Spent to 0 (Figure 8–58b). This change will take place automatically, regardless of whether the user changes the values in Datasheet view, with a form, in an update query, or in any other fashion.

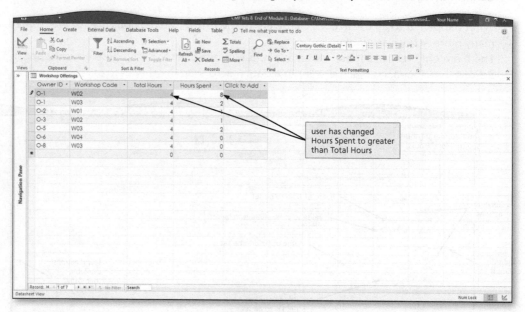

Figure 8–57a

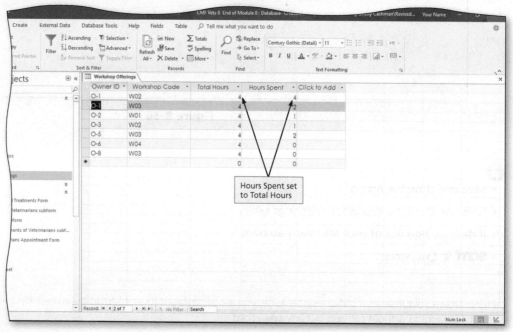

Figure 8–57b

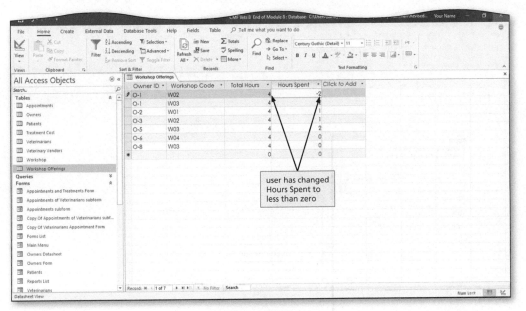

Figure 8–58a

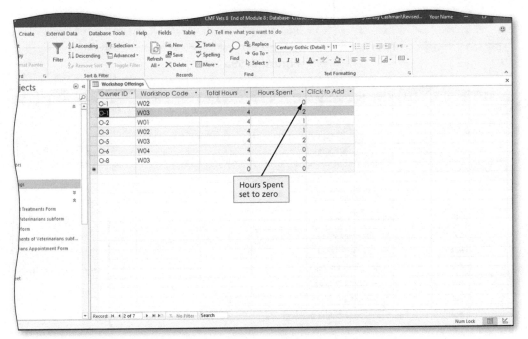

Figure 8–58b

Using Control Layouts on Forms and Reports

In earlier modules, you worked with control layouts in forms and reports. In a control layout, the data is aligned either horizontally or vertically. The two types of layouts are stacked layouts, which are most commonly used in forms, and tabular layouts, which are most commonly used in reports (Figure 8–59). Using a control layout gives you more options for moving rows or columns than you would have without the layout.

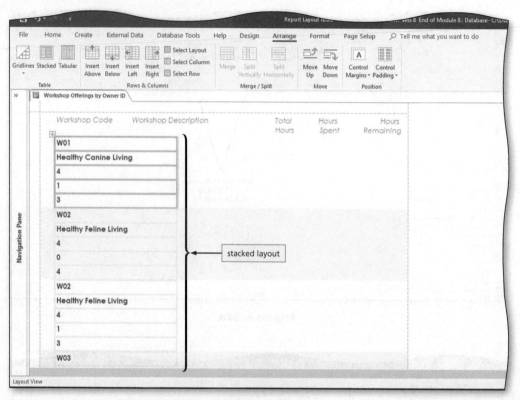

Figure 8–59a

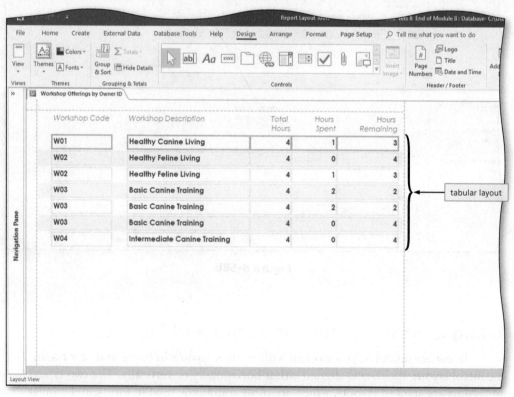

Figure 8–59b

In working with control layouts, there are many functions you can perform using the Form Layout Tools Arrange tab. You can insert rows and columns, delete rows and columns, split and merge cells, and move rows. You can also change margins, which affects spacing within cells, and padding, which affects spacing between rows and columns. You can split a layout into two layouts and move layouts. Finally, you can anchor controls so that they maintain the same distance between the control and the anchor position as the form or report is resized. Table 8–6 gives descriptions of the functions available on the Form Layout Tools Arrange tab.

Table 8–6 Arrange Tab	
Button	**Enhanced ScreenTip**
Gridlines	Gridlines
Stacked	Create a layout similar to a paper form, with labels to the left of each field.
Tabular	Create a layout similar to a spreadsheet, with labels across the top and data in columns below the labels.
Insert Above	Insert Above
Insert Below	Insert Below
Insert Left	Insert Left
Insert Right	Insert Right
Select Layout	Select Layout
Select Column	Select Column
Select Row	Select Row
Merge	Merge Cells
Split Vertically	Split the selected layout into two rows.
Split Horizontally	Split the selected layout into two columns.
Move Up	Move Up
Move Down	Move Down
Control Margins	Control Margins
Control Padding	Control Padding
Anchoring	Tie a control to a section or another control so that it moves or resizes in conjunction with movement or resizing of the parent.

TO CREATE A LAYOUT FOR A FORM OR REPORT

If you create a form using the Form button (Create tab | Forms group), Access automatically creates a stacked layout. If you create a report using the Report button (Create tab | Reports group), Access automatically creates a tabular layout. In other cases, you can create a layout using the Form Layout Tools Arrange tab for forms or the Report Layout Tools Arrange tab for reports. If you no longer want controls to be in a control layout, you can remove the layout.

To create a layout in either a form or report, you would use the following steps.

1. Select all the controls that you want to place in a layout.
2. Click the Stacked button (Form Layout Tools Arrange tab | Table group) to create a stacked layout or the Tabular button (Form Layout Tools Arrange tab | Table group) to create a tabular layout.

TO REMOVE A LAYOUT FOR A FORM OR REPORT

To remove a layout from either a form or report, you would use the following steps.

1. Right-click any control in the layout you want to remove to produce a shortcut menu.
2. Point to Layout on the shortcut menu and then click Remove Layout on the submenu to remove the layout.

BTW

Quick Styles for Controls
To make a navigation form more visually appealing, you can change the style of a command button and/or tabs. Quick styles change how the different colors, fonts, and effects are combined. To change the style of a command button or tab, open the navigation form in Layout view. Select the control(s) for which you want to change the style and then click Quick Styles. When the Quick Styles gallery appears, select the desired style. You also can change the style of a control in Design view.

BTW

Change the Shape of a Control
Command buttons and tabs have a default shape. For example, both command buttons and tabs have a rounded rectangle shape as the default shape. You can change the shape of a button or tab control on a navigation form. To do so, open the navigation form in Layout view. Select the control(s) for which you want to change the shape and click Change Shape. When the Change Shape gallery appears, select the desired shape. You also can change the shape of a command button or tab in Design view.

Using Undo

When making changes with the Form Layout Tools Arrange tab buttons, it is not uncommon to make a change that you did not intend. Sometimes taking appropriate action to reverse the change can prove difficult. If so, remember that you can undo the change by clicking the Undo button on the Quick Access Toolbar. It is also a good idea to save your work frequently. That way, you can always close the form or report without saving. When you reopen the form or report, it will not have any of your most recent changes.

TO INSERT A ROW

You can insert a blank row either above or below a selected row (Figure 8–60). You can then fill in the row by either typing a value or dragging a field from a field List. In a similar fashion, you can insert a blank column either to the left or right of a selected column.

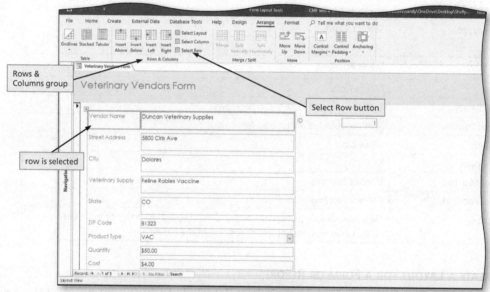

Figure 8–60a

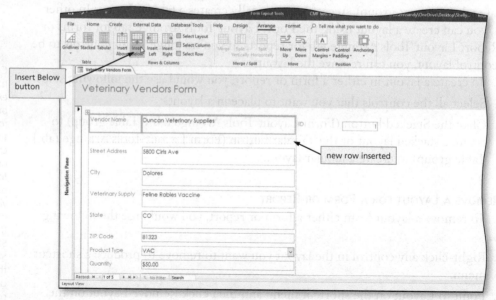

Figure 8–60b

You would use the following steps to insert a blank row.

1. Select any control in the row above or below where you want to insert a new row.
2. Click the Select Row button (Form Layout Tools Arrange tab | Rows & Columns group) to select the row.
3. Click the Insert Above button (Form Layout Tools Arrange tab | Rows & Columns group) to insert a blank row above the selected row or the Insert Below button (Form Layout Tools Arrange tab | Rows & Columns group) to insert a blank row below the selected row.

As you have seen earlier in the text, you also can insert a row containing a field by simply dragging the field from the field List to the desired location.

To Insert a Column

You would use the following steps to insert a new column.

1. Select any control in the column to the right or left of where you want to insert a new column.
2. Click the Select Column button (Form Layout Tools Arrange tab | Rows & Columns group) to select the column.
3. Click the Insert Left button (Form Layout Tools Arrange tab | Rows & Columns group) to insert a blank column to the left of the selected column or the Insert Right button (Form Layout Tools Arrange tab | Rows & Columns group) to insert a blank column to the right of the selected column.

To Delete a Row

You can delete any unwanted row or column from a control layout. You would use the following steps to delete a row.

1. Click any control in the row you want to delete.
2. Click Select Row (Form Layout Tools Arrange tab | Rows & Columns group).
3. Press DELETE to delete the row.

To Delete a Column

You would use the following steps to delete a column.

1. Click any control in the column you want to delete.
2. Click Select Column (Form Layout Tools Arrange tab | Rows & Columns group).
3. Press DELETE to delete the column.

Splitting and Merging Cells

You can split a cell into two cells either horizontally, as shown in Figure 8–61, or vertically. You can then enter contents into the new cell. For example, in Figure 8–61, you could type text into the new cell that gives information about Veterinarian IDs. You can also merge two cells into one.

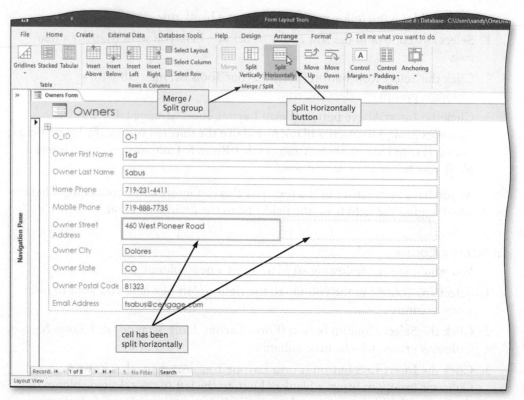

Figure 8–61

To Split a Cell

To split a cell, you would use the following steps.

1. Click the cell to be split.
2. Click the Split Vertically button (Form Layout Tools Arrange tab | Merge / Split group) to split the selected cell vertically or the Split Horizontally button (Form Layout Tools Arrange tab | Merge / Split group) to split the selected cell horizontally.

To Merge Cells

You would use the following steps to merge cells.

1. Select the first cell to be merged.
2. While holding down the CTRL key, CLICK all the other cells to be merged.
3. Click the Merge button (Form Layout Tools Arrange tab | Merge / Split group) to merge the cells.

BTW

Control Padding
The term, padding, refers to the amount of space between a control's border and its contents. Effectively, you can increase or decrease the amount of white space in a control.

Moving Cells

You can move a cell in a layout by dragging it to its new position. Most often, however, you will not want to move individual cells, but rather whole rows (Figure 8–62). You can move a row by selecting the row and then dragging it to the new position or you can use the Move buttons on the Form Layout Tools Arrange tab.

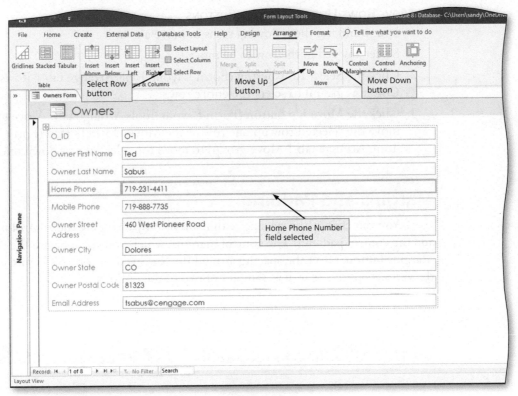

Figure 8–62a

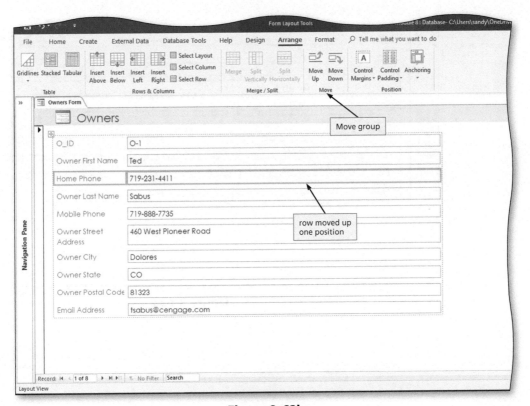

Figure 8–62b

To Move Rows Using the Move Buttons

You would use the following steps to move a row.

1. Select any cell in the row to be moved.

2. Click the Select Row button (Form Layout Tools Arrange tab | Rows & Columns group) to select the entire row.

3. Click the Move Up button (Form Layout Tools Arrange tab| Move group) to move the selected row up one row or the Move Down button (Form Layout Tools Arrange tab | Move group) to move the selected row down one row.

Margins and Padding

You can change the spacing within a layout by changing the control margins and the control padding. The control margins, which you change with the Control Margins button, affect the spacing around the text inside a control. Figure 8–63 shows the various options as well as samples of two of the options.

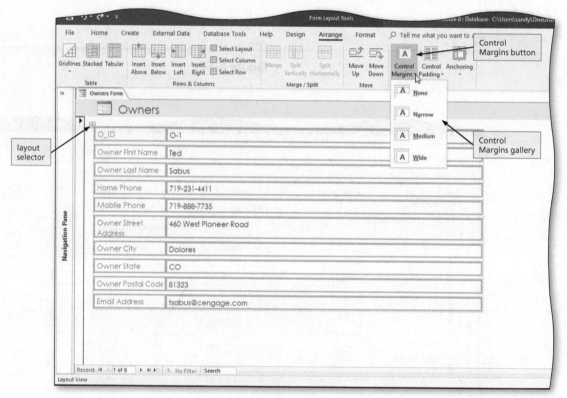

Figure 8–63a

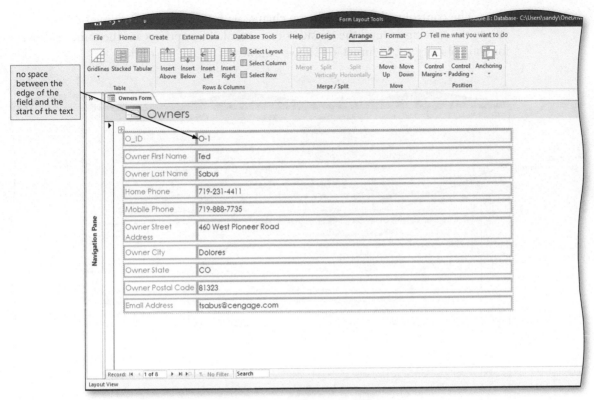

Figure 8–63b

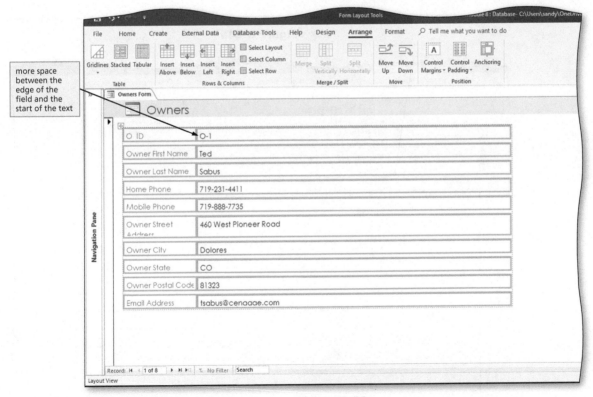

Figure 8–63c

The control padding, which you change with the Control Padding button, affects the spacing around the outside of a control. The options are the same as those for control margins. Figure 8–64 shows samples of two of the options.

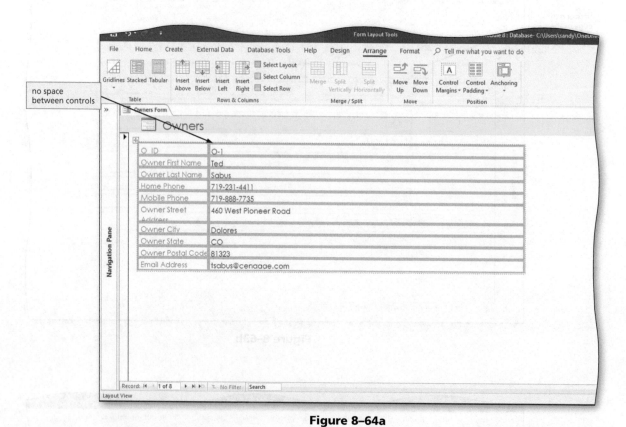

Figure 8–64a

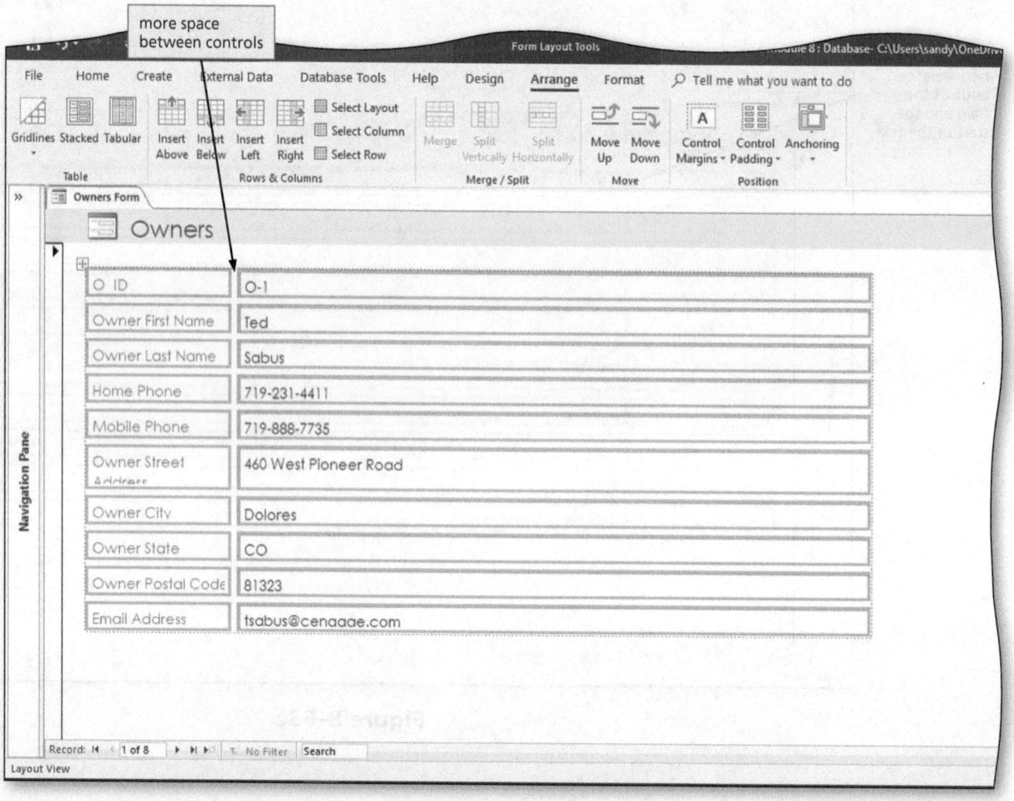

Figure 8–64b

TO CHANGE CONTROL MARGINS

You would use the following steps to change a control's margins.

1. Select any cell in the layout.
2. Click the Select Layout button (Form Layout Tools Arrange tab | Rows & Columns group) to select the entire layout. (You also can select the layout by clicking the layout selector.)
3. Click the Control Margins button (Form Layout Tools Arrange tab | Position group) to display the available margin settings.
4. Click the desired margin setting.

TO CHANGE CONTROL PADDING

You would use the following steps to change control padding.

1. Select the layout.
2. Click the Control Padding button (Form Layout Tools Arrange tab | Position group) to display the available padding settings.
3. Click the desired padding setting.

Although you can make the margin and padding changes for individual controls, it is much more common to do so for the entire layout. Doing so gives a uniform appearance to the layout.

Splitting a Layout

You can split a single control layout into two separate layouts (Figure 8–65) and then modify each layout separately. They can be moved to different locations and formatted differently.

BTW
Gridlines
You can also add gridlines to a form. To do so, select the control(s) for which you want to add gridlines, then click the Gridlines button. When the Gridlines menu appears, select the desired option. You also can change the color, border, style, and width of gridlines using the Gridlines menu.

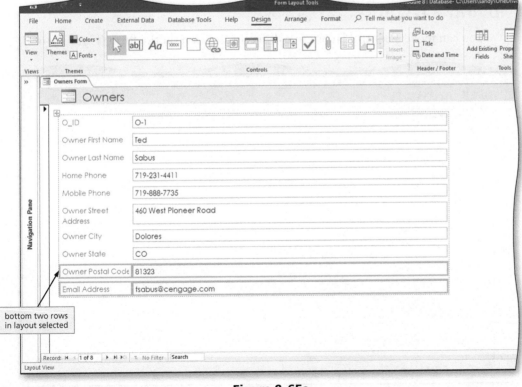

Figure 8–65a

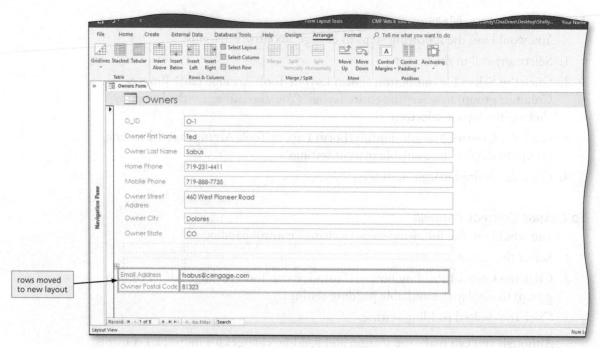

Figure 8–65b

TO SPLIT A LAYOUT

To split a layout, you would use the following steps.

1. Select all the cells that you want to move to a new layout.

2. Click the Stacked button (Form Layout Tools Arrange tab | Table group) to place the cells in a stacked layout or the Tabular button (Form Layout Tools Arrange tab | Table group) to place the cells in a tabular layout.

Moving a Layout

You can move a control layout to a different location on the form (Figure 8–66).

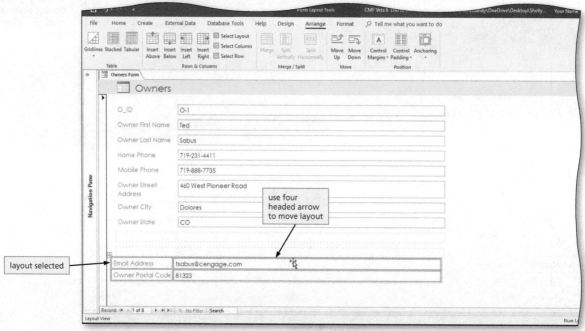

Figure 8–66

TO MOVE A LAYOUT

You would use the following steps to move a layout.

1. Click any cell in the layout to be moved and then click the Select Layout button (Form Layout Tools Arrange tab | Rows & Columns group) to select the layout.

2. Drag the layout to the new location.

Anchoring Controls

The Anchoring button allows you to tie (anchor) controls to a section or to other controls so that they maintain the same distance between the control and the anchor position as the form is resized. To anchor the controls you have selected, you use the Anchoring gallery (Figure 8–67).

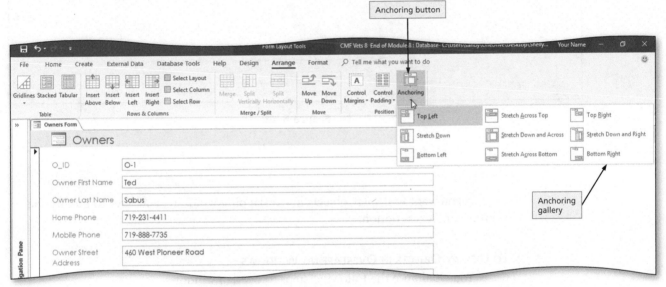

Figure 8–67

The Top Left, Top Right, Bottom Left, and Bottom Right options anchor the control in the indicated position on the form. The other five operations also stretch the controls in the indicated direction.

TO ANCHOR CONTROLS

You would use the following steps to anchor controls.

1. Select the control or controls to be anchored.

2. Click the Anchoring button (Form Layout Tools Arrange tab | Position group) to produce the Anchoring gallery.

3. Select the desired Anchoring option from the Anchoring gallery.

To see the effect of anchoring you need to display objects in overlapping windows rather than standard tabbed documents. With overlapping windows, you can resize the object by dragging the border of the object. Anchored objects keep their same relative position (Figure 8–68).

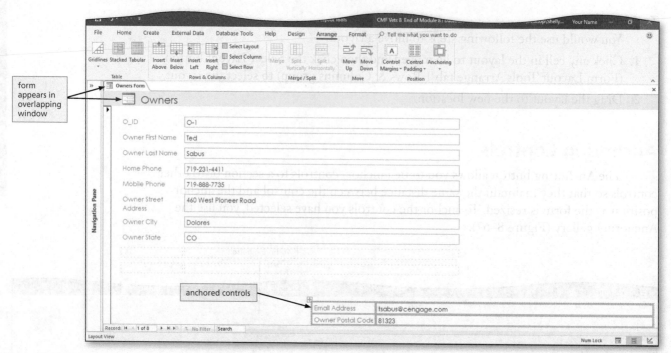

Figure 8–68

Window

If you want to display objects in overlapping windows, you have to modify the appropriate Access option.

TO DISPLAY OBJECTS IN OVERLAPPING WINDOWS

You would use the following steps to overlap windows.

1. Click File on the ribbon to open the Backstage view.
2. Click Options to display the Access Options dialog box.
3. Click Current Database to display the Current Database options.
4. In the Application Options area, click the Overlapping Windows option button.
5. Click the OK button to close the Access Options dialog box.
6. For the changes to take effect, you will need to close and then reopen the database.

You use a similar process to return to displaying objects in tabbed documents.

BTW
Overlapping Windows
When you display objects in overlapping windows, each database object appears in its own window. When multiple objects are open, these windows overlap each other. By default, Access 2019 displays database objects in a single pane separated by tabs.

TO DISPLAY OBJECTS IN TABBED DOCUMENTS

You would use the following steps to display tabbed documents.

1. Click File on the ribbon to open the Backstage view.
2. Click Options to display the Access Options dialog box.
3. Click Current Database to display the Current Database options.
4. In the Application Options area, click the Tabbed Documents option button.
5. Click the OK button to close the Access Options dialog box.
6. For the changes to take effect, you will need to close and then reopen the database.

Summary

In this module you have learned to create and use macros, create a menu form that uses command buttons for the choices, create a menu form that uses an option group for the choices, create a macro that implements the choices in the option group, create datasheet forms that utilize user interface macros, create a navigation form, add tabs to a navigation form, and create data macros. You also learned to modify control layouts.

CONSIDER THIS

What decisions will you need to make when creating your own macros and navigation forms?
Use these guidelines as you complete the assignments in this module and create your own macros and navigation forms outside of this class.

   1. Determine when it would be beneficial to automate tasks in a macro.

      a. Are there tasks involving multiple steps that would be more conveniently accomplished by running a macro than by carrying out all the individual steps? For example, opening a form in read-only mode could be accomplished conveniently through a macro.

      b. Are there tasks that are to be performed when the user clicks buttons on a menu form?

      c. Are there tasks to be performed when a user clicks a control on a form?

      d. Are there tasks to be performed when a user updates a table? These tasks can be placed in a macro that can be run when the button is clicked.

   2. Determine whether it is appropriate to create a navigation form.

      a. If you want to make it easy and convenient for users to perform a variety of tasks just by clicking tabs and buttons, consider creating a navigation form.

      b. You can associate the performance of the various tasks with the tabs and buttons in the navigation form.

   3. Determine the organization of the navigation form.

      a. Determine the various tasks that need to be performed by clicking tabs and buttons.

      b. Decide the logical grouping of the tabs and buttons.

CONSIDER THIS

How should you submit solutions to questions in the assignments identified with a symbol?
Every assignment in this book contains one or more questions identified with a symbol. These questions require you to think beyond the assigned database. Present your solutions to the questions in the format required by your instructor. Possible formats may include one or more of these options: write the answer; create a document that contains the answer; present your answer to the class; discuss your answer in a group; record the answer as audio or video using a webcam, smartphone, or portable media player; or post answers on a blog, wiki, or website.

Apply Your Knowledge

Reinforce the skills and apply the concepts you learned in this module.

Creating UI Macros and a Navigation Form

Note: To complete this assignment, you will be required to use the Data Files. Please contact your instructor for information about accessing the Data Files.

Instructions: Start Access. Open the Support_AC_Financial Services database and enable the content. (If you do not have the database, see your instructor for a copy of the modified database.)

Perform the following tasks:

1. Create a datasheet form for the Client table and name the form Client. Create a UI macro for the Client form. Use CN as the temporary variable name. When a user clicks a client number on a row in the datasheet form, the Client form should appear in a pop-up form in read-only mode.

2. Create a datasheet form for the Advisor table and name the form Advisor Datasheet. Create a UI macro for the Advisor Datasheet form. Use AN as the temporary variable name. When a user clicks an advisor number on a row in the datasheet form, the Advisor Datasheet form should appear in a pop-up form in read-only mode.

3. Create the navigation form shown in Figure 8–69. The purpose of the form is to display the two datasheet forms in the database as horizontal tabs. Name the form Main Menu and change the title to Financial Services Main Menu.

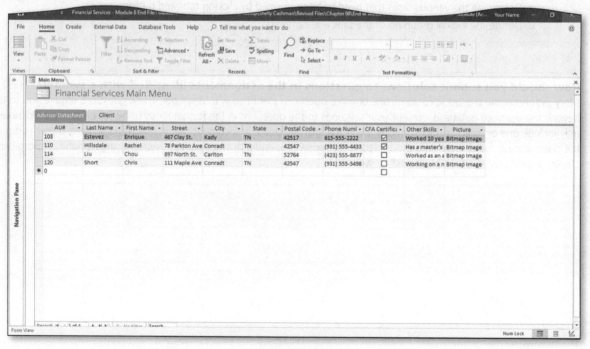

Figure 8–69

4. If requested to do so by your instructor, open the Advisor datasheet form and change the first and last names of advisor 110 to your first and last name.

5. Submit the revised database in the format specified by your instructor.

6. ✳ How could you add a Services Data form to the navigation form?

Extend Your Knowledge

Extend the skills you learned in this module and experiment with new skills. You may need to use Help to complete the assignment.

Creating and Modifying Navigation Forms

Note: To complete this assignment, you will be required to use the Data Files. Please contact your instructor for information about accessing the Data Files. Start Access, and then open the Support_AC_Healthy Pets database. (If you do not have this database, see your instructor for a copy of the modified database).

Instructions: Healthy Pets is a veterinary practice that is being closed due to retirements. CMF is thinking of buying the practice to expand their client base. Before the management makes any decisions on this, the Healthy Pets database needs to be updated so that it is compatible with CMF Vets and so their files may be imported into CMF Vets database. Perform the following tasks:

1. Create a form named Forms List form that contains macros to open the Clients by Technician form and the Technician form.
2. Create a form named Reports List form that contains macros to open the Client Amount Due Summary report and the Revised Client Summary report.
3. Create a Main Menu form for forms and reports. The Forms List menu should include the command buttons for the Clients and Technicians form and the Technician form. The Reports List menu should include Command Buttons for both summary reports. Test the macros and then save the changes.
4. Research how to import database objects from one database into another database. Note what changes would need to be made to the Healthy Pets database before it is imported into the CMF Vets database.
5. Open the Main Menu navigation form in Layout view. Change the shape of the Forms List tab to Oval and the shape of the Reports List tab to Snip Single Corner Rectangle.
6. If requested to do so by your instructor, add a label to the form header for the Main Menu form with your first and last name.
7. Submit the revised database in the format specified by your instructor.
8. ✳ Why would you convert a macro to Visual Basic code?

Expand Your World

Create a solution, which uses cloud and web technologies, by learning and investigating on your own from general guidance.

Problem: Support_AC_Physical Therapy is a database of clients and therapists. Therapists are required to update their national physical therapy certification annually with the American Physical Therapy Association. You will need to find colleges in the city of Madison, Wisconsin that offers these classes. Madison is the major city closest to the Wisconsin communities of Portage, Empeer, and Grant City. You will create images that display the course name and hyperlinks for these classes that you download from the Internet. Finally, you will modify the Therapist table by adding a field for these hyperlinks and images. In addition, you will add another field that displays either Yes or No to indicate whether the therapist has met the annual certification requirement.

Expand Your World *continued*

Note: To complete this assignment, you will be required to use the Data Files. Please contact your instructor for information about accessing the Data Files. Start access, and then open the Support_ AC_Physical Therapy database that you used in previous modules. (If you do not have database, see your instructor for a copy of the modified database).

Instructions: Perform the following tasks:

1. Search the Internet to locate continuing education courses for physical therapy in Madison, Wisconsin.

2. Create hyperlinks to the course information on the school's website. Enter the hyperlinks into the Therapist table.

3. Find images to enter for the courses for the Attachment field in the Therapist table. You can use images that you have found online or photos that you have taken. Note: make sure you have the appropriate permissions to use the images.

4. Add a Yes/No field into the Therapist table indicating whether the therapist has completed the annual certification.

5. Create a form based on the updated Therapist table for easy reference concerning the new fields and name the form Therapist Certification.

6. Save your changes.

7. Submit the revised database in the format specified by your instructor.

8. ✺ How did you create the images you included in the Therapist table? Why did you make those choices?

In the Labs

Design, create, modify and/or use a database following the guidelines, concepts, and skills presented in this module.

Lab: Adding a Navigation Form to the Lancaster College Database

Instructions: Open the Support_AC_Lancaster College database. (If you do not have the database, see your instructor for a copy of the modified database.)

Part 1:   The sports department of Lancaster College would like you to create a main menu that allows easy access to forms and reports.

   a.   Create a form with macro buttons that opens the Coach subform and the Sport subform. Name the form List of Available Forms.

   b.   Create a form with macro buttons that opens the Sport Teams and Captains report and the Sports table report. Name the form List of Available Reports.

   c.   Create a Main Menu navigation form that includes the List of Available Forms form and the List of Available Reports form.

   d.   Save the changes and test the navigation form.

Submit your assignment in the format specified by your instructor.

Part 2:   You made several decisions while adding the macro buttons and creating the form for this assignment. What was the rationale behind your decisions? Would you add any additional macro buttons to The Form List or The Report List?

   a.   Research and document how you can have the Navigation form open automatically when the database is opened.

   b.   Submit the revised database in the format specified by your instructor.

9 | Administering a Database System

Objectives

You will have mastered the material in this module when you can:

- Convert a database to and from earlier versions of Access
- Use the Table Analyzer, Performance Analyzer, and Documenter
- Create custom categories and groups in the Navigation Pane
- Use table, database, and field properties
- Create indexes

- Enable and use automatic error checking
- Create custom data type parts
- Create a database for a template
- Create a custom template
- Encrypt a database and set a password
- Lock a database and split a database

Introduction

Administering a database system is an important activity that has many facets. Administration activities are an important aspect of database management because they improve the usability, accessibility, security, and efficiency of the database.

Project — Administering a Database System

CMF Vets realizes the importance of database administration, that is, the importance of administering its database system properly. An important activity in administering databases is the creation of custom templates, application parts, and data type parts. A custom template is a customized database application that can be used as a basis for additional databases. The template contains tables, forms, queries, and other objects that can be used by others to create a database based on that template. Application parts and data type parts are templates included in Access that you can add to your database to extend its functionality. Clicking an application part adds to your database a predetermined collection of objects such as tables, queries, forms, reports, and /or macros. Clicking a data type part adds a predetermined collection of fields to a table. Creating an understandable startup form gives database users easy access to the forms when the database is opened.

CMF Vets have recognized a need for a pet sitting business. Many of their clients travel and want to have their pets cared for at home during their absence. The veterinary clinic decides to organize a pet sitting database system that links the available pet sitters with those owners in need of pet care. The personnel organizing the pet sitting business at CMF Vets realize that some of pet sitters might not be familiar with operating a database and a startup menu would be extremely helpful. Figure 9-1 shows a startup form that is automatically opened when the database is opened.

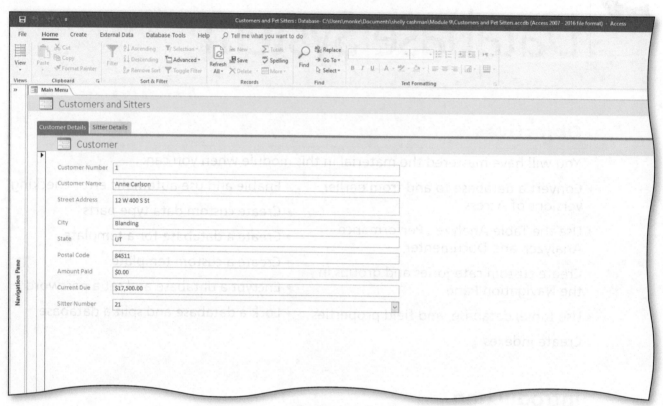

Figure 9–1

BTW

Enabling the Content
For each of the databases you use in this module, you will need to enable the content.

BTW

The Ribbon and Screen Resolution
Access may change how the groups and buttons within the groups appear on the ribbon, depending on the computer's screen resolution. Thus, your ribbon may look different from the ones in this book if you are using a screen resolution other than 1366 x 768.

Figure 9–2 illustrates the range of activities involved in database administration, including the conversion of an Access database to an earlier version of Access. Database administration usually includes such activities as analyzing tables for potential problems, analyzing performance to see if changes could make the system perform more efficiently, and documenting the various objects in the database. It can include creating custom categories and groups in the Navigation Pane as well as changing table and database properties. It can also include the use of field properties in such tasks as creating a custom input mask and allowing zero-length strings. It can include the creation of indexes to speed up retrieval. The inclusion of automatic error checking is part of the administration of a database system. Understanding the purpose of the Trust Center is critical to the database administration function. Another important area of database administration is the protection of the database. This protection includes locking the database through the creation of an ACCDE file to prevent unauthorized changes from being made to the VBA source code or to the design of forms and reports. Splitting the database into a front-end and a back-end database is another way to protect the functionality and improve the efficiency of a database.

File   Home   Create   External Data   Database Tools   Help   Fields   Table   Tell me what you wa...

Table Tools   Database13 : D

Figure 9–2

In this module, you will learn how to perform a variety of database administration tasks.

Converting Databases

Access 2007, Access 2010, Access 2013, Access 2016, and Access 2019 all use the same file format, the .accdb format. The format is usually referred to as the Access 2007 file format. Thus, in Access 2019, you can use any database created in Access 2007. You should be aware of the following changes in Access 2013, Access 2016, and Access 2019 from the earlier versions.

1. Unlike previous versions, these versions do not support PivotTables or PivotCharts.
2. The Text data type is now Short Text, and the Memo data type is now Long Text.
3. Smart Tags are no longer supported.
4. Replication is no longer available.

To convert an Access 2007 database to an earlier version, the database cannot contain any features that are specific to Access 2007, 2010, 2013, 2016, or 2019. These include attachments, multivalued fields, offline data, or links to external files not supported in earlier versions of Access. They also include objects published to the web, data macros, and calculated columns. Provided the database does not contain such features, you can convert the database by clicking the Save As tab in the Backstage view (Figure 9–3). You can then choose the appropriate format.

BTW
Converting Databases
If you try to convert a database that contains features specific to a later version of Access, Access displays an error message alerting you that you cannot save the database as an earlier version because it contains features that require the current file format.

BTW
Maintaining Backward Compatibility
If you plan to share your database with users who may have an earlier version of Access, be sure to maintain backward compatibility. Do not include multivalued fields, attachment fields, or calculated fields in your database design. For example, if there is a calculation that is used frequently, create a query with the calculated field and use the query as the basis for forms and reports rather than adding the field to the table design.

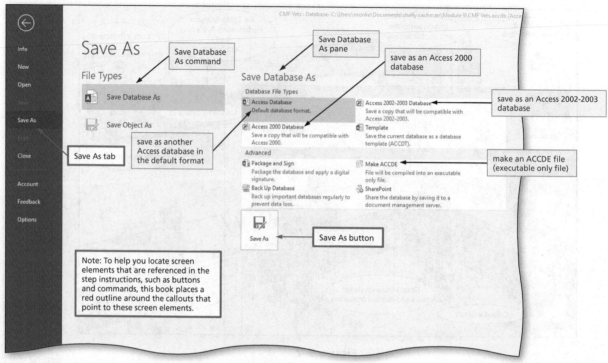

Figure 9–3

TO CONVERT AN ACCESS 2007–2016 DATABASE TO AN EARLIER VERSION

Specifically, to convert an Access 2007–2019 database to an earlier version, you would use the following steps.

1. With the database to be converted open, click File on the ribbon to open the Backstage view.
2. Click the Save As tab.
3. With the 'Save Database As' command selected, click the desired format, and then click the Save As button.
4. Type the name you want for the converted database, select a location in which to save the converted database, and click the Save button.

TO CONVERT AN ACCESS 2000 OR 2002–2003 DATABASE TO AN ACCESS 2019 DATABASE

To convert an Access 2000 or Access 2002–2003 database to the default database format for Access 2019, you open the database in Access 2019. Initially, the database is open in compatibility mode, where features that are new to Access 2019 and that cannot easily be displayed or converted are disabled. In this mode, the database remains in its original format. If you want to convert it so that you can use it in Access 2019, you use the Access Database command on the Backstage view. Once the database is converted, the disabled features will be enabled. You will no longer be able to share the database with users of Access 2000 or Access 2002–2003, however.

Specifically, to convert an Access 2000 or 2002–2003 database to the default database format for Access 2019, you would use the following steps.

1. With the database to be converted open, click File on the ribbon to open the Backstage view.
2. Click the Save As tab.

3. With the Save Database As command selected, click Access Database and then click the Save As button.

4. Type the name you want for the converted database, select a location, and click the Save button.

BTW
Creating Databases in Older Formats
To create a database in an older format, create a database and browse to select a location for the database, then click the Save As Type arrow in the File New Database dialog box, and select either 2002–2003 format or 2000 format.

Microsoft Access Analysis Tools

Microsoft Access has a variety of tools that are useful in analyzing databases. Analyzing a database gives information about how the database functions and identifies opportunities for improving functionality. You can use the Access analysis tools to analyze tables and database performance, and to create detailed documentation.

To Use the Table Analyzer

Access contains a Table Analyzer tool that performs three separate functions. This tool can analyze tables while looking for potential redundancy (duplicated data). The Table Analyzer can also analyze performance and check for ways to make queries, reports, or forms more efficient. Then, the tool will make suggestions for possible changes. The final function of the analyzer is to produce detailed documentation describing the structure and content of the various tables, queries, forms, reports, and other objects in the database.

The following steps use the Table Analyzer to examine the Account table for **redundancy,** or duplicated data. **Why?** *Redundancy is one of the biggest potential sources of problems in a database.* If redundancy is found, the Table Analyzer will suggest ways to split the table in order to eliminate the redundancy.

1

- **sam** ↓ Start Access and open the database named CMF Vets from your hard disk, OneDrive, or other storage location.

- If necessary, close the Navigation Pane.

- Display the Database Tools tab (Figure 9–4).

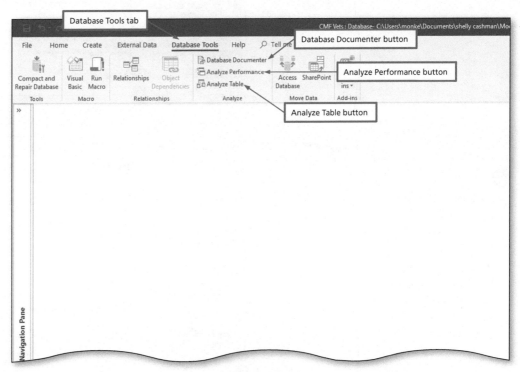

Figure 9–4

● Click the Analyze Table button (Database Tools tab | Analyze group) to display the Table Analyzer Wizard dialog box (Figure 9–5).

Q&A

Where did the data in the figure come from? It does not look like my data. The data is fictitious. It is just intended to give you an idea of what the data might look like.

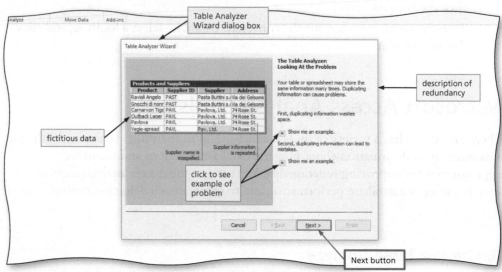

Figure 9–5

● Click Next to display the next Table Analyzer Wizard screen (Figure 9–6).

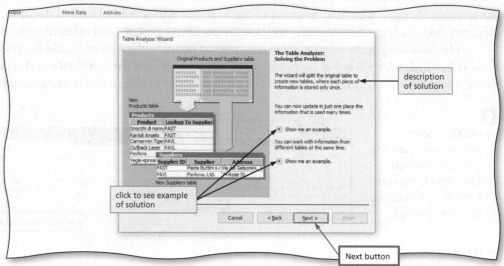

Figure 9–6

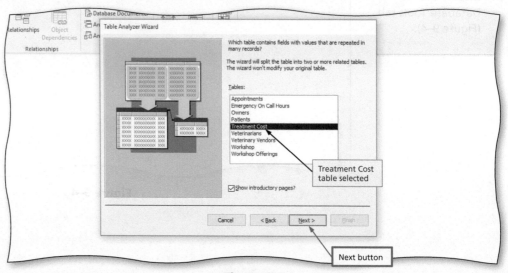

● Click Next to display the next Table Analyzer Wizard screen.

● If necessary, select the Treatment Cost table (Figure 9–7).

Figure 9–7

• Click Next.

• Be sure the 'Yes, let the wizard decide.' option button is selected (Figure 9–8) to let the wizard determine what action to take.

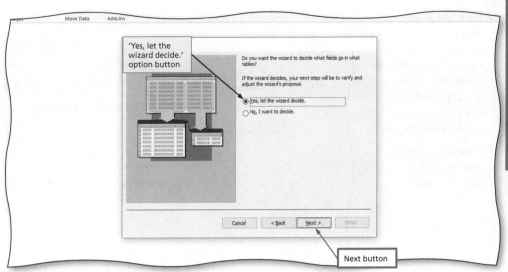

Figure 9–8

• Click Next to run the analysis (Figure 9–9), which indicates redundancy in the database.

Q&A I do not really want to put the Animal Type in a different table, even though I realize that this data does appear to be duplicated. Do I have to follow this advice?
Certainly not. This is only a suggestion.

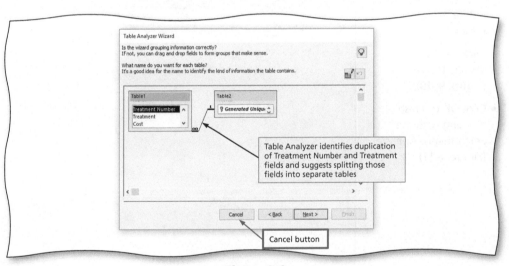

Figure 9–9

• Because the type of duplication identified by the analyzer does not pose a problem, click the Cancel button to close the analyzer.

To Use the Performance Analyzer

The Performance Analyzer examines the database's tables, queries, reports, forms, and other objects in your system, looking for ways to improve the efficiency of database operations. These improvements could include modifications to the way data is stored, as well as changes to the indexes created for the system. (You will learn about indexes later in this module.) The following steps use the Performance Analyzer. *Why? The Performance Analyzer identifies possible areas for improvement in the CMF Vets database. Users then can determine whether to implement the suggested changes.*

● Click the Analyze
Performance
button, shown in
Figure 9–4 (Database
Tools tab | Analyze
group), to display
the Performance
Analyzer dialog box.

● If necessary, click
the Tables tab
(Figure 9–10).

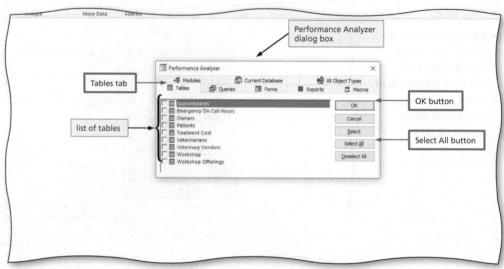

Figure 9–10

● Click the Select All
button to select all
tables.

● Click OK to
display the results
(Figure 9–10).

● Click OK to finish
working with the
Performance Analyzer
(Figure 9–11).

Q&A

What do the results
mean?
The data is stored
correctly to optimize
efficiency. If this had
not been the case,
you would see a set
of suggestions for
efficiency improvement
such as changing the data types of the fields.

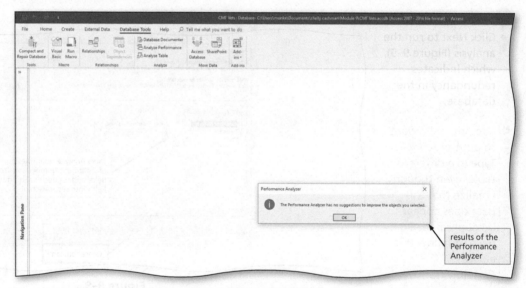

Figure 9–11

To Use the Database Documenter

The Database Documenter allows you to produce detailed documentation of the various tables, queries, forms, reports, and other objects in your database. Documentation is required by many organizations. It is used for backup, disaster recovery, and planning for database enhancements. Figure 9–12 shows a portion of the documentation for the Appointments table. The complete documentation is much lengthier than the one shown in the figure.

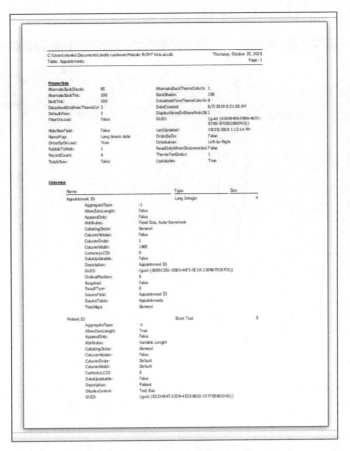

Figure 9–12

The following steps use the Database Documenter. *Why? The Database Documenter is the easiest way to produce detailed documentation for the Appointments table.*

- Click the Database Documenter button, shown in Figure 9–4 (Database Tools tab | Analyze group), to display the Documenter dialog box.

- If necessary, click the Tables tab and then click the Appointments check box to specify documentation for the Appointments table (Figure 9–13).

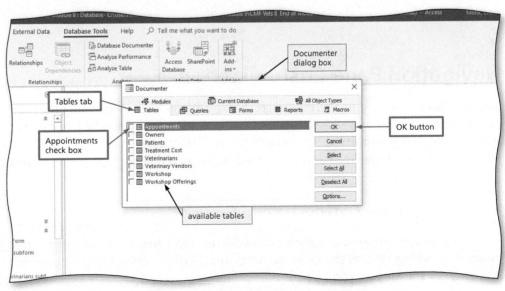

Figure 9–13

- Click OK to produce a preview of the documentation (Figure 9–14).

Q&A

What can I do with this documentation?
You could print it by clicking the Print button (Print Preview tab | Print group). You could create a PDF or XPS file containing the documentation by clicking the PDF or XPS button (Print Preview tab | Data group) and following the directions. You could create a Word (RTF) file by clicking the More button (Print Preview tab | Data

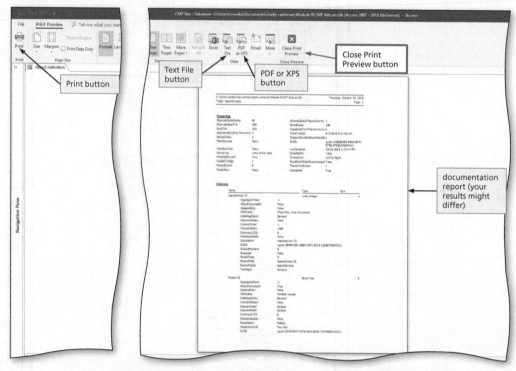

Figure 9–14

group), and then clicking Word and following the directions. Whatever option you choose, you might need to use this documentation later if you make changes to the database design.

- Click the 'Close Print Preview' button (Print Preview tab | Close Preview group) to close the preview of the documentation.

Experiment

- Try other options within the Database Documenter to see the effect of your choice on the documentation produced. Each time, close the preview of the documentation.

Navigation Pane Customization

You have already learned how to customize the Navigation Pane by selecting the category and the filter as well as how to use the Search Bar to restrict the items that appear in the Navigation Pane. You can also create custom categories and groups that you can use to categorize the items in the database in ways that are most useful to you.

To Create Custom Categories and Groups

You can create custom categories in the Navigation Pane. You can further refine the objects you place in a category by adding custom groups to the categories. Why? Custom categories and groups allow you to tailor the Navigation Pane for your own specific needs. The following steps create a custom category called Veterinarian Tasks. They then add two custom groups, Appointments and Emergency and On Call, to the Veterinarian Tasks category.

BTW
Touch Screen Differences
The Office and Windows interfaces may vary if you are using a touch screen. For this reason, you might notice that the function or appearance of your touch screen differs slightly from this module's presentation.

1

- Display the Navigation Pane.

- Right-click the Navigation Pane title bar to display a shortcut menu (Figure 9–15).

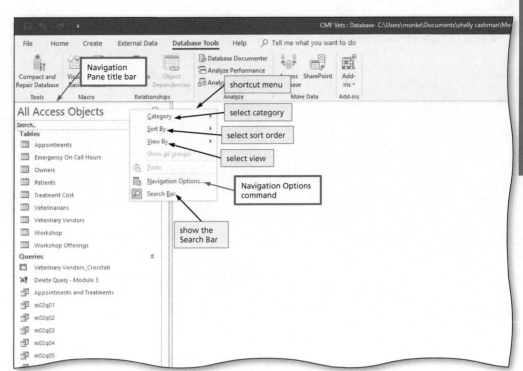

Figure 9–15

2

- Click the Navigation Options command on the shortcut menu to display the Navigation Options dialog box (Figure 9–16).

Q&A What else could I do with the shortcut menu?
You could select a category, select a sort order, or select how to view the items within the Navigation Pane.

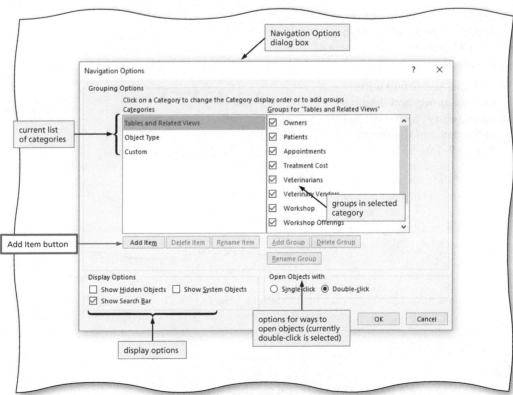

Figure 9–16

● Click the Add Item button to add
a new category (Figure 9–17).

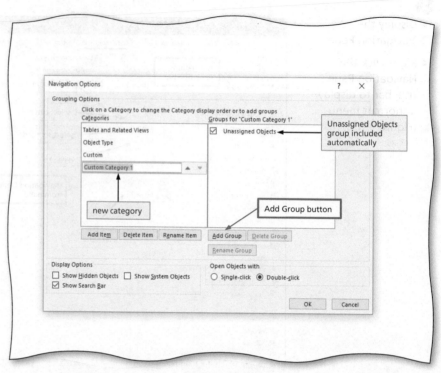

Figure 9–17

● Type **Veterinarian Tasks**
as the name of the category.

● Click the Add Group button
to add a group and then type
Appointments as the name of
the group.

● Click the Add Group button
to add a group and then type
Emergency and On Call
as the name of the group
(Figure 9–18).

Q&A

I added the groups in the wrong
order. How can I change the
order?
Select the group that is in the
wrong position. Click the Move Up
or Move Down arrow to move the
group to the correct location.

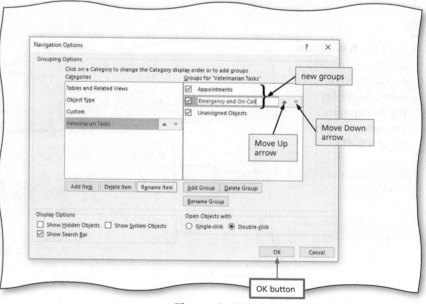

Figure 9–18

If I made a mistake in creating a new category, how can I fix it?
Select the category that is incorrect. If the name is wrong, click the Rename Item button and change the name
appropriately. If you do not want the category, click the Delete Item button to delete the category and then
click OK.

● Click OK to create the new category and groups.

To Add Items to Groups

Once you have created new groups, you can move existing items into the new groups. The following steps add items to the Appointments and Emergency and On Call groups in the Veterinarian Tasks category. **Why?** *These items are all related to the veterinarians.* Note: Before beginning this task, import the table Emergency On Call Hours from the database file called Emergency On Call Extra Table, if you did not already import it in completing Module 7. The Emergency On Call Hours database is stored with the Data Files. See your instructor for if you do not have the required files.

1

- Click the Navigation Pane arrow to produce the Navigation Pane menu and then scroll as necessary to display the Veterinarian Tasks category (Figure 9–19).

Q&A

Do I have to click the arrow?
No. If you prefer, you can click anywhere in the title bar for the Navigation Pane. Clicking arrows is a good habit, however, because there are many situations where you must click the arrow.

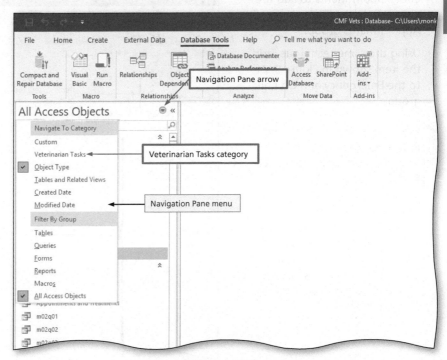

Figure 9–19

2

- Click the Veterinarian Tasks category to display the groups within the category. Because you created the Appointments and Emergency and On Call groups but did not assign items, the table objects all appear in the Unassigned Objects area of the Navigation Pane.

- Right-click Appointments table to display the shortcut menu.

- Point to the 'Add to group' command on the shortcut menu to display the list of available groups (Figure 9–20).

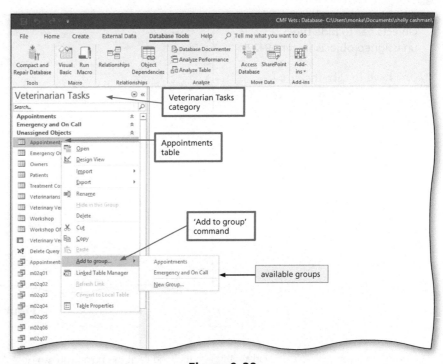

Figure 9–20

Q&A ◁ I did not create an Unassigned Objects group. Where did it come from?
Access creates the Unassigned Objects group automatically. Until you add an object to one of the groups you created, it will be in the Unassigned Objects group.

What is the purpose of the New Group on the submenu?
You can create a new group using this submenu. This is an alternative to using the Navigation Options dialog box. Use whichever approach you find most convenient.

3

- Click Appointments to add the Appointments table to the Appointments group.

- Using the same technique, add the item shown in Figure 9–21 to the Emergency and On Call group.

Q&A ◁ What is the symbol that appears in front of the items in the Appointments and Emergency and On Call groups?
It is the link symbol. You do not actually add an object to your group. Rather, you create a link to the object. In practice, you do not have to worry about this. The process for opening an object in one of your custom groups remains the same.

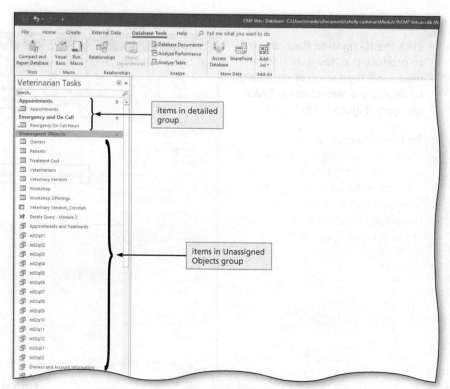

Figure 9–21

4

- Click the arrow in the Unassigned Objects bar to hide the unassigned objects (Figure 9–22).

Q&A ◁ Do I have to click the arrow?
No. Just as with the Navigation Pane, you can click anywhere in the Unassigned Objects bar.

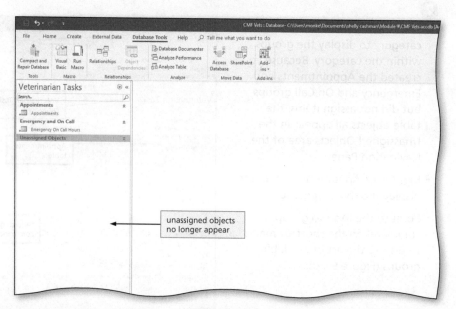

Figure 9–22

Break Point: If you wish to stop working through the module at this point, you can close Access now. You can resume the project at a later time by starting Access, opening the CMF Vets database, and continuing to follow the steps from this location forward.

What issues do you consider in determining the customization of the Navigation Pane?

The types of issues to consider are the following:

• Would a new category be useful?

• If so, are there new groups that would be useful to include in the new category?

• If you have created a new category and new groups, which items should be included in the new groups, and which should be left uncategorized?

Table and Database Properties

You can assign properties to tables. For example, you could assign a validation rule and validation text to an entire table. You can also assign properties to the database, typically for documentation purposes.

Touch and Pointers
Remember that if you are using your finger on a touch screen, you will not see the pointer.

To Create a Validation Rule for a Table

Previously, you created validation rules that applied to individual fields within a table. Some, however, apply to more than one field. In the Workshop Offerings table, you created a macro that would change the value of the Hours Spent field in such a way that it could never be greater than the Total Hours field. You can also create a validation rule that ensures this will never be the case; that is, the validation rule would require that the hours spent must be less than or equal to the total hours. To create a validation rule that involves two or more fields, you need to create the rule for the table using the table's Validation Rule property. The following steps create a **table validation rule**. *Why? This rule involves two fields, Hours Spent and Total Hours.*

1

• If necessary, click the arrow for Unassigned Objects to display those objects in the Navigation Pane.

• Open the Workshop Offerings table in Design view and close the Navigation Pane.

• If necessary, click the Property Sheet button (Table Tools Design tab | Show /Hide group) to display the table's property sheet.

• Click the Validation Rule property and type [Hours Spent] < = [Total Hours] as the validation rule.

• Click the Validation Text property and type Hours spent cannot exceed total hours as the validation text (Figure 9–23).

Figure 9–23

Q&A Could I use the Expression Builder to create the validation rule?
Yes. Use whichever method you find the most convenient.

- Close the property sheet.

- Click the Save button on the Quick Access Toolbar to save the validation rule and the validation text.

- When asked if you want to test existing data, click the No button.

- Close the Workshop Offerings table.

To Create Custom Properties

In addition to the general database property categories, you can also use custom properties. *Why? You can use custom properties to further document your database in a variety of ways. If you have needs that go beyond the custom properties, you can create your own original or unique properties.* The following steps **populate** the Status custom property; that is, they set a value for the property. In this case, they set the Status property to Live Version, indicating this is the live version of the database. If the database were still in a test environment, the property would be set to Test Version. The steps also create and populate a new property, Production, which represents the date the database was placed into production.

- Click File on the ribbon to open the Backstage view.

- Ensure the Info tab is selected (Figure 9–24).

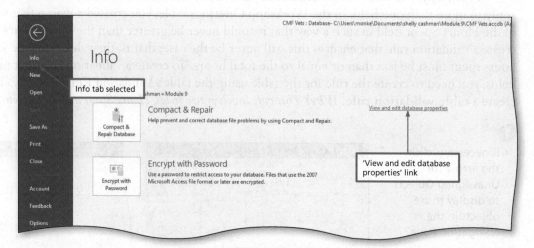

Figure 9–24

- Click the 'View and edit database properties' link to display the CMF Vets.accdb Properties dialog box.

- Click the Custom tab.

- Scroll down in the Name list so that Status appears, and then click Status.

- If necessary, click the Type arrow to set the data type to Text.

- Click the Value box and type **Live Version** as the value to create the custom property (Figure 9–25).

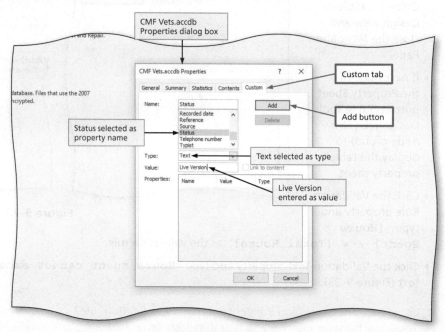

Figure 9–25

- Click the Add button to add the property.
- Type **Production** in the Name box.
- If requested to do so by your instructor, type your first and last name in the Name box.
- Select Date as the Type.
- Type **10/25/2021** as the value (Figure 9–26) to indicate that the database went into production on October 25, 2021.

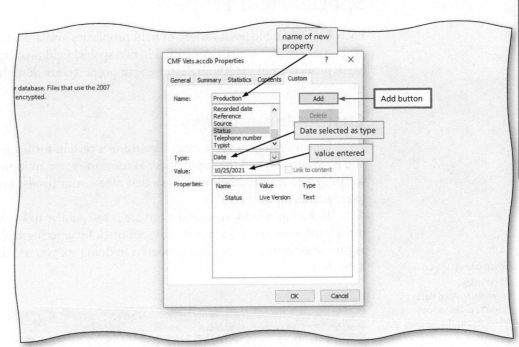

Figure 9–26

- Click the Add button to add the property (Figure 9–27).

Q&A What if I add a property that I decide I do not want?

You can delete it. To do so, click the property you no longer want and then click the Delete button.

- Click OK to close the CMF Vets.accdb Properties dialog box.

Q&A How do I view these properties in the future?

The same way you created them. Click File on the ribbon, click the Info tab, and then click the 'View and edit database properties' link. Click the desired tab to see the properties you want.

Figure 9–27

Special Field Properties

Each field in a table has a variety of field properties available. Recall that field properties are characteristics of a field. Two special field properties, the Custom Input Mask property and the Allow Zero Length property, are described in this section.

Custom Input Masks

One way to help users enter data using a certain format is to use an input mask. You have already used the Input Mask Wizard to create an input mask. Using the wizard, you can select the input mask that meets your needs. This is often the best way to create the input mask.

If the input mask you need to create is not similar to any in the list provided by the wizard, you can create a custom input mask by entering the appropriate characters as the value for the Input Mask property. In doing so, you use the symbols from Table 9-1.

BTW
Changing Data Formats
To create custom data formats, enter various characters in the Format property of a table field. The characters can be placeholders (such as 0 and #), separators (such as periods and commas), literal characters, and colors. You can create custom formats for short text, date, number, and currency fields. Date, number, and currency fields also include a number of standard data formats.

Table 9–1	Input Mask Symbols	
Symbol	**Type of Data Accepted**	**Data Entry**
0	Digits 0 through 9 without plus (+) or minus (−) sign are accepted. Positions left blank appear as zeros.	Required
9	Digits 0 through 9 without plus (+) or minus (−) sign are accepted. Positions left blank appear as spaces.	Optional
#	Digits 0 through 9 with plus (+) or minus (−) sign are accepted. Positions left blank appear as spaces.	Optional
L	Letters A through Z are accepted.	Required
?	Letters A through Z are accepted.	Optional
A	Letters A through Z or digits 0 through 9 are accepted.	Required
a	Letters A through Z or digits 0 through 9 are accepted.	Optional
&	Any character or a space is accepted.	Required
C	Any character or a space is accepted.	Optional
<	Symbol converts any letter entered to lowercase.	Does not apply
>	Symbol converts any letter entered to uppercase.	Does not apply
!	Characters typed in the input mask fill it from left to right.	Does not apply
\	Character following the slash is treated as a literal in the input mask.	Does not apply

BTW
Table Descriptions
To add a description for a table, right-click the table in the Navigation Pane and then click Table Properties on the shortcut menu. When the Properties dialog box for the table appears, enter the description in the Description property and then click OK. To enter a description for a table in Design view, click the Property Sheet button, and then enter a description in the Description property on the property sheet (see Figure 9–23).

For example, to indicate that account numbers must consist of two letters followed by three numbers, you would enter LL999. The Ls in the first two positions indicate that the first two positions must be letters. Using L instead of a question mark indicates that the users are required to enter these letters. If you had used the question mark instead of the L, they could leave these positions blank. The 9s in the last three positions indicate that the users can enter only digits 0 through 9. Using 9 instead of 0 indicates that they could leave these positions blank; that is, they are optional. Finally, to ensure that any letters entered are displayed as uppercase, you would use the > symbol at the beginning of the input mask. The complete mask would be > LL999.

To Create a Custom Input Mask

The following step creates a custom input mask for the Account Number field. Why? None of the input masks in the list meet the specific needs for the Account Number field.

1

- Open the Navigation Pane, open the Owners table in Design view, and then close the Navigation Pane.

- With the Owner ID field selected, click the Input Mask property, and then type `>L-999` as the value (Figure 9–28). Access adds a backslash to your custom input mask, like this >L\-999.

- Save the changes and close the table.

Q&A

What is the difference between the Format property and the Input Mask property?
The Format property ensures that data is displayed consistently, for example, always in uppercase. The Input Mask property controls how data is entered by the user.

What is the effect of this input mask?
From this point on, anyone entering an owner ID will be restricted to a letter in the first position, followed by a dash and numeric digits in the last three. Further, any letter entered in the first position will be displayed as uppercase.

Can you have a field that has both a custom input mask and a format. Is this a problem?
Technically, you do not need both. When the same field has both an input mask and a format, the format takes precedence. However, if the format specified for the field is the same as the input mask (uppercase), it will not affect the data.

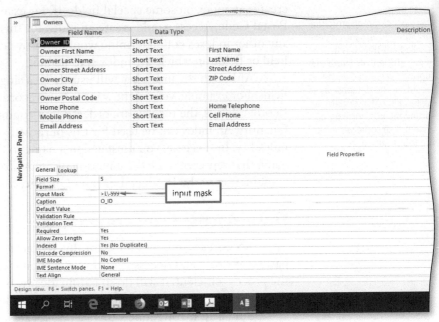

Figure 9–28

Creating and Using Indexes

You are already familiar with the concept of an index. The index in the back of a book contains important words or phrases along with a list of pages on which the given words or phrases can be found. An index for a table is similar. An index is a database object that is created based on a field or combination of fields. An index on the Vendor Name field, for example, would enable Access to rapidly locate a record that contains a particular veterinary vendor. In this case, the items of interest are vendor names instead of keywords or phrases, as is the case for the index in the back of this book. The field or fields on which the index is built is called the index key. Thus, in the index on account names, the Vendor Name field is the index key.

Each name occurs in the index along with the number of the record on which the corresponding account is located. Further, the names appear in the index in alphabetical order, so Access can use this index to rapidly produce a list of vendors alphabetized by account name.

BTW
Changing Default Sort Order
To display the records in a table in an order other than the primary key (the default sort order), use the Order By property on the table's property sheet (see Figure 9–23).

Another benefit of indexes is that they provide an efficient way to order records. That is, if the records are to appear in a certain order in a database object, Access can use an index instead of physically having to rearrange the records in the database. Physically rearranging the records in a different order can be a very time-consuming process.

To gain the benefits of an index, you must first create one. Access automatically creates an index on some special fields. If, for example, a table contains a field called Postal Code, Access would create an index for this field automatically. You must create any other indexes you determine would improve database performance, indicating the field or fields on which the index is to be built.

Although the index key will usually be a single field, it can be a combination of fields. For example, you might want to sort records by quantity within product type. In other words, the records are ordered by a combination of fields: Product Type and Quantity. An index can be used for this purpose by using a combination of fields for the index key. In this case, you must assign a name to the index. It is a good idea to assign a name that represents the combination of fields. For example, an index whose key is the combination of the Product Type and Quantity fields might be called TypeQuantity.

BTW
Indexes
The most common structure for high-performance indexes is called a B-tree. It is a highly efficient structure that supports very rapid access to records in the database as well as a rapid alternative to sorting records. Virtually all systems use some version of the B-tree structure.

How Access Uses Indexes

Access uses indexes automatically. If you request that data be sorted in a particular order and Access determines that an index is available that it can use to make the process efficient, it will do so automatically. If no index is available, it will still sort the data in the order you requested; it will just take longer than with the index.

Similarly, if you request that Access locate a particular record that has a certain value in a particular field, Access will use an index if an appropriate one exists. If not, it will have to examine each record until it finds the one you want.

To Create a Single-Field Index

The following steps create a single-field index on the Vendor Name field in the Veterinary Vendors table. *Why? This index will make finding vendors based on their name more efficient than it would be without the index. It will also improve the efficiency of sorting by vendor name.*

- Open the Navigation Pane, open the Veterinary Vendors table in Design view, and then close the Navigation Pane.

- Select the Vendor Name field.

- Click the Indexed property box in the Field Properties pane to select the property.

- Click the arrow that appears to display the Indexed list.

- Click Yes (Duplicates OK) in the list to specify that duplicates are to be allowed (Figure 9–29).

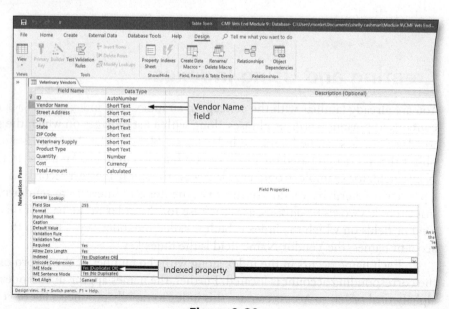

Figure 9–29

To Create a Multiple-Field Index

Creating **multiple-field indexes** — that is, indexes whose key is a combination of fields — involves a different process than creating single-field indexes. To create multiple-field indexes, you will use the Indexes button, enter a name for the index, and then enter the combination of fields that make up the index key. The following steps create a multiple-field index on the combination of Product Type and Quantity. *Why? CMF Vets needs to sort records on the combination of Product Type and Quantity and wants to improve the efficiency of this sort.* The steps assign this index the name TypeQuantity.

- Click the Indexes button, shown in Figure 9–29 (Table Tools Design tab | Show/Hide group), to display the Indexes: Veterinary Vendors window (Figure 9–30).

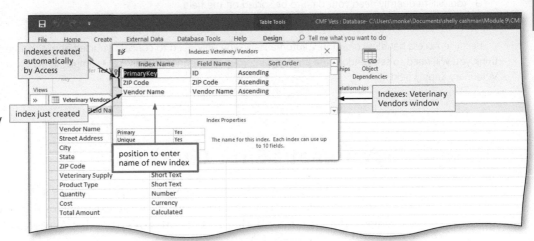

Figure 9–30

- Click the blank row (the row below Vendor Name) in the Index Name column in the Indexes: Veterinary Vendors window to select the position to enter the name of the new index.

- Type **TypeQuantity** as the index name, and then press TAB.

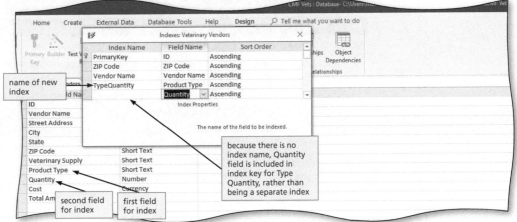

Figure 9–31

- Click the arrow in the Field Name column to produce a list of fields in the Veterinary Vendors table, and then select Product Type to enter the first of the two fields for the index.

- Press TAB three times to move to the Field Name column on the following row.

- Select the Quantity field in the same manner as the Product Type field (Figure 9–31).

- Close the Indexes: Veterinary Vendors window by clicking its Close button.

- Save your changes and close the table.

How do you determine when to use an index?

An index improves efficiency for sorting and finding records. On the other hand, indexes occupy space on your storage device. They also require Access to do extra work. Access must keep current all the indexes that have been created. The following guidelines help determine how and when to use indexes to their fullest advantage.

Create an index on a field (or combination of fields) if one or more of the following conditions are present:

1. The field is the primary key of the table. (Access creates this index automatically.)

2. The field is the foreign key in a relationship you have created.

3. You will frequently need your data to be sorted on the field.

4. You will frequently need to locate a record based on a value in this field.

Because Access handles condition 1 automatically, you only need to concern yourself about conditions 2, 3, and 4. If you think you will need to see vendor data arranged in order of veterinary supply, for example, you should create an index on the Veterinary Supply field.

Automatic Error Checking

Access can automatically check for several types of errors in forms and reports. When Access detects an error, it warns you about the existence of the error and provides you with options for correcting it. The types of errors that Access can detect and correct are shown in Table 9–2.

Table 9–2 Types of Errors	
Error Type	**Description**
Unassociated label and control	A label and control are selected and are not associated with each other.
New unassociated labels	A newly added label is not associated with any other control.
Keyboard shortcut errors	A shortcut key is invalid. This can happen because an unassociated label has a shortcut key, there are duplicate shortcut keys assigned, or a blank space is assigned as a shortcut key.
Invalid control properties	A control property is invalid. For example, the property contains invalid characters.
Common report errors	The report has invalid sorting or grouping specifications, or the report is wider than the page size.

To Enable Error Checking

Why? For automatic error checking to take place, it must be enabled. The following steps ensure that error checking is enabled and that errors are found and reported.

- Click File on the ribbon and then click the Options tab to display the Access Options dialog box.

- Click Object Designers to display the options for creating and modifying objects.

- Scroll down so that the Error checking area appears.

- Ensure the 'Enable error checking' check box is checked (Figure 9–32).

Q&A
What is the purpose of the other check boxes in the section?
All the other check boxes are checked, indicating that Access will perform all the various types of automatic error checking that are possible. If there were a particular type of error checking that you would prefer to skip, you would remove its check mark before clicking OK.

2
- Click OK to close the Access Options dialog box.

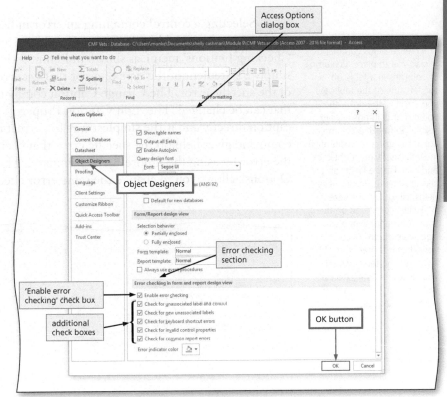

Figure 9–32

Error Indication

With error checking enabled, if an error occurs, a small triangle called an **error indicator** appears in the appropriate field or control. For example, you could change the label for Patient ID in the Appointments Master Form to include an ampersand (&) and letter A, making it a keyboard shortcut for this control. This would be a problem because A is already a shortcut for Appointment to Find. If this happens, an error indicator appears in both controls in which A is the keyboard shortcut, as shown in Figure 9–33.

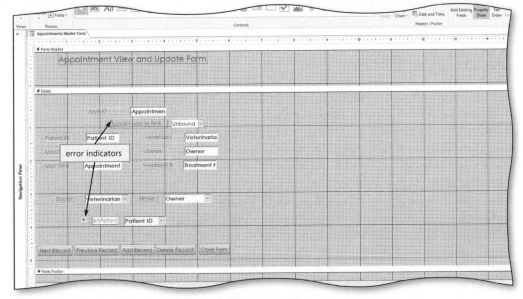

Figure 9–33

BTW
Freezing Fields
The Freeze Fields command allows you to place a column or columns in a table on the left side of the table. As you scroll to the right, the column or columns remain visible. To freeze a column or columns, select the column(s) in Datasheet view, right-click and click Freeze Fields on the shortcut menu. To unfreeze fields, click the `Unfreeze All Fields' command on the shortcut menu. When you freeze a column, Access considers it a change to the layout of the table. When you close the table, Access will ask you if you want to save the changes.

Selecting a control containing an error indicator displays an 'Error Checking Options' button. Clicking the 'Error Checking Options' button produces the 'Error Checking Options' menu, as shown in Figure 9–34. The first line in the menu is simply a statement of the type of error that occurred, and the second is a description of the specific error. The Change Caption command gives a submenu of the captions that can be changed. The 'Edit Caption Property' command allows you to change the caption directly and is the simplest way to correct this error. The 'Help on This Error' command gives help on the specific error that occurred. You can choose to ignore the error by using the Ignore Error command. The final command, 'Error Checking Options', allows you to change the same error checking options shown in Figure 9–34.

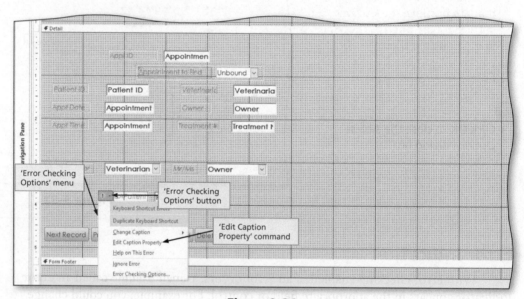

Figure 9–34

The simplest way to fix the duplicate keyboard shortcut error is to edit the caption property. Clicking the 'Edit Caption Property' command produces a property sheet with the Caption property highlighted. You could then change the Caption property of one of the controls.

Data Type Parts

Access contains data type parts that are available on the More Fields gallery. Some data type parts, such as the Category part, consist of a single field. Others, such as the Address part, consist of multiple fields. In addition to the parts provided by Access, you can create your own parts. Quick Start fields act as a framework that lets you rapidly add several fields to a table in a single operation. For example, you could create a quick start field called Name-Address that consists of a Last Name field, a First Name field, a Street field, a City field, a State field, and a Postal Code field. Once you have created this quick start field, you can use it when creating tables in the future. By simply selecting the Name-Address quick start field, you will immediately add the Last Name, First Name, Street, City, State, and Postal Code fields to a table.

To Create Custom Data Parts

CMF Vets has decided that combining several address-related fields into a single data part would make future database updates easier. To create data parts in the Quick Start category from existing fields, you select the desired field or fields and then select the Save Selection as New Data Type command in the More Fields gallery. If you select multiple fields, the fields must be adjacent.

The following steps create a Quick Start field consisting of the Owner First Name, Last Name, Street, City, State, and Postal Code fields in the Owners table. *Why? Once you have created this Quick Start field, users can add this collection of fields to a table by simply clicking the Quick Start field.*

1

- Open the Navigation Pane, open the Owners table in Datasheet view, and then close the Navigation Pane.

- Click the column heading for the Owner First Name field to select the field.

- Hold the SHIFT key down and click the column heading for the Owner Postal Code field to select all the fields from the Owner First Name field to the Owner Postal Code field.

- Display the Table Tools Fields tab.

- Click the More Fields button (Table Tools Fields tab | Add & Delete group) to display the More Fields gallery (Figure 9–35).

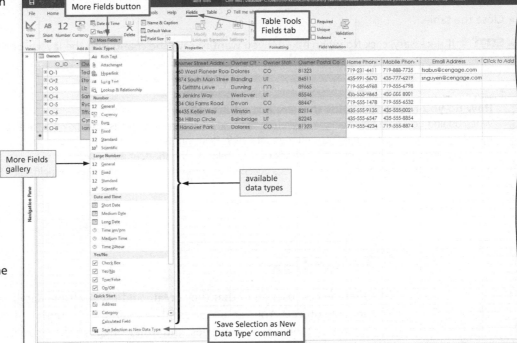

Figure 9–35

2

- Click 'Save Selection as New Data Type' to display the Create New Data Type from Fields dialog box.

- Enter **Name-Address** as the name.

- Enter **First Name, Last Name, Street Address, City, State, Postal Code** as the description.

Q&A
What is the purpose of the description?
When a user points to the Quick Start field you created, a ScreenTip will appear containing the description you entered.

- Click the Category arrow to display a list of available categories (Figure 9–36).

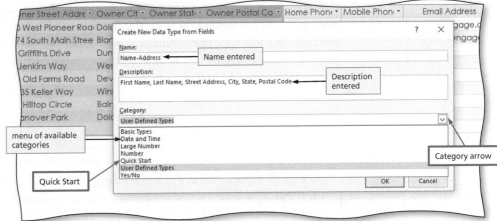

Figure 9–36

• Click Quick Start to indicate the new data type will be added to the Quick Start category.

Q&A What is the difference between the Quick Start and User Defined Types category?

If you select the Quick Start category, the data type you create will be listed among the Quick Start data types that are part of Access. If you select the User Defined Types category, the data type you create will be in a separate category containing only those data types you create. In either case, however, clicking the data type will produce the same result.

• Click OK (Create New Data Type from Fields dialog box) to save the data type.

• When Access indicates that your template (that is, your Quick Start field) has been saved, click OK (Microsoft Access dialog box).

• Close the table.

• **sam** ↑ If necessary, click No when asked if you want to save the changes to the layout of the table.

CONSIDER THIS

How do you rearrange fields that are not adjacent?

When adding new data type fields, you can hide the fields that keep your fields from being adjacent. To hide a field, right-click the field to display a shortcut menu, and then click Hide Fields on the shortcut menu. To later unhide a field you have hidden, right-click any column heading and then click Unhide Fields on the shortcut menu. You will see a list of fields with a check box for each field. The hidden field will not have a check mark in the check box. To unhide the field, click the check box for the field.

Templates

BTW

Templates and Application Parts

By default, user-created templates and application parts are stored in the C:\Users\user name\AppData\Roaming\Microsoft\Templates\Access folder.

Often, Access users find that they create and use multiple databases containing the same objects. You can use a template to create a complete database application containing tables, forms, queries, and other objects. There are many templates available for Access.

You can create your own template from an existing database. To do so, you must first ensure that you have created a database with all the characteristics you want in your template. In this module, the database you create will have two tables, a query, two single-item forms, two datasheet forms that use macros, and a navigation form that will serve as the main menu. In addition, the navigation form will be set to appear automatically whenever you open the database. Once you have incorporated all these features, you will save the database as a template. From that point on, anyone can use your template to create a new database. The database that is created will incorporate all the same features as your original database.

To Create a Desktop Database

The following steps create the Customers and Pet Sitters **desktop database**, that is, a database designed to run on a personal computer. *Why? This database will become the basis for a template.*

- Click File on the ribbon to open the Backstage view.
- Click the New tab.
- Click the 'Blank database' button.
- Type **Customers and Pet Sitters** as the name of the database file.
- Click the 'Browse for a location to put your database' button to display the File New Database dialog box, navigate to the desired save location (for example, the Access folder in the CIS 101 folder), and then click OK to return to the Backstage view (Figure 9–37).

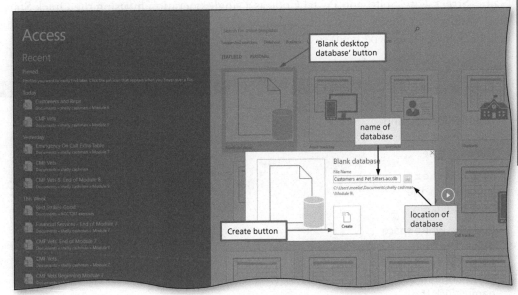

Figure 9–37

- Click the Create button to create the database (Figure 9–38).

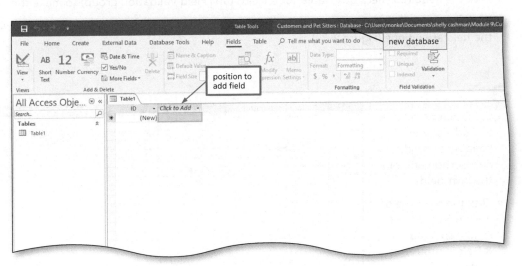

Figure 9–38

To Add Fields to the Table

The tables will have an autonumber ID field as the primary key. The field that would normally be the primary key will be designated both required and unique, two characteristics of the primary key.

The following steps add the Sitter Number, Last Name, First Name, Street, City, State, Postal Code, Rate, and Commission to a table. The Rate field is a Number field and the Commission field is a Currency field.

The steps designate the Sitter Number field as both required and unique. They add the Last Name, First Name, Street, City, State, and Postal Code as a single operation by using the Quick Start field created earlier. After adding the fields, they save the table using the name, Sitter. They also change the field size for the Rate field (a Number data type field) to Single so that the field can contain decimal places.

1

- **sam ↓** Click the 'Click to Add' column heading and select Short Text as the data type.

- Type **Sitter Number** as the field name.

- Click the white space below the field name to complete the change of the name. Click the white space a second time to select the field.

- Change the field size to 2.

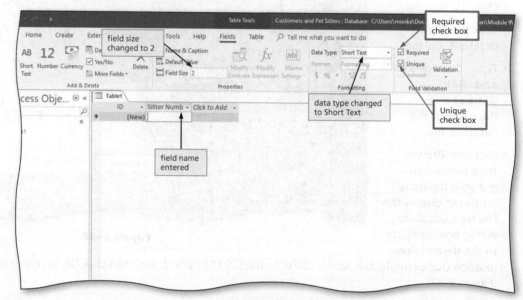

Figure 9–39

- Click the Required check box (Table Tools Fields tab | Field Validation group) to make the field a required field.

- Click the Unique check box (Table Tools Fields tab | Field Validation group) so that Access will ensure that values in the field are unique (Figure 9–39).

2

- Click under the 'Click to Add' column heading to produce an insertion point in the next field.

- Click the More Fields button (Table Tools Fields tab | Add & Delete group) to display the More Fields menu (Figure 9–40).

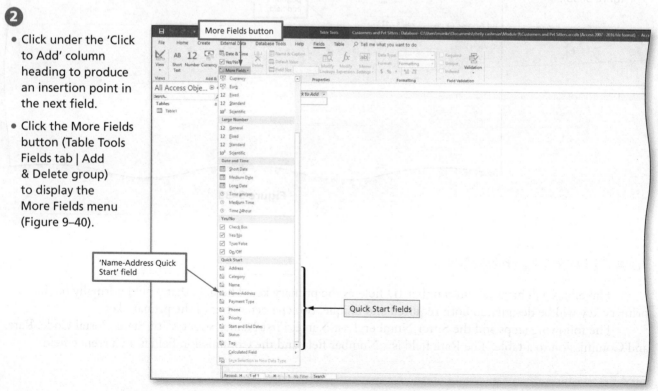

Figure 9–40

3

- Scroll as necessary to display the Name-Address Quick Start field you created earlier and then click the Name-Address Quick Start field to add the Owner First Name, Owner Last Name, Owner Street Address, Owner City, Owner State, and Owner Postal Code fields (Figure 9–41).

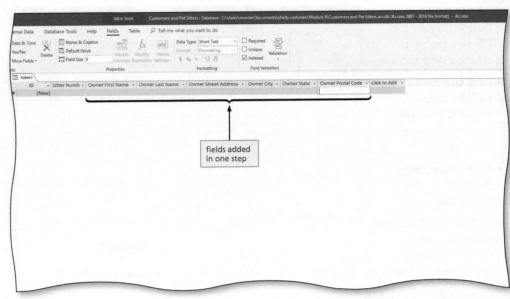

fields added in one step

Figure 9–41

4

- Delete the word "Owner" from the fields. Add the Rate and Commission fields as the last two fields. The Rate field has the Number data type and the Commission field has the Currency data type.

- Save the table, assigning `Sitter` as the table name.

- Switch to Design view, select the Rate field, and change the field size to Single so that the Rate field can include decimal places.

- Save and close the table.

Q&A

What if I don't see the quick start field?

If you have switched computers since you created the custom data parts, you may not see the quick start field Name-Address. Go back and recreate that quick start field before continuing.

To Create a Second Table

The following steps create the Customer table. The steps add a lookup field for Sitter Number to relate the two tables. **Why?** *Because no existing field links the two tables, the relationship between the tables needs to be implemented using a lookup field.*

1

- Display the Create tab (Figure 9–42).

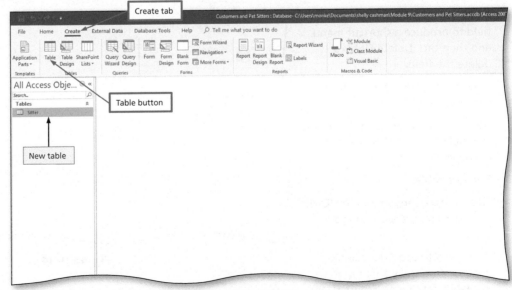

Create tab

Table button

New table

Figure 9–42

- Click the Table button (Create tab | Tables group) to create a new table.

- Click the 'Click to Add' column heading and select Short Text as the data type.

- Type **Customer Number** as the field name.

- Click the white space below the field name to complete the change of the name. Click the white space a second time to select the field.

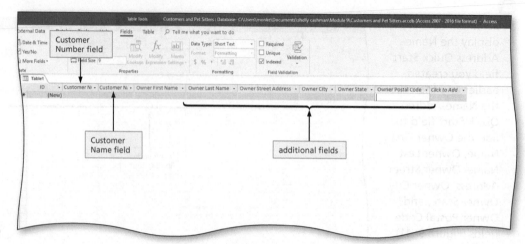

Figure 9–43

- Change the field size to 5.

- Save the table, assigning **Customer** as the table name.

- Switch to design view, make the Customer Number the key field and delete the ID field. Save your changes to the table.

- Switch back to the datasheet view.

- In a similar fashion, add the Customer Name field and change the field size to 50. Do not check the Required or Unique check boxes.

- Click under the 'Click to Add' column heading to produce an insertion point in the next field.

- Click the More Fields button (Table Tools Fields tab | Add & Delete group) to display the More Fields menu (see Figure 9–41).

- Click the Name-Address Quick Start field that you added earlier to add the Owner First Name, Owner Last Name, Owner Street Address, Owner City, Owner State, and Owner Postal Code fields (Figure 9–43).

- Right-click the Owner Last Name field to produce a shortcut menu, and then click Delete Field to delete the field.

- Right-click the Owner First Name field to produce a shortcut menu, and then click Delete Field to delete the field.

- Delete the word "Owner" from the other fields.

- Add the Amount Paid and Current Due fields. Both fields have the Currency data type.

- Save the table.

- Scroll, if necessary, so that the 'Click to Add' column appears on your screen.

- Click the 'Click to Add' column heading to display a menu of available data types (Figure 9–44).

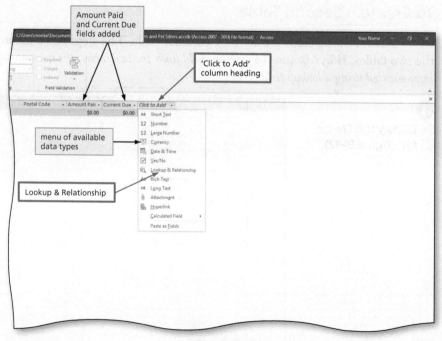

Figure 9–44

4

• Click Lookup & Relationship to display the Lookup Wizard dialog box (Figure 9–45).

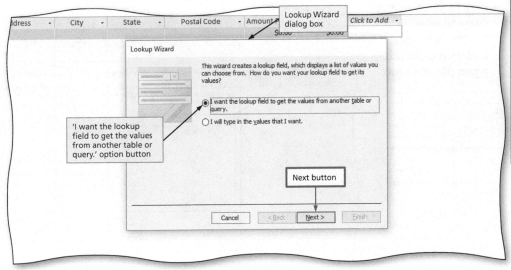

Figure 9–45

5

• Click the Next button to display the next Lookup Wizard screen, and then click the Sitter table to select it so that you can add a lookup field for the Sitter Number to the Customer table (Figure 9–46).

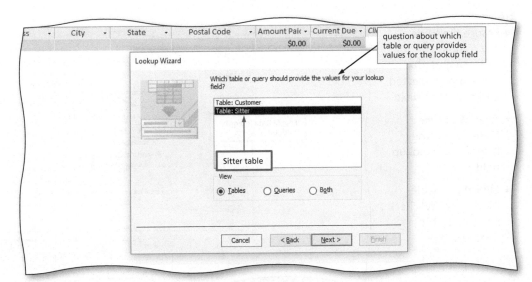

Figure 9–46

6

• Click the Next button, and then select the Sitter Number, First Name, and Last Name fields for the columns in the lookup field (Figure 9–47).

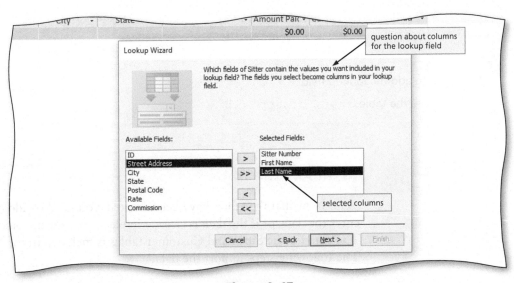

Figure 9–47

● Click Next, select the
Sitter Number field
for the sort order,
and then click Next
again (Figure 9–48).

Q&A I see the ID field
listed when I am
selecting the Sitter
Number field for the
sort order. Did I do
something wrong?
No. Access
automatically
included the ID field.

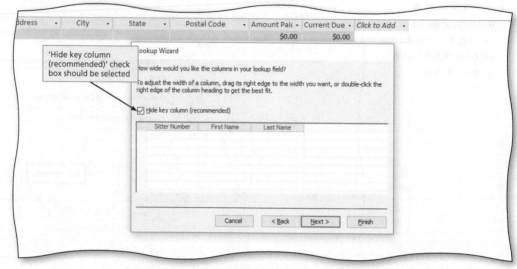

Figure 9–48

● Ensure the 'Hide
key column
(recommended)'
check box is selected,
and then click Next.

● Type **Sitter
Number** as the
label for the lookup
field.

● Click the 'Enable
Data Integrity' check
box to select it
(Figure 9–49).

Q&A What is the effect
of selecting Enable
Data Integrity?
Access will enforce
referential integrity for the Sitter Number. That is, Access will not allow a Sitter number in a customer record that
does not match the number of a Sitter in the Sitter table.

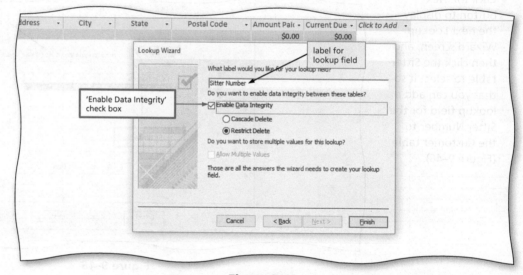

Figure 9–49

● Click Finish to add the lookup field.

● Save and close the table.

To Import the Data

Now that the tables have been created, you need to add data to them. You could
enter the data, or if the data is already in electronic form, you could import the data.
The data for the Sitter and Customer tables is included in the Data Files as text files.
The following steps import the data.

1 With the Customers and Pet Sitters database open, display the External Data tab, and then choose the New Data Source button (External Data tab | Import & Link group), point to From File and then click the Text File command.

2 Click the Browse button (Get External Data – Text File dialog box) and browse to select the location of the files to be imported (for example, the Access folder in the CIS 101 folder).

3 Select the Sitter text file, and then click the Open button.

4 Click the 'Append a copy of records to the table' option button to select it, select the Sitter table, and then click OK.

5 Ensure that the Delimited option button is selected, and then click the Next button.

6 Ensure that the Comma option button is selected, click the Next button, and then click the Finish button.

7 Click Close to close the Get External Data – Text File dialog box without saving the import steps.

8 Use the technique shown in Steps 1 through 7 to import the Customer text file into the Customer table.

BTW
Importing Tables from Other Databases
You can import tables from other Access databases. To do so, click the Access button (External Data tab | Import & Link group) then navigate to the location containing the database and select the database. Click the Open button. Ensure that the 'Import tables, queries, forms, reports, macros, and modules into the current database' option button is selected and click OK. When the Import Object dialog box appears, select the table or tables you want to import and then click OK. You also can import other objects by clicking the appropriate object tabs.

To Create a Query Relating the Tables

The following steps create a query that relates the Customer and Sitter tables.

1 Display the Create tab and then click the Query Design button (Create tab | Queries group) to create a new query.

2 Click the Customer table, click the Add button, click the Sitter table, click the Add button, and then click the Close button to close the Show Table dialog box.

3 Double-click the Customer Name, and Sitter Number fields from the Customer table. Double-click the First Name and Last Name fields from the Sitter table to add the fields to the design grid.

4 Click the Save button on the Quick Access Toolbar to save the query, type `Customer-Sitter Query` as the name of the query, and then click OK.

5 Close the query.

BTW
Rearranging Fields in a Query
If you add fields to a query in the wrong order, you can select the field in the design grid, and drag it to the appropriate location.

Creating Forms

There are several types of forms that need to be created for this database. The Customer and Sitter detail forms show a single record at a time. The Customer and Sitter forms are intended to look like the corresponding table in Datasheet view. Finally, the main menu is a navigation form.

To Create Single-Item Forms

The following steps create two single-item forms, that is, forms that display a single record at a time. The first form, called Customer Details, is for the Customer table. The second form is for the Sitter table and is called Sitter Details.

1 Select the Customer table in the Navigation Pane and then display the Create tab.

2 Click the Form button (Create tab | Forms group) to create a single-item form for the Customer table.

3 Click the Save button on the Quick Access Toolbar, type `Customer Details` as the name of the form, click OK (Save As dialog box) to save the form, and then close the form.

4 Select the Sitter table, display the Create tab, and then click the Form button (Create tab | Forms group) to create a form for the Sitter table that shows the customers using that particular sitter.

5 Save the form, using Sitter Details as the form name.

6 Close the form.

To Create a Navigation Form

The following steps create a navigation form containing a single row of horizontal tabs. The steps save the form using the name, Main Menu. *Why? This form is intended to function as a menu.* The steps change the form title and add the appropriate tabs.

- Display the Create tab and then click the Navigation button (Create tab | Forms group) to show the menu of available navigation forms.

- Click Horizontal Tabs in the menu to create a form with a navigation control in which the tabs are arranged in a single row, horizontally.

- If a field list appears, click the 'Add Existing Fields' button (Form Layout Tools Design tab | Tools group) to remove the field list.

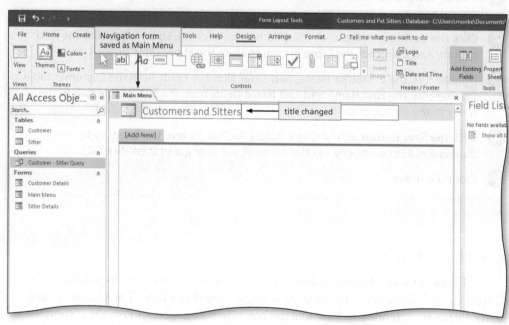

Figure 9–50

- Save the navigation form, using Main Menu as the form name.

- Click the form title twice, once to select it and the second time to produce an insertion point.

- Erase the current title and then type `Customers and Sitters` as the new title (Figure 9–50).

2

- One at a time, drag the Customer Details form, and the Sitter Details form to the positions shown in Figure 9–51.

- Save and close the form.

Q&A What should I do if I made a mistake and added a form to the wrong location? You can rearrange the tabs by dragging. However, the simplest way to correct a mistake is to click the Undo button to reverse your most recent action. You can also choose to simply close the form without saving it and then start over.

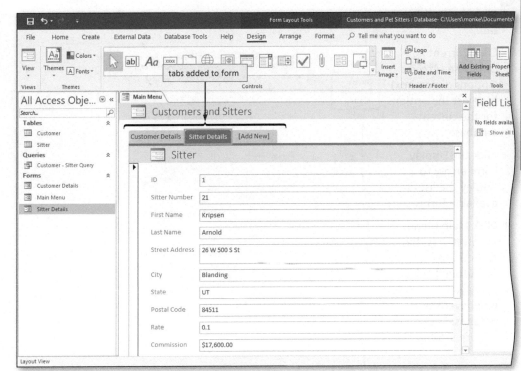

Figure 9–51

To Select a Startup Form

If the database includes a navigation form, it is common to select the navigation form as a **startup form,** which launches when the user opens the database. ***Why?*** *Designating the navigation form as a startup form ensures that the form will appear automatically when a user opens the database.* The following steps designate the navigation form as a startup form.

1

- Click File on the ribbon to display the Backstage view (Figure 9–52).

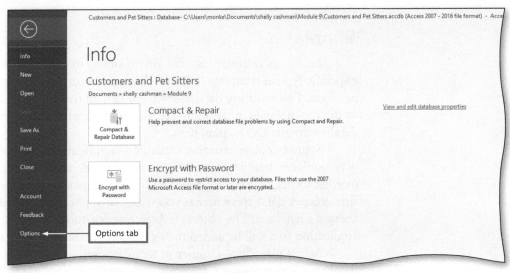

Figure 9–52

2

- Click the Options tab.

- Click Current Database (Access Options dialog box) to select the options for the current database.

- Click the Display Form arrow to display the list of available forms.

- Click Main Menu to select it as the form that will be automatically displayed whenever the database is opened (Figure 9–53).

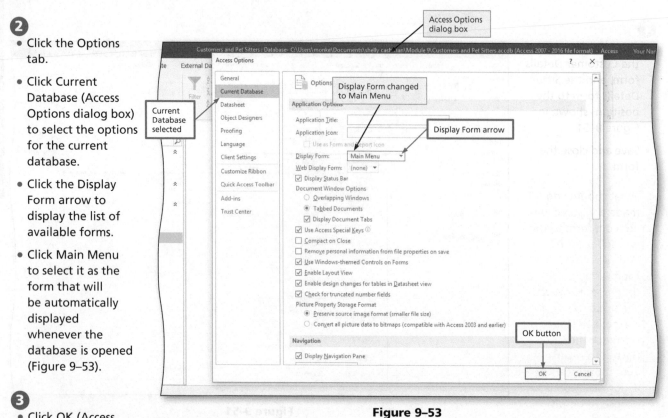

Figure 9–53

3

- Click OK (Access Options dialog box) to save your changes.

- Click OK (Microsoft Access dialog box) when Access displays a message indicating that you must close and reopen the database for the change to take effect.

- Close the database.

Break Point: If you wish to stop working through the module at this point, you can close Access now. You can resume the project at a later time by starting Access, and continuing to follow the steps from this location forward.

Templates

An Access **template** is a file that contains the elements needed to produce a specific type of complete database. You can select a template when you create a database. The resulting database will contain all the tables, queries, forms, reports, and/ or macros included in the template. In addition, with some templates, the resulting database might also contain data.

Some templates are also available as **application parts.** Application parts are very similar to templates in that selecting a single application part can create tables, queries, forms, reports, and macros. The difference is you select a template when you first create a database, whereas you select an application part after you have already created a database. The objects (tables, queries, forms, reports, and macros) in the application part will be added to any objects you have already created.

Access provides a number of templates representing a variety of types of databases. You can also create your own template from an existing database. When you create a template, you can choose to create an application part as well. When creating templates and application parts, you can also include data if desired.

To Create a Template and Application Part

The following steps create a template from the Customers and Pet Sitters database. *Why? The Customers and Pet Sitters database now contains all the tables, queries, and forms you want in the template. You will then be able to use the template when you want to create similar databases.* The steps also create an application part from the database so that you can reuse the parts in other databases.

1
- Open the Customers and Pet Sitters database and enable the content (Figure 9–54).

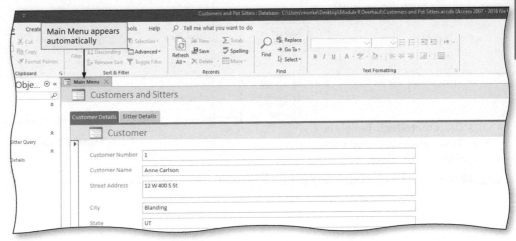

Figure 9–54

2
- Close the Main Menu form.
- Open the Backstage view.
- Click the Save As tab.
- Click the Template button in the Save Database As area to indicate you are creating a template (Figure 9–55).

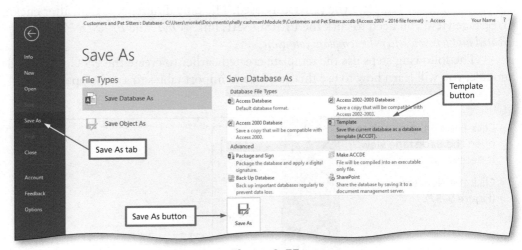

Figure 9–55

3
- Click the Save As button to display the Create New Template from This Database dialog box.
- Type `Customers and Pet Sitters` as the name for the new template.
- Type `Database of customers and pet sitters with navigation form menu.` as the description.
- Click the Application Part check box to indicate that you also want to create an application part.
- Click the 'Include All Data in Package' check box to indicate you want to include the data in the database as part of the template (Figure 9–56).

Q&A

Why include data?
Anytime a user creates a database using the template, the database will automatically include data. This enables the users to see what any reports, forms, or queries look like with data in them. Once the users have the reports, forms, and queries the way they want them, they can delete all this data. At that point, they can begin adding their own data to the database.

4

- Click OK (Create New Template from This Database dialog box) to create the template.

- **sam**⬆ When Access indicates that the template has been successfully saved, click OK (Microsoft Access dialog box).

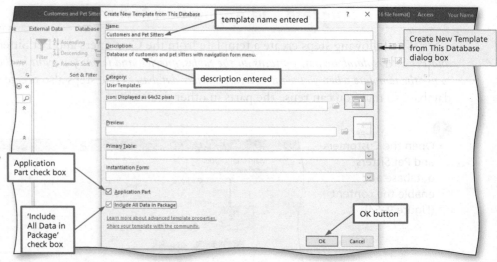

Figure 9–56

To Use the Template

You can use the Customers and Pet Sitters template just as you would use any other template, such as the Blank database template you previously used. The only difference is that, after clicking the New tab in the Backstage view, you need to click the PERSONAL link. *Why? The PERSONAL link displays any templates you created and lets you select the template you want.*

The following steps use the template created earlier to create the ES Customers database. Later in the module, you will learn how to use this database to import tables to a web app.

1

- Click File on the ribbon to open the Backstage view, if necessary.

- Click the New tab (Figure 9–57).

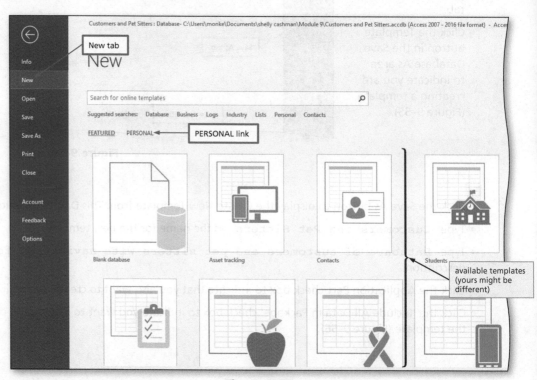

Figure 9–57

2
- Click the PERSONAL link to display the templates you have created (Figure 9–58).

3
- Click the Customers and Pet Sitters template that you created earlier.

- Type **ES Customers** as the name of the database and then navigate to the location where you will store the new database (for example, the Access folder in the CIS 101 folder).

- Click the Create button to create the database from the template.

- Close the database.

- If desired, sign out of your Microsoft account.

- Exit Access.

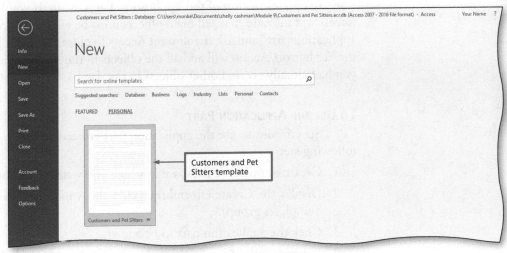

Figure 9–58

Note: Unless your instructor indicates otherwise, you are strongly encouraged to simply read the material in this module from this point on without carrying out any operations. If you decide to try it for yourself, it is important to make a backup copy of your database and store it in a secure location before performing the operation. That way, if something damages your database or you can no longer access your database, you still can use the backup copy.

Using an Application Part

To use the application part you created, you first need to create a database. After doing so, you click the Application Parts button (Create tab | Templates group) to display the Application Parts menu (Figure 9–59).

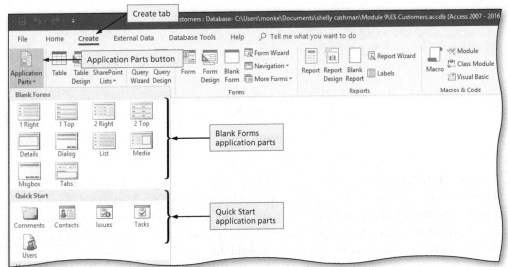

Figure 9–59

You can then click the application part you created, which will be located in the User Templates section of the Application Parts menu. If you have any open objects, Access will indicate that "all open objects must be closed before instantiating this application part" and ask if you want Access to close all open objects. After you click the Yes button, Access will add all the objects in the Application part to the database. If you had already created other objects in the database, they would still be included.

TO USE THE APPLICATION PART

Specifically, to use the application part created earlier, you would use the following steps.

1. Create or open the database in which you want to use the application part.
2. Display the Create tab and then click the Application Parts button (Create tab | Templates group).
3. Click the application part to be added.
4. If Access indicates that open objects must be closed, click the Yes button.

Blank Forms Application Parts

Blank Forms application parts (see Figure 9–59) represent a way to create certain types of forms. To do so, you click the Application Parts button to display the gallery of application part styles, and then click the desired type of form, for example, 1 Right. Access then creates a form with the desired characteristics and assigns it a name. It does not open the form, but you can see the form in the Navigation Pane (Figure 9–60).

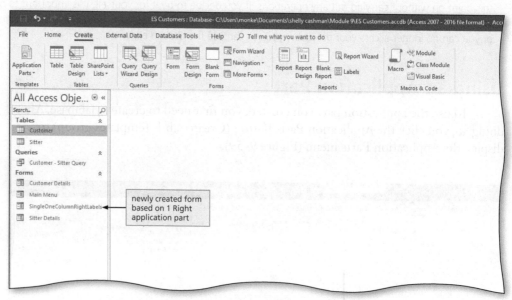

Figure 9–60

You can modify the form by opening the form in Layout or Design view (Figure 9–61). This particular form automatically creates a Save button. Clicking this button when you are using the form will save changes to the current record. The form also automatically includes a Save & Close button. Clicking this button will save changes to the current record and then close the form.

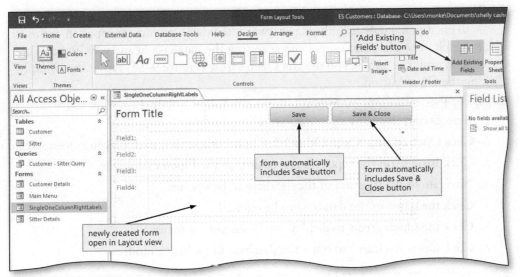

Figure 9–61

To add the specific fields you want to the form, display a field list. You can then drag a field onto the form (Figure 9–62). Once you have added the field, you can change the corresponding label by clicking the label to select it, clicking the label a second time to produce an insertion point, and then making the desired change.

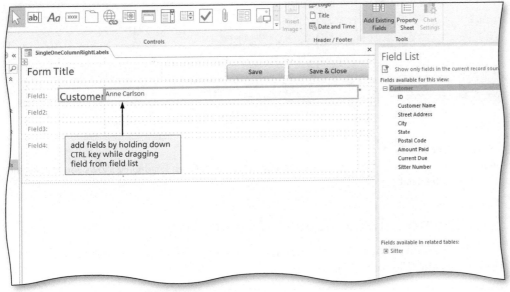

Figure 9–62

Encrypting a Database

Encrypting refers to the storing of data in the database in an encoded, or encrypted, format. Anytime a user stores or modifies data in the encrypted database, the database management system (DBMS) will encode the data before actually updating the database. Before a legitimate user retrieves the data using the DBMS, the data will be decoded. The whole encrypting process is transparent to a legitimate user; that is, he or she is not even aware it is happening. If an unauthorized user attempts to bypass all the controls of the DBMS and get to the database through a utility program or a word processor, however, he or she will only be able to see the encoded, and unreadable, version of the data. In Access, you encrypt a database and set a password as part of the same operation.

BTW
Encryption and Passwords
Encryption helps prevent unauthorized use of an Access database. Consider using encryption when the database contains sensitive data, such as medical records or employee records. Passwords should be eight or more characters in length. The longer the length of the password and the more random the characters, the more difficult it is for someone to determine. Use a combination of uppercase and lowercase letters as well as numbers and special symbols when you create a password. Make sure that you remember your password. If you forget it, there is no method for retrieving it. You will be unable to open the encrypted database.

To Open a Database in Exclusive Mode

To encrypt a database and set a password, the database must be open in exclusive mode, which prevents other users from accessing the database in any way. To open a database in exclusive mode, you use the Open arrow (Figure 9–63) rather than simply clicking the Open button.

To open a database in exclusive mode, you would use the following steps.

1. If necessary, close any open databases.
2. Click Open or click 'Open Other Files' in Backstage view to display the Open screen.
3. Click Browse on the Open screen to display the Open dialog box.
4. Navigate to the location of the database to be opened.
5. Click the name of the database to be opened.
6. Click the Open arrow to display the Open button menu.
7. Click Open Exclusive to open the database in exclusive mode.

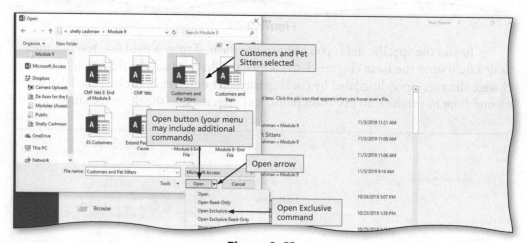

Figure 9–63

CONSIDER THIS

What is the purpose of the other modes?

The Open option opens the database in a mode so that it can be shared by other users. Open Read-Only allows you to read the data in the database, but not update the database.

Encrypting a Database with a Password

If you wanted to encrypt the database with a password, you would open the Backstage view (Figure 9–64).

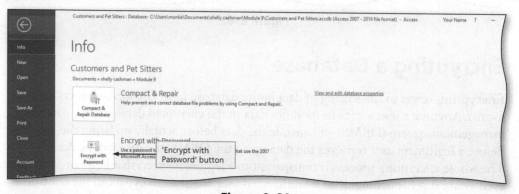

Figure 9–64

You would then click 'Encrypt with Password' to display the Set Database Password dialog box, and then enter the password you have chosen in both the Password text box and Verify text box (Figure 9–65).

Set Database
Password dialog box

Customers and Sitters

Set Database Password   ?   ×

Password:

Password text box ▭ ********

r Details

password appears
as asterisks (*)

Verify:

Verify text box ▭ ********

Cust

OK   Cancel

1

OK button

Figure 9–65

To Encrypt a Database with a Password

With the database open in exclusive mode, you would use the following steps to encrypt the database with a password.

1. Click File on the ribbon to open the Backstage view and ensure the Info tab is selected.
2. Click the 'Encrypt with Password' button to display the Set Database Password dialog box.
3. Type the desired password in the Password text box in the Set Database Password dialog box.
4. Press the TAB key and then type the password again in the Verify text box.
5. Click OK to encrypt the database and set the password.
6. If you get a message indicating that row level locking will be ignored, click OK.
7. Close the database.

Is the password case sensitive?
Yes, you must enter the password using the same case you used when you created it.

Opening a Database with a Password

When you open a database that has a password, you will be prompted to enter your password in the Password Required dialog box. Once you have done so, click OK. Assuming you have entered your password correctly, Access will then open the database.

Decrypting a Database and Removing a Password

If the encryption and the password are no longer necessary, you can decrypt the database. The database will no longer have a password. If you later found you needed the database to be encrypted, you could repeat the steps to encrypt the database and add a password. The button to encrypt a database with a password has changed to Decrypt Database (Figure 9–66).

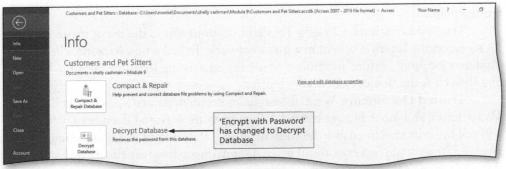

Figure 9–66

TO DECRYPT THE DATABASE AND REMOVE THE PASSWORD

To decrypt a database that you have previously encrypted and remove the password, you would use the following steps.

1. Open the database to be decrypted in exclusive mode, entering your password when requested.
2. Open the Backstage view and ensure the Info tab is selected.
3. Click the Decrypt Database button to display the Unset Database Password dialog box.
4. Type the password in the Password dialog box.
5. Click OK to remove the password and decrypt the database.
6. Close the database.

The Trust Center

The Trust Center is a feature within Access where you can set security options and also find the latest information on technology related to privacy, safety, and security. To use the Trust Center, you click File on the ribbon and then click the Options tab to display the Access Options dialog box. You then click Trust Center to display the Trust Center content (Figure 9–67). You would then click the 'Trust Center Settings' button to display the Trust Center dialog box in which you can make changes in the following categories.

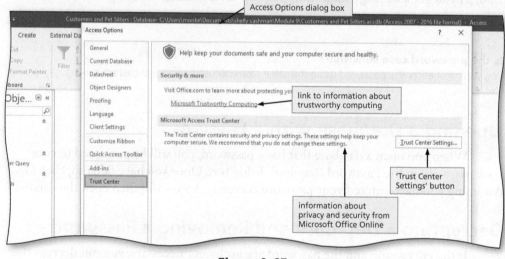

Figure 9–67

Trusted Publishers. Clicking Trusted Publishers in the Trust Center dialog box shows the list of trusted software publishers. To view details about a trusted publisher, click the publisher and then click the View button. To remove a trusted publisher from the list, click the publisher and then click the Remove button. Users may also add trusted publishers.

Trusted Locations. Clicking Trusted Locations shows the list of trusted locations on the Internet or within a user's network. To add a new location, click the 'Add new location' button. To remove or modify an existing location, click the location and then click the Remove or Modify button.

Trusted Documents. You can designate certain documents, including database, Word, Excel, and other files, as trusted. When opening a trusted document, you will not be prompted to enable the content, even if the content of the document has changed. You should be very careful when designating a document as trusted and only do so when you are absolutely sure the document is from a trusted source.

Add-ins. Add-ins are additional programs that you can install and use within Access. Some come with Access and are typically installed using the Access Setup program. Others can be purchased from other vendors. Clicking Add-ins gives you the opportunity to specify restrictions concerning Add-ins.

ActiveX Settings. When you use ActiveX controls within an Office app, Office prompts you to accept the controls. The ActiveX settings allow you to determine the level of prompting from Office.

Macro Settings. Macros written by other users have the potential to harm your computer; for example, a macro could spread a virus. The Trust Center uses special criteria, including valid digital signatures, reputable certificates, and trusted publishers, to determine whether a macro is safe. If the Trust Center discovers a macro that is potentially unsafe, it will take appropriate action. The action the Trust Center takes depends on the Macro Setting you have selected. Clicking Macro Settings enables you to select or change this setting.

Message Bar. Clicking Message Bar lets you choose whether the message bar should appear when content has been blocked.

Privacy Options. Clicking Privacy Options lets you set security settings to protect your personal privacy.

Trusted Add-in Catalogs. Use this option to specify trusted catalogs of web add-ins. You can also indicate whether Access will allow web add-ins to start.

BTW
Active X controls
Active X controls are small programs that can run within an Office app. The calendar control is an example of an Active X control.

Locking a Database

By locking a database, you can prevent users from viewing or modifying VBA code in your database or from making changes to the design of forms or reports while still allowing them to update records. When you lock the database, Access changes the file name extension from .accdb to .accde. To do so, you would use the Make ACCDE command shown in Figure 9–3.

BTW
Locked Databases
When you create a locked database, the original database remains unchanged and is still available for use.

TO CREATE A LOCKED DATABASE (ACCDE FILE)
To lock a database, you would use the following steps.

1. With the database open, click File on the ribbon to open the Backstage view.
2. Click the Save As tab.
3. Click Make ACCDE in the Advanced area.
4. Click the Save As button.
5. In the Save As dialog box, indicate a location and name for the ACCDE file.
6. Click the Save button in the Save As dialog box to create the file.

Using the Locked Database

You would use an ACCDE file just as you use the databases with which you are now familiar, with two exceptions. First, you must select ACCDE files in the 'Files of type' box when opening the file. Second, you will not be able to modify any source code or change the design of any forms or reports. If you right-clicked the Customer form, for example, you would find that the Design View command on the shortcut menu is dimmed, as are many other commands (Figure 9–68).

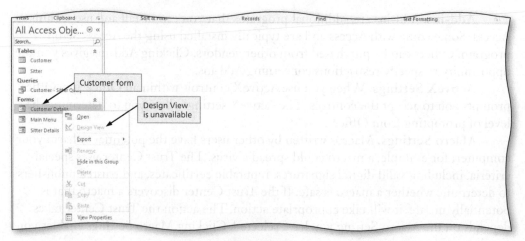

Figure 9–68

It is very important that you save your original database in case you ever need to make changes to VBA code or to the design of a form or report. You cannot use the ACCDE file to make such changes, nor can you convert the ACCDE file back to the ACCDB file format.

Record Locking

You can indicate how records are to be locked when multiple users are using a database at the same time. To do so, click File on the ribbon, click the Options tab, and then click Client Settings. Scroll down so that the Advanced area appears on the screen (Figure 9–69).

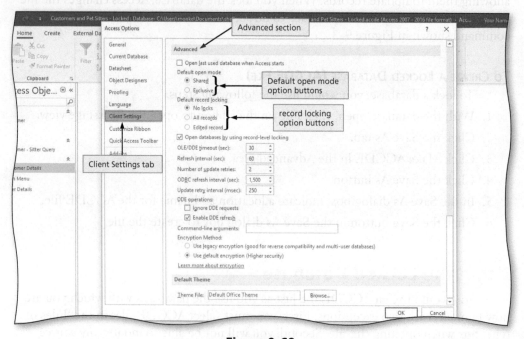

Figure 9–69

If you wanted the default open mode to be exclusive (only one user can use the database at a time) rather than shared (multiple users can simultaneously use the database), you could click the Exclusive option button. You can also select the approach you want for record locking by clicking the appropriate record locking option button. The possible approaches to record locking are shown in Table 9–3.

Table 9–3	Record Locking Approaches
Locking Type	**Description**
No locks	When you edit a record, Access will not lock the record. Thus, other users also could edit the same record at the same time. When you have finished your changes and attempt to save the record, Access will give you the option of overwriting the other user's changes (not recommended), copying your changes to the clipboard, or canceling your changes.
All records	All records will be locked as long as you have the database open. No other user can edit or lock the records during this time.
Edited record	When you edit a record, Access will lock the record. When other users attempt to edit the same record, they will not be able to do so. Instead, they will see the locked record indicator.

Database Splitting

You can split a database into two databases, one called the back-end database containing only the table data, and another database called the front-end database containing the other objects. Only a single copy of the back-end database can exist, but each user could have his or her own copy of the front-end database. Each user would create the desired custom reports, forms, and other objects in his or her own front-end database, thereby not interfering with any other user.

When splitting a database, the database to be split must be open. In the process, you will identify a name and location for the back-end database that will be created by the Access splitter. In the process, you would display the Database Splitter dialog box (Figure 9–70).

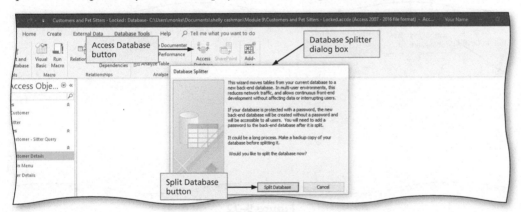

Figure 9–70

You would also have to select a location for the back-end database (Figure 9–71). Access assigns a name to the back-end database that ends with an underscore and the letters, be. You can override this name if you prefer.

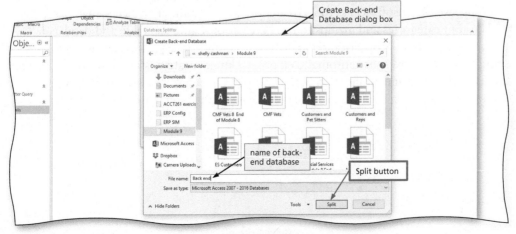

Figure 9–71

To Split the Database

To split a database, you would use the following steps.

1. Open the database to be split.
2. Display the Database Tools tab.
3. Click the Access Database button (Database Tools tab | Move Data group) to display the Database Splitter dialog box.
4. Click the Split Database button to display the Create Back-end Database dialog box.
5. Type a file name to the one you want.
6. Select a location for the back-end database.
7. Click the Split button to split the database.
8. Click OK to close the dialog box reporting that the split was successful.

The Front-End and Back-End Databases

The database has now been split into separate front-end and back-end databases. The front-end database is the one that you will use; it contains all the queries, reports, forms, and other components from the original database. The front-end database only contains links to the tables, however, instead of the tables themselves (Figure 9–72). The back-end database contains the actual tables but does not contain any other objects.

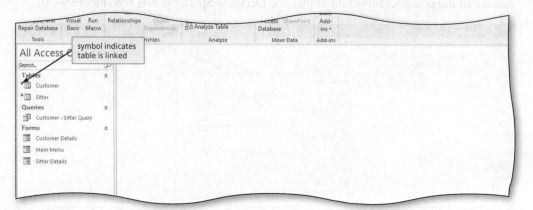

Figure 9–72

Summary

In this module you have learned to convert Access databases to and from earlier versions; use Microsoft Access tools to analyze and document an Access database; add custom categories and groups to the Navigation Pane; use table and database properties; use field properties to create a custom input mask; allow zero-length strings; create indexes; use automatic error checking; create custom data parts; create and use templates and application parts; encrypt a database and set a password; understand the Trust Center; lock a database; and split a database.

What decisions will you need to make when administering your own databases?

Use these guidelines as you complete the assignments in this module and administer your own databases outside of this class.

1. Determine whether you should create any templates, application parts, or data type parts.

    a. Is there a particular combination of tables, queries, forms, reports, and/or macros that you would like to enable users to easily include in their databases? If so, you could create a template and an application part containing the specific objects you want them to be able to include.

    b. Is there a particular collection of fields that you would like to enable users to include in a table with a single click? If so, you could create a data type part containing those fields.

2. Determine whether a database needs to be converted to or from an earlier version.

    a. Do users of a previous version of Access need to be able to use the database? If so, you will need to be sure the database does not contain any features that would prevent it from being converted.

    b. Do you use a database that was created in an earlier version of Access that you would like to use in Access 2019? If so, you can convert the database for use in Access 2019.

3. Determine when to analyze and/or document the database.

    a. Once you create a database, you should use the table and performance analyzers to determine if any changes to the structure are warranted.

    b. You should also document the database.

4. Determine the most useful way to customize the Navigation Pane.

    a. Would it be helpful to have custom categories and groups?

    b. What objects should be in the groups?

    c. Would it be helpful to restrict the objects that appear to only those whose names contain certain characters?

5. Determine any table-wide validation rules.

    a. Are there any validation rules that involve more than a single field?

6. Determine any custom database properties.

    a. Are there properties that would be helpful in documenting the database that are not included in the list of database properties you can use?

7. Determine indexes.

    a. Examine retrieval and sorting requirements to determine possible indexes. Indexes can make both retrieval and sorting more efficient.

8. Determine whether the database should be encrypted.

    a. If you need to protect the security of the database's contents, you should strongly consider encryption.

    b. As part of the process, you will also set a password.

9. Determine whether the database should be locked.

    a. Should users be able to change the design of forms, reports, and/or macros?

10. Determine whether the database should be split.

    a. It is often more efficient to split the database into a back-end database, which contains only the table data, and a front-end database, which contains other objects, such as queries, forms, and reports.

How should you submit solutions to questions in the assignments identified with a symbol?

Every assignment in this book contains one or more questions identified with a symbol. These questions require you to think beyond the assigned database. Present your solutions to the questions in the format required by your instructor. Possible formats may include one or more of these options: write the answer; create a document that contains the answer; present your answer to the class; discuss your answer in a group; record the answer as audio or video using a webcam, smartphone, or portable media player; or post answers on a blog, wiki, or website.

Apply Your Knowledge

Reinforce the skills and apply the concepts you learned in this module.

Administering the Financial Services Database

Instructions: Start Access. Open the Support_AC_Financial Services database. (If you did not complete the exercise, see your instructor for a copy of the modified database.)

Perform the following tasks:

1. Open the Client table in Design view and create a custom input mask for the Client Number field. The first two characters of the client number must be uppercase letters and the last two characters must be numerical digits.

2. Create an index on the combination of Client Type and Advisor Number. Name the index TypeAdv.

3. Save the changes to the Client table.

4. Use the Database Documenter to produce detailed documentation for the Services table. Export the documentation to a Word RTF file. Change the name of the file to LastName _Documentation.rtf where LastName is your last name.

5. Use the Table Analyzer to analyze the table structure of the Client table. Open the Word RTF file that you created in Step 4 and make a note of the results of the analysis at the end of the file.

6. Use the Performance Analyzer to analyze all the tables in the database. Describe the results of your analysis in your RTF file.

7. Populate the Status custom property for the database to a Live version.

8. Add a Production version with today's date.

9. Submit the revised Financial Services database and the RTF file in the format specified by your instructor.

10. ✷ Can you convert the Financial Services database to an Access 2002–2003 database? Why or why not?

Extend Your Knowledge

Extend the skills you learned in this module and experiment with new skills. You may need to use Help to complete the assignment.

Instructions: Start Access. Open the Support_AC_Healthy Pets database. (If you did not complete the exercise, see your instructor for a copy of the modified database.)

Perform the following tasks:

1. Create a Navigation Form that is called Clients and Technicians that contains a single row with two horizontal tabs. Add two forms to the Navigation Form: Clients by Technician Form and Technician Form.

2. Change the Current Database options to ensure that the Clients and Technicians navigation form opens automatically.

3. Currently, when you open the Potential Clients table in Datasheet view, the table is ordered by Client Number. Change the property for the table so the table is in order by Client Name.

4. Create an additional table called Potential Technicians. Add the Name-Address Quick Start fields to easily create the fields. Remove the word Owner from each field name. Save the table and close it.

5. Customize the Navigation Pane by adding a custom category called Clients. Then add two custom groups, Detailed and Summary, to the Clients category.

6. Add the Client table, the Potential Clients table, and the Clients by Technician Form to the Detailed custom group under the Clients category. Add both client summary reports to the Summary custom group under the Clients category.

7. Submit the revised database in the format specified by your instructor.

8. ✸ What advantages are there to using a custom Navigation Pane as opposed to the standard Navigation Pane?

Expand Your World

Create a solution which uses cloud and web technologies by learning and investigating on your own from general guidance.

Problem: There are many ways to share an Access database. Some ways require each user to have Microsoft Access installed on their computer, while others do not. The method you select depends on factors such as need and available resources.

Instructions: Perform the following tasks:

1. Create a blog, a Google document, or a Word document on OneDrive on which to store your findings.

2. Use the web to research different ways to share an Access database such as CMF Vets with others. Be sure to note any specific resources needed, such as an Access database or a SharePoint server, any costs involved, and provide examples of different reasons for sharing a database such as CMF Vets. Record your findings in your blog, Google document, or Word document, being sure to appropriately reference your sources.

3. Submit the assignment in the format specified by your instructor.

4. ✸ Based on your research, what method would you choose to share your Access databases?

In the Labs

Design, create, modify, and/or use a database following the guidelines, concepts, and skills presented in this module.

Lab: Administering the Lancaster College Database

Part 1: The administration at Lancaster College has asked you to perform a number of tasks. Open the Support_AC_Lancaster College database. (If you did not complete the exercise, see your instructor for a copy of the modified database.) Use the concepts and techniques presented in this module to perform each of the following tasks.

a. Create a main menu navigation form that includes all the forms in the database. Give the main menu an appropriate title.

b. Change the Current Database options to ensure that the Main Menu form opens automatically when the user opens the database.

c. Open the Coach table in Design view and Create an index for the LastName field that allows duplicates. Save the changes.

d. Open the Participation table in Design view and create an index named StudentIDSportName on the StudentID and the SportName.

e. Open the Sport table in Design view and create a validation rule to ensure that the minimum players are always less than the maximum players. Include validation text.

f. Open the Student table in Datasheet view and add the Quick Start Status field to the table.

g. Create a template of the database (with an application part) and call it Lancaster College Template.

h. From that template, create a new database called your initials college. Close the database.

Submit your assignment in the format specified by your instructor.

Part 2: You made several decisions while completing this project, including using an input mask and validation rule. What was the rationale behind your decisions? Would you add other input masks or validation rules to the Lancaster College database?

10 | Using SQL

Objectives

You will have mastered the material in this module when you can:

- Understand the SQL language and how to use it
- Change the font or font size for queries
- Create SQL queries
- Include fields in SQL queries
- Include simple and compound criteria in SQL queries
- Use computed fields and built-in functions in SQL queries
- Sort the results in SQL queries

- Use aggregate functions in SQL queries
- Group the results in SQL queries
- Join tables in SQL queries
- Use subqueries
- Compare SQL queries with Access-generated SQL
- Use INSERT, UPDATE, and DELETE queries to update a database
- Link table to outside data source
- Change tab order in a form

Introduction

The language called **SQL (Structured Query Language)** is a very important language for querying and updating databases. It is the closest thing to a universal database language, because the vast majority of database management systems, including Access, use it in some fashion. Although some users will be able to do all their queries through the query features of Access without ever using SQL, those in charge of administering and maintaining the database system should be familiar with this important language. You can also use Access as an interface to other database management systems, such as SQL Server. Using or interfacing with SQL Server requires knowledge of SQL. Virtually every DBMS supports SQL.

BTW
Distributing a Document
Instead of printing and distributing a hard copy of a document, you can distribute the document electronically. Options include sending the document via email; posting it on cloud storage (such as OneDrive) and sharing the file with others; posting it on a social networking site, blog, or other website; and sharing a link associated with an online location of the document. You also can create and share a PDF or XPS image of the document, so that users can view the file in Acrobat Reader or XPS Viewer instead of in Access.

Project—Using SQL

CMF Vets wants to be able to use the extended data management capabilities available through SQL. As part of becoming familiar with SQL, CMF Vets would like to create a wide variety of SQL queries.

Similar to creating queries in Design view, SQL provides a way of querying relational databases. In SQL, however, instead of making entries in the design grid, you type commands into SQL view to obtain the desired results, as shown in Figure 10–1a. You can then click the View button to view the results just as when you are creating queries in Design view. The results for the query in Figure 10–1a are shown in Figure 10–1b.

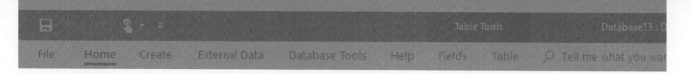

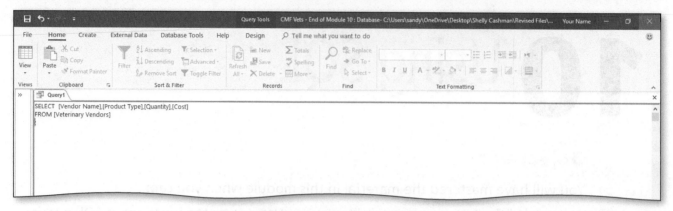

Figure 10–1a Query in SQL

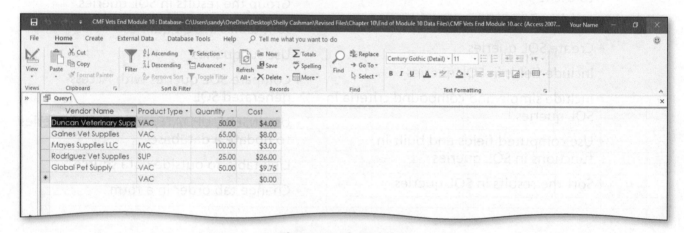

Figure 10–1b Results

In this module, you will learn how to create and use SQL queries like the one shown in Figure 10–1a.

BTW
The Ribbon and Screen Resolution
Access may change how the groups and buttons within the groups appear on the ribbon, depending on the computer's screen resolution. Thus, your ribbon may look different from the ones in this book if you are using a screen resolution other than 1366 × 768.

BTW
Enabling the Content
For each of the databases you use in this module, you will need to enable the content.

SQL Background

In this module, you query and update a database using the language called SQL (Structured Query Language). Similar to using the design grid in the Access Query window, SQL provides users with the capability of querying a relational database. Because SQL is a language, however, you must enter **commands** to obtain the desired results, rather than completing entries in the design grid. SQL uses commands to update tables and to retrieve data from tables. The commands that are used to retrieve data are usually called **queries**.

SQL was developed under the name SEQUEL at the IBM San Jose research facilities as the data manipulation language for IBM's prototype relational model DBMS, System R, in the mid-1970s. In 1980, it was renamed SQL to avoid confusion with an unrelated hardware product called SEQUEL. Most relational DBMSs, including Microsoft Access and Microsoft SQL Server, use a version of SQL as a data manipulation language.

Some people pronounce SQL by pronouncing the three letters, that is, "ess-que-ell." It is very common, however, to pronounce it as the name under which it was developed originally, that is, "sequel."

To Change the Font Size

You can change the font and/or the font size for queries using the Options button in the Backstage view and then Object Designers in the list of options in the Access Options dialog box. There is not usually a compelling reason to change the font, unless there is a strong preference for some other font. It often is worthwhile to change the font size, however. *Why? With the default size of 10, the queries can be hard to read. Increasing the font size to 11 can make a big difference.* The following steps change the font size for queries to 11.

1

- Start Access and open the database named CMF Vets from your hard drive, OneDrive, or other storage location.

- Click File on the ribbon to open the Backstage view.

- Click Options to display the Access Options dialog box.

- Click Object Designers to display the Object Designer options.

- In the Query design area, click the Size box arrow, and then click 11 in the list to change the size to 11 (Figure 10–2).

2

- Click OK to close the Access Options dialog box.

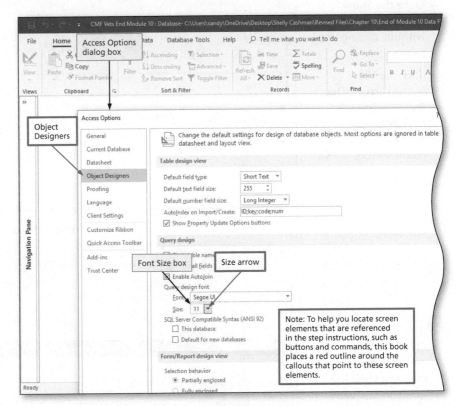

Figure 10–2

SQL Queries

When you query a database using SQL, you type commands in a blank window rather than filling in the design grid. When the command is complete, you can view your results just as you do with queries you create using the design grid.

To Create a New SQL Query

You begin the creation of a new **SQL query**, which is a query expressed using the SQL language, just as you begin the creation of any other query in Access. The only difference is that you will use SQL view instead of Design view. *Why? SQL view enables you to type SQL commands rather than making entries in the design grid.* The following steps create a new SQL query.

1

- Close the Navigation Pane.
- Display the Create tab.
- Click the Query Design button (Create tab | Queries group) to create a query.
- Close the Show Table dialog box without adding any tables.
- Click the View button arrow (Query Tools Design tab | Results group) to display the View menu (Figure 10–3).

Q&A Why did the icon on the View button change to SQL, and why are there only two items on the menu instead of the usual five?

Without any tables selected, you cannot view any results. You can only use the normal Design view or SQL view. The change in the icon indicates that you could simply click the button to transfer to SQL view.

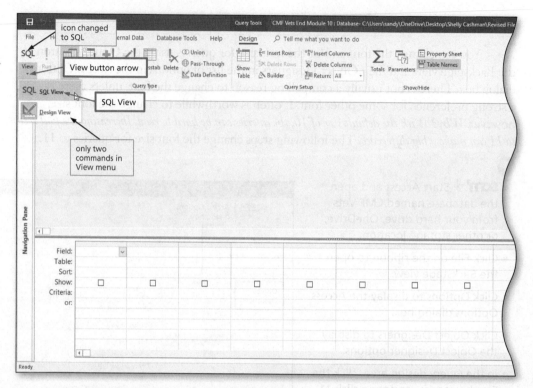

Figure 10–3

2

- Click SQL View on the View menu to view the query in SQL view (Figure 10–4).

Q&A What happened to the design grid?

In SQL view, you specify the queries by typing SQL commands rather than making entries in the design grid.

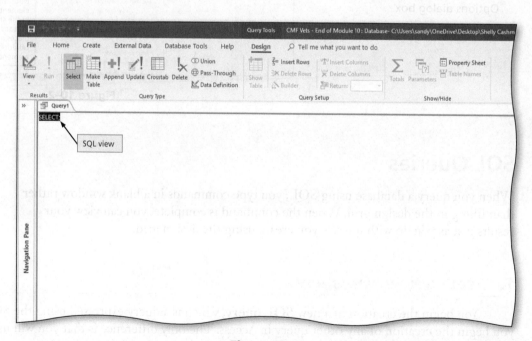

Figure 10–4

SQL Commands

The basic form of SQL expressions is quite simple: SELECT-FROM-WHERE. The command begins with a **SELECT clause**, which consists of the word, SELECT, followed by a list of those fields you want to include. The fields will appear in the results in the order in which they are listed in the expression. Next, the command contains a **FROM clause**, which consists of the word FROM followed by a list of the table or tables involved in the query. Finally, there is an optional **WHERE clause**, which consists of the word WHERE followed by any criteria that the data you want to retrieve must satisfy. The command ends with a semicolon (;), which in this text will appear on a separate line.

SQL has no special format rules for placement of terms, capitalization, and so on. One common style is to place the word FROM on a new line, and then place the word WHERE, when it is used, on the next line. This style makes the commands easier to read. It is also common to show words that are part of the SQL language in uppercase and others in a combination of uppercase and lowercase. This text formats SQL terms in uppercase letters. Because it is a common convention, and necessary in some versions of SQL, you will place a semicolon (;) at the end of each command.

Microsoft Access has its own version of SQL that, unlike some other versions of SQL, allows spaces within field names and table names. There is a restriction, however, to the way such names are used in SQL queries. When a name containing a space appears in SQL, it must be enclosed in square brackets. For example, Vendor Name must appear as [Vendor Name] because the name includes a space. On the other hand, Cost does not need to be enclosed in square brackets because its name does not include a space. For consistency, all names in this text are enclosed in square brackets. Thus, the Cost field would appear as [Cost] even though the brackets are not technically required by SQL.

To Include Only Certain Fields

To include only certain fields in a query, list them after the word, SELECT. If you want to list all rows in the table, you do not include the word, WHERE. **Why?** *If there is no WHERE clause, there is no criterion restricting which rows appear in the results. In that case, all rows will appear.* The following steps create a query for CMF Vets that will list the vendor name, product type, quantity, and cost of all vendors.

- Click to the right of the word, SELECT, delete the semicolon, type `[Vendor Name],[Product Type],[Quantity],[Cost]` as the first line of the command, and then press ENTER.

Q&A What is the purpose of the SELECT clause?
The SELECT clause indicates the fields that are to be included in the query results. This SELECT clause, for example, indicates that the Vendor Name, Product Type, Quantity, and Cost fields are to be included.

- Type `FROM [Veterinary Vendors]` as the second line to specify the source table, press ENTER, and then type a semicolon (;) on the third line (Figure 10–5a).

Q&A What is the purpose of the FROM clause?
The FROM clause indicates the table or tables that contain the fields used in the query. This FROM clause indicates that all the fields in this query come from the Veterinary Vendors table.

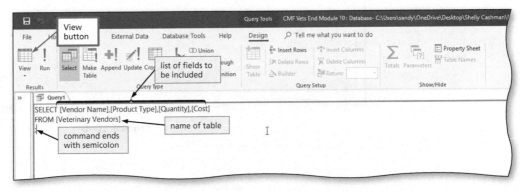

Figure 10–5a

• Click the View button (Query Tools Design tab | Results group) to view the results (Figure 10–5b).

My screen displays a dialog box that asks me to enter a parameter value. What did I do wrong?
You typed a field name incorrectly. Click Cancel to close the dialog box and then correct your SQL statement.

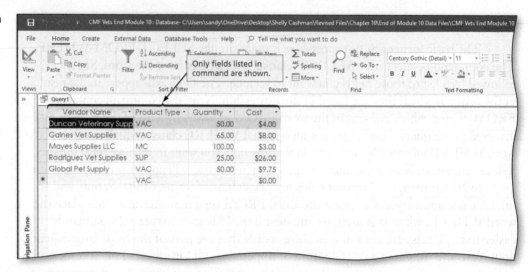

Figure 10–5b

2

• Click the Save button on the Quick Access Toolbar, type `m10q01` as the name in the Save As dialog box, and then click OK to save the query as m10q01.

To Prepare to Enter a New SQL Query

To enter a new SQL query, you could close the window, click the No button when asked if you want to save your changes, and then begin the process from scratch. A quicker alternative is to use the View menu and then select SQL View. ***Why?*** *You will be returned to SQL view with the current command appearing. At that point, you could erase the current command and then enter a new one. If the next command is similar to the previous one, however, it often is simpler to modify the current command instead of erasing it and starting over.* The following step shows how to prepare to enter a new SQL query.

1

• Click the View button arrow (Home tab | Views group) to display the View menu (Figure 10–6).

• Click SQL View to return to SQL view.

Could I just click the View button, or do I have to click the arrow?
Because the icon on the button is not the icon for SQL view, you must click the arrow.

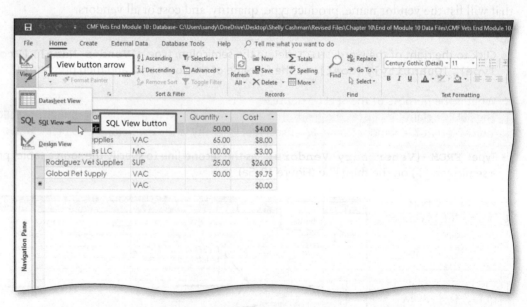

Figure 10–6

To Include All Fields

To include all fields, you could use the same approach as in the previous steps, that is, list each field in the Veterinary Vendors table after the word SELECT. There is a shortcut, however. Instead of listing all the field names after SELECT, you can use the asterisk (*) symbol. *Why? Just as when working in the design grid, the asterisk symbol represents all fields.* This indicates that you want all fields listed in the order in which you described them to the system during data definition. The following steps list all fields and all records in the Veterinary Vendors table.

1

- Delete the current command, type **SELECT *** as the first line of the command, and then press ENTER.

- Type **FROM [Veterinary Vendors]** as the second line, press ENTER, and type a semicolon (;) on the third line.

- View the results (Figure 10–7b).

Q&A
Can I use copy and paste commands when I enter SQL commands?
Yes, you can use copy and paste as well as other editing techniques, such as replacing text.

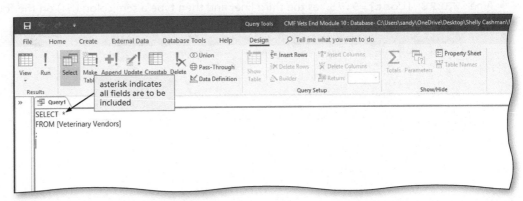

Figure 10–7a Query to List All Fields and All Records in the Veterinary Vendors Table

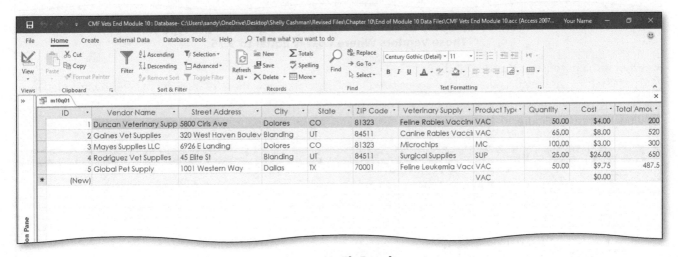

Figure 10–7b Results

2

- Click File on the ribbon to open the Backstage view, click the Save As tab to display the Save As gallery, click Save Object As in the File Types area, click the Save As button to display the Save As dialog box, type **m10q02** as the name for the saved query, and then click OK to save the query as m10q02 and return to the query.

Q&A
Can I just click the Save button on the Quick Access Toolbar as I did when I saved the previous query?
If you did, you would replace the previous query with the version you just created. Because you want to save both the previous query and the new one, you need to save the new version with a different name. To do so, you must use Save Object As, which is available through the Backstage view.

To Use a Criterion Involving a Numeric Field

To restrict the records to be displayed, include the word WHERE followed by a criterion as part of the command. If the field involved is a numeric field, you simply type the value. In typing the number, you do not type commas or dollar signs. *Why? If you enter a dollar sign, Access assumes you are entering text. If you enter a comma, Access considers the criterion invalid.* The following steps create a query to list the name of all vendors whose current cost amount is greater than $20.00 so other lesser cost options may be reviewed.

- Return to SQL view and delete the current command.
- Type `SELECT [Vendor Name],[Product Type],[Cost]` as the first line of the command.
- Type `FROM [Veterinary Vendors]` as the second line.
- Type `WHERE [Cost]=9.75` as the third line, and then type a semicolon (`;`) on the fourth line.

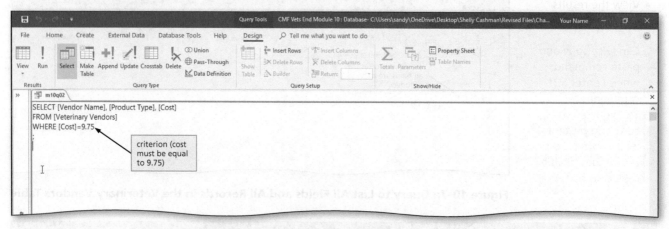

Figure 10–8a Query to List the Vendor Name and Product Type for Those Vendors Where Cost is Equal to 9.75

Q&A What is the purpose of the WHERE clause?

The WHERE clause restricts the rows to be included in the results to only those that satisfy the criteria included in the clause. With this WHERE clause, for example, only those rows on which Cost is equal to 9.75 will be included.

- View the results (Figure 10–8b).

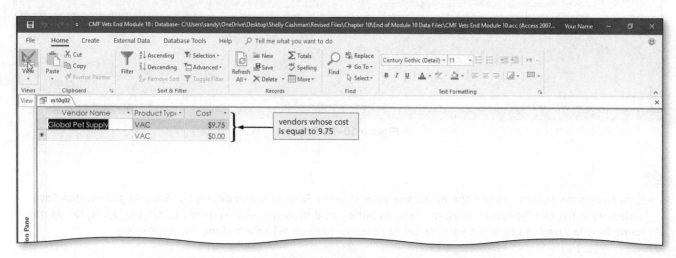

Figure 10–8b Results

- Save the query as m10q03.

Access Module 10

Simple Criteria

The criterion following the word WHERE in the preceding query is called a simple criterion. A **simple criterion** has the form: field name, comparison operator, then either another field name or a value. The possible comparison operators are shown in Table 10–1.

BTW
Context-Sensitive Help in SQL
When you are working in SQL view, you can obtain context-sensitive help on any of the keywords in your query. To do so, click anywhere in the word about which you wish to obtain help and press the F1 key.

Table 10–1 Comparison Operators

Comparison Operator	Meaning
=	equal to
<	less than
>	greater than
<=	less than or equal to
>=	greater than or equal to
<>	not equal to

To Use a Comparison Operator

In the following steps, CMF Vets uses a comparison operator to list the vendor name, product type, and cost for all vendors who have a product cost greater than $20. *Why? A comparison operator allows you to compare the value in a field with a specific value or with the value in another field.*

- Return to SQL view and delete the current command.
- Type `SELECT [Vendor Name],[Product Type],[Cost]` as the first line of the command.
- Type `FROM [Veterinary Vendors]` as the second line.
- Type `WHERE ([Veterinary Vendors].[Cost]>20)` as the third line.

Q&A Why are there parentheses in the WHERE clause?
Because this is the second time that Veterinary Vendors is shown in the query, SQL requires parentheses before the table name.

- Type a semicolon (`;`) on the fourth line.

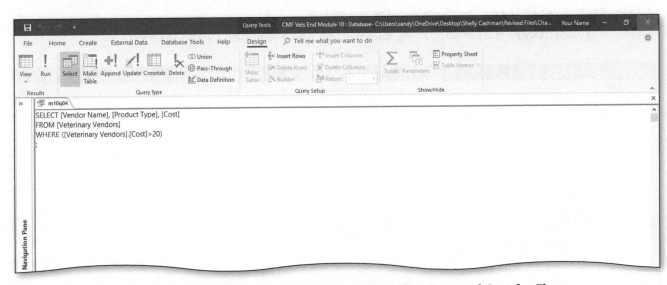

Figure 10–9a Query to List the Vendor Name. Product Type and Cost for Those Vendors Where Cost is Greater Than $20

- View the results (Figure 10–9b).

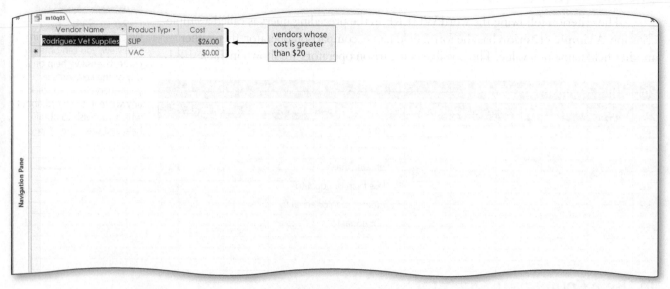

Figure 10–9b Results

- Save the query as m10q04.

To Use a Criterion Involving a Text Field

If the criterion involves a text field, the value must be enclosed in quotation marks. *Why? Unlike when you work in the design grid, Access will not insert the quotation marks around text data for you in SQL view. You need to include them.* The following example lists the Vendor Name and Product Name of all of CMF Vets' vendors located in Dolores, that is, all Vendors for whom the value in the City field is Dolores.

- Return to SQL view, delete the current command, and type `SELECT [Vendor Name],[Product Type],[City]` as the first line of the command.

- Type `FROM [Veterinary Vendors]` as the second line.

- Type `WHERE [City]='Dolores'` as the third line and type a semicolon (`;`) on the fourth line.

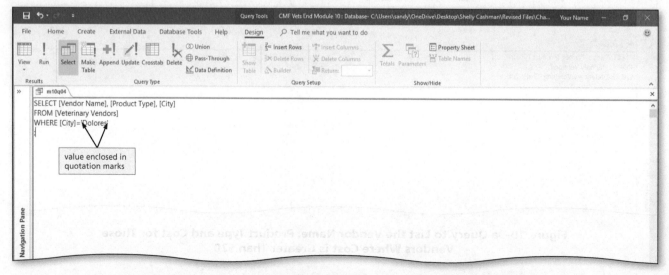

Figure 10–10a Query to List the Vendors Located in the City of Dolores

• View the results (Figure 10–10b).

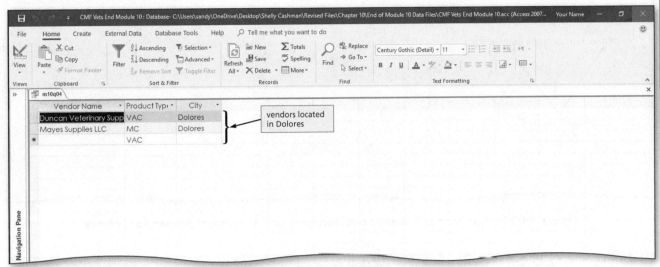

Figure 10–10b Results

Q&A Could I enclose the text field value in double quotation marks instead of single quotation marks?
Yes. It is usually easier, however, to use single quotes when entering SQL commands.

2

• Save the query as m10q05.

To Use a Wildcard

In most cases, the conditions in WHERE clauses involve exact matches, such as retrieving rows for each account located in the city of Dolores. In some cases, however, exact matches do not work. *Why? You might only know that the desired value contains a certain collection of characters.* In such cases, you use the LIKE operator with a wildcard symbol.

Rather than testing for equality, the LIKE operator uses one or more wildcard characters to test for a pattern match. One common wildcard in Access, the **asterisk** (*), represents any collection of characters. Thus, D* represents the letter, D, followed by any string of characters. Another wildcard symbol is the question mark (**?**), which represents any individual character. Thus, T?m represents the letter T, followed by any single character, followed by the letter, m, such as Tim or Tom.

The following steps use a wildcard to display the treatment number and treatment name for every treatment in the Treatment Cost table in CMF Vets for Felines. In case there are possible incorrect spellings, you will search for animal types starting with the letter F To be sure that Access associates the field and table correctly, you must place the table and field names in parentheses.

1

• Return to SQL view, delete the previous query, and type `SELECT [Treatment Number], [Treatment], [Animal Type]`.

• Type `FROM [Treatment Cost]` as the second line.

• Type `WHERE ([Treatment Cost].[Animal Type]) Like 'F*'` as the third line, and then type a semicolon (`;`) on the fourth line.

• View the query (Figure 10–11a) and the results (Figure 10–11b).

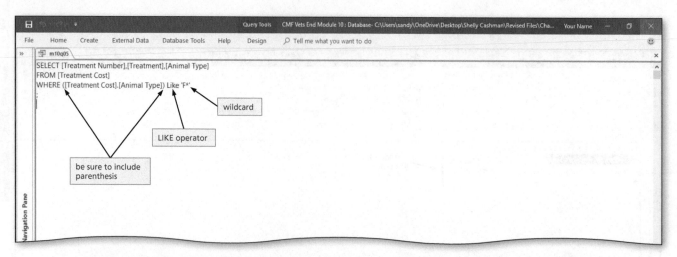

Figure 10–11a Query to List Treatment Numbers and Treatment Names for Felines

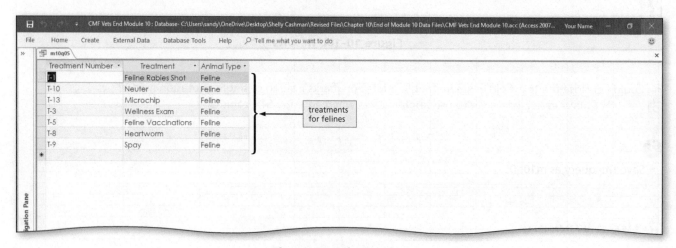

Figure 10–11b Results

• Save the query as m10q06.

Break Point: If you wish to stop working through the module at this point, you can close Access now. You can resume the project later by starting Access, opening the database called CMF Vets, creating a new query in SQL view, and continuing to follow the steps from this location forward.

Compound Criteria

BTW
Entering Field Names
Be sure to enclose field names in square brackets. If you accidentally use parentheses or curly braces, Access will display a syntax error (missing operator) message.

You are not limited to simple criteria in SQL. You can also use compound criteria. **Compound criteria** are formed by connecting two or more simple criteria using AND, OR, and NOT. When simple criteria are connected by the word AND, all the simple criteria must be true in order for the compound criterion to be true. When simple criteria are connected by the word OR, the compound criterion will be true whenever any of the simple criteria are true. Preceding a criterion by the word NOT reverses the truth or falsity of the original criterion. That is, if the original criterion is true, the new criterion will be false; if the original criterion is false, the new one will be true.

To Use a Compound Criterion Involving AND

The following steps use a compound criterion. *Why? A compound criterion allows you to impose multiple conditions.* In particular, these steps enable CMF Vets to display the treatments for felines whose treatment cost is greater than $20.

 1

- Return to SQL view, delete the previous query, and type `SELECT [Treatment Number], [Treatment], [Animal Type]` as the first line.

- Type `FROM [Treatment Cost]` as the second line.

- Type `WHERE ([Treatment Cost].[Animal Type]) Like 'F*'` as the third line.

- Type `AND ([Treatment Cost].Cost)>20` on the fourth line.

- Type a semicolon (**;**) on the fifth line.

Q&A
What is the purpose of the AND clause?
The AND clause indicates that there are multiple criteria, all of which must be true. With this AND clause, only rows on which BOTH Animal Type is Feline AND Cost of the treatment is greater than 20 will be included.

- View the query (Figure 10–12a) and the results (Figure 10–12b).

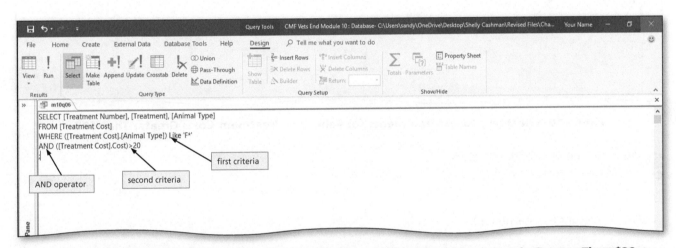

Figure 10–12a Query to List Treatments for Felines and Whose Treatment Cost is Greater Than $20

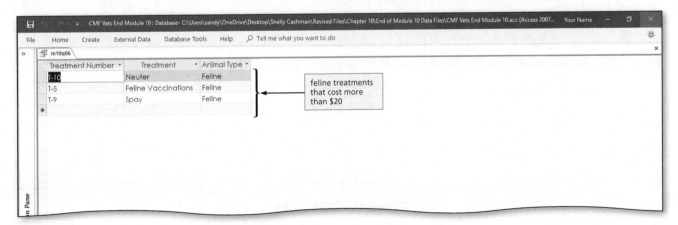

Figure 10–12b Results

 2

- Save the query as m10q07.

To Use a Compound Criterion Involving OR

The following steps use a compound criterion involving OR to enable CMF Vets to display felines or where the treatment cost is greater than $25.00. *Why? In an OR criterion only one of the individual criteria needs to be true in order for the record to be included in the results.*

- Return to SQL view, delete the previous query, and type `SELECT [Treatment Number], [Treatment], [Animal Type]` as the first line.
- Type `FROM [Treatment Cost]` as the second line.
- Type `WHERE ([Treatment Cost].[Animal Type]) Like 'F*'` as the third line.
- Type `OR ([Treatment Cost].Cost)>25` as the fourth line.
- Type a semicolon (`;`) on the fifth line (Figure 10–13a).

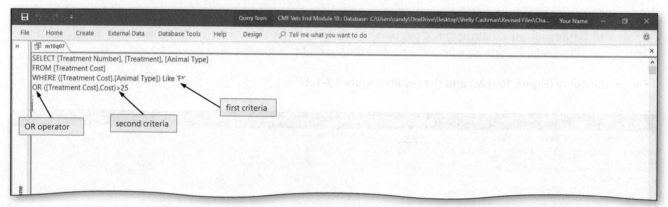

Figure 10–13a Query to List Treatments for Felines or Treatment Costs Greater Than $25

Q&A What is the purpose of the OR clause?
The OR clause indicates that there are multiple criteria, only one of which needs to be true. With this OR clause, those rows on which EITHER Animal Type is Feline OR Treatment Cost is less than $25 (or both) will be included.

- View the results (Figure 10–13b).

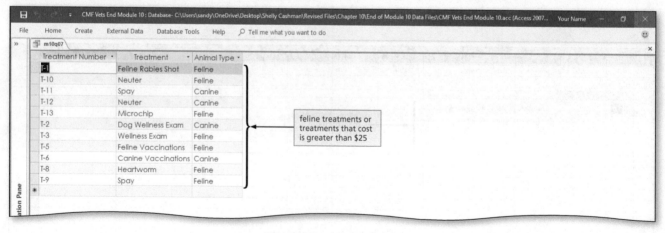

Figure 10–13b Results

- Save the query as m10q08.
- Close the query.

To Use NOT in a Criterion

Why? *You can negate any criterion by preceding the criterion with the word NOT.* The following steps use NOT in a criterion to list the first names and last names of the pet owners in CMF Vets that not located in the city of Dolores.

①

- Click the Create tab, and then click the Query Design button (Create tab | Queries group) to create a query.
- Close the Show Table dialog box without adding any tables.
- Click the View button arrow (Query Tools Design tab | Results group) to display the View menu.

②

- Click SQL View on the View menu.
- Delete SELECT; and then type **SELECT [Owner First Name], [Owner Last Name], [Owner City]** as the first line.
- Type **FROM Owners** on the second line.
- Type **WHERE NOT [Owner City]='Dolores'** as the third line and type a semicolon (**;**) on the fourth line (Figure 10–14a).

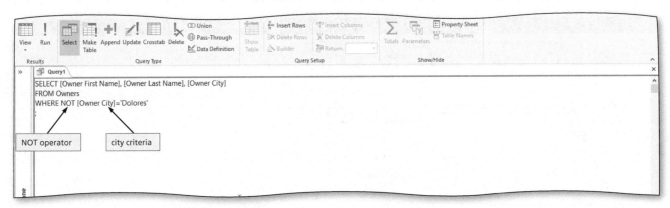

Figure 10–14a Query to List the Names of Pet Owners that Do Not Live in Dolores

- View the results (Figure 10–14b).

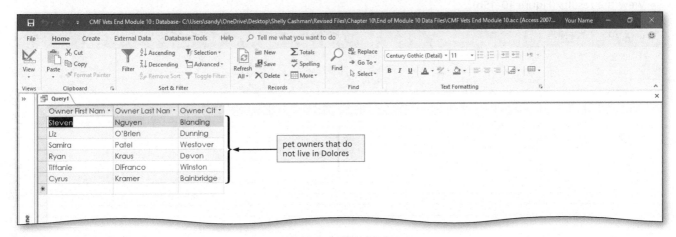

Figure 10–14b Results

③

- Save the query as m10q09.

To Use a Computed Field

Just as with queries created in Design view, you can include fields in queries that are not in the database, but that can be computed from fields that are. Such a field is called a **computed** or **calculated field**. Computations can involve addition (+), subtraction (-), multiplication (*), or division (/). The query in the following steps computes the hours remaining, which is equal to the total hours minus the hours spent.

To indicate the contents of the new field (the computed field), you can name the field by following the computation with the word AS and then the name you want to assign the field. *Why? Assigning the field a descriptive name makes the results much more readable.* The following steps calculate the hours remaining for each workshop offered by subtracting the hours spent from the total hours and then assigning the name Remaining to the calculation. The steps also list the Owner ID, Workshop Code, Total Hours, and Hours Spent for all workshop offerings for which the number of hours spent is greater than 0.

- Return to SQL view and delete the previous query.

- Type SELECT [Owner ID], [Workshop Code], [Total Hours], [Hours Spent], [Total Hours]-[Hours Spent] AS Remaining as the first line.

- Type FROM [Workshop Offerings] as the second line.

- Type WHERE [Hours Spent]>0 as the third line, and then type a semicolon on the fourth line (Figure 10–15a).

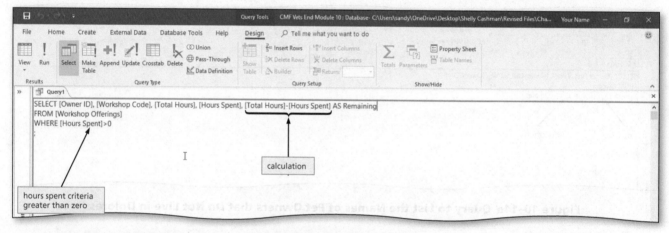

Figure 10–15a Query to List the Total Hours for a Workshop Less the Hours Already Spent

- View the results (Figure 10–15b).

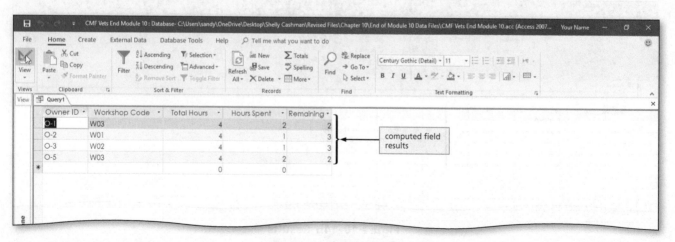

Figure 10–15b Results

- Save the query as m10q10.

Sorting

Sorting in SQL follows the same principles as when using Design view to specify sorted query results, employing a sort key as the field on which data is to be sorted. SQL uses major and minor sort keys when sorting on multiple fields. By following a sort key with the word DESC with no comma in between, you can specify descending sort order. If you do not specify DESC, the data will be sorted in ascending order.

To sort the output, you include an **ORDER BY clause**, which consists of the words ORDER BY followed by the sort key. If there are two sort keys, the major sort key is listed first. Queries that you construct in Design view require that the major sort key is to the left of the minor sort key in the list of fields to be included. In SQL, there is no such restriction. The fields to be included in the query are in the SELECT clause, and the fields to be used for sorting are in the ORDER BY clause. The two clauses are totally independent.

To Sort the Results on a Single Field

The following steps list the treatment number, treatment, animal type, and cost for all treatments sorted by animal type. *Why? CMF Vets wants this data to appear in alphabetical order by treatment.*

- Return to SQL view and delete the previous query.
- Type `SELECT [Treatment Number],[Treatment], [Animal Type],[Cost]` as the first line.
- Type `FROM [Treatment Cost]` as the second line.
- Type `ORDER BY [Treatment]` as the third line and type a semicolon on the fourth line (Figure 10–16a).

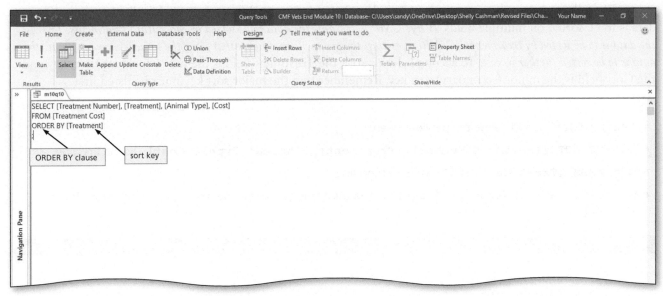

Figure 10–16a Query to List the Treatment Number, Treatment, Animal Type, and Cost Sorted by Treatment

Q&A What is the purpose of the ORDER BY clause?

The ORDER BY clause indicates that the results of the query are to be sorted by the indicated field or fields. This ORDER BY clause, for example, would cause the results to be sorted by Treatment.

- View the results (Figure 10–16b).

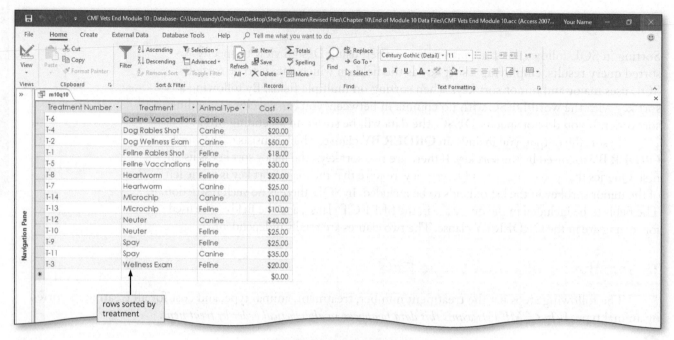

Figure 10–16b Results

• Save the query as m10q11.

To Sort the Results on Multiple Fields

The following steps list the treatment number, treatment, animal type, and cost for all treatments. The data is to be sorted on multiple fields. *Why? CMF Vets wants the data to be sorted by cost within treatments. That is, the data is to be sorted by treatment. In addition, within the group of treatments that have the same treatment name, the data is to be sorted further by cost.* To accomplish this sort, the Treatment field is the major (primary) sort key and the Cost field is the minor (secondary) sort key. Remember that the major sort key must be listed first.

• Return to SQL view and delete the previous query.

• Type `SELECT [Treatment Number],[Treatment], [Animal Type],[Cost]` as the first line.

• Type `FROM [Treatment Cost]` as the second line.

• Type `ORDER BY [Treatment],[Cost]` as the third line, and then type a semicolon on the fourth line (Figure 10–17a).

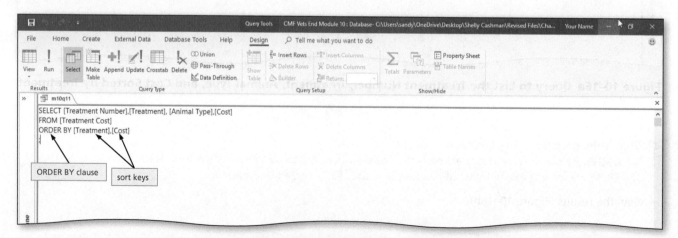

Figure 10–17a Query to List the Treatment Number, Treatment, Animal Type, and Cost Sorted by Treatment and Cost

- View the results (Figure 10–17b).

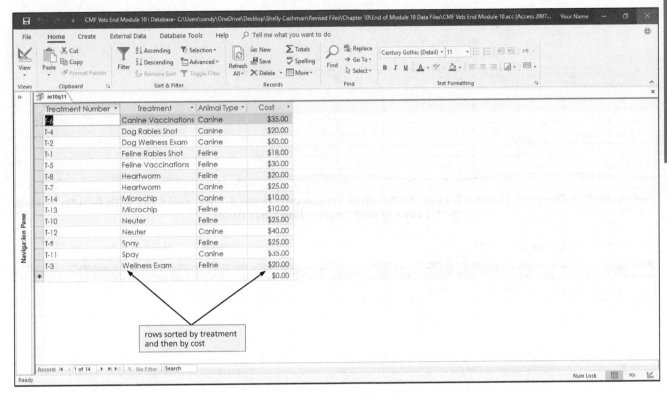

Figure 10–17b Results

 Experiment

- Try reversing the order of the sort keys to see the effect. View the results to see the effect of your choice. When finished, return to the original sorting order for both fields.

2

- Save the query as m10q12.

To Sort the Results in Descending Order

Why? *To show the results in high-to-low rather than low-to-high order, you sort in descending order.* To sort in descending order, you follow the name of the sort key with the DESC operator. The following steps list the treatment number, treatment, animal type, and cost for all treatments. CMF Vets wants the data to be sorted by descending cost within treatment. That is, within the treatments having the same name, the data is to be sorted further by cost in descending order.

1

- Return to SQL view and delete the previous query.

- Type `SELECT [Treatment Number],[Treatment], [Animal Type],[Cost]` as the first line.

- Type `FROM [Treatment Cost]` as the second line.

- Type `ORDER BY [Treatment],[Cost] DESC` as the third line, and then type a semicolon on the fourth line (Figure 10–18a).

 Do I need a comma between [Cost] and DESC?

No. In fact, you must not use a comma. If you did, SQL would assume that you want a field called DESC. Without the comma, SQL knows that the DESC operator indicates that the sort on the Cost field is to be in descending order.

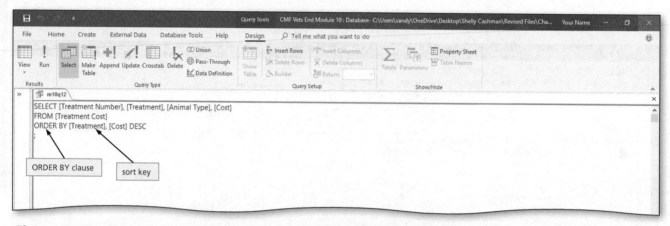

Figure 10–18a Query to List the Treatment Number, Treatment, Animal Type, and Cost with Results Sorted by Treatment and Descending Cost Order

- View the results (Figure 10–18b).

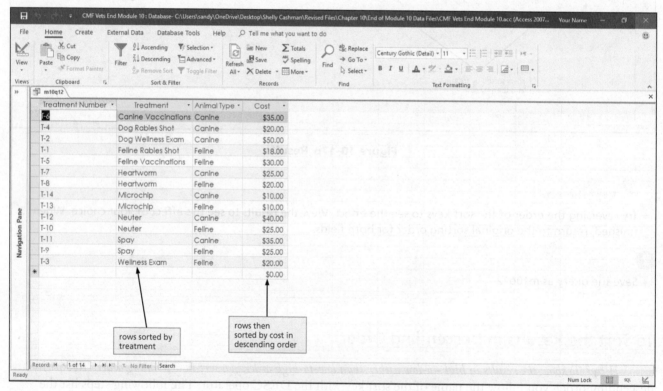

Figure 10–18b Results

- Save the query as m10q13.

To Omit Duplicates When Sorting

When you sort data, duplicates are normally included. For example, the query in Figure 10–19 sorts the Product Types in the Veterinary Vendors table. Because there are several vendors that supply vaccination products, CMF Vets does not find this useful and would like to eliminate these duplicate product types in this list. To do so, use the DISTINCT operator in the query. *Why? The DISTINCT operator eliminates duplicate values in the results of a query.* To use the operator, you follow the word DISTINCT with the field name in parentheses.

The following steps display the Product Types in the Veterinary Vendors table in Product ID order, but with any duplicates removed.

1

- Return to SQL view and delete the previous query.
- Type **SELECT DISTINCT ([Product Type])** as the first line of the command.
- Type **FROM [Veterinary Vendors]** as the second line.
- Type **ORDER BY [Product Type]** as the third line, and then type a semicolon on the fourth line (Figure 10–19a).

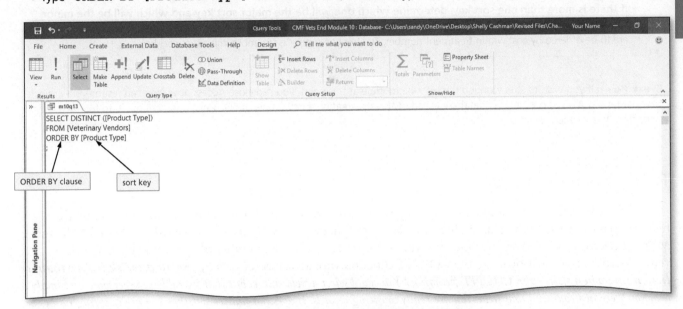

Figure 10–19a Query to List Product Types

- View the results (Figure 10–19b).

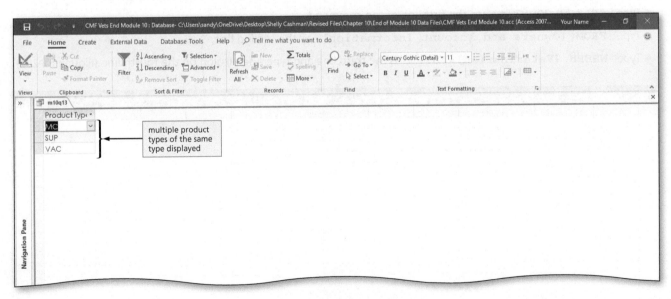

Figure 10–19b Results

2

- Save the query as m10q14. Return to the query.

How do you determine sorting when creating a query?

Examine the query or request to see if it contains words such as *order* or *sort* that would imply that the order of the query results is important. If so, you need to sort the query.

- **Determine whether data is to be sorted.** Examine the requirements for the query looking for words like *sorted by, ordered by, arranged by,* and so on.

- **Determine sort keys.** Look for the fields that follow sorted by, ordered by, or any other words that signify sorting. If the requirements for the query include the phrase, ordered by vendor name, then vendor name is a sort key.

- **If there is more than one sort key, determine which one will be the major sort key and which will be the minor sort key.** Look for words that indicate which field is more important. For example, if the requirements indicate that the results are to be ordered by cost within treatment number, Treatment Number is the more important sort key.

Break Point: If you wish to stop working through the module at this point, you can close Access now. You can resume the project later by starting Access, opening the database called CMF Vets, creating a new query in SQL view, and continuing to follow the steps from this location forward.

To Use a Built-In Function

SQL has built-in functions, also called aggregate functions, to perform various calculations. Similar to the functions you learned about in an earlier module, these functions in SQL are COUNT, SUM, AVG, MAX, and MIN, respectively. CMF Vets uses the following steps to determine the number of appointments assigned to veterinarian number B01 by using the COUNT function with an asterisk (*). *Why use an asterisk rather than a field name when using the COUNT function? You could select a field name, but that would be cumbersome and imply that you were just counting that field. You are really counting records. It does not matter whether you are counting names or street addresses or anything else.*

1

- Return to SQL view and delete the previous query.

- Type **SELECT COUNT(*)** as the first line of the command.

- Type **FROM [Owners and Account Information]** as the second line.

- Type **WHERE [Veterinarian]='B01'** as the third line and type a semicolon on the fourth line (Figure 10–20a).

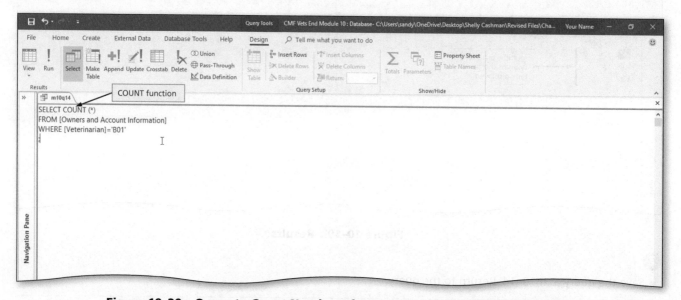

Figure 10–20a Query to Count Number of Appointments for Veterinarian B01

- View the results (Figure 10–20b).

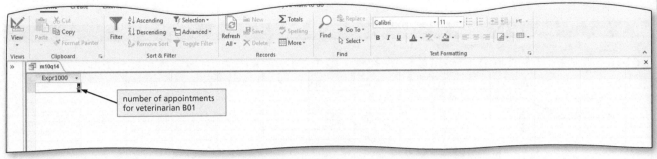

Figure 10–20b Results

Q&A

Why does Expr1000 appear in the column heading of the results?
Because the field is a computed field, it does not have a name. Access assigns a generic expression name. You can add a name for the field by including the AS clause in the query, and it is good practice to do so.

- Save the query as m10q15.

To Assign a Name to the Results of a Function

CMF Vets would prefer to have a more meaningful name than Expr1000 for the results of counting appointments. *Why? The default name of Expr1000 does not describe the meaning of the calculation.* Fortunately, just as you can assign a name to a calculation that includes two fields, you can assign a name to the results of a function. To do so, follow the expression for the function with the word AS and then the name to be assigned to the result. The following steps assign the name, Veterinarian Appointments, to the expression in the previous query.

1

- Return to SQL view and delete the previous query.
- Type `SELECT COUNT(*) AS [Veterinarian Appointments]` as the first line of the command.
- Type `FROM [Owners and Account Information]` as the second line.
- Type `WHERE [Veterinarian]='B01'` as the third line and type a semicolon on the fourth line (Figure 10–21a).

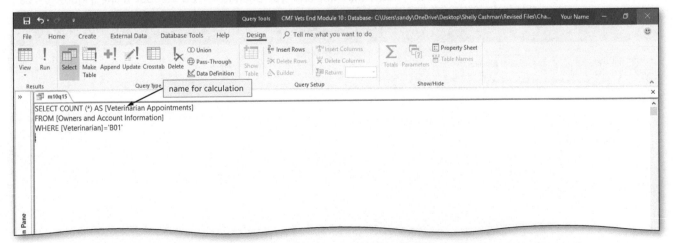

Figure 10–21a Query to Count Number of Appointments for Veterinarian B01 with Results Called Veterinarian Appointments

● View the results (Figure 10–21b). If necessary, increase the width of the Veterinarian Appointments: Count column to view the entire field name.

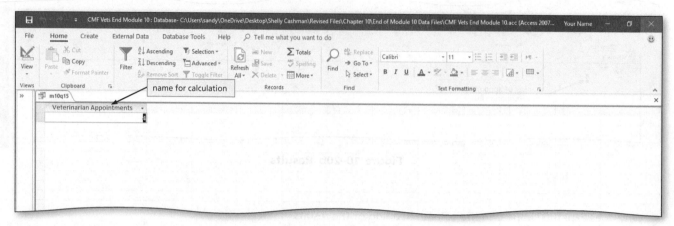

Figure 10–21b Results

● Save the query as m10q16.

To Use Multiple Functions in the Same Command

There are two differences between COUNT and SUM, other than the obvious fact that they are computing different statistics. First, in the case of SUM, you must specify the field for which you want a total, instead of an asterisk (*); second, the field must be numeric. *Why? If the field is not numeric, it does not make sense to calculate a sum. You could not calculate a sum of names or addresses, for example.* The following steps use both the COUNT and SUM functions to count the number of appointments whose veterinarian number is B01 and calculate the sum (total) of the appointment costs. The steps use the word AS to name COUNT(*) as Veterinarian Appointments and to name SUM([Cost]) as Total Due.

● Return to SQL view and delete the previous query.

● Type `SELECT COUNT(*) AS [Veterinarian Appointments], SUM([Cost]) AS [Total Due]` as the first line of the command.

● Type `FROM [Owners and Account Information]` as the second line.

● Type `WHERE [Veterinarian]='B01'` as the third line and type a semicolon on the fourth line (Figure 10–22a).

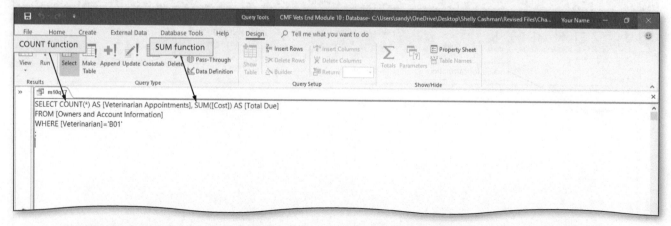

Figure 10–22a Query to Count Number of Appointments for Veterinarian B01 with Results Called Veterinarian Appointments and Calculate Cost with Results Called Total Due

- View the results (Figure 10–22b).

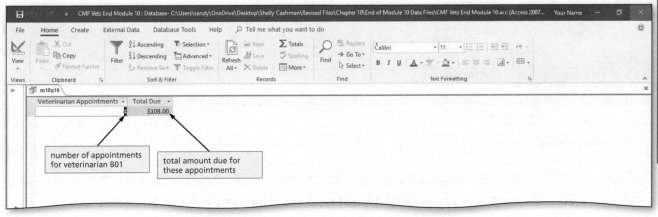

Figure 10–22b Results

 Experiment

- Try using the other functions in place of SUM. The use of AVG, MAX, and MIN is similar to SUM. The only difference is that a different statistic is calculated. In each case, view the results to see the effect of your choice. When finished, once again select SUM.

2

- Save the query as m10q17.

Grouping

Recall that grouping means creating groups of records that share some common characteristic. When you group rows, any calculations indicated in the SELECT command are performed for the entire group.

To Use Grouping

CMF Vets wants to calculate the totals of the Cost field, for Animal Types in the Appointments and Treatments table. To calculate the totals, the command will include the calculations, SUM([Cost]). To get totals for each animal type, the command will also include a **GROUP BY clause**, which consists of the words, GROUP BY, followed by the field used for grouping, in this case, Animal Type. *Why? Including GROUP BY Animal Type will cause the types of each animal to be grouped together; that is, all costs with the same animal type will form a group. Any statistics, such as animal type totals, appearing after the word SELECT will be calculated for each of these groups.* Using GROUP BY does not mean that the information will be sorted.

The following steps use the GROUP BY clause to produce the results CMF Vets wants. The steps also rename the cost as Animal Type Total.

1

- Return to SQL view and delete the previous query.

- Type `SELECT [Animal Type], SUM ([Cost]) AS [Animal Type Total]` as the first line.

- Type `FROM [Appointments and Treatments]` as the second line.

- Type `GROUP BY [Animal Type]` as the third line.

- Type `;` as the fourth line (Figure 10–23a).

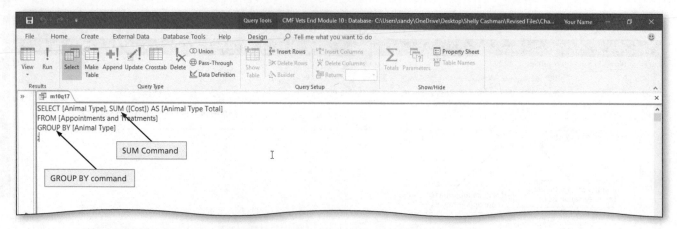

Figure 10–23a Query to Group By Animal Type and Display Cost Totals for Each Group

Q&A

What is the purpose of the GROUP BY clause?

The GROUP BY clause causes the rows to be grouped by the indicated field. With this GROUP BY clause, the rows will be grouped by Account Manager Number.

- View the results (Figure 10–23b). If necessary, increase the width of the Animal Type Total column to display the entire field name.

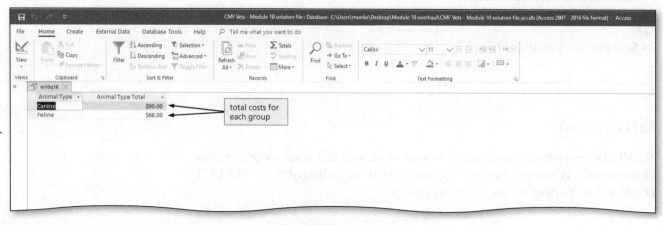

Figure 10–23b Results

- Save the query as m10q18.

Grouping Requirements

BTW

Wildcards

Other implementations of SQL do not use the asterisk (*) and question mark (?) wildcards. In SQL for Oracle and for SQL Server, the percent sign (%) is used as a wildcard to represent any collection of characters. In Oracle and SQL Server, the WHERE clause shown in Figure 10-11a would be WHERE [City] LIKE 'G%'.

When rows are grouped, one line of output is produced for each group. The only output that SQL can display is statistics that are calculated for the group or fields whose values are the same for all rows in a group. For example, when grouping rows by animal type as in the previous query, it is appropriate to display the animal type, because the type in one row in a group must be the same as the type in any other row in the group. It is appropriate to display the sum of the Costs because they are statistics calculated for the group. It would not be appropriate to display a treatment, however, because the treatment varies on the rows in a group; the animal type is associated with many accounts. SQL would not be able to determine which treatment to display for the group. SQL will display an error message if you attempt to display a field that is not appropriate, such as the treatment.

To Restrict the Groups That Appear

In some cases, CMF Vets might want to display only certain groups. For example, management may want to display only the animal type for which the sum of the current due amounts are less than $200. This restriction does not apply to individual rows, but instead to groups. You cannot use a WHERE clause to accomplish this restriction. *Why? WHERE applies only to rows, not groups.*

Fortunately, SQL provides the **HAVING clause**, which functions with groups similarly to the way WHERE functions with rows. The HAVING clause consists of the word HAVING followed by a criterion. It is used in the following steps, which restrict the groups to be included to those for which the sum of the cost is less than $200.

- Return to SQL view.
- Click the end of the third line (GROUP BY [Animal Type]) and press the ENTER key to insert a new blank line.
- Click the beginning of the new blank line, and then type **HAVING SUM([Cost]) <200** as the new fourth line. See Figure 10–24a.

Q&A | What is the purpose of the HAVING clause?
The HAVING clause restricts the groups that will be included to only those satisfying the indicated criteria.

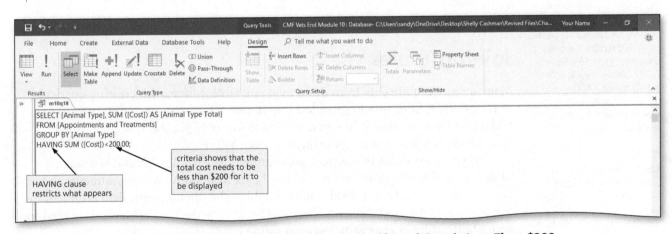

Figure 10–24a Query to Display Total Cost if Total Cost is Less Than $200

- View the results (Figure 10–24b).

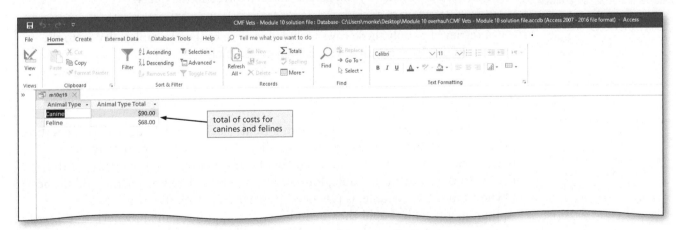

Figure 10–24b Results

- Save the query as m10q19.

How do you determine grouping when creating a query?

Examine the question or request to determine whether records should be organized by some common characteristic.

- **Determine whether data is to be grouped in some fashion.** Examine the requirements for the query to see if they contain individual rows or information about groups of rows.

- **Determine the field or fields on which grouping is to take place.** By which field is the data to be grouped? Look to see if the requirements indicate a field along with several group calculations.

- **Determine which fields or calculations are appropriate to display.** When rows are grouped, one line of output is produced for each group. The only output that can appear are statistics that are calculated for the group or fields whose values are the same for all rows in a group. For example, it would make sense to display the manager number, because all the accounts in the group have the same manager number. It would not make sense to display the account number, because the account number will vary from one row in a group to another. SQL could not determine which account number to display for the group.

BTW

Inner Joins

A join that compares the tables in the FROM clause and lists only those rows that satisfy the condition in the WHERE clause is called an inner join. SQL has an INNER JOIN clause. You could replace the query shown in Figure 10–26a with FROM Owners INNER JOIN Appointments ON Owners.[Owner ID] = Appointments. Owner to get the same results as shown in Figure 10–26b.

BTW

Outer Joins

Sometimes you need to list all the rows from one of the tables in a join, regardless of whether they match any rows in the other table. For example, you can perform a join on the Owners and Appointments tables but display all records in Appointments—but display only those records from Owners where the joined fields are equal. This type of join is called an outer join. In a left outer join, all rows from the table on the left (the table listed first in the query) will be included regardless of whether they match rows from the table on the right (the table listed second in the query). Rows from the right will be included only if they match. In a right outer join, all rows from the table on the right will be included regardless of whether they match rows from the table on the left. The SQL clause for a left outer join is LEFT JOIN and the SQL clause for a right outer join is RIGHT JOIN.

Break Point: If you wish to stop working through the module at this point, you can close Access now. You can resume the project later by starting Access, opening the database called CMF Vets, creating a new query in SQL view, and continuing to follow the steps from this location forward.

Joining Tables

Many queries require data from more than one table. Just as with creating queries in Design view, SQL should provide a way to **join** tables, that is, to find rows in two tables that have identical values in matching fields. In SQL, this is accomplished through appropriate criteria following the word WHERE.

If you want to list the owners, appointment date, owner ID, and last name of the owner for all appointments, you need data from both the Appointments and Owners tables. The Owner field is in both tables, the Appointment field is only in the Appointment table, and the Last Name field is only in the Owners table. You need to access both tables in your SQL query, as follows:

1. In the SELECT clause, you indicate all fields you want to appear.

2. In the FROM clause, you list all tables involved in the query.

3. In the WHERE clause, you give the criterion that will restrict the data to be retrieved to only those rows included in both of the two tables, that is, to the rows that have common values in matching fields.

Qualifying Fields

If there is a problem with matching fields, such as a field named Owners that exists in both tables, it is necessary to **qualify** Owners, that is, to specify to which field in which table you are referring. You do this by preceding the name of the field with the name of the table, followed by a period. The Owner ID field in the Owners table, for example, is [Owners].[Owner ID]. And, the owner field in the Appointments table would then be indicated as Appointments.[Owner]. In this case given the fact that one field name is Owner and the other field name is Owner ID, it is not necessary to qualify the fields, however, it is also permissible to qualify fields, even if there is no confusion. For example, instead of [Owner Last Name], you could type [Owners].[Owner Last Name] to indicate the Last Name field in the Owners table. Some people prefer to qualify all fields, and this is not a bad approach. In this text, you will only qualify fields when it is necessary to do so and for learning purposes.

To Join Tables

CMF Vets wants to list the appointment dates, owner, owner ID, and last name of the owner for all appointments. The following steps create a query to join the tables using an INNER JOIN. *Why? The data comes from two tables.* The steps also order the results by appointment date.

- Return to SQL view and delete the previous query.

- Type `SELECT Appointments.[Owner], Appointments.[Appointment Date], Owners.[Owner  ID], Owners.[Owner Last Name]` as the first line of the command (be sure to type two spaces between Owner and ID).

- Type `FROM Appointments INNER JOIN Owners ON Appointments.Owner = Owners.[Owner ID]` as the second line (include two spaces between Owner and ID).

Q&A Why does the FROM clause contain more than one table?
The query involves fields from both tables.

- Type `ORDER BY Appointments.[Appointment Date]` as the third line, and then type a semicolon on the fourth line (Figure 10–25a).

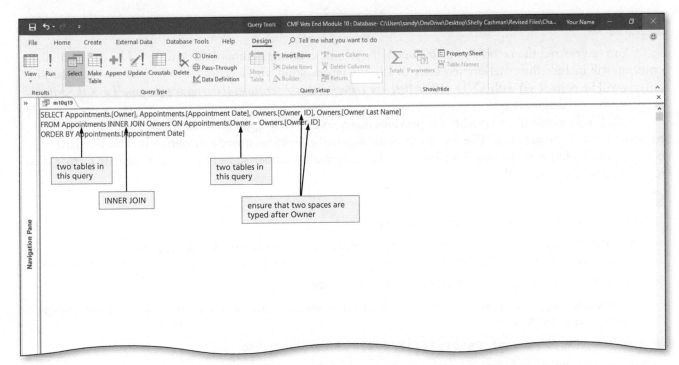

Figure 10–25a Query to Join Tables and Order by Appointment Date

• View the results (Figure 10–25b).

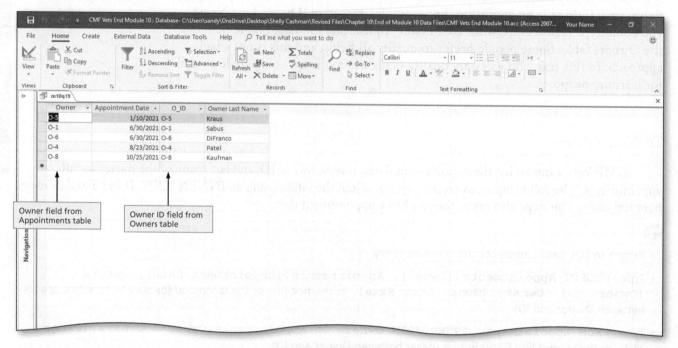

Figure 10–25b Results

• Save the query as m10q20.

To Restrict the Records in a Join

You can restrict the records to be included in a join by creating a compound criterion. The compound criterion will include the criterion necessary to join the tables along with a criterion to restrict the records. The criteria will be connected with AND. *Why? Both the criterion that determines the records to be joined and the criterion to restrict the records must be true.*

CMF Vets would like to modify the previous query so that only appointments whose start date is prior to June 15, 2021, are included. The following steps modify the previous query appropriately. The WHERE command be included as the join. The date is enclosed between number signs (#), which is the date format used in the Access version of SQL.

• Return to SQL view and delete the previous query.

• Type `SELECT Appointments.Owner, Appointments.[Appointment Date], Owners.[Owner ID], Owners.[Owner Last Name]` for the first line (include two spaces between Owner and ID).

• Type `FROM Appointments, Owners` for the second line.

• Type `WHERE [Appointments].[Owner]=Owners.[Owner  ID]` as the third line (include two spaces between Owner and ID).

• Type `AND [Appointment Date]>#6/15/2021#` for the fourth line.

• Type `ORDER BY Appointments.[Appointment Date]` as the fifth line, and then type a semicolon on the sixth line (Figure 10–26a).

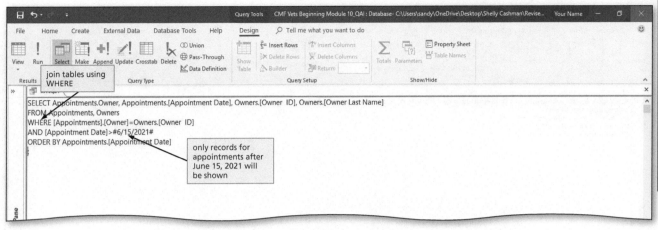

Figure 10–26a Query to Display Appointments After June 15, 2021

Q&A Could I use other formats for the date in the criterion?
Yes. You could type #June 15, 2021# or #15-June-2021#.

● View the results (Figure 10–26b).

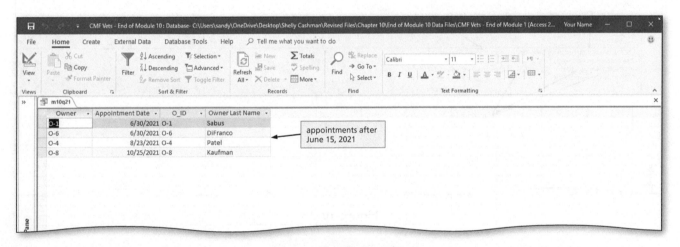

Figure 10–26b Results

2

● Save the query as m10q21.

Aliases

When tables appear in the FROM clause, you can give each table an **alias**, or an alternative name, that you can use in the rest of the statement. You create an alias by typing the name of the table, pressing the spacebar and then typing the name of the alias. No commas or periods are necessary to separate the two names.

You can use an alias for two basic reasons: for simplicity or to join a table to itself. Figures 10–27 and 10–28 show the same query, but Figure 10–28 assigns the letter A as an alias for the Appointment table and the letter O is assigned as an alias for the Owners table. The query in Figure 10–28 is less complex. Whenever you need to qualify a field name, you can use the alias. Thus, you only need to type A.[Owner] rather than Appointments.Owner.

BTW
Qualifying Fields
There is no space on either side of the period that is used to separate the table name from the field name. Adding a space will result in an error message.

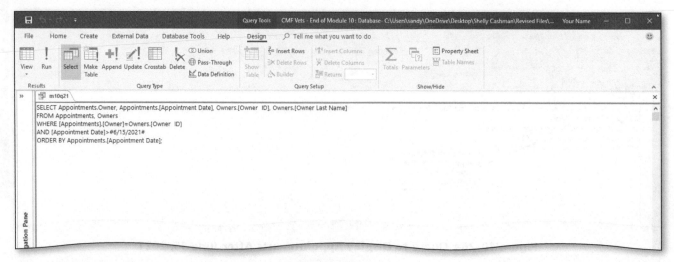

Figure 10–27

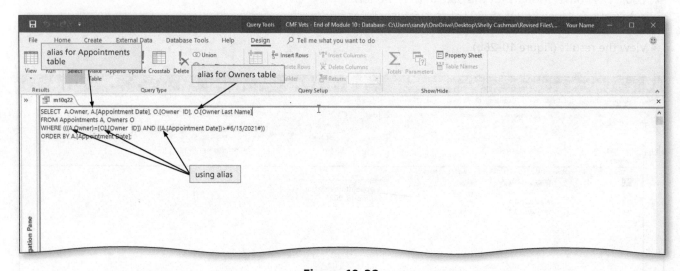

Figure 10–28

To Join a Table to Itself

The other use of aliases is in joining a table to itself. An example of this type of join would enable CMF Vets to find vendor ID numbers and names for every vendor located in the same city. One such pair, for example, would be vendor ID 1 (Duncan Veterinary Supply) and vendor ID 3 (Mayes Supply LLC) because both accounts are located in the same city (Dolores). Because there are two vendors in Dolores, you will see the vendors for Dolores appear on more than one line in the results.

Another example of a pair would be vendor ID 4 (Rodriquez Vet Supplies) and vendor ID 2 (Gaines Pet Supplies) because both accounts are also located in the same city (Blanding). If there were two Veterinary Vendors tables in the database, CMF Vets could obtain the results they want by simply joining the two Veterinary Vendors tables and looking for rows where the cities were the same. Even though there is only one Veterinary Vendors table, you can actually treat the Veterinary Vendors table as two tables in the query by creating two aliases. You would change the FROM clause to:

```
FROM [Veterinary Vendors] D, [Veterinary Vendors] B
```

SQL treats this clause as a query of two tables. The clause assigns the first Veterinary Vendors table the letter, D, as an alias. It also assigns the letter, B, as an alias for the Veterinary Vendors table. The fact that both tables are really the single Veterinary Vendors table is not a problem. The following steps assign two aliases (D and B) to the Veterinary Vendors table and list the vendor ID number and vendor name of both accounts as well as the city in which both are located. The steps also include a criterion to ensure D.[ID Number] < B.[ID Number].

Why? *If you did not include this criterion, the query would contain four times as many results. On the first row in the results, for example, the first vendor ID number is 1 and the second is 3. Without this criterion, there would be a row on which both the first and second vendor ID numbers are 1, a row on which both are 3, and a row on which the first is 1 and the second is 3. This criterion only selects the one row on which the first vendor ID number (1) is less than the second vendor number (3).*

- Return to SQL view and delete the previous query.

- Type `SELECT D.ID, D.[Vendor Name], B.ID, B.[Vendor Name], D.City` as the first line of the command to select the fields to display in the query result.

- Type `FROM [Veterinary Vendors]AS D,[Veterinary Vendors]AS B` as the second line to create the aliases for the first and second Veterinary Vendor tables.

- Type `WHERE D.[City]=B.[City]` as the third line to indicate that the cities in each table must match.

- Type `AND D.[ID]<B.[ID]` as the fourth line to indicate that the account number from the first table must be less than the account number from the second table.

- Type `ORDER BY D.[ID], B.[ID]` as the fifth line to ensure that the results are sorted by the account number from the first table and further sorted by the account number from the second table.

- Type a semicolon on the sixth line (Figure 10–29a).

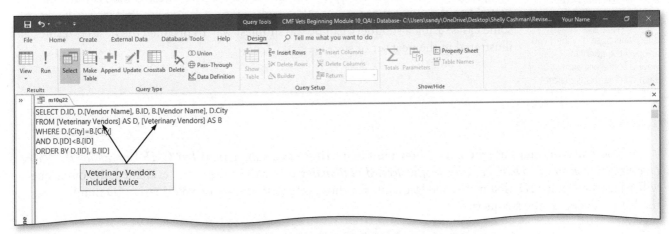

Figure 10–29a Query for Vendors in the Same City

- View the results (Figure 10–29).

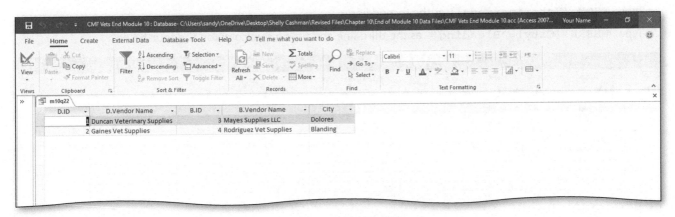

Figure 10–29b Results

- Save the query as m10q22.

How do you determine criteria when creating a query?

Examine the query or request to determine any restrictions or conditions that records must satisfy to be included in the results.

- **Determine the fields involved in the criteria.** For any criterion, determine the fields that are included. Determine the data types for these fields. If the criterion uses a value that corresponds to a Text field, enclose the value in single quotation marks. If the criterion uses a date, enclose the value between number signs (for example, #6/15/2021#).

- **Determine comparison operators.** When fields are being compared to other fields or to specific values, determine the appropriate comparison operator (equals, less than, greater than, and so on). If a wildcard is involved, then the query will use the LIKE operator.

- **Determine join criteria.** If tables are being joined, determine the fields that must match.

- **Determine compound criteria.** If more than one criterion is involved, determine whether all individual criteria are to be true, in which case you will use the AND operator, or whether only one individual criterion needs to be true, in which case you will use the OR operator.

BTW
SELECT clause
When you enter field names in a SELECT clause, you do not need to enter a space after the comma. Access inserts a space after the comma when you save the query and close it. When you re-open the query in SQL view, a space will appear after each comma that separates fields in the SELECT clause.

Subqueries

It is possible to place one query inside another. You will place the query shown in Figure 10–30 inside another query. When you have done so, it will be called a **subquery**, which is an inner query, contained within parentheses, that is evaluated first. Then the outer query can use the results of the subquery to find its results. In some cases, using a subquery can be the simplest way to produce the desired results, as illustrated in the next set of steps.

To Use a Subquery

The following steps use the query shown in Figure 10–30 as a subquery. *Why? CMF Vets can use this query to select veterinarians who have at least one office located in Blanding.* After the subquery is evaluated, the outer query will select the vendor ID, first name, and last name for those veterinarians whose veterinarian ID number is in the list produced by the subquery.

1

- Return to SQL view and delete the previous query.

- Type `SELECT [Veterinarian ID], [First Name], [Last Name],[City]` as the first line of the command.

- Type `FROM [Veterinarians]` as the second line.

- Type `WHERE [City]='Blanding'` as the third line and type a semicolon on the fourth line.

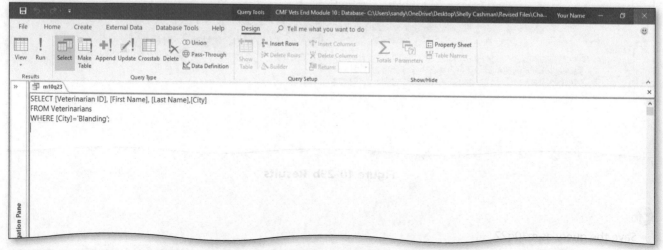

Figure 10–30a Query for Veterinarians in the Same City

• View the results (Figure 10–30b).

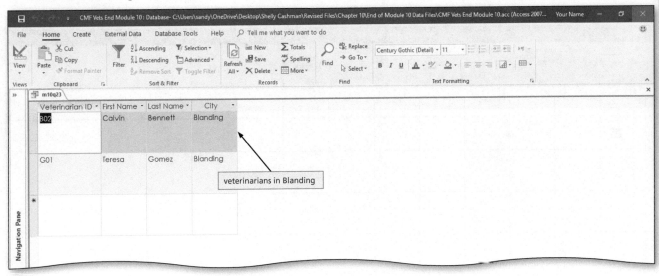

Figure 10–30b Results

②

• Return to SQL view and delete the previous query.

• Type **SELECT [Veterinarian ID],[First Name],
  [Last Name]** as the first line of the command.

• Type **FROM [Veterinarians]** as the second line.

• Type **WHERE [Veterinarian ID] IN** as the third line.

• Type **(SELECT [Veterinarian ID]** as the fourth line.

• Type **FROM [Veterinarians]** as the fifth line.

• Type **WHERE [City]='Blanding')** as the sixth line and type a semicolon on the seventh line.

BTW

SQL Standards

The International Standards Organization (ISO) and the American National Standards Institute (ANSI) recognize SQL as a standardized language. Different relational database management systems may support the entire set of standardized SQL commands or only a subset.

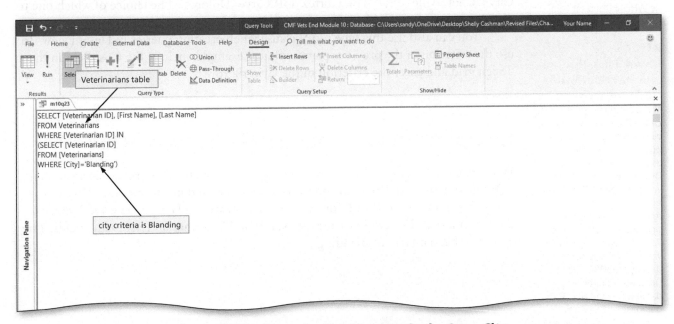

Figure 10–31a Query for Veterinarians in the Same City

• View the results (Figure 10–31).

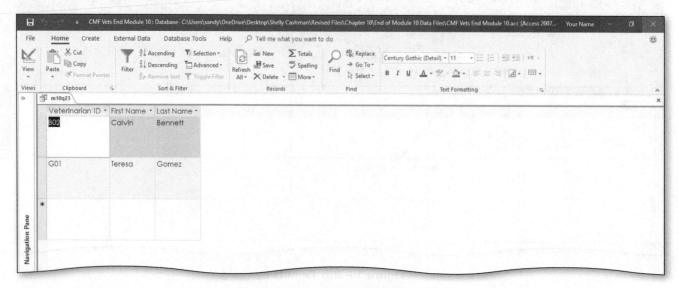

Figure 10–31b Results

• Save the query as m10q23.

Using an IN Clause

The query in Figure 10–31 uses an IN clause with a subquery. You can also use an IN clause with a list as an alternative to an OR criterion when the OR criterion involves a single field. For example, to find accounts whose city is Blanding, Dolores, Centerville, or Cortez, the criterion using IN would be City IN ('Blanding', 'Dolores', 'Centerville', 'Cortez'). The corresponding OR criterion would be City='Blanding' OR City= 'Centerville' OR City= 'Cortez' OR City= 'Dolores'. The choice of which one to use is a matter of personal preference.

You can also use this type of IN clause when creating queries in Design view. To use the criterion in the previous paragraph, for example, include the Cost field in the design grid and enter the criterion in the Criteria row.

Comparison with Access-Generated SQL

When you create a query in Design view, Access automatically creates a corresponding SQL query that is similar to the queries you have created in this module. The Access query shown in Figure 10–32, for example, was created in Design view and includes the Veterinarian ID, Veterinarian First Name, and Veterinarian Last Name fields. The City field has a criterion (Blanding).

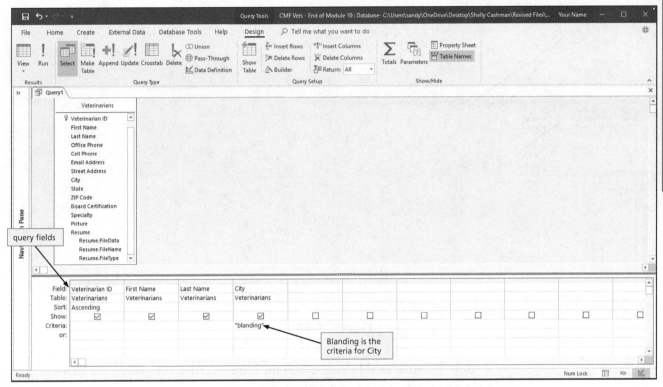

Figure 10–32a Query to List the Veterinarian ID Number, First Name, and Last Name for Vendors in Blanding

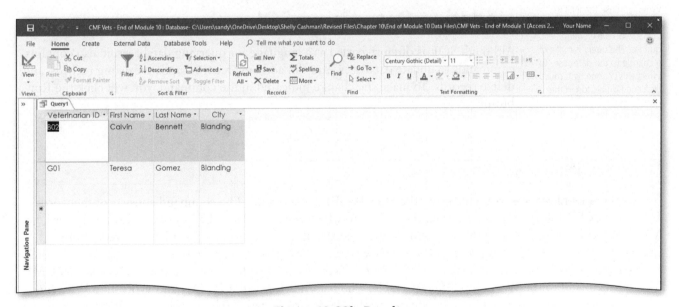

Figure 10–32b Results

The SQL query that Access generates in correspondence to the Design view query is shown in Figure 10–33. The query is very similar to the queries you have entered, but there are three slight differences. First, the Veterinarian.[Vendor ID] Veterinarian.[First Name] and Veterinarian.[Last Name] fields are qualified, even though they do not need to be; only one table is involved in the query, so no qualification is necessary. Second, the City field is not enclosed in square brackets. The field is legitimately not enclosed in square brackets because there are no spaces or other special characters in the field name. Finally, there are extra parentheses in the criteria.

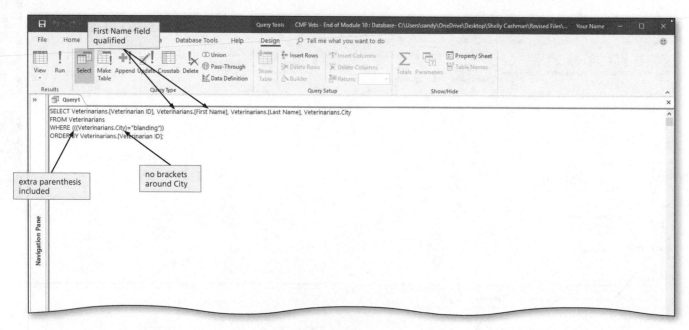

Figure 10–33

Both the style used by Access and the style you have been using are legitimate. The choice of style is a personal preference.

BTW
Action Queries
When you use the INSERT, UPDATE, or DELETE commands in SQL, you are creating action queries. The query is making a change to the database. To effect this change, you must click the Run button in the Results group.

Updating Data Using SQL

Although SQL is often regarded as a language for querying databases, it also contains commands to update databases. You can add new records, update existing records, and delete records. To make the change indicated in the command, you will click the Run button.

To Use an INSERT Command

You can add records to a table using the SQL INSERT command. The command consists of the words INSERT INTO followed by the name of the table into which the record is to be inserted. Next is the word VALUE, followed by the values for the fields in the record. Values for text fields must be enclosed within quotation marks. *Why? Just as you needed to type the quotation marks when you used text data in a criterion, you need to do the same when you use text values in an INSERT INTO command.* The following steps add a record that CMF Vets wants to add to the Workshop Offerings table. The record is for owner ID O-4 and Workshop W01 and indicates that the workshop will be offered for a total of 04 hours, of which 0 hours have already been spent.

- If necessary, return to SQL view and delete the existing query.
- Type `INSERT INTO [Workshop Offerings]` as the first line of the command.
- Type `VALUES ('O-4', 'W01',04,0)` as the second line.
- Type a semicolon on the third line (Figure 10–34).

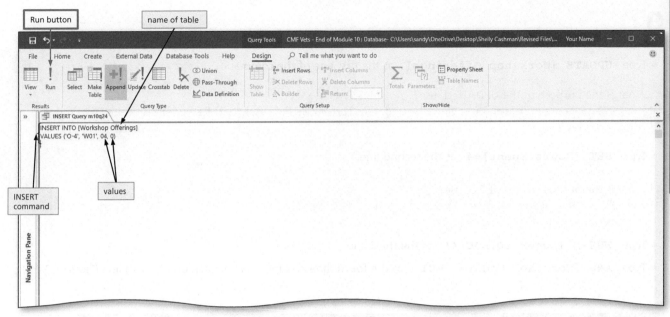

Figure 10–34

Q&A

What is the purpose of the INSERT INTO clause?
The clause indicates the table into which data is to be inserted.

What is the purpose of the VALUES clause?
The VALUES clause, which typically extends over two lines, indicates the values that are to be inserted into a new record in the table. For readability, it is common to place the word VALUES on one line and the actual values on a separate line.

- Run the query by clicking the Run button (Query Tools Design tab | Results group).
- When Access displays a message indicating the number of records to be inserted (appended), click the Yes button to insert the records.

Q&A

I clicked the View button and did not get the message. Do I need to click the Run button?
Yes. You are making a change to the database, so you must click the Run button, or the change will not be made.

How can I see if the record was actually inserted?
Use a SELECT query to view the records in the Workshop Offerings table or you can just open the table and view the records.

- Save the query as INSERT Query m10q24.

To Use an UPDATE Command

You can update records in SQL by using the UPDATE command. The command consists of UPDATE, followed by the name of the table in which records are to be updated. Next, the command contains one or more SET clauses, which consist of the word SET, followed by a field to be updated, an equal sign, and the new value. The SET clause indicates the change to be made. Finally, the query includes a WHERE clause. *Why? When you execute the command, all records in the indicated table that satisfy the criterion will be updated.* The following steps use the SQL UPDATE command to perform an update requested by CMF Vets. Specifically, they change the Hours Spent to 4 on all records in the Workshop Offerings table on which the account number is O-4 and the workshop code is W01. Because the combination of the Account Number and Workshop Code fields is the primary key, only one record will be updated.

- Delete the existing query.

- Type **UPDATE [Workshop Offerings]**   as the first line of the command.

Q&A
What is the purpose of the UPDATE clause?
The UPDATE clause indicates the table to be updated. This clause indicates that the update is to the Workshop Offerings table.

- Type **SET [Hours Spent]=4**   as the second line.

Q&A
What is the purpose of the SET clause?
The SET clause indicates the field to be changed as well as the new value. This SET clause indicates that the hours spent is to be set to 4.

- Type **WHERE [Owner ID]='O-4'**   as the third line.

- Type **AND [Workshop Code]= 'W01'**   as the fourth line and type a semicolon on the fifth line (Figure 10–35).

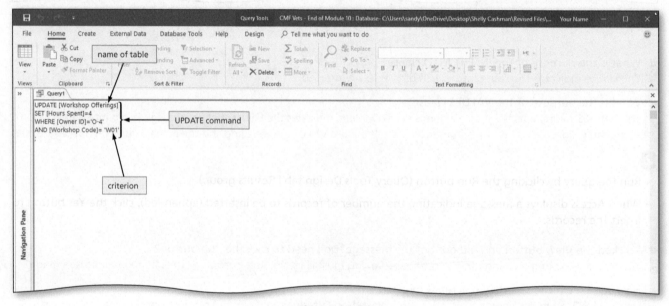

Figure 10–35

Q&A
Do I need to change a field to a specific value such as 4?
No. You could use an expression. For example, to add $100 to the Current Due amount, the SET clause would be SET [Current Due]=[Current Due]+100.

- Run the query.

- When Access displays a message indicating the number of records to be updated, click the Yes button to update the records.

Q&A
How can I see if the update actually occurred?
Use a SELECT query to view the records in the Workshop Offerings table or open the table and view the results.

- Save the query as m10q25.

To Use a DELETE Command

You can delete records in SQL using the DELETE command. The command consists of DELETE FROM, followed by the name of the table from which records are to be deleted. Finally, you include a WHERE clause to specify the criteria. ***Why?*** *When you execute the command, all records in the indicated table that satisfy the criterion will be deleted.* The following steps use the SQL DELETE command to delete all records in the Workshop Offerings table on which the Owner ID is O-4 and the workshop code is W01, as CMF Vets has requested. Because the combination of the Account Number and Workshop Code fields is the primary key, only one record will be deleted.

- Delete the existing query.

- Type `DELETE FROM [Workshop Offerings]` as the first line of the command.

◄ What is the purpose of the DELETE clause?
Q&A The DELETE clause indicates the table from which records will be deleted. This DELETE clause indicates that records will be deleted from the Workshop Offerings table.

- Type `WHERE [Owner ID]='O-4'` as the second line.

- Type `AND [Workshop Code]='W01'` as the third line and type a semicolon on the fourth line (Figure 10–36).

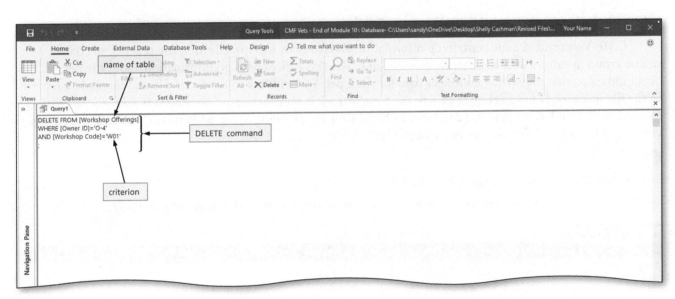

Figure 10–36

- Run the query.

- When Access displays a message indicating the number of records to be deleted, click the Yes button to delete the records.

◄ How can I see if the deletion actually occurred?
Q&A Use a SELECT query to view the records in the Workshop Offerings table.

- Save the query as m10q26.

- Close the query.

CONSIDER THIS

How do you determine any update operations to be performed?
Examine the database to determine if records must be added, updated, and/or deleted.

- **Determine INSERT operations.** Determine whether new records need to be added. Determine to which table they should be added.

- **Determine UPDATE operations.** Determine changes that need to be made to existing records. Which fields need to be changed? Which tables contain these fields? What criteria identify the rows that need to be changed?

- **Determine DELETE operations.** Determine which tables contain records that are to be deleted. What criteria identify the rows that need to be deleted?

Linking a Table to an Another File

Linking an Access database to data in other programs, such as an Excel worksheet, lets you work with this data in Access without having to maintain a copy of the Excel data in the database. When linking to an Excel workbook, or a named range in Excel, Access creates a new table in the database that is linked to the source cells. New records can be added, records edited, and records deleted in the Excel file, but only in Excel. You cannot make changes to the Excel data in the linked Access table.

To Link a Table to an Outside Data Source

CMF Vets created a file containing information about rescue groups, allowing the practice to contact a rescue group in case an animal is left outside one of CMF Vets offices with no information about the pet, or if a client indicated that they could no longer care for their pet. You will link to the Excel file and then add a record to the file in Excel. *Why? Linking to an external file allows you to store and access information in other file formats.* When you link an Excel file in the database, an Excel icon appears next to the table name. The following steps create a link to the CMF Vets Rescue Groups file.

1

- With the CMF Vets database open, click the External Data tab.

- Click the New Data Source button arrow and point to From File, and then click Excel (Figure 10–37).

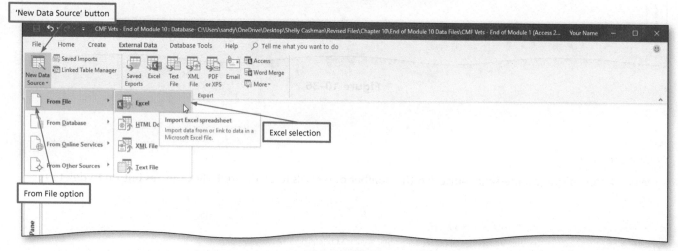

Figure 10–37

2

- Click the Browse button in the Get External Data—Excel Spreadsheet dialog box, navigate to the CMF Vets Rescue Groups Excel file, click to select it, and then click Open.

- Click the 'Link to the data source by creating a linked table.' option button (Figure 10–38).

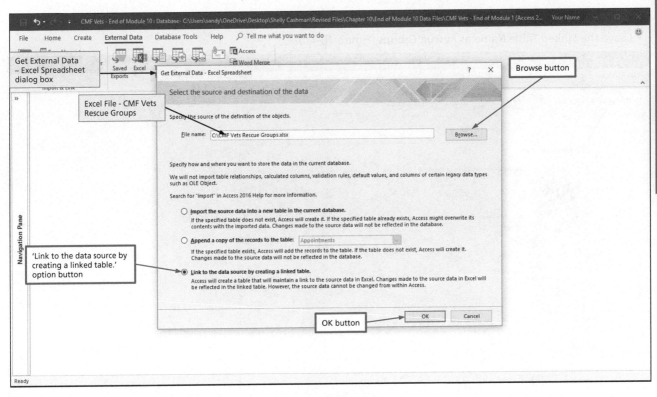

Figure 10–38

3

- Click OK.
- Check the First Row Contains Column Headings check box to select it and then click Next (Figure 10–39).

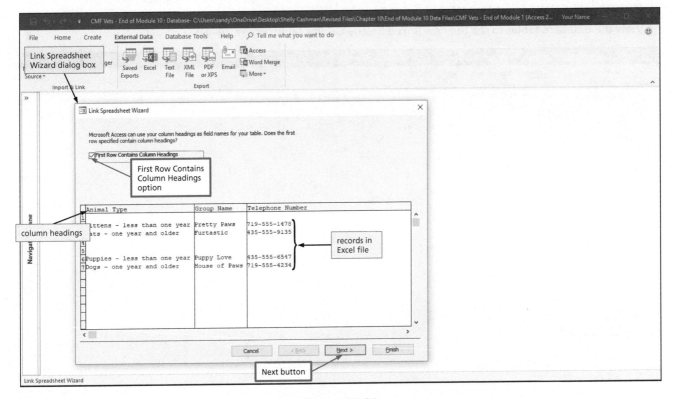

Figure 10–39

• Leave the Linked Table Name as Rescue Groups (Figure 10–40).

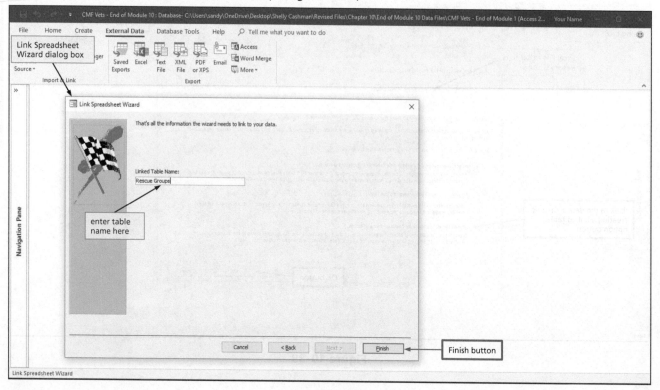

Figure 10–40

• Click Finish.
• Click OK in the Link Spreadsheet Wizard dialog box.
• View the database tables to see the new linked Rescue Groups table (Figure 10–41).

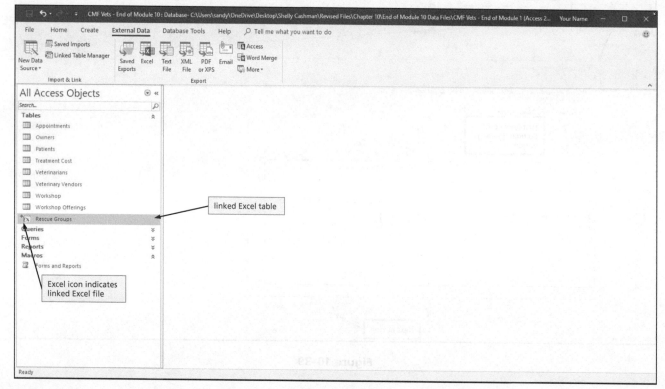

Figure 10–41

6

• Open the table to view the four records (Figure 10–42).

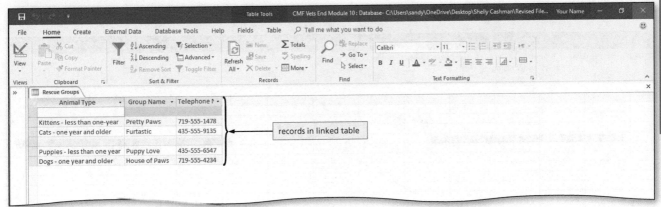

Figure 10–42

7

• Click in a cell with no data and try to add a record. Notice that Access prohibits you from entering data.

• Click the Rescue Groups table Close button to close the table in Access.

• Open Excel, navigate to the Data Files, open the CMF Vets Rescue Groups spreadsheet, and add the following record to the worksheet as the fifth row:

Kittens – less than one-year   Tall Tails Rescue   888-553-2713

• Save the Excel file and exit Excel.

8

• Open the Rescue Groups table and view the revised file in Access (Figure 10–43).

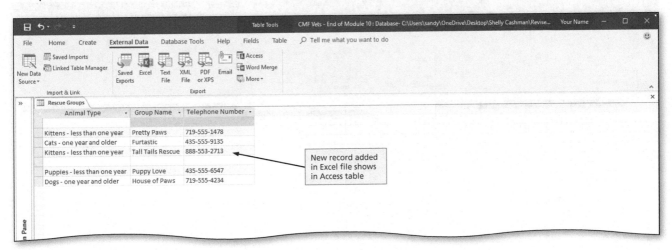

Figure 10–43

To Change Tab Order in a Form

A form created with a form tool or the Form Wizard places the fields in the order they appear in the table design. In many cases, this field order is sufficient. However, if the fields are rearranged for a more logical data entry, the form needs modification to arrange the order of movement through the fields in the form. This order is called the tab order. The following steps change the order of the tab stops in the Veterinarians form. *Why? CMF Vets wants users to tab to the Cell Phone field before the Office Phone field.*

- Open the Veterinarians form in Design view.
- Display the Design tab and in the Tools group, click the Tab Order button to display the dialog box (Figure 10–44).

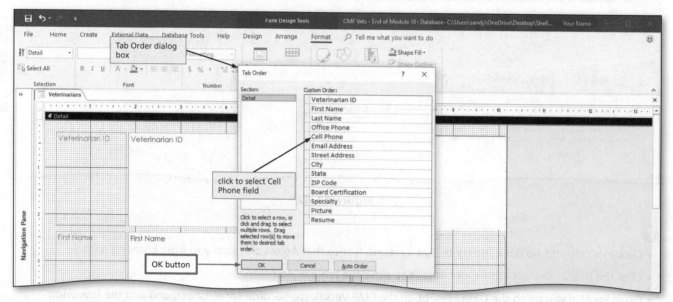

Figure 10–44

- Click the gray box to the left of Cell Phone to select the Cell Phone field.
- Drag the Cell Phone field by pointing to the gray box to the left of the field name and dragging it below the Last Name field (Figure 10–45).

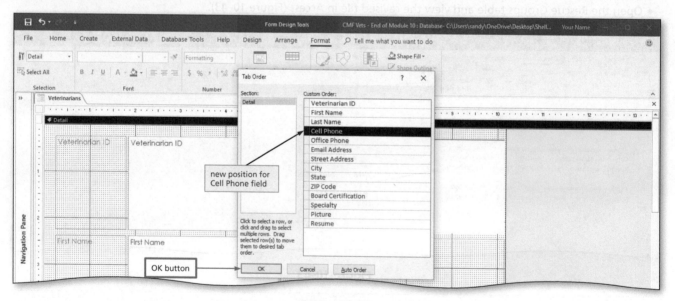

Figure 10–45

- Click OK to close the Tab Order dialog box.
- Save the changes to the Veterinarians form.

- Switch to Design view to test the results by clicking in the first field and pressing Tab to move to the other fields. If necessary, use the procedure described in the previous step to modify the tab order.

To Restore the Font Size

BTW
Datasheet Font Size
You also can use the Access Options dialog box to change the default font and font size for datasheets. To do so, click Datasheet in the Access Options dialog box and make the desired changes in the Default font area.

Earlier you changed the font size from its default setting of 10 to 11 so the SQL queries would be easier to read. Unless you prefer to retain this new setting, you should change the setting back to the default. The following steps restore the font size to its default setting.

1 Click File on the ribbon to open the Backstage view.

2 Click Options to display the Access Options dialog box.

3 If necessary, click Object Designers to display the Object Designer options.

4 In the Query design area, click the Size box arrow, and then click 10 in the list that appears to change the size back to 10.

5 Click the OK button to close the Access Options dialog box.

6 If desired, sign out of your Microsoft account.

7 sam⬆ Exit Access.

Summary

In this module you have learned to create SQL queries, include fields in a query, use criteria involving both numeric and text fields as well as use compound criteria, use computed fields and rename the computation, sort the results of a query, use the built-in functions, group records in a query and also restrict the groups that appear in the results, join tables and restrict the records in a join, and use subqueries. You looked at a SQL query that was generated automatically by Access. Then, you used the INSERT, UPDATE, and DELETE commands to update data. You learned how to create a table in Access that is linked to an Excel spreadsheet. Finally, you learned to change the Tab Order in a form.

CONSIDER THIS: PLAN AHEAD

What decisions will you need to make when creating your own SQL queries?
Use these guidelines as you complete the assignments in this module and create your own queries outside of this class.

1. Select the fields for the query.

a. Examine the requirements for the query you are constructing to determine which fields are to be included.

2. Determine which table or tables contain these fields.

a. For each field, determine the table in which it is located.

3. Determine criteria.

a. Determine any criteria that data must satisfy to be included in the results.

b. If there are more than two tables in the query, determine the criteria to be used to ensure the data matches correctly.

4. Determine sort order.

a. Is the data to be sorted in some way?

b. If so, by what field or fields is it to be sorted?

5. Determine grouping.

a. Is the data to be grouped in some way?

b. If so, by what field is it to be grouped?

c. Identify any calculations to be made for the group.

6. Determine any update operations to be performed.

a. Determine whether rows need to be inserted, changed, or deleted.

b. Determine the tables involved.

STUDENT ASSIGNMENTS

CONSIDER THIS

How should you submit solutions to questions in the assignments identified with a symbol?

Every assignment in this book contains one or more questions identified with a symbol. These questions require you to think beyond the assigned database. Present your solutions to the questions in the format required by your instructor. Possible formats may include one or more of these options: write the answer; create a document that contains the answer; present your answer to the class; discuss your answer in a group; record the answer as audio or video using a webcam, smartphone, or portable media player; or post answers on a blog, wiki, or website.

Apply Your Knowledge

Reinforce the skills and apply the concepts you learned in this module.

Using Criteria, Joining Tables, and Sorting in SQL Queries in the Financial Services Database

Note: To complete this assignment, you will be required to use the Data Files. Please contact your instructor for information about accessing the Data Files.

Instructions: Start Access and then open the Support_AC_Financial Services database. (If you do not have the database, see your instructor for a copy of the modified database.) Use SQL to query the Financial Services database.

Perform the following tasks:

1. Find all clients whose client type is RET. Display all fields in the query result. Save the query as AYK Step 1 Query.

2. Find all clients whose amount paid or current due is $0.00. Display the Client Number, Client Name, Amount Paid, and Current Due fields in the query result. Save the query as AYK Step 2 Query.

3. Find all clients in the Client table who are not located in Carlton. Display the Client Number, Client Name, and City in the query results. Save the query as AYK Step 3 Query.

4. Display the Client Number, Client Name, Advisor Number, First Name, and Last Name for all clients. Sort the records in ascending order by advisor number and client number. Save the query as AYK Step 4 Query.

5. Display the Advisor Number, First Name, Last Name, and Other Skills for all advisors who are CFA certified. Save the query as AYK Step 5 Query.

6. If requested to do so by your instructor, rename the AYK Step 5 Query as Last Name Query where Last Name is your last name.

7. Submit the revised database in the format specified by your instructor.

8. ✳ What WHERE clause would you use if you wanted to find all clients located in cities beginning with the letter K?

Extend Your Knowledge

Extend the skills you learned in this module and experiment with new skills. You may need to use Help to complete the assignment.

Creating Queries to Find Specific Criteria

Note: To complete this assignment, you will be required to use the Data Files. Please contact your instructor for information about accessing the Data Files.

Start Access and then open the Support_AC_Healthy Pets database. (If you do not have the database, see your instructor for a copy of the modified database.)

Instructions: CMF Vets would like more information about some of the clients of the Healthy Pets practice. Use SQL queries to find specific information.

Perform the following tasks:

1. Find all clients where the client's first name is either Saul or Ira. Display the Client Number, First Name, Last Name, and Address fields in the query result. Save the query as EYK Step 1 Query.

2. Find all clients who live in Cortez. Use the IN operator. Display the Client Number, First Name, Last Name, and City field in the query result. Save the query as EYK Step 2 Query.

3. Find all clients whose amount paid is greater than or equal to $500.00 and less than or equal to $600.00. Use the BETWEEN operator. Display the Client Number, First Name, Last Name, and Amount Paid fields in the query result. Save the query as EYK Step 3 Query.

4. Use an INNER JOIN in a query to find all technicians who are located in Cortez with clients that are also located in Cortez. Display the Client Name, Technician Number, First Name, Last Name, and City fields in the query result. Save the query as EYK Step 4 Query.

5. If requested to do so by your instructor, rename the EYK Step 4 Query as First Name City Query where First Name is your first name and City is the city where you currently reside.

6. Submit the revised database in the format specified by your instructor.

7. ✷ What WHERE clause would you use to find the answer to Step 2 without using the IN operator?

Expand Your World

Create a solution, which uses cloud and web technologies, by learning and investigating on your own from general guidance.

Problem: Many SQL tutorials are available on the web. One site, www.w3schools.com/sql, has an online SQL editor that allows you to edit SQL commands and then run commands. You will use this editor to create and run queries in the following steps.

Perform the following tasks:

1. Create a blog, Google document, or Word document on OneDrive on which to store your SQL statements and the number of results obtained from the query. Include your name and the current date at the beginning of the blog or document.

2. Access the www.w3schools.com/sql website and spend some time becoming familiar with the tutorial and how it works.

3. Using the website, explain how you would create a query to find records in a table where the Customer name in the table begins with the letter P. Note which section of this website where you located the answer.

4. Submit the document containing your statements and results in the format specified by your instructor.

5. ✷ Based on your research would you use online SQL research? Why?

In the Labs

Design, create, modify, and/or use a database following the guidelines, concepts, and skills presented in this module.

Lab: **Using SQL in the Lancaster College Database**

Instructions: Open the Support_AC_Lancaster College database. (If you do not have the database, see your instructor for a copy of the modified database.)

Part 1:   The administration at Lancaster College has asked you to perform a number of tasks. Use the concepts and techniques presented in this module to perform each of the following tasks.

    a.   Create queries using SQL. Find all the Orders where the quantity ordered was less than 75. Show all fields in the results and save the query as ITL Step 1 Query.

    b.   Create a query using the WHERE command to identify the Coaches with offices in the SM building. Save the query as ITL Step 2 Query.

    c.   Use the AND command to identify all the students who have waivers and are qualified academically for sports. Show the Student ID field in the query. Save the query as ITL Step 3 Query.

    d.   Using the NOT command, find all coaches that do not have offices in the JK building. Show the Coach ID field in the query. Save the query as ITL Step 4 Query.

    e.   Using the ORDER BY command, sort the students that are participating in sports by their student ID and then by the name of the sport they are participating in. Sort both in ascending order. Save the query as ITL Step 5 Query.

    f.   Use the AND command to find the football fields that are available in the Fall and sort the results in descending order by FieldID. Save the query as ITL Step 6 Query.

    g.   Group the Orders by Equipment ID and Count the number of orders with quantity ordered of greater than 30. Save the query as ITL Step 7 Query.

    h.   Close the database.

Submit your assignment in the format specified by your instructor.

Part 2:   You made several decisions while creating these queries, including the decision of which fields to include in the results. What was the rationale behind your decisions? What other queries would you create that you that you think would be relevant?

11 | Database Design

Objectives

You will have mastered the material in this module when you can:

- Understand the terms entity, attribute, and relationship
- Understand the terms relation and relational database
- Understand functional dependence and identify when one column is functionally dependent on another
- Understand the term primary key and identify primary keys in tables

- Design a database to satisfy a set of requirements
- Convert an unnormalized relation to first normal form
- Convert tables from first normal form to second normal form
- Convert tables from second normal form to third normal form
- Understand how to represent the design of a database using diagrams

Introduction

This module presents a method for determining the tables and fields necessary to satisfy a set of requirements. **Database design** is the process of determining the particular tables and fields that will comprise a database. In designing a database, you must identify the tables in the database, the fields in the tables, the primary keys of the tables, and the relationships between the tables.

The module begins by examining some important concepts concerning relational databases and then presents the design method. To illustrate the process, the module presents the requirements for the CMF Vets database. It then applies the design method to those requirements to produce the database design. The module applies the design method to a second set of requirements, which are requirements for a company called Car First Insurers. It next examines normalization, which is a process that you can use to identify and fix potential problems in database designs. The module concludes by explaining how to use a company's policies and objectives — which are typically addressed in existing documentation — to plan and design a database. Finally, you will learn how to represent a database design with a diagram.

Project — Design a Database

This module expands on the database design guidelines presented earlier. Without a good understanding of database design, you cannot use a database management system such as Access effectively. In this module, you will learn how to design two databases by using the database design process shown in Figure 11–1.

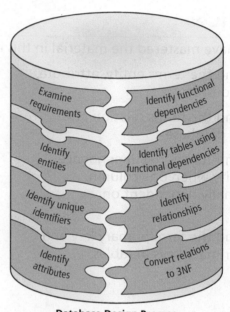

Database Design Process

Figure 11–1

You will design a database for CMF Vets that is similar to the database you have used in the previous modules. You will also design a database for Car First Insurers, a car insurance company.

Entities, Attributes, and Relationships

Working in the database environment requires that you be familiar with some specific terms and concepts. The terms *entity*, *attribute*, and *relationship* are fundamental when discussing databases. An **entity** is like a noun: it is a person, place, thing, or event. The entities of interest to CMF Vets, for example, are such things as owners, patients, veterinarians, and appointments. The entities that are of interest to a college include students, faculty, and classes; a real estate agency is interested in buyers, sellers, properties, and agents; and an automobile dealer is interested in vehicles, accounts, salespeople, and manufacturers. When creating a database, an entity is represented as a table.

An **attribute** is a property of an entity. The term is used here exactly as it is used in everyday English. For the entity *person*, for example, the list of attributes might include such things as eye color and height. For CMF Vets, the attributes of interest for the entity *patient* are such things as name, animal type, breed, and so on. For the entity *faculty* at a school, the attributes would be such things as faculty number, name, office number, phone, department, and so on. For the entity *vehicle* at an automobile dealership, the attributes are such things as the vehicle identification number, model, price, year, and so on. In databases, attributes are represented as the fields in a table or tables.

A **relationship** is an association between entities. There is an association between patients and appointments, for example, at CMF Vets. A patient is associated with all of its appointments, and an appointment is associated with the one patient to whom the appointment is assigned. Technically, you say that a patient is *related* to all of its appointments, and an appointment is *related* to a specific patient.

The relationship between patients and appointments is an example of a one-to-many relationship because one patient is associated with many appointments, but each appointment is associated with only one patient. In a **one-to-many relationship**, a table's record can be related to many records in another table. The other table's records are only related to one record in the first table. In this type of relationship, the word *many* is used in a way that is different from everyday English; it might not always mean a large number. In this context, for example, the term *many* means that a patient might be associated with *any* number of appointments. That is, one patient can be associated with zero, one, or more appointments.

There is also a relationship between veterinarians and patients. Each veterinarian sees many patients, and each patient can be seen by many different veterinarians. This is an example of a **many-to-many relationship**.

How does a relational database handle entities, attributes of entities, and relationships between entities? Entities and attributes are fairly simple. Each entity has its own table; in the CMF database, there is one table for patients, one table for appointments, and so on. The attributes of an entity become the columns in the table. In the table for patients, for example, there is a column for the patient ID, a column for the patient name, and so on.

What about relationships? Relationships are implemented through matching fields. One-to-many relationships, for example, are implemented by including matching fields in the related tables. Patients and appointments are related, for example, by including the Patient ID field in both the Patients table and the Appointments table.

Many-to-many relationships are implemented through an additional table that contains matching fields for both of the related tables. Patients and veterinarians are related, for example, through the Appointments table. The appointments table contains the veterinarian and the patient ID. This table links the two tables, patients and veterinarians, together in the many-to-many relationship.

BTW
Relationships
One-to-one relationships also can occur but they are not common. To implement a one-to-one relationship, treat it as a one-to-many relationship. You must determine which table will be the one table and which table will be the many table. To do so, consider what may happen in the future. In the case of one project that has one employee assigned to it, more employees could be added. Therefore, the project table would be the one table and the employee table would be the many table.

Relational Databases

A relational database is a collection of tables similar to the tables for CMF Vets that appear in Figure 11–2. In the CMF Vets database, the Appointments table contains information about the daily appointments that owners have booked (Figure 11–2a).

Appointments						
Appointment ID	Patient ID	Appointment Date	Appointment Time	Veterinarian	Owner	Treatment Number
1	P-3	6/30/2021	10:00:00 AM	B01	O-6	T-3
2	P-7	10/25/2021	9:00:00 AM	B01	O-8	T-4
3	P-2	1/10/2021	10:00:00 AM	B01	O-5	T-2
4	P-4	6/30/2021	10:00:00 AM	B01	O-1	T-1
5	P-5	8/23/2021	10:00:00 AM	G01	O-4	T-4
7	P-3	6/15/2021	10:00:00 AM	S01	O-6	T-5

Figure 11–2a Appointments Table

CMF Vets assigns each appointment to a specific patient. The Patients table contains information about the patients to whom these appointments are assigned (Figure 11–2b).

Patients				
Patient ID	Patient Name	Animal Type	Breed	Owner ID
P-1	Pepper	Canine	Weimaraner	O-2
P-10	Paws	Feline	Calico	O-2
P-11	Ranger	Canine	Labrador	O-1
P-12	Fluffy	Feline	Tabby	O-1
P-2	Hooper	Canine	Terrier	O-6
P-3	Oliver	Feline	Tabby	O-6
P-4	Chloe	Feline	Calico	O-1
P-5	Max	Feline	Mixed	O-4
P-6	Elvis	Feline	Siamese	O-3
P-7	Milo	Canine	Beagle	O-8
P-8	Millie	Canine	Mixed	O-5
P-9	Skippy	Feline	Mixed	O-1

Figure 11–2b Patients Table

The formal term for a table is relation. If you study the tables shown in Figure 11–2, you might see that there are certain restrictions you should place on relations. Each column in a table should have a unique name, and entries in each column should match this column name. For example, in the Appointment Date column, all entries should in fact *be* appointment dates. In addition, each row should be unique. After all, if two rows in a table contain identical data, the second row does not provide any information that you do not already have. In addition, for maximum flexibility, the order in which columns and rows appear in a table should be immaterial. Finally, a table's design is less complex if you restrict each position in the table to a single entry, that is, you do not permit multiple entries, often called **repeating groups**, in the table. These restrictions lead to the following definition:

A **relation** is a two-dimensional table in which:

1. The entries in the table are single-valued; that is, each location in the table contains a single entry.

2. Each column has a distinct name, technically called the *attribute name*.

3. All values in a column are values of the same attribute; that is, all entries must correspond to the column name.

4. Each row is distinct; that is, no two rows are identical.

Figure 11–3a shows a table with repeating groups, which violates Rule 1. Figure 11–3b shows a table in which two columns have the same name, which violates Rule 2. Figure 11–3c shows a table in which one of the entries in the Appointment Date column is not a date, which violates Rule 3. Figure 11–3d shows a table with two identical rows, which violates Rule 4.

repeating group (more than one entry in a single table location)

Appointments

Appointment ID	Patient ID	Appointment Date	Appointment Time	Veterinarian	Owner	Treatment Number
1	P-3	6/30/2021 7/15/2021 8/14/2021	10:00:00 AM 8:30:00 AM 2:00:00 PM	B01 G01 B01	O-6	T-3 T-5 T-8
2	P-7	10/25/2021	9:00:00 AM	B01	O-8	T-4
3	P-2	1/10/2021	10:00:00 AM	B01	O-5	T-2
4	P-4	6/30/2021	10:00:00 AM	B01	O-1	T-1
5	P-5	8/23/2021	10:00:00 AM	G01	O-4	T-4
7	P-3	6/15/2021	10:00:00 AM	S01	O-6	T-5

Figure 11–3a Appointments Table Violation of Rule 1 — Table Contains Repeating Groups

two columns with the same name

Patients

Patient ID	Patient Name	Animal Type	Animal Type	Owner ID
P-1	Pepper	Canine	Weimaraner	O-2
P-10	Paws	Feline	Calico	O-2
P-11	Ranger	Canine	Labrador	O-1
P-12	Fluffy	Feline	Tabby	O-1
P-2	Hooper	Canine	Terrier	O-6
P-3	Oliver	Feline	Tabby	O-6
P-4	Chloe	Feline	Calico	O-1
P-5	Max	Feline	Mixed	O-4
P-6	Elvis	Feline	Siamese	O-3
P-7	Milo	Canine	Beagle	O-8
P-8	Millie	Canine	Mixed	O-5
P-9	Skippy	Feline	Mixed	O-1

Figure 11–3b Patients Table Violation of Rule 2 — Each Column Should have a Distinct Name

Appointments						
Appointment ID	Patient ID	Appointment Date	Appointment Time	Veterinarian	Owner	Treatment Number
1	P-3	6/30/2021	10:00:00 AM	B01	O-6	T-3
2	P-7	Monday AM	9:00:00 AM	B01	O-8	T-4
3	P-2	1/10/2021	10:00:00 AM	B01	O-5	T-2
4	P-4	6/30/2021	10:00:00 AM	B01	O-1	T-1
5	P-5	8/23/2021	10:00:00 AM	G01	O-4	T-4
7	P-3	6/15/2021	10:00:00 AM	S01	O-6	T-5

value does not correspond to column name: that is, it is not an Appointment Date

Figure 11–3c Appointments Table Violation of Rule 3 — All Entries in a Column Must Correspond to the Column Name

Patients				
Patient ID	Patient Name	Animal Type	Breed	Owner ID
P-1	Pepper	Canine	Weimaraner	O-2
P-10	Paws	Feline	Calico	O-2
P-11	Ranger	Canine	Labrador	O-1
P-12	Fluffy	Feline	Tabby	O-1
P-2	Hooper	Canine	Terrier	O-6
P-2	Hooper	Canine	Terrier	O-6
P-3	Oliver	Feline	Tabby	O-6
P-4	Chloe	Feline	Calico	O-1
P-5	Max	Feline	Mixed	O-4
P-6	Elvis	Feline	Siamese	O-3
P-7	Milo	Canine	Beagle	O-8
P-8	Millie	Canine	Mixed	O-5
P-9	Skippy	Feline	Mixed	O-1

identical rows

Figure 11–3d Patients Table Violation of Rule 4 — Each Row Should be Distinct

In addition, in a relation, the order of columns is immaterial. The order of rows is also immaterial. You can view the columns or rows in any order you want.

A **relational database** is a collection of relations. Rows in a table (relation) are often called **records** or **tuples**. Columns in a table (relation) are often called **fields** or **attributes**. Typically, the terms *record* and *field* are used in Access.

To depict the structure of a relational database, you can use a commonly accepted shorthand representation: you write the name of the table and then within parentheses list all of the fields in the table. Each table should begin on a new line. If the entries in the table occupy more than one line, the entries that appear on the next line should be indented so it is clear that they do not constitute another table. Using this method, you would represent the CMF Vets database as shown in Figure 11–4.

Appointments (Appointment ID, Patient ID, Appointment Date, Appointment Time, Veterinarian, Owner, Treatment Number)

Patients (Patient ID, Patient Name, Animal Type, Breed, Owner ID)

Figure 11–4

The CMF Vets database contains some duplicate field names. For example, the Street Address field appears in *both* the Veterinarians table *and* the Veterinary Vendors table. This duplication of names can lead to possible confusion. If you write Street Address, it is not clear to which Street Address field you are referring.

When duplicate field names exist in a database, you need to indicate the field to which you are referring. You do so by writing both the table name and the field name, separated by a period. You would write the Street Address field in the Veterinarians table as Veterinarians.Street Address and the Street Address field in the Veterinary Vendors table as Veterinary Vendors.Street Address. As you learned previously, when you combine a field name with a table name, you say that you **qualify** the field names. It is *always* acceptable to qualify field names, even if there is no possibility of confusion. If confusion might arise, however, it is *essential* to qualify field names.

Functional Dependence

In the CMF Vets database (Figure 11–2), a given patient ID in the database will correspond to a single patient because patient ID numbers are unique. Thus, if you are given patient ID in the database, you could find a patient name that corresponds to it. No ambiguity exists. The database terminology for this relationship between patient ID numbers and patient names is that Patient ID determines Patient Name, or, equivalently, that Patient Name is functionally dependent on Patient ID. Specifically, if you know that whenever you are given a value for one field, you will be able to determine a single value for a second field, the first field is said to **determine** the second field. In addition, the second field is said to be **functionally dependent** on the first.

There is a shorthand notation that represents functional dependencies using an arrow. To indicate that Patient ID determines Patient Name, or, equivalently, that Patient Name is functionally dependent on Patient ID, you would write Patient ID → Patient Name. The field that precedes the arrow determines the field that follows the arrow.

If you were given a breed and asked to find a patient's name, you could not do it. Given tabby as the breed, for example, you would find two patient names, Fluffy and Oliver (Figure 11–5). Formally, you would say the breed does *not* determine Patient Name, or that Patient Name is *not* functionally dependent on breed.

BTW
Functional Dependence
To help identify functional dependencies, ask yourself the following question. If you know a unique value for an attribute, do you know the unique values for another attribute? For example, when you have three attributes — Patient ID, Patient Name, and Breed — and you know a unique value for Patient ID, do you also know a unique value for Animal Type and Owner? If so, then Animal Type and Owner are functionally dependent on Patient ID.

In the Patients table, is Owner ID functionally dependent on Patient ID?
Yes. If you are given a value for Patient ID, for example P-3, you will always find a *single* Owner ID, in this case O-6, associated with it.

In the Appointments table, is Veterinarian functionally dependent on Patient ID?
No. A given Veterinarian occurs on multiple rows. Veterinarian B01, for example, occurs on many rows and treats patients P-3, P-7, P-2, and P-4. Veterinarian S01 also treats P-3. Thus, veterinarians are associated with more than one appointment.

CONSIDER THIS

Patients				
Patient ID	Patient Name	Animal Type	Breed	Owner ID
P-1	Pepper	Canine	Weimaraner	O-2
P-10	Paws	Feline	Calico	O-2
P-11	Ranger	Canine	Labrador	O-1
P-12	Fluffy	Feline	Tabby	O-1
P-2	Hooper	Canine	Terrier	O-6
P-3	Oliver	Feline	Tabby	O-6
P-4	Chloe	Feline	Calico	O-1
P-5	Max	Feline	Mixed	O-4
P-6	Elvis	Feline	Siamese	O-3
P-7	Milo	Canine	Beagle	O-8
P-8	Millie		Mixed	O-5
P-9	Skippy		Mixed	O-1

breed is Tabby; name is Fluffy

breed is also Tabby, but name is Oliver (same breed but different name)

Figure 11–5

In the Appointments table, is Treatment Number functionally dependent on Patient ID?
No. There is a row, for example, in which the Patient ID is P-7 and the Treatment Number is T-4. There is another row in which the Patient ID is P-5 and the Treatment Number is T-4.

In the Appointments table, is the Veterinarian functionally dependent on the Patient ID?
No. There is a row, for example, in which the Patient ID P-3 is seen by Veterinarian B01 and another row in which the Patient ID P-3 is seen by Veterinarian S01.

On which fields is Treatment Number functionally dependent?
To determine the Treatment Number, you need the Appointment ID.

On which field is Veterinarian functionally dependent?
To determine the Veterinarian, you need the Appointment ID.

Primary Key

The **primary key** of a table is the field or minimum collection of fields — the fewest number of fields possible — that uniquely identifies a given row in that table. In the Appointments table, the Appointment ID uniquely identifies a given row. Any appointment ID appears on only one row of the table. Thus, Appointment ID is the primary key. Similarly, Patient ID is the primary key of the Patients table.

Is the Patient Name another possibility for the key field in the Patients table?
No, because there may be two patients with the same name. A key field must be unique for each row.

Could the combination of the Patient ID and the Appointment Date fields be the primary key for the Appointments table?
Yes, the combination of the two fields, Patient ID and Appointment Date, make each row unique. This would be an alternative to using the current key field, Appointment ID, assuming that each patient had only one appointment each day.

What if some patients had more than one appointment in any day?
In this case, you would need to use three fields, Patient ID, Appointment Date, and Appointment Time, to be key fields. Those three fields are a unique combination for each row.

The primary key provides an important way of distinguishing one row in a table from another. In the shorthand representation, you underline the field or collection of fields that comprise the primary key for each table in the database. Thus, the complete shorthand representation for the CMF Vets database is shown in Figure 11–6.

Appointments (<u>Appointment ID</u>, Patient ID, Appointment Date, Appointment Time, Veterinarian, Owner, Treatment Number)

Patients (<u>Patient ID</u>, Patient Name, Animal Type, Breed, Owner ID)

Figure 11–6

Occasionally, but not often, there might be more than one possibility for the primary key. For example, if the CMF Vets database included the veterinarian's Social Security number in the Veterinarians table, either the Veterinarian ID or the Social Security number could serve as the primary key. In this case, both fields are referred to as candidate keys. Similar to a primary key, a **candidate key** is a field or combination of fields on which all fields in the table are functionally dependent. Thus, the definition for primary key really defines candidate key as well. There can be many candidate keys, although having more than one is very rare. By contrast, there is only one primary key. The remaining candidate keys are called **alternate keys**.

BTW
Candidate Keys
According to the definition of a candidate key, a Social Security number is a legitimate primary key. Many databases use a person's Social Security number as a primary key. However, many institutions and organizations are moving away from using Social Security numbers because of privacy issues. Instead, many institutions and organizations use unique student numbers or employee numbers as primary keys.

Database Design

This section presents a specific database design method, based on a set of requirements that the database must support. The section then presents a sample of such requirements and illustrates the design method by designing a database to satisfy these requirements.

Design Process

The following is a method for designing a database for a set of requirements.

1. Examine the requirements and identify the entities, or objects, involved. Assign names to the entities. The entities will become tables. If, for example, the design involves the entities departments and employees, you could assign the names, Department and Employee. If the design involves the entities accounts, orders, and parts, you could assign the names, Account, Orders, and Part.

NOTE: The word, Order, has special meaning in SQL. If you use it for the name of a table, you will not be able to use SQL to query that table. A common approach to avoid this problem is to make the name plural. That is the reason for choosing Orders rather than Order as the name of the table.

2. Assign a unique identifier to each entity. For example, if one of the entities were "item," you would determine what it takes to uniquely identify each individual item. In other words, what enables the organization to distinguish one item from another? For an item entity, it might be Item Number. For an account entity, it might be Account Number. If there is no such unique identifier, it is a good idea

to add one. Perhaps the previous system was a manual one where accounts were not assigned numbers, in which case this would be a good time to add Account Numbers to the system. If there is no natural candidate for a primary key, you can add an AutoNumber field, which is similar to the ID field that Access adds automatically when you create a new table.

3. Identify the attributes for all the entities. These attributes will become the fields in the tables. It is possible that more than one entity has the same attribute. At CMF Vets, for example, veterinarians and veterinary vendors both have the attributes of street address, city, state, and zip code. To address this duplication, you can follow the name of the attribute with the corresponding entity in parentheses. Thus, Street (Veterinarians) would be the street address of a veterinarian, whereas Street (Veterinary Vendors) would be the street address of an veterinary vendor.

4. Identify the functional dependencies that exist among the attributes.

5. Use the functional dependencies to identify the tables. You do this by placing each attribute with the attribute or minimum combination of attributes on which it is functionally dependent. The attribute or attributes on which all other attributes in the table are dependent will be the primary key of the table. The remaining attributes will be the other fields in the table. Once you have determined all the fields in the table, you can assign an appropriate name to the table.

6. Determine and implement relationships among the entities. The basic relationships are one-to-many and many-to-many.

   One-to-many. You implement a one-to-many relationship by including the primary key of the "one" table as a foreign key in the "many" table. A **foreign key** is a field in one table whose values are required to match the *primary key* of another table. In the one-to-many relationship between appointments and patients, for example, you include the primary key of the Patients Table, which is Patient ID, as a foreign key in the Appointments table. You might have already included this field in the earlier steps. If so, you would simply designate it as a foreign key. If you had not already added it, you would need to add it at this point, designating it as a foreign key.

   Many-to-many. A many-to-many relationship is implemented by creating a new table whose primary key is the combination of the keys of the original tables.

   You may have already identified such a table in the earlier steps, in which case, all you need to do is to be sure you have designated each portion of the primary key as a foreign key that is required to match the primary key of the appropriate table. If you have not, you would add the table at this point. The primary key will consist of the primary keys from each of the tables to be related. If there are any attributes that depend on the combination of fields that make up the primary key, you need to include them in this table. (*Note:* There may not be any other fields that are dependent on this combination. In that case, there will be no fields besides the fields that make up the primary key.)

   The following sections illustrate the design process by designing the database for CMF Vets. The next section gives the requirements that this database must support, and the last section creates a database design based on those requirements.

Requirements for the CMF Vets Database

Systems analysts have examined the needs and organizational policies at CMF Vets and have determined that the CMF Vets database must support the following requirements:

1. For a patient, CMF Vets needs to maintain the patient's name, type of animal and breed, and the owner of the patient.

2. For an owner, the CMF Vets needs the owner's full name and address, both home and mobile phone numbers, and the owner's email address.

3. For veterinarians, similar information as for the owners needs to be recorded along with board certification and specialty of the vet.

4. Each appointment must be recorded as well. Information for appointments indicates when the appointment is scheduled, the procedure, the patients, and the vet who is handling the appointment.

5. Any given patient can have many appointments, and any vet can also have many appointments.

Design of the CMF Vets Database

The following represents the application of the design method for the CMF Vets requirements.

1. There appear to be four entities: owners, patients, veterinarians, and appointments. Reasonable names for the corresponding tables are Owners, Patients, Veterinarians, and Appointments.

2. The unique identifier for owners is the owner ID. The unique identifier for patients is the patient ID. The unique identifier for veterinarians is veterinarian ID. The unique identifier of appointments is appointment ID. Reasonable names for the unique identifiers are Owner ID, Patient ID, Veterinarian ID, and Appointment ID, respectively.

3. The attributes are:

> **Owner ID**
>
> **First Name (Owners)**
>
> **Last Name (Owners)**
>
> **Street Address (Owners)**
>
> **City (Owners)**
>
> **State (Owners)**
>
> **Postal Code (Owners)**
>
> **Home Phone**
>
> **Mobile Phone (Owners)**
>
> **Email Address (Owners)**
>
> **Patient ID**
>
> **Patient Name**
>
> **Animal Type**
>
> **Breed**

> **Owner ID**
>
> **Veterinarian ID**
>
> **First Name (Veterinarians)**
>
> **Last Name (Veterinarians)**
>
> **Street Address (Veterinarians)**
>
> **City (Veterinarians)**
>
> **State (Veterinarians)**
>
> **Zip Code (Veterinarians)**
>
> **Office Phone**
>
> **Mobile Phone (Veterinarians)**
>
> **Email Address (Veterinarians)**
>
> **Board Certified**
>
> **Specialty**
>
> **Appointment ID**
>
> **Patient ID**
>
> **Appointment Date**
>
> **Appointment Time**
>
> **Veterinarian**
>
> **Treatment Number**

Remember that parentheses after an attribute indicate the entity to which the attribute corresponds. Thus, Street Address (Owners) represents the street address of an owner in a way that distinguishes it from Street Address (Veterinarians), which represents the street address of a veterinarian.

4. The functional dependencies among the attributes are:

> **Owner ID → First Name (Owners), Last Name (Owners), Street Address (Owners), City (Owners), State (Owner), Postal Code (Owners), Home Phone, Mobile Phone (Owners), Email Address (Owners)**
>
> **Patient ID → Patient Name, Animal Type, Breed, Owner ID**
>
> **Veterinarian ID → First Name (Veterinarians), Last Name (Veterinarians), Street Address (Veterinarians), City (Veterinarians), State (Veterinarians), Postal Code (Veterinarians), Work Phone, Mobile Phone (Veterinarians), Email Address (Veterinarians), Board Certified, Specialty**
>
> **Appointment ID → Patient ID, Appointment Date, Appointment Time, Veterinarian, Treatment Number**

The patient ID, appointment date, appointment time, and treatment number are dependent only on appointment ID. Because an appointment has a single veterinarian, the veterinarian is dependent on appointment ID as well. The patient's name, animal type, breed, and owner ID are dependent only on the patient ID. The owner's name, address, phone numbers, and email are dependent only on the owner ID. Similarly, the veterinarian's name, address, phone numbers, email, and other attributes are dependent only on the veterinarian ID. The shorthand representation for the tables is shown in Figure 11–7.

Appointments (<u>Appointment ID</u>, Patient ID, Appointment Date, Appointment Time, Veterinarian, Owner, Treatment Number)

Patients (<u>Patient ID</u>, Patient Name, Animal Type, Breed, Owner ID)

Owners (<u>Owner ID</u>, Last Name, First Name, Street Address, City, State, Postal Code, Home Phone, Mobile Phone, Email Address)

Veterinarians (<u>Veterinarian ID</u>, Last Name, First Name, Street Address, City, State, Postal Code, Work Phone, Mobile Phone, Email Address, Board Certified, Specialty)

Figure 11–7

5. The following are the relationships between the tables:

   a. The Owners and Patients tables are related using the Owner ID fields, which is the primary key of the Owners table. The Owner ID field in the Patients table is a foreign key.

   b. The Appointments, Patients, and Veterinarians tables are related using the Patient ID field, which is the primary key of the Patients table and the Veterinarian ID field, which is the primary key of the Veterinarians table. The Patient ID and Veterinarian ID fields in the Appointments table are both foreign keys.

Does a many-to-many relationship exist between patients and veterinarians?
Yes. The Appointments table is the link between this many-to-many relationship.

CONSIDER THIS

NOTE: In the shorthand representation for a table containing a foreign key, you would represent the foreign key by using the letters FK, followed by an arrow, followed by the name of the table in which that field is the primary key. For example, to indicate that the Patient ID in the Appointments table is a foreign key that must match the primary key of the Patients table, you would write FK Patient ID → Patients.

   The shorthand representation for the tables and foreign keys is shown in Figure 11–8. It is common to list a table containing a foreign key after the table that contains the corresponding primary key, when possible. Thus, in the figure, the Appointments table comes after the other tables because it contains foreign keys from the tables listed above.

Owners (<u>Owner ID</u>, Last Name, First Name, Street Address, City, State, Postal Code, Home Phone, Mobile Phone, Email Address)

Patients (<u>Patient ID</u>, Patient Name, Animal Type, Breed, Owner ID)

FK Owner ID Owners

Veterinarians (<u>Veterinarian ID</u>, Last Name, First Name, Street Address, City, State, Postal Code, Work Phone, Mobile Phone, Email Address, Board Certified, Specialty)

Appointments (<u>Appointment ID</u>, Patient ID, Appointment Date, Appointment Time, Veterinarian, Owner, Treatment Number)

FK Patient ID Patient

FK Veterinarian ID Veterinarians

Figure 11–8

Car First Insurers

The management of Car First Insurers, a budget car insurance company, has determined that the company's rapid growth requires a database to maintain policy holders, drivers, and vehicles. With the data stored in a database, management will be able to ensure that the data is current and more accurate. In addition, managers will be able to obtain answers to their questions concerning the data in the database quickly and easily, with the option of producing a variety of reports. Note that the cost of the policies and the payments to the Car First Insurers are handled by a third party and are not requirements of this database design.

Requirements for the Car First Insurers Database

A system analyst has interviewed users and examined documents at Car First Insurers and has determined that the company needs a database that will support the following requirements:

1. For a customer, store the customer's first name, last name, street address, city, state, postal code, telephone number, and email address.

2. For a driver, store the driver's number, first name, last name, street address, city, state, postal code, telephone number, and email address. (Note that there might be many drivers under one customer. For example, a parent could have three teenage drivers.)

3. For an insured vehicle, store the vehicle identification number, make, model, and year. The database also should store the policy number under which each vehicle is registered.

4. The driver and vehicle must be associated; the database must include a table that links these two entities.

5. The analyst also obtained the following information concerning insurance:

   a. A customer could hold more than one policy.

   b. There could be multiple drivers associated with one policy.

   c. A driver can drive multiple cars.

Design of the Car First Insurers Database

BTW
Line Items
A line item is a unit of information that appears on its own line. For example, when you purchase groceries, each grocery item appears on its own line. Line items also can be referred to as order line items or item detail lines.

The following steps apply the design process to the requirements for Car First Insurers to produce the appropriate database design:

1. Assign entity names. There appear to be four entities: customers, drivers, policies, and vehicles. The names assigned to these entities are Customers, Drivers, Policies, and Vehicles, respectively.

2. Determine unique identifiers. From the collection of entities, review the data and determine the unique identifier for each entity. For the Customers, Drivers, and Policies entities, the unique identifiers are the customer ID, driver ID, and policy number, respectively. These unique identifiers are named Customer ID, Driver ID, and Policy Number, respectively. For the Vehicles, the unique identifier is the vehicle identification number, known as VIN, which is unique for each vehicle worldwide.

3. Assign attribute names. The attributes mentioned in the first requirement all refer to customers. The specific attributes mentioned in the requirement are the customer ID, first name, last name, street address, city, state, postal code,

telephone number, and email address. Assigning appropriate names to these attributes produces the following list:

Customer ID

First Name

Last Name

Street

City

State

Postal Code

Telephone

Email Address

The attributes mentioned in the second requirement refer to drivers. The specific attributes are the driver ID, name, street address, city, state, postal code, telephone number, and email address. Assigning appropriate names to these attributes produces the following list:

Driver ID

First Name

Last Name

Street

City

State

Postal Code

Telephone

Email Address

Do you need to include the policy associated with the driver in the list of attributes for the second requirement?

There is no need to include them in this list, because that information will be determined with linkages between tables later on.

CONSIDER THIS

There are attributes named Street, City, State, and Postal Code for customers as well as attributes named Street, City, State, and Postal Code for drivers. To distinguish these attributes in the final collection, the name of the attribute is followed by the name of the corresponding entity. For example, the street for a customer is Street (Customer) and the street for a driver is Street (Driver).

The attributes mentioned in the third requirement refer to the policy. The specific attributes are the policy number, effective date, expire date, and customer, who is the policy holder. Assigning appropriate names to these attributes produces the following list:

Policy Number

Effective Date

Expire Date

Customer ID

The attributes mentioned in the fourth requirement refer to vehicles. The specific attributes include the vehicle identification number, make, model, year, and policy number associated with the vehicle. Assigning appropriate names to these attributes produces the following list:

> **VIN**
>
> **Make**
>
> **Model**
>
> **Year**
>
> **Policy Number**

The statement concerning the linkage of driver to vehicle indicates that there are specific attributes to be stored for each vehicle. These attributes are the vehicle and driver. Assigning appropriate names to these attributes produces the following list:

> **VIN**
>
> **Driver ID**

The complete list grouped by entity is as follows:

> **Customer**
>> **Customer ID**
>>
>> **First Name**
>>
>> **Last Name**
>>
>> **Street**
>>
>> **City**
>>
>> **State**
>>
>> **Postal Code**
>>
>> **Telephone**
>>
>> **Email Address**
>
> **Driver**
>> **Driver ID**
>>
>> **First Name**
>>
>> **Last Name**
>>
>> **Street**
>>
>> **City**
>>
>> **State**
>>
>> **Postal Code**
>>
>> **Telephone**
>>
>> **Email Address**
>
> **Policy**
>> **Policy Number**
>>
>> **Effective Date**
>>
>> **Expire Date**
>>
>> **Customer ID**

> **Vehicle**
>> **VIN**
>> **Make**
>> **Model**
>> **Year**
>> **Policy Number**

For drivers of vehicles:
>> **VIN**
>> **Driver ID**

4. Identify functional dependencies. The fact that the unique identifier for customers is Customer ID gives the following functional dependencies:

> **Customer ID → First Name (Customer), Last Name (Customer), Street (Customer), City (Customer), State (Customer), Postal Code (Customer), Telephone (Customer), Email Address (Customer)**

The fact that the unique identifier for drivers is Driver ID gives the following preliminary list of functional dependencies:

> **Driver ID → First Name (Driver), Last Name (Driver), Street (Driver), City (Driver), State (Driver), Postal Code (Driver), Telephone (Driver), Email Address (Driver)**

The fact that the unique identifier for policies is Policy Number gives the following functional dependencies:

> **Policy Number → Effective Date, Expire Date, Customer ID**

The fact that the unique identifier for vehicles is VIN gives the following functional dependencies:

> **VIN → Make, Model, Year, Policy Number**

Do you need to include the name of a customer in the list of attributes determined by the policy number?
There is no need to include the customer name in this list because you can determine them from the customer ID, and they are already included in the list of attributes determined by customer ID.

The final attributes to be examined are those associated with the drivers and vehicles: VIN, Driver ID.

Why is Driver ID not included in the Vehicle table?
There could be multiple drivers for each vehicle, so this requires an additional table.

CONSIDER THIS

CONSIDER THIS

The following shorthand representation indicates that the combination of VIN and Driver ID. There are no functionally dependent fields in this table.

> **VIN, Driver ID →**

The complete list of functional dependencies with appropriate revisions is as follows:

> **Customer ID → First Name (Customer), Last Name (Customer), Street (Customer), City (Customer), State (Customer), Postal Code (Customer), Telephone (Customer), Email Address (Customer)**

> **Driver ID → First Name (Driver), Last Name (Driver), Street (Driver), City (Driver), State (Driver), Postal Code (Driver), Telephone (Driver), Email Address (Driver)**

> **Policy Number → Effective Date, Expire Date, Customer ID**

> **VIN → Make, Model, Year, Policy Number**

> **VIN, Driver ID →**

5. Create the tables. Using the functional dependencies, you can create tables with the attribute(s) to the left of the arrow being the primary key and the items to the right of the arrow being the other fields. For tables corresponding to those entities identified in Step 1, you can simply use the name you already determined. Because you did not identify any entity that had a unique identifier that was the combination of VIN and Driver ID, you need to assign a name to the table whose primary key consists of these two fields. Because this table represents the individual drivers within one vehicle, the name Vehicle Driver is a good choice. The final collection of tables for Car First Insurers is shown in Figure 11–9.

Customer (<u>Customer ID</u>, First Name, Last Name, Address, City, State, Postal Code, Telephone, Email Address)

Driver (<u>Driver ID</u>, First Name, Last Name, Address, City, State, Postal Code, <u>Telephone</u>, Email Address)

Policies (<u>Policy Number</u>, Effective Date, Expire Date, Customer ID)

Vehicle (<u>VIN</u>, Make, Model, Year, Policy Number)

Vehicle Driver (<u>VIN, Driver ID</u>)

Figure 11–9

6. Identify relationships.

   a. The Customer and Policy tables are related using the Customer ID fields. The Customer ID field in the Customer table is the primary key. The Customer ID field in the Policy table is a foreign key.

   b. The Policy and Vehicle tables are related using the Policy Number fields. The Policy Number field in the Policy table is the primary key. The Policy Number field in the Vehicle table is a foreign key.

   c. The Vehicle and Driver tables are related using the VIN and Driver ID fields. Both the VIN and the Driver ID are key fields together.

Does a many-to-many relationship exist between vehicles and drivers?
Yes. The Vehicle Driver table will implement a many-to-many relationship between vehicles and drivers. You identified this table as Vehicle Driver in the database design process.

In the Vehicle Driver table, the primary key consists of two fields, VN and Driver ID. Do you need both fields to be key fields?
Yes, because this table implements the many-to-many relationship between vehicles and drivers. It is perfectly legitimate for the table that implements a many-to-many relationship to contain only the two columns that constitute the primary key.

The shorthand representation for the tables and foreign keys is shown in Figure 11–10.

Customer (Customer ID, First Name, Last Name, Address, City, State, Postal Code,
   Telephone, Email Address)
Driver (Driver ID, First Name, Last Name, Address, City, State, Postal Code, Telephone,
   Email Address)
Policy (Policy Number, Effective Date, Expire Date, Customer ID)
FK Customer ID → Customer
Vehicle (VIN, Make, Model, Year, Policy Number)
FK Policy → Number Policy
Vehicle Driver (VIN, Driver ID)
FK VIN → Vehicles
FK Driver ID → Driver

Figure 11–10

Sample data for the Car First Insurers database is shown in Figure 11–11.

Customer

Customer ID	Customer First Name	Customer Last Name	Customer Street Address	Customer City	Customer State	Customer Postal Code	Customer Phone	Email Address
M9835	Tricia	Morris	460 West Longberg Road	Gainesville	FL	32603	352-231-4411	tmorris@cengage.com
N7453	Susan	Niack	9874 South Main Street	Gainesville	FL	32605	352-991-5670	sniack@cengage.com

Driver

Driver ID	Driver First Name	Driver Last Name	Driver Street Address	Driver City	Driver State	Driver Postal Code	Driver Phone	Email Address
C010	Steve	Chen	3 Hanover Park	Newberry	FL	32618	352-555-4234	schen@cengage.com
D340	Tiffanie	D'Vivo	14435 Keller Way	Gainesville	FL	32602	352-555-9135	tdvivo@cengage.com
K009	Cyrus	Killigan	784 Hilltop Circle	Gainesville	FL	32602	352-555-6547	ckilligan@cengage.com
K324	Ryan	Kraut	334 Old Farms Road	Gainesville	FL	32604	352-555-1478	rkraut@cengage.com
O543	Liz	O'Leary	13 Griffiths Drive	Gainesville	FL	32602	352-555-6968	loleary@cengage.com
P543	Sana	Patel	76 Jenkins Way	Live Oak	FL	32064	352-555-9865	spatel@cengage.com

Figure 11–11 (Continued)

Policy

Policy Number	Effective Date	Expire Date	Customer ID
123	2/13/2021	2/13/2022	M9835
124	4/1/2021	4/1/2022	N7453

Vehicle

VIN	Make	Model	Year	Policy Number
1ALLDVAF7HA470011	Ford	F150	2021	124
1ALSK2D47DA761712	Chevrolet	Cruze	2017	123
JM1BL1H64A1138112	Mazda	3	2016	123

Vehicle Driver

VIN	Driver ID
1ALLDVAF7HA470011	O543
1ALSK2D47DA761712	C010
JM1BL1H64A1138112	D340
JM1BL1H64A1138112	K009
1ALSK2D47DA761712	K324
1ALLDVAF7HA470011	P543

Figure 11–11

Normalization

After you create your database design, you should analyze it using a process called **normalization** to make sure the design is free of potential update, redundancy, and consistency problems. This process also supplies methods for correcting these problems.

The normalization process involves converting tables into various types of **normal forms**. A table in a particular normal form possesses a certain desirable set of properties. Several normal forms exist, the most common being first normal form (1NF), second normal form (2NF), and third normal form (3NF). The forms create a progression in which a table that is in 1NF is better than a table that is not in 1NF, a table that is in 2NF is better than one that is in 1NF, and so on. The goal of normalization is to take a table or collection of tables and produce a new collection of tables that represents the same information but is free of problems.

First Normal Form

A table that contains a **repeating group**, or multiple entries for a single row, is called an **unnormalized table**. Recall from the definition of relation that an unnormalized table actually violates the definition of relation.

Removal of repeating groups is the starting point in the goal of having tables that are as free of problems as possible. In fact, in most database management systems, tables cannot contain repeating groups. A table (relation) is in **first normal form (1NF)** if it does not contain repeating groups.

In designing a database, you may have created a table with a repeating group. For example, you might have created an Hours Worked table in which the primary key is the Veterinarian ID and there is a repeating group consisting of Treatment Number and Total Hours. In the example, each veterinarian appears on a single row and Treatment Number and Total Hours are repeated as many times as necessary for each account (Figure 11–12).

Hours Worked

Veterinarian ID	Treatment Number	Total Hours
B01	T-3	.25
B02	T-8 T-15 T-12	.25 .75 1.25
E01	T-2	.5
K01	T-1 T-2 T-8 T-9	.25 .50 .25 1.25
G01	T-4	.25
S01	T-5	.5
H03	T-7	.25

repeating group (more than one entry in a single table location)

fourth row indicates that Veterinarian K01 is performing four different treatments

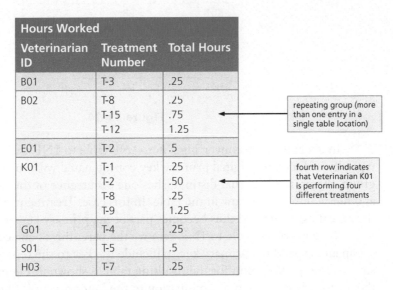

Figure 11–12

In the shorthand representation, you represent a repeating group by enclosing the repeating group within parentheses. The shorthand representation for the Hours Worked table from Figure 11–12 is shown in Figure 11–13.

Hours Worked (<u>Veterinarian ID</u>, Treatment Number, Total Hours)

Figure 11–13

Conversion to First Normal Form

Figure 11–14 shows the normalized version of the table. Note that the second row of the unnormalized table (Figure 11–12) indicates that veterinarian B02 is currently performing treatments T-8, T-15, and T-12. In the normalized table, this information is represented by *three* rows: the second, third, and fourth. The primary key for the unnormalized Hours Worked table was the Veterinarian ID only. The primary key for the normalized table is now the combination of Veterinarian ID and Treatment Number

Hours Worked		
Veterinarian ID	Treatment Number	Total Hours
B01	T-3	.25
B02	T-8	.25
B02	T-15	.75
B02	T-12	1.25
E01	T-2	.50
K01	T-1	.25
K01	T-2	.50
K01	T-8	.25
K01	T-9	1.25
G01	T-4	.25
S01	T-5	.5
H03	T-7	.25

second, third, and fourth rows indicate Veterinarian B02 is performing treatments T-8, T-15, and T-12

Figure 11–14

In general, when converting a non-1NF table to 1NF, the primary key will typically include the original primary key concatenated with the key of the repeating group, that is, the field that distinguishes one occurrence of the repeating group from another within a given row in the table. In this case, Treatment Number is the key to the repeating group and thus becomes part of the primary key of the 1NF table.

To convert the table to 1NF, remove the parentheses enclosing the repeating group and expand the primary key to include the key to the repeating group. The shorthand representation for the resulting table is shown in Figure 11–15. Notice that the primary key is now the combination of the Veterinarian ID field and the Treatment Number field.

Hours Worked (<u>Veterinarian ID</u>, <u>Treatment Number</u>, Total Hours)

Figure 11–15

Second Normal Form

Even though the following table is in 1NF, problems may exist that will cause you to want to restructure the table. In the database design process, for example, you might have created the Hours Worked table shown in Figure 11–16.

Hours Worked (<u>Veterinarian ID</u>, Veterinarian Last Name, <u>Treatment Number</u>, Treatment Name, Total Hours)

Figure 11–16

This table contains the following functional dependencies:

Veterinarian ID → Veterinarian Last Name

Treatment Number → Treatment Name

Veterinarian ID, Treatment Number → Total Hours

This notation indicates that Veterinarian ID alone determines Veterinarian Last Name, and Treatment Number alone determines Treatment Name, but it requires *both* a Veterinarian ID *and* a Treatment Number to determine Total Hours. Figure 11–17 shows a sample of this table.

Hours Worked

Veterinarian ID	Veterinarian Last Name	Treatment Number	Treatment Name	Total Hours
	Black	T-3	Feline Wellness Exam	.25
B02	Black	T-8	Feline Heartworm	.25
B02	Black	T-15	Recheck	.75
B02	Black	T-12	Canine Neuter	1.25
E01	Edwards	T-2	Canine Wellness Exam	.50
K01	Konig	T-1	Feline Rabies Shot	.25
K01	Konig	T-2	Canine Wellness Exam	.50
K01	Konig	T-8	Feline Heartworm	.25
K01	Konig	T-9	Feline Spay	1.25
G01	Gomez	T-4	Canine Rabies Shot	.25
S01	Schwartz	T-5	Feline Vaccinations	.5
H03	Heller	T-7	Canine Heartworm	.25

name of Veterinarian appears more than once

treatment name appears more than once

Figure 11–17

The name of a specific veterinarian, B02 for example, occurs multiple times in the table, as does the description of a treatment. This redundancy causes several problems. It is certainly wasteful of space, but that is not nearly as serious as some of the other problems. These other problems are called **update anomalies**, and they fall into four categories:

1. **Update.** A change to the name of veterinarian B02 requires not one change to the table, but several: you must change each row in which B02 appears. This certainly makes the update process much more cumbersome; it is logically more complicated and takes longer to update.

2. **Inconsistent data.** There is nothing about the design that would prohibit account B02 from having two or more different names in the database. The first row, for example, might have Black as the name, whereas the second row might have Blacks, a typo.

3. **Additions.** There is a real problem when you try to add a new treatment ID and its name to the database. Because the primary key for the table consists of both Veterinarian ID and Treatment Number, you need values for both of these to add a new row. If you have a new treatment to add (new offerings at the vet clinic to attract new patients) but there are so far no veterinarians scheduled for it, what do you use for a Treatment Number? The only solution would be to make up a placeholder Treatment Number and then replace it with a real Treatment Number once the account requests a workshop. This is certainly not an acceptable solution.

4. **Deletions.** In Figure 11–17, if you delete Treatment Number T-7 from the database, you would need to delete all rows on which the Treatment is T-7. In the process, you will delete the only row on which treatment T-7 appears, so you would also *lose* all the information about treatment T-7. You would no longer know that the last name of the veterinarian H03 is Heller.

These problems occur because there is a field, Veterinarian Last Name, that is dependent only on Veterinarian ID, which is just a portion of the primary key. There is a similar problem with Treatment Name, which depends only on the Treatment Number, not the complete primary key. This leads to the definition of second normal form. Second normal form represents an improvement over first normal form because it eliminates update anomalies in these situations. In order to understand second normal form, you need to understand the term, nonkey field.

A field is a **nonkey field**, also called a **nonkey attribute**, if it is not a part of the primary key. A table (relation) is in **second normal form (2NF)** if it is in first normal form and no nonkey field is dependent on only a portion of the primary key.

Note that if the primary key of a table contains only a single field, the table is automatically in second normal form. In that case, there could not be any field dependent on only a portion of the primary key.

Conversion to Second Normal Form

To correct the problems, convert the table to a collection of tables in second normal form, and then name the new tables. The following is a method for performing this conversion.

1. Take each subset of the set of fields that make up the primary key and begin a new table with this subset as its primary key. The result of applying this step to the Hours Worked table is shown in Figure 11–18.

(<u>Veterinarian ID</u>,

(<u>Treatment Number</u>,

(<u>Veterinarian ID</u>, <u>Treatment Number</u>,

Figure 11–18

2. Place each of the other fields with the appropriate primary key; that is, place each one with the minimal collection of fields on which it depends. The result of applying this step to the Hours Worked table is shown in Figure 11–19.

(<u>Veterinarian ID</u>, Veterinarian Last Name)

(<u>Treatment Number</u>, Treatment Name)

(<u>Veterinarian ID</u>, <u>Treatment Number</u>, Total Hours)

Figure 11–19

3. Give each of these new tables a name that is descriptive of the meaning of the table, such as Veterinarians, Treatments, and Hours Worked.

Veterinarian	
Veterinarian ID	**Veterinarian Last Name**
B01	Black
E01	Edwards
K01	Konig ←
G01	Gomez
S01	Schwartz
H03	Heller

veterinarian name appears only once

Figure 11–20 (Continued)

Treatments	
Treatment Number	**Treatment Name**
T-3	Feline Wellness Exam
T-8	Feline Heartworm
T-15	Recheck
T-12	Canine Neuter
T-2	Canine Wellness Exam
T-1	Feline Rabies Shot
T-9	Feline Spay
T-4	Canine Rabies Shot
T-5	Feline Vaccinations
T-7	Canine Heartworm

treatment name appears only once

Hours Worked		
Veterinarian ID	**Treatment Number**	**Total Hours**
B01	T-3	.25
B02	T-8	.25
B02	T-15	.75
B02	T-12	1.25
E01	T-2	.50
K01	T-1	.25
K01	T-2	.50
K01	T-8	.25
K01	T-9	1.25
G01	T-4	.25
S01	T-5	.5
H03	T-7	.25

Figure 11–20

The new design eliminates the update anomalies. A veterinarian last name occurs only once for each veterinarian ID, so you do not have the redundancy that occurred in the earlier design. Changing the name of veterinarian is now a simple process involving a single change. Because the name of veterinarian occurs in a single place, it is not possible to have multiple names for the same account in the database at the same time.

To add a new veterinarian, you create a new row in the Veterinarians table, and thus there is no need to have a treatment already scheduled for that veterinarian. In addition, deleting treatment T-7 has nothing to do with the Veterinarians table and, consequently, does not cause account H01 to be deleted. Thus, you still have her last name, Heller, in the database. Finally, you have not lost any information in the process.

Third Normal Form

Problems can still exist with tables that are in 2NF, as illustrated in the Patients table whose shorthand representation is shown in Figure 11–21.

Patients (<u>Patient ID</u>, Patient Name, Animal Type, Breed, Owner ID, Owner First Name, Owner Last Name)

Figure 11–21

BTW

3NF
The definition given for third normal form is not the original definition. This more recent definition, which is preferable to the original, is often referred to as Boyce-Codd normal form (BCNF) when it is important to make a distinction between this definition and the original definition. This text does not make such a distinction but will take this to be the definition of third normal form.

The functional dependencies in this table are:

**Patient ID → Patient Name, Animal Type, Breed, Owner ID,
    Owner First Name, Owner Last Name**
Owner ID → Owner First Name, Owner Last Name

As these dependencies indicate, Patient ID determines all the other fields. In addition, Owner ID determines Owner First Name and Owner Last Name.

Because the primary key of the table is a single field, the table is automatically in second normal form. As the sample of the table shown in Figure 11–22 demonstrates, however, this table has problems similar to those encountered earlier, even though it is in 2NF. In this case, it is the first name and last name of an owner that can occur many times in the table; see owner O-1, Ted Sabus, for example.

Patients						
Patient ID	Patient Name	Animal Type	Breed	Owner ID	Owner First Name	Owner Last Name
P-11	Ranger	Canine	Labrador	O-1	Ted	Sabus
P-12	Fluffy	Feline	Tabby	O-1	Ted	Sabus
P-4	Chloe	Feline	Calico	O-1	Ted	Sabus
P-9	Skippy	Feline	Mixed	O-1	Ted	Sabus
P-1	Pepper	Canine	Weimaraner	O-2	Steven	Nguyen
P-10	Paws	Feline	Calico	O-2	Steven	Nguyen
P-6	Elvis	Feline	Siamese	O-3	Liz	O'Brien
P-5	Max	Feline	Mixed	O-4	Samira	Patel
P-8	Millie	Canine	Mixed	O-5	Ryan	Kraus
P-2	Hooper	Canine	Terrier	O-6	Tiffanie	DiFranco
P-3	Oliver	Feline	Tabby	O-6	Tiffanie	DiFranco
P-7	Milo	Canine	Beagle	O-8	Ian	Kaufman

owner Sabus appears more than once

Figure 11–22

This redundancy results in the same set of problems described previously with the Hours Worked table. In addition to the problem of wasted space, you have similar update anomalies, as follows:

1. **Updates.** A change to the name of an owner requires not one change to the table, but several changes. Again, the update process becomes very cumbersome.

2. **Inconsistent data.** There is nothing about the design that would prohibit an owner from having two different names in the database. On the first row, for example, the name for owner O-1 might read Ted Sabus, whereas on the second row (another row on which the owner is O-1), the name might be Theodore Sabus.

3. **Additions.** In order to add a new owner to the database, she must have at least one pet (which most likely would be the case). For example, consider the situation in which Maryanne Webb, who is not currently an owner, would like to register with the veterinary clinic now because she is about to adopt a dog, but you could not input her owner information without the patient

information. Perhaps you could create a fictitious pet for her to represent while she waits for her adoption. Again, this is not a desirable solution to the problem.

4. **Deletions.** If a pet such as Elvis, P-6, dies, you might delete all the accounts of owner O-3 from the database, then you would also lose all information concerning owner O-3. This could be problematic if she owns another pet in the future.

These update anomalies are due to the fact that Owner ID determines First Name and Last Name, but Owner ID is not the primary key. As a result, the same Owner ID and consequently the same First Name and Last Name can appear on many different rows.

You have seen that 2NF is an improvement over 1NF, but to eliminate 2NF problems, you need an even better strategy for creating tables in the database. Third normal form provides that strategy.

Before looking at third normal form, you need to become familiar with the special name that is given to any field that determines another field, like Owner ID in the Patients table. Any field or collection of fields that determines another field is called a **determinant**. Certainly the primary key in a table is a determinant. Any candidate key is a determinant as well. (Remember that a candidate key is a field or collection of fields that could function as the primary key.) In this case, Owner ID is a determinant, but because several rows in the Patients table could have the same Owner ID, that field is not a candidate key for the Account table shown in Figure 11–22, and that is the problem.

A table is in **third normal form** (3NF) if it is in second normal form and if the only determinants it contains are candidate keys.

Conversion to Third Normal Form

You have now identified the problem with the Patients table: it is not in 3NF. You need a way to correct the deficiency in the Patients table and in all tables having similar deficiencies. Such a method follows.

First, for each determinant that is not a candidate key, remove from the table the fields that depend on this determinant, but do not remove the determinant. Next, create a new table containing all the fields from the original table that depend on this determinant. Finally, make the determinant the primary key of this new table.

In the Patients table, for example, First Name and Last Name are removed because they depend on the determinant Owner ID, which is not a candidate key. A new table is formed, consisting of Owner ID as the primary key, First Name, and Last Name. Specifically, you would replace the Patients table in Figure 11–22 with the two tables shown in Figure 11–23.

Patients (<u>Patient ID</u>, Patient Name, Animal Type, Breed, Owner ID)

Owners (<u>Owner ID</u>, Owner First Name, Owner Last Name)

Figure 11–23

Figure 11–24 shows samples of the tables.

Patients				
Patient ID	**Patient Name**	**Animal Type**	**Breed**	**Owner ID**
P-11	Ranger	Canine	Labrador	O-1
P-12	Fluffy	Feline	Tabby	O-1
P-4	Chloe	Feline	Calico	O-1
P-9	Skippy	Feline	Mixed	O-1
P-1	Pepper	Canine	Weimaraner	O-2
P-10	Paws	Feline	Calico	O-2
P-6	Elvis	Feline	Siamese	O-3
P-5	Max	Feline	Mixed	O-4
P-8	Millie	Canine	Mixed	O-5
P-2	Hooper	Canine	Terrier	O-6
P-3	Oliver	Feline	Tabby	O-6
P-7	Milo	Canine	Beagle	O-8

Owners		
Owner ID	**Owner First Name**	**Owner Last Name**
O-1	Ted	Sabus ← owner Sabus appears only once
O-2	Steven	Nguyen
O-3	Liz	O'Brien
O-4	Samira	Patel
O-5	Ryan	Kraus
O-6	Tiffanie	DiFranco
O-8	Ian	Kaufman

Figure 11–24

This design corrects the previously identified problems. An owner's name appears only once, thus avoiding redundancy and making the process of changing an owner's name a very simple one. With this design, it is not possible for an owner to have two different names in the database. To add a new owner to the database, you add a row in the Owners table; it is not necessary to have a preexisting patient for the owner. Finally, deleting all the patients of a given owner will not remove the owner's record from the Owners table, so you retain the owner's name; all the data in the original table can be reconstructed from the data in the new collection of tables. All previously mentioned problems have indeed been solved.

Special Topics

In addition to knowing how to design a database and how to normalize tables, there are two other topics with which you should be familiar. First, you may be given a requirement for a database in the form of a document that the database must be capable of producing; for example, an insurance policy. In addition, you should know how to represent your design with a diagram.

Obtaining Information from Existing Documents

Existing documents can often furnish helpful information concerning the database design. You need to know how to obtain information from the document that you will then use in the design process. An existing document, like the car insurance card for the company named Car First Insurers shown in Figure 11–25, will often provide the details that determine the tables and fields required to produce the document.

The first step in obtaining information from an existing document is to identify and list all fields and give them appropriate names. You also need to understand the business policies of the organization. For example, in the order shown in Figure 11–25, the information on Car First Insurers is preprinted on the form, and it is not necessary to describe the company. The following is a list of the fields you can determine from the document shown in Figure 11–25.

Policy Number
Policy Effective Date
Policy Expire Date
Customer Name
Street (Customer)
City (Customer)
State (Customer)
Postal Code (Customer)
Car Insured VIN
Car Make
Car Model
Car Year

Car First Insurance

INVOICE

2099 East Boulevard
Gainesville, FL 32601
1-800-999-9999

Policy Number: P59-7628749274950

Insured:
Carmen Delgado
523 Main Street
Gainesville, FL 32601

Policy Period:
12/31/2021-12/31/2022 12:01 a.m. standard time at the address of the Named Insured 12/31/2021

Vehicle Insured:

VIN	MAKE	MODEL	YEAR
1ALSK2D47DA761712	Chevrolet	Cruze	2017

Figure 11–25

Next, you need to identify functional dependencies. If the document you are examining is unfamiliar to you, you might have difficulty determining the dependencies and might need to get all the information directly from the user. On the other hand, you can often make intelligent guesses based on your general knowledge of the type of document you are studying. You might make mistakes, of course, and these should be corrected when you interact with the user. After initially determining the functional dependencies, you may discover additional information. The following are possible initial functional dependencies:

> **Customer ID → First Name (Customer), Last Name (Customer), Street (Customer), City (Customer), State (Customer), Postal Code (Customer)**
>
> **Policy Number → Effective Date, Expire Date, Customer ID**
> **VIN → Make, Model, Year, Policy Number**

You might realize that other attributes of the Customer may be required. For example, you may want to include the customer's telephone number and email address. If that is the case, then telephone number and email address are functionally dependent on the customer.

You might also realize that the insurance card does not include any information about approved drivers. For example, the insured shown in Figure 11–25 could have a husband and two teenage dependents who are allowed to drive the vehicle. In that case, you will need to add all information about the driver entity, and then also have an entity that combines the vehicle (VIN) with the drivers that are allowed to operate that specific vehicle.

Given these corrections, a revised list of functional dependencies might look like the following:

> **Customer ID → First Name (Customer), Last Name (Customer), Street (Customer), City (Customer), State (Customer), Postal Code (Customer), Telephone (Customer), Email Address (Customer)**
>
> **Driver ID → First Name (Driver), Last Name (Driver), Street (Driver), City (Driver), State (Driver), Postal Code (Driver), Telephone (Driver), Email Address (Driver)**
>
> **Policy Number → Effective Date, Expire Date, Customer ID**
> **VIN → Make, Model, Year, Policy Number**
>
> **VIN, Driver ID →**

After you have determined the preliminary functional dependencies, you can begin determining the tables and assigning fields. You could create tables with the determinant—the field or fields to the left of the arrow — as the primary key and with the fields to the right of the arrow as the remaining fields. This would lead to the following initial collection of tables shown in Figure 11–26.

Customer (<u>Customer ID</u>, First Name, Last Name, Address, City, State, Postal Code, Telephone, Email Address)

Driver (<u>Driver ID</u>, First Name, Last Name, Address, City, State, Postal Code, Telephone, Email Address)

Policies (<u>Policy Number</u>, Effective Date, Expire Date, Customer ID)

Vehicle (<u>VIN</u>, Make, Model, Year, Policy Number)

Vehicle Driver (<u>VIN, Driver ID</u>)

Figure 11–26

Adding the foreign key information produces the shorthand representation shown in Figure 11–27.

Customer (<u>Customer ID</u>, First Name, Last Name, Address, City, State, Postal Code, Telephone, Email Address)

Driver (<u>Driver ID</u>, First Name, Last Name, Address, City, State, Postal Code, Telephone, Email Address)

Policy (<u>Policy Number</u>, Effective Date, Expire Date, Customer ID)

FK Customer ID → Customer

Vehicle (<u>VIN</u>, Make, Model, Year, Policy Number)

FK Policy → Number Policy

Vehicle Driver (<u>VIN, Driver ID</u>)

FK VIN → Vehicles

FK Driver ID → Driver

Figure 11–27

At this point, you would need to verify that all the tables are in third normal form. If any are not in 3NF, you need to convert them. If you had not determined the functional dependency of Effective Date and Expire Date on Policy Number earlier, for example, you would have had Effective Date and Expire Date as fields in the Customer table. These fields are dependent on Policy Number, making Policy Number a determinant that is not a primary key, which would violate third normal form. Once you converted that table to 3NF, you would have the tables shown in Figure 11–27.

You may have already created some tables in your database design. For example, you may have obtained financial data on customers from the Accounting department concerning the credit card that is used to renew the car insurance policy each year. If so, you would need to merge the tables in Figure 11–27 with those tables you already created. To merge tables, you combine tables that have the same primary key. The new table contains all the fields in either individual table and does not repeat fields that are present in both tables. Figure 11–28, for example, illustrates the merging of two tables that both have the Customer Number field as the primary key. In addition to the primary key, the result contains the Customer Name and credit card information fields, which are included in both of the original tables; the Street, City, State, and Postal Code, Telephone, Email Address fields which are only in the first table; and the Credit Card Number, Expiration Date, and CVV fields, which are only in the second table. The order in which you decide to list the fields is immaterial.

Merging

Customer (<u>Customer ID</u>, First Name, Last Name, Address, City, State, Postal Code, Telephone, Email Address)

And

Customer (<u>Customer ID</u>, credit card number, expiration date, CVV code)

Gives

Customer (<u>Customer ID</u>, First Name, Last Name, Address, City, State, Postal Code, Telephone, Email Address, credit card number, expiration date, CVV code)

Figure 11–28

BTW
Merging Entities
When you merge entities, do not assume that the merged entities will be in 3NF. Apply normalization techniques to convert all entities to 3NF.

Diagrams for Database Design

You have now seen how to represent a database design as a list of tables, fields, primary keys, and foreign keys. It is often helpful to also be able to represent a database design with a diagram. If you have already created the database and relationships in Access, the Relationships window and Relationships report provide a helpful diagram of the design. Figure 11–29 shows the Access Relationship diagram and report for the CMF Vets database. In these diagrams, rectangles represent tables. The fields in the table are listed in the corresponding rectangle with a key symbol appearing in front of the primary key. Relationships are represented by lines with the "one" end of the relationship represented by the number, 1, and the "many" end represented by the infinity symbol (∞).

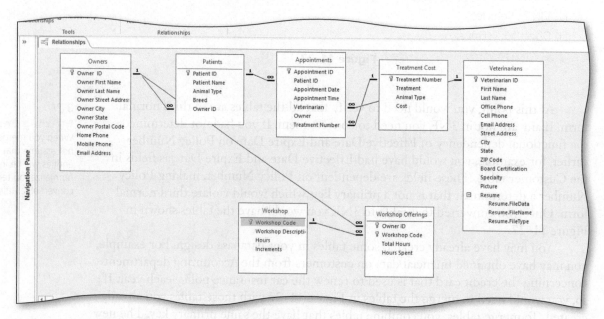

Figure 11–29a Access Relationship Diagram for CMF Vets Database

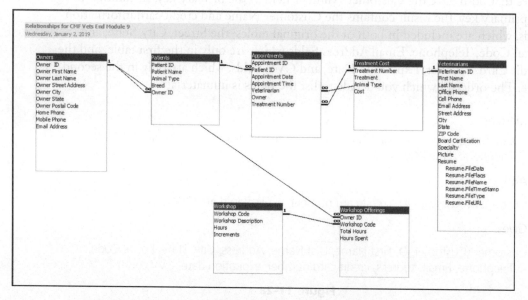

Figure 11–29b Access Relationship Report for CMF Vets Database

Figure 11–30 shows the Access Relationship diagram and report for the Car First Insurers database.

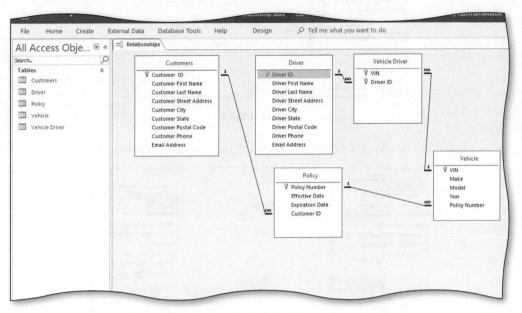

Figure 11–30a Access Relationship Diagram for Car First Insurers Database

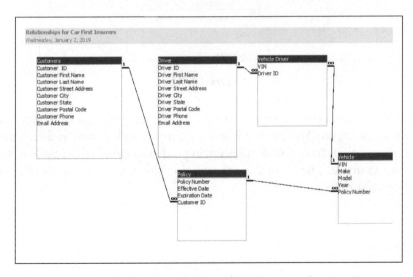

Figure 11–30b Access Relationship Diagram for Car First Insurers Database

Another popular option for diagramming a database design is the **entity-relationship diagram (ERD)**. Figure 11–31 shows a sample ERD for a portion of the CMF Vets database. In this type of diagram, rectangles represent the tables. The primary key is listed within the table above a line. Below the line are the other fields in the table. The arrow goes from the rectangle that represents the many part of the relationship to the one part of the relationship.

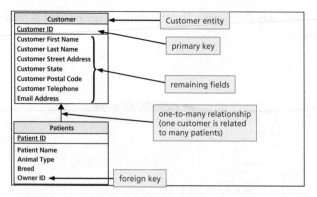

Figure 11–31

Figure 11–32 shows a similar diagram for the full Car First Insurers database.

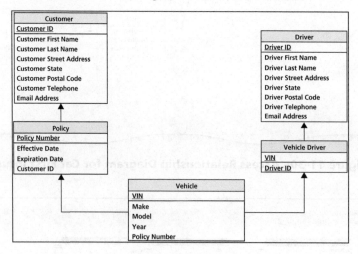

Figure 11–32

There are many options for such diagrams. Some options include more detail than shown in the figure. You can include, for example, such details as data types and indexes. Other options have less detail, showing only the name of the table in the rectangle, for example. There are also other options for the appearance of the lines representing relationships.

Summary

In this module, you have learned the following concepts.

1. An entity is a person, place, thing, or event. An attribute is a property of an entity. A relationship is an association between entities.

2. A relation is a two-dimensional table in which the entries in the table are single-valued, each column has a distinct name, all values in a column are values of the same attribute (that is, all entries must correspond to the column name), and each row is distinct.

3. In a relation, the order of columns is immaterial. You can view the columns in any order you want. The order of rows is also immaterial. You can view the rows in any order you want.

4. A relational database is a collection of relations.

5. Rows in a table (relation) are often called records or tuples. Columns in a table (relation) are often called fields or attributes. Typically, the terms *record* and *field* are used in Access.

6. If you know that whenever you are given a value for one field, you will be able to determine a single value for a second field, then the first field is said to determine the second field. In addition, the second field is said to be functionally dependent on the first.

7. The primary key of a table is the field or minimum collection of fields that uniquely identifies a given row in that table.

8. The following is a method for designing a database for a set of requirements.

   a. Examine the requirements and identify the entities (objects) involved. Assign names to the entities.

   b. Identify a unique identifier for each entity.

   c. Identify the attributes for all the entities. These attributes will become the fields in the tables.

   d. Identify the functional dependencies that exist among the attributes.

   e. Use the functional dependencies to identify the tables.

   f. Identify any relationships between tables by looking for matching fields where one of the fields is a primary key. The other field will then be a foreign key. In the shorthand representation for the table containing the primary key, represent the foreign key by using the letters FK, followed by an arrow, followed by the name of the table containing the primary key.

9. A table (relation) is in first normal form (1NF) if it does not contain repeating groups.

10. To convert a table to 1NF, remove the parentheses enclosing the repeating group and expand the primary key to include the key to the repeating group.

11. A field is a nonkey field (also called a nonkey attribute) if it is not a part of the primary key. A table (relation) is in second normal form (2NF) if it is in first normal form and no nonkey field is dependent on only a portion of the primary key.

12. To convert a table to 2NF, take each subset of the set of fields that make up the primary key and begin a new table with this subset as its primary key. Place each of the other fields with the appropriate primary key; that is, place each one with the minimal collection of fields on which it depends. Give each of these new tables a name that is descriptive of the meaning of the table.

13. Any field (or collection of fields) that determines another field is called a determinant. A table is in third normal form (3NF) if it is in second normal form and if the only determinants it contains are candidate keys.

14. To convert a table to 3NF, for each determinant that is not a candidate key, remove from the table the fields that depend on this determinant, but do not remove the determinant. Create a new table containing all the fields from the original table that depend on this determinant and make the determinant the primary key of this new table.

15. An entity-relationship diagram (ERD) is a diagram used to represent database designs. In ERDs, rectangles represent tables and lines between rectangles represent one-to-many relationships between the corresponding tables. You can also diagram a database design by using the Access relationship window.

How should you submit solutions to questions in the assignments identified with a symbol?

Every assignment in this book contains one or more questions identified with a ✳ symbol. These questions require you to think beyond the assigned database. Present your solutions to the questions in the format required by your instructor. Possible formats may include one or more of these options: write the answer; create a document that contains the answer; present your answer to the class; discuss your answer in a group; record the answer as audio or video using a webcam, smartphone, or portable media player; or post answers on a blog, wiki, or website.

Apply Your Knowledge

Reinforce the skills and apply the concepts you learned in this module.

Understanding Keys and Normalization

Instructions: Answer the following questions in the format specified by your instructor.

1. Figure 11–33 contains sample data for a Student table that could have been used for a college. Use this figure to answer the following:
   a. Is the table in first normal form (1NF)? Why or why not?
   b. Is the table in second normal form (2NF)? Why or why not?
   c. Is the table in third normal form (3NF)? Why or why not?
   d. Identify candidate keys for the table.

Student				
SID	FirstName	LastName	Team ID	SportName
23483	Corey	Gomez	BASK-1	Basketball
23423	Michael	Black	SOC-1	Soccer
23480	Kathy	Reid	SOF-1	Softball
23468	Matthew	Stone	TEN-1	Tennis

Figure 11–33

2. Figure 11–34 contains sample data for pet sitters and customers who hire those sitters. In discussing the data with users, you find that customer IDs — but not customer names — uniquely identify customers and their offered pay rate, and that sitter numbers uniquely identify pet sitters. Multiple customers can use the same sitter and customers can use more than one sitter. For example, Carl Rogers pet sits for Eileen Anderson and Anne Carlson.

   a. Convert the data in Figure 11–34 into a relation in first normal form (1NF) using the shorthand representation used in this module.
   b. Identify all functional dependencies using the notation demonstrated in the module.

Pet Sitters				
Sitter Number	FirstName	LastName	Customer Name	Amount Paid Per Hour
21	Arnold	Kripsen	Anne Carlson	$20
			Eileen Anderson	$21
			Fabio Lopez	$19
24	Carl	Rogers	Eileen Anderson	$21
			Anne Carlson	$20
27	Jaime	Fernandez	Barb Lenton	$15
34	Jose	Lorenz	Fabio Lopez	$19

Figure 11–34

3. ✺ Using only the data in Figure 11–33, how could you identify the entities and attributes that would be the starting point for a database design?

Extend Your Knowledge

Extend the skills you learned in this module and experiment with new skills. You may need to use Help to complete the assignment.

Modifying a Database Design and Understanding Diagrams

Instructions: Answer the following questions in the format specified by your instructor.

1. Using the shorthand representation illustrated in this module, indicate the changes you would need to make to the CMF Vets database design shown in Figure 11–8 in order to support the following requirements:

   a. A given appointment may be assigned to more than one veterinarian.
   b. However, only one treatment is given by one veterinarian at a time.

2. Using the shorthand representation illustrated in this module, indicate the changes you would need to make to the Car First Insurers data design shown in Figure 11–10 to support the following requirements:

   a. Car First Insurers is expanding its business to insure recreational vehicles (RVs).
   b. In this expansion, the class of RV must be recorded along with any indication of ownership, loan, or rental.

3. Use the Access Relationships Report for the Financial Services database shown in Figure 11–35 to answer the following:

   a. Identify the foreign keys in the Client table.
   b. What is the purpose of the Services table?
   c. What are the primary keys of the Services table?

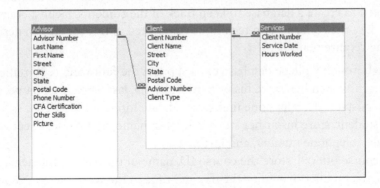

Figure 11–35

4. ✺ Financial Services has decided to add two tax advisors to the database. One tax advisor can service many clients and clients may use different tax advisors during the year, depending on their needs. What changes would you need to make to the database design for Financial Services?

Expand Your World

Create a solution which uses cloud and web technologies, by learning and investigating on your own from general guidance.

Instructions: There are several websites that provide examples of database models, such as www.databaseanswers.org/data_models/index.htm. These models provide a good starting point for creating your own database design.

1. Create a blog, a Google document, or a Word document on OneDrive on which to store your assignment. Include your name and the current date at the beginning of the blog or document.

2. Access the www.databaseanswers.org/data_models/index.htm website or another website of your choice that provides data models.

3. Browse the different database models and select one in which you have an interest.

4. In your own words, create a scenario for which the database model would work. Study the model to see if you need to modify it to make it applicable to your scenario. If changes are necessary, document the required modifications.

5. ✸ Why did you select the model that you did? How easy was it to understand the entities, attributes, and relationships? Were the relations in 3NF?

In the Labs

Design, create, modify, and/or use a database following the guidelines, concepts, and skills presented in this module.

Lab: **Designing a Database for Longborough Community College**

Instructions: Longborough Community College is a new educational institution in the Midwest. You have been asked to create a database to keep track of the students, faculty, course offerings, and class registration. Use the concepts and techniques presented in this module to design a database to meet the following requirements:

Part 1: The Longborough College database must support the following requirements:
   a. For each faculty member, store his or her faculty ID, last name, first name, street address, city, state, postal code, telephone number, and date hired.
   b. For each student, store his or her student ID, last name, first name, street address, city, state, postal code, telephone number, and birthdate.
   c. For each course offered, store the course ID, name of the course, the department the course resides in, the number of credits, the day and time of the week the course meets and the faculty teaching the course. To simplify the design, assume that only one section of each course is run, as this is a startup college.
   d. For each course registration, store student ID and the course ID.

Based on these requirements:
   a. Identify and list the entities and attributes of those entities.
   b. Identify and list the functional dependencies.
   c. Create a set of third normal form (3NF) relations using the shorthand notation given in this module. Be sure to identify all primary keys and foreign keys appropriately.

Submit your database design in the format specified by your instructor.

Part 2: ✸ You made several decisions while designing this database. What was the rationale behind these decisions? Are there other requirements that would have been helpful to you in the design process?

Index

Note: **Bold** page numbers refer to pages where key terms are defined.